T0301445

The Handbook of
European Fixed
Income Securities

THE FRANK J. FABOZZI SERIES

The Handbook of
European Fixed
Income Securities

FRANK J. FABOZZI
MOORAD CHOUDHRY

EDITORS

John Wiley & Sons, Inc.

Contents

SECTION THREE

Interest Rate and Credit Derivatives   493

SECTION FOUR

Portfolio Management   723

Preface

The *Handbook of European Fixed Income Securities* provides extensive and in-depth coverage of every aspect of the European fixed income markets and their derivatives. It includes a description of products and conventions as well as quantitative coverage of valuation and analysis of each instrument. Its focus is on the diversity of the product range across the markets, which presents features of interest for institutional investors worldwide. The emphasis is on both developed markets, such as the United Kingdom and Germany government and corporate bond markets as well as emerging markets in Eastern Europe, and includes instruments and institutions. Both plain "vanilla" and structured finance bond instruments are discussed in detail. There is also an extensive coverage of ancillary areas of importance such as trust and agency services, and legal documentation issues. The audience is primarily European institutional investors and portfolio managers worldwide who are diversifying into European instruments, as well as US-based researchers and academics. A secondary audience is students and market practitioners based in Europe, for whom no one book covering all aspects of the European market currently exists.

This last point was behind the motivation for compiling this book. We feel that there is no one book, aimed at both investors and practitioners, that covers every aspect of the European debt capital markets, which in terms of diversity, if not size, is the key capital market in the world. In our view there is a dearth of books written by European authors and aimed at market practitioners that cover this market. To facilitate this, we have assembled a field of over 30 authors, all leading names in their field, who have contributed chapters to this book. They represent investment bankers, traders, researchers, academics, and legal counsel. With only a few exceptions, all contributors are based in Europe. The diversity of contributors' backgrounds reflects the nature of our topic and helps us serve two different markets at once, practitioners (including investors and bankers) and students, each having their own reason for buying this book.

Another motivation for this book was the importance of the market itself. The advent of the euro currency has created a bond market of roughly equal size to the US dollar market; this is an important market for global investors. There is also a growing interest in European markets among US and Asian investors: for instance, market statistics show an increasing share of European issues held by US portfolio managers, generating greater need for market information in this field. This we hope we have achieved.

The book is grouped into the following sections:

Section One: Background
Section Two: Products
Section Three: Interest Rate and Credit Derivatives
Section Four: Portfolio Management
Section Five: Legal Considerations

Within this broad field there is detailed coverage of specific areas of importance to institutional investors.

We would like to thank all authors for their contributions, as well as Ruth Kentish and Paula Jacobsen for assistance with the editorial process, and Dr. Chee Hau at JPMorgan Chase for reviewing drafts of Moorad Choudhry's chapters. Special thanks to Professor Steven Mann at the University of South Carolina, for assisting us in several aspects of this project, in addition to his contribution of four chapters to this book.

Frank Fabozzi
Moorad Choudhry

About the Editors

Frank J. Fabozzi, Ph.D., CFA, CPA is the Frederick Frank Adjunct Professor of Finance in the School of Management at Yale University. Prior to joining the Yale faculty, he was a Visiting Professor of Finance in the Sloan School at MIT. Professor Fabozzi is a Fellow of the International Center for Finance at Yale University and the editor of the *Journal of Portfolio Management*. He earned a doctorate in economics from the City University of New York in 1972. In 1994 he received an honorary doctorate of Humane Letters from Nova Southeastern University and in 2002 was inducted into the Fixed Income Analysts Society's Hall of Fame. He is the honorary advisor to the Chinese Asset Securitization Web site.

Moorad Choudhry is Head of Treasury at KBC Financial Products (UK) Limited in London. He previously worked as a government bond trader and Treasury trader at ABN Amro Hoare Govett Limited and Hambros Bank Limited, and in structured finance services at JPMorgan Chase Bank. Moorad is a Fellow of the Centre for Mathematical Trading and Finance, CASS Business School, and a Fellow of the Securities Institute. He is author of *The Bond and Money Markets: Strategy, Trading, Analysis*, and editor of the *Journal of Bond Trading and Management*.

Contributing Authors

Phil Adams	Barclays Capital
Ludovic Breger	Barra, Inc.
Moorad Choudhry	CASS Business School, London
Graham "Harry" Cross	YieldCurve.com
Brian A. Eales	London Metropolitan University
Frank J. Fabozzi	Yale University
Lawrence Galitz	ACF Consultants Ltd.
Greg Gentile	Lehman Brothers
Mats Gustavsson	Barclays Capital
Claus Huber	Deutsche Bank
Inflation-Linked Research Team	Barclays Capital
David Jefferds	CREDITEX, Inc.
Helmut Kaiser	Deutsche Bank
Christoph Klein	Deutsche Asset Management
Edmond Leedham	JPMorgan Chase Bank
William T. Lloyd	Barclays Capital
Bharath K. Manium	Barclays Capital
Steven V. Mann	University of South Carolina
Lionel Martellini	University of Southern California and EDHEC Risk and Asset Management Research Center
Oldrich Masek	JPMorgan Securities Ltd.
David Munves	Lehman Brothers International
Markus Niemeier	Barclays Capital
Trusha Patel	CIBC World Markets PLC
Richard Pereira	Dresdner Kleinwort Wasserstein, London
Rod Pienaar	Deutsche Bank AG, London
Philippe Priaulet	HSBC-CCF and University of Evry Val d'Essonne
Stéphane Priaulet	AXA Investment Managers
Nick Procter	JPMorgan Chase Bank
Uri Ron	Bank of Canada

Warren Saft   CREDITEX, Inc.
Radu Tunaru   London Metropolitan University
Mariarosa Verde   Fitch Ratings
Lourdes Villar-Garcia   CIBC World Markets PLC
Antonio Villarroya   Merrill Lynch

Background

One

Background

CHAPTER 1

Introduction to European Fixed Income Securities and Markets

Moorad Choudhry
Senior Fellow
Centre for Mathematical Trading and Finance
CASS Business School, London

Frank J. Fabozzi, Ph.D., CFA
Frederick Frank Adjunct Professor of Finance
School of Management
Yale University

Steven V. Mann, Ph.D.
Professor of Finance
Moore School of Business
University of South Carolina

A *bond* is a debt capital market instrument issued by a borrower, who is then required to repay to the lender/investor the amount borrowed plus interest, over a specified period of time. Bonds are also known as *fixed income* instruments, or *fixed interest* instruments in the sterling markets. Usually bonds are considered to be those debt securities with terms to maturity of over one year. Debt issued with a maturity of less than one year is considered to be *money market* debt. There are many different types of bonds that can be issued. The most common bond is the *conventional* (or *plain vanilla* or *bullet*) *bond*. This is a bond paying periodic interest payments at a fixed rate over a fixed period to maturity or redemption, with the return of *principal* (the par or nominal value of the bond) on the maturity date. All other bonds will be variations of this basic structure.

A bond is therefore a financial contract from the person or body that has issued the bond, that is, the borrowed funds. Unlike shares or equity capital, bonds carry no ownership privileges. The bond remains an interest-bearing obligation of the issuer until it is repaid, which is usually on its maturity date.

There is a wide range of participants involved in the European fixed-income markets. We can group them broadly into borrowers and investors, plus the institutions and individuals who are part of the business of bond trading. Borrowers access the bond markets as part of their financing requirements; hence borrowers can include sovereign governments, local authorities, public sector organisations and corporations. Virtually all businesses operate with a financing structure that is a mixture of debt and equity finance. The debt finance may well contain a form of bond finance, so it is easy to see what an important part of the global economy the bond markets are.

The different types of bonds in the European market reflect the different types of issuers and their respective requirements. Some bonds are safer investments than others. The advantage of bonds to an investor is that they represent a fixed source of current income, with an assurance of repayment of the loan on maturity. Bonds issued by developed country governments are deemed to be guaranteed investments in that the final repayment is virtually certain. For a corporate bond, in the event of default of the issuing entity, bondholders rank above shareholders for compensation payments. There is lower risk associated with bonds compared to shares as an investment, and therefore almost invariably a lower return in the long term.

In this chapter, we will provide a basic description of the various types of fixed-income instruments encountered in the European markets as well as the definitions of some key terms and concepts that will assist the reader throughout the remainder of the book. Important groups of investors in these markets are briefly discussed in the last section of the chapter.

DESCRIPTION OF THE BASIC FEATURES

A bond, like any security, can be thought of as a package of cash flows. A bond's cash flows come in two forms—coupon interest payments and the *maturity value* or *par value*. In European markets, many bonds deliver annual cash flows. As an illustration, consider a 6% coupon

EXHIBIT 1.1   Bloomberg Security Description Screen for a Spanish Government Bond

```
GRAB                                                           Corp  DES
SECURITY DESCRIPTION            Redenominates on  1/ 1/99
SPANISH GOV'T    SPGB 6 01/31/08    114.7900/114.8500  (2.57/2.55) BGN  @11:13
ISSUER INFORMATION          IDENTIFIERS              1) Euro Redenomination
Name BONOS Y OBLIG DEL ESTADO   Common   007815719   2) Additional Sec Info
Type Sovereign              ISIN     ES0000011652    3) Identifiers
Market of Issue EURO-ZONE   BB number  GG7340209     4) Ratings
SECURITY INFORMATION        RATINGS                  5) Sec. Specific News
Country ES      Currency EUR   Moody's    Aaa        6) Involved Parties
Collateral Type BONDS       S&P        AA+           7) Custom Notes
Calc Typ(1029)SPAIN:GOVT BONDS Composite AA1         8) Issuer Information
Maturity   1/31/2008 Series  ISSUE SIZE              9) ALLQ
NORMAL                      Amt Issued               10) Pricing Sources
Coupon     6     FIXED      EUR 18,802,600   (M)     11) Related Securities
ANNUAL         ACT/ACT      Amt Outstanding
Announcement Dt  6/20/97    EUR 18,802,600   (M)
Int. Accrual Dt  1/31/98    Min Piece/Increment
1st Settle Date  7/15/97          0.01/    0.01
1st Coupon Date  1/31/99    Par Amount        60.10
Iss Pr  93.8670             BOOK RUNNER/EXCHANGE
                                                     65) Old DES
NO PROSPECTUS               MADRID                    66) Send as Attachment
PSTA 299.418BLN ISS'D 7/15/97; PSTA 156.806BLN 8/18/97; PSTA 147.491BLN 9/15/97;
PSTA 118.07BLN ISS'D BY EXCH 9/29/97. O/S AMT=PSTA 2.759014TLN EFF 6/5/98.
Australia 61 2 9777 8600      Brazil 5511 3048 4500      Europe 44 20 7330 7500       Germany 49 69 920410
Hong Kong 852 2977 6000 Japan 81 3 3201 8900 Singapore 65 6212 1000 U.S. 1 212 318 2000 Copyright 2003 Bloomberg L.P.
                                                                    G274-147-0 11-Jun-03 11:17:20
```

Source: Bloomberg Financial Markets.

bond issued by the Spanish government that matures on 31 January 2008. Exhibit 1.1 presents the Bloomberg Security Description Screen for this issue. The *coupon rate* is the rate of interest that is multiplied by the maturity value to determine the size of the bond's coupon payments. Note that this bond delivers annual coupon payments. Suppose one owns this bond in June 2003, what cash flows can the bondholder expect between now and the maturity date assuming the maturity value is €100? On each 31 January for the years 2004 through 2008, the bondholder will receive annual coupon payments of €6. Moreover, on the maturity date, the bondholder receives the maturity value of €100, which is the bond's terminal cash flow.

Type of Issuer

A primary distinguishing feature of a bond is its issuer. The nature of the issuer will affect the way the bond is viewed in the market. There are four issuers of bonds: sovereign governments and their agencies, local government authorities, supranational bodies such as the World Bank, and corporations. Within the corporate bond market there is a wide

EXHIBIT 1.2 Bloomberg Screen of the Benchmark Government Bonds of The Netherlands

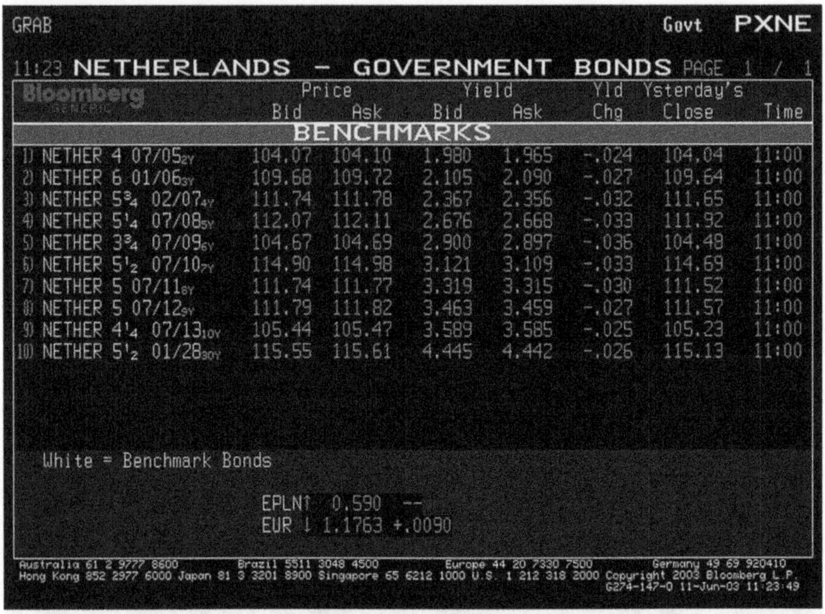
GRAB Govt PXNE

11:23 NETHERLANDS – GOVERNMENT BONDS PAGE 1 / 1

BENCHMARKS

	Price Bid	Price Ask	Yield Bid	Yield Ask	Yld Chg	Ysterday's Close	Time
1) NETHER 4 07/05 2Y	104.07	104.10	1.980	1.965	-.024	104.04	11:00
2) NETHER 6 01/06 3Y	109.68	109.72	2.105	2.090	-.027	109.64	11:00
3) NETHER 5¾ 02/07 4Y	111.74	111.78	2.367	2.356	-.032	111.65	11:00
4) NETHER 5¼ 07/08 5Y	112.07	112.11	2.676	2.668	-.033	111.92	11:00
5) NETHER 3¾ 07/09 6Y	104.67	104.69	2.900	2.897	-.036	104.48	11:00
6) NETHER 5½ 07/10 7Y	114.90	114.98	3.121	3.109	-.033	114.69	11:00
7) NETHER 5 07/11 8Y	111.74	111.77	3.319	3.315	-.030	111.52	11:00
8) NETHER 5 07/12 9Y	111.79	111.82	3.463	3.459	-.027	111.57	11:00
9) NETHER 4¼ 07/13 10Y	105.44	105.47	3.589	3.585	-.025	105.23	11:00
10) NETHER 5½ 01/28 30Y	115.55	115.61	4.445	4.442	-.026	115.13	11:00

White = Benchmark Bonds

EPLN↑ 0.590 --
EUR ↓ 1.1763 +.0090

Australia 61 2 9777 8600 Brazil 5511 3048 4500 Europe 44 20 7330 7500 Germany 49 69 920410
Hong Kong 852 2977 6000 Japan 81 3 3201 8900 Singapore 65 6212 1000 U.S. 1 212 318 2000 Copyright 2003 Bloomberg L.P.
G274-147-0 11-Jun-03 11:23:49

Source: Bloomberg Financial Markets.

range of issuers, each with differing abilities to satisfy their contractual obligations to investors. The largest bond markets are those of sovereign borrowers, the government bond markets.

The most actively traded government securities for various maturities are called *benchmark issues*. Yields on these issues serve as reference interest rates which are used extensively for pricing other securities.[1] Exhibit 1.2 is a Bloomberg screen of the benchmark bonds issued by the government of the Netherlands. European government bonds will be discussed in Chapter 5. As an illustration of a corporate bond, Exhibit 1.3 shows a Bloomberg Security Description screen for 4.875% coupon bond issued by Pirelli SPA that matures on 21 October 2008.

Term to Maturity

The *term to maturity* of a bond is the number of years after which the issuer will repay the obligation. During the term the issuer will also

[1] In some European countries, swap curves are used as a benchmark for pricing securities.

EXHIBIT 1.3 Bloomberg Security Description Screen for a Corporate Bond Issued by Pirelli

```
GRAB                                                     Corp   DES
SECURITY DESCRIPTION                     Redenominates on  1/ 1/99
PIRELLI SPA        PIREL 4 ⅞ 10/08  101.6628/101.9128  (4.51/4.46) BGN  @13:07
ISSUER INFORMATION                 IDENTIFIERS           1) Euro Redenomination
Name PIRELLI SPA                   Common   009142991    2) Additional Sec Info
Type Rubber-Tires                  ISIN    XS0091429919  3) Identifiers
Market of Issue EURO-ZONE          Wertpap. 176008       4) Ratings
SECURITY INFORMATION               RATINGS               5) Fees/Restrictions
Country IT         Currency EUR    Moody's    NA         6) Sec. Specific News
Collateral Type NOTES              S&P        NA         7) Involved Parties
Calc Typ(  1)STREET CONVENTION     Fitch      NA         8) Custom Notes
Maturity  10/21/2008 Series        ISSUE SIZE            9) Issuer Information
CALLABLE                           Amt Issued           10) ALLQ
Coupon     4 ⅞    FIXED            EUR 500,000.00  (M)  11) Pricing Sources
ANNUAL          ACT/ACT            Amt Outstanding      12) Prospectus Request
Announcement Dt 10/ 1/98           EUR 500,000.00  (M)  13) Related Securities
Int. Accrual Dt 10/21/98           Min Piece/Increment  14) Issuer Web Page
1st Settle Date 10/21/98             1,000.00/ 1,000.00
1st Coupon Date 10/21/99           Par Amount   1,000.00
Iss Pr 101.5360 Reoffer    99.961 BOOK RUNNER/EXCHANGE
                                   JPM,MEDBCA,PAR        65) Old DES
HAVE PROSPECTUS                    LUXEMBOURG            66) Send as Attachment
ALL PYMTS MADE IN ECU UNTIL INTRO OF EURO (EURO 1=ECU 1). UNSEC'D. CALL @ MAKE
WHOLE +10BP FROM 4/21/00. ALSO FRANKFURT & TLX SE.
Australia 61 2 9777 8600        Brazil 5511 3048 4500    Europe 44 20 7330 7500        Germany 49 69 920410
Hong Kong 852 2977 6000 Japan 81 3 3201 8900 Singapore 65 6212 1000 U.S. 1 212 318 2000 Copyright 2003 Bloomberg L.P.
                                                                      G274-147-0 12-Jun-03 13 34:37
```

Source: Bloomberg Financial Markets.

make periodic interest payments on the debt. The *maturity* of a bond refers to the date that the debt will cease to exist, at which time the issuer will redeem the bond by paying the principal. The practice in the market is often to refer simply to a bond's "term" or "maturity." The provisions under which a bond is issued may allow either the issuer or investor to alter a bond's term to maturity after a set notice period, and such bonds need to be analysed in a different way. The term to maturity is an important consideration in the makeup of a bond. It indicates the time period over which the bondholder can expect to receive the coupon payments and the number of years before the principal will be paid in full. The bond's *yield* also depends on the term to maturity. Finally, the price of a bond will fluctuate over its life as yields in the market change and as it approaches maturity. As we will discover later, the *volatility* of a bond's price is dependent on its maturity; assuming other factors constant, the longer a bond's maturity the greater the price volatility resulting from a change in market yields.

One common way to distinguish between different sectors of the debt markets is by the maturity of the instruments. The *money market* is the market for short-term debt instruments with original maturities of one year or less. This market includes such instruments as short-term government debt, commercial paper, some medium-term notes, bankers' acceptances, most certificates of deposit, and repurchase agreements. According to the European Central Bank, as March 2003, the total short-term debt outstanding (maturities of one year or less) in the Euro area was €783.6 billion. Although this is an important sector of the debt market, money market instruments are not covered in this book.[2] Instead, our focus is on the *capital market,* which includes debt instruments that have original maturities of greater than one year.

Coupon Types

As noted, the coupon rate is the interest rate the issuer agrees to pay each year. The coupon rate is used to determine the annual coupon payment which can be delivered to the bondholder once per year or in two or more equal installments. As noted, for bonds issued in European bond markets and the Eurobond markets, coupon payments are made annually. Conversely, in the United Kingdom, United States, and Japan, the usual practice is for the issuer to pay the coupon in two semiannual installments. An important exception is structured products (e.g., asset-backed securities) which often deliver cash flows more frequently (e.g., quarterly, monthly).

Certain bonds do not make any coupon payments at all and these issues are known as *zero-coupon bonds.* A zero-coupon bond has only one cash flow which is the maturity value. Zero-coupon bonds are issued by corporations and governments. Exhibit 1.4 shows a Bloomberg Security Description screen of a zero-coupon bond issued by the French bank BNP Paribus that matures March 11, 2005. Since the maturity value is €1,000, the price will be at a discount to €1,000. The difference between the price paid for the bond and the maturity value is the interest realized by the bondholder. One important type of zero-coupon bond is called *strips.* In essence, strips are government zero-coupon bonds. However, strips are issued by governments directly but are created by dealer firms. Conventional coupon bonds can be stripped or broken apart into a series of individual cash flows which would then trade separately as zero-coupon bonds. This is a common practice in European government bond markets. Exhibit 1.5 presents a Bloomberg screen of some German government coupon strips. Since zero-coupon bonds can created from coupon payments or the maturity value, a distinction is made between the two.

---

[2] For a complete treatment of the money markets, see Frank J. Fabozzi, Steven V. Mann, and Moorad Choudhry, *The Global Money Markets* (Hoboken, NJ: John Wiley & Sons, Inc., 2002).

EXHIBIT 1.4   Bloomberg Security Description Screen for a Zero-Coupon Bond Issued by BNP Paribus

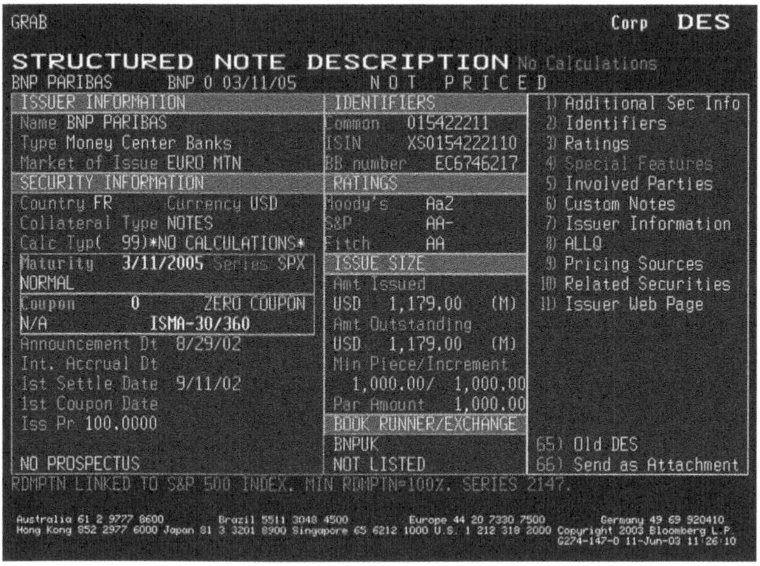

Source: Bloomberg Financial Markets.

EXHIBIT 1.5   Bloomberg Screen of German Government Coupon Strips

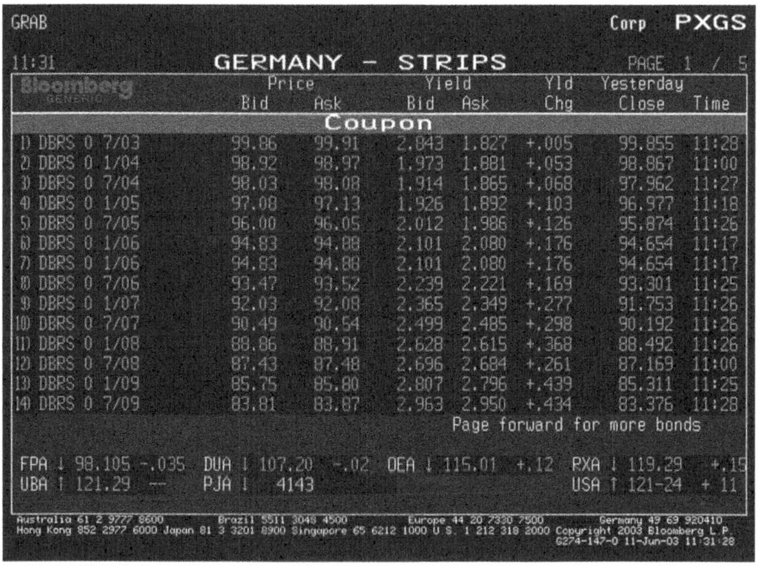

Source: Bloomberg Financial Markets.

In contrast to a coupon rate that remains unchanged for the bond's entire life, a *floating-rate security* or *floater* is a debt instrument whose coupon rate is reset at designated dates based on the value of some reference rate. Thus, the coupon rate will vary over the instrument's life. The coupon rate is almost always determined by a coupon formula. For example, a floater issued by Aareal Bank AG in Denmark (due in May 2007) has a coupon formula equal to three month EURIBOR plus 20 basis points and delivers cash flows quarterly.

There are several features about floaters that deserve mention. First, a floater may have a restriction on the maximum (minimum) coupon rate that be paid at any reset date called a *cap* (*floor*). Second, while a floater's coupon rate normally moves in the same direction as the reference rate moves, there are floaters whose coupon rate moves in the opposite direction from the reference rate. These securities are called *inverse floaters*. As an example, consider an inverse floater issued by the Republic of Austria. This issue matures in April 2005 and delivers semi-annual coupon payments according to the following formula:

$$12.125\% - \text{6-month EURIBOR.}$$

An *index-linked* bond has its coupon or maturity value or sometimes both linked to a specific index. When governments issue index-linked bonds, the cash flows are linked to a price index such as consumer or commodity prices. Corporations have also issued index-linked bonds that are connected to either an inflation index or a stock market index. For example, Kredit Fuer Wiederaufbau, a special purpose bank in Denmark, issued a floating-rate note in March 2003 whose coupon rate will be linked to the Eurozone CPI (excluding tobacco) beginning in September 2004. Inflation-indexed bonds are detailed in Chapter 8.

Currency Denomination

The cash flows of a fixed-income security can be denominated in any currency. For bonds issued by countries within the European Union, the issuer typically makes both coupon payments and maturity value payments in euros. However, there is nothing that prohibits the issuer from making payments in other currencies. The bond's indenture can specify that the issuer may make payments in some other specified currency. There are some issues whose coupon payments are in one currency and whose maturity value is in another currency. An issue with this feature is called a *dual-currency issue*.

NONCONVENTIONAL BONDS

The definition of bonds given earlier in this chapter referred to conventional or *plain vanilla* bonds. There are many variations on vanilla bonds and we can introduce a few of them here.

Securitised Bonds

There is a large market in bonds whose interest and principal payments are backed by an underlying cash flow from another asset. By securitising the asset, a borrower can provide an element of cash flow backing to investors. For instance, a mortgage bank can use the cash inflows it receives on its mortgage book as asset backing for an issue of bonds. Such an issue would be known as a *mortgage-backed security* (MBS). Because residential mortgages rarely run to their full term, but are usually paid off earlier by homeowners, the notes that are backed by mortgages are also prepaid ahead of their legal final maturity. This feature means that MBS securities are not bullet bonds like vanilla securities, but are instead known as *amortising bonds*. Other asset classes that can be securitised include credit card balances, car loans, equipment lease receivables, nursing home receipts, museum or leisure park receipts, and so on. Securitised bonds are usually called structured finance products or *structured products*, and the market in MBS, asset-backed securities (ABS), collateralised debt obligations (CDOs), and asset-backed commercial paper (AB-CP) is known as the structured finance market. Some of the more popular structured products are described in later chapters.

Bonds with Embedded Options

Some bonds include a provision in their offer particulars that gives either the bondholder and/or the issuer an option to enforce early redemption of the bond. The most common type of option embedded in a bond is a *call feature*. A call provision grants the issuer the right to redeem all or part of the debt before the specified maturity date. An issuing company may wish to include such a feature as it allows it to replace an old bond issue with a lower coupon rate issue if interest rates in the market have declined. As a call feature allows the issuer to change the maturity date of a bond it is considered harmful to the bondholder's interests; therefore the market price of the bond at any time will reflect this. A call option is included in all asset-backed securities based on mortgages, for obvious reasons.

A bond issue may also include a provision that allows the investor to change the maturity of the bond. This is known as a *put feature* and gives the bondholder the right to sell the bond back to the issuer at par on specified dates. The advantage to the bondholder is that if interest

EXHIBIT 1.6

Euro Corporate Index by Structure 1998 through 31 May 2003

| | Market Value Percent (%) of Euro Corporate Index | | | |
	Bullets	Callables	Putables	Total
1998	94.0%	5.7%	0.4%	100.0%
1999	98.4%	1.5%	0.1%	100.0%
2000	98.8%	1.1%	0.1%	100.0%
2001	99.5%	0.5%	0.1%	100.0%
2002	99.1%	0.8%	0.1%	100.0%
May 31, 2003	99.3%	0.6%	0.1%	100.0%

Pan-Euro Corporate Index by Structure 1999 through 31 May 2003

| | Market Value Percent (%) of Pan-Euro Corporate Index | | | |
	Bullets	Callables	Putables	Total
1999	98.2%	1.7%	0.1%	100.0%
2000	97.9%	2.0%	0.1%	100.0%
2001	99.4%	0.5%	0.1%	100.0%
2002	99.1%	0.9%	0.1%	100.0%
May 31, 2003	99.1%	0.8%	0.1%	100.0%

Source: Lehman Brothers Fixed Income Research.

rates rise after the issue date, thus depressing the bond's value, the investor can realise par value by *putting* the bond back to the issuer.

Bonds with embedded call and put options comprise a relatively small percentage of the European bond market. Exhibit 1.6 shows the percentage of the market value of the Euro Corporate Index and Pan-Euro Corporate Index attributable to bullets (i.e., option-free bonds), callable and putable bonds from the late 1990s through 31 May 2003. Accordingly, our discussion of bonds with embedded options in the remainder of the book will be confined to structured products.

A *convertible* bond is an issue giving the bondholder the right to exchange the bond for a specified amount of shares (equity) in the issuing company. This feature allows the investor to take advantage of favourable movements in the price of the issuer's shares. Exhibit 1.7 shows a Bloomberg Security Description screen of a convertible bond issued by Siemens Finance BV that matures in June 2010. This bond is convertible into 1,780.37 shares as can be seen in the upper left-hand corner of the screen in the box labeled "Convertible Information."

EXHIBIT 1.7 Bloomberg Security Description Screen of a Convertible Bond Issued by Siemens Financial BV

```
GRAB                                                        Corp  DES
SECURITY DESCRIPTION                        Page 1/ 1
SIEMENS FINAN    SIEM 1 ³₈ 06/10   103.6498/103.8998  (0.83/0.80) BGN @ 6/10
 CONVERTIBLE INFORMATION       IDENTIFIERS           1) Additional Sec Info
 CONV TO        1780.3700 SHARES  Common    016953458  2) Softcall Schedule
 PER    100000.00 NOMINAL        ISIN    XS0169534582  3) Convertible Info.
 SIE   (GR ) €42.65 ( 1.00)      BB number  EC9891507  4) Identifiers
 CONVERTIBLE UNTIL  5/28/10       RATINGS             5) Ratings
 PARITY   75.93 PREMIUM   36.83% Moody's     Aa3       6) Fees/Restrictions
 ISSUER INFORMATION             S&P         AA-        7) Sec. Specific News
 Name SIEMENS FINANCE BV        Composite   AA3        8) Involved Parties
 Market of Issue EURO-ZONE       ISSUE SIZE           9) Custom Notes
 SECURITY INFORMATION           Amt Issued            10) ALLQ
 Coupon     1 ³₈  FIXED         EUR  2,500,000  (M)   11) Pricing Sources
 ANNUAL       ACT/ACT           Amt Outstanding       12) Related Securities
 Maturity    6/ 4/2010 Series SIE  EUR  2,500,000  (M)
 CONVERTIBLE                    Min Piece/Increment
 Country NL      Currency EUR   100,000.00/100,000.00
 1st Coupon Date  6/ 4/04       Par Amount  100,000.00
 Price @ Issue   100.0000        BOOK RUNNER/EXCHANGE
 Calc Typ (   1)STREET CONVENTION  MS,UBS               65) Old DES
 NO PROSPECTUS                  LUXEMBOURG            66) Send as Attachment
PROV CALL. PRX/SHR=€56.168. INIT CV PREM=46%. SR. SUBJ TO CONTINGENT CVR.
HLDR OPT TO CVT UPON CHANGE OF CONTROL @ HIGHER CV RATIO. ALSO EBS.
Australia 61 2 9777 8600       Brazil 5511 3048 4500       Europe 44 20 7330 7500       Germany 49 69 920410
Hong Kong 852 2977 6000 Japan 81 3 3201 8900 Singapore 65 6212 1000 U.S. 1 212 318 2000 Copyright 2003 Bloomberg L.P.
                                                           G274-147-0 11-Jun-03 13 05 29
```

Source: Bloomberg Financial Markets.

The presence of embedded options in a bond makes valuation more complex compared to plain vanilla bonds.

PRICING A CONVENTIONAL BOND

The principles of pricing in the bond market are exactly the same as those in other financial markets, which states that the price of any financial instrument is equal to the net present value today of all the future cash flows from the instrument. In Chapter 3, bond pricing will be explained. In this chapter we will just present the basic elements of bond pricing.

A bond price is expressed as per 100 nominal of the bond, or "per cent." So for example if the all-in price of a euro-denominated bond is quoted as "98.00", this means that for every €100 nominal of the bond a buyer would pay €98. The interest rate or discount rate used as part of the present value (price) calculation is key to everything, as it reflects where the bond is trading in the market and how it is perceived by the market. All the determining factors that identify the bond—those discussed earlier in this chapter and including the type of issuer, the maturity, the coupon, and the currency—influence the interest rate at which a bond's cash flows are discounted, which will be roughly similar to the rate used for comparable bonds.

Since the price of a bond is equal to the present value of its cash flows, first we need to know the bond's cash flows before then determining the appropriate interest rate at which to discount the cash flows. We can then compute the price of the bond.

A conventional bond's cash flows are the interest payments or coupons that are paid during the life of the bond, together with the final redemption payment. It is possible to determine the cash flows with certainty only for conventional bonds of a fixed maturity. So for example, we do not know with certainty what the cash flows are for bonds that have embedded options and can be redeemed early.

The interest rate that is used to discount a bond's cash flows (therefore called the *discount rate*) is the rate required by the bondholder. It is therefore known as the bond's *yield*. The required yield for any bond will depend on a number of political and economic factors, including what yield is being earned by other bonds of the same class. Yield is always quoted as an annualised interest rate.

The *fair price* of a bond is the present value of all its cash flows. The formulas that can be used for determining the fair price are presented in Chapter 3.

The date used as the point for calculation is the *settlement date* for the bond, the date on which a bond will change hands after it is traded. For a new issue of bonds the settlement date is the day when the bond stock is delivered to investors and payment is received by the bond issuer. The settlement date for a bond traded in the *secondary market* is the day that the buyer transfers payment to the seller of the bond and when the seller transfers the bond to the buyer. Different markets will have different settlement conventions; for example, UK gilts normally settle one business day after the trade date (the notation used in bond markets is $T + 1$) whereas Eurobonds settle on $T + 3$. The term *value date* is sometimes used in place of settlement date, however the two terms are not strictly synonymous. A settlement date can only fall on a business date, so that a gilt traded on a Friday will settle on a Monday. However a value date can sometimes fall on a nonbusiness day.

ACCRUED INTEREST, CLEAN PRICE, AND DIRTY PRICE

All bonds coupon-paying bonds accrue interest on a daily basis, and this is then paid out on the coupon date. In determination of the fair price for a bond that is not purchased on a coupon date, *accrued interest* must be incorporated into the price. Accrued interest is the amount of interest earned by the bond's seller since the last coupon payment date. The calculation of accrued interest will differ across bonds due to day count conventions that will be discussed shortly.

In all major bond markets the convention is to quote price as a *clean price*. This is the price of the bond as given by the present value of its cash flows, but excluding coupon interest that has accrued on the bond since the last dividend payment. As all bonds accrue interest on a daily basis, even if a bond is held for only one day, interest will have been earned by the bondholder. However, we have referred already to a bond's *all-in* price, which is the price that is actually paid for the bond in the market. This is also known as the *dirty price* (or *gross price*), which is the clean price of a bond plus accrued interest. In other words, the accrued interest must be added to the quoted price to get the total consideration for the bond.

Accruing interest compensates the seller of the bond for giving up all of the next coupon payment even though they will have held the bond for part of the period since the last coupon payment. The clean price for a bond will move with changes in market interest rates; assuming that this is constant in a coupon period, the clean price will be constant for this period. The dirty price, however, for the same bond will increase steadily from one interest payment date until the next one. On the coupon date the clean and dirty prices are the same and the accrued interest is zero. Between the coupon payment date and the next *ex-dividend* date the bond is traded *cum dividend*, so that the buyer gets the next coupon payment. The seller is compensated for not receiving the next coupon payment by receiving accrued interest instead. This is positive and increases up to the next ex-dividend date, at which point the dirty price falls by the present value of the amount of the coupon payment. The dirty price at this point is below the clean price, reflecting the fact that accrued interest is now negative. This is because after the ex-dividend date the bond is traded "ex-dividend"; the seller not the buyer receives the next coupon and the buyer has to be compensated for not receiving the next coupon by means of a lower price for holding the bond.

The net interest accrued since the last ex-dividend date is determined as follows:

$$AI = C \times \left[\frac{N_{xt} - N_{xc}}{\text{Day Base}} \right]$$

where

AI	=	next accrued interest
C	=	bond coupon
N_{xc}	=	number of days between the ex-dividend date and the coupon payment date (seven business days for UK gilts)
N_{xt}	=	number of days between the ex-dividend date and the date for the calculation
Day Base	=	day count base (usually 365 or 360)

Interest accrues on a bond from and including the last coupon date up to and excluding what is called the *value date*. The value date is almost always the *settlement* date for the bond, or the date when a bond is passed to the buyer and the seller receives payment. Interest does not accrue on bonds whose issuer has subsequently gone into default. Bonds that trade without accrued interest are said to be trading *flat* or *clean*. By definition therefore,

$$\text{Clean price of a bond} = \text{Dirty price} - AI$$

For bonds that are trading ex-dividend, the accrued coupon is negative and would be subtracted from the clean price. The calculation is given below:

$$AI = -C \times \frac{\text{Days to next coupon}}{\text{Day Base}}$$

Certain classes of bonds, for example US Treasuries and Eurobonds, do not have an ex-dividend period and therefore trade cum dividend right up to the coupon date.

Accrual Day Count Conventions

The accrued interest calculation for a bond is dependent on the day-count basis specified for the bond in question. We have already seen that when bonds are traded in the market the actual consideration that changes hands is made up of the clean price of the bond together with the accrued that has accumulated on the bond since the last coupon payment; these two components make up the dirty price of the bond. When calculating the accrued interest, the market will use the appropriate day-count convention for that bond. A particular market will apply one of five different methods to calculate accrued interest; these are:

EXHIBIT 1.8   Government Bond Market Conventions

Market	Coupon Frequency	Day Count Basis	Ex-dividend Period
Austria	Annual	actual/actual	No
Belgium	Annual	actual/actual	No
Denmark	Annual	30E/360	Yes
Eurobonds	Annual	30/360	No
France	Annual	actual/actual	No
Germany	Annual	actual/actual	No
Ireland	Annual	actual/actual	No
Italy	Annual	actual/actual	No
Norway	Annual	actual/365	Yes
Spain	Annual	actual/actual	No
Sweden	Annual	30E/360	Yes
Switzerland	Annual	30E/360	No
United Kingdom	Semi-annual	actual/actual	Yes

actual/365	Accrued = Coupon × days/365
actual/360	Accrued = Coupon × days/360
actual/actual	Accrued = Coupon × days/actual number of days in the interest period
30/360	See below
30E/360	See below

When determining the number of days in between two dates, include the first date but not the second; thus, under the actual/365 convention, there are 37 days between 4 August and 10 September. The last two conventions assume 30 days in each month, so, for example, there are "30 days" between 10 February and 10 March. Under the 30/360 convention, if the first date falls on the 31st, it is changed to the 30th of the month, and if the second date falls on the 31st and the first date is on the 30th or 31st, the second date is changed to the 30th. The difference under the 30E/360 method is that if the second date falls on the 31st of the month it is automatically changed to the 30th.

Exhibit 1.8 shows the conventions (coupon frequency, Day count basis, and ex-dividend period) for the the government bond market of major European countries.

EXHIBIT 1.9   Price/Yield Relationship for an Option-Free Bond

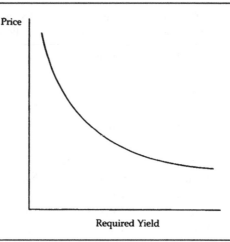

Required Yield

RISKS ASSOCIATED WITH INVESTING IN FIXED INCOME SECURITIES

Risk can thought of as the possibility of unpleasant surprise. Fixed-income securities expose the investor to one or more of the following types of risk: (1) interest rate risk; (2) credit risk; (3) call and prepayment risk; (4) exchange rate risk; (5) liquidity risk; and (6) inflation or purchasing power risk.

Interest Rate Risk

A fundamental property is that an upward change in a bond's price results in a downward move in the yield and vice versa. This result makes sense because the bond's price is the present value of the expected future cash flows. As the required yield decreases, the present value of the bond's cash flows will increase. The price/yield relationship for an option-free bond is depicted in Exhibit 1.9. This inverse relationship embodies the major risk faced by investors in fixed-income securities—*interest rate risk*. Interest rate risk is the possibility that the value of a bond or bond portfolio will decline due to an adverse movement in interest rates.

Bonds differ in their exposure to interest rate risk so investors want to know the sensitivity of a bond to change in interest rates. This sensitivity is first approximated by a bond's duration. There are various measures of duration (e.g., Macaulay, modified, effective, etc.) that will be discussed in Chapter 4. For the time being, a workable definition for duration is that it is the approximate percentage change in the bond's value for a 100 basis point change in the interest rates. As an illustration, suppose a bond has a duration of six and has a market price of €100. If rates increase by 100 basis points, this bond's value will fall be approximately 6%. The opposite is true for a decrease in interest rates.

Credit Risk

There are two main types of credit risk that a bond portfolio or position is exposed to. They are credit default risk and credit spread risk. *Credit default risk* is defined as the risk that the issuer will be unable to make timely payments of interest and principal. Typically, investors rely on the ratings agencies—Fitch Ratings, Moody's Investors Service, Inc., and Standard & Poor's Corporation—who publish their opinions in the form of ratings.

The *credit spread* is the excess premium over the government or risk-free rate required by the market for taking on a certain assumed credit exposure. Accordingly, *credit spread risk* is the risk of a financial loss resulting from changes in the level of credit spreads used in the marking-to-market of a fixed income product. Changes in observed credit spreads affect the value of the portfolio and can lead to losses for traders or underperformance for portfolio managers.

Call and Prepayment Risk

As noted, a bond may contain an embedded option which permits the issuer to call or retire all or part of the issue before the maturity date. The bondholder, in effect, is the writer of the call option. From the bondholder's perspective, there are three disadvantages of the embedded call option. First, relative to bond that is option-free, the call option introduces uncertainty into the cash flow pattern. Second, since the issuer is more likely to call the bond when interest rates have fallen, if the bond is called, then the bondholder must reinvest the proceeds received at the lower interest rates. Third, a callable bond's upside potential is reduced because the bond price will not rise above the price at which the issuer can call the bond. Collectively, these three disadvantages are referred to as *call risk*. MBS and ABS that are securitized by loans where the borrower has the option to prepay are exposed to similar risks. This is called *prepayment risk,* which is discussed in Chapter 11.

Exchange Rate Risk

If a European investor buys a bond whose cash flows are denominated in a currency other than euros, they are exposed to an additional risk. Namely, the euro-denominated cash flows are dependent on the exchange rate at the time the payments are received. For example, suppose a European investor purchases a US corporate bond whose payments are denominated in US dollars. If the dollar depreciates relative to the euro, then fewer euros will be received. This risk is called *exchange rate risk*. Thus, if an investor buys a bond in a currency other than her own, she is, in essence, making two investments—an investment in the bond and an investment in the currency.

Liquidity Risk

Liquidity involves the ease with which investors can buy or sell securities quickly at close to their perceived true values. *Liquidity risk* is the risk that the investor (who must trade at short notice) will have to buy/ sell at security at a price above/below its true value. One widely used indicator of liquidity is the size of the spread between the bid price (i.e., the price at which the dealer is willing to buy a security) and the ask price (i.e., the price at which a dealer is willing to sell a security). Other things equal, the wider the bid-ask spread, the greater the liquidity risk. For investors who buy bonds with the intent of holding them until maturity, liquidity risk is of secondary importance.

Inflation or Purchasing Power Risk

Inflation or *purchasing power risk* reflects the possibility of the erosion of the purchasing power of bond's cash flows due to inflation. Bonds whose coupon payments are fixed with long maturities are especially vulnerable to this type of risk. Floaters and inflation-indexed bonds have relatively low exposures to inflation risk.

INVESTORS

There is a large variety of players in the bond markets, each trading some or all of the different instruments available to suit their own purposes. We can group the main types of investors according to the time horizon of their investment activity.

Short-Term Institutional Investors

Short-term institutional investors include banks and building societies, money market fund managers, central banks and the treasury desks of some types of corporates. Such bodies are driven by short-term investment views, often subject to close guidelines, and will be driven by the total return available on their investments. Banks will have an additional requirement to maintain *liquidity*, often in fulfilment of regulatory authority rules, by holding a proportion of their assets in the form of easily-tradeable short-term instruments.

Long-Term Institutional Investors

Typically *long-term institutional investors* include pension funds and life assurance companies. Their investment horizon is long-term, reflecting the nature of their liabilities. Often they will seek to match these liabilities by holding long-dated bonds.

Mixed Horizon Institutional Investors

Mixed horizon institutional investors are possibly the largest category of investors and will include general insurance companies and most corporate bodies. Like banks and financial sector companies, they are also very active in the primary market, issuing bonds to finance their operations.

Market Professionals

Market professionals include the banks and specialist financial intermediaries mentioned above, firms that one would not automatically classify as "investors," although they will also have an investment objective. Their time horizon will range from one day to the very long term. They include the proprietary trading desks of investment banks, as well as bond market makers in securities houses and banks who are providing a service to their customers. Proprietary traders will actively position themselves in the market in order to gain trading profit, for example, in response to their view on where they think interest rate levels are headed. These participants will trade direct with other market professionals and investors, or via brokers. Market makers or *traders* (also called *dealers* in the United States) are wholesalers in the bond markets; they make two-way prices in selected bonds. Firms will not necessarily be active market makers in all types of bonds; smaller firms often specialise in certain sectors.

CHAPTER 2

Bondholder Value versus Shareholder Value

Claus Huber, Ph.D.
Corporate Bond Strategist
Private Asset Management
Portfolio Engineering Group
Deutsche Bank

The increasing internationalization of the European financial markets, a broader investor base, and the rising equity markets in the late 1990s have led more people in the European countries to deal with the equity markets. "Shareholder value" became the buzzword and got access to everyday language.

With the start of the European Monetary Union in 1999, new issuance volume of corporate bonds in the euro area has risen significantly. Apart from globalization, the structural change of the debt markets has contributed to this development: Until far into the 1990s, the European bond markets consisted basically only of obligations from governmental or semi-governmental issuers and financial institutions. Corporations virtually did not ask for debt as bank loans were the dominating way to raise capital. While the whole European bond market in 1999 was half of the size of the US debt market, the volume of corporate bonds only made up for 5% of the US market.[1] Since the start of the European Monetary Union this situation has changed dramatically. Europe's capital markets gained in breadth and depth. Exhibit 2.1 depicts the new issuance volume of euro-denominated corporate bonds from 1998 to

---

[1] Claus Huber, Helmut Kaiser, and Christoph Klein, *High Yield-Anleihen—Eine attraktive Depotbeimischung für Privatanleger*, Deutsche Bank Private Banking, ASP Analysetools, 2001.

EXHIBIT 2.1   New Issuance of Euro Corporate Bonds from 1998 to 2002

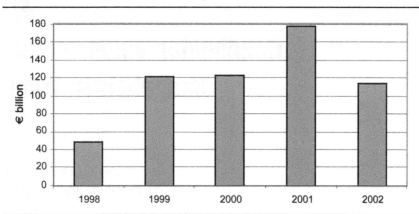

2002. Clearly, the interest group of bond creditors has become more and more important. Bondholder value has gained prominence in the capital markets.

This chapter defines the term bondholder value and contrasts it with shareholder value. In a second step, the different viewpoints of shareholders and bondholders are examined respectively. The discussion of both parties' conflicts of interests concentrates on capital structure, share buybacks, dividend policy, and corporate strategy. As there are also similarities between shareholders and bondholders, instruments of the shareholder value concept that can be used to create bondholder value are described. That includes investor relations, risk management and the balanced scorecard.

SHAREHOLDER AND BONDHOLDER— DEFINITION AND INTERESTS

Key to comprehending the motives of shareholders and bondholders is to understand how shareholder value and bondholder value are measured and how this translates into different claims of both stakeholder groups. This is discussed in the section below.

Shareholder Value

The approaches to shareholder value include all aspects of corporate governance that aim at the shareholder's property. The value of the corporation can be computed as its expected cash flows discounted with its average capital costs.[2] According to the original definition, shareholder value focuses on increasing the market value of equity. Meanwhile the orientation towards enhancing the market value of the corporation as a whole is generally accepted.[3] A common feature of all approaches to shareholder value is their secular orientation to cash flows, where the expectations of investors play a central role.[4] Shareholders require a return of at least the opportunity costs of investing in the company's stock. Claims of the shareholders on the assets of the corporation are subordinated to the bondholders. As shareholders take a higher risk, they demand a higher return than the bondholders.

Managing the corporation in the context of the shareholder value framework means "value oriented corporate governance" and is conducted via accounting figures. The company's value can be computed as follows:[5]

$$\text{Company value} = \text{Shareholder value} + \text{Debt value}$$

Company value can be enhanced by measures increasing shareholder value. The value of debt should not be diminished. The most effective way to increase the company's value is to simultaneously raise shareholder value and debt value. Both shareholders and bondholders are important. The question is how bondholder value can be defined analogously to shareholder value. This is discussed next.

Bondholder Value

There is no generally accepted definition of bondholder value. It could be set equal to the market value of a company's debt.[6] The market value of outstanding debt could be increased by issuing more bonds. This would adversely affect the market value of existing debt. Alternatively, bondholder value is based on the yield spread to government bonds: the wider the spread, the higher the risk associated with the issuer. A spread widening due to the company's activities leads to a reduction of bondholder value.

---

[2] Andrew Black, Philip Wright, and John Bachman, *In Search of Shareholder Value* (FT Prentice Hall, 2000).
[3] Ivo Welch, *A Primer on Capital Structure* (working paper, University of California, 1996).
[4] Rolf Bühner, "Shareholder Value," *Die Betriebswirtschaft* (1993), pp. 749–769.
[5] Alfred Rappaport, *Creating Shareholder Value* (Simon & Schuster, Inc., 1997).
[6] Werner Krämer, *Shareholder und Bondholder—Ein grundsätzlicher Antagonismus?* (working paper, Lazard Asset Management, 2001).

The spread does not only reflect idiosyncratic features of the company but depends on general market factors: a change of the political and/ or economic situation can alter the risk attitude of the market participants. Due to time varying risk components, the risk premium changes.

Research studies found that risk premiums fall in an environment of economic prosperity and rise when conditions are poor.[7] Lower-rated corporations usually have less diversified sources of income and thus are more sensitive to changes in the macroeconomic situation than higher-rated ones. Risk aversion increases with rising uncertainty and leads to higher expected compensation in the form of additional yield versus government bonds. Hence the effects of a company's individual actions to increase bondholder value can only inaccurately be measured. On the other hand, the spreads based on prices of the financial markets have anticipative character and reflect the expectations of a broad average of market participants.

Bondholder value can be understood as measures of a corporation raising the probability of timely payment of interest and principal,[8] although this is a quite general definition. It can be operationalized using the corporation's rating. The rating mirrors risk: the better the rating, the lower the credit risk of the issuer's bonds. Bondholder value increases by enhancing ratings and vice versa. A disadvantage with the rating-based definition of bondholder value is the fact that the rating agencies often react with considerable delay to a change in creditworthiness. Financial markets have usually processed a rating change before the change is publicly announced. Moreover, a corporation's rating needs not only depend on measures to create bondholder value, but is influenced, for example, by the macroeconomic environment.[9] Applying this concept, bondholder value of companies without a rating cannot be determined at all.

Apart from a rating one could target the balance sheet as an indicator for bondholder value.[10] Many evaluations of creditworthiness are based on financial ratios (e.g., debt to equity ratio, liquidity or profitability ratios).[11] Measuring bondholder value in this way is always due to delay: Balance sheets of listed corporations are published quarterly at

---

[7] James C. Van Horne, *Function and Analysis of Capital Market Rates* (Englewood Cliffs, NJ: Prentice Hall, 1970).

[8] Siegfried Utzig, "Shareholder versus Bondholder—Partner oder Konkurrenten?" *Die Bank* (July 1999), pp. 468–471.

[9] Volker Heinke, *Bonitätsrisiko und Credit Rating festverzinslicher Wertpapiere* (Bad Soden/Ts.: Uhlenbruch Verlag, 1998).

[10] Krämer, *Shareholder und Bondholder—Ein grundsätzlicher Antagonismus?*

[11] Claus Huber, Helmut Kaiser, and Christoph Klein, "Analysis and Evaluation of Corporate Bonds," *Economic & Financial Review* 8, no. 1 (Spring 2001), pp. 3–44.

EXHIBIT 2.2   Possible Definitions of Bondholder Value

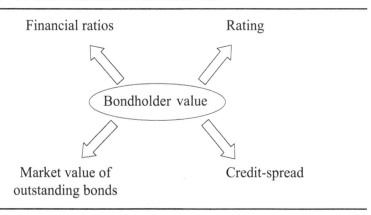

best or not published at all by small and medium enterprises. Balance sheets and financial ratios have retrospective character. Ratios are influenced by changes in the macroeconomic environment: In weaker times there is a tendency towards higher default probabilities and worse financial ratios. It is a sign of strength if the corporation manages to keep the financial ratios stable in a difficult economic environment. Qualitative factors, such as strategy, cannot be considered with the accounting related perspective: if a corporation moves away from its domestic market towards a debt-financed international expansion (e.g., European telecom companies), the risk of a worsening capital structure increases and bondholder value declines. Exhibit 2.2 presents an overview of possible definitions of bondholder value.

The most reasonable way to measure bondholder value appears to look at the spread versus government bonds: financial markets process information in a fast and anticipative way. Additionally, considering the spread to an index or benchmark bond representing the sector of the corporation allows to largely eliminate sector specific and general interest market related factors.

Shareholder value focuses on increasing the value of equity and of the corporation, while bondholder value concentrates on timely payment of coupons and principal. Exhibit 2.3 displays further differences between shareholders and bondholders.

It can be seen from Exhibit 2.3 that bonds bear a smaller upside potential compared to stocks, for example, bond price increases after an upbeat earnings report of a company are usually smaller than share price advances. Shareholders also risk total loss but profit from theoretically unlimited increases in the company's value. The next section

EXHIBIT 2.3   Claims of Shareholders and Bondholders

	Stocks	Corporate Bonds
Maturity	Infinite	Limited (EUR bonds mostly 2–10 years)
Revenues	Performance-related dividends, return on equity after interest payment for debt	(Fix) coupons, independent of performance
Chance	Share price increase, participation in growth of the company	Small price increases (relative to shares), no participation in growth of the company
Risk	Share price losses, total loss	Bond price losses, total loss
Participation in salvage value	Usually none	Dependent on pecking order of claims, satisfied prior to shareholders
Corporate governance	Vote in shareholders' assembly	Generally no vote. Possibly defined in covenants (e.g., maintaining a certain debt to equity ratio). In case of bankruptcy debtors can take over the company.

shows possible conflicts of interest resulting from the differing views of shareholders and bondholders.

CONFLICTS OF INTEREST BETWEEN SHAREHOLDERS AND BONDHOLDERS

Conflicts of interest between shareholders and bondholders often relate to capital structure, share buybacks or dividend policy, and strategy.[12] This section discusses these items.

Capital Structure

The question of determining the optimal capital structure has been subject to intensive discussions over the last few decades. Here, we briefly review the theses of Modigliani and Miller (expressed as MM), who proved the irrelevance of capital structure on a theoretical basis, and the traditional point of view, which postulates the existence of an optimal

---

[12] Utzig, "Shareholder versus Bondholder—Partner oder Konkurrenten?"

capital structure. An overview of the theoretical and empirical background of capital structure can be found in several studies.[13] Ramb investigates the capital structure of listed and unlisted European companies.[14]

MM showed in their seminal paper that—under a set of assumptions, for example, the absence of transaction costs and taxes—a company's capital structure is irrelevant for its value.[15] The foundation of their theoretical proof is the assumption that two companies with different levels of debt, but the same generation of cash flows, should have the same price. Otherwise, arbitrage would set in.[16] Consequently the market provides a company with capital for realizing its projected investments as far as its return exceeds the market return for equal risks.

The capital costs of a company are used to discount its future cash flows. The discount rate often is proxied by the weighted average cost of capital (WACC).[17] The company's value can be computed from the sum of the discounted cash flows. The company's value increases with higher cash flows or a lower discount rate. The *WACC* is calculated by weighting the costs for debt and equity with their proportions of total capital:

$$WACC = r_{\text{equity}} \times \frac{\text{Equity}}{\text{Equity} + \text{Debt}} + r_{\text{Debt}} \times \frac{\text{Debt}}{\text{Equity} + \text{Debt}} \qquad (2.1)$$

From equation (2.1) the expected return of the equity owners according to MM can be derived by rearranging

$$r_{\text{equity}}(MM) = WACC + \frac{\text{Debt}}{\text{Equity}} \times (WACC - r_{\text{Debt}}) \qquad (2.2)$$

---

[13] See, for example, Michael J. Barclay, Clifford W. Smith, and Ross L. Watts, "The Determinants of Corporate Leverage and Dividend Policies," *Journal of Applied Corporate Finance* (Winter 1995), pp. 4–19; and Milton Harris and Artur Raviv, "The Theory of Capital Structure," *Journal of Finance* 46 (1991), pp. 297–355.

[14] Fred Ramb, "Verschuldungsstrukturen im Vergleich—Eine Analyse europäischer Unternehmen," *Kredit und Kapital* 1 (2000), pp. 1–38.

[15] Franco Modigliani and Merton H. Miller, "The Cost of Capital, Corporation Finance and the Theory of Investment," *American Economic Review* 48 (1958), pp. 261–297.

[16] The basic statement of MM with respect to the capital structure can be transferred to the structure of a company's debt: the mixture of short- and long-term liabilities, secured and unsecured, subordinated and unsubordinated debt is irrelevant, too.

[17] Richard A. Brealey and Stewart C. Myers, *Principles of Corporate Finance 6th ed.* (McGrawHill, 2000).

EXHIBIT 2.4 Capital Structure and Expected Return

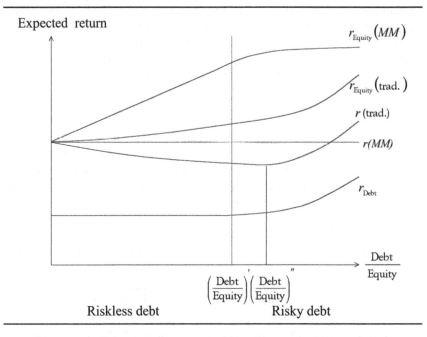

Equation (2.2) implies that the equity owners demand a higher compensation for increased gearing (= Debt/Equity). For the time being the required return on equity, r_{Equity}, increases linearly (Exhibit 2.4). At low debt levels the company is assessed as risk free.[18] If gearing exceeds a certain level (Debt/Equity)$'$, the required return on debt is no longer judged as risk free. The demanded minimum return on equity increases more slowly because a part of the additional risk can be transferred to the bondholders. The bondholders' demanded return r_{Debt} rises. On a net basis, the required return $r(MM)$ remains unchanged. Consequently there is no optimal debt level in the world of MM: The capital structure is irrelevant for the company's value.

The traditional school similarly assumes higher expected returns of the shareholders with rising indebtness. But the increase of expected return is not as distinct as with MM. If gearing exceeds a certain threshold (point (Debt/Equity)$''$ in Exhibit 2.4), the shareholders' expected returns rise significantly due to the increased risk sensitivity. Thus, according to the traditional view a capital structure can be determined which minimizes the cost of capital *WACC* and maximizes the company's value.

---

[18] Brealey and Myers, *Principles of Corporate Finance 6th ed.*

In practice, gearing often is created after "cosmetic" considerations (e.g., to fulfill the requirements of the rating agencies or the financial ratios of (benchmark) competitors or to optimize the effect of financing costs on profit per share).[19] There is no (theoretical) model connecting those components to shareholder value.

Equation (2.1) shows an incentive for shareholders to substitute equity by debt to increase the company's value: As interest on debt often is less than interest on equity, the substitution of equity by debt reduces the discount rate of the cash flows. Additionally, debt has a tax advantage unlike dividends expenses on debt diminish income. Moreover, external financing through a rights issue can be interpreted as a signal that management considers the share price as overvalued.[20] In most cases the share price drops after the announcement of a rights issue.[21]

From a creditor's perspective, equity serves as a risk cushion: higher equity better secures the claims of the creditors. If the profit situation proves to be unsatisfying, equity can be used to fulfill the payments of interest and principal to the creditors. Therefore, the capital structure is of significant importance for an issuer's rating: If gearing increases, the rating goes down.

The portion of the company's income exceeding the cost of debt belongs to the shareholders. From their perspective an increase of the debt level is not always welcome because volatility of the stock increments due to stronger deviations of shareholders' income after subtracting the expenses for debt.[22] Exhibit 2.5 displays an example assuming a total capital of €10,000.

In scenario 1, debt amounts to €2,500 (debt portion 25%). After interest expense of 10% (= €250), the remainder of the operating income (€1,000) goes to the shareholders (€750). This equals a return of 10% on the invested equity. The same return can be achieved with higher gearing (scenario 2). This transfers a part of business risk to the creditors. Stronger deviations of shareholders' income are shown in scenarios 3 and 4: if operating income falls to €500, a return on equity of 3.3% results when the debt portion is 25%, while the shareholders real-

---

[19] Tim C. Opler, Michael Saron, and Sheridan Titman, "Designing Capital Structure to Create Shareholder Value," *Journal of Applied Corporate Finance* 10, no. 1 (1997), pp. 21–32.

[20] Opler, Saron, and Titman, "Designing Capital Structure to Create Shareholder Value."

[21] Wolfgang Bessler and Stefan Thies, "Kapitalstruktur, Kapitalkosten und Informationseffekte," Chapter 3.4 in Ann-Kristin Achleitner and Georg F. Thoma (eds.), *Handbook Corporate Finance* (Verlagsgruppe Deutscher Wirtschaftsdienst, 2000).

[22] Opler, Saron, and Titman, "Designing Capital Structure to Create Shareholder Value."

EXHIBIT 2.5 Deviations of Shareholders' Income Depending on the Company's Income

	1	2	3	4
Operating income	1,000	1,000	500	500
Debt	2,500	5,000	2,500	5,000
Equity	7,500	5,000	7,500	5,000
Total capital	10,000	10,000	10,000	10,000
Interest expenses (10%)	250	500	250	500
Shareholders' income	750	500	250	0
Shareholders' return (in %)	10	10	3.3	0

EXHIBIT 2.6 Median Rating of European Issuers 1981–2001 (Standard & Poor's) versus MSCI Europe

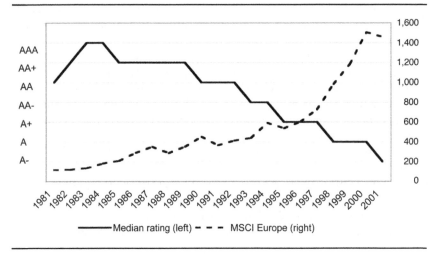

ize 0% return with a debt portion of 50%. Comparing scenarios 1 with 3 and 2 with 4 reveals the higher deviations of returns: from scenario 1 to 3 (= low debt portion) the return on equity is reduced from 10% to 3.3%, while it sinks from 10% in scenario 2 to 0% in scenario 4.

If the concentration on shareholder value came at the expense of bondholders, some empirical evidence should be available. Exhibit 2.6 can serve as an indication depicting the median rating of European issuers versus the stock index MSCI Europe.

The median rating declined from its peak AAA in 1983 and 1984 to only A– in 2001. The MSCI Europe, on the other hand, rose significantly. In 1981 and 1989 the median rating was AA. During this period the MSCI Europe tripled from 115 to 351 index points. Between 1990 and 2001, the rating went down substantially by four notches while the European stock market index quadrupled from the level of 1989.

The increasing relevance of shareholder value and the corresponding awareness of the problem of an optimized capital structure has led to the significant rise of corporate bond issuance since the start of the European Monetary Union. Investors are able to diversify more broadly, maximize returns and invest beyond formerly existing frontiers. Issuers can reduce financing costs and increase the company's value, which benefits bondholders. Thus concentration on shareholder value also generates bondholder value.

A conclusion is that the question of an optimal capital structure cannot be answered generally. Although high gearing neither serves the interest of shareholders (higher volatility of returns) nor bondholders (equity is a risk cushion), empirical data indicate that focussing on shareholder value comes at the expense of bondholders.

Stock Buybacks

Under a stock buyback program the company utilizes cash to buyback its own shares. Academic literature distinguishes between two alternative hypotheses to explain the impact of stock buybacks on bonds:[23] The *signaling hypothesis* states that management considers the company undervalued and believes a higher market price for stocks and bonds would be adequate. On the other hand, according to the *wealth transfer hypothesis*, the market price of the bonds sinks upon announcement of a share buyback program: stock buybacks, dividends, and other payments to the shareholders reduce the company's funds to fulfill its liabilities.[24] Moreover, a buyback can raise gearing, increasing bondholders' risk.

A share buyback can be an advantage for bondholders, if a low stock price is lifted, thus reducing the danger of a takeover and a change of management. A stock buyback lowers future dividend payments. This may be advantageous for bondholders if there are, for example, high dividends on preferred stock which are *de facto* paid independently of the economic situation and thereby have the character of a fixed interest rate. Sometimes a share buyback can turn out to be more pleasant than invest-

---

[23] Mark Klock and William F. Maxwell, *Do Large Dividend Changes Convey Information or Appropriate Wealth? Evidence from the Noninvestment Grade Bond Market* (working paper, Texas Tech University, 2000).
[24] William F. Maxwell and Clifford P. Stephens, *The Wealth Effects of Repurchases on Bondholders* (working paper, 2001).

ing the capital and changing the risk profile of the company. On the other hand, a high stock price represents an acquisition currency increasing the likelihood of buying another company. In the long run there could be a positive impact if an acquisition opens up new business areas that help to secure cash flows. Altogether the impact of a share buyback is not always clear: At least for the short term, the announcement leads to a spread widening, maybe a rating deterioration, and higher financing costs that have to be equalized by a higher market value of the stock.

Some empirical studies conclude that stock prices rise on the announcement of a share buyback program, while the value of bonds declines.[25] The magnitude of the price movement depends on the extent of the program. High-yield bonds react more strongly than investment grade bonds.[26] Other studies found out that the signaling effect over-compensates the wealth transfer effect.[27] Thus evaluating the impact of share buyback programs or dividend policy on bondholder value cannot be answered in a general way.

Corporate Strategy and Business Policy

The example in the preceding section showed that shareholders earn the residual income after satisfying the fixed claims of the bondholders. Creditors only want to cover their interest claims and avoid risky investments. From the shareholders' perspective, risky investments promising high returns conform with their interests, because shareholders and not bondholders decide on further employment of management. Thus management will decide in favor of shareholders. Bondholders bear a similar risk but are excluded from participation in the growth of the company's value.

A strategy to increment shareholder value at the expense of bondholder value could be implemented by wealth transfer from bondholders to shareholders (e.g., by issuing a bond and paying out the proceeds as a dividend).[28] Intended investments could be omitted and saved expenses paid out to shareholders. By analogy this could happen with the sale of core assets. In these situations bondholders lose if they did not already demand a compensation when the bonds were issued.

Debt financed acquisitions may come at the expense of the creditors because higher gearing corresponds with an increased risk assessment of

---

[25] Maxwell and Stephens, *The Wealth Effects of Repurchases on Bondholders*; Upinder Dhillon and Herb Johnsson, "The Effect of Dividend Changes on Stock and Bond Prices," *Journal of Finance* 49 (1994), pp. 281–289.
[26] Maxwell and Stephens, *The Wealth Effects of Repurchases on Bondholders*.
[27] J. Randall Woolridge, "Dividend Changes and Security Prices," *Journal of Finance* 38 (1983), pp. 1607–1615.
[28] Avner Kalay, "Stockholder-Bondholder Conflict and Dividend Constraints," *Journal of Financial Economics* 10 (1982), pp. 211–233.

the company. Acquisitions of this kind occurred in European business sectors which until the mid-1990s were characterized by state regulation (e.g., the utility and the telecommunication sectors). Formerly focussed on their regulated domestic markets, those companies were able to realize opulent profits. Liberalization brought new competitors. Additionally they recognized that eroding margins in the domestic markets are not sufficient to obtain critical size for international competition by organic growth. They changed strategy from domestically focussed companies to internationally or globally acting players. The necessary critical size was achieved by debt financed acquisitions.

Takeovers do not automatically come at bondholders' expense: if an acquisition secures and enhances the own market position or opens up new business areas, bondholders profit as well. Only a competitive company can generate the cash flows necessary to pay interest and principal. If an acquisition is cautiously financed (e.g., neutral with respect to debt ratios) or the issuer is bought by another company with a higher rating, bondholders will also benefit.[29]

It is common practice to link management's salary to the corporation's success. Stock options are an example. This increases the management focus on measures for raising the stock price, while bondholders' interests are of secondary importance. Linking management's salary to the company's rating could counter this problem.

After a bond is issued bondholders can do little to counter management's activities contrary to their interests. One possibility to commit management to bondholders' interests is to include covenants in the bonds' indentures. A covenant may restrain certain actions (e.g., forbid to sell part of the assets[30]). Covenants intend to protect investors from objectionable actions, e.g., a debt financed takeover of another company.

Apart from covenants, instruments of shareholder value can be used to increase bondholder value. These are discussed in the next section.

INSTRUMENTS OF SHAREHOLDER VALUE TO ENHANCE BONDHOLDER VALUE

Instruments for implementing shareholder value concepts are investor relations, risk management and the balanced scorecard.[31] These three

---

[29] Utzig, "Shareholder versus Bondholder—Partner oder Konkurrenten?"

[30] Clifford W. Smith and Jerold B. Warner, "On Financial Contracting: An Analysis of Bond Covenants," *Journal of Financial Economics* 7 (1979), p. 117–161.

[31] Heinz-Jürgen Weiss and Matthias Heiden, "Shareholder und Bondholder—Zwei Welten oder Partner?" *Betriebs-Berater 55* Jahrgang, issue 1 (2000), pp. 35–39.

instruments and their applicability to increase bondholder value are discussed below.

Investor Relations Not Only for Shareholders

The company's success not only has to be achieved, but has to be communicated to investors to have an impact on the company's securities prices. Communication is the central task of investor relations (IR). Many companies are aware of its significance and set up IR departments. Essential is the timely, regular, and transparent presentation of the company which is of interest to shareholders and bondholders: Market participants have to understand how the company works. And the company should know about investors' interests.

Successful IR can contribute to build up confidence in the company.[32] Simultaneously the principal-agent conflict between management and shareholders or bondholders can be mitigated. This depends on regular and extensive reporting to make the company's operations understandable, because uncertainty means risk. Information can significantly reduce the risk sensitivity of investors: the higher the quantity and quality of the information published by the company, the smaller the premium for uncertainty should be (see Exhibit 2.7).

Continuous financial communication can pay off if even in a difficult market environment stocks and bonds can be sold. Up to this point there is much scope for further improving the information flow from European companies to investors including setting up a balance sheet according to international standards (e.g., International Accounting Standards).

Risk Management

Risk management includes identification, quantification, reporting, and controlling the risks connected with the company's activities.[33] It can be distinguished between the perspective of an issuer and the perspective of an investor. The issuer is concerned, for example, about currency and interest rate risk and the development of turnover and prices for goods. These risks can be made transparent by scenario analyses and Monte Carlo simulations to sensitize the company and adopt measures for controlling those risks. Risk management creates shareholder value because management can prepare for current and future situations. This can

---

[32] Walter Paul and Matthias Zieschang, "Wirkungsweise der Investor Relations," *Die Betriebswirtschaft* 30 (1994), pp. 1485–1487.

[33] Michael Pfennig, "Shareholder Value durch unternehmensweites Risikomanagement," in Lutz Johanning and Bernd Rudolph (eds.), *Handbuch Risikomanagement Vol. 2* (Bad Soden Ts.: Uhlenbruch Verlag, 2000), pp. 1295–1332.

EXHIBIT 2.7   Relationship Between Information and Risk from Information Uncertainty

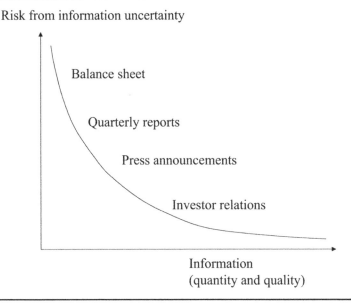

Risk from information uncertainty

Balance sheet

Quarterly reports

Press announcements

Investor relations

Information
(quantity and quality)

Source: Modified from Walter Paul, "Rating als Instrument des Finanzmarketing," in Hans E. Büschgen and Oliver Everling (eds.), *Handbuch Rating* (Wiesbaden: Gabler Verlag, 1996), pp. 373–419.

reduce volatility of cash flows and the probability of financial turmoil.[34] Moreover, the proactive use enhances capital allocation and the realization of entrepreneurial chances in crises. Consequently risk management creates bondholder value as well.

From the investor's perspective, risk management can be implemented by credit research, which focuses on the analysis of creditworthiness of a company.[35] As a first step, the company's sector(s) is screened. If a sector is sensitive to economic changes, it is strongly affected by a slowdown. So cyclical sectors tend to have lower average creditworthiness than more resistant sectors. Additionally, the competitive situation within the sector is of interest. To assess this situation criteria like the number of competitors, their market shares, their strategies, and strengths have to be scrutinized.

---

[34] Gummar Pritsch and Ulrich Hommel, "Hedging im Sinne des Aktionärs," *Die Betriebswirtschaft* 57 Jahrgang, no. 5 (1997), pp. 672–693.

[35] Anja Heilenkötter and Christoph Klein, *Unternehmensanleihen—neue attraktive Anlagechancen*, Deutsche Bank Private Banking (special publication, June 1999).

After evaluating the sector, the individual company comes to the fore. Here financial risk, business risk as well as the collateral of the bond (with covenants) is analyzed. To determine financial risk, financial statements are helpful. Relevant are, for example, ratios like gearing and profitability of the company. Apart from the absolute level of the company's results and cash flows, their stability over the course of time is important. Stable revenues in the past (e.g., producers of consumer goods with strong brands), give rise to the expectation of future stable sales. The assessment of a company's financial risk includes payout policy. High dividends and special payments indulge shareholders but mean reduced cash for fulfilling creditors' claims.

Hence financial ratios are oriented to the past and allow only limited forecasts about the future development of the company, they are not sufficient for assessing creditworthiness. Business risk has to be examined as well: this includes success factors, growth potential, and possible risks diminishing the solvency of the company. Criteria are, for example, quality of products, ability to innovate, strategy, and dependency on big customers or suppliers. Additionally the judgement of quality and trustworthiness of management is critical: special actions (e.g., a change of strategy), an acquisition or a special dividend to shareholders can lead to an immediate change of the assessment of an issuer's creditworthiness. Thus it is not sufficient to provide credit research only when a bond is issued or a report is published. To protect investors from negative developments, credit research should be conducted regularly.

Balanced Scorecard

The balanced scorecard, introduced by Kaplan and Norton, can be used to translate the company's strategy into a system of financial ratios.[36] Utilizing those ratios, the success of the strategy can directly be measured. Ratios oriented to the past and future as well as financial and non-financial figures (e.g., customer satisfaction) can be integrated.[37] General targets are four perspectives: financial, customer, innovation and learning, and internal business perspective. A parameter with the financial perspective could be shareholder value augmented with a ratio to measure bondholder value. Thus bondholder value becomes an integral part of the company's strategy.

---

[36] Robert S. Kaplan and David P. Norton, *The Balanced Scorecard* (Boston, MA: Harvard Business School Press, 1992).

[37] Iris Frick, "Visionen und strategische Ziele sind messbare Größen des Erfolgs," *Industrieanzeiger* 45 (2000), pp. 22–25.

SUMMARY

Contrasting the positions of shareholders and bondholders has shown that the latter focus on the risks of an investment rather than on the opportunities of an investment.

Due to its characteristic as a risk cushion, bondholders are interested in a high equity portion. On the other hand, the costs for debt are below the costs for equity. Thus shareholders target high gearing to optimize return on equity. But high gearing corresponds with higher dividend volatility. The concept of shareholder value not solely aims at achieving higher gearing, but generally at increasing capital efficiency and communicating a clear strategy. In this respect it conforms with bondholder value.

The effect of share buybacks on bondholder value cannot be answered unequivocally. Although there is a risk of wealth transfer from creditors to shareholders, an increased stock price can for example avoid a takeover of the company. Empirical studies come to contradictory results.

Again motivated by their diverging interests, shareholders favor riskier investments. This includes for example debt financed acquisitions of other companies that squeeze up gearing. The increased risk is mirrored in higher financing costs of the issuer when capital markets are tapped again. Over the longer term shareholder value sinks, too. Acquisitions to keep the issuer competitive are equally of interest for bondholders. However, they should be cautiously financed.

In the long run the aims of shareholders and bondholders are largely congruent. This is punctuated by the fact that instruments of shareholder value (investor relations, risk management, and balanced scorecard) can be used to enhance bondholder value. Thus it does not make sense to pursue short-term maximization of the stock price at the expense of the company's creditors.

CHAPTER 3

Bond Pricing and Yield Measures

Frank J. Fabozzi, Ph.D., CFA
Frederick Frank Adjunct Professor of Finance
School of Management
Yale University

Steven V. Mann, Ph.D.
Professor of Finance
Moore School of Business
University of South Carolina

Valuation is the process of determining the fair value of a financial asset. Once this process is complete, we can compare a financial asset's fair value to its market price in order to determine whether it is overvalued (i.e., rich) or undervalued (i.e., cheap). After this comparison, we can then take the appropriate position (short or long) in order to benefit from any differences. In well-functioning markets, however, fair values and market prices should be reasonably close.

GENERAL PRINCIPLES OF VALUATION

The fundamental principle of valuation is that the value of any financial asset is equal to the present value of its expected future cash flows. This principle holds for any financial asset from zero-coupon bonds to interest rate swaps. Thus, the valuation of a financial asset involves the following three steps:

Step 1: Estimate the expected future cash flows.

Step 2: Determine the appropriate interest rate or interest rates that should be used to discount the cash flows.

Step 3: Calculate the present value of the expected future cash flows found in Step 1 by the appropriate interest rate or interest rates determined in Step 2.

Estimating Cash Flows

Cash flow is simply the cash that is expected to be received in the future from owning a financial asset. For a fixed-income security, it does not matter whether the cash flow is interest income or repayment of principal. A security's *cash flows* represent the sum of each period's expected cash flow. Even if we disregard default, the cash flows for some fixed-income securities are simple to forecast accurately. Noncallable benchmark government securities possess this feature since they have known cash flows. For benchmark government securities, the cash flows consist of the coupon interest payments every year up to and including the maturity date and the principal repayment at the maturity date.

Many fixed-income securities have features that make estimating their cash flows problematic. These features may include one or more of the following:

1. The issuer or the investor has the option to change the contractual due date of the repayment of the principal.
2. The coupon and/or principal payment is reset periodically based on a formula that depends on one or more market variables (e.g., interest rates, inflation rates, exchange rates, etc.).
3. The investor has the choice to convert or exchange the security into common stock or some other financial asset.

Callable bonds, putable bonds, mortgage-backed securities, and asset-backed securities are examples of (1). Floating-rate securities and inflation-indexed bonds are examples of (2). Convertible bonds and exchangeable bonds are examples of (3).

For securities that fall into the first category, a key factor determining whether the owner of the option (either the issuer of the security or the investor) will exercise the option to alter the security's cash flows is the level of interest rates in the future relative to the security's coupon rate. In order to estimate the cash flows for these types of securities, we must determine how the size and timing of their expected cash flows will change in the future. For example, when estimating the future cash flows of a callable bond, we must account for the fact that when interest rates change the expected cash flows change. This introduces an additional layer of complexity to the valuation process. For bonds with embedded options, estimating cash flows is accomplished by introducing a parameter that reflects the expected volatility of interest rates.

Determining the Appropriate Interest Rate or Rates

Once we estimate the cash flows for a fixed-income security, the next step is to determine the appropriate interest rate for discounting each cash flow. Before proceeding, we pause here to note that we will once again use the terms "interest rate," "discount rate," and "required yield" interchangeably throughout the chapter. The interest rate used to discount a particular security's cash flows will depend on three basic factors: (1) the level of benchmark interest rates; (2) the risks that the market perceives the securityholder is exposed to; and (3) the compensation the market expects to receive for these risks.

The minimum interest rate that an investor should require is the yield available in the marketplace on a default-free cash flow. For bonds whose cash flows are denominated in euros, yields on European government securities serve as benchmarks for default-free interest rates. In some European countries, the swap curve serves as a benchmark for pricing spread product (e.g., corporate bonds). For now, we can think of the minimum interest rate that investors require as the yield on a comparable maturity benchmark security.

The additional compensation or spread over the benchmark yield that investors will require reflects the additional risks the investor faces by acquiring a security that is not issued by a sovereign government. These yields spreads (discussed later in the chapter) will depend not only on the risks an individual issue is exposed to but also on the level of benchmark yields, the market's risk aversion, the business cycle, and so on.

For each cash flow estimated, the same interest rate can be used to calculate the present value. This is the traditional approach to valuation and it serves as a useful starting point for our discussion. We discuss the traditional approach in the next section and use a single interest rate to determine present values. By doing this, however, we are implicitly assuming that the yield curve is flat. Since the yield curve is almost never flat and a coupon bond can be thought of as a package of zero-coupon bonds, it is more appropriate to value each cash flow using an interest rate specific to that cash flow. After the traditional approach to valuation is discussed, we will explain the proper approach to valuation using multiple interest rates and demonstrate why this must be the case.

Discounting the Expected Cash Flows

Once the expected (estimated) cash flows and the appropriate interest rate or interest rates that should be used to discount the cash flows are determined, the final step in the valuation process is to value the cash flows. The present value of an expected cash flow to be received t years from now using a discount rate i is

$$\text{Present value}_t = \frac{\text{Expected cash flow in period } t}{(1+i)^t}$$

The value of a financial asset is then the sum of the present value of all the expected cash flows. Specifically, assuming that there are N expected cash flows:

$$\text{Value} = \text{Present value}_1 + \text{Present value}_2 + \ldots + \text{Present value}_N$$

DETERMINING A BOND'S VALUE

Determining a bond's value involves computing the present value of the expected future cash flows using a discount rate that reflects market interest rates and the bond's risks. A bond's cash flows come in two forms—coupon interest payments and the repayment of principal at maturity.

To illustrate the process, let's value a 4-year, 6% coupon bond with a maturity value of €100. The coupon payments are €6 for the next four years. In addition, on the maturity date, the investor receives the repayment of principal (€100). The value of a nonamortizing bond can be divided in two components: (1) the present value of the coupon payments (i.e., an annuity) and (2) the present value of the maturity value (i.e., a lump sum). Therefore, when a single discount rate is employed, a bond's value can be thought of as the sum of two presents values—an annuity and a lump sum.

We now have everything in place to value an annual coupon-paying bond. Recall, the present value of an annuity is equal to

$$\text{Annuity payment} \times \left[\frac{1 - \dfrac{1}{(1+r)^{\text{no. of years}}}}{r} \right]$$

where r is the *annual* discount rate.

The present value of the maturity value is just the present value of a lump sum and is equal to

$$\text{Present value of the maturity value } = \frac{\$100}{(1 + i)^{\text{no. of years}}}$$

We will value our 4-year, 6% coupon bond under three different scenarios. These scenarios are defined by the relationship between the discount rate or required yield and the coupon rate. In the first scenario, we will consider the case when the annual discount rate and the coupon rate are equal. For the second scenario, we will value the bond when the discount rate is greater than the coupon rate. The last scenario assumes the discount rate is less than the coupon rate.

Valuing a Bond When the Discount Rate and Coupon Rate Are Equal

Now let's turn our attention to the 4-year 6% coupon bond and assume the annual discount is 6% and will be applicable for calculating the present value to all of the cash flows. Note that the coupon rate and the discount rate are the same. The relevant data are summarized below:

Annual coupon payment   = €6 (per €100 of par value)
Annual discount rate (i)   = 6%
Number of years to maturity = 4

To determine the present value of the coupon payments, we compute the following expression:

$$\text{€}6 \times \left[\frac{1 - \dfrac{1}{(1.06)^4}}{0.06} \right] = \text{€}20.79$$

Simply put, this number tells us how much the coupon payments contribute to the bond's value. In addition, the bondholder receives the maturity value when the bond matures so the present value of the maturity value must be added to the present value of the coupon payments. The present value of the maturity value is

$$\text{Present value of the maturity value } = \frac{\text{€}100}{(1.06)^4} = \text{€}79.21$$

This number (€79.21) tells us how much the bond's maturity value contributes to the bond's value. The bond's value is the sum of these two present values which in this case is €100 (€20.79 + €79.21).

When an option-free bond is issued, the coupon rate and the term to maturity are fixed. Consequently, as yields change in the market, bond prices will move in the opposite direction, as we will see in the next two scenarios. Generally, a bond's coupon rate at the time of issuance is set at approximately the required yield demanded by the market for comparable bonds. By comparison, we mean bonds that have the same maturity and the same risk exposure. The price of an option-free coupon bond at issuance will then be approximately equal to its par value. In the example presented above, when the required yield is equal to the coupon rate, the bond's price is its par value (€100).

Valuing a Bond When the Discount Rate Is Greater Than the Coupon Rate

We now take up the case when the discount rate is greater than the coupon rate. Suppose now that the relevant discount rate for our 4-year, 6% coupon bond is 7%. The data are summarized below:

Annual coupon payment = €6 (per €100 of par value)
Annual discount rate (i) = 7%
Number of years to maturity = 4

Note that the only number that has changed from the previous scenario is the annual discount rate which has increased from 6% to 7%. We compute the present value of the coupon payments in the same manner as before:

$$€6 \times \left[\frac{1 - \dfrac{1}{(1.07)^4}}{0.07} \right] = €20.2371$$

This number tells us that the coupon payments contribute €20.2371 to the bond's value.

The present value of the maturity value is

$$\text{Present value of the maturity value} = \frac{€100}{(1.07)^4} = €76.2895$$

This number (€76.2895) tells us how much the maturity value contributes to the bond's value. The bond's value is then €96.5266 (€20.2371

+ €76.2895). The price is less than par value and the bond is said to be trading at a *discount*. This will occur when the fixed coupon rate a bond offers (6%) is less than the required yield demanded by the market (the 7% discount rate). A discount bond has an inferior coupon rate relative to new comparable bonds being issued at par so its price must drop so as to bid up to the required yield of 7%. If the discount bond is held to maturity, the investor will experience a capital gain that just offsets the lower the current coupon rate so that it appears equally attractive to new comparable bonds issued at par.[1]

Valuing a Bond When the Discount Rate is Less Than the Coupon Rate

The final scenario is when the discount rate is less than the coupon rate. Suppose that the relevant discount rate for our 4-year, 6% coupon bond is 5%. The data are summarized below:

Annual coupon payment   = €6 (per €100 of par value)
Annual discount rate (i)   = 5%
Number of years to maturity = 4

Once again the only number that has changed for the scenario presented above is the annual discount rate, 5%. We compute the present value of the coupon payments in the same manner as before:

$$€6 \times \left[\frac{1 - \dfrac{1}{(1.05)^4}}{0.05} \right] = €21.276$$

This number tells us that the coupon payments contribute €21.276 to the bond's value.

The present value of the maturity value is

$$\text{Present value of the maturity value} = \frac{€100}{(1.05)^4} = €82.270$$

Once again, this number (€82.270) tells us how much the bond's maturity value contributes to the bond's value. The bond's value is then €103.546 (€21.276 + €82.270). That is, the price is greater than par value and the bond is said to be trading at a *premium*. This will occur

---

[1] We are ignoring the differential tax treatment of interest and capital gains/losses.

when the fixed coupon rate a bond offers (6%) is greater than the required yield demanded by the market (the 5% discount rate). Accordingly, a premium bond carries a higher coupon rate than new bonds (otherwise the same) being issued today at par so the price will be bid up and the required yield will fall until it equals 5%. If the premium bond is held to maturity, the investor will experience a capital loss that just offsets the benefits of the higher coupon rate so that it will appear equally attractive to new comparable bonds issued at par.[2]

THE PRICE/DISCOUNT RATE RELATIONSHIP

The preceding three scenarios illustrate an important general property of present value. The higher (lower) the discount rate, the lower (higher) the present value. Since the value of a security is the present value of the expected future cash flows, this property carries over to the value of a security: the higher (lower) the discount rate, the lower (higher) a security's value. We can summarize the relationship between the coupon rate, the required market yield, and the bond's price relative to its par value as follows:

> Coupon rate = Yield required by market ⇒ Price = Par value
> Coupon rate < Yield required by market ⇒ Price < Par value (discount)
> Coupon rate > Yield required by market ⇒ Price > Par value (premium)

Exhibit 3.1 depicts this inverse relationship between an option-free bond's price and its discount rate (i.e., required yield). There are two things to infer from the price/discount rate relationship depicted in the exhibit. First, the relationship is downward sloping. This is simply the inverse relationship between present values and discount rates at work. Second, the relationship is represented as a curve rather than a straight line. In fact, the shape of the curve in Exhibit 3.1 is referred to as *convex*. By convex, it simply means the curve is "bowed in" relative to the origin. This second observation raises two questions about the convex or curved shape of the price/discount rate relationship. First, why is it curved? Second, what is the import of the curvature?

The answer to the first question is mathematical and lies in the denominator of the bond pricing formula. Since we are raising one plus the discount rate to powers greater than one, it should not be surprising that the relationship between the level of the price and the level of the discount rate is not linear.

---

[2] We are ignoring the differential tax effects once again.

EXHIBIT 3.1   Price/Discount Rate Relationship for an Option-Free Bond

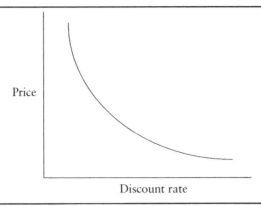

As for the importance of the curvature to bond investors, let's consider what happens to bond prices in both falling and rising interest rate environments. First, what happens to bond prices as interest rates fall? The answer is obvious: bond prices rise. How about the rate at which they rise? If the price/discount rate relationship was linear, as interest rates fell, bond prices would rise at a constant rate. However, the relationship is not linear, it is curved and curved inward. Accordingly, when interest rates fall, bond prices *increase* at an *increasing* rate. Now, let's consider what happens when interest rates rise. Of course, bond prices fall. How about the rate at which bond prices fall? Once again, if the price/discount rate relationship were linear, as interest rates rose, bond prices would fall at a constant rate. Since it curved inward, when interest rates rise, bond prices *decrease* at a *decreasing* rate. In Chapter 4, we will explore more fully the implications of the curvature or convexity of the price/discount rate relationship.

TIME PATH OF BOND

As a bond moves towards its maturity date, its value changes. More specifically, assuming that the discount rate does not change, a bond's value:

1. Decreases over time if the bond is selling at a premium.
2. Increases over time if the bond is selling at a discount.
3. Is unchanged if the bond is selling at par value.[3]

---

[3] We are assuming the bond is valued on its coupon anniversary dates.

At the maturity date, the bond's value is equal to its par or maturity value. So, as a bond's maturity approaches, the price of a discount bond will rise to its par value and a premium bond will fall to its par value— a characteristic sometimes referred to as "pull to par value."

Time Path of a Premium Bond

To illustrate what happens to a bond selling at a premium, consider once again the 4-year, 6% coupon bond. When the discount rate is 5%, the bond's price is €103.546. Suppose that one year later, the discount rate is still 5%. There are only three cash flows remaining since the bond is now a 3-year security. We compute the present value of the coupon payments in the same way as before:

$$\text{€}6 \times \left[\frac{1 - \dfrac{1}{(1.05)^3}}{0.05} \right] = \text{€}16.344$$

The present value of the maturity value is

$$\text{Present value of the maturity value} = \frac{\text{€}100}{(1.05)^3} = \text{€}86.3838$$

The bond's value is then €102.7278 (€16.344 + €86.3838).

As the bond moves toward maturity with no change in the discount rate, the price has declined from €103.546 to €102.7278. What are the mechanics of this result? The value of a coupon bond can thought of as the sum of two present values—the present value of the coupon payments and the present value of the maturity value. What happens to each of these present values as the bond moves toward maturity with no change in the discount rate? The present value of the coupon payments falls for the simple reason that there are fewer coupon payments remaining. Correspondingly, the present value of the maturity value rises because it is one year closer to the present. What is the net effect? The present value of the coupon payments fall by more than the present value of the maturity value rises so the bond's value declines or is pulled down to par.

The intuition for the result reveals a great deal about bond valuation. Why does the present value of the coupon payments fall by more than the present value of the maturity value rises? Recall why a coupon bond sells at a premium in the first place. The answer is because it offers a higher coupon rate (6%) than new comparable bonds issued at par (5%). So, a premium bond's value is driven by its relatively high coupon payments. As the premium bond marches toward maturity and these coupon payments are delivered to investors, there are fewer and fewer "high coupon" payments remaining. So, the bond's premium must shrink and the bond price declines toward par.

Time Path of a Discount Bond

Now suppose our 4-year, 6% coupon bond is selling at a discount. When the discount rate is 7%, the bond's price is €96.5266. Suppose that one year later, the discount rate is still 7%. We compute the present value of the coupon payments as shown below:

$$\text{€}6 \times \left[\frac{1 - \dfrac{1}{(1.07)^3}}{0.07} \right] = \text{€}15.7457$$

The present value of the maturity value is

$$\text{Present value of the maturity value} = \frac{\text{€}100}{(1.07)^3} = \text{€}81.6298$$

The bond's price increases from €96.5266 to €97.3755. Let's review the present value mechanics for this result. The present value of a discount bond's coupon payments falls for the same reason as before—as we march toward maturity, there are fewer coupon payments remaining so the present value of the remaining coupon payments must decline. As for the present value of the maturity value, it rises just like before and for the same reason—it is closer to the present. What is the net effect of these two forces for a discount bond? The present value of the maturity value rises by more than the present value of the coupon payments declines so the bond's value rises.

Why does the present value of the maturity value rise by more than the present value of the coupon payments falls? A coupon bond sells at a discount because it offers a lower coupon rate (6%) than new comparable bonds issued at par (7%). So, relative to a bond selling at par, the repayment of the principal at maturity is a relatively more important cash flow. To be sure, it is the capital gain we obtain from this payment if the bond is held to maturity that offsets the below current coupon interest payments. As the discount bond moves toward maturity, the receipt of the maturity value gets closer and closer. So, the discount must shrink and the bond's value rises toward par.

The Pull to Par Value

To illustrate how the value of a bond changes as it moves towards maturity, consider the following three 10-year bonds for which the yield required by the market is 7%: a premium bond (8% coupon selling for 107.0236), a discount bond (6% coupon selling for 92.9764), and a par bond (7% coupon). Exhibit 3.2 shows the value of each bond as it moves towards maturity assuming that the 7% yield required by the market does not change. Notice the pull downward to par value for the premium bond and the pull upward to par value for the discount bond. Exhibit 3.3 is a graph showing how each bond's value changes as the maturity date approaches assuming the yield remains at 7%. Note that if the discount rate does not change, a par bond's value does not change as the bond marches towards maturity. We want to emphasize this is only true if we value the bond on coupon payment dates.

EXHIBIT 3.2   Movement of a Premium, Discount, and Par Bond as a Bond Moves Toward Maturity[a]

Term to Maturity in Years	Premium Bond 8% Coupon	Discount Bond 6% Coupon	Par Bond 7% Coupon
10	107.0236	92.9764	100.00
9	106.5152	93.4848	100.00
8	105.9713	94.0287	100.00
7	105.3893	94.6107	100.00
6	104.7665	95.2335	100.00
5	104.1002	95.8998	100.00
4	103.5460	96.5266	100.00
3	102.6243	97.3757	100.00
2	101.8081	98.1921	100.00
1	100.9346	99.0654	100.00
0	100.0000	100.0000	100.00

[a] All bonds selling to yield 7%.

EXHIBIT 3.3   Time Path of Three Bonds

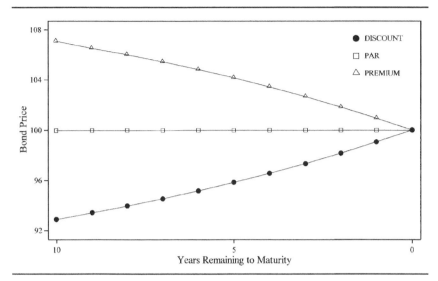

The Impact of Changing Discount Rates

In practice, of course, the discount rate will change over time. So the bond's value will change due to both the change in the discount rate and the change in the bond's cash flows as it marches toward maturity. For example, suppose that the discount rate for the 4-year, 6% coupon bond is 7% so that the bond is selling for €96.61. One year later, suppose that the discount rate appropriate for a 3-year, 6% coupon bond increases from 7% to 8%. The bond's price will decline from €96.61 to €94.85. If the discount rate had not increased, the price would have increased to €97.38. The price decline of €1.76 (€96.61 – €94.85) can be decomposed as follows:

Price change attributable to moving to maturity (no change in discount rate)	€0.77 (97.38 – 96.61)
Price change attribute to an increase in the discount rate from 7% to 8%	–€2.53 (94.85 – 97.38)
Total price change	–€1.76

VALUING A BOND BETWEEN COUPON PAYMENTS

In our discussion of bond valuation to this point, we have assumed that the bonds are valued on their coupon payment dates (i.e., the next coupon payment is one year away).

In order to value a bond with the settlement date between coupon payments, we must answer three questions. First, how many days are there until the next coupon payment date? From Chapter 1, we know the answer depends on the day count convention for the bond being valued. Second, how should we compute the present value of the cash flows received over the fractional period? Third, how much must the buyer compensate the seller for the coupon earned over the fractional period? This is accrued interest that we computed in Chapter 1. In the next two sections, we will answer these three questions in order to determine the full price and the clean price of a coupon bond.

Computing the Full Price

When valuing a bond purchased with a settlement date between coupon payment dates, the first step is to determine the fractional periods between the settlement date and the next coupon date. Using the appropriate day count convention, this is determined as follows:

$$w \text{ periods} = \frac{\text{Days between settlement date and next coupon payment date}}{\text{Days in the coupon period}}$$

Then the present value of each expected future cash flow to be received t years from now using a discount rate i assuming the next coupon payment is w years from now (settlement date) is:

$$\text{Present value}_t = \frac{\text{Expected cash flow}}{(1 + i)^{t - 1 + w}}$$

Note for the first coupon payment subsequent to the settlement date, $t = 1$ so the exponent is just w. This procedure for calculating the present value when a bond is purchased between coupon payments is called the "Street method." In the Street method, as can be seen in the expression above, coupon interest is compounded over the fractional period w.

To illustrate this calculation, suppose that a German government bond maturing 17 June 2005 is purchased with a settlement date of 8 July 2003. This bond's coupon rate is 2% and has a coupon date of 17 June. As a result, the next coupon payment date is 17 June 2004, while the previous coupon payment was 17 June 2003. There are two cash flows remaining: 17 June 2004 and 17 June 2005.

The final cash flow represents the last coupon payment and the maturity value of $100. Also assume the following:

1. Actual/actual day count convention.
2. 345 days between the settlement date and the next coupon payment date.
3. 366 days in the coupon period.

Then w is 0.9426 years (345/366). The present value of each cash flow assuming that each is discounted at a 2.122% annual discount rate is

$$Period\ 1: \text{Present value}_1 = \frac{€2}{(1.02122)^{0.9426}} = €1.9608$$

$$Period\ 2: \text{Present value}_2 = \frac{€102}{(1.02122)^{1.9426}} = €99.8858$$

The sum of the present values of the cash flows is €101.8466. This price is referred to as the *full price* (or the *dirty price*).

It is the full price the bond's buyer pays the seller at delivery. However, the very next cash flow received and included in the present value calculation was not earned by the bond's buyer. A portion of the next coupon payment is the *accrued interest*. From Chapter 1, we know that accrued interest is the portion of a bond's next coupon payment that the bond's seller is entitled to depending on the amount of time the bond was held by the seller. Recall, the buyer recovers the accrued interest when the next coupon payment is delivered.

Computing the Accrued Interest and the Clean Price

The last step in this process is to find the bond's value without accrued interest (called the *clean price* or simply *price*). To do this, the accrued interest must be computed. The first step is to determine the number of days in the accrued interest period (i.e., the number of days between the last coupon payment date and the settlement date) using the appropriate day count convention. For ease of exposition, we will assume in the example that follows that the actual/actual calendar is used. We will also assume there are only two bondholders in a given coupon period—the buyer and the seller.

As an illustration, we return to the previous example with the 2% German government bond. Since there are 366 days in the coupon period and 345 days from the settlement date to the next coupon period, there are 21 days (366 − 345) in the accrued interest period. Therefore, the percentage of the next coupon payment that is accrued interest is

$$\frac{21}{366} = 0.0574 = 5.74\%$$

Of course, this is the same percentage found by simply subtracting w from 1. In our example, w was 0.9426. Then, $1 - 0.9426 = 0.0574$.

Given the value of w, the amount of accrued interest (AI) is equal to

$$AI = \text{semiannual coupon payment} \times (1 - w)$$

Accordingly, using a 2% German government bond with a settlement date of 8 July 2003, the portion of the next coupon payment that is accrued interest is

$$\text{€2} \times (1 - 0.9426) = \text{€0.1147 (per €100 of par value)}$$

Once we know the full price and the accrued interest, we can determine the clean price. The clean price is the price that quoted in the market and represents the bond's value to the new bondholder. The clean price is computed as follows

$$\text{Clean price} = \text{Full price} - \text{Accrued interest}$$

In our illustration, the clean price is

$$\text{€99.7711} = \text{€99.8858} - \text{€0.1147}$$

It should be noted that the convention in the European bond markets is to quote the clean price and then calculate the accrued interest to obtain the dirty price. However, we want to emphasize that the answer is the same regardless of the order in which clean and dirty prices are calculated.[4]

SPOT RATES AND ARBITRAGE-FREE VALUATION

The approach described above for valuing a bond is to discount every cash flow using the same interest or discount rate. The fundamental flaw of this approach is that it views each security as the same package of cash flows. For example, consider a 5-year French government bond with a 4% coupon rate. The cash flows per €100 of par value would be four payments of €4 every year and €104 five years from now. In the

---

[4] See the discussion on day count conventions and accrued interest in Chapter 1.

procedure described thus far in this chapter, one discounts every cash flow using the same discount rate regardless of when the cash flows are delivered in time and the shape of the yield curve. Finance theory tells us that any security should be thought of as a package or portfolio of zero-coupon bonds.

The proper way to view the 5-year, 4% coupon French government security is as a package of zero-coupon instruments whose maturity value is the amount of the cash flow and whose maturity date coincides with the date the cash flow is to be received. Thus, the 5-year 4% coupon bond should be viewed as a package of five zero-coupon instruments that mature every year for the next five years. This approach to valuation does not allow a market participant to realize an arbitrage profit by breaking apart or "stripping" a bond and selling the individual cash flows (i.e., stripped securities) at a higher aggregate value than it would cost to purchase the security in the market. Simply put, arbitrage profits are possible when the sum of the parts is worth more than the whole or vice versa. Because this approach to valuation precludes arbitrage profits, we refer it as the *arbitrage-free valuation approach*.

By viewing any security as a package of zero-coupon bonds, a consistent valuation framework can be developed. Viewing a security as a package of zero-coupon bonds means that two bonds with the same maturity and different coupon rates are viewed as different packages of zero-coupon bonds and valued accordingly. Moreover, two cash flows that have identical risk delivered at the same time will be valued using the same discount rate even though they are attached to two different bonds.

To implement the arbitrage-free approach it is necessary to determine the theoretical rate that a government would have to pay on a zero-coupon security. We say "theoretical" because the only zero-coupon securities issued by most European governments are very short-term with original maturities of one year or less. Zero-coupon bonds are, however, created by dealer firms. The name given to the zero-coupon rate is the *spot rate*. There are various techniques for computing spot rates with coupon government bonds trading at par (i.e., a par coupon yield curve). The most common technique used is called bootstrapping. There are also econometric techniques that can be used.

Given the spot rates for each maturity, the arbitrage-free value of a government bond for which the spot rates apply is found as follows:

$$\text{Price} = \frac{C}{(1+z_1)^1} + \frac{C}{(1+z_2)^2} + \ldots + \frac{C+M}{(1+z_N)^N}$$

EXHIBIT 3.4 Determination of the Arbitrage-Free Value of an 8%, 10-Year Government Bond

Period	Years	Cash Flow (€)	Spot Rate (%)	Present Value (€)
1	0.5	€4.00	3.0000	€3.9409
2	1.0	4.00	3.3000	3.8712
3	1.5	4.00	3.5053	3.7968
4	2.0	4.00	3.9164	3.7014
5	2.5	4.00	4.4376	3.5843
6	3.0	4.00	4.7520	3.4743
7	3.5	4.00	4.9622	3.3694
8	4.0	4.00	5.0650	3.2747
9	4.5	4.00	5.1701	3.1791
10	5.0	4.00	5.2772	3.0828
11	5.5	4.00	5.3864	2.9861
12	6.0	4.00	5.4976	2.8889
13	6.5	4.00	5.6108	2.7916
14	7.0	4.00	5.6643	2.7055
15	7.5	4.00	5.7193	2.6205
16	8.0	4.00	5.7755	2.5365
17	8.5	4.00	5.8331	2.4536
18	9.0	4.00	5.9584	2.3581
19	9.5	4.00	6.0863	2.2631
20	10.0	104.00	6.2169	56.3828
			Total	€115.2619

where C is the periodic coupon payment, M is the maturity value, N is the number of periods to maturity, and z_t is the zero-coupon rate applicable to period t.

For example, consider a 10-year government bond denominated in euros with an 8% coupon rate. Suppose that coupon payments are delivered semiannually and the annual spot rates are shown in the fourth column of Exhibit 3.4. The third column of the exhibit shows the cash flow every six months. The last column shows the present value of each cash flow discounted at the corresponding spot rate. The total in the last column is the arbitrage-free value of the bond, €115.2619.

To value a nongovernment bond, the arbitrage-free value is found by adding a suitable spread to the government spot rates. A spot rate curve can be created using any benchmark such as LIBOR.

VALUING A CREDIT-RISKY FLOATER

Thus far our coverage of valuation has been on fixed-rate coupon bonds. In this section we look at how to value credit-risky floaters. We begin our valuation discussion with the simplest possible case—a default risk-free floater with no embedded options. Suppose the floater pays cash flows quarterly and the coupon formula is 3-month LIBOR flat (i.e., the quoted margin is zero).[5] The coupon reset and payment dates are assumed to coincide. Under these idealized circumstances, the floater's price will always equal par on the coupon reset dates. This result holds because the floater's new coupon rate is always reset to reflect the current market rate (e.g., 3-month LIBOR). Accordingly, on each coupon reset date, any change in interest rates (via the reference rate) is also reflected in the size of the floater's coupon payment.

The discussion is easily expanded to include risky floaters (e.g., corporate floaters) without a call feature or other embedded options. A floater pays a spread above the reference rate (i.e., the quoted margin) to compensate the investor for the risks (e.g., default, liquidity, etc.) associated with this security. The quoted margin is established on the floater's issue date and is fixed to maturity. If the market's evaluation of the risk of holding the floater does not change, the risky floater will be repriced to par on each coupon reset date just as with the default-free floater. This result holds as long as the issuer's risk can be characterized by a constant markup over the risk-free rate.

The more likely scenario, however, is that the market's perception of the security's risk will change over time. A perceived change in the floater's risk manifests itself in a divergence between the quoted margin (which is fixed at issue) and the spread the market requires for bearing the security's risks—henceforth, the required margin. When this divergence occurs, the risky floater will not be repriced to par on the coupon reset date. If the required margin increases (decreases) relative to the quoted margin, the floater will be repriced at a discount (premium) to par value.

Intuitively, the pricing expression for a risky floater can be thought of as possessing two components:

1. A floater whose quoted margin and required margin are the same; and
2. A "differential risk annuity" that delivers payments equal to the difference between the quoted margin and the required margin multiplied by the par value.

Note it is the differential risk annuity that causes the floater's price to deviate from par on a coupon reset date. Specifically, if the required

---

[5] Quoted margin is also called the "index spread."

margin is above (below) the quoted margin, then the differential risk annuity will deliver negative (positive) cash flows and the floater's price will be reset at a discount (premium) to its par value.

We will illustrate this process using a hypothetical 4-year floater that deliver cash flows quarterly with a coupon formula equal to 3-month LIBOR plus 15 basis points and does not possess a cap or a floor. The coupon reset and payment dates are assumed to be the same. For ease of exposition, we will invoke some simplifying assumptions. First, the issue will be priced on a coupon reset date. Second, although floaters typically use an ACT/360 day-count convention, for simplicity we will assume that each quarter has 91 days. Third, we will assume initially that the LIBOR yield curve is flat such that all implied 3-month LIBOR forward rates are the same. (We will relax this assumption shortly.) Note the same principles apply with equal force when these assumptions are relaxed.

Since this floater matures in four years, there are 16 coupon payments to be made. Assume that 3-month LIBOR is 5% and will remain at that level until the floater's maturity. Finally, suppose the required margin is also 15 basis points so the quoted margin and the required margin are the same. Exhibit 3.5 illustrates the valuation process.

The first column in Exhibit 3.5 simply lists the quarterly periods. Next, Column (2) lists the number of days in each quarterly coupon period assumed to be 91 days. Column (3) indicates the assumed current value of 3-month LIBOR. In period 0, 3-month LIBOR is the current 3-month spot rate. In periods 1 through 16, these rates are implied 3-month LIBOR forward rates derived from the current LIBOR yield curve. For ease of exposition, we will call these rates forward rates. Recall for a floater, the coupon rate is set at the beginning of the period and paid at the end. For example, the coupon rate in the first period depends on the value of 3-month LIBOR at period 0 plus the quoted margin. In this first illustration, 3-month LIBOR is assumed to remain constant at 5%. Column (4) is the quoted margin of 15 basis points and remains fixed to maturity.

The cash flow is found by multiplying the coupon rate and the maturity value (assumed to be 100). However, the coupon rate (the forward rate in the previous period plus the quoted margin) must be adjusted for the number of days in the quarterly payment period. The formula to do so is

$$\frac{\text{Coupon rate} \times \text{Number of days in period}}{360} \times 100$$

In addition to the projected cash flow, in period 16 the investor receives the maturity value of 100. The projected cash flows four our hypothetical 4-year floater are shown in Column (5).

EXHIBIT 3.5 Valuing a Risk Floater When the Market's Required Margin Equals the Quoted Margin[a]

(1) Coupon Period	(2) Day Count	(3) Forward Rate (%)	(4) Quoted Margin (%)	(5) Cash Flow (€)	(6) Required Margin (%)	(7) Discount Factor	(8) PV of Cash Flow (€)
0	91	5.00				1.000000	
1	91	5.00	0.15	€1.301806	0.15	0.987149	€1.285076
2	91	5.00	0.15	1.301806	0.15	0.974464	1.268562
3	91	5.00	0.15	1.301806	0.15	0.961941	1.252260
4	91	5.00	0.15	1.301806	0.15	0.949579	1.236168
5	91	5.00	0.15	1.301806	0.15	0.937377	1.220282
6	91	5.00	0.15	1.301806	0.15	0.925331	1.204600
7	91	5.00	0.15	1.301806	0.15	0.913439	1.189120
8	91	5.00	0.15	1.301806	0.15	0.901701	1.173839
9	91	5.00	0.15	1.301806	0.15	0.890113	1.158755
10	91	5.00	0.15	1.301806	0.15	0.878675	1.143864
11	91	5.00	0.15	1.301806	0.15	0.867383	1.129164
12	91	5.00	0.15	1.301806	0.15	0.856237	1.114654
13	91	5.00	0.15	1.301806	0.15	0.845233	1.100329
14	91	5.00	0.15	1.301806	0.15	0.834371	1.086189
15	91	5.00	0.15	1.301806	0.15	0.823649	1.072231
16	91	5.00	0.15	101.301800	0.15	0.813065	82.264910

Price = €100.000000

[a] Assumes 3-month LIBOR remains constant at 5%.

It is from the assumed values of 3-month LIBOR (i.e., the current spot rate and the implied forward rates) and the required margin in Column (6) that the discount rate that will be used to determine the present value of the cash flows will be calculated. The discount factor is found as follows:

$$\frac{\text{Discount factor in the previous period}}{1 + (\text{Fwd. rate in previous period} + \text{Required margin}) \times \text{No. of days in period}/360}$$

The discount factors are shown in Column (7).

Finally, Column (8) is the present value of each of the cash flows and is computed by taking the product of the cash flow in Column (5) and the dis-

EXHIBIT 3.6 Valuing a Risk Floater When the Market's Required Margin Equals the Quoted Margin[a]

(1)	(2)	(3)	(4)	(5)	(6)	(7)	(8)
Coupon Period	Day Count	Forward Rate (%)	Quoted Margin (%)	Cash Flow (€)	Required Margin (%)	Discount Factor	PV of Cash Flow (€)
0	91	5.00%				1.000000	
1	91	5.01	0.15%	€1.301806	0.15%	0.987149	€1.285076
2	91	5.02	0.15	1.304333	0.15	0.974439	1.270994
3	91	5.03	0.15	1.306861	0.15	0.961869	1.257029
4	91	5.04	0.15	1.309389	0.15	0.949437	1.243182
5	91	5.05	0.15	1.311917	0.15	0.937143	1.229453
6	91	5.06	0.15	1.314444	0.15	0.924984	1.215840
7	91	5.07	0.15	1.316972	0.15	0.912961	1.202344
8	91	5.08	0.15	1.319500	0.15	0.901071	1.188963
9	91	5.09	0.15	1.322028	0.15	0.889314	1.175698
10	91	5.10	0.15	1.324556	0.15	0.877689	1.162547
11	91	5.11	0.15	1.327083	0.15	0.866194	1.149511
12	91	5.12	0.15	1.329611	0.15	0.854828	1.136588
13	91	5.13	0.15	1.332139	0.15	0.843590	1.123779
14	91	5.14	0.15	1.337194	0.15	0.832458	1.113159
15	91	5.15	0.15	1.339722	0.15	0.821453	1.100519
16	91	5.16	0.15	101.342300	0.15	0.810573	82.145320

Price = €100.000000

[a] Assumes 3-month LIBOR increases 1 basis point per quarter until maturity.

count factor in Column (7). The floater's value is the sum of these present values and appears at the bottom of Column (8). Thus, a floater whose quoted margin and market's required margin are the same trades at par.

It is important to stress that this result holds regardless of the path 3-month LIBOR takes in the future. To see this, we replicate the process described in Exhibit 3.5 once again with one important exception. Rather than remaining constant, we assume that 3-month LIBOR forward rates increase by 1 basis point per quarter until the floater's maturity. These calculations are displayed in Exhibit 3.6. As before, the present value of the floater's projected cash flows is 100. When the market's required margin equals the quoted margin, any increase/decrease in the floater's projected cash flows will result in an offsetting increase/

decrease in the floater's discount factors leaving the total present value of the cash flow equal to par.

Now let's consider the case when the required margin does not equal the quoted margin. A risky floater can be separated into two components. Namely, a floater selling at par (i.e., the required margin equals the floater's quoted margin) and a "differential risk annuity" that causes the floater to deviate from par. A differential risk annuity is a series of constant payments (until a floater's maturity date) equal to the difference between the quoted margin and the required margin multiplied by the par value. A position in a risky floater can be described as a long position in a par floater and a long (short) position in a differential risk annuity. A long (short) position in the differential risk annuity indicates that the required margin has decreased (increased) since the floater's issue date. Accordingly, the price of a risky floater is equal to par plus the present value of the differential risk annuity when the required margin and the quoted margin are not the same.

To illustrate, we will value the same hypothetical 4-year floater assuming that the required margin is now 20 basis points. For this to occur, some dimension of the floater's risk or the market must have increased since the floater's issuance. Now in order to be reset to par, our floater would hypothetically have to possess a coupon rate equal to 3-month LIBOR plus 20 basis points. Since the quoted margin is fixed, the floater's price must fall to reflect the market's perceived increase in the security's risk.

Exhibit 3.7 illustrates the calculation. Once again for simplicity, we assume that 3-month LIBOR remains unchanged at 5% and there are 91 days in each coupon period. Since a risky floater can be thought of as par plus the differential risk annuity, all that is necessary is to take the present value of the annuity. Each annuity payment is computed as follows:

Differential risk annuity payment

$$= \frac{[(\text{Quoted margin} - \text{Required margin}) \times \text{Number of days in period}]}{360} \times 100$$

The quoted margin and required margin are in Columns (4) and (5), respectively. These cash flows are contained in Column (6). The discount factors are computed as described previously with the exception of the larger required margin. The discount factors appear in Column (7). The present value of the each cash flow is in Column (8) and is just the product of the cash flow (Column (6)) and its corresponding discount factor (Column (7)). The present value of the differential risk annuity is −0.1813 and is shown at the bottom of Column (8).

EXHIBIT 3.7 Valuing the Differential Risk Annuity When the Market's Required Margin Is Greater Than the Quoted Margin[a]

(1)	(2)	(3)	(4)	(5)	(6)	(7)	(8)
Coupon Period	Day Count	Forward Rate (%)	Quoted Margin (%)	Required Margin (%)	Cash Flow (€)	Discount Factor	PV of Cash Flow (€)
0	91	5.00%				1.000000	
1	91	5.00	0.15%	0.20%	−€0.01264	0.987026	−€0.01247
2	91	5.00	0.15	0.20	−0.01264	0.974221	−0.01231
3	91	5.00	0.15	0.20	−0.01264	0.961581	−0.01215
4	91	5.00	0.15	0.20	−0.01264	0.949106	−0.01200
5	91	5.00	0.15	0.20	−0.01264	0.936792	−0.01184
6	91	5.00	0.15	0.20	−0.01264	0.924638	−0.01169
7	91	5.00	0.15	0.20	−0.01264	0.912642	−0.01153
8	91	5.00	0.15	0.20	−0.01264	0.900801	−0.01139
9	91	5.00	0.15	0.20	−0.01264	0.889115	−0.01124
10	91	5.00	0.15	0.20	−0.01264	0.877579	−0.01109
11	91	5.00	0.15	0.20	−0.01264	0.866194	−0.01095
12	91	5.00	0.15	0.20	−0.01264	0.854956	−0.01081
13	91	5.00	0.15	0.20	−0.01264	0.843864	−0.01067
14	91	5.00	0.15	0.20	−0.01264	0.832915	−0.01053
15	91	5.00	0.15	0.20	−0.01264	0.822109	−0.01039
16	91	5.00	0.15	0.20	−0.01264	0.811443	−0.01026

Total Present Value = −€0.1813

[a] Assumes 3-month LIBOR remains constant at 5%.

Once the present value of the differential risk annuity is determined, the price of our hypothetical 4-year floater is simply the sum of 100 (price of the floater per 100 of par value when the quoted margin and required margin are the same) and the present value of the differential risk annuity. In our example,

Price of risky floater = 100 + (−0.1813) = 99.8187

When the required margin exceeds the quoted margin, the floater will be priced at a discount to par value. However, the size of the discount will depend on the assumed path 3-month LIBOR will take in the future.

Let's discuss the case when the required margin is less than the quoted margin. Assume the required margin is now 10 basis points and everything else remains the same. In this instance, it can be demonstrated that the price of the 4-year floater is given by

$$\text{Price of risky floater} = 100 + 0.1817 = 100.1817$$

As can be seen, when the required margin is less than the quoted margin, the floater will be priced at a premium to par value.

YIELD MEASURES

A bond's yield is a measure of its *potential* return. Market participants commonly assess a security's relative value by calculating a yield or some yield spread. There are a number of yield measures that are quoted in the market. These measures are based on certain assumptions necessary to carry out the calculation. However, they also limit effectiveness of a yield measure in gauging relative value. In this section, we will explain the various yield and yield spread measures as well as document their limitations.

SOURCES OF RETURN

The dollar return an investor expects to receive comes from three potential sources:

1. The periodic interest payments made by the issuer (i.e., coupon payments).
2. Any capital gain (or capital loss, which is a negative euro return) when the bond matures, is sold by the investor, or is called by the issuer.
3. Income earned from reinvestment of the bond's interim cash flows (i.e., coupon payments and principal repayments).

In order to be a useful indicator of a bond's potential return, a yield measure should account for all three of these potential sources of euro return in a reasonable way. We will begin our discussion by examining the three return sources in more detail.

We will illustrate the sources of euro returns using an example. In early July 2003, the 5-year German government bond (i.e., bund) was trading at 100.103 assuming a settlement date of 9 July 2003. The security description screen from Bloomberg is presented in Exhibit 3.8. This bond carries a coupon rate of 3% and matures on 11 April 2008. Cou-

EXHIBIT 3.8   Bloomberg Security Description Screen for a 5-Year German
Government Bond

```
GRAB                                                        Corp   DES
SECURITY DESCRIPTION                       Page 1/ 1
BUNDESOBL-142    OBL 3 04/08 #142   100.0530/100.1030   (2.99/2.97) BGN  @ 7/04
 ISSUER INFORMATION             IDENTIFIERS               1) Additional Sec Info
 Name BUNDESOBLIGATION          Common   016866261        2) Identifiers
 Type Sovereign                 ISIN     DE0001141422      3) Ratings
 Market of Issue EURO-ZONE      Wertpap. 114142            4) Fees/Restrictions
 SECURITY INFORMATION           RATINGS                    5) Sec. Specific News
 Country DE       Currency EUR  Moody's      Aaa           6) Custom Notes
 Collateral Type BONDS          S&P          NA            7) Issuer Information
 Calc Typ( 60)GERMAN BONDS      Composite    AAA           8) ALLQ
 Maturity  4/11/2008 Series  142  ISSUE SIZE               9) Pricing Sources
 NORMAL                         Amt Issued               10) Related Securities
 Coupon    3       FIXED        EUR 14,000,000   (M)
 ANNUAL          ACT/ACT        Amt Outstanding
 Announcement Dt  5/ 6/03       EUR 14,000,000   (M)
 Int. Accrual Dt  4/11/03       Min Piece/Increment
 1st Settle Date  5/16/03            100.00/       0.01
 1st Coupon Date  4/11/04       Par Amount         0.01
 Iss Pr  99.6700                BOOK RUNNER/EXCHANGE
                                                      65) Old DES
 NO PROSPECTUS                  ALL GERMAN SE        66) Send as Attachment
 €3.583BLN RETAINED FOR MKT INTERVENTION. ADD'L €7BLN ISS'D 6/03 @101.56%.
 Australia 61 2 9777 8600      Brazil 5511 3048 4500     Europe 44 20 7330 7500     Germany 49 69 920410
 Hong Kong 852 2977 6000 Japan 81 3 3201 8900 Singapore 65 6212 1000 U.S. 1 212 318 2000 Copyright 2003 Bloomberg L.P.
                                                                              G274-147-0 05-Jul-03 15:18:29
```

Source: Bloomberg Financial Markets.

pon payments are delivered annually on 11 April. Suppose a €1,000,000
of par value of these 5-year bonds are purchased and held to maturity.
What are the three sources of euro returns? These numbers can be found
on the yield analysis (YA) screen from Bloomberg in Exhibit 3.9.

Periodic Interest Payments

The most obvious source of dollar return is the annual coupon interest
payments. For the €1 million par value of this 5-year bond, the annual
coupon payments consist of five payments of €30,000 with the first
occurring on April 11, 2004. Since this bond has a settlement date that
does not fall on a coupon payment date, the buyer pays the seller
accrued interest. There are 89 days the first interest accrual date (11
April 2003) and the bond's settlement date of 9 July 2003. In addition,
there are 366 days in the annual coupon period. At settlement, the
buyer will pay the seller €7,295.08 (per €1 million in par value) in
accrued interest which is calculated as follows:

$$€30,000 \times (89/366) = €7,295.08$$

EXHIBIT 3.9 Bloomberg Yield Analysis Screen for a 5-Year German Government Bond

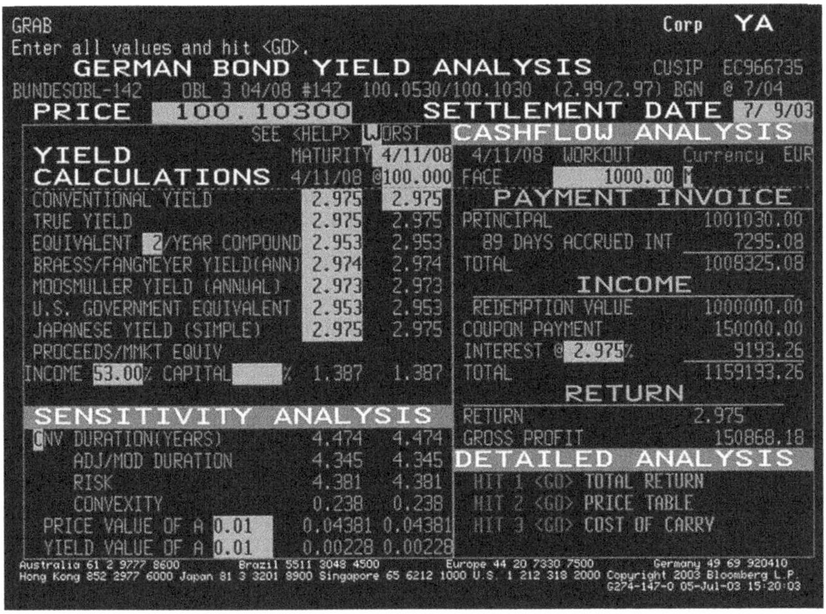

Source: Bloomberg Financial Markets.

The accrued interest is located on the right-hand side of the screen under "Payment Invoice" and is labeled "89 days accrued int."

Capital Gain or Loss[6]

The investor's tenure as a bond's owner ends as a result of one of the following circumstances. First, the investor may simply sell the bond and will receive the bond's prevailing market price plus accrued interest. Next, the issuer may call the bond in which case the investor receives the call price plus accrued interest or the investor may put the bond and receive the put price plus accrued interest. Lastly, if the bond matures, the investor will receive the maturity value plus the final coupon payment. Regardless of the reason, if the proceeds received are greater than the investor's initial purchase price, a capital gain is generated, which is an additional source of dollar return. Similarly, if the proceeds received are less than the investor's initial purchase price, a capital loss is gener-

---

[6] The definition of capital gain or loss here is different from that defined for tax purposes.

ated which is a negative dollar return. For the 5-year bond described above, the purchase price is €1,008,325.08 (i.e., the clean price plus the accrued interest). Thus, if the investor holds this bond until the maturity date of 11 April 2009, the investor will realize a capital loss of €8,325 (€1,000,000 × €1,008,325.08).

Reinvestment Income

The source of dollar return called *reinvestment income* represents the interest earned from reinvesting the bond's interim cash flows (interest and/or principal payments) until the bond is removed from the investor's portfolio. With the exception of zero-coupon bonds, fixed income securities deliver coupon payments that can be reinvested. Moreover, amortizing securities (e.g., mortgage-backed and asset-backed securities) make periodic principal repayments which can also be invested.

As an example, if a €1 million par value position of this 5-year bond is held to maturity, the investor will receive €150,000 in coupon payments over the next five years. The total coupon payments can be found on the left-hand side of the YA screen in Exhibit 3.9 and are labeled "Coupon payment." Suppose an investor can reinvest each of these five annual coupon payments at say 2.975% compounded annually.[7] Recall the general formula for the future value of an ordinary annuity when payments occur m times per year is

$$FV_n = A\left[\frac{(1+i)^n - 1}{i}\right]$$

where

A = Annual annuity of payment (€)
i = Annual interest rate (in decimal form)
N = Number of payments

Accordingly, the future value of five annual payments of €30,000 to be received plus the interest earned by investing the payments at 2.975% compounded annually is found as follows:

A = 30,000
i = 0.03
N = 5

Therefore,

---

[7] The interest rate was not chosen arbitrarily; the 5-year bond's yield to maturity (discussed shortly) is 2.975%.

$$FV_5 = €30,000\left[\frac{(1.02975)^5 - 1}{0.02975}\right]$$
$$= €30,000(5.3064) = €159.193.26$$

Thus the coupon payments and reinvestment income together are €159,194.49. The reinvestment income alone is €9,193.26, which is found by subtracting the total coupon payments (€159,193,26 − €150,000). This number matches the reinvestment income (labeled as "Interest 2.975%") presented in the yield analysis screen in Exhibit 3.9.

TRADITIONAL YIELD MEASURES

There are several yield measures commonly quoted by dealers and traders in the bond market. Among the more prominent are *current yield*, *yield to maturity*, *yield to call*, *yield to worst*, and *cash flow yield*. In this section, we will demonstrate how to compute various yield measures for a bond given its price. We will also highlight their limitations as measures of potential return.

Current Yield

The *current yield* of a bond is calculated by dividing the security's annual dollar coupon payment by the market price. The formula for the current yield is

$$\text{Current yield} = \frac{\text{Annual dollar coupon payment}}{\text{Price}}$$

To illustrate the calculation, consider a 5.25% coupon bond issued by BMW Finance NV in February 2001 that matures on 1 September 2006. The Security Description screen is presented in Exhibit 3.10. Moreover, the Bloomberg Yield Analysis screen is displayed in Exhibit 3.11. The market price of this bond is 107.299377. The current yield is located underneath the price and is 4.893%. The current yield calculation is shown below:

Annual dollar coupon payment = €100 × 0.0525 = €5.25

$$\text{Current yield} = \frac{€5.25}{€107.244377} = 0.04893 = 4.893\%$$

EXHIBIT 3.10   Bloomberg Security Description Screen for a BMW Finance Bond

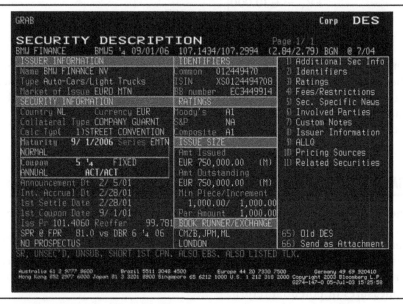

Source: Bloomberg Financial Markets.

EXHIBIT 3.11   Bloomberg Yield Analysis Screen for a BMW Finance Bond

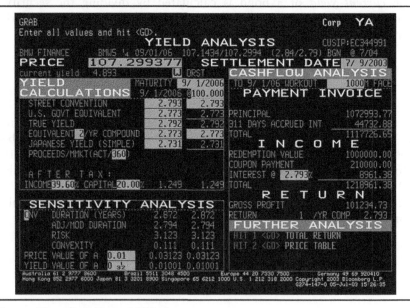

Source: Bloomberg Financial Markets.

Current yield possesses a number of drawbacks as a potential return measure. Current yield considers only coupon interest and no other source of return that will affect an investor's yield. To see this, assume the current yield is a yield to perpetuity, the annual euro coupon payment is a perpetual annuity payment, and the security's price is the present value of the perpetual annuity. By rearranging terms such that the price equals the annual coupon payment divided by the current yield, we obtain the present value of a perpetual annuity formula as shown below

$$€107.299377 = \frac{€5.25}{0.04893}$$

Simply put, the current yield assumes that the bond delivers a perpetual annuity. As such, current yield ignores the capital gain that the investor will realize if the bond is held to maturity as well as any reinvestment income.

Yield to Maturity

The most common measure of yield in the bond market is the *yield to maturity*. The yield to maturity is simply a bond's internal rate of return. Specifically, the yield to maturity is the interest rate that will make the present value of the bond's cash flows equal to its market price plus accrued interest (i.e., the full price). To find the yield to maturity, we must first determine the bond's expected future cash flows. Then we search by trial and error for the interest rate that will make the present value of the bond's cash flows equal to the market price plus accrued interest.

To illustrate, consider once again the 5.25% coupon BMW Finance described in Exhibit 3.10. From the yield analysis screen in Exhibit 3.11, we can locate the bond's full price under the heading "Payment Invoice" on the right-hand side of the screen. The full price is €1,117,726.69 (labeled "Total") for a €1 million par value position. The cash flows of the bond are (1) annual payments of €5,250 for the next four years and (2) a payment of €1,000,000 at maturity. The interest rate that makes these cash flows equal to the full price is 2.793%.

Limitations of the Yield to Maturity Measure

At first blush, the yield to maturity appears to be an informative measure of a bond's potential return. It considers not only the coupon income but any capital gain or loss that will be realized by holding the bond to maturity. The yield to maturity recognizes the timing of the cash flows. It also considers the third source of euro return that we discussed earlier: reinvestment income. However, when calculating yield to maturity, we are implicitly assuming that the coupon payments can be reinvested at an interest equal to the semiannual yield to maturity.[8]

The following illustration demonstrates this. In what follows, the analysis will be cast in terms of euros. Be sure to keep in mind the distinction between *total future euros* which are equal to all euros that the bond investor expects to receive (including the recovery of the principal) and the *total euro return* which is equal to the euros the investor expects to realize from the three sources of return, namely, coupon payments, capital gain/loss, and reinvestment income.

Let's illustrate the distinction between total future euros and total euro return with a simple example. Suppose one invested €100 for 10 years at 7% compounded annually. What are the total future euros that will result from this investment? This is nothing more than asking for the future value invested of €100 at 7% for 10 years. The total future euros generated are €196.72, as shown below

$$\text{Total future euros} = €100(1.07)^{10} = €196.72$$

The total future euros of this investment (€196.72) are comprised of the return of principal €100 and the total interest of €96.72. If we subtract the amount invested (€100) from the total future euros, the difference is €96.72, which is the total euro return.

Consider a hypothetical 10-year bond selling at par (€100) with a coupon rate of 7%. Assume the bond delivers coupon payments annually. The yield to maturity for this bond is 7%. Suppose an investor buys this bond, holds it to maturity, and receives the maturity value of €100. In addition, the investor receives 10 annual coupon payments of €7 and can reinvest them every year that they received at an annual rate of 7%. What are the total future euros assuming a 7% reinvestment rate? As demonstrated above, an investment of €100 must generate €196.72 in order to generate a yield of 7% compounded semiannually. Alternatively, the bond investment of €100 must deliver a total euro return of €96.72.

Let us partition the total dollar return for this bond into its three components: coupon payments, capital gain/loss, and reinvestment income. The coupon payments contribute €70 of the total euro return. The capital gain/loss component is zero because the bond is purchased at par and held to maturity. Lastly, the remainder of the total euro return (€26.72) must be due to reinvestment income.

---

[8] This assumes that the bond in question pays semiannual cash flows. If the bond pays annual cash flows, the cash flows must be reinvested at the annual yield to maturity.

To verify this, this par bond's total euro return of €96.72 is driven by two sources of euro return: coupon payments and reinvestment income. Recall from the beginning of the chapter, the reinvestment income can be determined using the future value of an ordinary annuity formula. Accordingly, the future value of 10 annual payments of €7 to be received plus the interest earned by investing the payments at 7% compounded annually is found as follows:

A = €7
i = 0.07
N = 10

Therefore,

$$FV_{10} = €7\left[\frac{(1.07)^{10} - 1}{0.07}\right]$$
$$= €7(13.8171) = €96.72$$

Thus, the coupon payments and reinvestment income together are €96.72 which agrees with total euro return from our earlier calculation. The reinvestment income alone is €26.72 (€96.72 − €70).

Clearly, the investor will only realize the yield to maturity that is computed at the time of purchase if the following two assumptions hold:

Assumption 1: The coupon payments can be reinvested at the yield to maturity.
Assumption 2: The bond is held to maturity.

With respect to the first assumption, the risk that an investor faces is that future interest rates will be less than the yield to maturity at the time the bond is purchased. This risk is called *reinvestment risk.* As for the second assumption, if the bond is not held to maturity, it may have to be sold for less than its purchase price, resulting in a return that is less than the yield to maturity. This risk is called *interest rate risk.*

Factors Affecting Reinvestment Risk

There are two characteristics of a bond that affect the degree of reinvestment risk. First, for a given yield to maturity and a given nonzero coupon rate, the longer the maturity the more the bond's total return is dependent on reinvestment income to realize the yield to maturity at the time of purchase. The implication is that the yield to maturity measure for long-term coupon bonds tells us little about the potential return an investor may realize if the bond is held to maturity. For long-term bonds, the reinvestment income component will be the most important source of total dollar return.

The second bond characteristic that affects reinvestment income is the coupon rate. For a coupon bond of a given maturity and yield to maturity, the higher the coupon rate, the more dependent the bond's total dollar return will be on the reinvestment of the coupon payments in order to produce the yield to maturity at the time of purchase. In other words, holding maturity and yield to maturity constant, a bond selling at a premium will be more dependent on reinvestment income than a bond selling at par. This is true because the reinvestment income must offset the capital loss realized by holding the premium bond to maturity. Conversely, a bond selling at a discount depends less on reinvestment income than a bond selling at par because a portion of the return is derived from the capital gain that is realized from maturing the bond. For a zero-coupon bond, none of the bond's total dollar return is dependent on reinvestment income. Hence, a zero-coupon bond has no reinvestment risk if held to maturity.

YIELD TO CALL

For callable bonds, the market convention is to calculate a yield to call in addition to a yield to maturity. A callable bond may be called at more than one price and these prices are specified in a call price schedule. The yield to call assumes that the issuer will call the bond at some call date and the call price is then specified in the call schedule

The procedure for calculating the yield to call is the same as that for the yield to maturity: determine the interest rate that will make the present value of the expected cash flows equal to the market price plus accrued interest. The expected cash flows are the coupon payments to a particular call date in the future and the call price.

To illustrate the various yield to call measures, consider a callable bond with a 5.75% coupon issued by DZ Bank. The Security Description screen from Bloomberg is presented in Exhibit 3.12. The bond matures on 10 April 2012 and is callable on coupon anniversary dates until maturity at a call price of 100. Exhibit 3.13 present the Yields to Call screen. Using a settlement date of 22 July 2003, the various yield to call measures are presented.

Yield to Custom

Yield to custom computes a yield to call for a call date and a price specified by the user. Typically, a bond does not have one call price but a call schedule which sets forth the call price based on when the issuer can

EXHIBIT 3.12 Bloomberg Security Description Screen for a DZ Bank Bond

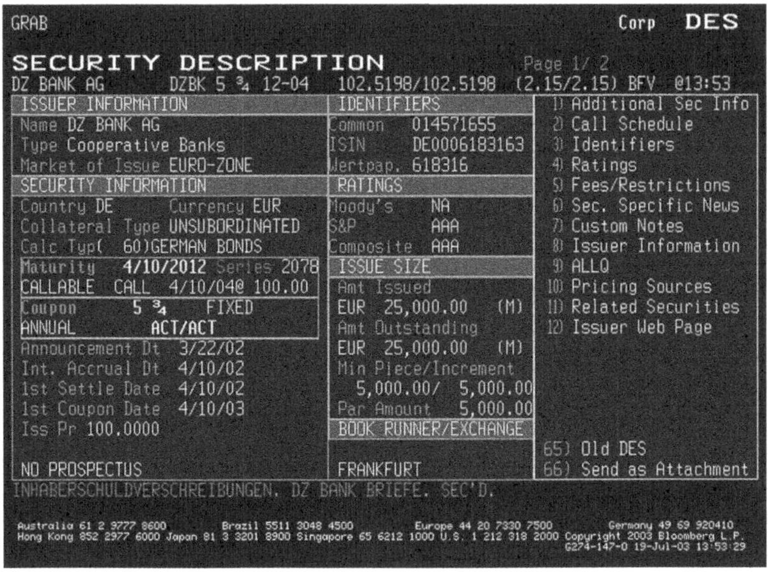

Source: Bloomberg Financial Markets.

EXHIBIT 3.13 Bloomberg Yields to Call Screen for a DZ Bank Bond

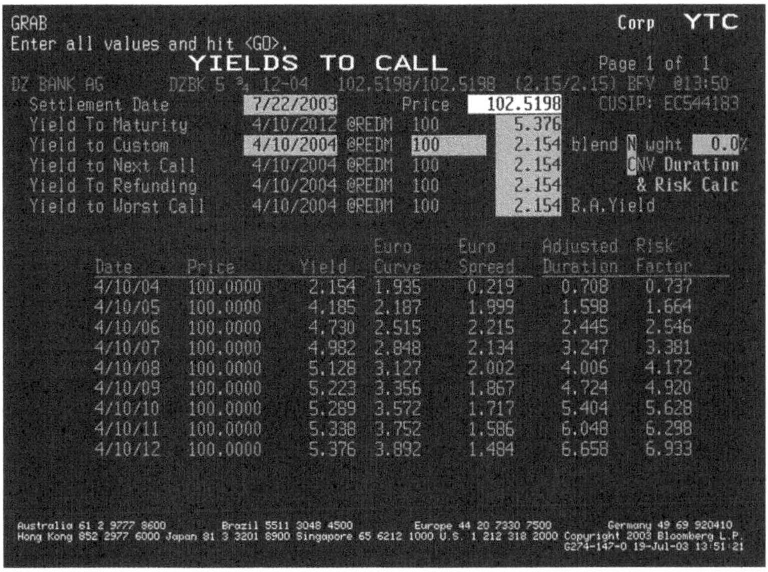

Source: Bloomberg Financial Markets.

exercise the call option. Bloomberg's YTC screen allows the user to select any call date in the future to compute a yield to call for the designated bond. The call price according to the call schedule for the particular date selected will be used in the yield calculation.

Yield to Next Call

Yield to next call is the yield to call for the next call date after the current settlement date. For the DZ Bank bond, the next call date is 10 April 2004. The yield to next call is 2.154%. Specifically, an annual interest of 2.154% makes the present value of the next coupon payment and the call price of €100 (i.e., the bond's cash flows assuming it will be called on 10 April 2004) equal to the current market price of 102.5198 plus the accrued interest.

Yield to Refunding

Yield to refunding is employed when bonds are currently callable but have some restrictions on the source of funds used to buyback the debt when a call is exercised. Namely, if a debt issue contains some refunding protection, bonds cannot be called for a certain period of time with the proceeds of other debt issues sold at a lower cost of money. As a result, the bondholder is afforded some protection if interest rates decline and the issuer can obtain lower cost funds to pay off the debt. It should be stressed that the bonds can be called with funds derived from other sources (e.g., cash on hand) during the refunded-protected period. The refunding date is the first date the bond can be called using lower cost debt. Given this backdrop, the yield to refunding is the discount rate (appropriately annualized) that discounts the cash flows to the first refunding date back to the bond's market price. For the DZ Bank bond shown in Exhibit 3.13, the yield to worst is 2.154%.

YIELD TO WORST

A yield can be calculated for every possible call date. Additionally, a yield to maturity can be calculated. The lowest of all these possible yields is called the *yield to worst*.

CASH FLOW YIELD

Mortgage-backed and asset-backed securities are backed by a pool of loans or receivables. For example, mortgage-backed securities are backed by a pool of mortgage loans. The cash flows for these securities include principal repayment as well as interest. Uncertainty in the cash flows arises because the individual borrowers whose loans comprise the pool usually have the option to prepay the loan in whole or in part usually without penalty prior to the scheduled principal repayment date. Thus, a mortgaged-backed or asset-backed security has an embedded short position in a prepayment option. Owing to this prepayment option, it is necessary to assume the rate at which prepayments will occur in order to project the security's cash flows. The assumed rate is called the *prepayment rate* or *prepayment speed*.

A yield can be calculated given the projected cash flows based on an assumed prepayment rate. The yield is the interest rate that will make the present value of the assumed cash flows equal to the clean price plus accrued interest. A yield calculated in this manner is called a *cash flow yield*.

Although it is commonly quoted by market participants, the cash flow yield suffers from limitations similar to the yield to maturity. These shortcomings include: (1) the projected cash flows assume that the prepayment speed will be realized; (2) the projected cash flows are assumed to be reinvested at the cash flow yield; and (3) the mortgage-backed or asset-backed security is assumed to be held until the final payoff of all the loans in the pool based on some prepayment assumption. If the cash flows are reinvested at rate lower than the cash flow yield (i.e., reinvestment risk) or if actual prepayments differ from those projected, then the cash flow yield will not be realized. Mortgage-backed and asset-backed securities are particularly sensitive to reinvestment risk since payments are usually monthly and include principal repayments as well as interest.

YIELD SPREAD MEASURES RELATIVE TO A SPOT RATE CURVE

Traditional yield spread analysis for a nongovernment bond involves calculating the difference between the risky bond's yield and the yield on a comparable maturity benchmark government security. As an illustration, let's use a 5.25% coupon BMW Finance bond described in Exhibit 3.10 that matures on 1 September 2006. Bloomberg's Yield & Spread Analysis screen is presented in Exhibit 3.14. The yield spreads against various benchmarks appear in a box at the bottom left-hand corner of the screen. Using a settlement date of 9 July 2003, the yield spread is 31 basis points versus the interpolated 3.1-year rate on the Euro Benchmark Curve. This yield spread measure is referred to as the *nominal spread*.

EXHIBIT 3.14 Bloomberg Yield and Spread Analysis Screen for a BMW Finance Bond

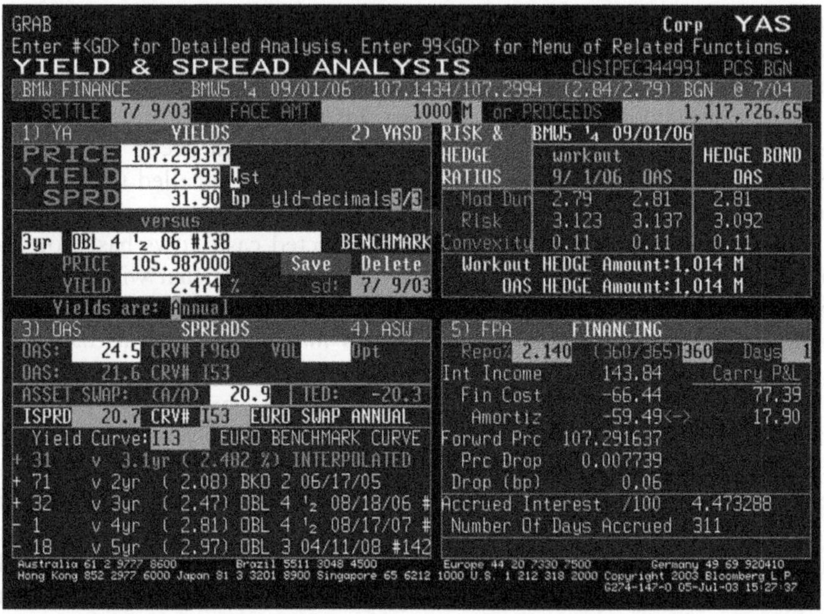

Source: Bloomberg Financial Markets.

The nominal spread measure has several drawbacks. For now, the most important is that the nominal spread fails to account for the term structure of spot rates for both bonds. We will pose an alternative spread measure that incorporates the spot rate curve.

Zero-Volatility Spread

The *zero-volatility spread*, also referred to as the *Z-spread* or *static spread,* is a measure of the spread that the investor would realize over the entire benchmark spot rate curve if the bond were held to maturity. Unlike the nominal spread, it is not a spread at one point on the yield curve. The Z-spread is the spread that will make the present value of the cash flows from the nongovernment bond, when discounted at the benchmark rate plus the spread, equal to the nongovernment bond's market price plus accrued interest. A trial-and-error procedure is used to compute the Z-spread.

To illustrate how this is done, consider the following two 5-year bonds:

EXHIBIT 3.15   Determination of the Z-Spread for a 7% 5-Year Bond

Years	Cash Flow (€)	Spot Rate (%)	Present value (€) assuming a spread of		
			100 bp	120 bp	150 bp
1	7	4.33	6.6458	6.6332	6.6144
2	7	4.44	6.2963	6.2725	6.2370
3	7	4.54	5.9545	5.9208	5.8707
4	7	4.73	5.6015	5.5593	5.4968
5	107	5.11	79.5430	78.7976	77.6952
		Total	104.0412	103.1835	101.9141

Issue	Coupon	Price	Yield to Maturity
Benchmark	5.058%	100.0000	5.058%
Nongovernment	7.000%	101.9141	6.5389%

The nominal spread for the nongovernment bond is 148.09 basis points. Let's use the information presented in Exhibit 3.15. The second column in Exhibit 3.15 shows the cash flows for the 7%, 5-year nongovernment issue. The third column is a hypothetical benchmark spot rate curve that we will employ in this example. The goal is to determine the spread that, when added to all the Treasury spot rates, will produce a present value for the non-government bond equal to its market price of €101.9141.

Suppose we select a spread of 100 basis points. To each benchmark spot rate shown in column 3 of Exhibit 3.15, 100 basis points are added. So, for example, the 1-year spot rate 5.33% (4.33% plus 1%). This spot rate is used to calculate the present values shown in the fourth column. Because the present value is not equal to the nongovernment issue's price of €101.9141, the Z-spread is not 100 basis points. If a spread of 120 basis points is tried, it can be seen from the next-to-last column of Exhibit 3.15 that the present value is €103.1835; again, because this is not equal to the nongovernment issue's price, 120 basis points is not the Z-spread. The last column shows the present value of the cash flows is equal to the nongovernment issue's price. Accordingly, 150 basis points is the Z-spread, compared to the nominal spread of 148.09 basis points.

What does the Z-spread represent for this nongovernment security? Since the Z-spread is relative to the benchmark euro spot rate curve, it represents a spread required by the market to compensate for all the risks of holding the nongovernment bond versus a government bond with the same maturity. These risks include credit risk, liquidity risk, and the risks associated with any embedded options.

Divergence Between Z-Spread and Nominal Spread

Generally, the divergence between the Z-spread and the nominal spread is a function of the term structure's shape and the security's characteristics. Among the relevant security characteristics are coupon rate, term to maturity, and type of principal repayment provision—nonamortizing versus amortizing. The steeper the term structure, the greater will be the divergence. For standard coupon-paying bonds with a bullet maturity (i.e., a single payment of principal), the Z-spread and the nominal spread will usually not differ significantly. For monthly-pay amortizing securities the divergence can be substantial in a steep yield curve environment.

Z-Spread Relative to Any Benchmark

A Z-spread can be calculated relative to any benchmark spot rate curve in the same manner. The question arises: what does the Z-spread mean when the benchmark is not the euro benchmark spot rate curve (i.e., default-free spot rate curve)? This is especially true in Europe where swaps curves are commonly used as a benchmark for pricing.[9] When the government spot rate curve is the benchmark, we indicated that the Z-spread for nongovernment issues captured credit risk, liquidity risk, and any option risks. When the benchmark is the spot rate curve for the issuer, for example, the Z-spread reflects the spread attributable to the issue's liquidity risk and any option risks. Accordingly, when a Z-spread is cited, it must be cited relative to some benchmark spot rate curve. This is essential because it indicates the credit and sector risks that are being considered when the Z-spread is calculated. Vendors of analytical systems such Bloomberg commonly allow the user to select a benchmark.

Option-Adjusted Spread

The spread measures discussed thus far fail to recognize any embedded options that may be present in a bond. A spread measure that takes into account embedded options is the *option-adjusted spread* or *OAS*. A discussion of how this spread measure is computed is beyond the scope of this chapter.[10] Basically, it is a byproduct of a model that is used for val-

---

[9] Swaps and swap rates are discussed in Chapter 19.

[10] See Chapter 6 in Frank J. Fabozzi and Steven V. Mann, *Introduction to Fixed Income Analytics* (Hoboken, NJ: John Wiley & Sons, Inc., 2001).

uing a security with one or more embedded options. The spread is referred to as "option adjusted" because the valuation model adjusts the cash flows based on how changes in the reference rates might be expected to change the cash flows of the security, taking into account any embedded options.

Despite its widespread use, the OAS has a number of limitations. Specifically, the OAS is model-dependent. Changing the assumptions of the valuation model may produce substantial differences in the computed OAS.

MARGIN MEASURES FOR FLOATING-RATE SECURITIES

There are several yield spread measures or margins that are routinely used to evaluate floaters. The four margins commonly used are spread for life, adjusted simple margin, adjusted total margin, and discount margin. To illustrate these measures, we will assume a floater that has a coupon formula equal to 3-month LIBOR plus 45 basis points and delivers cash flows quarterly.

Spread for Life

When a floater is selling at a premium/discount to par, a potential buyer of a floater will consider the premium or discount as an additional source of return. *Spread for life* (also called *simple margin*) is a measure of potential return that accounts for the accretion (amortization) of the discount (premium) as well as the constant index spread over the security's remaining life.

Spread for life is calculated using the following formula:

$$\text{Spread for life} = \left[\frac{100(100 - P)}{\text{Maturity}} + \text{Quoted margin} \right] \frac{100}{P}$$

where P is the market price (per 100 of par value) and Maturity is in years using the appropriate day-count convention. The quoted margin is measured in basis points.

To illustrate this calculation, suppose our hypothetical floater has a current coupon of 5.45%, matures in 345 days or 0.9583 of a year using an ACT/360, and is selling for 99.99 (i.e., P = 99.99). The simple margin is calculated as follows

$$\text{Spread for life} = \left[\frac{100(100 - 99.99)}{0.9583} + 45 \right] \frac{100}{99.99} = 46.0481 \text{ basis points}$$

Note that spread for life considers only the accretion/amortization of the discount/premium over the floater's remaining term to maturity but does not consider the level of the coupon rate or the time value of money.

Adjusted Simple Margin

The *adjusted simple margin* (also called *effective margin*) is an adjustment to spread for life. This adjustment accounts for a one-time cost of carry effect when a floater is purchased with borrowed funds. Suppose a security dealer has purchased €10 million of a particular floater. Naturally, the dealer has a number of alternative ways to finance the position—borrowing from a bank, repurchase agreement, etc. Regardless of the method selected, the dealer must make a one-time adjustment to the floater price to account for the cost of carry from the settlement date to the next coupon reset date. Given a particular financing rate, a carry-adjusted forward price can be determined as of the next coupon reset date. Once the carry-adjusted price is determined, the floater's adjusted price is simply the carry-adjusted price discounted to the settlement date by the reference rate. As before, the reference rate is assumed to remain constant until maturity. Note the cost of carry adjustment is simply an adjustment to the purchase price of the floater. If the cost of carry is positive (negative), the purchase price will be adjusted downward (upward). A floater's adjusted price is calculated as below:

$$\text{Adjusted price} = P - \frac{[(\text{Coupon rate})100 - (P + AI)rf]w}{[1 + (w)(rr_{\text{avg}})]}$$

where

Coupon rate	= current coupon rate of the floater (in decimal)
P	= market price (per 100 of par value)
AI	= accrued interest (per 100 of par value)
rf	= financing rate (e.g., the repo rate) (in decimal)

$$w = \frac{\text{Number of days between settlement and the next coupon payent}}{\text{Number of days in a year using the appropriate day-count}}$$

rr_{avg} = assumed (average) value for the reference rate until maturity (in decimal)

To illustrate this calculation, we use our hypothetical floater with a coupon rate of 0.0545 (in decimal) assuming a market price is 99.99. Assume the accrued interest is 0.3179 (per 100 of par value) and the repo rate to the next coupon reset date is 4.9755% (0.049755). Assume also that there are 71 days between the settlement date and the next coupon reset date and the day count is ACT/360. Given this information, w = 71/360 or 0.1972. We will also assume the value of the reference rate until maturity (rr_{avg}) is 0.05 (in decimal).

Given these assumptions, the adjusted price is 99.90031 as shown below:

$$\text{Adjusted price} = 99.99 - \frac{[(0.0545)100 - (99.99 + 0.3179)0.049755]0.1972}{[1 + (0.1972)(0.05)]}$$

$$= 99.90033$$

Once the adjusted price is determined, the adjusted simple margin is computed using the formula below:

$$\text{Adjusted simple margin} = \left[\frac{100(100 - P_A)}{\text{Maturity}} + \text{Quoted margin}\right]\frac{100}{P_A}$$

where P_A is the adjusted price, Maturity is measured in years using the appropriate day-count convention, and Quoted margin is measured in basis points.

To compute the adjusted simple margin for our floater, we use the following information:

Adjusted price = 99.90031
Days between the settlement date and the maturity date = 345
Quoted marging = 45 basis points
w = 345/360

Plugging this information into the equation for the adjusted simple margin we find that it is 55.458 basis points as shown below:

$$\text{Adjusted simple margin} = \left[\frac{100(100 - 99.90031)}{0.9583} + 45\right]\frac{100}{99.90031}$$

$$= 55.458 \text{ basis points}$$

Adjusted Total Margin

The *adjusted total margin* (also called *total adjusted margin*) adds one more refinement to the adjusted simple margin. Specifically, the adjusted total margin is the adjusted simple margin plus the interest earned by investing the difference between the floater's par value and the adjusted price. The current value of the reference rate (i.e., the assumed index) is assumed to be the investment rate. The adjusted total margin is calculated using the following expression:

Adjusted total margin

$$= \left[\frac{100(100 - P_A)}{\text{Maturity}} + \text{Quoted margin} + 100(100 - P_A)rr_{\text{avg}} \right] \frac{100}{P_A}$$

The notation used is the same as given above.

For our hypothetical floater we used in previous illustrations, the adjusted total margin is

Adjusted total margin

$$= \left[\frac{100(100 - 99.90031)}{0.9583} + 45 + 100(100 - 99.90031)0.05 \right] \frac{100}{99.90031}$$

$$= 55.957 \text{ basis points}$$

Discount Margin

One common method of measuring potential return that employs discounted cash flows is *discount margin*. This measure indicates the average spread or margin over the reference rate the investor can expect to earn over the security's life given a particular assumption of the path the reference rate will take to maturity. The assumption that the future levels of the reference rate are equal to today's level is the usual assumption. The procedure for calculating the discount margin is as follows:

Step 1. Determine the cash flows assuming that the reference rate does not change over the security's life.

Step 2. Select a margin.

Step 3. Discount the cash flows found in Step 1 by the current value of the reference rate plus the margin selected in Step 2.

Step 4. Compare the present value of the cash flows as calculated in Step 3 to the price. If the present value is equal to the security's price, the discount margin is the margin assumed in Step 2. If the present value is not equal to the security's price, go back to Step 2 and select a different margin.

For a security selling at par, the discount margin is simply the quoted margin.

EXHIBIT 3.16   Calculation of the Discount Margin for a Floater

Floater: Maturity   = 6 years
          Coupon rate   = Reference rate + 80 basis points
                             Resets every 6 months
          Maturity value = €100

(1)	(2)	(3)	(4)	(5)	(6)	(7)	(8)
	Rate	Flow	Assumed Margin				
Period	(%)	(€)[a]	80	84	88	96	100
1	10	€5.40	€5.1233	€5.1224	€5.1214	€5.1195	€5.1185
2	10	5.40	4.8609	4.8590	4.8572	4.8535	4.8516
3	10	5.40	4.6118	4.6092	4.6066	4.6013	4.5987
4	10	5.40	4.3755	4.3722	4.3689	4.3623	4.3590
5	10	5.40	4.1514	4.1474	4.1435	4.1356	4.1317
6	10	5.40	3.9387	3.9342	3.9297	3.9208	3.9163
7	10	5.40	3.7369	3.7319	3.7270	3.7171	3.7122
8	10	5.40	3.5454	3.5401	3.5347	3.5240	3.5186
9	10	5.40	3.3638	3.3580	3.3523	3.3409	3.3352
10	10	5.40	3.1914	3.1854	3.1794	3.1673	3.1613
11	10	5.40	3.0279	3.0216	3.0153	3.0028	2.9965
12	10	105.40	56.0729	55.9454	55.8182	55.5647	55.4385
	Present value = €100.00			€99.8269	€99.6541	€99.3098	€99.1381

[a] For periods 1–11: Cash flow = 100(Reference rate + 80 basis points) (0.5)
   For period 12: Cash flow = 100(Reference rate + 80 basis points) (0.5) + 100

For example, suppose that a 6-year floater selling for $99.3098 pays the reference rate plus a quoted margin of 80 basis points. The coupon resets every six months. Assume that the current value of the reference rate is 10%.

Exhibit 3.16 presents the calculation of the discount margin for this security. Each period in the security's life is enumerated in Column (1), while the Column (2) shows the current value of the reference rate. Column (3) sets forth the security's cash flows. For the first 11 periods, the cash flow is equal to the reference rate (10%) plus the quoted margin of 80 basis points multiplied by 100 and then divided by 2. In last 6-month period, the cash flow is €105.40—the final coupon payment of €5.40 plus the maturity value of €100. Different assumed margins appear at the top of the last five columns. The rows below the assumed margin indicate the present value of each period's cash flow for that particular value of assumed margin. Finally, the last row gives the total present value of the cash flows for each assumed margin.

For the five assumed margins, the present value of the cash flows is equal to the floater's price (€99.3098) when the assumed margin is 96 basis points. Accordingly, the discount margin on a semiannual basis is 48 basis points and correspondingly 96 basis points on an annual basis. (Notice that the discount margin is 80 basis points (i.e., the quoted margin) when the floater is selling at par.)

There are several drawbacks of the discount margin as a measure of potential return from holding a floater. First and most obvious, the measure assumes the reference rate will not change over the security's life. Second, the price of a floater for a given discount margin is sensitive to the path that the reference rate takes in the future except in the special case when the discount margin equals the quoted margin.

To see the significance of the second drawback, it is useful to partition the value of an option-free floater into two parts: (1) the present value of the security's cash flows (i.e., coupon payments and maturity value) if the discount margin equals the quoted margin and (2) the present value of an annuity which pays the difference between the quoted margin and the discount margin multiplied by 100 and divided by the number of periods per year.

$$P = 100 + \sum_{i=1}^{n} \frac{100(qm - dm)/m}{(1 + y_i + dm)^i}$$

where

P = price of the floater (per 100 of par value)
qm = quoted margin
dm = discount margin
y_i = assumed value of the reference rate in period i
n = number of periods until maturity
m = number of periods per year

In this framework, one can see as before that if the quoted margin is equal to the discount margin, the second term is zero and the floater will be valued at par. If the index spread is greater than (less than) the discount margin, the second term is positive (negative) and the floater will be valued at a premium (discount).

This framework is also quite useful for addressing the question: For a given discount margin, how does the present value of the floater's cash flows change given different assumptions about how the reference rate is

EXHIBIT 3.17   Bond Values Assuming Different Discounted Margins and Alternative Interest Rate Paths

Discounted Margin	Assumed Interest Rate Path	
	6-month LIBOR remains constant at 5.25%	6-month LIBOR increases 10 bp each period
100	98.6512	98.6549
50	100.0000	100.0000
0	101.3713	101.3676

expected to change in the future? Consider a floater that pays interest semiannually with the following characteristics:

Maturity   = 3 years
Coupon rate   = 6-month LIBOR + 50 bps
Maturity value = $100

For ease of exposition, assume that we value the security on its coupon anniversary date. Let's consider two paths that 6-month LIBOR can take in the next three years. In the first path, we assume that 6-month LIBOR will remain unchanged at say, 5.25%. In the second path, we assume that 6-month LIBOR will increase by 10 basis points each period for the next three years (i.e., 5.25%, 5.35%, 5.45%, 5.55%, 5.65%, 5.75%). Finally, we will value the floater assuming three different values (in basis points) for the discount margin: 0, 50 and 100. The values for the floaters associated with each discount margin and under each interest rate path are given in Exhibit 3.17.

There are several implications that we can draw from the results in Exhibit 3.17. First, as discussed previously, when the discount margin equals the quoted margin, the value of the floater equals 100 regardless of the assumed interest rate path. This result holds because any change in the discount rate is exactly offset by a corresponding increase/decrease in the coupon. However, when the discount margin differs from the quoted margin, the present value of the security's cash flows will depend on the assumed interest rate path.

What happens to the size of the discount/premium of a floater? When the discount margin is less than the quoted margin, the effect will be smaller because the cash flows are growing at a slower rate than the discount rate. If this occurs, the security will have a smaller premium than under the assumption of an unchanged reference rate. Conversely, when the discount margin is larger than the quoted margin, the effect is reversed. A smaller discount and a higher price will result owing to the fact that the cash flows are growing at a faster rate than the discount rate. These effects are even more pronounced as the term to maturity increases. This illustration clearly demonstrates that the discount margin possesses an important shortcoming as a measure of relative value.

CHAPTER 4

Measuring Interest Rate Risk

Frank J. Fabozzi, Ph.D., CFA
Frederick Frank Adjunct Professor of Finance
School of Management
Yale University

Steven V. Mann, Ph.D.
Professor of Finance
Moore School of Business
University of South Carolina

A general principle of valuation is the present value of expected future cash flow changes in the opposite direction from changes in the interest rate used to discount the cash flows. This inverse relationship lies at the heart of the major risk faced by fixed-income investors: *interest rate risk*. Interest rate risk involves the possibility that the value of a bond position or a bond portfolio's value will decline due to an adverse interest rate movement. Specifically, a long bond position's value will decline if interest rates rise, resulting in a loss. Conversely, for a short bond position, a loss will be realized if interest rates fall. To effectively control interest rate risk, a portfolio manager must be able to quantify the portfolio's interest rate risk exposure. The purpose of this chapter is to understand the dimensions of interest rate risk and explain how it is measured. Interest rate risk can be divided into two types of risk: level risk and yield curve risk. *Level risk* focuses on a change in a bond's value due to a parallel shift in the yield curve. Conversely, *yield curve risk* refers to the price impact due to changes in the shape, as opposed to a parallel shift, of the yield curve.

We will discuss two approaches for assessing the interest rate risk exposure of a bond or a portfolio. The first approach is the *full valuation approach* that involves selecting possible interest rate scenarios for how interest rates and yield spreads may change and revaluing the bond position. The second approach entails the computation of measures that approximate how a bond's price or the portfolio's value will change when interest rates change. The most commonly used measures are *duration* and *convexity*. We will discuss duration/convexity measures for bonds and bond portfolios. Finally, we discuss measures of yield curve risk.

THE FULL VALUATION APPROACH

The most obvious way to measure the interest rate risk exposure of a bond position or a portfolio is to revalue it when interest rates change. The analysis is performed for a given scenario with respect to interest rate changes. For example, a manager may want to measure the interest rate exposure to a 50 basis point, 100 basis point, and 200 basis point instantaneous change in interest rates. This approach requires the re-valuation of a bond or bond portfolio for a given interest rate change scenario and is referred to as the *full valuation approach*. It is sometimes referred to as *scenario analysis* because it involves assessing the exposure to interest rate change scenarios.

To illustrate this approach, suppose that a portfolio manager has a $50 million par value position in UK gilt principal strip (i.e., zero-coupon) that matures on June 7, 2021.[1] Exhibit 4.1 presents Bloomberg's Yield Analysis screen for this security. With a settlement date of May 30, 2003, the price is 45.36 with a corresponding yield of 4.435%. The market value of the position is £22,680,000 (45.36% × £50,000,000). Since the manager has a long position in this issue, she is concerned with a rise in yields since this will decrease the position's market value. To assess the portfolio's exposure to a rise in yields, the manager decides to examine how the strip's value will change if yields change instantaneously for the following four scenarios: (1) 50 basis point increase, (2) 100 basis point increase, (3) 150 basis point increase, and (4) 200 basis point increase. In other words, the manager wants to assess the consequences to the portfolio's value if the bond's yield increases from its current level at 4.435% to (1) 4.935%, (2) 5.435%, (3) 5.935%, and (4) 6.435%. Because this zero-coupon bond is option-free, valuation is straightforward. The strip's price per £100 of par value and the market value of the £50 million par position are shown in Exhibit 4.2. Also presented are the change in the market value and percentage change.

---

[1] A principal strip is a zero-coupon bond created from a bond's principal payment.

EXHIBIT 4.1   Bloomberg Yield Analysis Screen for a UK Gilt Principal Strip

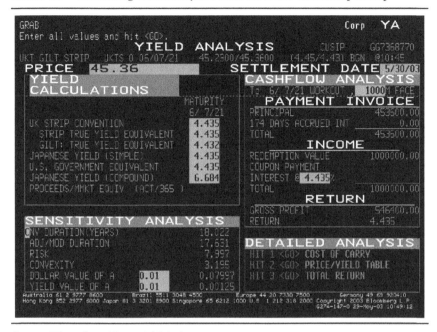

Source: Bloomberg Financial Markets.

EXHIBIT 4.2   Illustration of Full Valuation Approach to Assess the Interest Rate Risk of a Bond Position for Four Scenarios

Current bond position: UK gilt strip that matures 7 June 2021
Price: 45.36
Yield to maturity: 4.435%
Par value owned: £50 million
Market value of position: £22,680,000

Scenario	Yield Change (bp)	New Yield (%)	New Price	New Market Value (£)	Percentage Change in Market Value
1	50	4.935	41.5369	20,768,450	−8.043
2	100	5.435	38.0442	19,022,100	−16.130
3	150	5.935	34.8526	17,426,300	−23.160
4	200	6.435	31.9356	15,967,800	−29.600

EXHIBIT 4.3   Bloomberg Yield Analysis Screen for a 2-Year Italian Government Bond

```
GRAB                                                         Corp   YA
Enter all values and hit <GO>,
               YIELD  ANALYSIS                              CUSIP EC5262166
BTPS              BTPS 4 03/01/05   103.1330/103.1730  (2.17/2.15) BGN  @13:12
PRICE        103.173000        SETTLEMENT DATE 6/ 3/03
YIELD                       MATURITY  CASHFLOW  ANALYSIS
CALCULATIONS                  3/ 1/05  To   3/ 1/05WORKOUT      1000.00 M
  GROSS TRUE YIELD               2.147    GROSS PAYMENT INVOICE
  NET TRUE YIELD                 1.610  CURRENCY  EUR
  GROSS YIELD                    2.147  PRINCIPAL                  1031730.00
  NET YIELD                      1.610   94 ACCRUED DAYS             10217.40
  GROSS SEMI-ANNUAL TRUE YIELD   2.136  TOTAL                      1041947.40
  NET SEMI-ANNUAL TRUE YIELD     1.603    GROSS INCOME
  PROCEEDS/MMKT EQUIVALENT GROSS 2.135  REDEMPTION VALUE           1000000.00
  PROCEEDS/MMKT EQUIVALENT NET   1.640  COUPON PAYMENT               80000.00
                                        INTEREST @   2.147%          1295.24
                                        TOTAL                      1081295.24
                                          GROSS RETURN
GROSS SENSITIVITY ANALYSIS              GROSS PROFIT                 39347.84
  DURATION(YEARS)                1.688  RETURN                       2.135
  ADJ/MOD DURATION               1.652  DETAILED  ANALYSIS
  RISK                           1.722   HIT 1 <GO> COST OF CARRY
  CONVEXITY                      0.044   HIT 2 <GO> PRICE/YIELD TABLE
  DOLLAR VALUE OF A    0.01      0.01722 HIT 3 <GO> TOTAL RETURN
  YIELD VALUE OF A     0.01      0.00581
Australia 61 2 9777 8600      Brazil 5511 3048 4500   Europe 44 20 7330 7500      Germany 49 69 920410
Hong Kong 852 2977 6000 Japan 81 3 3201 8900 Singapore 65 6212 1000 U.S. 1 212 318 2000 Copyright 2003 Bloomberg L.P.
                                                                      G274-147-0 29-May-03 14:04:12
```

Source: Bloomberg Financial Markets.

In the case of a portfolio, each included bond is valued and the port-folio's total value is computed for a given scenario. For example, suppose that a portfolio manager has a portfolio that consists of the following two Italian government bonds: (1) a 4% coupon bond that matures on March 1, 2005 and (2) a 5.75% coupon bond that matures on February 1, 2033. Exhibits 4.3 and 4.4 present Bloomberg's Yield Analysis screens for these two securities. For the 2-year security, €10,000,000 of par value is owned. With a settlement date of June 3, 2003, the security's full price is 104.1947 with a yield of 2.147%. For the 30-year security, €20,000,000 of par value is owned. With a settlement date of June 3, 2003, the security's full price is 119.1198 with a yield of 4.727%. Suppose that the manager wants to assess the portfolio's interest rate risk for a 50, 100, 150, and 200 basis point increases in interest rates, assuming both the 2-year yield and the 30-year yield change by the same number of basis points. Exhibit 4.5 shows the exposure. Panel A of the exhibit shows the market value of the 2-year security for the four scenarios. Panel B does the same for the 30-year security. Panel C shows the total market value of the portfolio and the percentage change in the market value for the four outcomes.

EXHIBIT 4.4   Bloomberg Yield Analysis Screen for a 30-Year Italian Government Bond

```
GRAB                                                    Corp   YA
Enter all values and hit <GO>.
              YIELD ANALYSIS                        CUSIP EC5346845
BTPS          BTPS 5 ¾ 02/33   117.1220/117.1820  (4.73/4.73) BGN  @13:12
PRICE    117.182000         SETTLEMENT DATE 6/ 3/03
YIELD                  MATURITY  CASHFLOW ANALYSIS
CALCULATIONS           2/ 1/33  To   2/ 1/33WORKOUT      1000.00
  GROSS TRUE YIELD         4.727    GROSS PAYMENT INVOICE
  NET TRUE YIELD           4.073  CURRENCY  EUR
  GROSS YIELD              4.728  PRINCIPAL              1171820.00
  NET YIELD                4.073  122 ACCRUED DAYS         19378.50
  GROSS SEMI-ANNUAL TRUE YIELD 4.673  TOTAL             1191198.50
  NET SEMI-ANNUAL TRUE YIELD   4.032    GROSS INCOME
                                 REDEMPTION VALUE       1000000.00
                                 COUPON PAYMENT         1725000.00
                                 INTEREST @    4.727%   2002223.22
                                 TOTAL                  4727223.22
                                   GROSS RETURN
GROSS SENSITIVITY ANALYSIS       GROSS PROFIT           3536024.72
  DURATION(YEARS)          15.419  RETURN                    4.697
  ADJ/MOD DURATION         14.723  DETAILED ANALYSIS
  RISK                     17.538  HIT 1 <GO> COST OF CARRY
  CONVEXITY                 3.300  HIT 2 <GO> PRICE/YIELD TABLE
  DOLLAR VALUE OF A  0.01  0.17538  HIT 3 <GO> TOTAL RETURN
  YIELD VALUE OF A   0.01  0.00057
Australia 61 2 9777 8600     Brazil 5511 3048 4500   Europe 44 20 7330 7500      Germany 49 69 920410
Hong Kong 852 2977 6000 Japan 81 3 3201 8900 Singapore 65 6212 1000 U.S. 1 212 318 2000 Copyright 2003 Bloomberg L.P.
                                                                 G274-147-0 29-May-03 13:46:50
```

Source: Bloomberg Financial Markets.

In the illustration in Exhibit 4.5, it is assumed that both the 2-year and 30-year yields change by the same number of basis points. The full valuation approach can also handle scenarios where the yield curve does not change in a parallel fashion. Exhibit 4.6 illustrates this for our portfolio that includes the 2-year and the 30-year Italian government securities. The scenario analyzed is for a change in the yield curve's slope combined with changes in the level of yields. In the illustration in Exhibit 4.6, the following yield changes are assumed for the 2-year and the 30-year yields:

Scenario	Change in the 2-year rate (bp)	Change in the 30-year rate (bp)
1	40	20
2	60	40
3	80	60
4	100	80

The last panel in Exhibit 4.6 shows how the portfolio's market value changes for each scenario.

EXHIBIT 4.5 Illustration of Full Valuation Approach to Assess the Interest Rate Risk of a Bond Portfolio for Four Scenarios Assuming a Parallel Shift in the Yield Curve, 2-Bond Portfolio (both bonds option-free)

Panel A
Bond 1: 4% coupon Italian government bond maturing 1 March 2005
Full Price: 104.1947
Yield: 2.147%
Market value: €10,419,470
Par value: €10,000,000

Scenario	Yield Change (bp)	New Yield (%)	New Price	New Market Value (€)	Percentage Change in Market Value
1	50	2.647	103.3401	10,334,010	−0.820
2	100	3.147	102.4963	10,249,630	−1.630
3	150	3.647	101.6636	10,166,360	−2.430
4	200	4.147	100.8418	10,084,180	−3.220

Panel B
Bond 2: 5.75% coupon Italian government bond maturing 1 February 2033
Full Price: 119.1198
Yield: 4.727%
Market value: €23,823,960
Par value: €20,000,000

Scenario	Yield Change (bp)	New Yield (%)	New Price	New Market Value (€)	Percentage Change in Market Value
1	50	5.227	110.8284	22,165,680	−6.960
2	100	5.727	103.3936	20,678,720	−13.200
3	150	6.227	96.7185	19,343,700	−18.810
4	200	6.727	90.7126	18,142,520	−23.850

Panel C
Portfolio Market Value: €34,243,430

Scenario	Yield Change (bp)	Market Value of Bond 1 (€)	Bond 2 (€)	Portfolio (€)	Percentage Change in Market Value
1	50	10,334,010	22,165,680	32,499,690	−5.090
2	100	10,249,630	20,678,720	30,928,350	−9.680
3	150	10,166,360	19,343,700	29,510,060	−13.820
4	200	10,084,180	18,142,520	26,051,980	−23.920

EXHIBIT 4.6   Illustration of Full Valuation Approach to Assess the Interest Rate Risk of a Bond Portfolio for Four Scenarios Assuming a Nonparallel Shift in the Yield Curve, 2-Bond Portfolio (both bonds option-free)

Panel A
Bond 1: 4% coupon Italian government bond maturing 1 March 2005
Full Price: 104.1947
Yield: 2.147%
Market value: €10,419,470
Par value: €10,000,000

Scenario	Yield Change (bp)	New Yield (%)	New Price	New Market Value (€)	Percentage Change in Market Value
1	40	2.547	102.4885	10,248,850	−0.660
2	60	2.747	102.1488	10,214,880	−0.990
3	80	2.947	101.8108	10,181,080	−1.320
4	100	3.147	101.4746	10,147,460	−1.650

Panel B
Bond 2: 5.75% coupon Italian government bond maturing 1 February 2033
Full Price: 119.1198
Yield: 4.727%
Market value: €23,823,960
Par value: €20,000,000

Scenario	Yield Change (bp)	New Yield (%)	New Price	New Market Value (€)	Percentage Change in Market Value
1	20	4.927	113.7589	22,751,780	−4.530
2	40	5.127	110.4776	22,095,520	−8.680
3	60	5.327	107.3380	21,467,600	−9.920
4	80	5.527	104.3329	20,866,580	−12.440

Panel C
Portfolio Market Value: €34,243,430

Scenario	Market Value of Bond 1 (€)	Bond 2 (€)	Portfolio (€)	Percentage Change in Market Value
1	10,248,850	22,751,780	33,000,630	−3.629%
2	10,214,880	22,095,520	32,310,400	−5.645%
3	10,181,080	21,467,600	31,014,040	−7.577%
4	10,147,460	20,866,580	31,014,040	−9.431%

A common question that often arises when using the full valuation approach is which scenarios should be evaluated to assess interest rate risk exposure. For some regulated entities, there are specified scenarios established by regulators. For example, it is common for regulators of depository institutions to require entities to determine the impact on the value of their bond portfolio for a 100, 200, and 300 basis point instantaneous change in interest rates (up and down). (Regulators tend to refer to this as "simulating" interest rate scenarios rather than scenario analysis.) Risk managers and highly leveraged investors such as hedge funds tend to look at extreme shocks to assess exposure to interest rate changes. This practice is referred to as *stress testing*.

Of course, in assessing how changes in the yield curve can affect the exposure of a portfolio, there are an infinite number of scenarios that can be evaluated. The state-of-the-art technology involves using a complex statistical procedure[2] to determine a likely set of yield curve shift scenarios from historical data.

In summary, we can use the full valuation approach to assess the exposure of a bond or portfolio to interest rate shocks, assuming—and this cannot be stressed enough—that the manager has a good valuation model to estimate what the price of the bond will be in each interest rate scenario. Moreover, we recommend use of the full valuation approach for assessing the position of a single bond or a portfolio of a few bonds. For a portfolio with a large number of bonds and/or the bonds containing embedded options, the full valuation process may be too time consuming. In its stead, managers want a single measure that they can employ to estimate how a portfolio or even a single bond will change if interest rates change in a parallel fashion rather than having to revalue an entire portfolio to obtain that answer. Duration is such a measure and we will discuss it as well as a supplementary measure called *convexity* later in the chapter. Before we discuss the basic price volatility characteristics of bonds, we discuss a widely used interest rate risk measure: price value of a basis point. It should come as no surprise that there are limitations of using one or two measures to describe the interest rate exposure of a position or portfolio. Nevertheless, these measures provide us with some important intuition about assessing interest rate risk.

PRICE VALUE OF A BASIS POINT

Some managers use another measure of the price volatility of a bond to quantify interest rate risk—the *price value of a basis point* (PVBP). This mea-

---

[2] The procedure used is principal component analysis.

EXHIBIT 4.7   Bloomberg Yield Analysis Screen for a 10-Year Spanish
Government Bond

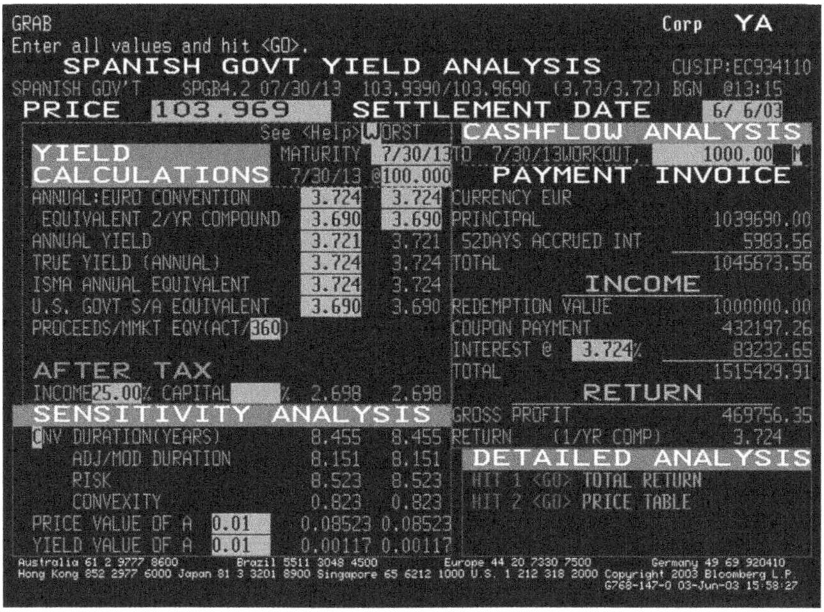

Source: Bloomberg Financial Markets.

sure, also called the *dollar value of an 01* (DV01), is the absolute value of the
change in the price of a bond for a 1 basis point change in yield. That is,

PVBP = | Initial price – Price if yield is changed by 1 basis point |

Does it make a difference if the yield is increased or decreased by 1
basis point? It does not because of Property 2—the change will be about
the same for a small change in basis points.

To illustrate the computation, let's examine a 4.2% coupon, 10-year
Spanish government security that matures on July 30, 2013. Bloomberg's
Yield Analysis Screen is presented in Exhibit 4.7. If the bond is priced to
yield 3.724% on a settlement date of June 6, 2003, we can compute the
PVBP by using the prices for either the yield at 3.734 or 3.714. The
bond's initial full price at 3.724% is 104.5673. If the yield is decreased by
1 basis point to 3.714%, the PVBP is 0.085 (|104.5673 – 104.6522|).
Note that our PVBP calculation agrees with Bloomberg's calculation
labeled "PRICE VALUE OF A 0.01" that is presented in the Sensitivity
Analysis box located in the lower left-hand corner of the screen.

EXHIBIT 4.8   Price/Yield Relationship for Four Hypothetical Option-Free Bonds

Yield (%)	Price (€)			
	7%, 10-year	7%, 30-year	9%, 10-year	9%, 30-year
5.00	115.5892	130.9087	131.1783	161.8173
6.00	107.4387	113.8378	122.3162	141.5133
6.50	103.6348	106.5634	118.1742	132.8171
6.90	100.7138	101.2599	114.9908	126.4579
6.99	100.0711	100.1248	114.2899	125.0947
7.00	100.0000	100.0000	114.2124	124.9447
7.01	99.9290	99.8754	114.1349	124.7950
7.10	99.2926	98.7652	113.4409	123.4608
7.50	96.5259	94.0655	110.4222	117.8034
8.00	93.2048	88.6883	106.7952	111.3117
9.00	86.9921	79.3620	100.0000	100.0000

PRICE VOLATILITY CHARACTERISTICS OF BONDS

There are four characteristics of a bond that affect its price volatility: (1) term to maturity, (2) coupon rate, (3) the level of yields, and (4) the presence of embedded options. In this section, we will examine each of these price volatility characteristics.

Price Volatility Characteristics of Option-Free Bonds

Let's begin by focusing on option-free bonds (i.e., bonds that do not have embedded options). A fundamental characteristic of an option-free bond is that the price of the bond changes in the opposite direction from a change in the bond's required yield. Exhibit 4.8 illustrates this property for four hypothetical bonds assuming a par value of €100.

When the price/yield relationship for any hypothetical option-free bond is graphed, it exhibits the basic shape shown in Exhibit 4.9. Notice that as the required yield decreases, the price of an option-free bond increases. Conversely, as the required yield decreases, the price of an option-free bond increases. In other words, the price/yield relationship is negatively sloped. In addition, the price/yield relationship is not linear (i.e., not a straight line). The shape of the price/yield relationship for any option-free bond is referred to as *convex*. The price/yield relationship is for an instantaneous change in the required yield.

Exhibit 4.10 shows the price/yield relationship for the UK gilt principal strip that is shown in Exhibit 4.1. Recall, using a settlement date of

EXHIBIT 4.9   Price/Yield Relationship for a Hypothetical Option-Free Bond

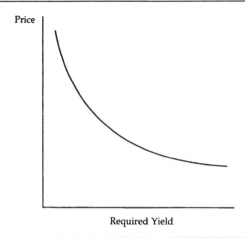

EXHIBIT 4.10   Price/Yield Relationship for a UK Gilt Principal Strip

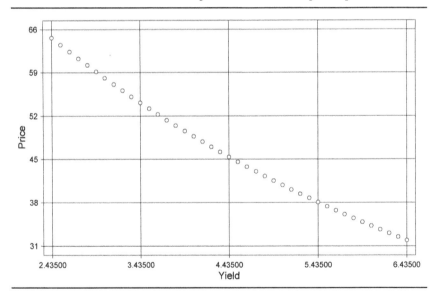

May 30, 2003, the yield is 4.435%. To construct the graph, the gilt strip was repriced using increments and decrements of 10 basis points from 2.435% to 6.435%. Exhibit 4.11 shows the two price/yield relationships for the 4% coupon, 2-year Italian government and 5.75% coupon, 30-year Italian government shown in Exhibits 4.3 and 4.4, respectively.

EXHIBIT 4.11   Price/Yield Relationship for a 2-Year and a 30-Year Italian
Government Bonds

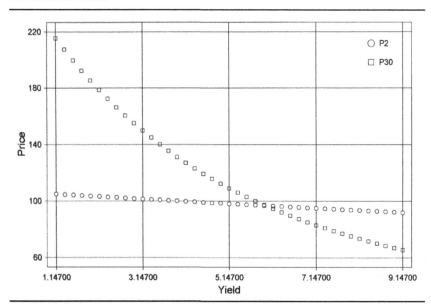

Note the 30-year security's price/yield relationship is more steeply sloped
and more curved than the price/yield relationship for the 2-year security.
The reasons for these differences will be discussed shortly.

The price sensitivity of a bond to changes in the required yield can
be measured in terms of the euro price change or the percentage price
change. Exhibit 4.12 uses the four hypothetical bonds in Exhibit 4.8 to
show the percentage change in each bond's price for various changes in
yield, assuming that the initial yield for all four bonds is 7%. An exami-
nation of Exhibit 4.12 reveals the following properties concerning the
price volatility of an option-free bond:

> *Property 1*: Although the price moves in the opposite direction from
> the change in required yield, the percentage price change is not the
> same for all bonds.
> *Property 2*: For small changes in the required yield, the percentage
> price change for a given bond is roughly the same, whether the
> required yield increases or decreases.
> *Property 3*: For large changes in required yield, the percentage price
> change is not the same for an increase in required yield as it is for a
> decrease in required yield.

EXHIBIT 4.12   Instantaneous Percentage Price Change for Four Hypothetical Bonds (Initial Yield for all four bonds is 7%)

Yield (%)	Price (€)			
	7%, 10-year	7%, 30-year	9%, 10-year	9%, 30-year
5.00	15.5892	30.9087	14.8547	29.5111
6.00	7.4387	13.8378	7.0954	13.2607
6.50	3.6368	6.5634	3.4688	6.3007
6.90	0.7138	1.2599	0.6815	1.2111
6.99	0.0711	0.1248	0.0679	0.1201
7.00	0.0000	0.0000	0.0000	0.0000
7.01	−0.0710	−0.1246	−0.0679	−0.1200
7.10	−0.0707	−1.2350	−0.6750	−1.1880
7.50	−3.4740	−5.9350	−3.3190	−5.7160
8.00	−6.7950	−11.3120	−6.4940	−10.9110
9.00	−13.0080	−20.6380	−12.4440	−19.9650

Property 4: For a given large change in basis points in the required yield, the percentage price increase is greater than the percentage price decrease.

While the properties are expressed in terms of percentage price change, they also hold for euro price changes.

An explanation for these two properties of bond price volatility lies in the convex shape of the price/yield relationship. Exhibit 4.13 illustrates this. The following notation is used in the exhibit

Y = initial yield
Y_1 = lower yield
Y_2 = higher yield
P = initial price
P_1 = price at lower yield Y_1
P_2 = price at higher yield Y_2

What was done in the exhibit was to change the initial yield (Y) up and down by the same number of basis points. That is, in Exhibit 4.13, the yield is decreased from Y to Y_1 and increased from Y to Y_2 such that the magnitude of the change is the same:

$$Y - Y_1 = Y_2 - Y$$

Also, the amount of the change in yield is a large number of basis points.

EXHIBIT 4.13   Impact of Convexity on Property 4: Less Convex Bond

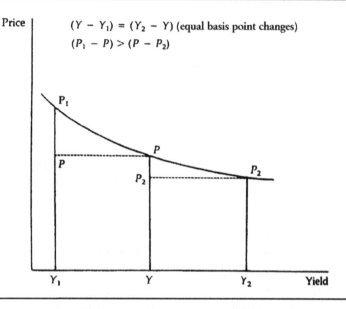

The vertical distance from the horizontal axis (the yield) to the intercept on the graph shows the price. The change in the initial price (P) when the yield declines from Y to Y_1 is equal to the difference between the new price (P_1) and the initial price. That is,

$$\text{Change in price when yield decreases} = P_1 - P$$

The change in the initial price (P) when the yield increases from Y to Y_2 is equal to the difference between the new price (P_2) and the initial price. That is,

$$\text{Change in price when yield increases} = P - P_2$$

As can be seen in the exhibit, the change in price when yield decreases is not equal to the change in price when yield increases by the same number of basis points. That is,

$$P_1 - P \neq P - P_2$$

This is what Property 3 states. Moreover, a comparison of the price change shows that the change in price when yield decreases is greater than the change in price when yield increases. That is,

EXHIBIT 4.14   Graphical Illustration of Properties 3 and 4 for an Option-Free Bond

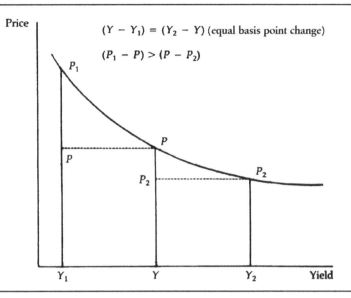

$$P_1 - P > P - P_2$$

This is Property 4.

The implication of Property 4 is that if an investor is long a bond, the price appreciation that will be realized if the required yield decreases is greater than the capital loss that will be realized if the required yield increases by the same number of basis points. For an investor who is short a bond, the reverse is true: the potential capital loss is greater than the potential capital gain if the yield changes by a given number of basis points.

To see how the convexity of the price/yield relationship impacts Property 4, look at Exhibits 4.14 and 4.15. Exhibit 4.14 shows a less convex price/yield relationship than Exhibit 4.13. That is, the price/yield relationship in Exhibit 4.14 is less bowed than the price/yield relationship in Exhibit 4.13. Because of the difference in the convexities, look at what happens when the yield increases and decreases by the same number of basis points and the yield change is a large number of basis points. We use the same notation in Exhibits 4.14 and 4.15 as in Exhibit 4.13. Notice that while the price gain when the required yield decreases is greater than the price decline when the required yield increases, the gain is not much greater than the loss. In contrast, Exhibit

EXHIBIT 4.15   Impact of Convexity on Property 4: Highly Convex Bond

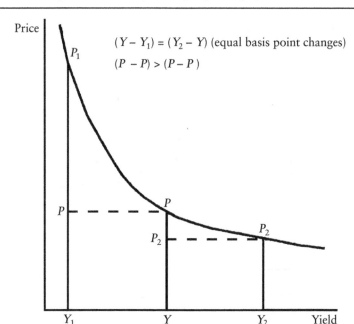

4.15 has much greater convexity than the bonds in Exhibits 4.13 and 4.14 and the price gain is significantly greater than the loss for the bonds depicted in Exhibits 4.13 and 4.14.

Price Volatility Characteristics of Bonds with Embedded Options

Now let's turn to the price volatility characteristics of bonds with embedded options. As explained in previous chapters, the price of a bond with an embedded option is comprised of two components. The first is the value of the same bond if it had no embedded option. That is, the price if the bond is option free. The second component is the value of the embedded option.

The two most common types of embedded options are call (or prepay) options and put options. As interest rates in the market decline, the issuer may call or prepay the debt obligation prior to the scheduled principal repayment date. The other type of option is a put option. This option gives the investor the right to require the issuer to purchase the bond at a specified price. Below we will examine the price/yield relationship for bonds with both types of embedded options (calls and puts) and implications for price volatility.

EXHIBIT 4.16   Price/Yield Relationship for a Callable Bond and an
Option-Free Bond

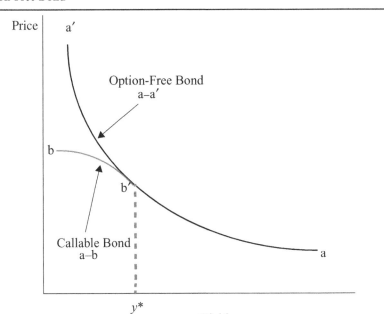

Bonds with Call and Prepay Options

In the discussion below, we will refer to a bond that may be called or is prepayable as a callable bond. Exhibit 4.16 shows the price/yield relationship for an option-free bond and a callable bond. The convex curve given by a-a′ is the price/yield relationship for an option-free bond. The unusual shaped curve denoted by a-b in the exhibit is the price/yield relationship for the callable bond.

The reason for the price/yield relationship for a callable bond is as follows. When the prevailing market yield for comparable bonds is higher than the coupon rate on the callable bond, it is unlikely that the issuer will call the issue. For example, if the coupon rate on a bond is 7% and the prevailing market yield on comparable bonds is 12%, it is highly unlikely that the issuer will call a 7% coupon bond so that it can issue a 12% coupon bond. Since the bond is unlikely to be called, the callable bond will have a similar price/yield relationship as an otherwise comparable option-free bond. Consequently, the callable bond is going to be valued as if it is an option-free bond. However, since there is still some value to the call option, the bond won't trade exactly like an option-free bond.

As yields in the market decline, the concern is that the issuer will call the bond. The issuer won't necessarily exercise the call option as soon as the market yield drops below the coupon rate. Yet, the value of the embedded call option increases as yields approach the coupon rate from higher yield levels. For example, if the coupon rate on a bond is 7% and the market yield declines to 7.5%, the issuer will most likely not call the issue. However, market yields are at a level at which the investor is concerned that the issue may eventually be called if market yields decline further. Cast in terms of the value of the embedded call option, that option becomes more valuable to the issuer and therefore it reduces the price relative to an otherwise comparable option-free bond.[3] In Exhibit 4.16, the value of the embedded call option at a given yield can be measured by the difference between the price of an option-free bond (the price shown on the curve a-a′) and the price on the curve a-b. Notice that at low yield levels (below y^* on the horizontal axis), the value of the embedded call option is high.

Let's look at the difference in the price volatility properties relative to an option-free bond given the price/yield relationship for a callable bond shown in Exhibit 4.16. Exhibit 4.17 blows up the portion of the price/yield relationship for the callable bond where the two curves in Exhibit 4.16 depart (segment b-b′ in Exhibit 4.16). We know from our discussion of the price/yield relationship that for a large change in yield of a given number of basis points, the price of an option-free bond increases by more than it decreases (Property 4 above). Is that what happens for a callable bond in the region of the price/yield relationship shown in Exhibit 4.17? No, it is not. In fact, as can be seen in the exhibit, the opposite is true! That is, for a given large change in yield, the price appreciation is less than the price decline.

The price volatility characteristic of a callable bond is important to understand. The characteristic of a callable bond—that its price appreciation is less than its price decline when rates change by a large number of basis points—is referred to as *negative convexity*.[4] But notice from Exhibit 4.16 that callable bonds do not exhibit this characteristic at every yield level. When yields are high (relative to the issue's coupon

---

[3] For readers who are already familiar with option theory, this characteristic can be restated as follows: When the coupon rate for the issue is below the market yield, the embedded call option is said to be "out-of-the-money." When the coupon rate for the issue is above the market yield, the embedded call option is said to be "in-the-the money."

[4] Mathematicians refer to this shape as being "concave."

EXHIBIT 4.17   Negative Convexity Region of the Price/Yield Relationship for a Callable Bond

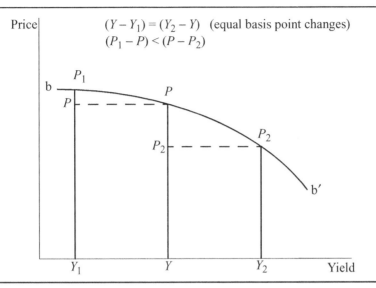

Price

$(Y - Y_1) = (Y_2 - Y)$ (equal basis point changes)
$(P_1 - P) < (P - P_2)$

rate), the bond exhibits the same price/yield relationship as an option-free bond and therefore at high-yield levels it also has the characteristic that the gain is greater than the loss. Because market participants have referred to the shape of the price/yield relationship shown in Exhibit 4.17 as negative convexity, market participants refer to the relationship for an option-free bond as *positive convexity*. Consequently, a callable bond exhibits negative convexity at low yield levels and positive convexity at high-yield levels. This is depicted in Exhibit 4.18.

As can be seen from the exhibits, when a bond exhibits negative convexity, the bond compresses in price as rates decline. That is, at a certain yield level there is very little price appreciation when rates decline. When a bond enters this region, the bond is said to exhibit "price compression."

Bonds with Embedded Put Options

Putable bonds may be redeemed by the bondholder on the dates and at the put price specified in the indenture. Typically, the put price is par value. The advantage to the investor is that if yields rise such that the bond's value falls below the put price, the investor will exercise the put option. If the put price is par value, this means that if market yields rise above the coupon rate, the bond's value will fall below par and the investor will then exercise the put option.

EXHIBIT 4.18   Negative and Positive Convexity Exhibited by a Callable Bond

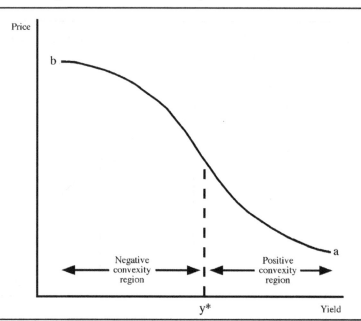

The value of a putable bond is equal to the value of an option-free bond plus the value of the put option. Thus, the difference between the value of a putable bond and the value of an otherwise comparable option-free bond is the value of the embedded put option. This can be seen in Exhibit 4.19 which shows the price/yield relationship for a putable bond (the curve a-b) and an option-free bond (the curve a-a′).

At low yield levels (low relative to the issue's coupon rate), the price of the putable bond is basically the same as the price of the option-free bond because the value of the put option is small. As rates rise, the price of the putable bond declines, but the price decline is less than that for an option-free bond. The divergence in the price of the putable bond and an otherwise comparable option-free bond at a given yield level is the value of the put option. When yields rise to a level where the bond's price would fall below the put price, the price at these levels is the put price.

DURATION

Given the background about a bond's price volatility characteristics, we can now turn our attention to an alternate approach to full valuation:

EXHIBIT 4.19 Price/Yield Relationship for a Putable Bond and an Option-Free Bond

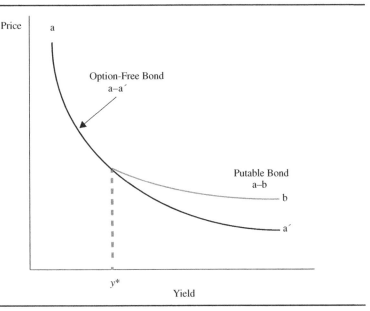

the duration/convexity approach. Simply put, *duration* is a measure of the approximate sensitivity of a bond's value to rate changes. More specifically, *duration is the approximate percentage change in value for a 100 basis point change in rates.* We will see in this section that duration is the first approximation (i.e., linear) of the percentage price change. To improve the estimate obtained using duration, a measure called "convexity" can be used. Hence, using duration and convexity together to estimate a bond's percentage price change resulting from interest rate changes is called the *duration/convexity approach.*

Calculating Duration

The duration of a bond is estimated as follows:

$$\frac{\text{Price if yields decline} - \text{Price if yields rise}}{2(\text{Initial price})(\text{Change in yield in decimal})}$$

If we let

Δy = change in yield in decimal
V_0 = initial price

$V-$ = price if yields decline by Δy
V_+ = price if yields increase by Δy

then duration can be expressed as

$$\text{Duration} = \frac{V_- - V_+}{2(V_0)(\Delta y)} \qquad (4.1)$$

For example, consider the UK gilt principal strip discussed earlier that matures on June 7, 2021 and on a settlement date of May 30, 2003 is priced to yield 4.435%. Exhibit 4.1 presents Bloomberg's Yield Analysis screen for this security. Let's change (i.e., shock) the note's required yield up and down by 20 basis points and determine what the new prices will be in the numerator of equation (4.1). If the required yield were decreased by 20 basis points from 4.435% to 4.235%, the strip's price would increase to 46.99. Conversely, if the yield increases by 20 basis points, the strip's price would decrease to 43.99. Thus,

Δy = 0.002
V_0 = 45.36
V_- = 46.99
V_+ = 43.79

$$\text{Duration} = \frac{46.99 - 43.79}{2 \times (45.36) \times (0.002)} = 17.636$$

Note that our calculation for duration of 17.636 agrees (within rounding error) with Bloomberg's calculation in Exhibit 4.1. Bloomberg's interest rate risk measures are located in a box titled "Sensitivity Analysis" in the lower left-hand corner of the screen. The duration measure we just calculated is labeled "Adj/Mod Duration" which stands for adjusted/modified duration.

Duration is interpreted as the approximate percentage change in price for a 100 basis point change in the required yield. The change in yield is the same change in yield for all maturities. This assumption is commonly referred to as a parallel yield curve shift assumption. Consequently, a duration of 17.636 means that the approximate percentage change in the bond's price will be 17.636% for a 100 basis point shift in the yield curve. Moreover, since duration is a linear approximation, the approximate percentage price change for a 50 basis point change in required yield is one-half the modified duration or in the case 8.818%. This result generalizes.

A common question often raised at this juncture is the consistency between the yield change that is used to compute duration (Δy) using equation (4.1) and the interpretation of duration. For example, recall that in computing the duration of the UK strip, we used a 20 basis point yield change to obtain the two prices used in the numerator in equation (4.1). Yet, we interpret the duration measure computed using equation (4.1) as the approximate percentage price change for a 100 basis point change in yield. The reason is that regardless of the yield change used to estimate duration in equation (4.1), the interpretation is unchanged. If we used a 30 basis point change in yield to compute the prices used in the numerator of equation, the resulting duration measure is interpreted as the approximate percentage price change for a 100 basis point change in yield. Simply put, the choice of Δy in equation (4.1) is arbitrary. Shortly, we will use different changes in yield to illustrate the sensitivity (or lack thereof) of the computed duration using equation (4.1).

Approximating the Percentage Price Change Using Duration

In order to approximate the percentage price change for a given change in yield and a given duration, we employ the following formula:

$$\text{Approximate percentage price change} = -\Delta\text{uration} \times \Delta y \times 100 \qquad (4.2)$$

The reason for the negative sign on the right-hand side of equation (4.2) is due to the inverse relationship between price change and yield change.

For example, consider once again the UK gilt principal strip whose duration we just computed is 17.636. The approximate percentage price change for a 10 basis point increase in the required yield (i.e., $\Delta y = +0.001$) is

$$\begin{aligned} \text{Approximate percentage price change} &= -17.636 \times (+0.001) \times 100 \\ &= -1.7636 \end{aligned}$$

How good is this approximation? The actual percentage price change is -1.74 (= $(44.57 - 45.36)/45.36$). Duration, in this instance, did an accurate job of estimating the percentage price change. We would reach the same conclusion if we used duration to estimate the percentage price change if the yield declined by 10 basis points (i.e., $\Delta y = -0.001$). In this case, the approximate percentage price change would be $+1.7636$ (i.e., the direction of the estimated price change is the reverse but the magnitude of the change is the same because it is a linear approximation).

In terms of estimating the new price, let's see how duration performs. The initial price is 45.36. For a 10 basis point increase in yield, duration estimates that the price will decline by −1.7636%. Thus, the price will decline to 44.56. The actual price if the yield increases by 10 basis points is 44.57. Thus, the price estimate using duration is very close to the actual price. For a 10 basis point decrease in yield, the actual price is 46.17 and the estimated price using duration is 46.16 (a price increase of 1.7636%).

Now let us examine how well duration does in estimating the percentage price change when the yield increases by 200 basis points rather than a 10 basis points. In this case, Δy is equal to +0.02. Substituting into equation (4.2) we have

$$\text{Approximate percentage price change} = -17.636 \times (+0.02) \times 100$$
$$= -35.272\%$$

How accurate is this estimate? The actual percentage price change when the yield increases by 200 basis points (4.435% to 6.435%) is −29.6%. Thus, the estimate is considerably less accurate than when we used duration to approximate the percentage price change for a change in yield of only 10 basis points. If we use duration to approximate the percentage price change when the yield decreases by 200 basis points, the approximate percentage price change in this scenario is +35.272 (remember only the sign changes). The actual percentage price change is +42.53%.

As before, let's examine the use of duration in terms of estimating the new price. Since the initial price is 45.36 and a 200 basis point increase in yield will decrease by −35.272%, the estimated new price using duration is 29.36. The actual price if the yield rises by 200 basis points (4.435% to 6.435%) is 31.94. Consequently, the estimate is not as accurate as the estimate for a 10 basis point change in yield. The estimated new price using duration for a 200 basis point decrease in yield (4.435% to 2.435%) is 61.36 compared to the actual price of 64.65. Once again, the estimation of the price using duration is not as accurate as for a 10 basis point change. Notice that whether the yield is increased or decreased by 200 basis points, duration underestimates what the new price will be. We will discover why shortly. Exhibit 4.20 summarizes what we found in our application to approximate the 10-year UK gilt principal strip's percentage price change.

This result should come as no surprise to careful readers of the last section on price volatility characteristics of bonds. Specifically equation (4.2) is somewhat at odds with the properties of the price/yield relationship. We are using a linear approximation for a price/yield relationship that is convex.

EXHIBIT 4.20   Application of Duration to Approximate the Percentage Price
Change

Yield Change (bp)	Initial Price	New Price		Percent Price Change		Comment
		Based on Duration	Actual	Based on Duration	Actual	
+10	45.36	44.56	44.57	−1.7636	−1.74	Estimated price close to new price
−10	45.36	46.16	46.17	+1.7636	+1.79	Estimated price close to new price
+200	45.36	29.36	31.94	−35.272	−29.60	Underestimates new price
−200	45.36	61.36	64.65	+35.272	+42.53	Underestimates new price

The PVBP discussed earlier is related to duration. In fact, PVBP is
simply a special case of a measure called *dollar duration*. Dollar duration is the approximate price change for a 100 basis point change in
yield. We know that a bond's duration is the approximate percentage
price change for a 100 basis point change in interest rates. We also
know how to compute the approximate percentage price change for any
number of basis points given a bond's duration using equation (4.2).
Given the initial price and the approximate percentage price change for
1 basis point, we can compute the change in price for a 1 basis point
change in rates.

For example, consider once again the 4.2% coupon, 10-year Spanish government bond. From Exhibit 4.7, the duration is 8.151. Using
equation (4.2), the approximate percentage price change for a 1 basis
point increase in interest rates (i.e., $\Delta y = 0.0001$) ignoring the negative
sign in equation (4.2) is

$$8.151 \times (0.0001) \times 100 = 0.08151\%$$

Given the initial full price of 104.5673, the euro price change estimated using duration is

$$0.08151\% \times 104.5673 = €0.0852$$

This is the same price change as shown above for a PVBP for this
bond.[5]

---

[5] Bloomberg's "Risk" measure is simply the PVBP × 100. For bonds that are trading
close to par, risk should be close to modified duration.

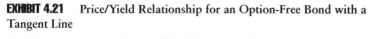

EXHIBIT 4.21   Price/Yield Relationship for an Option-Free Bond with a
Tangent Line

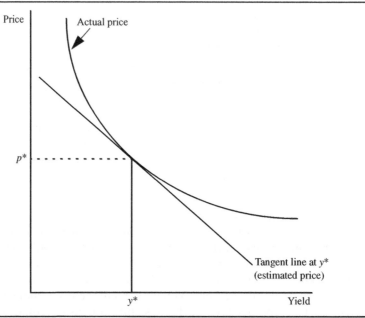

Graphical Depiction of Using Duration to Estimate Price Changes

Earlier we used the graph of the price/yield relationship to demonstrate
the price volatility properties of bonds. We can use graphs to illustrate
what we observed in our examples about how duration estimates the
percentage price change, as well as some other noteworthy points.

The shape of the price/yield relationship for an option-free bond is
convex. Exhibit 4.21 shows this relationship. In the exhibit a tangent
line is drawn to the price/yield relationship at yield y^*. (For those unfamiliar with the concept of a tangent line, it is a straight line that just
touches a curve at one point within a relevant (local) range. In Exhibit
4.21, the tangent line touches the curve at the point where the yield is
equal to y^* and the price is equal to p^*.) The tangent line is used to *estimate* the new price if the yield changes. If we draw a vertical line from
any yield (on the horizontal axis), as in Exhibit 4.21, the distance
between the horizontal axis and the tangent line represents the price
approximated by using duration starting with the initial yield y^*.

Now how is the tangent line, used to approximate what the new
price will be if yields change, related to duration? The tangent line tells

EXHIBIT 4.22   Estimating the New Price Using a Tangent Line

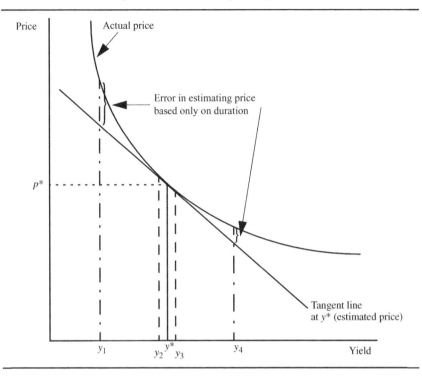

us the approximate new price of a bond if the yield changes. Given (1) the initial price and (2) the new price of a bond if the yield changes using the tangent line, the approximate percentage price change can be computed for a given change in yield. But this is precisely what duration (using equation (4.2)) gives us: the approximate percentage change for a given change in yield. Thus, using the tangent line one obtains the same approximate percentage price change as using equation (4.2).

This helps us understand why duration did an effective job of estimating the percentage price change or, equivalently, the new price when the yield changes by a small number of basis points. Look at Exhibit 4.22. Notice that for a small change in yield, the tangent line does not depart much from the price/yield relationship. Hence, when the yield changes up or down by 10 basis points, the tangent line does a good job of estimating the new price, as we found in our earlier numerical illustration.

Exhibit 4.22 also shows what happens to the estimate using the tangent line when the yield changes by a large number of basis points.

EXHIBIT 4.23   Estimating the New Price for a Large Yield Change for Bonds with Different Convexities

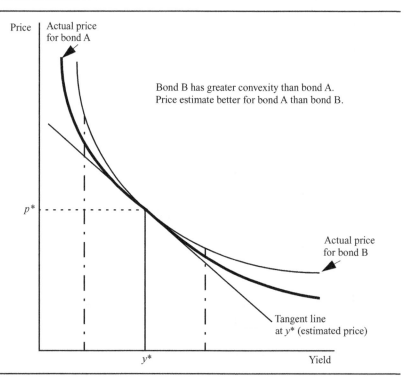

Notice that the error in the estimate gets larger the further one moves from the initial yield. The estimate is less accurate the more convex the bond. This is illustrated in Exhibit 4.23.

Also note that regardless of the magnitude of the yield change, the tangent line always underestimates what the new price will be for an option-free bond because the tangent line is below the price/yield relationship. This explains why we found in our illustration that when using duration we underestimated what the actual price will be.

Rate Shocks and Duration Estimate

In calculating duration using equation (4.1), it is necessary to shock interest rates (yields) up and down by the same number of basis points to obtain the values for V_- and V_+. In our illustration, 20 basis points was arbitrarily selected. But how large should the shock be? That is, how many basis points should be used to shock the rate? Looking at equation (4.1) it is relatively easy to discern why the size of the interest

EXHIBIT 4.24   Duration Estimates for Different Rate Shocks
Assumptions: The initial yields for the 2-year Italian government and UK gilt principal strip are 2.147% and 4.435% respectively.

Bond	1 bp	10 bp	20 bp	50 bp	100 bp
2-year, 4% coupon Italian Government security maturing 3/1/05	1.67	1.67	1.67	1.67	1.67
UK gilt principal strip maturing 6/7/21	17.64	17.64	17.64	17.66	17.74

rate shock should not matter too much. Specifically, the choice of Δy has two effects on equation (4.1). In the numerator, the choice of Δy affects the spread between V_- and V_+ in that the larger the interest rate shock, the larger the spread between the two prices. In the denominator, the choice of Δy appears directly and the denominator is larger for larger values of Δy. The two effects should largely neutralize each other, unless the price/yield relationship is highly convex (i.e., curved).

In Exhibit 4.24, the duration estimate for the securities from Exhibits 4.1 and 4.3 using equation (4.1) for rate shocks of 1 basis point to 100 basis points is reported. The duration estimates for the 2-year Italian government are unaffected by the size of the shock. If the duration estimates are ever going to be affected by the size of the interest rate shock, this should be evident when this exercise is performed on the UK gilt principal strip, which has large positive convexity relative to the 2-year coupon security (i.e., a price/yield relationship that is very curved). However, even in this case, the duration estimates are affected only marginally. It would appear that the size of the interest rate shock is unimportant for approximating the duration of option-free bonds using equation (4.1).

When we deal with more complicated securities, small rate shocks that do not reflect the types of rate changes that may occur in the market do not permit the determination of how prices can change because expected cash flows may change when dealing with bonds with embedded options. In comparison, if large rate shocks are used, we encounter the asymmetry caused by convexity. Moreover, large rate shocks may cause dramatic changes in the expected cash flows for bonds with embedded options that may be far different from how the expected cash flows will change for smaller rate shocks.

There is another potential problem with using small rate shocks for complicated securities. The prices that are inserted into the duration formula as given by equation (4.1) are derived from a valuation model. The duration measure depends crucially on a valuation model. If the rate shock is small and the valuation model used to obtain the prices for equation (4.1) is poor, dividing poor price estimates by a small shock in rates in the denominator will have a significant affect on the duration estimate.

What is done in practice by dealers and vendors of analytical systems? Each system developer uses rate shocks that they have found to be realistic based on historical rate changes.

Modified Duration versus Effective Duration

One form of duration that is cited by practitioners is *modified duration.* Modified duration is the approximate percentage change in a bond's price for a 100 basis point change in yield *assuming that the bond's expected cash flows do not change when the yield changes.* What this means is that in calculating the values of V_- and V_+ in equation (4.1), the same cash flows used to calculate V_0 are used. Therefore, the change in the bond's price when the yield is changed is due solely to discounting cash flows at the new yield level.

The assumption that the cash flows will not change when the yield is changed makes sense for option-free bonds. And, as noted in Chapter 1, most bonds in the European government and corporate bond markets are option free. However, for the minority of bonds that have an embedded option and for all mortgage-backed securities, the expected cash flow will change when interest rates change. Earlier in the chapter, we presented the price/yield relationship for callable and prepayable bonds. Failure to recognize how changes in yield can alter the expected cash flows will produce two values used in the numerator of equation (4.1) that are not good estimates of how the price will actually change. The duration is then not a good number to use to estimate how the price will change.

There are valuation models that can be used to value bonds with embedded options.[6] These models take into account how changes in yield will affect the expected cash flows. Thus, when V_- and V_+ are the values produced from these valuation models, the resulting duration takes into account both the discounting at different interest rates and how the expected cash flows may change. When duration is calculated in this manner, it is referred to as *effective duration* or *option-adjusted duration* or *OAS duration.* Below we explain how effective duration is calculated based on the lattice model and the Monte Carlo model.

---

[6] For a discussion of these models, see Chapters 6 and 8 in Frank J. Fabozzi and Steven V. Mann, *Introduction to Fixed Income Analytics* (Hoboken, NJ: John Wiley & Sons, Inc., 2001).

Macaulay Duration and Modified Duration

It is worth comparing the relationship between modified duration to another duration measure. Modified duration can also be written as:[7]

$$\frac{1}{(1+\text{yield}/k)}\left[\frac{1 \times \text{PVCF}_1 + 2 \times \text{PVCF}_2 + ... + n \times \text{PVCF}_n}{k \times \text{Price}}\right] \quad (4.3)$$

where

k = number of periods, or payments, per year (e.g., k = 2 for semiannual-pay bonds and k = 12 for monthly pay bonds)

n = number of periods until maturity (i.e., number of years to maturity times k)

yield = yield to maturity of the bond

PVCF_t = present value of the cash flow in period t discounted at the yield to maturity where t = 1, 2, ..., n

The expression in the brackets of the modified duration formula given by equation (4.3) is a measure formulated in 1938 by Frederick Macaulay.[8] This measure is popularly referred to as *Macaulay duration*. Thus, modified duration is commonly expressed as:

$$\text{Modified duration} = \frac{\text{Macaulay duration}}{(1 + \text{yield}/k)}$$

Bloomberg reports Macaulay duration on its YA (yield analysis) screen in the Sensitivity Analysis box in the lower left-hand corner of Exhibits 4.1, 4.3, and 4.4. Macaulay duration is labeled "CNV DURA-TION (YEARS)" where the CNV stands for "conventional."

The general formulation for duration as given by equation (4.1) provides a short-cut procedure for determining a bond's modified duration. Because it is easier to calculate the modified duration using the shortcut procedure, most vendors of analytical software will use equation (4.1) rather than equation (4.3) to reduce computation time.

However, it must be clearly understood that modified duration is a flawed measure of a bond's price sensitivity to interest rate changes for a bond with an embedded option and therefore so is Macaulay duration.

---

[7] More specifically, this is the formula for the modified duration of a bond on a coupon anniversary date.

[8] Frederick Macaulay, *Some Theoretical Problems Suggested by the Movement of Interest Rates, Bond Yields, and Stock Prices in the U.S. Since 1856* (New York: National Bureau of Economic Research, 1938).

The use of the formula for duration given by equation (4.3) *misleads* the user because it masks the fact that changes in the expected cash flows must be recognized for bonds with embedded options. Although equation (4.3) will give the same estimate of percent price change for an option-free bond as equation (4.1), equation (4.1) is still better because it acknowledges that cash flows and thus value can change due to yield changes.

Portfolio Duration

A portfolio's duration can be obtained by calculating the weighted average of the duration of the bonds in the portfolio. The weight is the proportion of the portfolio that a security comprises. Mathematically, a portfolio's duration can be calculated as follows:

$$w_1 D_1 + w_2 D_2 + w_3 D_3 + \dots + w_K D_K$$

where

w_i = market value of bond i/market value of the portfolio
D_i = duration of bond i
K = number of bonds in the portfolio

To illustrate the calculation, consider the following three-bond portfolio in which all three bonds are Irish government securities. Exhibit 4.25 presents a brief description for each bond that includes the following: full price per €100 of par value, its yield, the par amount owned, the market value and its duration assuming a settlement date of 6 June 2003. Since these securities are priced with a settlement date between coupon payments dates, the market prices reported are full prices. The

EXHIBIT 4.25   Summary of a Three-Irish-Government-Bond Portfolio

Bond	Full Price ($)	Yield (%)	Par Amount Owned ($)	Market Value ($)	Duration
3.50% coupon Irish Government security maturing 10/18/05	105.2950	2.148	1,000,000	1,052,950.68	2.221
3.25% coupon Irish Government security maturing 4/18/09	101.7551	3.000	5,000,000	5,087,755.46	5.259
4.6% coupon Irish Government security maturing 4/18/16	106.3398	4.020	3,000,000	3,190,195.41	9.638

market value for the portfolio is €9,330,901.55. Since each security is option-free, modified duration can be used.

In this illustration, K is equal to 3 and

w_1 = €1,052,950.68/9,330,901.55 = 0.113 D_1 = 2.221
w_2 = €5,087,755.46/9,330,901.55 = 0.545 D_2 = 5.259
w_3 = €3,190,195.41/9,330,901.55 = 0.342 D_3 = 9.638

The portfolio's duration is

$$0.113(2.221) + 0.545(5.259) + 0.342(9.638) = 6.413$$

A portfolio duration of 6.413 means that for a 100 basis point change in the yield for each of the three bonds, the portfolio's market value will change by approximately 6.413%. It is paramount to keep in mind that the yield for each of the three bonds must change by 100 basis points for this duration measure to be useful. This is a critical assumption and its importance cannot be overemphasized. Portfolio managers will find it necessary to be able to measure a portfolio's exposure to a reshaping of the yield curve. We will examine methods for doing later in the chapter when we discuss key rate duration.

An alternative procedure for calculating a portfolio's duration is to calculate the dollar price change for a given number of basis points for each security in the portfolio and then sum up all the changes in market value. Dividing the total of the changes in market value by the portfolio's initial market value produces a percentage change in market value that can be adjusted to obtain the portfolio's duration.

For example, consider the 3-bond portfolio given in Exhibit 4.25. Suppose that we calculate the dollar change in market value for each bond in the portfolio based on its respective duration for a 50 basis point change in yield. We would then have:

Bond	Market Value (€)	Duration	Change in Value for 50 bp Yield Change (€)
3.50% coupon Irish Government security maturing 18/10/05	1,052,950.68	2.221	11,604.13
3.25% coupon Irish Government security. maturing 18/4/09	5,087,755.46	5.259	131,588.46
4.6% coupon Irish Government security maturing 18/4/16	3,190,195.41	9.638	149,038.74
Total			292,231.33

Thus, a 50 basis point change in all rates will change the market value of the 3-bond portfolio by €292,231.33. Since the market value of the portfolio is 9,330,901.55, a 50 basis point change produced a change in value of 3.132% (€292,231.33 divided by 9,330,901.55). Since duration is the approximate percentage change for a 100 basis point change in rates, this means that the portfolio is 6.264 (found by doubling 3.132). This is very close to the value for the portfolio's duration as found earlier.

Contribution to Portfolio Duration

Some portfolio managers view their exposure to a particular issue or to a sector in terms of the percentage of that issue or sector in the portfolio. A better measure of exposure of an individual issue or sector to changes in interest rates is in terms of its *contribution to the portfolio duration*. Contribution to portfolio duration is computed by multiplying the percentage that the individual issues comprises of the portfolio by the duration of the individual issue or sector. Specifically,

$$\text{Contribution to portfolio duration} = \frac{\text{Market value of issue or sector}}{\text{Market value of portfolio}} \times \text{Duration of issue or sector}$$

This exposure can also be cast in terms of dollar exposure. To accomplish this, the dollar duration of the issue or sector is used instead of the duration of the issue or sector.

A portfolio manager who desires to determine the contribution to a portfolio of a sector relative to the contribution of the same sector in a broad-based market index can compute the difference between these two contributions.

OTHER DURATION MEASURES

Numerous duration measures are routinely employed by fixed-income practitioners that relate to both fixed-rate and floating-rate securities. Furthermore, there are more sophisticated duration measures that allow for nonparallel yield curve shifts. We discuss these measures in this section.

Spread Duration for Fixed-Rate Bonds

As we have seen, duration is a measure of the change in a bond's value when interest rates change. The interest rate that is assumed to shift is the government rate which serves as the benchmark interest rate. However, for nongovernment instruments, the yield is equal to the government yield plus a spread to the government yield curve. This is why nongovernment securities are often called "spread products." Of course, the price of a bond exposed to credit risk can change even though government yields are unchanged because the spread required by the market changes. A measure of how a nongovernment security's price will change if the spread sought by the market changes is called *spread duration*.

The problem is, what spread is assumed to change? There are three measures that are commonly used for fixed-rate bonds: nominal spread, zero-volatility spread, and option-adjusted spread. Each of these spread measures were defined earlier in this book.

The nominal spread is the traditional spread measure. The nominal spread is simply the difference between the yield on a nongovernment issue and the yield on a comparable maturity government. When the spread is taken to be the nominal spread, spread duration indicates the approximate percentage change in price for a 100 basis point change in the nominal spread holding the government yield constant.

The zero-volatility or static spread is the spread that when added to the government spot rate curve will make the present value of the cash flows equal to the bond's price plus accrued interest. When spread is defined in this way, spread duration is the approximate percentage change in price for a 100 basis point change in the zero-volatility spread holding the government spot rate curve constant.

Finally, the option-adjusted spread (OAS) is the constant spread that, when added to all the rates on the interest rate tree, will make the theoretical value equal to the market price. Spread duration based on OAS can be interpreted as the approximate percentage change in price of a nongovernment for a 100 basis point change in the OAS, holding the government rate constant.

A sensible question arises: How do you know whether a spread duration for a fixed-rate bond is a spread based on the nominal spread, zero-volatility spread, or the OAS? The simple answer is you do not know! You must ask the broker/dealer or vendor of the analytical system. To add further to the confusion surrounding spread duration, consider the term "OAS duration" that is referred to by some market participants. What does it mean? On the one hand, it could mean simply the spread duration that we just described. On the other hand, many market participants use the term "OAS duration" interchangeably with the term "effective duration." Once again, the only way to know what OAS is measuring is to ask the broker/dealer or vendor.

Spread Duration for Floaters

Two measures have been developed to estimate the sensitivity of a floater to each component of the coupon reset formula: the index (i.e., reference rate) and the spread (i.e., quoted margin). *Index duration* is a measure of the price sensitivity of a floater to changes in the reference rate holding the spread constant. *Spread duration* measures a floater's price sensitivity to a change in the spread assuming that the reference rate is unchanged.

Key Rate Durations

Duration measures the sensitivity of a bond's price to a given change in yield. The traditional formulation is derived under the assumption that the reference yield curve is flat and moves in parallel shifts. Simply put, all bond yields are the same regardless of when the cash flows are delivered across time and changes in yields are perfectly correlated. Several recent attempts have been made to address this inadequacy and develop interest rate risk measures that allow for more realistic changes in the yield curve's shape.[9]

One approach to measuring the sensitivity of a bond to changes in the shape of the yield curve is to change the yield for a particular maturity of the yield curve and determine the sensitivity of a security or portfolio to this change holding all other yields constant. The sensitivity of the bond's value to a particular change in yield is called *rate duration*. There is a rate duration for every point on the yield curve. Consequently, there is not one rate duration but a vector of rate durations representing each maturity on the yield curve. The total change in value if all rates move by the same number of basis points is simply the duration of a security or portfolio to a parallel shift in rates.

The most popular version of this approach was developed by Thomas Ho in 1992.[10] This approach examines how changes in US Treasury yields at different points on the spot curve affect the value of a bond portfolio. Ho's methodology has three basic steps. The first step is to select several key maturities or "key rates" of the spot rate curve. Ho's approach focuses on 11 key maturities on the spot rate curve. These rate durations are called *key rate durations*. The specific maturities on the spot rate curve for which a key rate duration is measured are 3 months, 1 year, 2 years, 3 years, 5 years, 7 years, 10 years, 15 years, 20 years, 25 years, and 30 years. However, in order to illustrate Ho's methodology, we will select only three key rates: 1 year, 10 years, and 30 years.

The next step is to specify how other rates on the spot curve change in response to key rate changes. Ho's rule is that a key rate's effect on

---

[9] For a discussion, see Steven V. Mann and Pradipkumar Ramanlal, "Duration and Convexity Measures When the Yield Curve Changes Shape," *Journal of Financial Engineering* (March 1998), pp. 35-58.

[10] Thomas S. Y. Ho, "Key Rate Durations: Measures of Interest Rate Risk," *Journal of Fixed Income* (September 1992), pp. 29-44.

neighboring rates declines linearly and reaches zero at the adjacent key rates. For example, suppose the 10-year key rate increases by 40 basis points. All spot rates between 10 years and 30 years will increase but the amount each changes will be different and the magnitude of the change diminishes linearly. Specifically, there are 40 semiannual periods between 10 and 30 years. Each spot rate starting with 10.5 years increases by 1 basis point less than the spot rate to its immediate left (i.e., 39 basis points) and so forth. The 30-year rate, which is the adjacent key rate, is assumed to be unchanged. Thus, only one key rate changes at a time. Spot rates between one year and 10 years change in an analogous manner such that all rates change but by differing amounts. Changes in the 1-year key rate affect spot rates between one and 10 years while spot rates 10 years and beyond are assumed to be unaffected by changes in the 1-year spot rate. In a similar vein, changes in the 30-year key rate affect all spot rates between 30 years and 10 years while spot rates shorter than 10 years are assumed to be unaffected by the change in the 30-year rate. This process is illustrated in Exhibit 4.26. Note that if we add the three rate changes together, we obtain a parallel yield curve shift of 40 basis points.

The third and final step is to calculate the percentage change in the bond's portfolio value when each key rate and neighboring spot rates are changed. There will be as many key rate durations as there are preselected key rates. Let's illustrate this process by calculating the key rate duration for a coupon bond. Our hypothetical 6% coupon bond has a maturity value of $100 and matures in five years. The bond delivers coupon payments semiannually. Valuation is accomplished by discounting each cash flow using the appropriate spot rate. The bond's current value is $107.32 and the process is illustrated in Exhibit 4.27. The initial hypothetical (and short) spot curve is contained in column (3).[11] The present values of each of the bond's cash flows is presented in the last column.

To compute the key rate duration of the 5-year bond, we must select some key rates. We assume the key rates are 0.5, 3, and 5 years. To compute the 0.5-year key rate duration, we shift the 0.5-year rate upwards by 20 basis points and adjust the neighboring spot rates between 0.5 and 3 years as described earlier. (The choice of 20 basis points is arbitrary.) Exhibit 4.28 is a graph of the initial spot curve and the spot curve after the 0.5-year key rate and neighboring rates are shifted. The next step is to compute the bond's new value as a result of the shift. This calculation is shown in Exhibit 4.29. The bond's value subsequent to the shift is $107.30. To

---

[11] The spot rates are annual rates and are reported as bond-equivalent yields. When present values are computed, we use the appropriate semiannual rates which are taken to be one half the annual rate.

EXHIBIT 4.26　　Graph of How Spot Rates Change when Key Rates Change

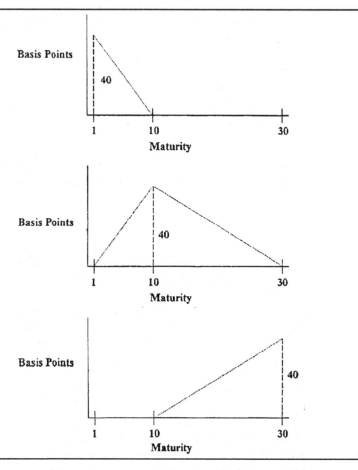

estimate the 0.5-year key rate duration, we divide the percentage change in the bond's price as a result of the shift in the spot curve by the change in the 0.5-year key rate. Accordingly, we employ the following formula:

$$\text{Key rate duration} = -\frac{P_0 - P_1}{P_0 \Delta y}$$

where

P_1 = bond's value after the shift in the spot curve
P_0 = bond's value using the initial spot curve
Δy = shift in the key rate (in decimal)

EXHIBIT 4.27 Valuation of 5-Year, 6% Coupon Bond Using Spot Rates

Years	Period	Spot Rate (in percent)	Cash Flow (in dollars)	Present Value (in dollars)
0.5	1	3.00	3	2.96
1.0	2	3.25	3	2.90
1.5	3	3.50	3	2.85
2.0	4	3.75	3	2.79
2.5	5	4.00	3	2.72
3.0	6	4.10	3	2.66
3.5	7	4.20	3	2.59
4.0	8	4.30	3	2.53
4.5	9	4.35	3	2.47
5.0	10	4.40	103	82.86
			Total	107.32

EXHIBIT 4.28 Graph of the Initial Spot Curve and the Spot Curve After the 0.5-Year Key Rate Shift

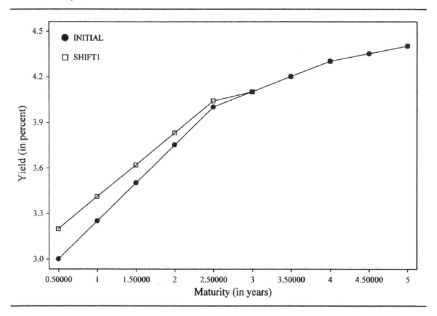

EXHIBIT 4.29   Valuation of the 5-Year, 6% Coupon Bond After 0.5-Year Key Rate and Neighboring Spot Rates Change

Years	Period	Spot Rate (in percent)	Cash Flow (in dollars)	Present Value (in dollars)
0.5	1	3.20	3	2.95
1.0	2	3.41	3	2.90
1.5	3	3.62	3	2.84
2.0	4	3.83	3	2.78
2.5	5	4.04	3	2.71
3.0	6	4.10	3	2.66
3.5	7	4.20	3	2.59
4.0	8	4.30	3	2.53
4.5	9	4.35	3	2.47
5.0	10	4.40	103	82.86
			Total	107.30

Substituting in numbers from our illustration presented above, we can compute the 0.5-year key rate duration as follows:

$$0.5\text{-year key rate duration} = \frac{107.32 - 107.30}{107.32(0.002)}$$

$$= 0.0932$$

To compute the 3-year key rate duration, we repeat this process. We shift the 3-year rate by 20 basis points and adjust the neighboring spot rates as described earlier. Exhibit 4.30 shows a graph of the initial spot curve and the spot curve after the 3-year key rate and neighboring rates are shifted. Note that in this case the only two spot rates that do not change are the 0.5-year and the 5-year key rates. Then, we compute the bond's new value as a result of the shift. The bond's postshift value is $107.25 and the calculation appears in Exhibit 4.31. Accordingly, the 3-year key rate duration is computed as follows:

$$3\text{-year key rate duration} = \frac{107.32 - 107.25}{107.32(0.002)}$$

$$= 0.3261$$

The final step is to compute the 5-year key duration. We shift the 5-year rate by 20 basis points and adjust the neighboring spot rates.

EXHIBIT 4.30   Graph of the Initial Spot Curve and the Spot Curve After the 3-Year Key Rate Shift

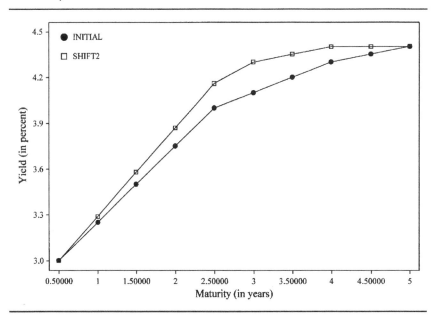

EXHIBIT 4.31   Valuation of the 5-Year, 6% Coupon Bond After 3-Year Key Rate and Neighboring Spot Rates Change

Years	Period	Spot Rate (in percent)	Cash Flow (in dollars)	Present Value (in dollars)
0.5	1	3.00	3	2.96
1.0	2	3.29	3	2.90
1.5	3	3.58	3	2.84
2.0	4	3.87	3	2.78
2.5	5	4.16	3	2.71
3.0	6	4.30	3	2.64
3.5	7	4.35	3	2.58
4.0	8	4.40	3	2.52
4.5	9	4.40	3	2.47
5.0	10	4.40	103	82.86
			Total	107.25

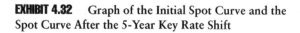

EXHIBIT 4.32   Graph of the Initial Spot Curve and the
Spot Curve After the 5-Year Key Rate Shift

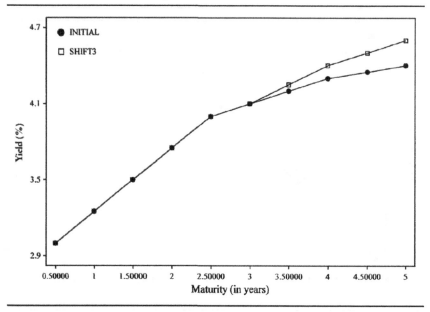

Exhibit 4.32 presents a graph of the initial spot curve and the spot curve after the 5-year key rate and neighboring rates are shifted. The bond's postshift value is $106.48 and the calculation appears in Exhibit 4.33. Accordingly, the 5 year key rate duration is computed as follows:

$$\text{5-year key rate duration} = \frac{107.32 - 106.48}{107.32(0.002)}$$
$$= 3.9135$$

What information can be gleaned from these key rate durations? Each key rate duration by itself means relatively little. However, the distribution of the bond's key rate durations helps us assess its exposure to yield curve risk. Intuitively, the sum of the key rate durations is approximately equal to a bond's duration.[12] As a result, it is useful to think of a set of key rate durations as a decomposition of duration into sensitivities to various portions of the yield curve. In our illustration, it is not surprising that the lion's share of the yield curve risk exposure of the

---

[12] The reason it is only approximate is because modified duration assumes a flat yield curve whereas key rate duration takes the spot curve as given.

EXHIBIT 4.33   Valuation of the 5-Year, 6% Coupon Bond After 5-Year Key Rate and Neighboring Spot Rates Change

Years	Period	Spot Rate (in percent)	Cash Flow (in dollars)	Present Value (in dollars)
0.5	1	3.00	3	2.96
1.0	2	3.25	3	2.90
1.5	3	3.50	3	2.85
2.0	4	3.75	3	2.79
2.5	5	4.00	3	2.72
3.0	6	4.10	3	2.66
3.5	7	4.25	3	2.59
4.0	8	4.40	3	2.52
4.5	9	4.50	3	2.46
5.0	10	4.60	103	82.05
			Total	106.48

coupon bond in our illustration is due to the bond's terminal cash flow, so the 5-year key rate duration is the largest of the three. Simply put, the 5-years bond's value is more sensitive to movements in longer spot rates and less sensitive to movements in shorter spot rates.

Key rate durations are most useful when comparing two (or more) bond portfolios that have approximately the same duration. If the spot curve is flat and experiences a parallel shift, these two bond portfolios can be expected to experience approximately the same percentage change in value. However, the performance of the two portfolios will generally not be the same for a nonparallel shift in the spot curve. The key rate duration profile of each portfolio will give the portfolio manager some clues about the relative performance of the two portfolios when the yield curve changes shape and slope.

CONVEXITY

The duration measure indicates that regardless of whether interest rates increase or decrease, the approximate percentage price change is the same. However, as we noted earlier, this is not consistent with Property 3 of a bond's price volatility. Specifically, while for small changes in yield the percentage price change will be the same for an increase or decrease in yield, for large changes in yield this is not true. This suggests that duration is only a good approximation of the percentage price change for small changes in yield.

We demonstrated this property earlier using a UK gilt principal strip priced to yield 4.435% with a duration of 17.631. For a 10 basis point change in yield, the estimate was accurate for both an increase and decrease in yield. However, for a 200 basis point change in yield the approximate percentage price change was off considerably.

The reason for this result is that duration is in fact a first (linear) approximation for a small change in yield.[13] The approximation can be improved by using a second approximation. This approximation is referred to as "convexity." *The use of this term in the industry is unfortunate since the term convexity is also used to describe the shape or curvature of the price/yield relationship.* The *convexity measure* of a security can be used to approximate the change in price that is not explained by duration.

Convexity Measure

The convexity measure of a bond is approximated using the following formula:

$$\text{Convexity measure} = \frac{V_+ + V_- - 2V_0}{2V_0(\Delta y)^2}$$

where the notation is the same as used earlier for duration as given by equation (4.4).

For the UK gilt principal strip priced to yield 4.435% with a settlement date of May 30, 2003, we know that for a 20 basis point change in yield ($\Delta y = 0.002$):

$$V_0 = 45.36, \ V_- = 46.99, \ V_+ = 43.79$$

Substituting these values into the convexity measure given by equation (4.4):

---

[13] Mathematically, any function can be estimated by a series of approximations referred to as a Taylor series expansion. Each approximation or term of the Taylor series is based on a corresponding derivative. For a bond, duration is the first-term approximation of the price change and is related to the first derivative of the bond's price with respect to a change in the required yield. The convexity measure is the second approximation and related to the second derivative of the bond's price.

$$\text{Convexity measure} = \frac{46.99 + 43.79 - 2(45.36)}{2(45.36)(0.002)^2} = 165.344$$

We'll see how to use this convexity measure shortly. Before doing so, there are three points that should be noted. First, there is no simple interpretation of the convexity measure as there is for duration. Second, it is more common for market participants to refer to the value computed in equation (4.4) as the "convexity of a bond" rather than the "convexity measure of a bond." Finally, the convexity measure reported by dealers and vendors will differ for an option-free bond. The reason is that the value obtained from equation (4.4) is often scaled for the reason explained after we demonstrate how to use the convexity measure.

Convexity Adjustment to Percentage Price Change

Given the convexity measure, the approximate percentage price change adjustment due to the bond's convexity (i.e., the percentage price change not explained by duration) is

$$\begin{aligned} &\text{Convexity adjustment to percentage price change} \\ &= \text{Convexity measure} \times (\Delta y)^2 \times 100 \end{aligned} \tag{4.4}$$

For example, for the UK gilt principal strip, the convexity adjustment to the percentage price change based on duration if the yield increases from 4.435% to 5.435% is

$$165.34 \times (0.01)^2 \times 100 = 1.65\%$$

If the yield decreases from 4.435% to 5.435%, the convexity adjustment to the approximate percentage price change based on duration would also be 1.65%.

The approximate percentage price change based on duration and the convexity adjustment is found by summing the two estimates. So, for example, if yields change from 4.435% to 5.435%, the estimated percentage price change would be

Estimated change using duration alone	=	−17.63
Convexity adjustment	=	+1.65
Total estimated percentage price change	=	−15.98%

The actual percentage price change is −16.14%.

For a decrease of 100 basis points, from 4.435% to 3.435%, the approximate percentage price change would be as follows:

Estimated change using duration alone   = +17.63
Convexity adjustment   =   +1.65
Total estimated percentage price change = +19.28%

The actual percentage price change is +19.33%. Thus duration combined with the convexity adjustment does a much better job of estimating the sensitivity of a bond's price change to large changes in yield. Accordingly, for large changes in required yield, duration and convexity used together deliver a more accurate estimate of how much a bond's price will change for a given change in required yield than duration used alone.

Notice that when the convexity measure is positive, we have the situation described earlier that the gain is greater than the loss for a given large change in rates. That is, the bond exhibits positive convexity. We can see this in the example above. However, if the convexity measure is negative, we have the situation where the loss will be greater than the gain. For example, suppose that a callable bond has an effective duration of 4 and a convexity measure of -30. This means that the approximate percentage price change for a 200 basis point change is 8%. The convexity adjustment for a 200 basis point change in rates is then

$$-30 \times (0.02)^2 \times 100 = -1.2$$

The convexity adjustment is -1.2% and therefore the bond exhibits the negative convexity property illustrated in Exhibit 4.18. The approximate percentage price change after adjusting for convexity is

Estimated change using duration   = −8.0%
Convexity adjustment   = −1.2%
Total estimated percentage price change = −9.2%

For a decrease of 200 basis points, the approximate percentage price change would be as follows:

Estimated change using duration   = +8.0%
Convexity adjustment   = −1.2%
Total estimated percentage price change = +6.8%

Notice that the loss is greater than the gain—a property called *negative convexity* that we discussed earlier and illustrated in Exhibit 4.18.

Scaling the Convexity Measure

The convexity measure as given by equation (4.4) means nothing in isolation. It is the substitution of the computed convexity measure into equation (4.5) that provides the estimated adjustment for convexity that is meaningful. Therefore, it is possible to scale the convexity measure in any way as long as the same convexity adjustment is obtained.

For example, in some books the convexity measure is defined as follows:

$$\text{Convexity measure} = \frac{V_+ + V_- - 2V_0}{V_0(\Delta y)^2} \tag{4.5}$$

Equation (4.6) differs from equation (4.4) since it does not include 2 in the denominator. Thus, the convexity measure computed using equation (4.6) will be double the convexity measure using equation (4.4). So, for our earlier illustration, since the convexity measure using equation (4.4) is 165.35, the convexity measure using equation (4.6) would be 330.68.

Which is correct, 165.35 or 330.68? The answer is both. The reason is that the corresponding equation for computing the convexity adjustment would not be given by equation (4.5) if the convexity measure is obtained from equation (4.6). Instead, the corresponding convexity adjustment formula would be

$$\begin{aligned} &\text{Convexity adjustment to percentage price change} \\ &= (\text{Convexity measure}/2) \times (\Delta y)^2 \times 100 \end{aligned} \tag{4.6}$$

Equation (4.7) differs from equation (4.5) in that the convexity measure is divided by 2. Thus, the convexity adjustment will be the same whether one uses equation (4.4) to get the convexity measure and equation (4.5) to get the convexity adjustment or one uses equation (4.6) to compute the convexity measure and equation (4.7) to determine the convexity adjustment.

Some dealers and vendors scale convexity in a different way. One can also compute the convexity measure as follows:

$$\text{Convexity measure} = \frac{V_+ + V_- - 2V_0}{2V_0(\Delta y)^2(100)} \tag{4.7}$$

Equation (4.8) differs from equation (4.4) by the inclusion of 100 in the denominator. In our illustration, the convexity measure would be 1.6535 rather than 165.35 using equation (4.4). The convexity adjustment formula corresponding to the convexity measure given by equation (4.8) is then

Convexity adjustment to percentage price change

$$= \text{Convexity measure} \times (\Delta y)^2 \times 10{,}000 \qquad (4.8)$$

Similarly, one can express the convexity measure as shown in equation (4.9):

$$\text{Convexity measure} = \frac{V_+ + V_- - 2V_0}{V_0(\Delta y)^2(100)} \qquad (4.9)$$

For the UK gilt principal strip we have been using in our illustrations, the convexity measure is 3.3068.

Convexity adjustment to percentage price change

$$= (\text{Convexity measure}/2) \times (\Delta y)^2 \times 10{,}000 \qquad (4.10)$$

Consequently, the convexity measure (or just simply "convexity" as it is referred to by some market participants) that could be reported for this UK strip are 165.35, 330.68, 1.6535, or 3.3068. All of these values are correct, but they mean nothing in isolation. To use them to obtain the convexity adjustment to the price change estimated by duration requires knowing how they are computed so that the correct convexity adjustment formula is used. *It is the convexity adjustment that is important—not the convexity measure in isolation.*

It is also important to understand this when comparing the convexity measures reported by dealers and vendors. For example, if one dealer shows a manager Bond A with a duration of 4 and a convexity measure of 50, and a second dealer shows the manager Bond B with a duration of 4 and a convexity measure of 80, which bond has the greater percentage price change response to changes in interest rates? Since the duration of the two bonds is identical, the bond with the larger convexity measure will change more when rates decline. However, not knowing how the two dealers computed the convexity measure means that the manager does not know which bond will have the greater convexity adjustment. If the first dealer used equation (4.4) while the second dealer used equation (4.6), then the convexity measures must be adjusted in terms of either equation. For example, the convexity measure of 80 computed using equation (4.6) is equal to a convexity measure of 40 based on equation (4.4).

Let's return to Exhibit 4.1 which is the Bloomberg Yield Analysis screen for the UK gilt principal strip in our illustration. Bloomberg's convexity measure is displayed in the Sensitivity Analysis box in lower left-hand corner of the screen. Specifically, the convexity measure reported is 3.195 which is the same number (within rounding error) we calculated using equation (4.10).

Modified Convexity and Effective Convexity

The prices used in equation (4.4) to calculate convexity can be obtained by either assuming that when the yield changes the expected cash flows either do not change or they do change. In the former case, the resulting convexity is referred to as *modified convexity*. (Actually, in the industry, convexity is not qualified by the adjective "modified.") In contrast, *effective convexity* assumes that the cash flows do change when yields change. This is the same distinction made for duration.

As with duration, there is little difference between modified convexity and effective convexity for option-free bonds. However, for bonds with embedded options there can be quite a difference between the calculated modified convexity and effective convexity measures. In fact, for all option-free bonds, either convexity measure will have a positive value. For bonds with embedded options, the calculated effective convexity measure can be negative when the calculated modified convexity measure is positive.

THE IMPORTANCE OF YIELD VOLATILITY

What we have not considered thus far is the volatility of interest rates. For example, as we explained earlier, all other factors equal, the higher the coupon rate, the lower the price volatility of a bond to changes in interest rates. In addition, the higher the level of yields, the lower the price volatility of a bond to changes in interest rates. This is illustrated in Exhibit 4.34, which shows the price/yield relationship for an option-free bond. When the yield level is high (Y_H in the exhibit) a change in interest rates does not produce a large change in the initial price (P_H in the exhibit). However, when the yield level is low (Y_L in the exhibit) a change in interest rates of the same number of basis points as shown when the yield is high does produce a large change in the initial price (P_L in the exhibit).

This can also be cast in terms of duration properties: the higher the coupon, the lower the duration; and the higher the yield level the lower the duration. Given these two properties, a 10-year noninvestment grade bond has a lower duration than a current coupon 10-year Treasury note since the former has a higher coupon rate and trades at a

EXHIBIT 4.34   The Effect of Yield Level on Price Volatility

$$(Y_H' - Y_H) = (Y_H - Y_H'') = (Y_L' - Y_L) = (Y_L - Y_L'')$$
$$(P_H - P_H') < (P_L - P_L') \text{ and}$$
$$(P_H - P_H'') < (P_L - P_L'')$$

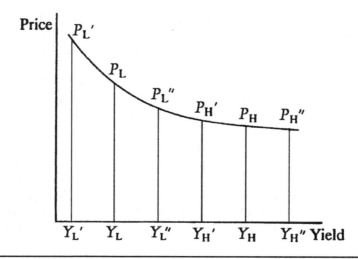

higher yield level. Does this mean that a 10-year noninvestment grade bond has less interest rate risk than a current coupon 10-year Treasury note? Consider also that a 10-year Swiss government bond has a lower coupon rate than a current coupon 10-year US Treasury note and trades at a lower yield level. Therefore, a 10-year Swiss government bond will have a higher duration than a current coupon 10-year Treasury note. Does this mean that a 10-year Swiss government bond has greater interest rate risk than a current coupon 10-year US Treasury note? The missing link is the relative volatility of rates which we shall refer to as *yield volatility* or *interest rate volatility.*

The greater the expected yield volatility, the greater the interest rate risk for a given duration and current value of a position. In the case of non-investment grade bonds, while their durations are less than current coupon Treasuries of the same maturity, the yield volatility is greater than that of current coupon Treasuries. For the 10-year Swiss government bond, while the duration is greater than for a current coupon 10-year US Treasury note, the yield volatility is considerably less than that of 10-year US Treasury notes.

Consequently, to measure the exposure of a portfolio or position to rate changes, it is necessary to measure yield volatility. This requires an understanding of the fundamental principles of probability distributions. The measure of yield volatility is the standard deviation of yield changes. As we will see, depending on the underlying assumptions, there could be a wide range for the yield volatility estimate. A framework that ties together the price sensitivity of a bond position to rate changes and yield volatility is the *value-at-risk (VaR) framework*.

Products

Two

Products

CHAPTER 5

The Euro Government Bond Market

Antonio Villarroya
Director of European Fixed Income Strategy
Merrill Lynch

Despite the appearance of many new fixed income assets, the government bond market continues to be, by far, the largest market in the Eurozone. In this chapter we analyse the recent trends in this market, its primary and secondary markets, and the key intracountry spread determinants.

RECENT EVOLUTION OF THE EURO GOVERNMENT BOND MARKET

The history of the government bond market in continental Europe is relatively short, as most of the countries in this region did not have a liquid government bond market until the early 1990s. Yet, after several years of steady growth, the key event for the European government market was the start of the European Monetary Union (EMU) in January 1999. Up to that moment, the excessive fragmentation among the different European bond markets and the embedded exchange rate risk had prevented the emergence of a deep, large government bond market in continental Europe. Before this consolidation process, the market could not be considered large and deep enough to compete with the US Treasury market as the asset of choice for investors looking for a liquid "risk-free" asset. The start of the EMU therefore made a much deeper government market possible, widening significantly this market's investor base.

EXHIBIT 5.1   Euro Government, Treasury, JGB, and Gilt Market in Percent Terms

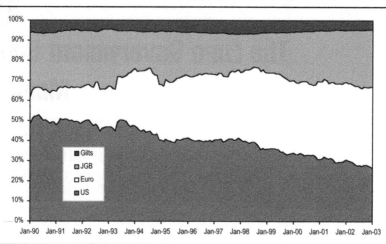

Source: ML Bond Index System.

Helped by the strong growth registered in recent years, the Euro government market has recently become the largest government bond market, due not only to the sizeable increase registered in the late 1990s, but also due to the decrease in the US Treasury market outstanding in this period. This recent growth has taken the Euro government market outstanding to €2.5 trillion[1] at the beginning of 2003 (i.e., around 40% larger than the Treasury market and 30% more than the outstanding amount of Japanese government bonds). In fact, taking only into consideration the four major government bond markets (US Treasuries, Euro govies, UK gilts, and Japanese JGBs), the Euro bond market has registered the largest increase among all these markets being currently close to 40% of this aggregate. As seen in Exhibit 5.1, this percentage was just around 13% of the G-4 combined market in 1990 and, by January 2003, nearly eight times its size in 1990. In the meantime the size of the US Treasury market has increased by "only" 40%, registering a sharp decrease in relative terms. The UK gilt and the JGB market were by January 2003 around twice the size they were in the early 1990s.

The Euro market has not only become the largest government bond market in size but also in number of issues. This market had in February 2003 over 250 liquid issues (over €1 billion outstanding and 1-year maturity), significantly more than the 108 issues in the Treasury market or the nearly 170 JGB issues. There are just around 25 liquid issues trading in the UK gilt market.

---

[1] According to Merrill Lynch (ML) indices, that is, without illiquid bonds (outstanding below €1 billion) or bonds shorter than a 1-year maturity.

EXHIBIT 5.2   Volumes Issued in the Euro-Denominated Bond Markets (1999 – 2002)

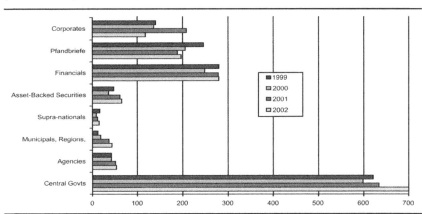

Source: European Commission.

This market's growth rate has been fairly steady in the last few years, with 1998 and 1999 registering the largest increases. Yet this growth pace subsequently decreased, mainly because of the large UMTS windfalls in some Euro countries and the Stability and Growth Pact limits. As a result, this market has registered single digit growth rates in the three years from 2000 to 2002. In this regard, in addition to the above mentioned factors, it should also be taken into account the relative increase in the Euro T-bill market. Helped by a low interest rate environment and a steep yield curve, many of these countries have noticeably increased their T-bill markets at the expense of the bond market.

The beginning of the Monetary Union also benefited the other Euro fixed income markets, i.e., quasi-sovereigns, high grade and high-yield credit bonds, ABS, etc. Yet although all these other markets have experienced a massive increase in the last few years (see Exhibit 5.2), they are still quite small compared with the government sector, being still very far from reaching the relative size they represent in the US fixed income market (see Exhibit 5.3). The government market continues to represent nearly 50% of all the euro-denominated bond supply, followed by the Pfandbfriefe market (around 13%), and the financial sector bond market (19%).

Country Breakdown

Within Euroland just three countries (Germany, Italy, and France) add up to over two thirds of the total Euro government market, increasing this percentage to nearly 90% of the total size if the Spanish, Dutch, and Belgian markets are included (see Exhibit 5.4). These relative

EXHIBIT 5.3   2002 Relative Bond Supply in Euro-Denominated Bonds

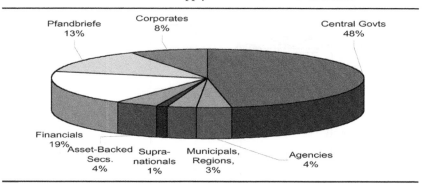

Source: European Commission.

EXHIBIT 5.4   Euro Government Bond Market Breakdown in Percentage Terms (2002)

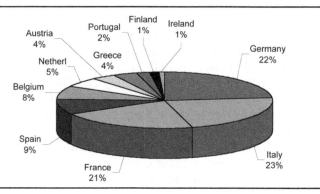

Source: ML Global Bond Indices.

weights have not changed significantly in the last few years although it is worth noticing how the relative weight of those countries following more strictly the Stability and Growth Pact (SGP) has diminished compared to those whose deficits have remained closer to the 3% threshold. In general terms, the amounts issued by each country are very close to their respective market weights, with the total amount of fixed-rate bond supply around €500 billion in both 2001 and 2002.

It is also interesting to notice how the average duration of the different Euro government bond markets has been converging in the last few years, with the duration of the lower rated countries increasing to almost match the stable or declining duration figures of the core Euro countries. This process has taken the modified duration of the Euro G-8 markets within a 0.4 range, with a range of just around 0.25 among the Euro G-4 countries.

EXHIBIT 5.5   Euro Government Bond Market Outstanding by Redemption Date
(€ million)

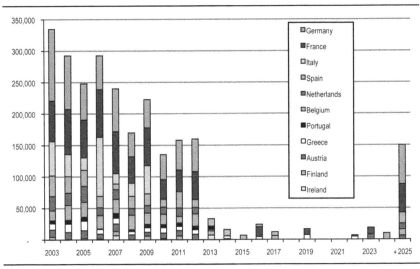

Source: ML, BBG.

Maturity Breakdown

As seen in Exhibit 5.5, due to the large percentage of the short-end supply
and the time decay of the longer-dated issuance, the bulk of the outstanding government debt is currently concentrated in short-end maturities,
with almost 50% of the total debt outstanding maturing before 2007. Also
significant are the large decline in outstanding terms above the 10-year
maturity and the large gap between this maturity and the 30-year sector. In
fact, until very recently, the Spanish Treasury was practically the only frequent borrower in the 15-year maturity. Between 1999 to 2002 the
French, Italian, and Austrian Debt Agencies have started (or come back) to
issue bonds in that area, helping to fill the gap between the 10-year and the
ultra-long end of the curve. We think this trend is likely to continue,
although mainly to the detriment of the very long end of the curve, whose
supply has remained fairly stable (in nominal terms) in the last few years,
despite the increase since 2000 in the total amount of bonds issued.

EURO GOVERNMENT BOND PRIMARY MARKET

The two main developments in the Euro government bond primary market since the inception of EMU have been the decline in the relative

amount of government sector supply within the Eurozone bond market and the increase in the competence among the Euro Debt Agencies.

The fiscal consolidation registered in the Eurozone countries in the late 1990s was the main driver behind the sizeable decrease in Euro government bond supply since 1999, although the economic downturn that started in 2000 has decelerated the previous trend. This decline has been specially patent in the Mediterranean countries, whose deficit and debt to GDP ratios fell significantly in the second half of the last decade (see Exhibit 5.6).

Forced by the Maastricht criteria, Euro countries' fiscal accounts registered a noticeable improvement in the late 1990s, thus diminishing significantly these countries' government bond supply in GDP terms. In fact, some of these countries had to undertake buyback programs and/ or bond exchanges to be able to give liquidity to their markets given their declining funding needs. This trend was exacerbated in the year 2000 by the sale of third generation telephone licenses (UMTS),[2] gener-

---

[2] In the year 2000, at the peak of the dot-com bubble, many governments around the world allocated or sold licenses to offer high-speed wireless (third generation) telephone services. The sales of these UMTS (Universal Mobile Telecommunications System) licenses produced in some of these countries large windfalls for their governments.

These one-off revenues added to the healthy and sustained economic growth in those years (the Euro economy grew 2.8% in 1999 and 3.5% in 2000) reduced significantly those countries' financing needs. Accordingly, the amount of Euro government bonds issued in 2000 was just around €475 billion, clearly below the €600 billion issued the previous year.

The amounts obtained by these governments varied significantly according to the timing and the procedure followed in the sale. In those Euro countries, where the licenses were allocated via "beauty contests," (Spain, Finland), the proceeds were not significant enough to affect these governments' funding needs. Yet in those countries where the 3G licenses were sold via auctions, the windfalls provided a large help to those governments' accounts, thus reducing significantly their funding needs that year. The United Kingdom aside, the clearest example of the "irrational exuberance" prevalent in those days was the more than €50 billion obtained by the German government in the sale of its UMTS licenses. To put things into perspective, this amount was equivalent to the 2.5% of that year's German GDP. More moderate, but still significant in relative terms, were the €2.7 billion paid in the Netherlands or the €13.5 billion in Italy.

Due to the sharp decline in their funding needs some of these governments, (especially the United States and the United Kingdom) had to become more active in buying back their own debt to be able to issue new bonds (thus providing liquidity to the market given the lack of funding needs).

As time proved, these declines were only temporary and a mirror image of the frenzied times. The subsequent downturn in the global economy increased the governments' funding needs significantly in the subsequent years, taking many of these countries back to 2–3% deficit to GDP ratios in 2002–2003.

EXHIBIT 5.6   Public Deficit and Debt to GDP Ratios

	2004	2003	2002	2001	2000	1999	1998	1998	1999	2000	2001	2002	2003	2004
Belgium	96.8	101.7	105.6	107.6	109.2	114.9	119.2	-0.7	-0.5	0.1	0.4	-0.1	0.0	0.3
Germany	61.1	61.8	60.9	59.5	60.2	61.2	60.9	-2.2	-1.5	1.1	-2.8	-3.8	-3.1	-2.3
Greece	98.5	102.0	105.8	107.0	106.2	105.1	105.8	-2.5	-1.9	-1.8	-1.2	-1.3	-1.1	-1.1
Spain	51.1	53.2	55.0	57.1	60.5	63.1	64.6	-2.7	-1.1	-0.6	-0.1	0.0	-0.3	0.1
France	59.3	59.3	58.6	57.3	57.3	58.5	59.5	-2.7	-1.6	-1.3	-1.4	-2.7	-2.9	-2.5
Ireland	34.5	35.0	35.3	36.4	39.1	49.7	55.2	2.4	2.2	4.4	1.5	-1.0	-1.2	-1.0
Italy	106.9	108.0	110.3	109.9	110.6	114.5	116.3	-2.8	-1.8	-0.5	-2.2	-2.4	-2.2	-2.9
Netherlands	48.8	50.1	51.0	52.8	55.8	63.1	66.8	-0.8	0.7	2.2	0.1	-0.8	-1.2	-0.9
Austria	62.3	63.0	63.2	63.2	63.6	64.9	63.9	-2.4	-2.3	-1.5	0.2	-1.8	-1.6	-1.5
Portugal	58.1	58.1	57.4	55.5	53.3	54.4	55.0	-2.6	-2.4	-2.9	-4.1	-3.4	-2.9	-2.6
Finland	41.1	41.9	42.4	43.4	44.0	46.8	48.8	1.3	1.9	7.0	4.9	3.6	3.1	3.5
Euro Area	68.2	69.1	69.6	69.3	70.1	72.5	73.7	-2.2	-1.3	0.1	-1.5	-2.3	-2.1	-1.8
Denmark	39.8	42.4	44.0	44.7	46.8	52.7	56.2	1.1	3.1	2.5	3.1	2.0	2.0	2.5
Sweden	50.3	51.7	53.8	56.6	55.3	65.0	70.5	1.9	1.5	3.7	4.8	1.4	1.2	1.5
UK	37.6	38.1	38.5	39.1	42.1	45.1	47.7	0.2	1.1	4.0	0.7	-1.1	-1.3	-1.4
EU-15	61.6	62.5	63.0	63.0	64.1	67.3	68.9	-1.6	-0.7	1.0	-0.8	-1.9	-1.8	-1.6
Luxemb.	5.4	3.9	4.6	5.6	5.6	6.0	6.3	3.1	3.6	5.6	6.1	0.5	-1.8	-1.9
United States								0.3	0.7	1.5	-0.5	-3.2	-3.6	-3.8
Japan								-10.7	-7.1	-7.4	-7.2	-8.0	-8.1	-8.2

Source: European Commission, November 2002 Forecasts.

149

ating sizeable fiscal surpluses that year in some of these countries. Yet from that moment onwards the economic deceleration has pushed financing needs higher and gross bond supply has increased again.

The decline in the amount of government bonds being issued in the late 1990s was partially filled by a sharp increase in corporate bond supply, especially within the high-grade spectrum. Yet, despite its significant growth, this market is still very far from the government market in outstanding terms. On the other hand, between 2000 and 2003 the low level of interest rates and the steepness of the yield curve have made most of the Euro Debt Agencies shift part of their bond supply to the T-bill market.

The broadening of the investor base caused by the start of the monetary union brought forward a significant increase in the competition between the different Eurozone sovereign issuers. This competition in search of the investors' preference was even more extreme in the Eurozone given the small difference in the credit risk component among all these similarly rated countries. If, before EMU, the currency risk helped these borrowers to have a quasi-monopoly situation in their own markets with the appearance of the euro currency, all these Treasuries had to compete for the same pool of funds. This increase in competition forced the Euro Debt Agencies to improve their transparency, predictability, and relationship with all market participants.

Another important factor that the EMU brought along was the standardisation of the bond markets, given the beneficial effect on these governments' debt from the exchangeability of that debt, thus increasing foreign investors' preference for these markets. To compete with other non-Euro government markets, it was second to none to have a market as homogeneous as possible among all the different Euro issuers. Accordingly, these Treasuries increased their coordination in the basic characteristics of their instruments, procedures, and coupon calculation convention (Actual/Actual).

The broadening in the fixed income managers' mandates since the EMU started (to track Eurozone bond indices), the redemption of long-held bonds, and the increase in the exchangeability between these markets helped to increase significantly the percentage of sovereign debt held by nonresidents. As an example of a middle-sized market, the percentage of nonresidents' holdings of Spanish bonos increased to 45% by the end of 2002 versus just 23% four years earlier.

Another area these Debt Agencies have had to focus on more has been their communication policy. Another of the obvious consequences of the above mentioned loss of the domestic edge was the necessary increase in the transparency and predictability of these Debt Agencies, especially in terms of issuance policy. In fact, most Euro Debt Agencies now publish periodical supply calendars providing as much details as possible regarding the amounts and maturities to be issued as well as any other useful information regarding new bond lines, swap operations, average duration targets, etc. These communications are not only held with their respective market makers but also via periodical bulletins and their Internet web sites. Another increasingly frequent method of keeping the market informed about their activities has been the pages these Debt Agencies have on several financial servers such as Bloomberg and Reuters.

Primary Market Measures to Improve Market Liquidity

Besides this improvement in the information provided to the market, the above-mentioned increase in competition has made the Debt Agencies improve as much as possible the liquidity of their bonds. As we mention earlier, liquidity, and credit rating are the key drivers of the relative performance of Euro countries' bonds and, therefore, the Debt Agencies will try to improve their bonds' liquidity as much as possible to decrease their funding costs. In the primary market this increase in *liquidity* has been patent as explained below.

Bond Auctions: Sizes, Maturities and Types of Bonds

The broadening of the investor base together with the desire to enhance the liquidity in the government bond secondary market have been the main reasons behind the continuous increase in the size of both the Euro bond outstandings as well as the amounts offered at every auction.

This has not only been the case for smaller issuers with low nominal funding needs. In fact some of the largest increases in both the outstanding size and the amounts offered at every auction have taken place in the Euro G-3 countries. A clear example is in the evolution of the Euro benchmark government bonds, that is, on 10-year Bunds. Those German 10-year bonds issued in 1998–1999 had an average outstanding of around €10 billion while this amount has more than doubled with the 5% Jul-12 Bund, which has reached a €27 billion outstanding (see Exhibit 5.7). With the largest BTPs also exceeding €20 billion and most of the new French OATs just slightly lower, these Euro government bond outstandings have become much closer to their US counterparts, where some Treasuries reach the $35 billion level.

A similar pattern has taken place not only in the other maturities of the German curve (the OBL 140 Aug-07 is €20 billion, whereas the OBLs 130 to 133 were between €5 billion and €8 billion) but also in practically all other Euro countries. This increase in the auctioned and outstanding sizes has been even more dramatic in the smaller countries.

The smaller Euro countries, given their low GDP levels and therefore reduced nominal funding needs, used to issue a large number of

EXHIBIT 5.7   2008–12 German Bunds Outstanding (€ billion)

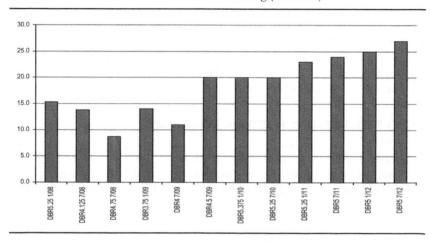

small bonds before EMU started. Yet the outstanding size of many of
these bonds (many of them below €2 billion) was not enough to reach
the critical mass to be considered a liquid asset where investors could
trade large amounts without significantly affecting its price. Therefore
these countries have had to concentrate most of their supply in just a
few bonds a year, having sometimes had to carry out exchange auctions
and/or buybacks to reach this critical mass. This situation was even
more extreme in the high-growth, late 1990s period and in the fiscally
stricter countries. Nowadays, practically only the Euro G-4 countries
and Greece launch and tap bonds across the entire yield curve while the
rest of the Euro countries just launch a few new bonds every year, tap-
ping them afterwards throughout the year.

The level that could be considered a minimum for liquidity purposes
could be the €5 billion Euro MTS threshold. Below this level bonds are
considered too easy to squeeze and therefore their liquidity is much
lower, creating a sort of vicious circle. This €5 billion level is actually
the target many smaller Euro countries have when they launch a new
bond, especially when they are issued via syndicate. Otherwise they
would try to reach this amount as fast as possible.

Exchange Auctions and Buybacks

To reach this minimum amount as soon as possible as well as to reduce
the level of their liabilities, smoothen their debt's redemption profile or
improve the liquidity of selected issues, many European Debt Agencies
carry out bond exchange auctions and/or buybacks. These operations

are even more important for those countries that, due to their small size or their strict fiscal policy, have low funding needs.

Bond Exchanges

The bond exchange procedure has been used profusely by many Euro Debt Agencies such as the Spanish Treasury, which has been exploiting this tool since 1996 to enhance the liquidity of its on-the-run bonds. France, Italy, Portugal, and Belgium have also been carrying out frequent bond exchange auctions, either as one-off operations or by opening exchange windows during a specific period of time. As mentioned above, the main target behind these exchanges is to provide liquidity to the new bonds as fast as possible. In fact, this procedure has been necessary for some small countries to provide liquidity to their markets since 1999. This was the case of Ireland that, after being absent from the market throughout 2001, carried a sizeable exchange program in 2002 to be able to issue its new 5- and 10-year bonds, as this country's funding needs were too small to issue new liquid bonds.

These operations have normally been concentrated in the last months of the year, as exchanging old (high coupon) bonds by new lower coupon bonds (closer to current market levels) has a cost given the difference between both prices. Accordingly, these Debt Agencies tend to wait to have as much information as possible regarding the evolution of their countries' fiscal deficits to evaluate the amount of cash they can allocate to these operations. In general terms, these operations are well perceived by the market as they allow investors to exchange their old, less liquid bonds for the new benchmarks. On top of this, the Debt Agency will be able to increase the liquidity of its new benchmarks faster than otherwise.

Bond Buybacks

The rationale behind bond buybacks is very similar to that behind the exchange auctions (i.e., to increase the country's funding needs to allow a larger—and faster—issuance of the current benchmark bonds). In fact, a buyback is just the first leg of an exchange auction, the other one being the actual bond issuance. The main difference is that buybacks tend to be concentrated in short maturity bonds, thus helping to smoothen the redemption profile by limiting upcoming years' redemptions and therefore supply.

A weaker than expected fiscal performance could cause the reduction or even the total disappearance of any scheduled buyback programs, as happened in France and Spain in 2002, which bought back a noticeably lower amount of bonds than previously announced in their funding programs.

The procedure for these buybacks could either be via OTC purchases or preannounced buyback windows, normally restricted to primary dealers.

Other Key Characteristics of the Primary Markets

Other key features of primary markets include (1) issuance maturities and techniques, (2) issuing procedure, and (3) primary dealers. Each characteristic is discussed below.

Issuance Maturities and Techniques

Although the introduction of the euro has helped to homogenise the characteristics and maturities of the bonds issued, there are still some differences between these countries' supplied assets. Euro-denominated fixed coupon bonds bear the brunt of these countries' issuance, but there are also some other types of bonds being issued by these countries.

In general terms the maturities issued are split between the short-end (2- and 3-year), the intermediate sector (5-year), the long end (10-year), and ultralong end bonds. Within this area the most frequently tapped maturity used to be the 30-year sector; but since 2001 many countries have joined Spain in issuing 15-year bonds, making this sector's supply in 2003 as large as that of the 30-year maturity. In the long end of the curve, some countries such as Greece have also issued 20-year maturity bonds. Historically there has not been a market for over-30-year bonds, although the Italian Treasury has announced its intention to start issuing bonds in the 40- and 50-year area.

Most of these bonds normally pay fixed-rate coupons, the main exception being the Italian CCTs. These bonds have a 7-year maturity and they pay a floating coupon related to the yield of the Italian 6-month T-bills. Other than these, floating-rate note supply has fallen significantly since 1998–1999, although some countries still issue a small part of their supply in floating-rate notes. Another noticeable exception to fixed coupon issuance are French TECs. These bonds' coupons, paid on a quarterly basis, are linked to the Tec10 index, an average yield of OATs with a constant maturity of 10 years. Yet these bonds' supply has also decreased significantly of the last few years.

Last, but not least, one sector that is increasingly gaining importance, not only in terms of amounts issued but also in investors' interest, is the *inflation-linked bond market*. Up to this moment the French Trésor has been the main issuer of these bonds, although some other treasuries have already issued small amounts in these type of bonds (Greece) or have expressed their desire to do it in the future (Italy).

Without getting into too much detail, these bonds pay a smaller fixed coupon (between 2% and 4%) to which the accumulated inflation in that period is added. By mid-2003 the French Trésor had already issued five different inflation-linked OATs, three of them referenced to French inflation[3] and two of them linked to Eurozone retail prices. The success of these bonds has recently permitted their launch via normal auctions, rather than syndicate issues. As of July 2003, they represent more than 10% of the French bond annual supply.

Issuing Procedure: Syndicate versus Auctions

Given some Euro countries' relatively low funding needs—even more as they stabilise their budgets—and due to the increase in the competitiveness for the investors' preference (and to achieve the above-mentioned critical mass) many countries are increasingly launching their new bonds via syndication. This method, used among others by the Finnish, Portuguese, Austrian, Greek, and Belgian Debt Agencies, allows them to allocate large sums in one go (€5 billion is the most usual amount) thus reaching a broader investor base and facilitating the good performance of these bonds after their launch. These syndicate issues, also used by quasisovereign issuers as EIB, FHLMC, or KfW, tend to be followed by subsequent taps.

Such syndicated issues have also been used by some of the larger Debt Agencies such as Spain and Italy, to distribute their long-term bonds more efficiently. The French Trésor has used this procedure for the launch of its inflation-linked bonds.

The main benefit of these syndications compared to the normal auctions is that the syndicate leading group will try to reach final and stable investors for the bonds, thus avoiding large sales in the secondary market after their launch.

In these syndicate issues the borrower tends to name several (three to four) lead managers who would allocate most of the expected amount to be issued with a co-lead group allocating the rest of this target amount. The lead group would in normal terms be formed by domestic and foreign banks, usually primary dealers in that market.

Primary Dealers

To ensure the good performance of the bond auctions and a constant pricing of their bonds, the Government Debt Agencies constitute a group of primary dealers for their bond markets. In general terms these institutions (normally investment banks) will have to bid in the auctions

---

[3] French ex-tobacco CPI.

and quote a certain number of bonds with a predetermined bid-offer spread. On the other hand, these banks would have access to the second round of the auctions (in better conditions) and should be the main beneficiaries of other deals with these Treasuries such as swap operations or the above mentioned syndicate issuance.

SECONDARY MARKET AND INTRA-EURO SPREAD DETERMINANTS

In general terms, within a Monetary Union, the spreads between same maturity bonds from different countries should be determined by the relative liquidity of these bonds and their credit status.

Bearing this in mind, yield differences among Euro countries should tend to diminish (or even disappear) in the long run. On the one hand, the decline in these countries' financing needs as they strengthen their fiscal positions, forced by the Stability and Growth Pact, tends to make these credit ratings converge, albeit slowly. On the other hand, the smaller countries, helped by a broader investor base within EMU and the above mentioned enhanced supply mechanisms and trading platforms, should see improved the liquidity of their bonds, thus helping to diminish the liquidity component of their spreads to the Euro core countries. This reduction in the liquidity premium and the relative credit worthiness among the Euro countries' should make bond spreads converge in the long run.

Yet it should be taken into account that a large part of this convergence had already taken place before the actual start of the monetary union (see Exhibit 5.8). Once the market had priced in a significant probability of a country getting into EMU, investors started to put on convergence trades, tightening significantly the peripheral spreads to the Euro core countries. These trades had a limited risk, as in most cases the final exchange rate parities were already known (mid rate of the previous ERM bands).

Sovereign Credit Ratings

Credit rating agencies (CRAs) try to encapsulate in the qualifications they assign to the different sovereign issuers the financial and economic conditions of the specific country, as well as their ability and willingness to pay their obligations. These ratings should therefore theoretically be a good indicator of the financial health of the issuer and these qualifications should be correlated to the yields and spreads within the Eurozone, as they should measure, to a certain extent, the borrowers' small-but-positive default probabilities.

EXHIBIT 5.8   German, French, Spanish, Italian, and Greek 10-Year Government
Yields (%)

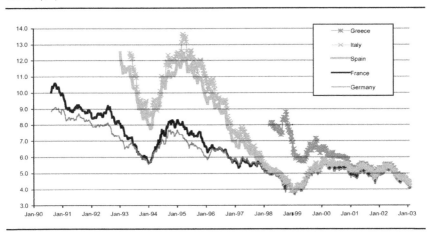

Source: ML, BBG. Greece joined the Euro in 2001.

In this regard the appearance of the EMU started an interesting discussion regarding the countries' ratings, as these qualifications used to
differentiate between domestic- and foreign-currency ratings. Sovereign
issuers usually enjoy the highest credit standing for obligations in their
own currency as they normally retain the right to print their own money
and therefore the possibility of default is very limited. On the other hand,
many of these countries, due to their specific financial and economic characteristics, do not have the highest qualification in a foreign currency.

As the Euro countries do not have the ability to print money inside
EMU, although the Euro is their domestic currency, the ratings these
countries were assigned at the beginning of the EMU were their former
foreign-currency ratings. Before January 1999 four of the countries in
this area already deserved the highest credit rating according to the
major three CRAs (Germany, France, the Netherlands and Austria).
From the start of the Monetary Union two more countries have joined
the top-notch club, namely Ireland (October 2001, S&P) and Finland
(February 2002, S&P). The rest of the countries are still below this category, with Greece being the lowest-rated country in this area (in EMU
since 2001). As seen in Exhibit 5.9, there are no significant divergences
between the ratings these three agencies assign to each specific country,
the only small difference being that S&P and Fitch appear to be slightly
stricter than Moody's in this regard.

As these ratings reflect the ability and willingness of the countries to
assume their obligations and, taking it to the extreme, the probability to

EXHIBIT 5.9 Euro Countries' Credit Rating (March 2003)

	Moody's	S&P	Fitch
Germany	Aaa	AAA	AAA
France	Aaa	AAA	AAA
Netherlands	Aaa	AAA	AAA
Austria	Aaa	AAA	AAA
Finland	Aaa	AAA	AAA
Ireland	Aaa	AAA	AAA
Spain	Aaa	AA+	AA+
Belgium	Aa1	AA+	AA
Portugal	Aa2	AA	AA
Italy	Aa2	AA	AA
Greece	A1	A	A

Source: Moody's, S&P, and Fitch.

EXHIBIT 5.10 10-Year Spread to Germany (Average 1999–2003) versus Credit Rating

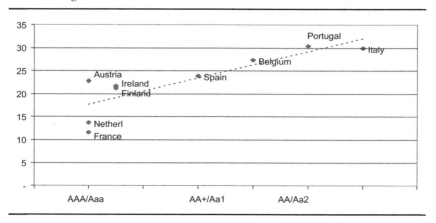

Source: ML, BBG. Greece not included given its late adhesion to the EMU.

default, there should be a direct relationship between the countries' ratings and their yields (or spreads to benchmark curve). This relationship is clearly shown in Exhibit 5.10, which represents each country's rating versus its average 10-year maturity yield spread versus Germany between January 1999 and February 2003. It seems clear from the exhibit that there is an almost linear relationship between spreads and ratings, with the distance between each country's spread to the regression line being a proxy of each country's liquidity premium. This

EXHIBIT 5.11 Spain versus Germany 10-Year Spread

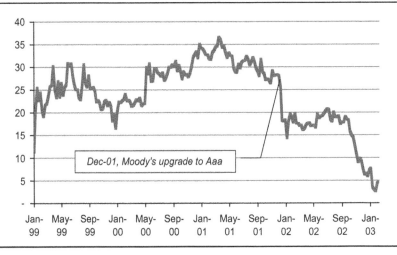

Source: ML, BBG.

"liquidity premium" is more evident in the AAA rated category, where the market has clearly differentiated between very liquid and deep markets, such as France, versus smaller less liquid countries such as Austria.

Changes in the rating of any of these Euro countries should obviously make its bonds under or outperform the rest of the markets. Yet most of the time these rating changes have been largely anticipated by the market either due to the improvement in that country's official rating outlook or just based on previous comments or reports from these agencies. A clear example of this relationship between spreads and credit ratings was seen in December 2001, when Moody's upgraded the Kingdom of Spain to Aaa. Prior to the announcement, based on the previous comments from this agency, the market was already speculating with the possibility of a rating upgrade. Yet Moody's decided to upgrade the Spain debt by two notches, taking its rating to the highest category. The extent of this shift surprised the market, which expected just a single notch increase, and therefore the Spanish debt outperformed all its Euro counterparties after the announcement, tightening its spread versus Germany and the other Euro core countries (see Exhibit 5.11).

As of March 2003 and since the inception of the Monetary Union no single country has been downgraded, with only one country having been given a negative outlook. In January 2003 S&P changed the outlook of the Republic of Italy to negative given "the persistence of large structural fiscal deficits and the lack of a well-defined medium-term fiscal strategy." Interestingly, Italy had been upgraded seven months earlier by Moody's, to Aa2.

The breach of the Stability and Growth Pact deficit threshold by several countries (Portugal in 2001 and Germany and France in 2002) could also endanger these countries' rating outlooks. Their fiscal evolution is therefore being closely watched by the market as they may have an impact on these countries' spreads to other Euro governments and interest rate swaps.

Other Intra-Euro Bond Spread Drivers

Credit ratings and the size and liquidity of each bond market are the main long-term drivers behind intra-Euro government bond spreads. Yet there are many other smaller and more microspread drivers, which are becoming increasingly more relevant given the above-mentioned credit and liquidity convergence among these countries.

Supply Dynamics, Fiscal Trends, and Issuance Policy

Although the credit rating and fiscal outlook are by far the two most important spread drivers in the Eurozone, the extent of the market impact of these fiscal features depend significantly on the assets chosen to fund those needs. Fiscal needs have a noticeable impact on bond markets when these gaps are funded via government bonds—their market impact is much more limited if this funding is obtained via other sources (T-bills, loans, privatisations, etc.). On top of this, these issued amounts are relevant not only in gross terms but also in net terms (*ex*-redemptions) as it is this second amount that better reflects each country's financial needs. Additionally, with most of the Euro markets still being quite domestic in terms of bond holdings, it can be assumed that a large part of the bonds being paid down may come back to the same market, helping this market to outperform the rest of its Euro counterparties.

In this regard, it is also important to add to the amounts due to mature the possible buybacks or exchange auctions. These targeted bonds would tend to trade rich as the market would assume that the Treasury buying back these bonds could be keen to pay a premium to retire the largest possible amount of those bonds.

Large coupon payments are another key factor to watch to assess each country's relative performance, as the investor's domestic bias could favour that part of these payments would come back to the same market. Additionally, by reinvesting these flows (coupons and redemptions) in the same market they come from, the country and credit composition of the bond portfolio would not be altered.

The breakdown between the funding by maturities and assets is also affected by market dynamics. In this regard, low short-term yields and steep yield curves have recently favoured the increase in T-bill issuance, with many Euro countries having increased since 2001 the percentage of their funding needs covered in the very short end of the curve. With this shift to the T-bill market, the Debt Agencies not only obtain a cheaper funding. They also avoid the negative impact on their bond markets that a sharp increase in this supply would have.

The maturity breakdown of the government bond issuance is also key in determining Euro government spreads. Accordingly, the announcement of an unexpected supply increase (or decrease) in a specific maturity could affect significantly the spreads and slope in the Euro curve. This feature was clearly seen by the end of 2001, when the German Debt Agency announced its intention to issue just €6 billion in 30-year Bunds in 2002, noticeably below the market expectations. The initial reaction was not only a clear outperformance of the German long end but also a sizeable flattening in the 30-/10-year slope and a widening in long German swap spreads. These dynamics increase the importance of an accurate forecasting of the amounts and maturity breakdown of each country's upcoming supply—even more in the present spread stability given the similarity between these countries' credit fundamentals. On top of this, when a bond auction takes place, the actual increase in the amount of paper in the market may affect its price just due to a supply-demand condition, although this possible impact would depend on the market conditions of that moment.

Bond Index Tracking

As in many other financial markets, many fixed income fund managers measure their performance against bond indices, formed by the most liquid bonds in each market. So, any noticeable deviation between the characteristics of the managed portfolio and the index tracked would involve a risk for the asset manager. Therefore, these indexed funds would tend to track (although to a different degree, depending on the risk characteristics of the portfolio) the evolution of these indices. In fact, the most passive funds managers should try to minimise their tracking error by replicating as much as possible the characteristics of the index in terms of average coupon, duration, and country breakdown.

One of the obvious consequences is that index tracking fund managers have to anticipate as much as possible any possible change in these indices to avoid increases in their tracking errors. The indices are usually rebalanced at the end of each month according to the bonds entering or leaving the index,[4] with those months with heavy long-term

---

[4] Many indices only include bonds over 1-year maturity and, therefore, the rebalancing would take into account the bonds falling below this threshold in the previous month. Accordingly, the larger the amount of bonds falling below this maturity, the larger the index extension.

supply and/or large drops from the index producing significant changes in the index duration at the month-end. Indexed investors would therefore have to buy or sell bonds around those days to match these duration changes. To minimise the tracking error further these managers would have to make their adjustments at the same time that the index is rebalanced, with the obvious consequences on the bond market around that period.

Bond Future Deliverability

Bond futures have become, due to their liquidity and leverage characteristics, the main hedging and investment instruments for many market participants. Their open interest and traded volumes have therefore increased sharply in the last few years. As the underlying of these bond futures are specific government bonds, these bonds tend to follow a similar evolution than the future they represent. Accordingly, the bonds included in an exchange traded future deliverable basket and, especially, the cheapest to deliver (CTD) tend to trade rich in their own curve, given the large amount of long and short positions in this future as well as the possibility of squeezes in the delivery dates.

The degree of this dearness will depend, among other factors, on the outstanding amount of the bond, the open interest of the future, bond market volatility, and that bond's supply dynamics. As discussed next, the Eurex victory in the Eurozone "battle of the futures" has made the German deliverable (and CTD) bonds trade richer than the other German and Euro bonds in their respective maturities.

Swap Spreads and their Relationship to Peripheral Spreads

The evolution of Euro government bond swap spreads has always been linked to the performance of the peripheral spreads (or vice versa). Yet this relationship should be taken with a pinch of salt as, having the German rate in both sides of the equation, a simple spike in the German market bond volatility will make this correlation increase spuriously.

That said, there are two reasons why the performance of German swap spreads are related to Euro peripheral spreads. The first one is that, flows apart, the bond-swap spread reflects the yield difference between a government rate and the composition of a string of EURIBOR rates (i.e., a swap fixed rate). As the average credit quality of the banks in the EURIBOR panel is A-AA, any increase in the investors' preference for credit quality will make both swap and peripheral spreads widen versus the core Euro government rate, thus increasing the correlation between both differentials. Yet this increase in the correlation will be mainly due to the outperformance of the benchmark asset

(German bonds in this case) rather than to any similarity between the swap rate and that of the peripheral country.

Yet there is another relationship between swap and peripheral spreads. The sharp swap spread tightening the Euro market has registered since 2001 has taken some peripheral bond yields over their respective maturity swap rate. At this point some investors have increased their purchases of non-German bonds, swapping them into floating. With these two actions investors will receive a string of EURIBOR flows during the life of the asset, but they would keep a high quality sovereign paper that they can use as collateral to get cheap financing conditions (for instance in the European Central Bank repo operations). These trades were seen first when long BTPs started to trade over EURIBOR rates, but after the recent large swap spread narrowing many medium and long-end Euro government bonds now trade over EURIBOR, thus making these trades less interesting. As these trades are not symmetrical (no need to undo the trade once/if the bond trades again through EURIBOR), the correlation between swap and peripheral spreads should be lower in a swap spread widening trend.

Other Related Markets

Government bond markets are closely related to other fixed income assets and interest rate and bond futures. This market is also increasingly related to the interest rate swap market.

Wholesale Electronic Markets and Trading Platforms

One of the most significant developments after the start of the EMU has been the success of EuroMTS, an electronic broking system launched in April 1999. Before 1999 most bond markets were telephone-based, but this platform has expanded rapidly to cover practically all the government markets; its market share has expanded significantly. The success of these trading platforms has been favoured by the large broadening of this market with the start of EMU and they have become very important to increase investors' confidence, market liquidity, and price transparency. This increase in platform trading has not only taken place in the Eurozone, being also the case in the US and other bond markets.

The other recent advance in bond trading has been the dealer-to-customer platforms, where institutional investors can compare the prices provided by several intermediaries simultaneously, with the obvious benefit for the final investor.

Strip Markets

Many Euro government bonds can be "stripped," breaking them down into each of the single payments that they involve, that is, one flow for each remaining coupon payment and another one for the principal. With this procedure an n-year maturity coupon-bearing bond is transformed into $n + 1$ strips (zero coupon bonds), which can be traded separately in the market. Yet this market is much less liquid in the Eurozone than in the United States.

Repo Markets

Despite the homogenisation among Euro government bond markets, repo markets have remained largely national and unevenly developed throughout the single-currency area, showing a scarce increase in cross-border transactions. Regulatory, legal, and tax specific issues as well as different market practices have been the main reason behind the lack of a truly unified repo market in the Euro area.

Euro Futures Market

The recent large increase in the size and number of investors in the Euro government bond has brought along a significant improvement in the depth and liquidity of the bond futures market. In fact, since 1999 Eurex has continued to confirm its status as the most active derivatives exchange globally, ahead of the Chicago Board of Trade (CBOT), while the Bund contract established itself firmly as the most actively traded futures contract in the world. This 10-year bond based future is actually most widely used hedging instrument for all euro-denominated issues. As an example, the Euro Bund future in January 2003 had an open interest of 973,000 contracts (just in the March-03 maturity) while the open interest of the CBOT US 10-year Note Future for the same maturity was around 750,000 contracts and 400,000 in the US long bond future.[5] In this regard, the winner-takes-all characteristic of a futures market (where liquidity is second to none) created at the beginning of EMU a dispute between the Eurex and the Matif future exchanges. While the characteristics are very similar (it could even be argued that Matif's future coupon is closer to current yields), the winner of this battle has been (at least up to March 2003) the Eurex future. In fact, Eurex futures are the main reference in all maturities (Euro Bunds, 5-year Bobl, and 2-year Schatze futures). These contracts only include German bonds in the deliverable baskets.

---

[5] Contract sizes are very similar being €100,000 in Eurex and $100,000 in the States.

Yet this superiority was not always that clear as the Matif future challenged this supremacy in 2000, when the large decrease in the German funding needs created a shortage of deliverable paper that made squeezes easier in these futures.[6] The particular features of the German debt in those days made the Matif contract a better hedge of a pan-Euro bond portfolio, given its higher correlation with the Euro government index. Yet the subsequent increase in the German funding needs, the changes in some Eurex rules (making squeezes less likely) and the large concentration of positions in these futures avoided the diversion of these positions to the Euro Notional Matif future.

---

[6] For many years some of the Euro countries' Debt Agencies have been fine tuning their liabilities, paydown calendars, and liability risks in the swap and other derivatives market. Yet since 2001 these Debt Agencies have increased their activity in these markets significantly. The main purpose behind this activity is twofold: to save money by managing their debt portfolios and to gain more freedom in their supply breakdown. This increased activity in IRS also helped to tighten long-term swap spreads because of (1) the interest of many of the Treasuries in reducing the average life of their debt, due in part to the steepness of the curve and (2) the small size of the funding needs of some of these countries and their desire to issue their bonds where liquidity is highest are forcing them to concentrate a large part of their supply on the 10-year maturity. Therefore, to offset the subsequent increase in their debt's average life, they become long-end receivers in the swap market, being sometimes helped by paying positions in short-end maturities.

In this respect the French Trésor (AFT) has attracted the most market attention, due to the large volumes used, the announcement of the maximum amounts eligible for these operations, and the aggressive average life targets set. The AFT announced in September 2001 a large reduction in its marketable debt average life by the end of that year and 2002 (6 and 5.5 years respectively). Yet after €60 billion done in swaps (between long receivers and short payers), the AFT cancelled this program temporarily in the third quarter of 2002, given the low levels in both yields and swap spreads. In theory, once swap spreads widen and/or yields rise again, the AFT could reopen this program as it still targets a significant duration reduction for its debt average life by the end of 2003.

The German Debt Agency (GDA) has seen increases in the maximum amount it can do in swaps from DM20 billion in 2001 (€10 billion) to €20 billion in 2002 and, at least, €30 billion in 2003. As stated by the GDA, "swap deals can play a very important role in present day portfolio management." Yet, due to stability, the GDA is trying to keep in its debt average life and the wide distribution of its supply across the yield curve, the GDA could not be considered a clear net receiver or payer in swaps.

Regarding other Euro countries, the Dutch and the Belgian Debt agencies are also players in this market trying to keep their respective debt's average duration close to their target of four, but the amounts involved are smaller than in France or Germany, between €5 billion and €10 billion per year. Some other countries (Portugal, Greece, Italy, etc.) have been active in this market for a very long time, although with no clear directional bias. Spain is expected to start this activity in the near future.

There is some trading in other Euro countries' futures (France, Spain, etc.) but the amounts traded in them are very small in relative terms to the Eurex, and they remain due to some market makers' commitment to continue giving liquidity to these products.

Interest Rate Swaps as the Benchmark Curve for Euro Govies

Given the absence of a single, clearly defined benchmark sovereign yield curve and the continuous expansion of the IRS market since the late 1990s, government bond market participants have increased the use of the swap curve as a reference for the valuation (and hedge) of government and nonsovereign bonds. Another factor that has enhanced the depth and liquidity of the swap market is the enlargement of the Euro corporate bond market, as both investors and issuers could use swaps to convert their fixed-rate liabilities into floating-rate ones or vice versa.

CHAPTER 6

The Eurobond Market

David Munves, CFA
Head of Lehman Brothers' European Index Group
Lehman Brothers International

Most inventions are born of necessity, and the Eurobond market is no exception. It grew out of the need to find a home for dollars that were accumulating overseas in the late 1950s. One source of these funds was Russian trade officials who were parking dollars in European banks. This was the time of the Cold War, and the Russians were reluctant to deposit their money in US institutions, where they would be subject to the vicissitudes of international politics. The offshore market was further boosted in the early 1960s by a series of regulations in the United States that encouraged dollar bank deposit growth and borrowing outside the country. The first generally recognized Eurobond was sold in 1963, and the market has grown more or less steadily ever since.

Since its beginnings, the Eurobond market has changed beyond all recognition. Even the way the term Eurobond is used has evolved. Forty years seems like a very long time, especially in the financial markets. Yet other sources of finance, such as banking and insurance, have been around for centuries. The US corporate bond market traces its roots to the 1840s. Moreover, in many ways the evolution of the Eurobond market can be divided into two distinct periods, one before, and one after, the introduction of the euro in January 1999. The market remains in a phase of evolution and growth. The limitations we describe later are significant.

Estefania Meana, Sally Cartwright, Filippo Lanza, CFA, Tom Howard, CFA, Morven Jones, and Mark Howard, CFA, all of Lehman Brothers, and Maurice Walraven of ABP Investments in the Netherlands, provided valuable insights and assistance in the writing of this chapter.

However, the economic rationale for its continued expansion remains intact. It might take longer than some of the original optimistic pundits predicted. But over time, the Eurobond market will develop the depth and liquidity to match the needs of both investors and issuers.

We have divided this chapter into five sections that chart the evolution of the Eurobond market: (1) the market's roots and growth through the end of 1998; (2) the first four years of the euro-denominated market (from 1999 to 2002), including a discussion of the motivations of investors and issuers for participating in the market; (3) trading and other practices of today's Eurobond market; (4) Eurobond market sectors other than fixed rate, high grade corporates; and (5) the outlook for the Eurobond market in the 21st century. The bulk of the chapter concerns itself with the high grade euro-denominated corporate market (in this chapter, "corporate" includes issues sold by industrial companies, utilities, and financial institutions). This is deliberate. High-grade corporates are the dominant market sector and look likely to remain so for some time. Nonetheless, other sectors are active and of considerable interest to market participants. Away from straight cash instruments, the euro-denominated spread product area also contains thriving credit derivatives and structured cash sectors. These are covered in other chapters of this book.

FOUNDING AND THE EARLY YEARS

For market practitioners, in the pre-EMU, era the term Eurobond meant a type of security rather than the currency of the obligation. Eurobonds could be sold in any convertible currency, by issuers domiciled in any country. A Eurobond had—and still has—the following features:[1]

- Usually issued in bearer form, that is, not registered in a way that makes ownership known to national authorities.
- Interest is paid free of withholding taxes.
- Underwritten and distributed by an international group of banks.
- Free from national regulations.
- Unsecured (usually).
- Listed on a stock exchange—usually Luxembourg or London. However, this is largely a formality. Almost all trading takes place over-the-counter. Most of this is over the telephone, but trading through electronic hubs is growing.

---

[1] Peter Gallant, *The Eurobond Market* (London: Woodhead-Faulkner Ltd., 1988), p. 54.

▨ Cleared through a pan-European clearing system, that is, Clearstream Banking Societe Anonyme or Euroclear Bank SA/NV, as operator of the Euroclear System.

Eurobonds are distinct from domestic bonds sold in a country's home market. Such issues are sold in the country's currency; listed on the national stock exchange; cleared through the domestic system; and subject to national regulation. Domestic issues tend to have less protection for creditors, in that they often carry very basic terms and lack features such as negative pledges. (We discuss bond covenants and other documentation issues later in the chapter.) In the Eurobond market's early days the distinction between a Eurobond and a domestic security was of some importance—particularly for questions of tax. "Foreign bonds" were also popular. These were bonds sold in a domestic market, but by nondomestic issuers. Hence the Bulldog market in the United Kingdom, Rembrandts in the Netherlands, and Yankees in the United States. The old distinctions have largely fallen by the wayside as the Eurobond format has triumphed. At least in Europe, domestic corporate securities are extremely rare.

Since the establishment of European Monetary Union on 1 January 1999, the word Eurobond has taken on an additional meaning—that of a euro-denominated security. In this chapter we generally use "Eurobond" both for issues that are in Eurobond format, and that are euro-denominated. There are, of course, markets for noneuro denominated corporate issues, chiefly in dollars and sterling. Noncorporate borrowers, such as sovereigns, supranationals, and agencies, are also big issuers of Eurobonds in all the major currencies.

Early Developments

For the first few years of its life, the Eurobond market was largely the preserve of the dollar. Why were the early issues in dollars rather than in European currencies? For a start, the money was there to be invested. We have already mentioned the prudent Russians, who had good reason to keep their hard-earned dollars "off-shore." The stock of dollars outside the United States was further built up by the country's dominant position in the post-war global economy.

On top of this, US regulations (specifically "Reg Q") limited the interest rate that could be paid on domestic depository accounts. So holders of overseas dollars were in no hurry to repatriate them. Borrowing in European currencies was made difficult by a web of exchange controls and other limitations hard to imagine for today's market participants. Indeed, the gradual relaxation of these controls allowed the Eurobond market to expand to other currencies.

The late 1960s saw issuance in French francs, Deutschmarks, and Dutch guilders, while in the 1970s issues denominated in Australian and Canadian dollars, sterling, and yen made their debuts.[2] However, dollar-denominated issues retained their predominant position, accounting for around two-thirds of activity through the 1980s.[3]

London quickly established itself as the effective center of the Eurobond market. It benefited from a good location in terms of time zones, overlapping for at least part of the business day with New York, the Continental centers, and Tokyo. Language was important. US banks were already established in the City of London, and the ability to work in an English-language location made growth there attractive. There was already a critical mass of expertise in ancillary areas such as law and accountancy, from the City's role as an arranger of syndicated loans. On the regulatory front, the Bank of England was prepared to take a relaxed view towards the growth of the new market. The United Kingdom was also largely free of market-limiting features such as turnover taxes and exchange controls on international transactions. And lest we forget, the United Kingdom's lighter tax regime for individuals—at least compared with most continental European countries—was and remains an attraction for well-paid bankers.[4]

Private clients formed a major part of the investor base in the early days of the market. The bearer nature of the obligations[5] was an important factor, as money could be invested without the tax authorities knowing the principal existed. As noted, interest on Eurobonds is paid free of tax, and it is up to the recipient to report the income earned to the authorities. Finally, many issuers are well-known, good quality names, just the sort of borrowers that appeal to individual investors. While private clients are not nearly as important as they used to be, the stereotypical "Belgian dentist" was indeed a key provider of funds during the market's early development.[6]

---

[2] Gallant, *The Eurobond Market*, p. 77.

[3] Gallant, *The Eurobond Market*, p. 79.

[4] Gallant, *The Eurobond Market*, p. 19.

[5] "Bearer" securities come in two forms. In the market's early days, bonds were physical definitive notes, with coupons attached. The owner, or more often, the custodial bank, would clip the coupons and present them to the paying agent for the issue to receive payment. Now global notes are more common. Global notes preserve the anonymity of the owner but are more efficient to manage than physical definitive notes, as they allow the owners to collect payments of interest and principal through the clearing systems. A global note represents the entire tranche of the issue. It is held by a depository on behalf of the clearing systems.

[6] For a good description of this and other aspects of the Eurobond market's sometimes colorful early days, see Ian Kerr, *A History of the Eurobond Market* (London: Euromoney Publications, 1984).

The final milestone to note in the Eurobond market's formative years was the creation of securities clearing systems in the late 1960s. The lack of such systems caused a number of problems for market participants at the time. The transfer of paper securities between buyers and sellers was cumbersome, and the process was subject to the risk of theft or loss. The same problems arose in the presentation of clipped coupons for payment to the issuers' paying agents. A far better alternative would be to keep the securities in one place, and transfer ownership and make coupon payments electronically. Settlement risk would also be reduced. These imperatives gave birth to Euroclear in 1968 and Cedel (since renamed Clearstream) in 1970. Both are owned by a consortium of banks.[7] Subsequently, the clearing systems have assumed key roles in the market for lending out Eurobonds under repurchase (repo) agreements.

The 1990s

Throughout the 1990s the Eurobond market grew at a slow but steady pace (see Exhibit 6.1). As the decade progressed, private clients formed a decreasing share of the investor base, reflecting the growth in demand from banks and big institutional investors. The expansion of the interest rate swap market in the early 1990s paved the way for banks to invest in fixed-rate securities. At the time, banks were looking for good quality corporate assets to offset the reduction in loan demand that was a consequence of the global recession. By combining an interest rate swap with a fixed-rate bond (an asset swap package), banks were able to create a floating-rate asset that matched their floating-rate liabilities.

EXHIBIT 6.1   Annual Eurobond Issuance by Currency

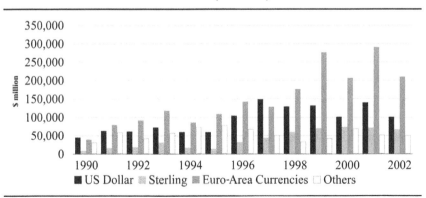

Source: Capital Data Bondware.

[7] Gallant, *The Eurobond Market*, p. 17.

EXHIBIT 6.2 The European Government Market Convergence Trade[a] versus US Single-B Credit Spreads

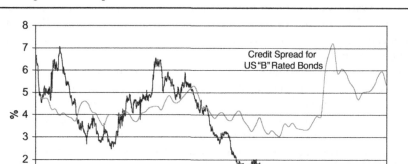

[a]Yield differential between 10-year Italian and German government debt.
Source: Bloomberg, Lehman Brothers.

The focus of institutional investors on corporate bonds rose as yields fell on government securities in the latter part of the 1990s. But demand was capped by the need for institutions such as insurance companies and pension funds to currency-match the bulk of their assets and liabilities. For example, Dutch pension funds, potentially important players in the international corporate bond market, had to place most of their funds in guilder-denominated assets. This largely limited their investment activities to government and local authority debt, since at the end of 1998 there was only €60 billion (equivalent) in guilder corporate bonds outstanding. The situation was a bit better for the bigger countries such as Germany and France; in 1998, euro-DM and euro-FFr bonds outstanding totaled €130 billion and €164 billion, respectively. But the point remains. Supply was artificially constrained, meaning higher prices and less choice.

The extremely attractive opportunities available in government bonds in the second half of the 1990s was a second factor that diverted investors' attention from the corporate sector. Foremost amongst these was the famous "convergence trade"—the bet that yields in the "peripheral" European Monetary Union (EMU) candidate countries (mainly Italy, Spain, and Portugal) would converge towards those of the "core," mainly meaning Germany. As we show in Exhibit 6.2, in 1995 Italian government yields posted their last peak at 625 bp over those for Germany. Since then they rallied in more or less a straight line, to reach a yield differential of less than 30 bp by the time the euro was launched. By way of comparison, in the United States the credit spread for single-B rated bonds—issuers with a significant risk of default, according to the rating agencies—was 429 bp over the Treasury curve in early 1995.[8] It has not traded inside 300 bp over Treasuries since then (as of early 2003). In contrast to the credit risk on single-B rated debt, in the mid-1990s Italy's local currency debt was rated A1 by Moody's and AAA by Standard & Poor's.

With the benefit of hindsight the Italy/Germany convergence play looks like the ultimate "no brainer" trade. But buying peripheral government debt against that of the core countries was not a risk-free proposition. Currency depreciation was a constant threat, as was the possibility that the countries would not qualify for EMU. But even with these risks, the convergence trade beat anything that the corporate market could offer, especially in Europe. It worked, of course, and proved to be an enormous money-maker for investors who had put it on. But by early 1998, it was largely over. Fund managers had to cast about for other ways to outperform the competition. For many, the expanded potential of the corporate Eurobond market looked like it would provide just the opportunity they needed.

THE EUROBOND MARKET POST-EMU: THE DRIVERS OF DEVELOPMENT

The Eurobond market changed significantly with the launch of European Monetary Union, which added a new impetus to its development.

The Eurobond Market at the Dawn of Monetary Union

Much as history is conventionally divided between the BC and AD eras, the development of the Eurobond market can be split between pre-euro and post-euro periods.

By the end of 1998, Eurobonds outstanding in EMU country currencies had reached the equivalent of €425 billion. The market was set to take off, and the launch of the euro provided the vital push. Investor demand reflected two factors, in addition to the need to boost portfolio performance. One was the expanded universe in which they could invest. Pension funds and insurance companies were still currency-constrained. But now they could buy securities across the Eurozone, rather than just in their home country's currency.

---

[8] Unless otherwise indicated, credit spread and bond volume data come from the Lehman Brothers Global Family of Indices

The euro-denominated Eurobond market also included bonds denominated in legacy currencies (i.e., in the currencies that became subsumed into the euro). A slightly legalistic note is in order at this point. With the launch of EMU, outstanding Eurobonds in legacy currencies (e.g., euro-Deutschmarks) have effectively been redenominated so that payments are made in euros. However, the market practice has been still to refer to them in their original currencies. Not surprisingly, they have become extremely illiquid, and are only rarely traded. Until the member states' currencies disappeared from circulation in early 2002, investors could elect to receive payment either in euros or in an issue's original currency. Most institutions chose euros.

Eurobond Market Composition at the Launch of the Euro

When the euro was launched in January 1999, the Eurobond market's composition was far from what would be expected from a "corporate" market. Some 75% of outstandings consisted of bank paper. This was due to the very tight credit spreads[9] at which banks could sell their paper. And this in turn reflected the influence of the Bank for International Settlements' (BIS) asset risk-weighting system. Banks could buy senior bonds issued by other banks, and need to set aside a much smaller amount of the capital (specifically, one-fifth the amount) than was required for debt issued by industrial companies. The dominance of banks helps to explain why the average rating for the investment grade market was so high—around Aa1, compared to A3 in the United States.

Why were there so few industrial or utility borrowers at the time of the market's launch? The reasons lie in the way the industrial and financial systems in Europe developed. It is worth digressing to explore these briefly, for they shape the market's direction even in the 21st century. A comparison with the very different history of the United States is also useful, since the American corporate market is often held out—sometimes too simplistically—as a model for Europe's future development.

A principal reason for the shortage of nonfinancial borrowers in the Eurobond market is the strength of the European banking system. Banks, rather than the bond market, have long been the major providers of credit in Europe. This stands in sharp contrast to the United States, where institutional investors are much more prominent. As can be seen in Exhibit 6.3, banks contribute 60% to 80% of national financial

---

[9] The terms "spread" or "credit spread" refer to the yield differential, usually expressed in basis points, between a corporate bond and an equivalent maturity government security or point on the government curve. It can also be expressed as a spread over the swap curve. In the former case, we refer to the fixed-rate spread. In the latter, we use the term spread over EURIBOR, or over the swap curve.

EXHIBIT 6.3   The Prominence of Banks in Different Countries

	Asset of Banks as a Percent of National Financial Assets
Austria	85
France	70
Germany	76
Italy	77
Netherlands	57
Spain	75
Switzerland	79
United Kingdom	53
United States	26

Source: BIS.

assets on the continent, compared to around 25% in the United States. The resulting deep relationships between European companies and their banks reduced the need for an active corporate bond market. And the small size of the institutional buyer base (compounded by the currency restraints noted above) meant that there were not many players to purchase the securities that might otherwise be sold.

The underlying reasons for these differences run deep. Largely for political reasons the American banking system is highly fragmented. Until recently, many states did not allow banks to have more than one branch. Even after a period of consolidation, there are still more than 9,000 banks and savings and loan institutions in America, according to the FDIC. As US industrial growth accelerated in the first half of the 19th century, the banks were not able to provide the required funding. Corporate bonds were sold instead—with many purchased by European investors.[10] In Europe, most countries have long featured large banking groups that were better able to provide the amounts of capital needed in the new industrial era.

What America lacked in banking critical mass it more than made up for in the pension fund area. The US pension system is "funded." That is, there are assets to meet the needs of retirees and to pay the future benefits of those still working. This is not to say that the funding is always adequate. Pension plan shortfalls frequently arise, especially during periods of market decline. But there are still huge amounts of cash to be invested in the equity and bond markets, as well as in alternative areas such as real estate.

---

[10] For a good history of this period, see Ron Chernow, *The House of Morgan* (London: Simon & Schuster, 1990).

In contrast to European's strength in banking, its pension system is a very limited provider of investment capital. The situation varies from country to country, but most national pension systems are largely unfunded. That is, the money paid in by workers goes directly to pay retirees' benefits. Exhibit 6.4 summarizes the situation across Europe, with a comparison to the United States. The only Eurozone country with an extensively funded system is the Netherlands. Outside of the EMU area, Switzerland, the United Kingdom, and the Nordic countries also have a good level of pension funding. This is slowly changing, as the demographic pressures on the existing system (more retirees living longer, fewer workers) prove unbearable. Moreover, the limits on national budget deficits mean that countries no longer have the flexibility to cover short-falls in pension plans, at least without making unpopular cuts in other benefits or raising social charges. The pension issue is highly charged politically, and change is slow. But change is coming nonetheless, and it provides a key driver of the Eurobond market's long-term development.

Eurobond Issuance Since the Start of EMU

On January 1, 1999, the average fixed-rate credit spread for the corporate Eurobond market was only 27 bp. This reflected the predominance of banks, the market's high average rating, the lack of credit differentiation by investors, and the rarity value of the outstanding issues. The situation did not last long. The big borrowers were anxious to diversify their funding away from the banks that had long been their major providers of credit. Banks were also not able to provide longer maturity, fixed-rate money. At the same time, issuers in sectors such as telecommunications had increased funding requirements stemming from mergers and acquisition activity and higher levels of capital investment.

Since the market's launch, diversification has increased at a fairly rapid pace, to the point that banks now make up only 33% of outstanding issues. However, the spread of activity by issuer type has been limited. The strongest growth has been in telecommunications and auto issuers, as shown in Exhibit 6.5. Bank, auto, and telecom issuers accounted for 62% of outstanding debt at the end of 2002. Again, the contrast with the United States is instructive. In the domestic dollar market, these three sectors make up 32% of outstanding debt. The growth of other industrial issuance in euros has been more muted, although it is beginning to accelerate.

Several drivers lie behind this pattern. For telecoms, the need to issue substantial amounts of long-term debt reflected the vast technological changes that swept over the industry at the end of the last millennium. The rapid spread of wireless communications led to the wave of partly debt-financed mergers among the major telecom service providers. In order to

EXHIBIT 6.4 Pension Assets and Population by Country

	Population (in millions)	Dependency Ratio[a] (%)	Value of Pension Assets ($ billion)	Pension Assets as a % of GDP	Pension Assets per Capita ($000s)
United States	267.6	19	5.571	78	21.4
EMU Members	281.1	22.4[b]	1,124	19	4.0[b]
Austria	8.1	N/A	8	4	1
Belgium	10.2	24.2	26	10	2.5
Finland	5.2	20.9	41	31	7.9
France	58.8	22.7	95	7	1.6
Germany	82.3	21.7	286	12	3.5
Ireland	3.7	19	35	43	9.7
Italy	57.4	23.2	195	19	4.3
Netherlands	15.7	18.8	558	141	35.5
Portugal	10	22.4	12	10	1.2
Spain	39.4	23.5	26	4	0.7
Other European Countries					
Denmark	5.3	22.4	166	89	31.2
Norway	4.4	25	39	24	8.9
Sweden	8.9	28.6	226	90	25.3
Switzerland	7.1	22.4	286	105	40.3
United Kingdom	59.1	24.6	1,241	86	21

[a] Population aged 65+ as a proportion of population aged 15–64.
[b] Weighted Averages for EMU member states.
Source: William M. Mercer, *US Statistical Abstracts, Pension and Investments.*

177

EXHIBIT 6.5   Euro Corporate Issuance by Major Sector

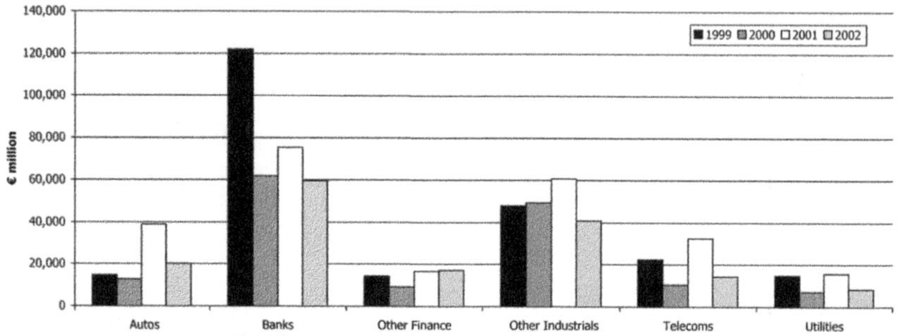

Source: Capital Data Bondware and Lehman Brothers Fixed Income Research.

provide capacity for the expected boom in wireless use, in 2000 European governments sold licences to provide "Third Generation" (3G) Universal Mobile Telephony Services. Nicely timed at the peak of the technology bubble, the licence auctions brought in a total of €117 billion to the larger countries in Europe, while adding substantially to the telecom service providers' debt levels. Much of this was refinanced in the bond market.

The story of auto company issuance is different. When discussing the auto sector, we include the finance subsidiaries of Ford, General Motors, and Daimler-Chrysler (DCX). These are commonly referred to as the US "Big Three" companies, despite DCX's German ownership. Auto manufacturers have always been heavy users of the bond market. This partly reflects the capital-intensive nature of the industry. But more important are the activities of the Big Three's finance subsidiaries (especially Ford Motor Credit and General Motors Acceptance Corp.). These provide lease and purchase financing (often at very low interest rates) for their parents' products, and are integral parts of their business models. The auto companies' large size and the short average maturities of the finance units' issues means they are among the largest corporate borrowers in the global debt markets. The growing depth of the Eurobond market provided an attractive new source of funds for them. For example, in 2001 DCX issued €7 billion in fixed-rate debt compared to €1 billion in 2000.

The steady rise of the "other industrial" (i.e., the nontelecom and nonauto sectors), reflected the aforementioned desire to diversify the companies' funding sources away from banks as well as the need to finance mergers. We should not take the bank disintermediation story too far, however. The idea seems attractive. Banks, as financial intermediaries, stand between lenders and borrowers of funds. To earn a profit out of these activities, they take a margin from the difference between their cost

EXHIBIT 6.6   Spread Differential between Bonds and Syndicated Loans[a]

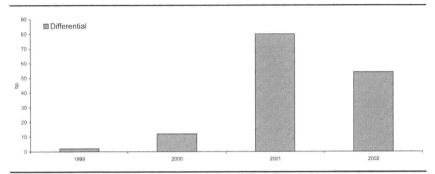

[a] Syndicated loans longer than two years. Bond LIBOR spreads measured the month of each loan signing, using bonds of similar tenors
Source: Dealogic Loanware, Lehman Brothers.

of funds and what they earn on their loans. Why not cut them out and use the bond market to connect lenders of funds directly with borrowers?

In reality, this has been slow to happen, at least for the big, profitable companies that have access to the public bond markets.[11] European banks have been reluctant to loosen their ties with long-standing customers. Also, for many institutions, their lending to prime customers has been done in the hope that it will lead to future capital markets or investment banking business. Thus, the spreads on loans to these favored borrowers are usually tighter than those on equivalent bond issues (see Exhibit 6.6). The spread differential shown in Exhibit 6.6 is not a true like-for-like comparison. Syndicated loans contain various fees that raise the total cost of borrowing. Offsetting this, spreads on bilateral loans (arranged directly between a bank and a borrower) are usually tighter than those on syndicated facilities. But even with these cautionary notes, the gap shown in Exhibit 6.6 remains substantial, and this results in a number of issuers avoiding the bond market in favor of bank borrowings.

The final reason for the slow rise of other industrial issuers is the more limited pool of potential companies to come to market. Exhibit 6.7 lists rated European companies by country as of early 2003, along with the number of potential rated entities, established by a broad screening approach. While the list is only a rough estimate, it does establish that the potential size of the ratings universe in Europe is significantly smaller

---

[11] Despite our focus on the public debt markets, banks still provide the bulk of corporate Europe's credit needs. Bank loans to commercial and industrial borrowers in Europe total €3,000 billion, compared to €651 billion of public fixed-rate investment grade debt.

EXHIBIT 6.7   Existing and Potential Rated European Issuers
Industrial and Utility Companies Only

Country/Region	Number of Companies		
	Rated	Potential Ratings Candidates[a]	Total
Benelux	11	11	22
Nordic Region	25	17	42
France	34	15	49
Germany	20	14	34
Italy	6	10	16
Iberian Peninsula	11	6	17
United Kingdom	97	32	129
Others	101	18	119
Total	305	123	428
United States	660		

[a] Unrated stock exchange listed companies with at least $500 million in equity and $150 million in operating profits.
Source: Lehman Brothers.

than the United States, which we include as a basis of comparison. The reasons for this are easy to discover. Industrial development in European countries followed different paths than the United States, which again is often held up as a model. Germany and Italy feature a (generally) thriving base of smaller, family-owned companies that are not the types to sell public market debt. The Iberian peninsula industrialized late. France's postwar economy was dominated by a small number of large state-owned or affiliated groups. And so on. Also, many companies are sized to serve their national markets, and not a pan-European one. This will no doubt change over time. But for the moment, it means that many of these entities are too small to access the public bond market.

Corporate Bonds: The Investors' Approach

So far we have focused on the issuers' view of the market—why they want to access it, and what are the barriers to their doing so. How about investors? What attractions does the European corporate bond market hold for them?

As we discussed above, one draw is the scope to outperform. With yields among government markets all tightly compressed, the only way to add alpha (fund manager-generated outperformance versus a benchmark) in the government sector is via a yield curve or duration call.

Making such "bets" offers significant possibilities, but the outcome is highly volatile. Agency and related debt trades at tight credit spreads, so there are few ways for a fund manager to distinguish himself or herself in this regard. Pfandbriefe (bonds issued by specified German entities and backed by public sector loans or mortgages) also offer only a small yield pick-up over government debt.

A second attraction is diversification. Excess returns on corporate bonds are inversely correlated with total returns on government instruments. A corporate bond's excess return is a common performance metric for the asset class. It measures the difference between a corporate bond's total return and that on an equivalent-maturity government bond (or equivalent-duration section of the government curve), usually on a monthly basis. A corporate bond's excess return "should" be positive, reflecting the additional risks (mainly default, downgrade, and liquidity), that an investor bears when buying a corporate bond rather than a default risk-free government bond. Excess return turns negative when a bond's credit spread widens (i.e., its yield increases) so its price falls in relation to a reference government bond or section of the government curve. Note that the price fall has to be enough to offset the "carry" (extra spread, or yield) earned on the corporate bond. Excess returns are usually calculated on a cumulative basis (i.e., adding the monthly figures over a period of time).

The benefits of diversification can be seen in Exhibit 6.8, which shows the relationship between the total return on government bonds and the spread on corporate assets. Their comovement (when the spread scale for the corporate market is inverted) means that when government bonds are

EXHIBIT 6.8 Euro Government Yields and Euro Corporate Spreads

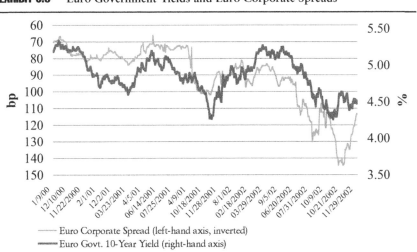

—— Euro Corporate Spread (left-hand axis, inverted)
━━ Euro Govt. 10-Year Yield (right-hand axis)

losing their value in price terms, corporate bonds are gaining in a relative sense (i.e., the tightening spreads will generate excess returns). The reverse is also true, underlining the obvious point that investors should avoid or underweight corporate bonds when credit spreads are widening. But we are discussing diversification benefits, not questions of market timing. And on this basis, the case for corporate bonds is clear.

Another factor that has driven the increased demand for corporate bonds has been changes in benchmarking practices. Bond indices have a long history in Europe as well as in the United States. Prior to EMU most indices consisted of government bonds. These were mainly calculated on a national basis, although pan-European indices were also common. Investors bought corporate bonds as an "overlay" strategy, that is, as a way to enhance performance. This changed considerably with the launch of the euro. The increased interest in corporate bonds, as well as improved data quality, gave rise to several aggregate (all asset class) indices. These could usually be provided on a component basis, such as corporate bonds only. They could also be customized according to an investor's needs. A life insurance company might want a longer duration index, for example. These benchmarks increasingly came to be adopted by fund managers looking to match more closely their benchmarks to the investment style for each portfolio, although funds using government benchmarks with corporate overlays still exist.

The effect of the aggregate indices has been to institutionalize the demand for corporate bonds. Before, it had fluctuated wildly. That is, when fund managers (usually with government benchmarks) thought that credit spreads would widen, they would divest their corporate bonds completely. Now, fund managers with aggregate indices might hold smaller corporate positions at times, but they are unlikely to eliminate them completely. To do so would be to incur an unacceptably high level of tracking error.[12]

The Euro-Denominated High-Yield Market

So far our discussion of the euro-denominated corporate Eurobond market has focused on the high grade sector, that is, on issuers rated Baa3/BBB– and above by Moody's and Standard & Poor's. This is only part of the corporate story. The high-yield, or subinvestment grade, sector has developed in parallel since the mid-1990s. The divide between the high grade and high-yield sectors is deeply rooted in US regulation and practice, particularly as it involves insurance companies. The split

---

[12] Tracking error, a common measure of portfolio risk, measures the expected volatility (in basis points of total return) of the portfolio against its benchmark over a specified period.

has carried over to Europe. But it is less strongly felt, given the lack of strong regulatory differentiation between high grade and high-yield issuers. Investor guidelines are also more loosely written in Europe, allowing some fund managers to buy both high-yield and high grade assets. A final point is the large number of "fallen angels" (issuers that have been downgraded from high grade to high yield) in 2001 and 2002 have reduced the divisions between the two sectors.

Nonetheless, a lot of high-yield investing is done by funds dedicated to the asset class. Drivers of market performance also differ. For these reasons, we have chosen to discuss the high-yield asset class separately from high grade.

Phases of the High-Yield Market's Development

The development of the high-yield market can be divided into three distinct phases. The market opened in earnest in 1997. Probably the first benchmark issue was sold by Geberit, a Swiss manufacturer of bathroom fixtures. A Deutschmark issue, it was in many ways a classic high-yield debt transaction. It was rated B2/B, and partly funded a leveraged buyout of the company sponsored by Doughty Hanson, a private equity firm. The company's strong competitive position and stable earnings record made it an attractive noninvestment grade issuer (the company's noninvestment grade ratings reflected its high gearing following the buyout).

Other similar deals followed, although market growth was slow; by 2000 the high-yield sector had outstandings of €20 billion. This was small compared to the high-grade market (€417 billion at the time), but still encouraging given that European high-yield debt represented an entirely new form of financing. Note that the high-yield data includes only issues rated Ba1/BB+ or below, and thus understates the true size of the market. Unrated issues, many of which would be high-yield if rated, have always been more common in Europe than in the United States, where they are almost unheard of in the public market. The ability to execute transactions without the involvement of the rating agencies is largely due to the more relaxed guidelines at many investment funds, as we noted above.

The second phase of the market's development began in early 1999, when emerging telecommunications companies began to sell debt. These included competitive local exchange companies (commonly known as CLECs); competitive long distance carriers; emerging markets wireless carriers; cable television companies; and, at the final stage, web hosting companies. This was, of course, at the height of the telecom and technology bubble. The subsequent failure of growth to meet expectations—combined with the companies' leveraged capital structures—placed them under severe strain. Downgrades and defaults mounted rapidly. By the end of 2002, most emerging telecom issuers had defaulted or restructured their debt, with recovery rates as low as zero. By contrast, issues sold by the "Phase 1" companies performed much better, with default rates no worse than for the US high-yield area. The result has been a heavily bifurcated market, with little issuance. Rated high-yield issuance has fallen from €9.4 billion in 1999 to €4.6 billion in 2002. However, towards the end of the year the market has shown a renewed level of activity, mainly in the form of refinancing of leveraged buyouts.

The third phase of the European high-yield market's evolution appears to be following the US market's model, with an increased focus on higher quality issuers, more investor-friendly debt structures, and expansion of the asset classes accessed by institutional investors.

Bondholders increasingly demand that issuers meet certain size parameters, that debt issues meet minimum liquidity requirements, and that noninvestment grade debt achieve strong rankings within the companies' capital structures. Structural enhancements to the issues themselves are also becoming more common.

Other market drivers are also changing. New types of noninvestment grade debt are coming to the market. Beyond the usual public securities, types of financing include mezzanine debt and private loans. The emergence of new asset pools with more flexible investment parameters, including collateralized debt obligations (CDOs),[13] has increasingly driven demand in the market and improved the flexibility of financing structures. Many CDOs can invest in bonds, mezzanine debt, and loans, and can make relative value investment decisions among these asset classes.

THE CORPORATE EUROBOND MARKET TODAY

Trading and origination practices have evolved over the life of the market, but would remain recognisable to market practitioners from earlier years. A much bigger change has come from the rise of the synthetic credit market, and its knock-on effect on how cash securities are valued.

Trading Practices

Although the Eurobond market has changed hugely over time, in some ways it remains close to its roots. The way bonds are traded is one of these. Most transactions are still done over the telephone between market professionals. Salespeople take orders from institutional investors and relay them to the traders.

---

[13] CDOs are covered in Chapter 15.

In the pre-euro days, traders were usually organized by currency. Now, sector specialization is the rule. For most issues, buy or sell indications are initially indicated on a spread basis. The spread can be either over the swap curve or over a specified government benchmark. A corporate bond issue keeps the same benchmark for its entire life; they "roll down the curve" together. This is in contrast to the United States, where the convention is to quote a corporate bond's spread over the nearest "on-the-run" (most recently issued) 2-, 5-, 10-, or 30-year maturity Treasury bond.

The bid or offer from a dealer (depending on whether the customer wants to sell or buy bonds) is usually in competition with at least one other intermediary. The transaction is done on a price basis. This is usually straightforward. Disputes around prices are rare, since the spread is agreed, the price of the underlying government security is known from marketwide information screens, and the price calculation method is a matter of market practice.

The size of each trade varies considerably, but amounts under €5 million are usually considered "odd lots." They are less efficient for dealers to handle and are priced accordingly. Trades above €50 million are rare.

Intermediaries trade either with customers or with each other. In the latter case, trading is conducted via interdealer brokers (IDBs). Like all brokers, they match up buyers and sellers, but do not take positions themselves. They provide a useful service by allowing intermediaries to adjust their positions without revealing them to other professionals. In the absence of a centralized exchange, IDBs provide dealers with market color around flows of securities. Related to this, they also provide information to allow dealers to price less liquid bonds.

Like most developments associated with the technology boom in the late 1990s, electronic trading systems have yet to live up to their earlier hype. That said, by late 2002 electronic trading platforms began to play useful roles, especially around buying and selling smaller positions. For larger blocks of bonds, investors still get better execution by dealing directly with a selected number of intermediaries. The leading electronic platform is Market Axess. It is owned by a consortium of dealers. Other single-dealer platforms are also in operation. Generally, electronic platforms provide listings of dealers' bids and offers of securities. Customers can then choose electronically which bid to hit or offer to lift, and the order is transmitted directly to the bank's back office ("straight through processing"). Alternately, an electronic or telephonic confirmation with the intermediary involved is required to execute the transaction. Market Axess and similar systems are designed to serve investors' needs. Platforms also exist to facilitate transactions and promote liquidity among intermediaries. These are usually owned by the interdealer brokers.

All active intermediaries keep inventories of bonds. That is to say, cash traders are naturally "long" securities. Corporate bond positions are usually financed in the repo market, and the interest rate risk is hedged out by shorting government bonds or futures. This leaves dealers exposed to "spread risk"—the risk that credit spreads will widen, causing losses. This can be covered by shorting very liquid corporate assets, although this practice is itself subject to risks. The principal one is that changes in the shorted bond's credit spread will not match that of the dealer's portfolio of positions. There is also the related risk of a squeeze in the repo market. That is, the bond might become more expensive to borrow, with a resulting rise in price on the short position. Dealer inventories will go up and down depending on a number of factors. These include the time of year (inventories tend to drop around banks' reporting periods); perceived market direction (dealers carry less inventory if they think credit spreads will widen); the state of the repo market; and the slope of the yield curve—steeply sloped curves allow dealers to carry inventory more profitably.

Market Liquidity

Regardless of the currency market, corporate bonds are less liquid than most other public market financial assets such as equities, government bonds, and most derivatives. At the end of November 2002 there were 861 fixed-rate investment-grade bonds outstanding in the Euro corporate market, compared to 3,535 in the United States.[14] Yet no more than 20% of these issues trade regularly. The rest are locked away in investors' portfolios, often not marked to market, and happily earning a rate of interest until they mature at par. For most investors, the transaction costs on such securities are too burdensome, particularly if they have to be replaced with alternative assets. Also, for many bank and insurance investors, securities held in nonmark-to-market accounts are not available for sale except in unusual circumstances. So trading tends to be concentrated in newer and larger issues.

The relative liquidity of the Eurobond market compared to the United States is a hotly debated question. The general impression is that the Eurobond market is less liquid than the US corporate sector. The average transaction size is greater in the United States, reflecting the market's larger size ($1,679 billion versus €651 billion) and the concentrated structure of the investor base. Other obvious liquidity metrics, such as bid/offer spreads are hard to track consistently. What is true is that secondary market trading conventions have converged over time.

---

[14] There are fixed-rate bonds with at least one year to maturity and minimum outstanding amounts (face value) of €300 million and $150 million.

In both markets, dealers will bid for most securities in most cases. In the United States this is often done through "bid lists." Big institutional investors send a selected group of dealers lists of securities on which the dealers are invited to bid. The timeframe for this "bid wanted in comp" (i.e., competition) approach is short—usually a few hours. Each dealer is then notified of the securities for which they are the highest bidder. For less liquid bonds, it is also common for dealers to "work an order." Under this approach, an investor leaves an order with a dealer to buy or sell a set amount of securities within a spread range. The dealer then has a limited amount of time (usually one or two days) to source the bonds. In working an order, a dealer is functioning more like a broker.

Intermediaries are usually reluctant to offer securities if they do not have them in inventory. Exceptions are highly liquid issues, where the dealer is confident he can obtain the bonds via the interdealer broker market. Generally, Eurobond dealers are more willing than their US counterparts to make "short offerings," that is, to sell bonds they do not have in inventory. This mostly reflects the more competitive nature of the market—there are more dealers with smaller market shares than in the United States. But with the market's increased volatility short offerings are less common, and the US-style order system is becoming more prevalent.

High Levels of Credit Spreads and Volatility: Marks of a Changed Valuation Paradigm

In the Euro corporate market's short life, the level of credit spreads and spread volatility have increased almost beyond recognition. As we show in Exhibit 6.9, with the exception of the recovery from the market shock of 11 September 2001, credit spreads moved out more or less in a straight

EXHIBIT 6.9 Euro Corporate Fixed-Rate Spread

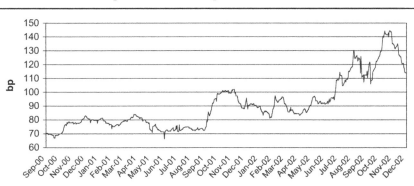

Source: Lehman Brothers.

EXHIBIT 6.10   Euro Corporate Market Monthly Spread Volatility
(12-month moving average)

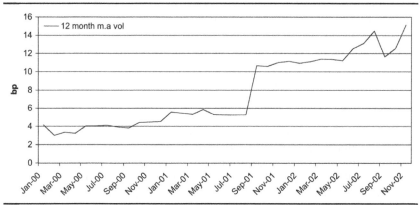

Source: Lehman Brothers.

EXHIBIT 6.11   US Credit Market Fixed-Rate Spread

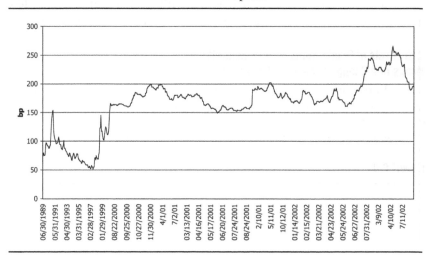

Source: Lehman Brothers—US credit market fixed-rate spread.

line before rallying with the bounce in equities in the fall of 2002. Spread
volatility is at near its all-time highs, as well (see Exhibit 6.10). We have
a longer time series of data for the United States, as shown in Exhibits
6.11 and 6.12. The data show a similar pattern to the Euro market, with
significant rises in the average market spread and its volatility. The
increase in the spread level is all the more remarkable when we consider
the survivorship bias at work in the data. That is, when the weaker cred-

EXHIBIT 6.12   US Corporate Market Spread Volatility

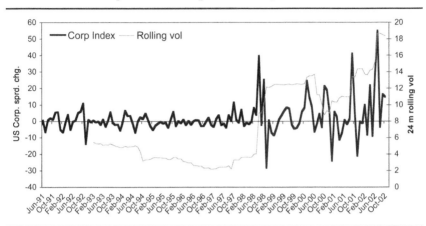

Source: Lehman Brothers.

its are downgraded to high yield, they are removed from the investment-grade index, improving its average credit quality.

What lies behind these trends? Two big—and related—factors are the decline in credit quality and the change in this composition of the index in terms of credit quality and issuer type. Baa rated debt has grown from 2% of the market at the end of 1998 to 26% as of early 2003. Similarly, banks, which used to trade at very tight spreads, have dropped sharply as a percent of the index, as we have discussed. (The bank data only includes senior and dated subordinated debt. Subordinated debt trades at wider spreads than senior paper, and has increased as a percent of the bank total.) 2002 has also seen a significant decline in credit quality. Fallen angel debt totaled a record €24 billion, and Eurozone downgrades outnumbered upgrades by 2.8 times through the first three quarters of the year. Of course, the large amount of fallen angel debt was itself a significant contributor to spread volatility in 2002.

But these developments do not explain everything. Spread volatility and the absolute level of credit spreads have also risen because of fundamental changes in the trading pattern in the market. Probably the biggest influence has been the rapid growth of the credit default swap market, which allows investors to take long and short positions in individual issuers. A number of new players, principally credit hedge funds, have taken advantage of this. The result has been a rise in selling pressure, and in credit spread volatility. The difficult conditions in the high-yield market, and the resulting impaired ability of high-yield investors to absorb fallen angel debt, has also played a big role.

Beyond this, the synthetic CDO[15] market has created a substantial bid for credit risk. This really only began in 1999. Synthetic CDOs substitute credit default swaps (CDS) for cash assets in all but the mezzanine and equity portions of their structures. Sponsors of synthetic CDOs are selling default protection (i.e., creating credit risk), just as if they were issuing bonds. This results in short positions for the parties on the other side of the trade (i.e., the buyers of protection). These are usually the investment banks that originated the transactions. By covering their short positions, investment banks increase the demand for credit—at least for the companies included in the structures. For issuers excluded from the structures, the synthetic CDO bid has the opposite effect. Lacking this crucial market support, credit spreads for such companies can widen hugely. The result is an increased bifurcation of the market, and greater spread volatility for the "have nots" excluded from the synthetic structures because of their deteriorating credit concerns.

The final piece of the puzzle is the merger of cash and credit derivatives trading desks at many intermediaries. This has changed fundamentally how trading desks view and manage credit risk. Before the rise of the CDS market, mark-to-market risk on trading desks chiefly came from credit spread fluctuations. And since cash desks are naturally long, their downside risk usually came from spread widening. Cash books are still "naturally" long credit. But this is offset by short positions on synthetic (i.e., CDS) positions on the same names, due to the origination of synthetic CDOs.

The upshot is that integrated trading desks now see their risk mainly as a portfolio of basis trades, the "basis" in this case being the differential between the spread on a company's CDS and the corresponding cash instrument (swapped to LIBOR or EURIBOR). Buying protection on a credit in the CDS market means essentially buying a put on the company. This is because on default, the buyer of protection delivers an asset of the defaulted entity to the protection seller in exchange for a payment equal to the par value of the CDS. So if a dealer is long a bond of the same issuer, that dealer is holding a covered put on the company. This becomes a bet that spread volatility will rise, since this will usually cause the spread on an issuer's CDS to widen more quickly than the spread on its bond. In other words, a rise in spread volatility will increase the basis, improving the profitability of the trade for the dealer. If a dealer believes that spreads will tighten, he will quickly cover many of his short positions, causing a rapid contraction in spread levels.

Credit quality levels will wax and wane, and credit spread levels will fluctuate accordingly. But many of the structural shifts in the mar-

---

[15] Synthetic CDOs are discussed in Chapter 15.

ket, in particular the growth of CDS activity, are here to stay. This means that the increase in credit spreads since 2001 represents a real regime shift. While spreads have tightened from the historically wide levels seen in the early fall of 2002, they are unlikely to revert back to their long-term average.

The Primary Market

So far in this section we have discussed the secondary market—transactions involving outstanding issues. Let's now turn to the primary sector, through which bond issues are originated and priced. The new issue sector provides the lifeblood of the Eurobond market by supplying new issues to replace those that have matured or been called. Also, bond issues become less liquid as time passes, so greater origination has a direct beneficial effect on the secondary market, as well.

Nonfinance companies sell bonds mainly as alternatives to bank finance. But there are also other advantages. Bond issues can be of longer maturities than bank loans, and serve to diversify a company's investor base.

Often in determining to use the bond market, an issuer will approach one or more investment banks to serve as advisors in the issuance process. In any event, in most cases new issues come to market through a syndicate, or group of banks. A common approach is a "negotiated transaction." This means an issuer invites a number of banks to present their ideas on how best to bring the company's bond issue to market. This "beauty contest" can go through several rounds, as the issuer narrows down the banks to a short list from which the lead managers are chosen. (These transactions are usually large, and sole lead mandates are rare.) The negotiated part refers to the fact that the level (in credit spread terms) at which the bonds are issued is negotiated between the underwriters and the issuer. The negotiation takes place after a marketing period, during which the issuer often embarks on a road show to present the company to investors. Following the marketing period, the lead managers solicit orders from investors and "build a book" for the issue within spread parameters. Other issue details, such as size and maturity, can also change as a result of investor feedback received during the marketing campaign. Before launch, the syndicate is usually enlarged to include banks with good placing power among specialized investor groups.

Alternately, "bought deals" are common in good market conditions, especially for smaller transactions. Under this structure, a small number of banks bid for the bonds being offered for sale by the company. The bank offering the highest price (i.e., the lowest yield) wins the mandate and owns the bonds. They are then offered out to the market, usually without the involvement of additional banks.

Occasionally, new issues are withdrawn prior to their scheduled launch, usually because of unfavorable market conditions. In most situations, the issuer returns to the market once things have settled down.

Regardless of the approach chosen, new issues are underwritten by the intermediaries. That is, once an issue is launched the intermediaries own the bonds and are responsible for placing them with investors. The underwriting risk is small with a negotiated transaction, but can be substantial with bought deals. The fee earned by the dealers for underwriting a deal is simply the difference between the price paid to an issuer for the bonds and the price at which they are re-offered (and hopefully sold) to investors. The "all-in rate" to the issuer is the yield (or spread) that reflects the price paid to the issuer.

If a deal clears "within fees" it means that the bonds were sold at a level that allowed the underwriters to earn their full fees. This is not always the case. Underwriters can suffer substantial losses if they misjudge the clearing level for a bought deal, or if the market suffers a disruption between the time a deal is underwritten and when it is fully placed.

Bond Covenants and Other Documentation Issues

The debate around bond prospectus covenant packages, in terms of the relatively poor protection they offer bondholders, has been one of the hardy perennials of the Eurobond market. The primary reason for the lack of strong covenants is the extremely diffuse investor base, which makes it difficult for bondholders to form a consensus on what covenants are truly desirable.

Linked to this is the absence of agreement on the part of investors on the topic of just how much they would be willing to pay for covenant protection. That is, companies can issue bonds with a standard covenant package at the current market spread. This is usually determined with reference to their existing issues, or those of similar companies. But how much would investors be willing to pay in the form of a tighter spread over the swap or government curve, in exchange for covenant protection? Except for some special situations like the jumbo telecom deals in 2000 and 2001, this question has never been answered.

Eurobond documentation for investment-grade issues is reasonably standardized, although the wording of some terms and conditions has varied over time. We list the key terms and conditions below. (Sterling issuers offer additional protection in some instances, as discussed separately.)

- **Governing law.** Most transactions are governed by UK law, although New York state law is an occasional alternative.
- **Security.** As a rule, issues are not secured by the company's assets.
- **Negative pledges.** Negative pledges are common. They prohibit an issuer from creating security interests on its assets, unless all bondholders receive the same level of security.
- **Subordination.** Except for bank or insurance capital issues, most bonds are sold on a senior basis.
- **Cross-default clauses.** Cross-default clauses state that if an issuer defaults on other borrowings, then the bonds will become due and payable. The definition of which borrowings are covered can vary. The cross-default clause usually carves out defaults in borrowings up to a certain threshold (e.g., €10,000) to prevent a minor trade dispute or overlooked invoice from allowing the bondholders to put the bonds back to the issuer.
- **Prohibition on the sale of material assets.** In order to protect bondholders, most documentation prohibits the sale or transfer of material assets or subsidiaries. The definition of "material" can vary considerably.

In addition, many of the jumbo telecom issues from 2000, 2001, and 2002 were sold with coupon step-ups or step-downs. That is, their coupons increased in the event of a ratings downgrade, and then stepped back if they were upgraded. For issuers, these inducements were necessary to sell huge amounts of debt (several of the multi-tranche transactions were in the €7 billion range) at a time when their credit outlooks were uncertain. A limited number of other issuers in the telecom and technology area also included step-ups in their documentation. However, step-ups and step-downs have not become widespread in the market. (Perpetual bank capital issues have long had coupon step-ups, but their structures are heavily influenced by regulatory considerations.) Indeed, since 2001 several telecom issuers with outstanding step-up step-down issues have since been able to do deals—albeit smaller—without this feature.

Sterling Market Documentation Forms an Exception

The sterling-denominated Eurobond market has an active long-dated (30 years or more) sector, and this has led to two important differences in documentation compared to the Euro market. Firstly, to provide additional comfort to investors in long maturity paper, the bonds are often secured by charges on the issuers' assets. It is worth noting in this connection that the common terminology can be inconsistent. Market participants have traditionally called long-dated bonds secured by a charge on the issuer's assets "debentures" or "debenture stock" although these are now sometimes called just "secured bonds." Unsecured issues were historically referred to as "loan stock" but became known simply as "bonds" after the inception of the sterling Eurobond market.

The other special feature of the sterling sector is that long-dated issues usually contain a mechanism for calling an issue at a price that is the greater of par or one set at a small spread over gilts. Issuers can use the mechanism to call an issue so as to avoid an event of default that might occur if they are in breach of a covenant in the bonds' terms and conditions. Since the call has to be at what is assumed to be a high price relative to the market level, the existence of this mechanism is generally positive for bondholders.

The original form of this call pricing mechanism was the Spens clause, which required the issuer to call in the bonds at an above-market price if certain events detrimental to the interests of the bondholders took place. Following a decision by the International Primary Markets Association (IPMA) in July 2001, the market convention is that the Spens clause is no longer used, although it remains in many outstanding issues. Instead, the market now uses a formula to calculate the redemption yield of a bond in the event it is called prior to maturity. This is set out in the UK Debt Management Office (DMO) paper dated 8 June 1998.

The Spens formula came spectacularly to the fore in the case of Stagecoach Group, which ran into financial difficulties in 2000 and tried to sell its Porterbrook subsidiary. The bondholders objected strenuously. Stagecoach had euro- and sterling-denominated Eurobonds outstanding. The former did not benefit from a Spens clause, while the latter did. The sterling issue also had stronger wording on what constituted an event of default on the question of the sale of a material subsidiary, and on the question of a material subsidiary ceasing or threatening to cease to carry on its business. As a result of these two factors, the sterling issue was called at a price of 111.82, while the euro-denominated bonds fell to around 86. The resulting furore led to renewed calls for strengthened covenants for euro-denominated Eurobonds, but in the end little has changed. The sterling market's experience reinforces how difficult it is for strong covenants to become the practice. Protection like the call option coupled with the Spens formula or DMO formula and security interests in assets are generally only found in longer-dated issues. Shorter maturity issues typically display the same lack of covenants as in the euro-denominated market.

BEYOND HIGH GRADE EURO CORPORATES: THE OTHER EUROBOND SECTORS

So far this chapter has mostly concerned itself with Eurobonds sold by corporates (including financial institutions). In this section we look at other sectors, such as sovereigns, supranationals, and agencies.

Eurodollar Bonds

As we noted before, dollar-denominated Eurobonds (usually referred to as Eurodollar bonds) were the original Eurobonds. The market is quite large—$1,731 billion in outstanding debt. This reflects two factors. One is that it includes almost all sectors; in addition to corporates, sovereign, agency, and supranational issuers are also big issuers (see Exhibit 6.13). The second development has been the rise of dollar-denominated global issues, that is, issues registered and sold in more than one country. These are often included in the Eurodollar bucket.

Exhibit 6.14 shows the breakdown of the two broad categories, and emphasizes the shrinkage of the classic Eurodollar sector. This mirrors the relative decline of the private client part of the investor base. Private clients have traditionally been big buyers of Eurodollar bonds because of the popularity of the currency and the bearer nature of the obligations. The European tranches of dollar-denominated global bonds sold by US entities—who account for most of the origination in this regard—do not carry the same tax advantages.

The Eurosterling Market

Sterling is the other main noneuro currency bucket. Most issues are in Eurobond form, as opposed to domestic market form, in order to broaden the potential investor base for new issues.

EXHIBIT 6.13   Eurodollar Market Breakdown

	Outstanding Amount ($ millions)
Industrials	311,721
Utilities	27,123
Financials	409,858
Sov/Agencies	981,845
Total	1,730,547

Source: Lehman Brothers.

EXHIBIT 6.14   Eurodollar Market—Dollar Global Issues and Eurodollar Bonds

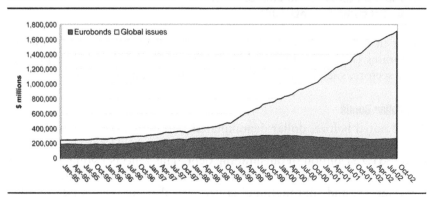

Source: Lehman Brothers.

EXHIBIT 6.15   Euros, Dollars, and Sterling Market Maturity Breakdown

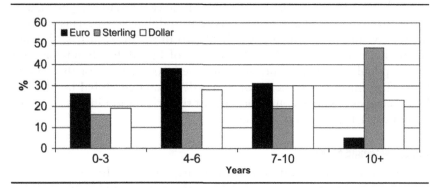

Source: Lehman Brothers.

In many ways the sterling market is most like the US domestic dollar market. It has a relatively long history and a good level of sector and quality differentiation. The investor base also has similarities to that of the United States, with the United Kingdom's tradition of funded pension plans providing a solid base of institutional demand that has only recently developed in the Eurozone. This is evident from the strength of the long-dated sterling market, which mirrors that of the United States. By contrast, until the 30-year sector of the market opened in January 2003, issuance beyond 10 years was almost unknown in euros (see Exhibit 6.15). Eurosterling investors often benefit from good covenant protection, particularly at the long end of the curve, as we discussed above.

EXHIBIT 6.16   Eurosterling Market

£ millions	Outstanding Amount
Industrials	31,088
Utilities	16,772
Financials	37,762
Sov/Agencies	64,951
Total	150,573

Source: Lehman Brothers.

Like the Eurodollar market, the Eurosterling sector is quite diversified by issuer type (Exhibit 6.16). Issuance of top quality paper with long maturities has been especially large, mainly because issuers can achieve very tight funding in LIBOR terms, given the relatively wide 30-year sterling swap rate.

Investors have had a very strong bid for 30-year paper due to the need to match their pension liabilities. In particular, the sterling bond sector generally has been boosted by two changes in UK pension regulations. The first was the Minimum Funding Requirement (MFR), which came into force in 1995. In addition to setting funding requirements for pensions, it established a long-end gilt benchmark for the fixed-rate portion of pension funds. Sales of longer maturity gilts soared as a result, causing the sterling yield curve to invert. The second development is the proposal to implement a new reporting standard for company pension fund obligations (FRS-17). For a UK company, this will require it to carry the net over-funded or under-funded position of its pension plan on either the asset or liability side of the balance sheet, depending on the plan's status. Changes in the net level of funding will be reported through the profit and loss statement on a three-year average basis. FRS-17's discount rate is the Aa long maturity corporate yield. The greater volatility of reported pension fund balances introduced by FRS-17 poses challenges for company managers. One way to reduce this is to buy more sterling corporate bonds. That way the yield on the assets will more closely match the Aa corporate yield used as a discount rate.

Sovereign, Supranational, Local Authority, and Agency Issuers

Top quality issuers have long been a part of Eurobond scene. But in euros, they have been eclipsed by the growth of the corporate market. Sovereign issuance in particular has fallen, as countries have shifted activity back to their domestic issuance mechanisms. This has mainly been done to increase liquidity and size in domestic market format, so as to compete better within the Eurozone.

EXHIBIT 6.17   Euro-Denominated Noncorporate Bonds Outstanding[a]

	€ millions
Local Governments[b]	131,517
Supranationals	74,889
Sovereigns	33,971
Pfandbriefe	426,317
Mortgage Securities	84,083
Total	750,777

[a] €300 million and above, rated investment grade, and with at least one year to maturity.
[b] Includes Landesbanken unsecured debt.
Source: Lehman Brothers.

Exhibit 6.17 provides a breakdown of issuance among the five principal sectors. The definition of what is an agency can be contentious. For our purposes, we count as agencies all issuers that are either 100% owned by a government, guaranteed by a government, or that are legal subunits or departments of a government.

Floating-Rate Notes

Floating-rate notes (FRNs) are Eurobonds that have their coupon levels reset periodically, with reference to a money market rate. For dollar-denominated assets, this is LIBOR (the London Inter-bank Offer Rate) as determined by a group of 16 reference banks. The mechanism is run by the British Bankers Association (BBA). The BBA also supervises LIBOR fixings in a number of other currencies. For euros, the most common reference rate is EURIBOR, as determined by a reference group of around 50 banks chosen by European Banking Federation. In both cases, most issues are priced off of the three-month rate, although one-month and six-month rates are also used.

Issues are initially priced and sold at a fixed spread over the reference rate. The price of an FRN can fluctuate considerably during the life of the issue, mainly depending on trends in the issuer's credit quality. The frequent resets in the reference rate means that changes in market interest levels have a minimal impact on an FRN's price. For investors, movements in an FRN's price are reflected in changes in the discount rate. The discount rate is effectively the yield needed to discount the future cash flows on the security to its current price. It thus functions in the same way as the yield to maturity for a fixed-rate instrument. And like a fixed-rate bond, the market convention is to use a constant spread

EXHIBIT 6.18   Euro FRNs Monthly Issuance

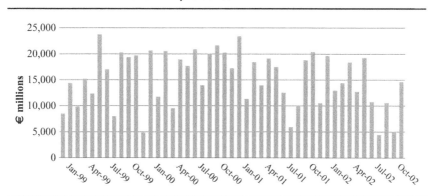

Source: Capital Data Bondware.

to a constant EURIBOR (or LIBOR) rate to discount future cash flows, rather than a forward curve.

Most FRNs have been issued by sovereign-type entities and financial institutions. Industrial and utility activity has been relatively low, although it picked up somewhat in early 2002, as the extremely unstable market conditions made it difficult for issuers to sell fixed-rate securities (see Exhibit 6.18).

THE OUTLOOK FOR THE EUROBOND MARKET

It is easy to focus on the Eurobond market's limitations at the expense of just how far it has come. From the perspective of its early days, the market has changed and grown beyond all recognition. As we have seen, the launch of the euro has provided a critical step up to a new level, upon which the market is still consolidating. Indeed, the strong recovery of investor demand in the late Autumn of 2002, following the shocks of WorldCom and the like, is an indication of the market's resilience.

Corporate bond valuations will always fluctuate, of course. But to stay in the market, investors have to believe that it offers a decent level of risk-adjusted reward compared to other sectors. It also needs to satisfy the related needs of diversification and liquidity. Particularly regarding the question of diversification, progress so far has fallen short of what investors require. But to return to the point made at the opening of this chapter, the market is still early in its evolution. Trends regarding growth are generally positive. Indeed, we expect issuance to accelerate going forward, as competing sources of funds (mainly bank loans) become more expensive for borrowers. On the demand side, the slow movement towards funded pension plans is creating new pools of investors, including insurance companies that manage many pension plans. Other fixed-income markets, such as governments and Pfandbriefe, provide neither the yield nor the volatility (away from yield curve movements) required by fund managers if they are to outperform their benchmarks. The fundamentals for growth are in place. All that is needed is time.

CHAPTER 7

The German Pfandbrief and European Covered Bonds Market

Graham "Harry" Cross
Research Partner
YieldCurve.com

This chapter describes the German mortgage-bonds or Pfandbriefe market, its institutions, and working practice. We also consider other aspects of the European covered bond market. The instruments themselves are essentially plain vanilla bonds, and while they can be analysed in similar ways to US agency bonds and mortgage-backed bonds, there are also key differences between them, which we highlight in this chapter. Mortgage-backed securities are described in Chapter 11.

THE PFANDBRIEF MARKET

Pfandbriefe[1] are bonds issued by German mortgage banks, which are subject to special governing legislation. These bonds are "covered" or backed by underlying asset pools, equating to at least the same nominal amount of the issue. The assets contained within these pools must be recorded into a cover register, maintained by the mortgage bank, to ensure that these are easily identifiable. In this regard, covered bonds such as Pfandbriefe are considered highly secure. In the event of the issuing mortgage bank becoming insolvent, the creditors would receive

---

[1] *Pfandbrief*—the literal translation is *Letter of pledge*.

a preferential claim over the assets in the cover pool, which is there solely to protect them.

Pfandbriefe are categorized into two types. *Öffentliche Pfandbriefe*, which are bonds fully collateralised by loans to public sector entities (also known as "Public" Pfandbriefe), while *Hypotheken Pfandbriefe* (Mortgage Pfandbriefe) are fully collateralised by residential and commercial mortgages, whose loan-to-value ratio must not exceed 60%. The former constitute just over 90% of the overall Pfandbrief market.

The market, with an overall volume of €1.1 trillion, has become the largest asset class on the European bond market and is ranked the sixth largest in the world. It is regulated within a stringent legal framework and is under special supervision.[2] The mortgage banks—the largest group of issuers on the Pfandbriefe market—are, in addition to be bound under the terms of the German Banking Act (KWG), by which all German banks are governed, are also subject to the provisions of the Mortgage Bank Act (HBG) as well. It is noteworthy that since the inception of the Mortgage Bank Act over 100 years ago, there has not been one case of insolvency. All of these factors have in the past assisted issuers in obtaining the highest possible ratings (AAA) for their Pfandbrief paper. This situation has in some cases, however, changed somewhat and this will be discussed in detail later.

Although the German Pfandbrief market has a history dating back well over 200 years, its recognition as an asset class by international investors has only occurred recently in the mid-1990s with the advent of the *Jumbo* Pfandbrief. The name "Jumbo" is derived from the large issue volume, with the size requirement of €500 million. This sector of the market, founded in the spring of 1995, and geared towards the liquidity criteria of large international investors, has managed to establish itself as Europe's fourth largest bond market—surpassed only by the government markets of Italy, Germany, and France—had an outstanding volume of well over €400 billion as of year-end 2001. Prior to the arrival of the first issue of this nature, a DM 1 billion Frankfurter Hypothekenbank bond, the Pfandbrief market had been an illiquid and highly fragmented sector comprising of some 17,000 individual issues with a very small average volume of around €80 million. Investors in these "Traditional" Pfandbriefe were almost exclusively domestic.

In this light, the main focus of this chapter shall be on the Jumbo sector as this has the most relevance to the investment community at large.

Exhibit 7.1 shows the size of the market compared to European sovereign government markets.

---

[2] Supervision conducted by the German Financial Supervisory Authority (BAFin).

EXHIBIT 7.1	Pfandbriefe versus Euro-In Government Bonds (End-2001)

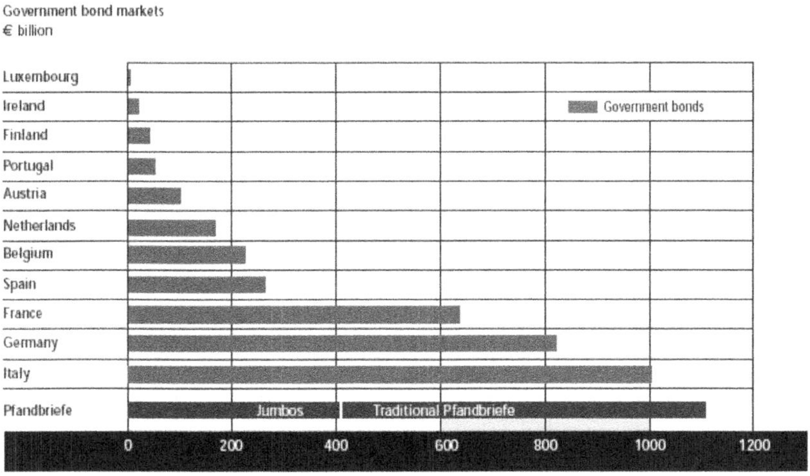

Government bond markets
€ billion

Source: Association of German Mortgage Banks. Used with permission.

HISTORY OF THE PFANDBRIEF

The origins of the German Pfandbrief system are widely regarded to lie within the "cabinets-ordre" of Frederick II of Prussia, back in August 29, 1767—the basis of which concerned the introduction of the of the Pfandbrief system in an attempt to remedy the aristocrats' shortage of credit in the areas of Prussia that had been ravaged during the Seven Years War (1756–1763)

On the basis of this royal decree, the Silesian Landschaft, an association of estates belonging to the aristocracy, churches, and monasteries, was set up in 1770. In time, more of these cooperations were set up throughout the individual provinces of Prussia, as compulsory law associations to the aristocratic landowners. These so-called "Landschaften" facilitated the refinancing of loans to their members by issuing debentures. Purchase of this paper ensured the creditor acquired a direct charge over the estate, which the landowner had put up as collateral. In the event of default, the estate named in the Pfandbrief, the Landschaft and all of the landowners belonging to the Landschaft served the Pfandbriefe holder as security. Understandably, this paper was also known as "estate Pfandbrief" and largely corresponds with today's Mortgage Pfandbrief.

The Pfandbrief system rapidly gained popularity throughout Europe and the development of the present day format was given a decisive boost from the foundation of organisations outside of Prussia, such as *Crédit Foncier de France* in 1852. Issuers of this second generation Pfandbriefe were not law associations but private real estate credit institutions, which adopted the system for the refinancing of loans to the public sector borrowers and loans guaranteed by public sector institutions and agencies (public sector loans).

Whereas in the early days Pfandbrief were used to finance agriculture, this new variation was used to finance the then rapidly expanding towns and cities of Europe. In the latter half of the 19th century, one of the major priorities facing European governments was the provision of housing to meet the widespread exodus from rural areas and the corresponding growth in urban population levels. Concentration from the outset was on real estate financing and, above all, the financing of construction of housing and commercial properties. In this respect, today's mortgage banks were among Europe's first large scale financial intermediaries and can very much be regarded as a by product of the industrial age.

The first German mortgage bank of the type familiar today was established, by the decree of the senate, on 8 December 1962 (*Frankfurter Hypothekenbank* in Frankfurt). From this moment, numerous other mortgage banks emerged in quick succession in almost all of the German federal states until, by the beginning of the twentieth century, a total of 40 private mortgage banks existed. Throughout the ensuing years of economic "boom and bust," the business sector occupied by these real estate credit institutions, understandably, became one of the biggest sectors in banking.

These developments led to the promulgation of the *German Mortgage Banks Act* (Hypothekenbankgesetz–HBG) of 1900, which was the first uniform law in the field of banking for the entire German Reich. This Act provided a legally prescribed, uniform organization framework for this group of institutions that has stood the test of time, right up until the present day.

The new generation of Pfandbrief had spread across Europe from France, through Germany to the United Kingdom, Italy, and Spain among others. In this respect, it is interesting to note that in the annex to the preamble to the Act[3] contained the laws from Germany's neighbouring countries, evidencing the influence of foreign laws on the lawmakers of Germany. However, during the 20th century with the onset of two World Wars, global economic crisis, inflation and the currency reform in 1948

---

[3] *100 Jahre Hypothekenbankgesetz, Textsammlung und Materialen*, Verband Deutscher Hypothekenbanken, Frankfurt/Main, 1999. (*100 Years Mortgage Bank Act, A Collection of Texts and Material*, published by the Association of Mortgage Banks, Frankfurt/Main, 1999.)

resulted in a curbing of cross border influence. This in turn caused the mortgage banks throughout Europe to develop in sharply divergent ways. Some countries chose to abandon the whole Pfandbriefe concept altogether, whereas others turned the mortgage banks into state monopoly institutions.

In Germany, no other group in the whole of the banking sector was as impacted by these factors as the mortgage banks, which had seen their business volumes fall drastically by the time of the currency reform. Nevertheless, Pfandbriefe proved an invaluable tool in the reconstruction programs that were set up to deal with the aftermath of the war and their popularity grew with each successive decade. The reunification in Germany after the fall of the Berlin Wall highlights this resurgence, as a demand for both commercial and residential property construction as well as for public infrastructure renewal had to be met in the new federal states in East Germany. With the advent of the euro and the recent amendments that were made to the German Mortgage Bank Act, new avenues of cross-border lending have opened up in Germany for the mortgage banks. They now have the ability to market Pfandbriefe internationally.

The market has grown considerably from the lowly position it found itself in, midcentury, a period when mortgage banks reported business volumes down to levels of 5% of those quoted just 30 years earlier, to it current status as one of the largest bond markets in the world.

KEY FEATURES OF INVESTOR INTEREST

Reduction of Credit Risk

The tight legal framework within which the participants of the Pfandbrief market must operate is one of the foremost reasons why Pfandbriefe appeal to both domestic and international investors. In addition to being bound by the general provisions set out in the German Banking Act (KWG), the law by which all German banks are governed, German mortgage banks are also subject to the requirements of the Mortgage Bank Act.

The *Hypothekenbankgesetz* (Mortgage Bank Act) states that mortgage banks may only be engaged in two types of business:

- Lending to public sector entities.
- The financing of mortgage-backed loans for residential and commercially used properties (i.e., mortgage loans).

In addition to what could be considered low risk fields of activity; a strict regional restriction is added in order to reduce risks in connection with cross-border business. Under this restriction, loans may only be granted to borrowers situated within the member states of the European Union, the EEA, the European OECD countries as well as the non-European G7 countries.

Further security is provided to the investor by the fact that Pfandbrief bonds are required to be covered by assets, which have at least the same value and bear the same interest rate.

It is necessary for these underlying assets to be segregated into two separate cover pools, one for mortgage loans and the other public sector loans, thus reflecting the two types of business within which the mortgage banks are involved. In the case of Mortgage Pfandbriefe, covering assets are "first-charge" mortgages.

In the event of a mortgage bank becoming insolvent, the Pfandbriefe creditor would receive a preferential claim over the assets in the respective cover pool, which is there solely to protect them. They would not be required to participate in the insolvency procedures, but instead have any claim satisfied on schedule in accordance with the terms of the respective issue out of the cover assets. However, if the claim cannot be satisfied on time, in respect of coupon payments and redemptions because the cover pool is insolvent, separate proceedings will then commence in regard to the pool affected.

It is worthwhile noting that there has not been a bankruptcy proceeding against a mortgage bank since the enactment of the Mortgage Bank Act over 100 years ago.

The Mortgage Bank Act contains further protective measures to safeguard investors in Mortgage Pfandbriefe. Namely, a limit imposed on those mortgages being used as cover to a maximum of 60% of the "prudently" calculated mortgage lending value. This provides a safety cushion against the potential cyclical fluctuations in the market value of the cover pool asset.

The comparatively low risk that a portfolio of both residential and commercial mortgages entails is also expressed in the equity weighting of 50% for mortgage loans with a lending limit of up to 60%.

These elements obviously offer exceptional safety to investors in the Pfandbrief market and should therefore limit the impact of any adverse market movements on the back of any detrimental news in regard to the parent companies.

Liquidity

The Jumbo Pfandbrief market—on its own it is Europe's fourth largest bond market, surpassed only by the government markets of Italy, Germany and France. The name is derived from the large issue volume, with the size requirement of €500 million. In comparison, the average size of the traditional Pfandbriefe is approximately €150 million, which tends to prohibit the trading-orientated investor and favour the "buy and hold" types.

The minimum issue size requirement for the Jumbos is only of theoretical significance as the majority of issues are launched in considerably larger sizes (the average volume is currently around €1.5 billion, however, some Jumbos have a volume of up to €5 billion). It can therefore be seen that the volume of Jumbo Pfandbriefe is equal to that of the bonds brought by medium-sized sovereign issuers within the Eurozone. The overall Pfandbrief market, with a volume outstanding of more than €1.1 trillion, is the biggest bond market within Europe. Of course, this figure includes *Structured* Pfandbriefe, the smaller traditional variety as well as the Jumbo sector.

The market-making obligations further enhance the liquidity of the Jumbo Pfandbriefe. Namely, that Jumbo Pfandbrief are syndicated by at least three market makers who pledge to quote two-way (bid/offer) prices simultaneously, for lots up to €15 million during the usual trading hours—9.00 A.M. to 5.00 P.M. (GMT + 1) for the life of the issue. The issuer itself may also perform the function of market maker and should obtain an undertaking from the assigned market makers not to exceed the following bid/offer spreads when quoting:

Up to and including 4 years	—	5 cents
Over 4 years up to and including 6 years	—	6 cents
Over 6 years up to and including 8 years	—	8 cents
Over 8 years up to and including 15 years	—	10 cents
Over 15 years up to and including 20 years	—	15 cents
Over 20 years	—	20 cents

The maximum bid/offer spread is adjusted according to the remaining life of the bond.

There are further nuances to the market that should be noted. Admission to either the official or the regulated market at one German stock exchange is compulsory for Jumbo Pfandbriefe; an official listing must be obtained immediately after issue or not later than 30 days after the settlement date. However, only a fraction of Pfandbrief trading is settled through the stock exchange. By far the greater share of trading is executed off the floor, for the most part via the telephone or, to an ever-greater extent, through the numerous electronic trading systems including the EuroCreditMTS. To be eligible to trade on this platform, bonds must fulfil stringent credit criteria. They must have a triple A rating from either Moody's or S&P and a minimum volume outstanding of €3 billion.

Jumbo Pfandbriefe are responsible for more than 80% of the issues traded on EuroCreditMTS.

Over and above this, there are certain recommendations in place regarding the issuance of Jumbos:

- The coupon should be expressed in fractions of not less than a quarter percentage point.
- In the event of an issue being tapped, the tap amount should not be less than €125 million per add-on.
- In the case of new issues or taps, a maximum of five days should separate pricing date and settlement date.

In addition, all Jumbo Pfandbriefe with a volume outstanding of €1.25 billion or greater and with a residual life of more than two years are greatly assisted by the market making pledge, given by 17 institutions, to provide a repo market in these issues.

Yield and Yield Spread

In addition to the safety and liquidity aspects, Pfandbriefe also offer investors an attractive yield pick-up over government bonds. For instance, the spread in the 10-year sector is as of March 2003 between 30 to 50 basis points above the relevant Bund issue. In 2000, this spread ballooned out to a high of almost 70 basis points, reflecting the uncertain environment in the credit markets, due to the decline in the equity markets witnessed around the world. As one might imagine, during these phases of increasing yield spreads, the Bund/Pfandbrief spread tends to widen to a considerably lesser extent than say the Bund spread versus "uncovered" bank bonds.

Exhibit 7.2 illustrates recent Bund/Pfandbriefe spread history from June 2000 to September 2002.

MARKET INSTRUMENTS

The Pfandbrief market is comprised of several types of issues; in addition to the aforementioned traditional and Jumbo Pfandbriefe, there are Global issues and a variety of Structured issues and the latest enhancements to the product range by the way of Medium-Term Note (MTN) and Commercial Paper (CP) programs.

As previously discussed, the major difference between traditional and Jumbo Pfandbriefe is the issue volume. Further distinctions are also evident in the issuing procedures of the two. Traditional Pfandbriefe are brought to the market in Tap form and individual series feature within one

EXHIBIT 7.2   5-Year/10-Year Jumbo Pfandbrief/Bund Spread

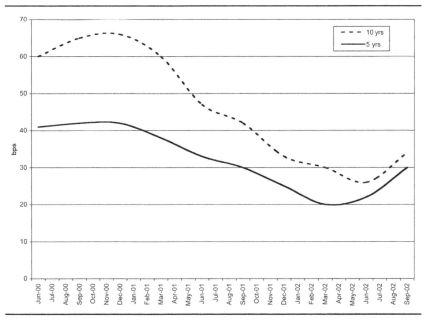

Source: Association of German Mortgage Banks (VDH). Used with permission.

issue. Jumbos, on the other hand, are issued via syndicates using the *fixed price reoffer* method. To guarantee the liquidity, Jumbos must have at least three market makers willing to make prices throughout normal trading hours. Some time ago, a book-building procedure with a premarketing phase was put in place, in line with standard practices within the international markets. A so-called "pot procedure," similar to the auction procedure, has been introduced as well. With this method, syndicate banks can put together an order book from which the respective issuer can decide on allocation. This places the issuer in a position to allot investor demand among the syndicate banks in the run-up to the issue, thus enabling greater control over the book and, of course, more precise pricing.

Traditional Pfandbriefe may be issued in either bearer or registered form, whereas Jumbos are only issuable as bearer bonds. For several years now, there has been a considerable shift in favour of the bearer paper, an indication of the growing share of Jumbo issues brought by the mortgages banks and their willingness to provide fungible bonds to their investors. Today, approximately 75% of all Pfandbriefe are bearer instruments.

As a rule, Pfandbriefe are issued with maturities of one to 10 years, and currently the most predominant incidence of issuance occurs in the medium term maturities of five to seven years. However, this predominance has been on the wane over the last few years and more and more bonds are appearing on the market with lives of less than one year or more than 10 years.

Global Pfandbriefe

These issues are aimed specifically at the large financial centres around the world. For example, in order to facilitate investor access to the market, particularly in the United States, the first Globals were issues almost exclusively in accordance with SEC Rule 144a. This prevents the need for investors to go through the costly SEC registration procedure and avoids the need for annual accounts in line with US accounting regulations. It does, however, restrict sales to so-called "qualified investors" with a portfolio of at least $100 million. A number of mortgage banks have gained a frequent issuer status in the United States, in accordance with Rule 12g 3-2 (b), which grants exemption from the extensive registration and reporting requirements. Under this rule, the publishing of a separate US prospectus is not required; the standard documents presented in the issuer's home country are sufficient. Despite these helpful measures, the process of marketing Pfandbriefe in the United States is still very much in its infancy and the competition for the attention of investors is huge.

By definition, Jumbo Pfandbriefe are always plain vanilla structures: Jumbos are fixed-interest bullet bonds, the coupon on which is payable annually in arrears. The calculation of interest accrued is done uniformly using the actual/actual method in line with international practice. While this standardisation helps to enhance the transparency of the market, it inhibits the ability for these issues to be targets to an investor's specific needs and this is where the structured issues come into their own.

Structured Pfandbrief

Aside from the traditional and Jumbo Pfandbriefe, the mortgage banks also offer structured Pfandbriefe for those investors that seek a more individually tailored product to suit their portfolios. These products are structured to particularly suit the investors' interest rate expectations and their desired risk/return profiles. Structured Pfandbriefe allow the mortgage banks to combine the asset quality of the Pfandbrief with the advantages offered by derivatives.

MTN and Commercial Paper Programs

A recent important addition to the range of refinancing tools has arrived in the form of Medium-Term Note and Commercial Paper programs. Pfandbriefe issued under these programs offer a greater range of maturities and can be denominated in different currencies. For the mortgage banks they offer a superior degree of flexibility in refinancing, as a variety of bonds can be issued as and when required. They offer a reduction in costs as the workload involved in issuance is much less and finally, they open the market to an increased range of investors with specific investment criteria.

Clearing

Transactions in Germany are usually settled through Clearstream Banking AG, Frankfurt, a subsidiary of Deutsche Börse AG, formed as a result of the merger of Deutsche Börse Clearing AG and Cedel International. The remainder are settled via Euroclear or Clearstream International.

KEY DIFFERENCES BETWEEN COVERED BONDS AND ABS OR MBS

While covered bonds are often regarded as similar to asset-backed securities (ABS) and mortgage-backed securities (MBS), many noteworthy differences exist between them:

- The assets behind the covered bonds assets remain on the originator's balance sheet, even though they may be maintained in distinct pools or lodged in special purpose affiliates. However, in the case of ABS or MBS, the assets are segregated from any other assets and are usually off balance sheet and placed in a special purpose vehicle (SPV).
- The covered bond issuer is the source of the principal and interest cash flows, whereas the actual assets provide those payments in the case of the ABS/MBS.
- In certain jurisdictions, covered bondholders have some recourse to "noneligible" assets and, in the case of the special purpose affiliates, may also rely on some form of parental support for the issuer. For ABS/MBS, in the event of insufficient proceeds from the pool assets to cover the claim, holders have no recourse above and beyond the collateral contained within the pools and the original ABS/MBS structure.
- Eligible assets for covered bonds are clearly defined by law and are substitutable. Therefore the asset mix varies over time and is relatively heterogeneous. For ABS/MBS, the assets are of the originator's discretion and once the structure is finalised, no asset adjustments can generally be made. The mix of assets can usually be regarded as quite homogeneous.

- Asset quality is a measure of the strengths of the specific structure created for the ABS/MBS. However, it is a function of the issuer and underwriting standards of the covered bond, as well as the features of each issues framework.
- Covered bondholders, in the event of issuer insolvency and provided that the covering assets continue to meet regulator requirements, will still receive interest and principal payments according to the contractual dates (with the exception of Spain). However, certain credit events such as deterioration in the quality of the underlying assets for example, would trigger the acceleration of ABS/MBS payments.

MARKET PARTICIPANTS

In August 2002, the real estate and public sector lending operations of Commerzbank Frankfurt (Rheinische Hypothekenbank AG), Deutsche Frankfurt (Deutsche Hypothekenbank AG), and Dresdner Frankfurt (Europäische Hypothekenbank der Deutschen Bank AG) merged to form Eurohypo AG,[4] Germany's largest mortgage bank, and in doing so, reduced the number of issuers of German Pfandbriefe to its current total of 40 institutions. This number consists of 20 private mortgage banks, 18 public sector credit institutions and two private ship mortgage banks. Nineteen private mortgage banks and one private ship mortgage bank form the *Verband Deutscher Hypothekenbanken* (The Association of German Mortgage Banks) and issue approximately 60% of the outstanding total volume in the Pfandbrief market.

Exhibit 7.3 is an outline of the structure of market participants. Of the 20 private mortgage banks, 17 are classed as "pure" mortgage banks and, as the name suggests, their lending operations are limited essentially to mortgage loans for commercial and residential property and to public sector lending. The latter includes loans to the federal government, the federal state governments or *Länder*, local authorities and public sector institutions.

Alongside these "pure" mortgage banks are three "mixed" mortgage banks (Eurohypo, HVB RE, and DEPFA). The difference between the two is that the "mixed" banks, in addition to conducting the same business conducting as the other mortgage banks, they are also licensed to engage in universal banking operations. Currently, only one mixed institution operates outside the regular remit of a German mortgage bank.

---

[4] The main shareholders continue to be Deutsche Bank (approximately 34.6%), Commerzbank (approximately 34.5%) and Dresdner Bank (approximately 28.7%).

EXHIBIT 7.3   Outline of Market Participants

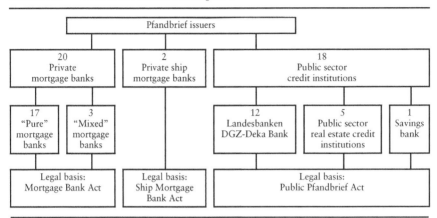

Source: Association of German Mortgage Banks. Used with permission.

The three mixed mortgage banks are now the exception; mortgage banks founded today may only be done so as pure mortgage institutions. The existing mixed institutions retain their status as they were engaged in other banking activities prior to the Mortgage Bank Act of 1900.

As mentioned previously, the mortgage banks are monitored by BAFin, in close collaboration with the Deutsche Bundesbank and are bound under the requirements of both the Mortgage Bank Act (HBG) and the German Banking Act (KWG).

The next group of Pfandbriefe issuers are classified as public sector credit institutions. The most significant of these are the *Landesbanks* and the DGZ-DekaBank (an umbrella organisation).

The state banks, or Landesbanks, are legally independent public sector entities. At present they benefit from the principles of *Gewährträgerhaftung* (guarantee obligation) and *Anstaltslast* (maintenance obligation). That is to say, that both the respective federal state and the regional savings banks or their regional associations guarantee them. This extra "guaranteed" status ensures that the issues brought by these institutions trade at a premium to their counterparts (see the relative value analysis discussion later in this chapter). However, under an agreement concluded between the European Union commission and the German federal government (on 18 July 2001), the Gewährträgerhaftung must be abolished by mid-2005, while the Anstaltslast support mechanism has to be modified. The European Union commission felt these guarantees from the public sector were anticompetitive and effectively amounted to a state subsidy, allowing the Landesbanks to fund themselves more cheaply.

EXHIBIT 7.4   The Ten Most Active Jumbo Issuers (as of 23 January 2003)

Issuer	Issues	Volume (€ millions)	Average size (€ millions)	Market share
Eurohypo	38	73,282	1,928	17.98%
AHBR	27	49,088	1,818	12.05%
DEPFA	16	39,715	2,482	9.75%
HypEssen	19	34,380	1,809	8.44%
HVB	18	29,453	1,636	7.23%
DG HYP	18	29,075	1,615	7.13%
HVB RE	16	16,636	1,040	4.08%
LB NRW	7	16,250	2,321	3.9%
LB Bad. Württ	5	10,750	2,150	2.64%
WestHyp	7	10,500	1,500	2.58%
Sum top 10	171	309,130	1,808	75.85%
Overall Market	252	407,538	1,617	100%

Source: DZ Bank. Used with permission.

In order to protect investors, outstanding bonds will stay guaranteed through a "grandfathering" agreement.

Completing this group of issuers are the public sector real estate lenders and one savings bank, the Public Pfandbrief Act (ÖPG) governs all. The regulations set out in the ÖPG are not comparable to the stringent legislation laid down in the HGB.

Deutsche Schiffsbank AG in Bremen and Schiffshypothekenbank zu Lübeck, the two ship mortgage banks, complete the list of Pfandbriefe issuers. They issue long-term credit against ship mortgages and fund their lending by issuing ship Pfandbrief and are regulated by the Ship Mortgage Act.

Exhibit 7.4 shows recent issue size from selected participants.

AMENDMENT TO THE MORTGAGE BANK ACT

On 1 July 2002, the amendments to the German Mortgage Bank Act finally came into force. The main ambition of these changes was to allow the Pfandbrief market to compete on a more level playing field with their up and coming foreign rivals.

The principal changes made were threefold. First and foremost, they allow the mortgage banks to engage in lending operations in previously restricted areas, namely outside of Europe in countries such as the United States, Canada, and Japan. Under the old law, German mortgage banks were only allowed to use public sector loans made in the European Union and euro-currency area as collateral for their bonds. This increasingly placed them at a distinct disadvantage when competing with banks in countries such as Luxembourg, which can use loans to any OECD country to cover their *Lettres de Gage*.

Secondly, German mortgage banks are now allowed to provide a broader range of services related to real estate and public sector lending, opening up new, fee-paying business opportunities.

The third major component of the new legislation related to the inclusion of derivatives in the cover pools and the net present value calculation of the respective pools. The total volumes of these derivatives are limited to 12% of both the total pool and Pfandbriefe outstanding and to maintain the Pfandbrief reputation for safety, the banks are still prohibited from assuming too much risk, by writing open-ended options and the like.

Collateral cover is now calculated with reference to market value as well as nominal value, enabling greater transparency and precision in the calculation of cover. Both these amendments benefit the Pfandbrief investor; in the event of the insolvency of a mortgage bank, there would be no netting of derivatives, which would therefore continue to protect the cover pools and allow the banks to hedge against adverse market conditions that could cause their paper to suffer credit deterioration.

HEDGING PFANDBRIEFE HOLDINGS

Players within the market have several options available to them when it comes to hedging their exposure to the Jumbo Pfandbrief. By far the simplest is to merely enter into an offsetting trade using the most relevant German government bond or futures contract and in periods of relative calm this can work reasonably well. There is a close correlation between Pfandbriefe and futures and the underlying Bunds have a well-developed repo market. For investors looking to capitalise on the pick-up in yield between Bunds and Pfandbriefe, then this method would certainly seem to be ideal, it is not without one major inherent problem: basis risk. It is difficult if not impossible to calculate one's basis risk in this scenario.

In 1998, with the global fixed income crisis that occurred after Russia's devaluation, the ensuing "flight to quality" caused the spreads to balloon some 30 to 35 basis points and this strategy proved to be ineffective and extremely costly. Many investment fund managers that use this hedging approach tend to wait to see extensive spread widening between the Bund and the Pfandbrief market before entering the market in anticipation of tightening.

In an attempt to attract foreign investors to the market by providing a truly homogenous hedging vehicle, Eurex launched the Jumbo Pfandbrief future on 6 July 1998. This followed a period of sustained issuance in Jumbos and it was felt at the time that this would provide a critical mass of underlying bonds of a size, around €50 billion, that would underpin sufficient volumes of deliverable paper. Eurex at the introduction, felt that the criteria for such a contract had been fully met and were quoted as saying that "a delivery commitment under a short position in a Pfandbrief futures contract can be fulfilled only by certain Jumbo Pfandbriefe, namely Mortgage Pfandbriefe and Public Pfandbriefe with a residual life on the delivery date of at least three and a half years and not more than five years, and a minimum issue size of DM1 billion. Further, the Jumbo Pfandbriefe must be rated AAA and structured in straight bond format. Also, at least three institutions must be named in the syndicate agreements of the issuers as market makers for the cash market."

The initial reaction to this new contract greatly exceeded most market participants' expectations with between 6,000 and 8,000 contracts being traded per day, but the enthusiasm was short-lived and by the end of July the volume traded had halved. The emerging market turmoil that began in the late summer dealt the faltering confidence in the new contract a further blow and as *Euroweek* reported in its 1998 Year End Review, "on one average day in October (1998), 214 Jumbo contracts were traded—a paltry figure compared to 133,000 Bobl contracts traded that day."

And so the Jumbo Pfandbrief contract had failed at its first major hurdle, and on 1 March 1999 Eurex suspended trading in both the Deutschmark- and euro-denominated contracts. It did however; indicate at the time, that the door remained open for a possible relaunch of the contract at a future date.

Several reasons as to why the liquidity in the contract failed to live up to expectations were offered. One, which many adhered to, was that the timing was extremely unfortunate, with the Russian crisis occurring so soon after the launch (although this type of situation is precisely the type of test that a genuinely liquid contract must be able to meet and surpass). In practice, however, the "flight to quality" proved this strategy very costly.

As at the start of 2003, no moves have be made to reinstate the Jumbo contract and presently the only way to effectively hedge ones exposure to the Pfandbrief market is via the swaps market, although many still favour the peripheral government bond route, particularly for trades conducted on a short-term horizon.

Exhibits 7.5 and 7.6 show relevant spreads for market participants who use Bunds or interest-rate swaps to hedge their holdings.

EXHIBIT 7.5   Jumbo–Bund Spreads

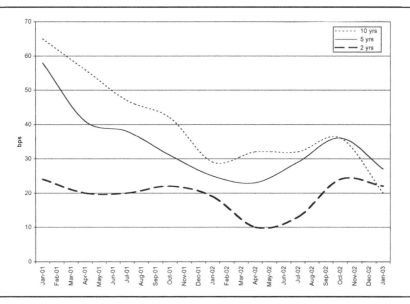

Rates Source: Bloomberg L.P.

EXHIBIT 7.6   Jumbo–Swap Spreads

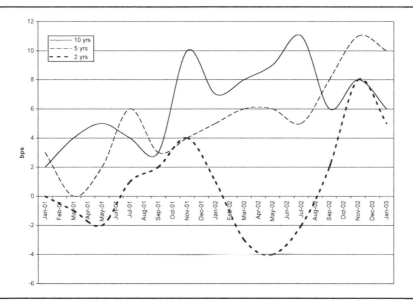

Rates Source: Bloomberg L.P.

THE CREDIT RATING APPROACH TOWARDS PFANDBRIEFE

With regard to credit rating, the Jumbo market has developed considerably from its inception in 1995. In that year, only three of the issuers were formally rated. During 2003 all issuers were rated by one or more of the public rating agencies.

The two main international ratings agencies, Moody's and Standard & Poor's, adopt different methodologies when approaching Pfandbriefe and this has caused some confusion among investors.

Moody's generally assume a strong link between the credit quality of the bonds and that of the issuer and this has lead to a "notching" approach. This method mirrors Moody's general opinion that the credit quality of a covered bond is a "function of the quality of the assets originator rather than that of the assets themselves." As a concession to the fact that these are "covered" bonds and as recognition of the tight legal framework within which these issues are bound, Moody's add three or four notches (for mortgage and public sector Pfandbriefe respectively) to the senior unsecured rating.

The approach applied by S&P is somewhat different. Although they too recognize the link between the creditworthiness of the issuer and its covered bonds, S&P operates on the basis that any potential weakness of the issuer can be overcome by the provision of a higher degree of overcollaterisation.[5] As a result, S&P's ratings are based essentially on an analysis of the collateral pool and therefore tend to be higher than those of Moody's.

This distinction between the two translated, until recently, into very little in practice. However, as the mortgage banks, in common with all German banks in the latter half of 2002, experienced significant credit deterioration these different approaches have become far more apparent. Pfandbrief paper from the same issuer is now rated differently by the two main rating agencies; for example, Moody's now rates AHBR's mortgage-backed bonds A1 whereas S&P still maintains a triple-A outlook.

The VDH consider this disparity to be unsatisfactory as it makes the job of marketing the product to an investor base, with ever-increasing risk awareness, more difficult. Their view is that the rigid notching approach adopted by Moody's creates a certain asymmetry as one moves down the credit scale, as it does not recognize the high quality of the assets in Pfandbrief cover pools.

At present any change in approach from Moody's is unlikely, given their view that Pfandbriefe are not bankruptcy-proof entities. Though

---

[5] The increasing of nominal cover for the Pfandbriefe outstanding, by way of appropriate assets to a level higher than the minimum required by law.

none has gone bankrupt yet, this does not mean that such an event is impossible. In the event of bankruptcy, investors will be exposed to a loss.

RELATIVE VALUE ANALYSIS

The yields of a single covered bond within one maturity band currently vary by as much as 20 to 25 basis points. This is a sharp increase from the 6 to 8 basis points variations seen in 1999 and preceding years. We now focus on the factors that can cause such differences.

As discussed in the previous section, a differential exists between the methods used by the two main ratings agencies to rate Pfandbriefe and this obviously has an impact on how the fair value of an issue is perceived. Also, given several prominent downgrades witnessed within the German market in the latter half of 2002, it is understandable to see that the level of yield spread variations has increased throughout the curve.

The type of issuer is naturally a major influence and as an example of the impact this can have, covered bonds issued by the Landesbanken, which profit from state guarantees and from the fact that they are eligible assets for the covered bonds of the private mortgage banks, trade on average 6 to 8 basis points more expensive than the other issues.

Under the tax legislation in Germany, domestic investors tend to favour low coupon bonds that are trading below par. Therefore one would expect to see these issues to trade rich to the curve. However, the impact of this has become more and more muted in recent years, perhaps a clear indication of a reduction in the influence of tax-driven domestic investors on the overall flows in the market. On this note, interest income earned in Germany by nonresidents is generally not subject either to income tax or to corporation tax. By analogy, withholding tax is not retained on interest income that nonresidents earn on Pfandbrief investments.

One could also assume that the size of issue may be a determining factor in the curve spreads; larger size would usually imply greater liquidity. The fact that volume has an almost negligible effect on spreads is testament to the market making obligations that are present in the Jumbo market.

Another factor to play its part is the collateral element of covered bonds. Mortgage loans are generally regarded as riskier than loans to the public sector, and hence, it has been noted that mortgage Pfandbriefe tend to trade some 1.5–2.5 basis points cheaper than public sector Pfandbriefe as investors tend to demand a slightly higher risk premium. The influence of collateral quality is obviously well covered by other aforementioned measures, such as the type of issuer and, of course, the bond's credit rating. These two variables have significantly increased their influence on curve spreads over the last couple of years and explain the majority of credit and spread differentiation in the world of covered bonds.

There is, therefore, a rationale behind the yield spread differential witnessed between two "like" issues occupying the same maturity band, and the above points must be factored in when assessing the fair value of a particular Pfandbrief. As of early 2003, it is generally felt that the market has found its echelon in regard to curve spread and that current relative valuations should remain to a large extent intact in the near term. In this context, any short-term deviations from fair value could represent profitable trading opportunities for investors.

THE EUROPEAN COVERED BOND MARKET

As more European countries aim to establish their own covered bond markets with updated legislation, investors are getting a larger choice of Pfandbrief-like products. Most of the laws are based on the established German framework and aim to provide the same high quality of asset, but slight differences still remain. Here we look at the differences between the main runners in the covered bond arena.

The European market volume share is shown in Exhibit 7.7.

France

The mortgage bond market in France dates back to 1852 when, on 28 February, the Decree of 1852 established mortgage banks that were authorized to lend funds to property owners. These loans were repay-

EXHIBIT 7.7   European Covered Bond Market as of 24 January 2003

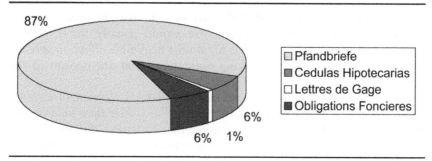

87%

☐ Pfandbriefe
■ Cedulas Hipotecarias
☐ Lettres de Gage
■ Obligations Foncieres

6%

6%   1%

able by long-term annual instalments. However, it was not until June 1999 when modifications to this law broadened the appeal of *Obligations Foncières* (OFs) for international investors. These modifications to the Mortgage Act had two main objectives: to lower refinancing costs for the issuer and to offer investors secure and liquid products.

France had seen Germany's mortgage banks, with the success of the Pfandbrief market, being able to raise refinancing facilities at considerably lower costs than their French counterparts. They wanted quickly to follow suit. The French banks realised that failing to do so could result in their domestic market share being eroded by aggressive competition from across the border.

Another major reason for amendments to the Mortgage Act was to attempt to restore a widespread confidence in the French mortgage-lending sector after the real estate crisis that occurred in the early 1990s. The new requirements set in place were successful in doing just that.

1999 saw the creation of a new type of financial institution in France, the Société de Credit Foncier (SCF) or mortgage loan company, provided for under the new law. Their creation sets the Obligations Foncières aside from other newly created European mortgage-backed sectors such as Spain's *Cédulas Hipotecarias* by the fact that their issuance is restricted solely to these Sociétés de Credit Foncier.

SCFs have the sole purpose of refinancing eligible assets, mainly through the issuance of OFs. While they have the legal status of banks, they are prohibited from engaging in traditional banking activities and from holding equity stakes in any subsidiaries, which mean that they operate very similarly to a SPV. French issuers also manage only one asset pool comprising both types of loans and whether the pool consists of public sector loans, mortgage loans or a mix of the both depends on the business model of the issuer.

Their bankruptcy remoteness is greatly enhanced through one of the most reassuring features of the French law and that is its specific exclusion of the SCF from any bankruptcy proceedings initiated at the level of its parent(s). The SCF is therefore less vulnerable to the default of its parent credit institution.

However, these legal provisions do not completely isolate the creditworthiness of the SCF from external factors, but only limit the extent to which credit risk contamination may occur. For this reason Moody's, when granting ratings, begin their analysis by assessing the creditworthiness of the SCF itself. They achieve this by principally analyzing:

- The strategic importance of the SCF to the refinancing of its parent credit institution(s).

- The support extended to the SCF by its shareholder(s) whether in terms of liquidity or capital.
- The nature and quality of the SCF's assets, underpinned by conservative loan-to-value thresholds.
- The capacity of the institution managing the SCF to adequately perform this role.
- Its asset and liability management practices, notably regarding interest rate mismatches.

The fact that the bankruptcy of a parent cannot be extended to an SCF is welcome, however, as a Moody's report published in October 1999 states

> ... the fact that OFs are issued by special purpose subsidiaries means that OF holders have no direct recourse to assets outside the SCF although they could reasonably expect some parent support. This is notably different from *Pfandbriefe* where bondholders have an eventual direct recourse to non-eligible assets if cover assets are insufficient to cover their claims and become *pari passu* with other senior unsecured creditors. Along similar lines, in case of insolvency of an originating credit institution, asset replenishment and/ or substitution is no longer possible, which leaves the SCF fully exposed to asset quality deterioration and repayment, and ensuing cashflow mismatches.

Although Moody's continues, "We consider that this element of weakness is mitigated by the strong likelihood that the French regulator would exert pressure on an SCF's shareholder(s) to extend support to this subsidiary."

Having thus arrived at a senior unsecured debt rating for the SCF, Moody's then turns its attention to the specific characteristics of the Obligations Foncières issued by the mortgage loan company. Given that the OFs exhibit a reduced frequency of default, a reflection of the "bankruptcy-remote" element of SCFs in regard to parent(s), and the lower loss potential due to their secured nature, Moody's grant a rating to Obligations Foncières of "up to three notches above the senior unsecured debt rating of the SCF."

Like Pfandbriefe, Obligations Foncières bondholders retain preferential rights with regard to the event of bankruptcy over any other claims. The similarities do not stop there. Issuers and market makers have agreed that the minimum size of issuance should be €500 million, that the issue is supported by a market making commitment from at least three banks, quoting continuous prices with bid/offer spreads of between 5 and 20 cents. Also, it almost goes without saying, all OFs must be rated by at least two of the internationally recognised ratings agencies.

While currently lacking in size in comparison to its German neighbour, the Obligations Foncières are rapidly proving to be a worthy competitor.

As of January 2003, there were 17 Jumbo OFs outstanding with a maturity greater than two years, totalling €29.2 billion.

Spain

The year 1999 also witnessed, again due to a modification of legislation, the debut of the first international issue of the Spanish *Cédulas Hipotecarias* or "Mortgage Notes."

Like other covered bonds, their initial existence dates back many years previous, in the case of Spain's offering, to 1869. A considerable number of cédulas have been issued in the domestic retail market since that time.

In 1981, the introduction of the "Ley del Mercado Hipotecario" (Mortgage Market Law) and its subsequent amendments allowed Cédulas Hipotecarias to be issued by almost any credit institution.

The first Jumbo-style issue was brought to the market in March 1999 and since then 12 more bonds have been launched. However, despite the enthusiastic start, only one bond was issued in 2000 and one of the existing issues was tapped. 2001 showed more promise, with a total of five new issues and the number of issuers increased from two to five.

Spanish cédulas are, so far, exclusively backed by mortgage loans; the legal framework for the issuance of "Cédulas Territoriales," public sector loans is still in the preparation stage.

Unlike the Obligations Foncières, cédulas do not possess the protection of bankruptcy remoteness in regard to their issuing entity; the probability of default between them is inextricably linked. Understandably, the ratings of these issues are therefore determined by the creditworthiness of the issuer and the whole process of rating is conducted on a case-by-case basis; analysing both the issuing institution as well as the specific characteristics of the security itself.

Under Spanish law, the underlying assets for the Cédulas Hipotecarias do not count as special assets. They are not separated from the bankrupt's assets in the event of the issuer becoming insolvent, as is the case with the German and French Pfandbrief-style bonds, and this obviously places the holder of cédulas in a much weaker position by comparison. However this weakness is considered to be largely offset by the fact that cédulas have the highest level of surplus cover (overcollateralisation) in Europe of at least 11%, which is imposed by law.

Cédulas have a "bond issuing ceiling" of up to 90% of the volume of "eligible mortgages" (loan-to-value ceiling of a maximum of 70% for commercial properties and 80% for residential properties). Even in the event of a full use of this ceiling, Cédulas Hipotecarias have an overcollaterisation of over 11%, as the mortgage loans also serve as collateral, although they cannot be included in the calculation of the maximum volume outstanding because of the higher loan to value levels. If this limit is exceeded at any time, the issuer has to restore the overcollateralisation limits by

- Depositing cash collateral of government bonds with the Bank of Spain within 10 working days.
- Buying back/amortising early outstanding cédulas.
- Adding new qualifying mortgages to the existing ones (e.g., by purchasing *Participaciones Hipotecarias*[6]).

It should be noted that due to the limited use of Cédulas Hipotecarias so far, the actual degree of overcollateralisation is at least within triple digits and this mandatory requirement is a major strength of the cédulas system.

The quality and size of the mortgage portfolio and the surplus cover are also subject to regular monitoring by the Bank of Spain.

All in all, the secured nature of this type of product strongly reduces the loss potential in a default scenario and to date, since their inception back in 1869, no Cédulas Hipotecarias has ever defaulted. In Moody's opinion these factors justify a rating of two notches above the senior unsecured debt rating for the issuer.

Although market makers provide a similar degree of liquidity for this product as for French and German Jumbos, the overall turnover in the cédulas has been somewhat limited. This is something that is likely to change in the near future. As of January 2003, the amount of Jumbo Cédulas Hipotecarias, with maturities exceeding two years, equals 16 with an outstanding volume of €30.05 billion.

Luxembourg

In November 1997 the Grand Duchy passed a new law that authorised the creation of a brand new financial entity known as the *Banque d'Emission de Lettres de Gage*, a mortgage-bond-issuing bank.

The Luxembourg law was modelled closely on the German Mortgage Bank Act governing the issuance of Pfandbriefe. Like Germany, the *Lettres de Gage* are subdivided into two categories: one backed by public sector loans (*Lettres de Gage Publiques*) and the other by mortgages (*Lettres de Gage Hypothecaires*). The bondholders also enjoy the same

---

[6] *Mortgage participations* are used for the securitisation of mortgages.

preferential rights over the covering assets which rank above all other existing claims, while the matching principal familiar in the German market also applies to the Luxembourg law.

There are, however, some key variances from Germany's mortgage law and perhaps the most important arises from the different geographical restrictions on lending business between the two. In the case of Luxembourg, public sector loans from the whole OECD area are eligible for refinancing via covered bonds without restrictions.

There are two diametrically opposing views as to the effect this difference has on the security aspect of the Lettres de Gage; the first is that the Luxembourg could be considered to be more secure than its German counterpart. This is thought to be due to the fact that in their search for diversified assets to use as collateral for their Pfandbrief-like product, Luxembourg banks will diversify their exposure to top-rated OECD sovereigns such as Australia and Japan.

However competition among the mortgage banks to deliver superior returns on investments will lead them to pursue assets in lower-rated OECD member countries such as Turkey and Mexico.

In the market we observe that German banks are keen to be involved in this wider business opportunity. This is borne out by the German mortgage bank involvement in the three main Luxembourg Pfandbrief banks. Pfandbriefbank International (PBI) is part of the HVB group, Europäische Hypothekenbank S.A is a 90%-owned subsidiary of the Eurohypo group and Erste Europäische Pfandbrief und Kommunalkreditbank (EPB), the third specialist bank to receive a Pfandbrief licence is owned jointly by Hypothekenbank in Essen AG, Düsseldorfer Hypothekenbank AG and a Geneva-based holding company of the financier Dr. Wolfgang Schuppli. The latter also holds a 49% stake in HypoEssen and, through another holding, a 100% stake in Düsseldorfer Hypothekenbank AG.

The Luxembourg market is still relatively small in comparison to its European cousins and has three Jumbo issues outstanding, as of January 2003, with a volume of €3.25 billion. With no issue with an individual volume of €3 billion, the Lettres de Gage are currently precluded from trading on the EuroCreditMTS platform.

Ireland

The Irish covered market is the most recent in Europe. When Ireland sought to create their covered bond market, they looked at all the relevant laws already in place throughout Europe, and cherry-picked the most attractive factors from an investor's perspective. What made this initiative even more impressive was the fact that Ireland has no history in issuing mortgage bonds.

Towards the end of 2001, the Irish Asset Covered Securities Act was passed allowing banks recognised by the Central Bank of Ireland as "Designated Credit Institutions" (DCIs) to issue *Irish Asset Covered Securities*.

When the legal framework was first put forward in early 2000, some of the proposed features of these issues were considered to be unique attractions from an investor's perspective. Their impact, however, has been somewhat nullified by progresses made in other markets, for example, the recent amendments to the German Mortgage Bank Act. Nevertheless, the concept of Irish covered bonds still represents an improved version of the German Pfandbrief. Ireland's rules for investor protection are the most stringent in the market—with strict supervision,[7] controls on assets eligible for cover pools and no possibility of risk from duration mismatching.

The Irish steering committee decided against adopting a policy such as that used by Luxembourg's Lettres de Gage with regard to "eligible-assets." They felt that allowing loans made in any OECD country as collateral for their bonds would compromise the credit quality of their Irish Asset Covered Securities. Instead, Ireland has limited the asset pool to the EEA, along with G7 countries and Switzerland.

A maximum of 10% of the cover pool can be commercial property loans and substitution assets cannot exceed 20%. To limit cash flow mismatching risk, the Irish bonds exhibit tight matching requirements. For example, the nominal value of the cover assets must at all times exceed the value of the corresponding securities. The aggregate interest from the assets must also exceed that of the covered bond and the currency of the cover assets must be similar to the related bonds. In addition to this, the duration of the cover assets must be greater than the duration of the bonds.

Critically, it is only in Ireland where the regulator has further stipulated that "the weighted average duration of the cover assets should not exceed the weighted average duration of the Irish covered bonds by a period greater than three years."

There is a loan-to-value limit imposed of 60% for residential mortgages and 100% for public sector loans and hedging contracts against interest rate risk are permitted in the collateral pool.

This new Irish product provides an interesting enhancement to the range of high quality products available in this sector. The legal framework combines all the traditional elements of covered bonds from existing European markets with innovative augmentations that serve to strengthen credit quality further.

The first issue in the Irish Asset Covered Securities market is due in March 2003 and will be brought by a well-known German name, the

---

[7] Supervision by the Central Bank of Ireland and an Independent Cover Asset Monitor approved by the regulator.

Deutsche Pfandbrief bank (DEPFA) under the guise of their Irish subsidiary, DEPFA ACS Bank.

Investors will thus benefit from a high degree of liquidity coupled with professional expertise in the placement and trading of these bonds.

CONCLUSION

Covered bonds offer high safety while at the same time granting the investor an enhanced yield in comparison to government bonds. The sheer size of the Pfandbrief market with its market-making obligations has the potential to offer good liquidity and it is gradually breaking away from its reputation as a German "closed shop." However, it still has some way to go to catch up with the very markets that it purports to challenge, the aforementioned government markets, in terms of professionalism and ability to provide a credible liquid marketplace. Mortgage banks have now been given the opportunities to operate beyond European borders and truly market their product globally. Failure to take advantage of this situation could prove extremely detrimental to their standing. One issuer in particular, DEPFA, has already tapped into the United States with a Pfandbrief issue denominated in US dollars. This offers US investors a high-quality investment alternative to US agencies and triple-A ABS and can give them much sort after diversification.

New and sophisticated covered bond laws, offering significant improvements to the original Pfandbrief model, have been introduced in France, Spain, Luxembourg, and now Ireland. Germany has responded with its amendments to the Mortgage Bank Act.

The development of these other markets comes at a time when the Pfandbrief market is experiencing a difficult period, featuring several prominent downgrades, as the whole German banking system has become embroiled in an economic crisis. Their introduction is, for the first time, representing increased competition for the German market, albeit still some way off posing a serious threat.

The legislation changes throughout the European covered bond markets, also bring another possibility a step closer—a European Pfandbrief.

It is not unforeseeable for further adaptation to take place that would create a truly homogenized product; an idea originally envisaged back in the 1980s. Currently, investors have to research the slight differences between the various covered bonds and although these can offer up some interesting opportunities, they require greater analysis. In the absence of any further concerted efforts to create such an attractive instrument, the different national laws seem likely to prevail for some time.

CHAPTER 8

European Inflation-Linked Bonds

Barclays Capital Inflation-Linked Research Team

Concern about the future purchasing power of money is probably as old as money itself. Periods where governments sought to fix money against real commodities, notably gold and silver, stemmed from the desire to foster certainty in the real value of their currencies. The inflation-linking of contracts and bonds is not new, and there has been a long line of academic luminaries supporting the principle of protecting both parties to a monetary obligation against unanticipated inflation. Books and papers often cite the debt issued by the State of Massachusetts in the eighteenth century, first linked to silver in 1742 and later to a broader basket of commodities in 1780, as the first instance of such assets.

Inflation-linked bonds indexed to consumer or wholesale prices have been issued by a number of countries since 1945—early issuers included Israel, Brazil, and Argentina. Those early markets normally came into existence out of a need to secure finance in environments characterised by high and volatile inflation. Sometimes, when a government's imperative to fund has confronted investors' unwillingness to trust nominal assets because of inflation, inflation-linked bond markets have been born out of necessity. In more recent times, countries with low and fairly stable inflation have still seen advantages in issuing these instruments. Even Japan, which is currently experiencing mild deflation, sees value in issuing inflation-linked bonds—Japan intends to launch its first "linker" in early 2004.

There have been many different structures of inflation-linked bonds issued over time, but the most widely used form is one where principal and income are adjusted for changes in the relevant consumer price index between issue date and cash flow payment date, subject to an indexation

EXHIBIT 8.1 Market Value Composition of the Barclays Capital Global Inflation-Linked Bond Index (€ billion)

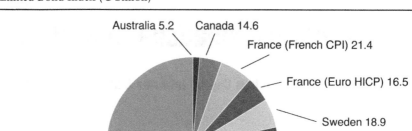

Australia 5.2   Canada 14.6

France (French CPI) 21.4

France (Euro HICP) 16.5

Sweden 18.9

US 161.9

UK 113.7

Total: €352.1 billion

Source: Barclays Capital.

lag. The modern inflation-linked bond market probably dates back to the UK government's launch of "index-linked gilts" in March 1981, and since then this essential bond structure has been common to all such bonds issued by governments globally, although precise linking methodologies, lengths of indexation lags, and market conventions for real yield calculations, and so on, do differ.

The European inflation-linked government bond market comprises three main issuers, the United Kingdom, France, and Sweden. France issues bonds linked to two different price indices, the French Consumer Price Index (CPI), excluding tobacco, and the Eurozone's Harmonised Index of Consumer Prices (HICP), excluding tobacco. In April 2003, these three markets had an aggregate market capitalisation of €170 billion, representing almost exactly half the €352 billion value of the Barclays Capital Global Inflation-Linked Government Bond Index. The non-European markets in the index are the United States, the largest single linker market, Australia, and Canada. Other countries have issued these bonds, but are not included in the index for reasons of issue size, market size, or credit rating. (See Exhibit 8.1.)

In March 2003, Greece launched its first bond linked to Eurozone HICP, ex-tobacco, and other Euro countries are understood to be investigating the possibility of joining the "real world." There is a small but rapidly growing nongovernment inflation bond market in Europe. Barclays Capital's nongovernment sterling linker index is capitalised at £6.7 billion and its euro equivalent at €9.2 billion. Inflation derivatives have proved particularly successful in the Eurozone. Although the euro-denominated inflation-linked bond market is still materially smaller than either that of the United States or United Kingdom, its inflation-derivatives market is easily the biggest, most active, and most diverse in terms of products traded.

Fans of inflation-linked bonds tend to be evangelical about the product. At the heart of this evangelism is a firm belief that the unique qualities of "linkers" make them optimal assets and liabilities for investors and borrowers, respectively. True, they are slightly more complicated than nominal instruments mathematically, but they are simpler than nominals in a valuation sense. They take a big worry—inflation risk—out of the equation. However, it is not all about risk reduction. Trading opportunities are there to be taken advantage of, and linkers offer new trading dimensions. If you think of nominal bond trading as one dimension—"nominal space"—then inflation-linked trading in "real space" is a second dimension, and trading between the two markets occurs in a third dimension—"inflation space." Why should active bond investors restrict themselves to one dimension when there are three?

The objectives of this chapter are to discuss the benefits of the inflation-linked asset class to both issuers and investors, to provide brief histories and salient characteristics of the different European inflation-linked markets (both bonds and derivatives), and to introduce key analytical and trading concepts.

THE CONTINUING NEED FOR THIS ASSET CLASS IN A LOW-INFLATION WORLD

In May 1996, when the US Treasury announced its intention to issue inflation-linked bonds, *Barron's* joked that it was "a good idea whose time has come ... and gone"—the message being that we had moved into an era of price stability, so why would anyone want or need the inflation-protection offered by such instruments? Is inflation dead, or is it just resting? It is worth mentioning that history records periods where prices saw fairly flat long-term trends, while still being volatile about those trends. Inflation volatility is always something worth insuring against, if you can.

It is true that the very recent history has been of low and relatively stable inflation, and if we look at the relationship between the first 30-year US Treasury Inflation-Indexed bond issued and an appropriate nominal "comparator" of similar date, the "implied" US inflation rate has ranged between a low of 1.2% and a high of 2.6%. However, inflation at those bounds would mean that US$100 paid in 30 years time would be worth either US\$70 of today's dollars or \$46 of today's dollars, respectively, in terms of its future buying power. To emphasise the point, the former amount would be worth 50% more than the latter. In short, even seemingly mild inflation uncertainty can play havoc with expectations of the future purchasing power of our savings, when it interacts with the forces of time and compound interest.

There is only one reason to save, sacrificing current spending, and that is in order that savers and their dependents can enjoy future consumption. The saver is predominantly, if not wholly, interested in the future real worth (purchasing power) of savings and not their future nominal price. To be interested in the future money price, over and above the real value, is to suffer from money illusion. It is true that this principle is complicated by the fact that individuals do enter nominal arrangements with institutions handling their savings, so those institutions become interested in meeting nominal liabilities (e.g., providing flat private pensions without cost of living adjustments, savings bonds, etc.). But the individual is still ultimately concerned with what that pension, endowment, or other intermediate vehicle will buy, nevertheless.

There are exceptions and provisos, but they are few. Possibly the only material exception is the need for the individual to pay down a nominal home loan over its life, so not all liabilities are ultimately real in the real world. A key proviso is that however well a linking index is constructed, there will be a "basis risk" between the inflation measured by the index and the "personal inflation" experienced by the unique basket of goods and services that each saver hopes to consume one day.

With these qualifications in mind, we feel we can still say that these instruments come closest to offering real value certainty for savers. If an inflation-linked bond exists with a term matching the saver's investment horizon, then it essentially is the risk-free asset by definition. So the question should not be "Why should I buy linkers?" The question should be "Why should I buy anything else?" The burden of proof falls on all other, riskier, asset classes to justify displacing linkers in a portfolio. Many argue that this inflation insurance is precious, deserving a "risk premium." If people are prepared to pay a premium to insure their possessions against a small chance of loss through theft and fire, why shouldn't they pay a premium to insure against the risk of loss of real wealth resulting from unanticipated inflation?

People tend to regard inflation as bad for savers and good for borrowers, but this is an oversimplification. Inflation that is higher than expected results in an unanticipated transfer of real wealth from nominal bond investor to borrower, while lower-than-expected inflation results in an unanticipated transfer of real wealth from borrower to investor. Therefore, inflation uncertainty is (or should be) as much of a concern for borrowers as for investors, and we hope to demonstrate that a large, vibrant, inflation-linked bond market is in the mutual interest of both issuer and investor. To be really provocative, we could go so far as to suggest that it is only money illusion that weds market participants to nominal fixed-rate debt, when inflation-linked bonds are available. There is a certain irony in knowing a nominal bond's yield to the third decimal place but only having the loosest perception of what it will be worth (in real terms) when it matures. If the markets had invented inflation-linked bonds first, would they have bothered to invent nominal bonds?

WHY ISSUE INFLATION-LINKED BONDS?

We have sketched out a couple of reasons why governments issue index-linked bonds already. We also said how the removal of inflation risk is valuable for the borrower, as it is for the investor, and earlier we described how in some countries rampant inflation resulted in a complete loss of investor confidence in nominal government debt, requiring the creation of an inflation-linked bond market out of necessity. However, there are other arguments why governments should issue linkers, and the reasons already given need to be added to, expanded upon and broken down into different subarguments.

We divide the arguments for inflation-linked government debt issuance into two historical sets: early arguments and new arguments.

Early Arguments

There are the early arguments, focusing on the potential to save money, and these dominated the original debate over issuance in the United Kingdom and have continued to be influential as other countries have entered the market.

Early Argument 1: Exploiting Market Inflation Expectations That Exceed Those of the Government

If a government, encompassing the central bank, has confidence in its own intent to operate a robust anti-inflation stance, but sceptical investors remain unconvinced, building high inflationary expectations into nominal yields, then a government issuing index-linked bonds will save money if it is right. It will deliver lower inflation than is priced into the relationship between inflation-linked and nominal bonds. The UK Treasury certainly saved an enormous amount of money for this reason, through a long period of falling inflationary expectations. Other countries have also managed to save money in this way.

UK linkers were often criticised in the 1980s and early 1990s for being poor performers relative to nominal gilts because of this. In truth, such criticism was unfair, and this becomes clear if the experience is thought of in real space, rather than nominal space. Index-linked, after all, delivered the real returns expected of them, and investors had little justification for griping about nominals returning windfall gains when inflation turned out to be lower than they were expecting. You cannot complain about not profiting from something you were surprised by.

Early Argument 2: Saving a Risk Premium

An argument that was also to the fore in early thinking was the notion that a government issuing these securities can save the aforementioned risk premium. If investors are primarily interested in the future real value of their savings, they should be prepared to pay an insurance premium for the privilege of owning a risk-free inflation hedge. Phrasing the argument slightly differently, we could say that a government that chooses to issue a nominal bond, when investors would prefer an inflation-indexed bond, is selling a suboptimal asset, as far as the investor is concerned at least. It should therefore expect to be penalised for it through higher expected debt-servicing costs. This is a complex area, deserving a chapter all to itself, but to the extent that investors will pay a price for inflation insurance, the government will cut its funding costs.

Early Argument 3: Positive Credibility Feedback

There were other, peripheral and often very intangible, arguments made in the early days. One commonly held opinion was that because a government issuing such bonds cannot debase the value of these liabilities with inflation, this demonstrated a strong anti-inflation commitment. This should, it was proposed, enhance credibility and reduce inflationary expectations, thereby enabling governments to issue *nominal* bonds on lower yields.

Early Argument 4: A Cash Flow Benefit

Issuing what is effectively a kind of deep discount bond—one which pays accumulated inflation on the principal at maturity—reduces the burden of immediate debt servicing costs. This is a questionable benefit, since the inflation experienced should really be accounted for as a cost in the fiscal year it accretes.

Early Argument 5: The Provision of a "Social Good"

The relationship between inflation-linked and nominal debt provides a market-based reading of inflationary expectations, although several things, such as the risk premium, tax and various regulatory factors, may distort this measure. Even if these distortions are estimated to be large, or if they cannot be measured, as long as they can be assumed to be stable, then at least we would have a measure of how inflationary expectations change through time. This inflation "barometer" should be valuable—for companies making business decisions, for investors, for public spending planning, for central banks gauging interest rate policy, and so on. Putting a price on this intangible social good would probably defy the economics fraternity's best academic brains. We can all probably agree that it is worth something, but not necessarily to the investor that buys such a bond.

Early Argument 6: Other Macroeconomic Benefits

There were several additional macroeconomic arguments, but they became increasingly obscure and intangible. These included the possibility that offering an instrument that removes (or minimises) inflation uncertainty will boost the saving rate, and the belief that taking inflation risk out of lending and borrowing improves economic efficiency by improving the allocation of resources.

How Do Those Early Arguments Stack Up Now?

Governments do not currently suffer the lack of anti-inflationary credibility of the past, it is true, and some countries have appeared, from time to time, to issue inflation-linked bonds on negative risk premiums. However, typically, either inflation has subsequently fallen to justify those seemingly low inflation expectations (i.e., the market was right and economists wrong), or break-even rates have firmed up as the market has matured, correcting the anomaly. Sometimes, in the early stages of a linker market's development, supply appears to grow a little faster than demand—the investor base can take time to climb the learning curve and embrace the new instrument. However, this tends to be a short-lived "growing pain."

The market's pure inflationary expectations and the risk premium, if any, are not strictly observable. They cannot be separated from one another. Whether existing or future linker issuance will save or cost a government money, relative to nominal bond or other alternative financing choices, will depend upon the future behaviour of inflation. We have said that the credibility feedback benefit is intangible, so cannot be valued, but one suspects that it is less meaningful for the major issuers of linkers than in the past. As we write, the central banks' anti-inflationary credibility seems more robust than ever, although this may be more a function of either microeconomic improvements in the working of economies or the stage of the global economic cycle than of the dogged adherence of central bankers to price stability.

These issues are still actively debated, and will continue to be. However, what we consider to be a much more powerful and sophisticated understanding of the benefits for governments has evolved as the global market for these securities has grown.

New Arguments

Then there are the more recent, more sophisticated, and (we would say) more powerful arguments, which focus on liability risk management for governments. Given that asset management is all about risk and return, it is only natural that liability management should be all about risk and cost.

New Argument 1: The Appropriate Nature of Liabilities

A government's future expenditures and revenues are almost all essentially real flows. We would regard its biggest single "asset" as its entitlement to a future stream of tax revenues, which will reflect both inflation and real economic activity. Having at least a portion of its liabilities linked to inflation should offer risk reduction benefits to the government borrower, matching its future debt servicing costs with its revenues.

The example of Japan, in the recent past, is one of a country that has suffered from unexpected disinflation and now deflation. This has resulted in an unanticipated real wealth transfer from issuers of nominal bonds to investors, resulting in a windfall loss to the government and windfall gains for investors. Had it issued inflation-linked JGBs, this would have tempered the escalation in Japan's public debt/GDP ratio a little. The unique economic structures and circumstances might not make Japan a particularly persuasive comparison to apply to other economies, the intention is simply to illustrate the risks of the unexpected.

New Argument 2: Risk Diversification

A government might decide to ignore the above, regarding itself instead as having no natural preference for either real or nominal liabilities. However, even such a government will not have a single-point forecast of future long-term inflation—its expectations are likely be described by a range of possible outcomes (i.e., a probability density function). A government should regard it as appropriate to have inflation-linked liabilities in proportion to the probability it ascribes to lower future inflation than the market expects.

The argument here is the need for a balanced liability portfolio in the face of an uncertain economic future. So even if inflation-linked funding sometimes appears expensive to issuers (because implicit inflation appears too low), it can still make sense from a risk reduction standpoint to have inflation-linked liabilities as part of a government's debt portfolio.

New Argument 3: Inflation and the Budget Balance

This argument is really a component part of New Argument 1, but it is worth elaborating, not least because it has been emphasised by the United Kingdom's Debt Management Office (DMO) in describing its own philosophy towards inflation-linked liabilities. It is based on the fact that both inflation and the budget surplus/deficit are likely to have correlated, cyclical, components. In times of strong growth, public finances will be more healthy but inflation will be higher—a government might have higher-than-expected debt servicing costs on its inflation-linked bonds, but it will be in a more comfortable fiscal position to pay those higher costs. Conversely, in an economic slump, the budget balance will deteriorate, but inflation will subside—the government will have lower-than-anticipated servicing costs on its inflation-linked debt at a time when its finances are in less good shape. Thus, linker debt-servicing costs should act as what the UK DMO calls "a fiscal stabiliser."

New Argument 4: Maximising Reach and Capturing the Consumer Surplus—the Economics of Discriminating Monopolies

In its original discussions with the market before launching the TIPS programme, the US Treasury recognised the potential advantage of being able to reach pools of potential investor demand with TIPS that nominal bonds do not. Expanding the universe of potential buyers for Treasury securities, accessing those with different needs, or different economic views, should reduce the average cost of funding.

This is all about the economics of "discriminating monopolies." A classic example of discriminating monopolies is where airlines regard it as optimal to offer different classes of plane travel to better target different market segments. The majority of airline passengers may not need the choice of first class travel, but that does not change the fact that it is optimal for an airline to make it available for those that want it.

Applying These Arguments to Corporate Borrowers

If you reread the four new arguments for issuing linkers, above, substituting the word "corporate" in place of the word "government," it becomes clear that they all support the idea that it should also be attractive for corporates to issue linkers.

Corporates' balance sheets are full of real assets, so real liabilities are intuitively appealing, and future corporate revenues may not be purely inflation-linked, but they still tend to be more real than nominal. And sometimes revenues are explicitly inflation-linked, as in the case of some utilities and infrastructure projects carried out for the public sector.

Risk diversification seems obvious—there are several examples of companies weighed down by long-term nominal debt that was taken on in more inflationary times, paying rates that are now painfully high. The notion of inflation-linked debt being a fiscal stabiliser for governments is easily transformed into an "earnings stabiliser" argument for companies.

And the argument that diversifying the range of debt instruments offered can reduce total funding costs is becoming increasingly understood in the United Kingdom. UK companies with a large block of debt funding planned will often issue a variety of different instruments of different terms, and it is no longer unusual to see one or more inflation-linked bond tranches within a programme.

Are There any Disadvantages in Issuing Inflation-linked Bonds?

Ahead of the launch of most index-linked markets, one fiercely argued view has repeatedly been presented. It is that any form of inflation indexation is insidious and pernicious. Inflation is an economic evil, and if you index goods, wages, or liabilities to it, the argument goes, thereby "inoculating" against it, people will cease to care about it. And if voters, businesses, and governments have no vested interest in price stability, then inflation will rampage once again. This view was behind Germany's former law prohibiting debt indexation and behind other countries with chequered inflation histories attempting to wean themselves off indexation (e.g., Israel and Iceland).

Our response to this has always been the same: A government with nominal liabilities has a vested interest in debasing the real value of the national debt with inflation, while a government with index-linked liabilities cannot escape them in this way. However, this does give us a better, if Machiavellian, reason for a government to prefer nominal issuance—it might wish to retain the option to inflate away its liabilities. However, even that is a trick you can only pull once. The likelihood would be that the market penalises you for it a later date—think how long it took bond markets to forgive governments for the inflation of the 1970s and 1980s. Index-linked bonds also provide a measure of inflationary expectations—an early warning indicator for everyone to see.

It is conceivable that the perception of inflation as irrelevant (which we would classify as money illusion), or the slightly greater complexity of these instruments, or their admittedly lower liquidity levels, might render inflation-linked bonds unpopular, but we doubt it. We have already shown how very modest mistakes in inflation estimation can still have a major cumulative impact on the real value of nominal assets in an era of supposed "price stability." The instruments may be more complex mathematically than nominal bonds, but they are simpler assets in worry terms—there is one less thing to worry about (inflation).

Inflation-linked bonds are a little less liquid than nominal bonds, but the possibility that this results in them trading cheaply—suffering "an illiquidity discount"—is contentious. We would propose that turnover is lower in linkers because they meet investor needs so well. They are natural buy-and-hold assets because they are worry-free core holdings. Thus, illiquidity, relative to nominals, is something investors in linkers understand and accept. It is not so much a penalty, more the price of success.

A government or company does need to assess all its assets, liabilities, and cash flows when arriving at a decision about the appropriate proportion of its bond obligations to be in inflation-linked form. It will already have other real liabilities, such as pension obligations, and real outgoings, such as salaries. Experience suggests that governments that have performed this sort of analysis with a view to issuing inflation-linked bonds have come down strongly in favour of doing so.

WHY INVEST IN INFLATION-LINKED BONDS?

Hopefully readers will need little convincing of the merits of investing in index-linked bonds based upon what has already been said. The key reasons are summarised below.

The True Purpose of Saving is to Defer Consumption

The purpose of saving is to provide for deferred consumption of the saver and the saver's dependents. There is no other rational reason to save, unless one regards a desire to display conspicuous wealth as an end in itself. Therefore, the only concern of savers is the future real purchasing power of their savings. To focus on future nominal certainty is to suffer from money illusion. Inflation-indexed government bonds are the lowest risk instruments for meeting long-term savings needs. Index-linked government bonds, where they exist, should be the first choice investment, from which you only depart because you see superior returns elsewhere.

Diversification Benefits

Inflation-linked bonds also have different behavioural characteristics to other assets. They form a distinct asset class offering portfolio diversification benefits. This can be demonstrated using efficient frontier analysis. However, we should bear in mind what has already been said in the previous point. Efficient frontiers can make linkers appear riskier than they really are. A standard efficient frontier typically analyses nominal returns against the variability (risk) of those nominal returns, and we would suggest that it is real risk and return that matters.

Efficient frontiers also invariably place Treasury bills as the risk-free asset. T-bills may be risk-free from a creditworthiness point of view, but it is not tenable that a three-month nominal asset is a risk-free instrument for someone with, say, a 30-year savings horizon. If you are investing for 30 years, over which time you are interested in your prospective real returns, then a 30-year linker (to be held to maturity) is your risk-free asset, almost by definition. 100% invested in that bond becomes the lowest risk portfolio on your frontier. Efficient frontier analysis starts to lose its impact once this premise is accepted, not least because you do not have a large data sample of consecutive, nonoverlapping 30-year periods (for any asset) to produce robust analysis.[1]

Textbook efficient frontiers using, say, one-year period returns suffer from a mismatch between the term of the observation period and the term of a typical investment horizon (for which there may well be a linker of appropriate term). For long-term investors, it is not a particularly good way to examine inflation-linked bonds.

New Trading Dimensions and Greater Trading Precision

We have already described the notion of bond trading in three dimensions, thanks to the availability of linkers. Perhaps the most important aspect of this "3D trading" is the ability to implement a view with much greater precision. Often, when trades are done in nominals, they really reflect a view on inflation, but because nominal yields do not just represent inflationary expectations, this is an imprecise enactment of that view. With inflation-linked bonds, investors can express a much purer inflation expectation.

THE MAIN EUROPEAN INFLATION-LINKED ISSUERS: FRANCE

On 3 December 1997, M. Dominique Strauss-Kahn, Minister of the Economy, announced France's intention to issue its first inflation-linked bond in 1998. Legislation needed to usher in the new asset was passed on 3 July 1998, paving the way for the 15 September 1998, launch of the 3% OAT*i* July 2009. The first sale was a syndicated deal, with sub-

---

[1] Even the Barclays *Equity Gilt Study*, published annually since 1956 and now with 103 years of UK and 77 years of US history, gives us only three complete observations for the former and two for the latter.

sequent reopenings of the same bond being handled by auctions (the two additional inflation-linked issues since then have both followed the same approach).

The market was widely consulted on the main decisions to be taken, such as choice of linking index, bond structure, and so on. It was decided that the bonds would adopt the linking methodology created by Canada in 1991—the Canadian model that was fast becoming the preferred global structure because of its elegance, simplicity, and the fact that it allowed a much shorter indexation lag than other models such as the United Kingdom's. The bonds would be linked to the measure of French national CPI, excluding tobacco, published by L'Institut National de la Statistique et des Etudes Economiques (INSEE). The reasons for this election are discussed below. In addition to the arguments for issuing these instruments already discussed in this document, France had a unique, additional reason. It was approaching monetary union, with the prospect of a merging of the nominal government bond markets under one currency umbrella. This would likely intensify competition for financing in the "nominal world," and the hope was that an instrument such as this would appeal to other Eurozone member investors, conferring upon France a first-mover advantage.

A second linker, the 3.4% OAT*i* 2029, was launched a year later in September 1999, again linked to French national CPI, ex-tobacco. Growth in the outstanding market value of these two bonds was slow but steady—in particular, there was some disappointment that the instruments did not seem to be capturing the imagination of investors in Eurozone countries other than France.

In October 2001, France addressed this issue head-on, in launching the 3% OAT*ei* 2012 linked to the Euro-zone Harmonised Index of Consumer Prices (HICP), ex-tobacco. Exchanges out of the OAT*i* 2009 issue were also accepted. There were good reasons why the French national CPI was chosen as the linking index the first time around (see below), and good reasons why the time was now ripe to take the next step in creating an index-linked market for the whole EMU area. Following the same pattern as with the OAT*i*s, France launched a 30-year "*ei*" (Eurozone inflation) linker a year later in October 2002—the 3.15% OAT*ei* 2032.

Anyone who thought that the advent of a Eurozone inflation-linked bond would cause the French CPI linked bonds to "wither on the vine" has been proved mistaken. Agence France Trésor (AFT) has continued to reopen the two OAT*i* issues, and demand for these, and the domestic inflation-linked bonds of CADES (a government-owned institution created to repay past social security liabilities), has been sufficiently strong for AFT to issue a new 10-year OAT (2.5% July 2013), in January 2003.

EXHIBIT 8.2   Market Capitalisation of France's Inflation-Linked Debt (€ billion)

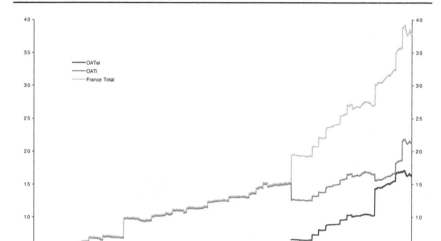

Source: Barclays Capital.

In short, the two inflation-linked markets coexist comfortably, affording cross-market trading opportunities. The introduction of the Euro HICP market gave a new lease of life to the sector, as the evolution of the market's captitalisation shows in Exhibit 8.2. The market goes from strength to strength in spite of the low inflation environment and the fact that Europe has a long way to go in the development of private pension provision.

The Linking Indices for OAT*i* and OAT*ei* Issues

Whether to select a French CPI index or a Euro-area one was an issue that saw intense debate before the launch of France's first issue. The arguments for the domestic index included the likelihood that using national inflation would be a better liability match for the government. The disadvantages of using France's CPI included the risk of narrower appeal outside France, although it was persuasively argued that some important countries (like Germany) might find that their own inflation proves to be more closely correlated with France's than with the Euro-zone as a whole. International trading accounts in particular probably had a preference for bonds linked to the same inflation measure that was targeted by the ECB.

EXHIBIT 8.3   French Inflation, Including and Excluding Tobacco (%)

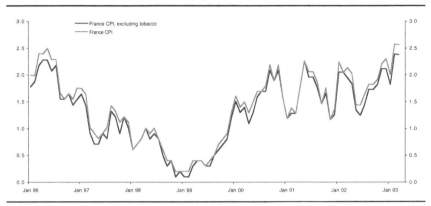

Source: Thomson Financial.

In 1998, the final decision almost certainly came down to practicalities. At the time, the disadvantages of Eurostat's European Harmonised Index of Consumer Prices (HICP) for the EMU area were material:

- It was a relatively new, untested index with no track record.
- Index coverage was far from complete, with components only able to be introduced as quickly as all member countries were able to deliver consistently calculated data, so the index was still evolving and compositionally in flux.
- There was an associated fear of revision risk.

The conclusion of the Trésor, and of the market consensus at the time, was that these issues rendered the Euro HICP undesirable; not least because of the revision risk problem, since contracts and payments cannot be changed retrospectively. The hope was that, particularly for longer dated issues, French inflation would be regarded as a good proxy for European inflation over the full term of the bonds, and this would encourage strong demand from other Euro-zone countries. After all, in this sense, what is important is the long-term *correlation* of inflation rates—it is not necessary for the inflation *levels* to be the same for these bonds to be appropriate hedging instruments. Tobacco's exclusion, a tiny influence that must be considered and valued but is not something material, was a legal matter—further difficult legislation would have had to be cleared away to change it. All other government contractual arrangements in France with an inflation element (minimum wages, social benefits, etc.) use the ex-tobacco series. Exhibits 8.3 and 8.4 com-

EXHIBIT 8.4 Eurozone Inflation, Including and Excluding Tobacco (%)

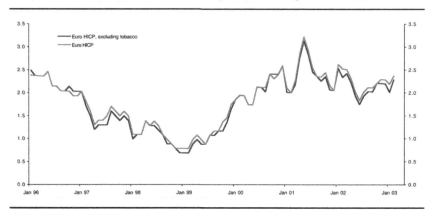

Source: Thomson Financial.

pare the inflation series including and excluding tobacco for France and for the Eurozone, respectively.

However, by October 2001, when OAT*ei* 2012 was launched, the Euro-zone HICP was well seasoned. The use of a Euro-zone index became possible, where it was less acceptable in 1998, because:

- The index had matured, with stable, extended coverage.
- The index is still subject to potential revisions, but should they occur, they can be expected to be sufficiently rare and small for the US ruling on this issue to be acceptable where bonds are indexed to the first published figure for each monthly HICP. This methodology works well in the United States, where CPI-U is also exposed to "revision risk."

So the prime obstacle to the development of a Euro-zone real yield curve was gone. And, as we have said, Greece has now joined the sector and other governments are understood to be considering entry, potentially adding points to the real yield curve and investor choice.

The French national and Euro HICP series both use geometric aggregation at the lowest strata subindices, and have long been innovative in the use of hedonic techniques for quality adjustments. It is generally felt that any Boskin-style inflation "overstatement" of inflation in either series is likely to be minimal, so there would appear to be little or no threat of inflation being materially affected by purely methodological changes, as happened in the United States through the early years of its inflation-linked market.

Calculations

The bond's quoted price is in real terms. Settlement values and cash flows are arrived at using the following formulas:

Each settlement day has its own distinct Reference Index. The first day of each month has a Reference Index equal to the CPI index of three calendar months earlier, for example, that for 1 September 2003 is the CPI for June 2003 and that for 1 October 2003 is the CPI for July 2003. Reference Indices for intervening days are calculated by straight-line interpolation on a standard Actual/Actual accrual rate.

$$\text{Index} = \text{CPI}_{m-3} + \frac{(\text{nd} - 1)}{\text{ND}_m} \times (\text{CPI}_{m-2} - \text{CPI}_{m-3})$$

where

CPI_{m-2} = price index for month m–2
CPI_{m-3} = price index for month m–3
ND_m = number of days in month m
m = month in which settlement takes place
nd = day of the month on which settlement takes place

This formula is used to calculate a CPI Reference Index for the issue date, or "Base Reference Index." For the settlement date or cash flow payment date, t, a Reference CPI is then calculated. These two indices provide an Index Ratio for the value date:

$$\text{Index ratio} = \text{Reference CPI}_t / \text{Reference CPI}_{\text{Base}}$$

For settlement amounts, real accrued interest is calculated as for ordinary OATs. Clean price and accrued are each multiplied by the Index Ratio to arrive at a cash settlement amount. For actual coupons paid, the (real) annual coupon rate is multiplied by the Index Ratio for the payment date, and likewise for the par redemption amount (with the cash value subject to a par floor).

Issuance Patterns

The AFT has steadily increased linker issuance since the product was launched, and currently targets approximately 10% of gross issuance in inflation-linked. Its commitment to a stable issuance pattern was re-emphasised prior to the launch of the OAT*ei* 12 in October 2001. AFT maintains some discretion over which issues to auction and when, and is sensitive to expected market demand for that issuance.

THE MAIN EUROPEAN INFLATION-LINKED ISSUERS: SWEDEN[2]

The Swedish government first issued inflation-linked bonds in 1994. According to the Swedish National Debt Office (SNDO), this was to supply those investors who demanded a large inflation premium when buying nominal bonds but who were not in need of the liquidity available in benchmark bonds. Taking a similar view to the UK government, it was expected that the asset class would create cheaper funding in the long run for the government and would diversify the risk of the government debt portfolio. It should also be noted that the Swedish Krona had devalued sharply in the year preceding the programme's inception, dramatically raising the value of foreign currency debt outstanding. Thus the SNDO needed an alternative source of funding at a time when inflation expectations were rising. Inflation-linked bonds were arguably the most suitable choice for further borrowing.

The first linker to be issued was a 20-year bond with a zero-coupon structure (No. 3001, 0% 2014). A selection of the eight Primary Dealers in the nominal market took responsibility to quote two-way prices for the new bond. The Debt Office held five common price auctions from April to June, which saw a face value of SEK16 billion being offered to the market. But demand for much higher real yields from the market meant that only SEK6.7 billion was allotted.

In 1995 the SNDO launched the second inflation-linked bond, another zero but with a shorter maturity of 10 years (No. 3002, 0% 2004). At this time the SNDO decided to replace the common price auctions with multiple price auctions. Moreover, the SNDO opened a non-competitive facility for small volumes in the auctions, so that small investors could enter the market. In February 1996 the SNDO launched two new bonds: a 5-year zero-coupon bond (3003, 0% 2001) and a 12-year coupon bond (3101, 4% 2008). In June 1996 the 24-year coupon bond (3102, 4% 2020) was launched. The market continued to grow rapidly in 1997 and 1998.

Since 1998 the growth in the market has slowed. This was to be expected given that the programme was maturing and the SNDO did not feel it necessary to pump the market with supply just for the sake of liquidity. The inflation rate fell sharply and this lowered the cost of funding the inflation-linked debt. However, it did not prevent the difference between nominal and real rates falling sharply, thus reducing the cost effectiveness of inflation-linked versus nominal debt from the Debt

---

[2] The authors would like to give special thanks to the Swedish National Debt Office for their assistance with this section. Of course, any views expressed and any errors and omissions are those of the authors.

Office's perspective. Low volumes were issued through this period of very low breakeven inflation spreads. In June 1998 the third coupon bond was issued (3103, 3.5% 2028), the first bond with a 30-year maturity.

In April 1999 the SNDO launched two new linkers, a new 30-year bond (3104, 3.5% 2028) and a new 16-year bond (3105, 3.5% 2015). These two bonds were issued with an inflation floor, meaning that the new bonds had a similar structure to United States and French inflation-indexed bonds. The format of issuing inflation linked bonds was changed, this time moving back to bid price auctions, every three months. The reason being that this type of auction was common at the international level, allowing clearer signals of the volume on offer. The primary dealers were permitted to switch linkers directly with the SNDO on a daily basis, in order to enhance the liquidity of the market.

In 2000, the SNDO decided to conduct monthly auctions. The SNDO focused on larger issue sizes in coupon linkers, which was to be achieved by outright auctions and switches from zero-coupon linkers. In early 2002, the SNDO held buybacks in the 3002, 0% 2004, to facilitate issuance because the projected budget surplus negated the need for new issuance.

The Swedish Consumer Price Index (CPI)

The Swedish Consumer Price Index is compiled monthly and is a good proxy for the consumption patterns of the entire country. The weights and sample of items are revised at the beginning of each year. The weights for the major groups are based on the Swedish National Accounts statistics.

The index uses regular prices paid by the public, Value-Added Tax is included in the prices and subsidies are excluded. The price collection is done in the middle of the month. Prices are collected from a random sample of 600 retail stores, restaurants, and so on.

The Consumer Price Index is chain-weighted with yearly links (each link with December of the preceding year, the weights being revised for each link). The links for the months January to December are computed with weights based on the value of private consumption during the preceding year recalculated to December prices of that year. For the month of December a revised link, the long-term link, is also calculated. The weights for this link are based on the value of private consumption during the year, recalculated to the price level in December of the previous year. The long-term link may differ from the short-term link due to better information on the price development. The index number of the Consumer Price Index is calculated for every month, from the two types of links. The short-term link is chained back, through the long-term link in each preceding year. This method of reweighting can lead to significant changes in the CPI index between December and January releases that do not correspond to price changes in that period.

Calculations

Swedish linkers are quoted on yield basis, but for pricing and inflation indexation purposes the bonds adopt a similar methodology to Canada, France, and the United States.

Real interest is accrued on a European 30/360 basis. To calculate settlement amounts, real accrued interest and clean price are multiplied by the indexation ratio for the settlement date, as for France's issues. Also, as in France, coupon and redemption amounts are calculated by multiplying the real value of the payment by the indexation ratio for the payment date. All five coupon-paying bonds pay on 1 December each year.

Swedish bonds, like Australian and UK bonds, have a short period before the coupon is paid where the buyer will not be entitled to receive that coupon. In Sweden this ex-dividend period is five working days, during which the accrued interest will be negative.

The settlement price and the accrued interest for Swedish inflation-linked bonds are calculated in the following way: A reference CPI value is calculated for every day of the year based upon the CPI values CPI_{t-3} and CPI_{t-2} for three months and two months prior to the month of settlement, respectively. These reference CPI values apply to the first day of the month containing the settlement date and the first day of the following month, respectively. The reference CPI for any day between these two dates is calculated by linear interpolation.

Reference CPI for day d is

$$d = \frac{\text{Minimum of } [d-1, 29]}{30}(CPI_{t-2} - CPI_{t-3}) + CPI_{t-3}$$

where

d = day of the month (e.g., 1st implies $d = 1$)

For settlement purposes there are separate rounding conventions applied to the zero-coupon and coupon-paying issues. For zero-coupon bonds there is no rounding in the calculation, but the settlement price is rounded to the nearest krona. Coupon bonds are rounded once before you get to the settlement price, the clean price is rounded to three decimal places before adding on accrued interest. The settlement price is then rounded to the nearest krona.

THE MAIN EUROPEAN INFLATION-LINKED ISSUERS: UNITED KINGDOM

After announcing its intent in the 10 March 1981 Budget, the UK Treasury issued its first index-linked gilt on 27 March 1981 with an auction of £1 billion 2% Index-Linked Treasury 1996. Through constant commitment to the asset class from both the Treasury and the investor base, the market had grown to £85 billion by April 2003, by market capitalisation, representing 26% of the total gilt market. Bond maturities are relatively evenly spaced along the real yield curve, out to the longest (2035) bond, and issue size by market value is less variable than for nominal gilts.

The creation of a linker market was formally recommended by the "Committee to Review the Functioning of Financial Institutions (1977–1980)"—known as the "Wilson Committee," after its Chairman Sir Harold Wilson. However, Mark Deacon's and Andrew Derry's excellent book *Inflation-Indexed Securities* cites a recommendation by Keynes to issue linkers as early as 1924. There was a domestic precursor for the market, inasmuch as the UK government's National Savings department had been issuing inflation-linked savings certificates for retail investors since 1975.

The launch certainly "caught the wave" in terms of the time and the place to start a linker market. The high and volatile UK inflation of the recent past made this an instrument that was very popular with academics and actuaries—investors had fresh experience of unanticipated inflation debasing the real value of assets. It would be wrong to call it opportunism, but the then relatively new Conservative administration certainly turned adverse prevailing economic circumstances to its advantage, in this respect. It wasn't just about the inflation background either, it should also be remembered that the economic rigidities of the time meant that the consensus was acutely pessimistic about trend GDP growth and the prospective real returns that the real economy could deliver. This encouraged the view that a 2% risk-free real rate of interest was attractive from an "opportunity cost" standpoint.

Long-dated real rates are back around that 2% level as we write, but the average real yield over the life of the market has been much higher. Rising real yields in the earlier years can be attributed to a variety of things, but we would include improving perceptions of the real returns the economy could deliver and a reducing scarcity value of index-linked. The scarcity of the asset, relative to nominal bonds, was reduced as the market capitalisation grew. A discussion point at the time was that early investors in linkers suffer a "first-mover-disadvantage" because of this, and it can be argued that this is a feature that seems to have been observable in other linker markets, in their developmental stages. To try and elaborate, rather than just label this "supply and demand," we could argue that the initial buyers of linkers will be either those who are most inflation risk-averse (so those for whom inflation-protection is most precious), or those who are the most pessimistic about inflation prospects. In fact, scarcity value took a double hit—they become less scarce and the value attributed to this scarcity reduced as the level and volatility of inflation fell.

The UK government was probably a little reticent about issuing these bonds to start with, perhaps explaining the initial restriction that they could only be held by pension funds, or the pensions accounts within other businesses (e.g., annuities at life companies). This restriction was lifted after one year.

No thumbnail sketch of the UK linker market's early days would be complete without a mention of the one-off innovation of an index-linked convertible gilt, nicknamed the "Maggie Mays." The 2% Index-Linked 1999 was convertible into a nominal bond (10.25% 1999) at three future conversion dates. At a time when inflation remained volatile, and with the term to option expiry spanning a general election whose outcome was uncertain, seldom has so much optionality been sold so cheaply. The bonds were all (or almost all) converted.

Although the degree to which this was envisaged by the government is debatable, the UK Treasury has saved money through issuing linkers rather than conventional gilts, thanks to the long-term decline in inflationary expectations from high levels. It has therefore capitalised on a "credibility gap" between its own resolve to bring inflation down and pessimistic market expectations about the likelihood of success.

The Choice of Linking Index

Index-linked gilts are linked to the "Retail Prices Index (All Items)," or RPI, with an eight-month lag. The inflation rate calculated from this index is often described as "headline" inflation, as a short-form name distinguishing it from the so-called "underlying" measure RPIX, which excludes mortgage interest payments and is the index subject to the Monetary Policy Committee's inflation target.

The debate about which index to choose for linking purposes is something every country goes through before it launches a linker market. In the United Kingdom, and elsewhere, a host of different indices were considered, including wages (the average earnings series) and the GDP deflator. Wage indexation was appealing for practical reasons, because defined benefit pensions are linked to salaries, and for "social inclusivity" reasons. It was thought socially desirable for retirees to share in the real income growth enjoyed by those in work, rather than see real income divergence between workers and pensioners as time passes.

The GDP deflator's attraction stems from it being perhaps the broadest possible measure of inflation, but the appeal of this is eclipsed by its shortcomings. A linking index needs to be transparent, widely and easily understood, robust, timely, and not prone to revision. Here the GDP deflator falls-down on most counts and problems also emerge with using wage and salary indices. RPI or CPI measures become the obvious choices.

In the United Kingdom, RPI raw data is collected in the middle of each month, with the new index for that month published in the middle of the following month. Weights are recalculated annually, with reweighting done in January.

A particularly important thing to understand is that, as a European Union member state, the United Kingdom also calculates a Harmonised Index of Consumer Prices (HICP) using goods and services coverage and methods consistent with other European countries' HICP indices. The HICP methodology and coverage are quite different from those for the RPI linking index, and the HICP inflation rate has been consistently below the RPI rate (lately by about 1%). These issues need to be borne in mind when comparing value between UK linkers and other markets, particularly France's.[3]

How Do They Work?

Index-linked gilts, like all other linkers covered in this chapter, are known as "capital indexed bonds," where the income and principal are adjusted for changes in a consumer price index, subject to a lag. In the United Kingdom, the index is the RPI and the lag is eight months. The market trades on a clean price basis, with the quoted price a cash price (not a real price), including inflation accretion.

For example, the eight month lag means that the principal value of the 2% IL 2006, issued in July 1981 and redeeming in July 2006, will actually be uplifted by the percentage increase in the RPI between November 1980 and November 2005. Investors should note that the RPI was rebased in January 1987 from 394.5 to 100.

The cash value of semi-annual coupons are calculated as follows:

$$\text{Coupon paid} = \frac{C}{2}\left(\frac{\text{RPI}_{r-8}}{\text{RPI}_{i\ 8}}\right)$$

---

[3] For a full description of the RPI, see the National Statistics publication, *The Retail Price Index Technical Manual*, 1998 edition, www.statistics.gov.uk/downloads/theme_economy/RPI_TECHNICAL_MANUAL.pdf

where

C   = quoted annual coupon
RPI_t = RPI for month t
m = payment month
i = issue month

The coupon arrived at, now in money terms, is truncated to two decimal places for the two oldest existing linkers (2006 and 2011), and truncated to four decimal places for all others bar one. The exception is the new 2035 issue, which uses natural rounding to six decimal places. Accrued interest is calculated on the money value, not real value, of the coupon to be paid on an actual/actual basis.

Similarly, the cash value of the redemption amount is

$$\text{Redemption value} = 100\left(\frac{RPI_{r-8}}{RPI_{i-8}}\right)$$

where r is the redemption month.

Unlike some other linker markets, there is no minimum redemption floor of 100 in the event of deflation over the entire life of a bond.

Why the Eight-Month Lag?

Here, and in the complexity of the real yield calculation, the United Kingdom suffers perhaps for being the "prototype" linker market. An eight-month lag is needed in order to always know with certainty the future money, or cash, value of the next coupon, so that the money value of that coupon can be accrued. The major innovation of the Canadian model is the use of a formula that accrues coupons on a real basis, removing the need to know precisely what will be paid in cash terms on the next coupon day.

So investors "lose" the inflation for the last eight months of a bonds life, but "gain" the inflation for the eight months prior to the bonds issue. This term mismatch might not seem a problem, but the history shows that the impact has been large. Exhibit 8.5 depicts the rolling difference between 10-year average inflation and the 10-year average inflation eight months earlier. Even as recently as October 2000, that average difference was as much as 0.6%. The average inflation over the ten years to October 2000 was 2.8%, while the average over the ten years to February 2000 was 3.4%. The impact of the lag was so great because prices rose by 8.4% in the eight months to October 1990 but only by 2.4% in the eight months to October 2000.

EXHIBIT 8.5   10-Year Average UK Inflation Less 10-Year Average UK Inflation Eight
Months Earlier (%)

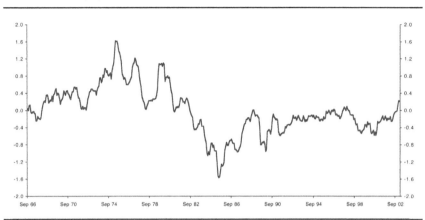

Source: Thomson Financial, Barclays Capital.

Because inflation has been falling for 20 years, the lag has almost
always been to the investor's advantage since the market came into being.

These matching "errors" are less alarming than they might appear,
because all known price information is built into the real yield formula
as soon as it is published. Two things really matter, in terms of the
achieved real yield relative to the quoted real yield at purchase: firstly,
the difference between future inflation over the life of the bond and the
3% inflation assumption used in the market convention for calculating
yields, and secondly (as with any coupon bond) reinvestment risk. However, we are getting ahead of ourselves—the next section handles the
market's yield conventions.

Yield Calculations

Because inflation-linked bonds all have indexation lags, they retain an
unavoidable nominal element. Unless you have perfect contemporane-
ous indexation—that is, a zero time lag—you cannot calculate a pure
real yield. For markets that use the Canadian model, the lag is sufficiently short for market to be happy to accept a degree of approximation to what you might call the "true real yield," in order to avoid over-
complicating a neat and simple real yield formula that keeps every input
in real terms (and one which is familiar, because it is the same formula
as that for nominals). However in the United Kingdom, the long lag and
the slightly different way the linking works mean the bonds require
something less "user-friendly."

The yield formula, expressed algebraically, is daunting, but readers should not worry unduly about it because we will go on to explain it in words that should make more sense. For practical purposes, it is often much less cumbersome to calculate these yields numerically on a spreadsheet, rather than algebraically.

The real yield formula below has been taken from the Debt Management Office's *Formulae for Calculating Gilt Prices from Yields*, 15 January 2002 update, and it covers bonds with two or more remaining cash flows. The term "quasi-coupon date," in the notes that follow the formula, means the theoretical cash flow dates determined by the redemption date—they are quasi dates because weekends and holidays may mean the true payment dates differ.

Any errors of duplication are ours and we have also trimmed and altered the wording of the explanatory notes. Readers should refer to the above official publication to see complete details, including the treatment of linkers with less than two cash flows remaining.

$$P = \left[d_1 + d_2(uw) + \frac{acw^2}{2(1-w)}(1 - w^{n-1}) \right](uw)^{\frac{r}{s}} + 100au\,w^{\frac{r}{s} + n}, \text{ for } n \geq 1$$

where

P	=	"dirty" price (i.e., including accrued) per £100 face
d_1	=	cash flow due on the next quasi-coupon date per £100 face (may be zero in the case of a long first coupon period or in the case of settlement in the ex-dividend period; or may be greater or less than $c/2$ during long or short first coupon periods)
d_2	=	cash flow due on the next but one quasi-coupon date per £100 face (may be greater or less than $c/2$ times the RPI Ratio during long first coupon periods)
c	=	(real) coupon per £100 face
r	=	number of days from settlement date to next quasi-coupon date
s	=	number of days in coupon run containing settlement date
g	=	semi-annual real yield
w	=	$\dfrac{1}{1 + \dfrac{g}{2}}$
f	=	assumed inflation rate (3% is the current convention)

$$u \quad = \left(\frac{1}{1+f}\right)^{\frac{1}{2}} = \left(\frac{1}{1.03}\right)^{\frac{1}{2}}$$

n =   number of coupon periods from next quasi-coupon date to redemption

RPIB = the Base RPI for the bond—that for the month eight months prior to issue date

RPIL = latest published RPI

k =   number of months from the month whose RPI determines the next coupon to the month of the latest RPI

$$a \quad = \frac{\mathrm{RPIL}}{\mathrm{RPIB}} u^{\frac{2k}{12}}$$

What is this Formula Doing?

With an eight-month lag, we will know the next coupon cash flow and possibly the subsequent one, but no others. The formula takes the latest known RPI value and from that month projects all future monthly RPI values using an inflation assumption (currently 3%), which is a market convention. So an unknown RPI in month t is given by

$$\mathrm{RPI}_t = \mathrm{RPI}_{t-1}(1+f)^{\frac{1}{12}}$$

Applying the indexation lag, this allows us to calculate estimated nominal values of all future cash flows which, knowing the current dirty nominal price, P, allows us to solve for an internal (nominal) rate of return—a nominal, semi-annual, gross redemption yield, y. Having applied our 3% inflation assumption, f, to get nominal future payments, we now remove it from the nominal yield using the simple formula

$$\left(1+\frac{g}{2}\right)^2 = \frac{\left(1+\frac{y}{2}\right)^2}{(1+f)}$$

to arrive at our real yield, g.

This is relatively simple to perform on a spreadsheet, setting up a "look-up table" of estimated RPI values to apply to future cash flows.

The process of assuming an inflation rate at the start, then taking it out at the end will seem odd to the newcomer. The inflation assumption

EXHIBIT 8.6   UK Real Yield Curves at Different Inflation Assumptions (%)

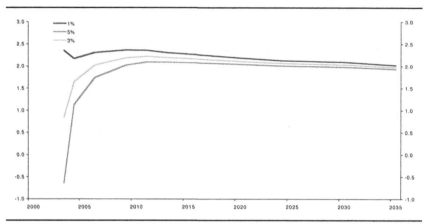

Source: Barclays Capital.

used still has a residual impact upon the real yield calculated, because of the lag, which is undesirable but unavoidable in this framework. The real yield varies inversely with the inflation assumption. This impact is small for the longest issues but can be quite large for the shortest linkers, as Exhibit 8.6 shows.

It would be wrong to believe that this is not a problem that affects markets that use the Canadian model. It does, in a smaller way, because the indexation lag is shorter. But the problem is hidden, so it emerges in a slightly different form. One advantage the UK formula does have is that it embodies the full effect of all the known RPI data immediately that is published. This does cause discontinuous jumps in real yields when a new RPI is announced; but intuitively people will understand that a yield measure should ideally include all known information that directly affects its future return. In the Canadian model, newly published CPI data is only incorporated in the price of the bond with a delay, which encourages a focus on "good carry months," when index increases are large, and "bad carry months," when they are small or negative. Roughly speaking, at the start of good carry months, "true" real yields are effectively understated—there is known favourable future price information that isn't captured by the yield. And the degree of understatement will increase for shorter-dated maturities.

Market Conventions and Practice

In 1988 auctions were replaced by taps (ad hoc sales of small amounts) for primary issuance of linkers, reverting to auctions in November 1998.

Auctions are single-price, rather than the multiple-price auctions used for nominal gilts, and have been smaller in size than for nominals. The approach has been to repeatedly reopen existing linker issues at each auction—the recent 2% 2035 issue was the first new bond in 10 years.

In 1998, the DMO removed the obligation for all gilt-edged market makers (GEMMs) to make prices in linkers, introducing a smaller grouping of index-linked market makers (IG GEMMs). The framework under which the DMO interacts with the market is quite involved, so readers should refer to the latest version of "Official Operations in the Gilt-Edged Market" on the DMO's website for a full understanding. The pertinent elements to look at for linkers include auction methodology, circumstances when the DMO might consider using taps and linker switch auctions (and how they would work), the DMO's "Shop Window" facility, and so on.

The repo market in linkers coexists alongside an old-style stock-lending system. Issues seldom stray far from general collateral rates. Index-linked gilts are not strippable, and there is no index-linked futures contract. There is a sterling inflation derivatives market, which we return to later in the chapter.

Government funding plans are laid out annually in a "gilt remit" within the Treasury's "Debt and Reserves Management Report." This generally coincides with the Budget, just ahead of the beginning of the new fiscal year in April. The remit contains an estimate of the total size of linker sales, by market value, to be carried out in the new fiscal year. In recent years, this has been subject to a minimum of £2.5 billion, which will remain in place until further notice. We are also told planned auction dates, and are often given guidance as to how plans might be altered in the event of changes to the health of public finances. Formal remit revisions can happen at any time, but two key times are firstly, early in the new fiscal year once the prior year's finances are known, and secondly, when the Autumn Pre-Budget Statement is announced.

The DMO has (twice) consulted on the possibility of adopting the Canadian model for future new issues of index-linked gilts. Opinion was divided in the latest consultation round, and the authorities felt there was insufficient support to justify the change.

Taxation

What is outlined below is the authors' general understanding of UK tax principles as they apply to index-linked bonds. It should not be construed as tax advice, and it may be incorrect, or out-of-date; it is certainly an incomplete synopsis. Where tax is an issue, no action should be taken without proper advice from a qualified tax expert.

For index-linked gilts, institutional investors that are taxed are treated in the following way. An inflation tax relief is granted based on the inflation experienced between tax year-ends. This relief is deducted from the total return (calculated on a mark-to-market basis or an accrual basis, according to the an election made by the investor), and the difference is taxed. This means that index-linked enjoy a material tax advantage over nominal gilts—the intent and effect is that investors are only taxed on their real return, not on inflation compensation.

This is essentially, but not precisely, the same as saying that the inflation increase in principal is not taxable. There are two reasons why it is not the same. Firstly, if an investor tax year end is, say, December, the relief will be based on the RPI change from December to December, without a lag, whereas indexation occurs with an eight month lag. Secondly, the starting value at the beginning of any tax year is unlikely to be exactly indexed par.

This tax treatment covers most taxed investors, but there are exceptions. It is also worth saying that most index-linked gilts are held by pension funds, or within the pension business lines of life assurance companies, which do not pay tax, so this is not relevant for them. This also means that tax is not a material influence on the market.

Corporate index-linked do not enjoy this inflation relief. The inflation uplift is taxable—that is, no inflation credit is applied. However, certain issuers might be able to obtain an exemption from this tax. The UK's Inland Revenue decided that since corporate issuers are allowed to offset the inflation uplift against taxable income, in the year that it accretes, then corporate linker investors should not receive inflation relief. As we have said, this is not an issue for pension funds who are the main holders.

Private individuals who hold UK index-linked gilts only pay tax on income accrued over the course of the financial year, so they do get all gains—inflation-linked or otherwise—tax free. This also means that losses, in the event of a falling RPI, are not allowable against tax.

Institutional Issues

The sterling securities markets are dominated by long-term institutional investors, namely pension funds and life assurance companies. This is particularly (we would say acutely) true of the index-linked market. Official statistics for pension fund investments are perceived to be of poor quality. They are now notorious after the suspension of pension fund statistics between January and May 2002, pending an investigation into a £105 billion downward revision to the value of end 1999 equity asset holdings (from £395 billion to £290 billion). Bearing this in mind, the balance sheet numbers for end 2000 suggest that of £75.2 billion index-linked outstanding by market value, life companies held £18.7 billion and pension funds held £41.2 billion. Collectively, those two sets of institutions held 80% of the linker market, and we would suspect that private holders' interest—for tax-efficiency reasons—is shorter on the curve, so the institutional holdings of over 5-year linkers is higher still, proportionally. We would also suggest that life company holdings are in effect pensions assets, matching real annuity obligations and pension fund obligations that have been "bought-out."

The majority of UK private pension liabilities are still of a defined benefit (DB), or final salary, type, although there is an inexorable shift towards defined contribution (DC), encouraged by the increase in the burden upon companies operating DB schemes. Within DB schemes, there are three broad classes of pensions liability—active (those in work and contributing to a scheme), deferred (those no longer contributing but not yet retired), and pensioners. Active liabilities rise with salaries, while, under the Pensions Act 1995, deferred and pensions-in-payment liabilities must rise by something called the Limited Price Index (LPI), which is inflation with a 5% cap and a zero floor. These schemes are very mature, with the majority of liabilities now LPI-linked, so the appropriateness of index-linked becomes obvious, and there is a growing nongovernment market in LPI bonds and swaps.

The rules governing how these liabilities should be valued under the Pensions Act, and how minimum scheme contributions should be determined, are set out in the Minimum Funding Requirement (MFR), an adjunct to the Pensions Act issued in 1996. The MFR has been widely criticised and a replacement for it is planned, but however its replacement works will not alter the essential nature of the liabilities, which are inflation-linked. The new accounting framework, FRS17, and the last few years market experience, also highlight the risks UK pension funds have been running by holding very high equity weightings against very mature liabilities. The need for UK pension funds to migrate to greater bond weightings (particularly index-linked) seems inescapable.

KEY ANALYTICAL CONCEPTS

The presence of a risk-free real asset is of great value to the study of finance, lending itself to theoretical and behavioural analysis. In this section, we examine the relationship between inflation-linked bonds and nominal bonds, then show how this framework can be applied to the relationship with equities.

The Fisher Equation

The Fisher equation, which predated the existence of inflation-linked bond markets, states that a nominal bond yield is made up of three components—inflationary expectations, a required real yield that investors demand over and above those inflationary expectations, and a "risk premium." The risk premium reflects the assumption that investors want additional compensation for accepting undesirable inflation risk when holding (therefore suboptimal) nominal bonds.

The presence of inflation-linked bonds allows the substitution of actual real yields for "required real yields" in the formula, to give

$$(1 + n) = (1 + r)(1 + f)(1 + p)$$

where

n = yield on nominal bond
r = real yield in index-linked bond
f = inflationary expectations
p = risk premium

This is often approximated by

$$n = r + f = p$$

leading to the market "shortcut":

$$n = r + \text{BEI}$$

where BEI is the "break-even inflation."

Later we will show that a similar equation can be constructed that relates inflation-linked bonds to equities.

Break-Even Inflation

So we have formally introduced the notion of "break-even inflation," a term at the heart of inflation-linked bond analysis and trading. In principle it is the rate of inflation that will equate the returns on an inflation-linked bond and a "comparator" nominal bond issue of the same term. In theory, calculating it by simply subtracting a real yield from a nominal yield is a crude form of a properly compounded calculation, particularly when bond market conventions are semi-annual and what you should want is an annual measure of inflation.

For a market with an annual yield convention, the following would be appropriate:

$$(1 + \text{BEI}) = \frac{(1 + n)}{(1 + r)}$$

while for a semi-annual market, we would use the following:

$$(1 + \text{BEI}) = \frac{\left(1 + \dfrac{n}{2}\right)^2}{\left(1 + \dfrac{r}{2}\right)^2}$$

However, the subtraction form is widely accepted. After all, there are other difficulties involved which have to be accepted—invariably there is a term mismatch between linker and comparator, there is reinvestment risk, and there is the fact that the real yield is not a "pure real yield" (as we explained in the UK section), because of the indexation lag. A truer measure of break-even inflation would be achieved if we were lucky enough to have zero coupon linkers with no lag and a zero coupon nominal of identical term.

Although there is no formal break-even calculation "convention," or way of selecting the best nominal comparator for that matter, historically break-even inflation in the United Kingdom has been calculated in a slightly more complicated way. Because UK real yields require an inflation assumption—3% is the market convention—there would be an inconsistency between the break-even inflation (BEI) rate and the inflation assumption used. The market tends to use the last formula above to arrive at a "first cut" BEI, then it uses that BEI rate as the new inflation assumption to calculate a new real yield. This is done iteratively until the assumed inflation rate and the BEI rate converge on a "final cut" BEI.

The Risk Premium

The search for the inflation risk premium is something of an academic "holy grail." Beware those that claim to have found it, because the path is fraught with difficulties. We do not question the logic that investors might be prepared to pay a risk premium for inflation protection. That is powerful, as is the argument that the premium should be a function of inflation uncertainty, which in turn, is likely to be correlated with the recent experience of inflation volatility. But these things get us no closer to attaching a value to the premium.

The problem is that true inflationary expectations are not observable. We cannot disaggregate break-even inflation into inflationary expectations and the risk premium. We might have an economists' consensus for this year's or next year's inflation. (Why do they call it a consensus, when it is an average, not a consensus?) However, there is no guarantee that the economists' consensus is either up-to-the-minute or in agreement with the market's consensus. And we certainly don't have good current data for long-term inflationary expectations.

Consider the following. Assume a two-asset world where there are only nominal bonds and inflation-linked bonds. If a government announced that the following day it would buy in a third of its nominal debt and replace it by issuing an equal amount of inflation-linked debt, would the market's average inflation expectations change? No. Would the average value the market places on inflation protection (the risk premium) change? It shouldn't. But we can all be sure that nominal yields would fall sharply and real yields would rise sharply. The risk premium would appear to collapse.

Does this violate the Fisher equation? It would appear to. However, if it is accepted that different investors have different inflation views and risk preferences (some may even have a preference for nominal certainty over real certainty), the paradox can be resolved, if you say that all market participants have their own Fisher equations. As the market mix of nominals and linkers change, the risk preferences and inflationary expectations of the marginal investor changes—the marginal investor here being the marginal "switcher" between nominals and linkers. Thus, the market clearing break-even inflation rate after the government has changed its debt mix will reflect the inflationary expectations and risk premium of a new marginal investor, not the market as a whole.

If you accept our theory, it probably makes the search for the risk premium an even more thankless task, but it does help to explain why the risk premium can seem to fall in the early stages of a linker market's development, as the bonds become less scarce.

We would also propose that there is a gaping hole in most learned texts about the inflation risk premium because they focus entirely on investors. If a market needs a buyer and a seller, then the other half of the picture must be that of the issuer(s) of nominal and inflation-linked debt. What are their inflationary expectations and risk preferences? Textbooks typically make government bond supply curves vertical—they are endogenous, a fixed amount of bonds determined by the budget balance, that must be sold at whatever price. However, if the government can issue either nominal or inflation-linked bonds, the mix can be varied at the government's discretion. So the government's own estimated probability density function of future inflation, and its own inflation risk preferences come into play in determining the mix. This would almost certainly have a dramatic effect on the market-clearing risk premium (if only we could observe it).

This may all seem rather convoluted, so a simple example might suffice to make the point clear. Let us assume that the average bond investor expects future long-term inflation to be 2.5%, and that the average investor is inflation risk averse, so be prepared to pay a 0.25% risk premium. On this basis alone, we would expect observed break-even inflation to be 2.75%. Now let us say that the government also has inflationary expectations of 2.5%, but it prefers real liabilities to nominal liabilities, and places a 0.25% yield value on that preference. It will prefer to sell inflation-linked bonds rather than nominal bonds until break-even inflation falls to 2.25%.

How would the market clear in our example? The government's preferences would exert themselves on the market, with much more than half the bonds sold being inflation-linked. The average investor's break-even inflation would be 2.75% but the marginal investor's would be 2.25%. If we knew that both investors and the government had average inflationary expectations of 2.5%, there would appear to be a 0.25% negative risk premium, but this would be a misleading number.

Needless to say, we do not live in a "two-asset world," and this complicates matters further. An investor might place a high inflation risk premium on an index-linked bond when only nominal alternatives are available, but the value attributed to the risk premium will also be influenced at least a little by the availability of competing assets offering some degree of inflation protection—the more classic inflation hedges such as real estate and land.

So, we have argued, the economics of supply and demand make the risk premium a slippery concept. Bond mathematics now makes matters worse. This new aspect centres on the issue of convexity. We know that a forward curve of implied future short-term nominal rates can be derived from the nominal government bond curve. In principle, a forward curve of implied future short-term real rates can be similarly derived from the inflation-linked bond real yield curve. These two curves, taken together, should imply a future path of inflation, if we can set aside the risk premium for the moment. Unfortunately, that is not the case.

The presence of convexity means that both our forward bond curves understate true expectations of the future paths of nominal and real short-term rates. However, the value placed on convexity is a function of volatility, which is much greater in nominals than in linkers. Therefore, an implied path of future inflation derived in this way will understate true inflationary expectations because of convexity, if there are no other influences, such as the risk premium.

Convexity differences between nominals and linkers create a systematic bias in break-even inflation, which is itself hard to quantify reliably (for instance, we have little objective current market-based information about prospective long-term real yield volatility). This makes the isolation of the risk premium even more difficult, if that's possible. The purpose of all of this is not to discourage the investigation of the risk premium, but rather to raise awareness of some important influences that need to be considered before you decide to begin your quest.

The Duration of Inflation-Linked Bonds and the Concept of the Beta

How does an investor measure the modified duration of linkers? It sounds like a straightforward question and there is an easy answer, but it is sadly not the answer that people generally want. The easy answer is that a linker's modified duration is the (normalised) first derivative of price with respect to real yield, just as a conventional bond's modified duration is that with respect to nominal yield. This answer is a flippant one, because what people really want to know is some empirical rule about the sensitivity of a linker's price with respect to nominal yields, either for hedging purposes or in order to calculate aggregate duration statistics for portfolios holding both nominal and real bonds.

On this basis, there is a huge urge to say "you can't do it," but we must try to offer something a little more constructive. Nobody ever asks what the duration of an equity is, but the question is almost equivalent—linkers, like equities, are a different asset class. There are equity duration measurements—price sensitivities with respect to changes in the earnings yield or dividend yield—and equities can be related to nominal bonds via a Fisher equation as we have shown, just as linkers are related to nominals via a Fisher equation. However, equity duration numbers are seldom calculated, and would never be used in a mixed portfolio of equities and bonds to give a total portfolio duration.

If we think about the simplified Fisher equation for linkers,

$$\text{Nominal yield } (y) = \text{real yield } (r) + \text{inflationary expectations } (f) + \text{risk premium } (p)$$

then a meaningful duration of linkers with respect to nominal yields can only be calculated if f and p are constant, or small enough to be irrelevant, or sufficiently strongly correlated with r. However, as Wesley Phoa states, if inflation-indexed bonds could be perfectly hedged with nominals, then there would be no point in issuing them because the market could replicate them if there was a need. It is only their distinct attributes as a separate asset class that make them worth having.[4]

Frustratingly, a duration of nominals with respect to real yield is easy to calculate, because it's just a partial derivative of the Fisher equation, but nobody wants to know that. Asking for the duration of a linker with respect to nominal yields is akin to asking how much the base of a triangle changes if its area doubles. You can only answer if you can assume something about the change in the triangle's height, or the proportionate relationship between its base and height. If its base and height are known to be random variables, then you are stuck.

The only mathematically correct way to report duration for a mixed portfolio of nominals and linkers, in a way that adds some useful information, is to drop the standard duration figure and instead show two new numbers: duration with respect to real yield and duration with respect to inflationary expectations. These are the two main partial derivatives of the Fisher equation.

There is still merit in trying to pin down a "beta"—the expected change in real yield for a given change in nominal yield. Bloomberg users will be familiar with the YA screen for linkers, which allows a beta to be entered and then uses it to scale modified duration in order to get some sort of risk measure relative to nominal yields. These betas can, of course, be calculated as long-term averages, but (because of all we've said above) they are notoriously unstable through time and should carry a wealth warning. We therefore need to have strong regard for the confidence intervals around our betas as well as the betas themselves.

By way of example, consider the first US inflation-linked issue, maturing January 2007, where the early experience was of rising real yields while nominal yields fell. Much depends on the time horizon used, and this just shows how unreliable these betas can be. Already, the European linker market has experienced betas well below 1, above 1, and negative.

To see why, let's reduce the Fisher equation to the more manageable form:

Nominal yield (y) = Real yield (r) + Break-even inflation (BEI)

We can now take variances of both sides:

Variance (y) = Variance (r) + Variance (BEI) + $\{2 \times$ Covariance $(r,\text{BEI})\}$

---

[4] Wesley Phoa, *Advanced Fixed Income Analytics* (New Hope, PA: Frank J. Fabozzi Associates, 1998).

EXHIBIT 8.7 Nominal Yield Volatility Composition in the United States, France, and the United Kingdom

	United States	France	United Kingdom
Variance of nominal yield	8.3	4.1	4.8
of which:			
Variance of real yield	3.8	2.1	2.2
Variance of BEI	4.5	2.0	3.7
2 × Covariance (real yield, BEI)	0.0	0.0	−1.0

N.B. Figures shown are for nonannualised monthly changes, and are in basis points. US and UK data since February 1997; France since September 1998. IL bonds used are TII 07, OATi 09, and UKT 2.5% 09, with appropriate nominal bond comparators.
Source: Barclays Capital.

What the formula tells us is that, theoretically, the variance of nominal yields could actually be lower than that for linker real yields if real yields and inflationary expectations were sufficiently highly negatively correlated, i.e., the beta could exceed one. We'd place heavy emphasis on the word "theoretically," and we mention it only because Wesley Phoa entertains the possibility in his book. He cites analysis suggesting that there is a long-term negative correlation between GDP and inflation, then (reasonably) argues that real yields are a function of real GDP, hence real yields and break-evens should be inversely related.

One must nevertheless dispute this argument, or at least dispute its usefulness for managing linker trading. Certainly the last 30 years has seen a trend decline in global inflation and a trend increase in global growth potential. However, we would question whether it is fair to assume the trends to ever-higher growth and ever-lower inflation will continue, and would also say that this emphasises the secular over the cyclical. Call us old-fashioned, but for practical purposes we believe that the positive cyclical relationship, whereby economic booms are associated with rising inflationary pressures and slowdowns are associated with disinflation, is likely to continue to dominate market sentiment. It shows through in the empirical experience of the variance decomposition in the formula above. Exhibit 8.7 shows that even though the United Kingdom has exhibited mild negative covariance between real yields and break-even inflation, real yields are still materially less volatile than nominal yields.

Exhibit 8.7 uses calendar month changes in real and nominal yields to demonstrate that the lion's share of nominal yield volatility has come

EXHIBIT 8.8   Monthly Changes in Real and Nominal Yields using UK IL 2009 and Nominal Bond of Similar Term (bp)

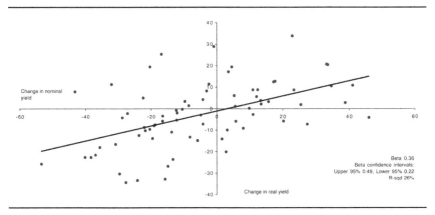

Source: Barclays Capital.

EXHIBIT 8.9   Monthly Changes in Real and Nominal Yields using OAT*i* 2009 and Nominal Bond of Similar Term (bp)

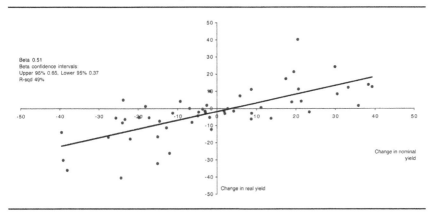

Source: Barclays Capital.

from the break-even inflation component for the United States, the United Kingdom and France. Real yield volatility has been much milder and this is reflected in the low betas shown in the charts. Exhibits 8.8 to 8.10 also show how unreliable these betas are, both in terms of the low R^2 and in the wide confidence intervals around the betas. For instance, for France with the highest R^2 of 0.49, the beta is 0.51, but the 95% confidence interval for this beta is between 0.37 and 0.65.

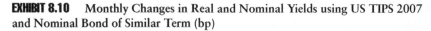

EXHIBIT 8.10   Monthly Changes in Real and Nominal Yields using US TIPS 2007 and Nominal Bond of Similar Term (bp)

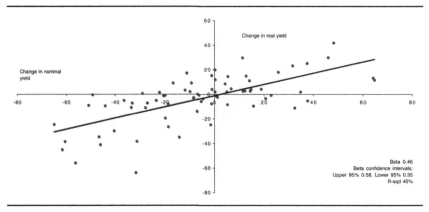

Source: Barclays Capital.

INFLATION-LINKED BONDS COMPARED TO EQUITIES

The relationship between linkers and equities is not written about as often as that between linkers and nominals. It doesn't lend itself to trading opportunities in the same way, perhaps partly because the market "players" are different people. In the United Kingdom, equity/index-linked yield gaps, using either the equity dividend yield or the earnings yield, are seen as classic "value touchstones." However, if they are followed, they are probably looked at as two among many indicators, as aids to long-term asset allocation. Nevertheless, it is always worth remembering that the standard Fisher equation relating nominal government bonds to inflation-linked bonds that we have just described, which quickly becomes second nature to anyone looking at linkers, has an equally valid equivalent which relates equities to index-linked.

The standard Fisher equation:

$$n = r + f + p$$

where

n = yield on nominal bond
r = real yield in index-linked bond
f = inflationary expectations
p = inflation risk premium

has an analogue, relating real yields to equity dividend yields:

$$r = dy + E(rdg) - edrp \qquad (8.1)$$

where

r = real yield in index-linked bond
dy = equity dividend yield
$E(rdg)$ = expected real equity dividend growth
$edrp$ = equity dividend risk premium,

or relating index-linked real yields to equity earnings yields:

$$r = ey + E(reg) - eerp \qquad (8.2)$$

where

ey = equity earnings yield
$E(reg)$ = expected real equity earnings growth
$eerp$ = equity earnings risk premium

Rearranging equation (8.1) gives

The "dividend yield gap" $= r - dy = E(rdg) - edrp$

Rearranging equation (8.2) gives:

The "earnings yield gap" $= r - ey = E(reg) - eerp$

In practical usage, the inflation risk premium in the standard nominal/real bond Fisher relationship is sidestepped when the formula is reduced to:

Nominal yield – Real yield = Break-even inflation

Likewise, our equity yield gaps have similar analogues:

The dividend yield gap = Break-even future real dividend growth

and

The earnings yield gap = Break-even future real earnings growth

Exhibit 8.11 charts the dividend yield gap for the European markets with inflation-linked bond sectors.

EXHIBIT 8.11   Long Inflation-Linked Bond Real Yields Less Equity Dividend Yields
(%)

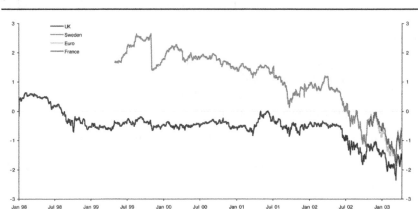

Source: Thomson Financial, Barclays Capital.

So we have removed the equity risk premium from the equation, just as we removed the inflation risk premium from the equation earlier. The equity risk premium is a huge, sprawling, monster of a subject all on its own, which we do not intend to dwell on here. However, people will have (at least) two concerns with the above simple algebra being presented as identities, or "fundamental truths," in this way. Firstly, standard dividend discount models sum the present values of future flows to a time horizon at infinity, so we should use the longest possible linker real yield and assume it represents some sort of fair real yield applicable beyond its maturity. Second, some might be concerned by the presentation of two alternative measures—one using equity dividends and one using equity earnings.

In older textbooks, such models always used dividends, making for a more tangible comparison with bonds because cash is returned to owners of assets in the same way. However, dividends are not very fashionable and have not been regarded as a tax efficient way to return cash to shareholders in recent years, and the tendency is to downplay dividends in valuation measurement.

It is certainly fair to use earnings, since those earnings do accrue to the owners of the company—the shareholders—even if they are not paid out to them. However, the earnings yield is almost always much higher than the dividend yield, because some earnings are retained, so how can both the dividend and the earnings relationship be true? We can "square this circle," if it is accepted that shareholders forfeit dividends today, allowing earnings to be retained, in anticipation of stronger dividend growth in the future (stronger than would otherwise be the case and stronger than earnings growth). This simplification of a fairly heavy debate, encompassing such issues as the treatment of equity buybacks, may not satisfy everyone but a full discourse would be lengthy and tedious here.

A QUICK SKETCH OF THE PERFORMANCE CHARACTERISTICS OF INFLATION-LINKED BONDS RELATIVE TO OTHER ASSET CLASSES

On a hold-to-maturity basis, as we've said, inflation-linked government bonds provide as close an approximation to a guaranteed real return as is currently available. If we can assume the government is credit risk-free, then there remain only two modest reasons for us to couch the above statement with the cautionary use of the word "approximation." There will inevitably always be a small coupon reinvestment risk and also a small degree of real value uncertainty because of the indexation lag.

However, when holding linkers in a performance-based portfolio, rather than as a passively matched investment, short-time horizons become paramount. Real yields on inflation-linked bonds do change, creating short-term volatility in their real and nominal returns.

UK index-linked gilts have existed since March 1981, with the FT All Index-Linked coming into existence at the end of that year. Unsurprisingly, index-linked have underperformed conventional gilts over their full history, given the collapse in inflation and inflationary expectations since the market's inception. In March 1981, the launch month of the first linker (2% IL 1996), headline UK inflation was 12.6%. We have seen inflation fall by 10%. (See Exhibit 8.12.)

In spite of the underperformance of index-linked over their full life, they have nevertheless proved a useful diversifying asset in low-risk portfolios, as Exhibits 8.13 to 8.15. If we can assume we have reached a level of inflation that central bankers regard as desirable, then the prospective future returns on inflation-linked bonds will not be disadvantaged as they were in an era of economic transformation, but linkers should retain their attractive low-risk attributes.

Exhibit 8.13 shows a scatterplot of average annual real returns against risk (the volatility of those real returns) since end-1981, for linkers, conventional gilts, equities, and gold. Gold has historically been regarded as the ultimate real asset.

EXHIBIT 8.12   Nominal Total Return Indices for UK Equities, Conventional Gilts
and Index-Linked Gilts, End-1981 = 100

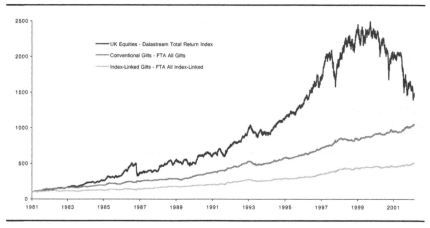

Source: Thomson Financial.

EXHIBIT 8.13   Risk Against Return—UK Equities, Gilts, Index-Linked and Gold,
Using Annual Data Since End-1981

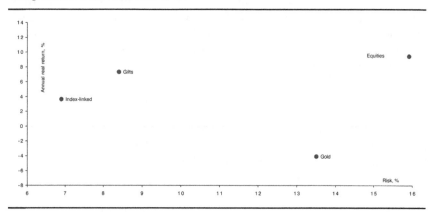

Source: Thomson Financial, Barclays Capital.

In Exhibits 8.14 and 8.15, we use the same data to construct two efficient frontiers of portfolios—one without index-linked gilts as an available
asset choice and one where index-linked can be selected. For the first frontier below, without linkers, gold is still selected for the lowest risk portfolios
because of its diversifying characteristics, in spite of its dreadful risk-return
trade-off over the 21 years. However, it quickly disappears from optimal
portfolios along the frontier if risk tolerance is raised a tiny bit. The asset
mixes of a selection of portfolios along the frontier are also detailed.

EXHIBIT 8.14 Efficient Frontier of Three-Asset Portfolios, When Equities, Gilts, and Gold Are Available

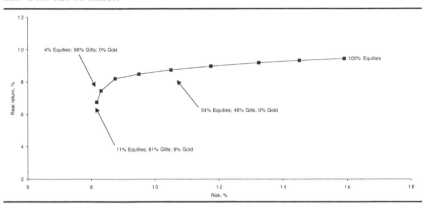

Source: Thomson Financial, Barclays Capital.

EXHIBIT 8.15 Efficient Frontier of Four-Asset Portfolios, When Equities, Gilts, Linkers, and Gold Are Available

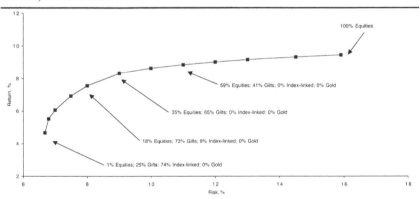

Source: Thomson Financial, Barclays Capital.

When you add index-linked gilts as an asset choice, this results in the deselection of gold in even the lowest risk portfolios and the extension of the efficient frontier into the low risk domain to the left, as can be seen in Exhibits 8.14 and 8.15.

WHAT DRIVES REAL YIELDS AND WHAT MAKES GLOBAL REAL YIELDS DIFFER?

Investors who are long-familiar with nominal bonds should probably not even ask the question, thinking back to the Fisher equation. If they are able form a view about where value lies in nominal bonds, then that must already embody views about both inflationary expectations and real yields. Anyone who has a view about nominal yields must implicitly have a view about real yields. Linkers may be more complex instruments than nominals mathematically, but they are simpler instruments economically—there is less to worry about, as we have said.

We have compared linkers with other investment assets already, and that is really at the root of the issue. It is a question of opportunity cost. Risk-free real yields are determined by the prospective returns that other, riskier, assets in an economy are perceived to offer.

Therefore, they are determined ultimately by the prospective returns on real investment (in plant and machinery) in the real economy. They will be influenced by competition between the governments' call on savings (the fiscal position) and the private sector's financing need, and the size of that savings pool. It is all about the flow of funds.

So there is inevitably a cyclical component. At times of weak activity, the private sector's call on capital tends to decline and the public sector's call tends to rise, but the former tends to fall faster than the latter rises The risk-free real yield (the risk-free real price of money) falls as prospective returns on economic activity decline.

Fisher—he of the famous Fisher equation—argued that the real yield should be constant. However, the evidence to support this much less well-known hypothesis is patchy to say the least.

In asking why real yields differ around the world, we have tended to turn the question on its head and ask instead: "What are the conditions necessary for real yields to be the same?" It is by creating model axioms necessary to deliver a common real yield that we see "imperfections" in that model, resulting in real yield divergence. Of course, real yields might coincide temporarily, but we feel that in order for them to be the same always:

- Investors must be "risk neutral" and completely global, with no preference for domestic or overseas habitats.
- Investors must believe that currencies will maintain their current real exchange rate in the future, moving in line with relative changes in the linking price indices in any two markets. This will ensure that equal real yields result in equal nominal returns when translated into any currency.
- Linking indices should measure inflation in a perfectly consistent way in different markets.
- There should be no creditworthiness, tax or other regulatory distortions.

EXHIBIT 8.16   Real Yields and Net External Assets/GDP, April 2003 (%)

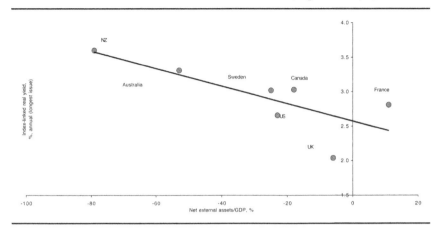

Source: Thomson Financial, Barclays Capital.

Investors are Not Risk Neutral

Investors tend to prefer their domestic habitat. When they have domestic liabilities, their first choice will probably be domestic assets. This is all the more likely in index-linked markets, where the inflation protection offered by an Australian linker is likely to be far more valuable to an Australian than to a Swede.

If you introduce preferred habitats, then real yields cease to "clear" in a completely global market between financing needs and savings. Domestic drivers can influence real yield differences—different fiscal positions, different stages of the economic cycle, and so on.

With preferred domestic habitats, countries with excess savings should require a higher real yield to be prepared to invest abroad. For example, although Switzerland does not have a linker market, we can observe persistently low real yields on its nominal bonds thanks to its enormous stock of net external assets (not just its long record of price stability). Conversely, countries with large net external liabilities will often have to pay higher real yields to attract and retain foreign capital. These net foreign assets or liabilities are accumulated through current account surpluses or deficits, respectively.

For those countries with linker markets, the relationship between their net external positions and their real yields is loose because there are other real yield influences (and it has been better in the past). But it seems valid, nevertheless. (See Exhibit 8.16.)

Relaxing the second "axiom," that investors must expect real exchange rates to be constant in order to accept a common real yield, would suggest that where currencies are cheap on purchasing parity grounds (like the euro, or the Canadian dollar, currently), real yields should be lower. The theory is powerful and persuasive, but finding supporting evidence has proved extremely difficult, at least for us.

The real yield divergences resulting from the breakdown of the last two axioms, referring to consistent linking indices and regulatory issues, are best highlighted by the situation in the United Kingdom. The UK's RPI overstates "true" inflation, at least relative to measures used in either the United States or Europe for reasons we have discussed, while UK linkers are tax advantaged (inflation escalation is tax-free), and pensions legislation encourages investment in the asset class. All these things, to a greater or lesser extent, currently justify lower quoted real yields in the United Kingdom than elsewhere.

TRADING INFLATION-LINKED BONDS

As we have said already, trading in "nominal space" has its analogue in "real space." So there are directional trades, real yield curve trades, and anomaly (or "relative value") trades between issues. There are also trades between the real and nominal markets, in "inflation space"—buying and selling break-even inflation, and expressing views on the term structure of break-even inflation. Exhibits 8.17 and 8.18 show histories of real yields and break-even inflation, respectively, for the three main European inflation-linked markets, while Exhibit 8.19 highlights the volatility in the UK's real yield and break-even inflation curves.

EXHIBIT 8.17   Real Yield Histories for Similarly Dated French, Swedish, and UK Inflation-Linked Issues—Maturity Year Shown (%)

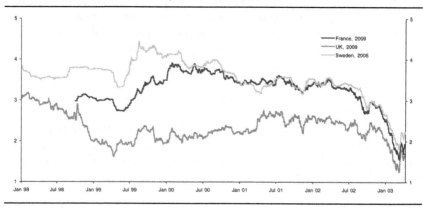

Source: Barclays Capital.

EXHIBIT 8.18   Break-Even Inflation Histories for Similarly Dated French, Swedish, and UK Inflation-Linked Issues—Maturity Year Shown (%)

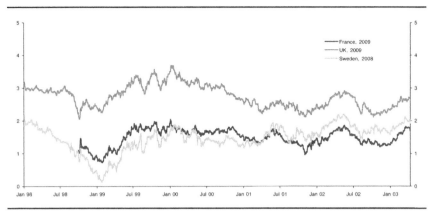

Source: Barclays Capital.

EXHIBIT 8.19   UK Real Yield Curve and Break-Even Inflation Curve Histories (%)

As with the nominal world, the variety of such trades are limited only by liquidity and imagination. For instance, France's issues and the newer Swedish issues have a "principal floor," that is, if a linking index is lower at maturity than at issue (under deflation), the investor will receive par back. This gives a trade where one is "long break-even inflation" (long a linker, short a nominal comparator), characteristics akin to that of a call option, and some investors seek ways of valuing that option and extracting its value, perhaps mixing linker trades with option trades in nominals.

Investors who perform break-even inflation trades may choose to weight them for expected differences in nominal and real yield volatility, or "beta-weight" them. Cross-market trades are also popular—selling break-even inflation in one market, and buying it in another, in order to express a view on future inflation differences between two economies. And market participants quickly become aware of seasonality in (unadjusted) CPI linking indices, trading into "good carry months" and out of "bad carry months."

Key trade types include:

- Directional real yield trades—outright buying/selling.
- Real yield curve trades.
- Break-even inflation (BEI) trades, either "one-for-one" (pure break-even) or "beta-adjusted."
- Forward real yield trades and forward BEI (inflation curve) trades.
- BEI trades employing derivatives, e.g., "buy-writes" with options/ swaptions.
- Real yield and BEI difference trades between two markets.
- Implied forward real yield and BEI difference trades between two markets.

An important aspect of trading these bonds is using expectations of future monthly changes in linking indices, provided by economists, to calculate expected forward real yields and expected forward break-even inflation. Making assumptions about future price index levels allows these forward aggregates to be calculated in the same way that forward nominal bond prices and yields are worked out.

INFLATION-LINKED DERIVATIVES

Inflation-linked derivative instruments are now widely traded in the capital markets divisions of investment banks that trade the sovereign inflation-linked bonds. Many smaller banks with regional dominance are also building up their trading capabilities as they rise to meet the increasing demand from their client base for inflation-linked products.

Why Inflation-Linked Derivatives?

These derivatives provide additional sources and destinations for inflation-linked flows, lower the barrier to entry, and bring in an expanded universe of market participants. This has, over time, enhanced and made more efficient the underlying bond market.

Derivatives in the inflation market offer various advantages and opportunities to market participants. These include structuring, portfolio hedging requirements, customizing cash flows, market timing advantages, increased liquidity, extracting value, arbitrage, hybrid structures (equity plus inflation), and risk transfer. These encompass strategies that are either cheaper and more efficient to execute than in the bond market or meet needs that the bond market is unable to satisfy.

The UK market in inflation-linked swaps has existed since the early 1990s. In the last five years, there has been a steady growth in volume and lengthening of maturities. The recent developments in the Eurozone inflation derivatives market show that we can very quickly move from a nonexistent market to a multi-billion Euro market in a matter of a few months.

Early History of the Market

In tracing the brief history of inflation-linked swaps (ILS), it is instructive to look at the development of the now ubiquitous interest-rate swap (IRS) market in the early 1980s. This is because we can note many similar aspects that can explain the ILS market's development thus far and also help chart its likely future course. The IRS market started in 1981. Initially, a few companies and banks were involved, and banks running swap books, did so on a "matched" basis whereby the bank acted as an intermediary, thus only taking counterparty credit risk. Over time, the marked moved towards the mismatched book approach and instead of matching swaps immediately, dealers warehoused risk until the swap could be matched at a later date and the banks hedged their portfolios with available exchange-traded instruments such as futures and government bonds.

The ILS market has developed in a similar fashion. Since a move towards running large unmatched books would normally necessitate the existence of tradable instruments with similar risk, the UK market was the first to go towards the running of unmatched books as it had the earliest and most developed market for government-issued inflation-linked bonds. Moreover, the existence of a real rate "curve" through a large range of maturities means that the banks running inflation swap books incur very little duration-related basis risk. Instead, managing the bond-swap spread risk as well as reset risks, repo spreads, and the like became the focus of risk managing an IL swap book.

The UK Market

In the UK ILS market, the main drivers are the usual payers and receivers of inflation, namely corporate debt issuers and insurance company/pension fund investors. IL swaps essentially perform a supporting role to the underlying IL bond market, providing payers and receivers with cheaper and more efficient routes to execution than in the bond market or meeting needs that the bond market is unable to satisfy (e.g., small projects that cannot issue bonds).

The Private Finance Initiative (PFI) in the United Kingdom has been a large and steady source of inflation-linked flows into the market. Typically, a central or local government entity guarantees an annuity flow (typically over 20–30 years) to the private sector for the development of the project. The project companies then fund their initial costs in the form of bond issues (typically credit wrapped) or through bank lending. PFI deals are usually associated with infrastructure projects such as roads, railroads, and bridges, or health, education, or defense building projects. However, only some projects (notably in the health sector) have consistently had guaranteed cash flows linked to UK RPI. In such cases, the project company hedges out some or all of these flows (e.g., issuing an RPI-linked bond, using an RPI-linked swap associated with fixed bank lending, or through real rate bank lending).

With the introduction of the gilt repo market in 1996, IL swap market participants have been able to more efficiently hedge IL swaps with IL and nominal gilts. Since then, the market has developed to a state where GBP50–100 million plus deals are now the norm in the long-dated maturities (15-year+).

In the summer of 2000, a large number of AAA issuers (IBRD, EBRD, EIB, NIB, RFF, CDC, and others) entered the IL issuance market in the United Kingdom with close to all of the investor demand coming from the UK pension and insurance sectors that hedged pension liabilities with eligible UK RPI-linked instruments that yielded higher real yields than IL gilts. These new issues were all swapped (i.e., the issuers were all getting LIBOR funding and hedging out the inflation-linked flows).

The European Market

Coinciding with the French Trésor's introduction of the 2009 OATi in 1998, some minor IL swap activity was started in the French market, mainly involving French counterparties. This market remained small and illiquid until the introduction of additional bonds linked to French inflation (CADESi, CNAi, OATi 2029). With six different maturities now trading, albeit some less liquidly, a reasonable break even "curve" can be constructed from 2006 out to 2029 which can provide some bounds on the levels that IL swaps can trade. Recently, cash flow matching swaps for pension funds have been dealt similar to the type observed in the UK market in the late 1990s (and continuing today) and the activity in the broker market indicates a more liquid market.

The Eurozone IL swap market started trading in May 2001, months before the Trésor issued the first Eurozone IL bond, the OATei 2012. The introduction and hedging of retail inflation protected equity products (e.g., those issued by the Italian Post Office and others) helped to kick off activity in the interbank Eurozone IL swap market, which has seen a steadily increasing uptrend in volumes traded per month. As of May 2003, pension related IL swaps and swaps from corporate payers are still a rarity, however some infrastructure driven hedging is taking place.

Future Trends in Inflation-Linked Derivatives

Pension reforms in Europe will be the main factor driving the development of the Eurozone market for inflation derivatives and for real assets in general beyond their current niche market state. As the natural demand for real assets grows in parallel with the development of a private pensions market, corporate payers will emerge, with associated issuance and swaps, that is, analogous to the current state in the UK market. However, the presence of a larger number of players (payers, receivers, and market makers) means that the market will likely be more liquid and more efficient than the current UK IL swap market.

Options (caps and floors), swaptions, and other derivatives are likely to start trading alongside the IL swap market on a more standardized basis, but are likely to develop in parallel with hedging requirements of the end users (e.g., the currently trading LPI swaps with 0% floor and 5% caps trading in the UK market) rather than a replication of what trades in the interest rate market.

CHAPTER 9

The United Kingdom Gilts Market

Moorad Choudhry
Senior Fellow
Centre for Mathematical Trading and Finance
CASS Business School, London

Securities issued by the government of the United Kingdom are known as gilts. The gilts market is the oldest government bond market in the world. In this chapter we present an overview of the gilts market, its structure, and institutions.

MARKET INSTRUMENTS

The gilts market is overwhelmingly plain vanilla in nature. We describe all the market instruments here.

Conventional Gilts

The gilts market is primarily a plain vanilla market, and the majority of gilt issues are conventional fixed interest bonds. Conventional gilts have a fixed coupon and maturity date. By volume they made up 82% of the market in June 2002. Coupon is paid on a semi-annual basis. The coupon rate is set in line with market interest rates at the time of issue, so the range of coupons in existence reflects the fluctuations in market interest rates. Unlike many government and corporate bond markets, gilts can be traded in the smallest unit of currency and sometimes nominal amounts change hands in amounts quoted down to one penny (£0.01) nominal size.

EXHIBIT 9.1   Gilt Ex-Dividend Trading

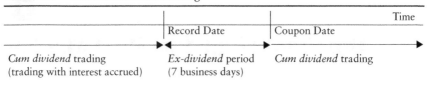

Individual gilts are given names such as the 5% Treasury 2012 or the 9% Conversion 2011. There is no significance attached to the name given to a gilt, they are all identical in makeup and credit quality, and they all trade in the same way. Most issues in existence are now "Treasury" issues, although in the past it was sometimes possible to identify the purpose behind the loan by its name. For example a "Conversion" issue usually indicates a bond converted from a previous gilt. The 3½% War Loan on the other hand was issued to help refinance loans raised to help pay for the 1914–18 war. The 3% Gas 1995/98 was issued to finance the nationalisation of the gas industry and was redeemed in 1998.

Gilts are registered securities. All gilts pay coupon to the registered holder as at a specified record date; the record date is seven business days before the coupon payment date. The period between the record date and the coupon date is known as the *ex-dividend* or "ex-div" ("xd") period; during the ex-dividend period the bond trades without accrued interest. This is illustrated in Exhibit 9.1.

The ex-dividend period was reduced from three weeks to seven business days for all gilts in 1995; the facility to trade *special ex-div*, which was a two-week period prior to the start of the ex-dividend period during which transactions could be traded ex-div on agreement between buyer and seller, was removed in 1998. The ex-dividend period for one issue, 3½% War Loan, was retained at three weeks (subsequently reduced to 10 business days) due to the large number of retail holders of this bond. Currently there are no floating-rate gilts in existence (the most recent was the floating-rate gilt 2001).[1] The 1999 floating-rate gilt also had an ex-dividend period.

Double-Dated Gilts

Although they have not been issued since 1987, there are currently eight double-dated gilts in existence, but they represent a small proportion of

---

[1] Floating-rate gilts paid coupon on a quarterly basis at a rate of LIBID minus 12.5 basis points. The Bank of England calculates the coupon level based on the LIBID fixing for the day before the coupon payment is due. The liquidity of floating-rate gilts was comparable to conventional gilts.

the gilts market. Double-dated gilts have two maturity dates quoted, and under the terms of issue the government may redeem them on any day between the first and second maturity dates, providing at least three months' notice is given. As with callable bonds in the corporate market, the government will usually redeem a double-dated bond early if it is trading above par, since this indicates that the coupon on the bond is above the prevailing market interest rate. When the price is below par, the bond will be allowed to run to the final redemption date. An example of the latter is the 3½% Funding 1999–2004, which trades well below par and therefore can be expected to run to its final maturity date of 14 July 2004, although the government can redeem it at any point between now and July 2004 if it so wishes, providing it gives at least three months' notice.

Double-dated issues are usually less liquid than conventional or index-linked gilts (I-L gilts), mainly because there is a relatively small amount in issue and also because a larger proportion are held by personal investors. They also tend to have high coupons, reflecting the market rates in existence at the time they were issued.

Gilt Strips

Gilt strips are zero-coupon bonds created from conventional coupon gilts. Only issues actually designated as strippable gilts may be stripped. They trade as conventional zero-coupon bonds and are deemed as conventional gilts in terms of their creditworthiness.

Undated Gilts

The most esoteric instruments in the gilts market are the undated gilts, also known as *irredeemable gilts* or *consols*. They are very old issues, indeed some date from the 19th century.[2] There are eight such issues, and they do not have a maturity date. Redemption is therefore at the discretion of the government. Some undated issues are very illiquid. The largest issue is the 3½% War Loan, with just over £1.9 billion in existence. In the past the Bank of England (BoE) undertook conversions of the less liquid irredeemable bonds into War Loan, so that for all but this stock and the 2½% Treasury bond there are only rump amounts remaining. The government can choose to redeem an undated gilt provided a requisite notice period is given (this varies for individual issues but generally is three months), but in practice—given that the coupon on these bonds is very low—it is unlikely to do so unless market interest

---

[2] For instance the 2½% Annuities gilt was issued in 1853. You won't find too many market makers who are keen to trade in it though!

rates drop below say, 3%. A peculiarity of three of the undated gilts is
that they pay interest on a quarterly basis.[3]

Treasury Bills

Strictly speaking Treasury bills (T-bills) are not part of the gilts market
but form part of the sterling money markets. They are short-term government instruments, issued at a discount and redeemed at par. The
most common bills are 3-month (91-day) maturity instruments,
although six-month bills are also issued. In theory any maturity between
1-month and 12-months may be selected. In the past the BoE has issued
1-month and 6-month bills in addition to the normal 3-month maturity
bills. Bills are issued via a weekly tender at which anyone may bid; generally clearing banks, building societies and discount houses take an
active part in the bill market.

In debt capital markets the yield on a domestic government T-bill is
usually considered to represent the risk-free interest rate, since it is a short-
term instrument guaranteed by the government. This makes the T-bill rate,
in theory at least, the most secure investment in the market. It is common
to see the 3-month T-bill rate used in corporate finance analysis and option
pricing analysis, which often refer to a risk-free money market rate.

The responsibility for bill issuance was transferred to the Debt
Management Office (DMO) from the BoE in 1999. The DMO set up a
slightly changed framework[4] in order to facilitate continued market
liquidity. The main elements of the framework included a wider range of
maturities and a larger minimum issue size at each weekly tender, plus a
guaranteed minimum stock in issue of £5 billion. The DMO also pre-
announces the maturities that will be available in the next quarter's ten-
ders. The settlement of Treasury bills has been fixed at the next working
day following the date of the tender.

Maturity Breakdown of Stock Outstanding

Gilts are classified by the DMO and the *Financial Times* as "shorts" if
maturing in 0–7 years, "mediums" if maturing in 7–15 years, and "longs"
if maturing in over 15 years time. Gilt-edged market makers (GEMMs)
usually apply a different distinction, with shorts being classified as 0–3
years, mediums as 4–10 years and longs as those bonds maturing in over
10 years. Of conventional gilts outstanding, the proportion of shorts to
mediums to longs has remained fairly constant in recent years; the ratio

[3] These are 2½% Consolidated stock, 2½% Annuities, and 2½% Annuities.
[4] This is set out in The Future of UK Government Cash Management: The New
Framework, Debt Management Office, 4 December 1998. Further detail is contained
in the DMO's Information Memorandum from September 2001.

was 46:35:19 in 1997; 45:35:20 in 1998; 44:30:26 in 1999; and 45:27:28 in June 2002 (DMO 2002).

Investor Holdings
By investor the distribution of gilt holdings as at June 2002 is shown below.

Insurance companies and pension funds	61%
Overseas holders	18%
Households	9%
Banks and building societies	2%
Other institutions	9%
Local authorities and public corporations	1%

Source: DMO.

Market Turnover
Exhibit 9.2 shows the annual turnover by value in gilts from the fiscal year 1993/94 to 2000/01. Average daily turnover in 2000/01 was £8.3 billion. The exhibit illustrates a general upward trend in market trading volumes, the trend being reversed temporarily during 1998. This reflects the contraction in global bond market trading in the aftermath of the financial crises of the second half of that year, typified by the technical default in a Russian long-dated bond and the Brazilian currency crisis.

Data on market turnover are published by the London Stock Exchange (LSE) and the DMO on a regular basis.

EXHIBIT 9.2   Average Daily Gilt Market Turnover

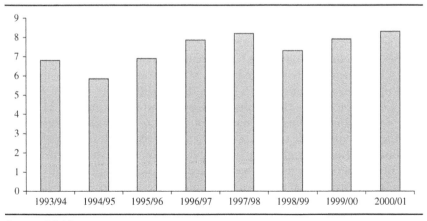

Source: DMO.

Market Trading Conventions

Gilts are quoted on a clean price basis, for next day settlement. This is known as "cash" settlement or $T + 1$. It is possible to trade for same day settlement ("cash-cash") if dealing is carried out before midday and with the agreement of the market maker. It is also possible to trade for forward settlement. During 1998 there were major changes to gilt market trading conventions designed to bring market conventions into line with major European bond markets. These changes are detailed below.

Price Quote

From 1 November 1998 gilt prices changed from pricing in ticks (½₂ of a point; a tick was therefore equal to 0.03125) to pricing in decimals. The tick price quote is employed in the US Treasury market. Prices are now displayed as £ and pence percent of stock. Auction bids are to two decimal places, as are GEMM reference prices. The bid-offer spread is very close in the gilt market, reflecting its liquidity and transparency. For bonds up to ten years in maturity it is possible to receive quotes as narrow as £0.01 between bid and offer; at the very short end institutional investors are often able to deal on "choice" prices (when the price for bid and offer is the same) if talking to two GEMMs simultaneously. For long-dated gilts the bid-offer spread can sometimes be as close as £0.06, roughly the equivalent of two ticks.

Daycount Convention

The daycount convention for the calculation of accrued interest was changed from actual/365 to actual/actual, from 1 November 1998. In addition, after 31 July 1998 the special ex-dividend period arrangement for gilts was ended. This mechanism had allowed trading whereby up to 21 calendar days prior to the ex-dividend date the parties to a gilt transaction could agree to trade on an ex-dividend basis. (This refers to a trade in which the purchaser takes delivery of the gilts without the right to the next coupon payment.) Although special ex-dividend arrangements have now been removed, gilts still automatically trade ex-dividend up to seven business days before the calendar date (except for the War Loan, for which the ex-dividend period was retained at 21 days, since reduced to 10 business days). There is no ex-dividend period for floating-rate gilts. Gilt strips trade on a yield basis and, of course, there is no accrued interest element in the calculation of settlement proceeds in a transaction. The DMO has published a yield-to-price conversion formula, to ensure that a uniform calculation is used by all market participants.

EXHIBIT 9.3   King & Shaxson Bond Brokers Ltd. Gilts Screen on 6 June 2003

```
GRAB                                               Corp   KSBB
12:36 KING & SHAXSON BOND BROKERS          PAGE  1 / 1
     UK Gilt Prices
     Benchmarks          Close    Current   Change    Gry     Time
 1) UKT  6¾  04         104.900   104.930    0.03     3.26    12:35
 2) UKT  8½  05         112.050   112.120    0.07     3.39    12:28
 3) UKT  7½  06         112.850   112.980    0.13     3.52    12:35
 4) UKT  7¼  07         114.730   114.890    0.16     3.63    12:35
 5) UKT  5   08         105.620   105.790    0.17     3.66    12:35
 6) UKT  5¾  09         111.000   111.170    0.17     3.79    12:35
 7) UKT  5   12         107.350   107.460    0.11     3.98    12:36
 8) UKT  8   15         137.300   137.420    0.12     4.14    12:36
 9) UKT  5   25         109.430   109.420   -0.01     4.33    12:36
10) UKT  4¼  32          98.730    98.620   -0.11     4.34    12:36



               Prices shown are indications only.
*Important*
          Prices will soon only be available to registered users.
          Please Contact KSBB on 020 7776 2630  to register.
Australia 61 2 9777 8600      Brazil 5511 3048 4500    Europe 44 20 7330 7500     Germany 49 69 920410
Hong Kong 852 2977 6000 Japan 81 3 3201 8900 Singapore 65 6212 1000 U.S. 1 212 318 2000 Copyright 2003 Bloomberg L.P.
                                                                       G797-57-0 06-Jun-03 12:36:53
```

Source: © Bloomberg L.P. © King & Shaxson Bond Brokers Ltd. Used with permission.

Market Screens

There are a number of news screens associated with the gilt market, which help to make it transparent. The DMO has screens on Reuters, Telerate, and Bloomberg. Many GEMMs also post prices of gilts on their own news screens, although some firms only make their screens available to selected customers. Brokers screens are usually available to the market as a whole. Prices are indicative only and must be checked on the telephone with the market maker or broker before dealing. A typical broker screen as appearing on Bloomberg, showing midprices for benchmark gilts, is shown at Exhibit 9.3. The screen also shows the most recent price change, the closing price, and the equivalent yield. This is the screen for King & Shaxson Bond Brokers Ltd. A Bloomberg DES screen showing the Treasury 5% 2012 gilt is shown in Exhibit 9.4.

EXHIBIT 9.4   Bloomberg Page DES, Showing Details of 5% Treasury 2012, 6 June 2003

```
GRAB                                                      Corp   DES
SECURITY DESCRIPTION                      Page 1/ 1
TREASURY          UKT 5 03/07/12    107.4200/107.4800  (3.99/3.98) BGN  @12:32
ISSUER INFORMATION            IDENTIFIERS            1) Additional Sec Info
Name TSY 5 2012               Common   013042586     2) Identifiers
Type Sovereign                ISIN     GB0030468747   3) Ratings
Market of Issue UK GILT STOCK Sedol    3046874        4) Sec. Specific News
SECURITY INFORMATION          RATINGS                5) Custom Notes
Country GB        Currency GBP Moody's     NA         6) Issuer Information
Collateral Type BONDS          S&P         AAA        7) ALLQ
Calc Typ( 26)UK:BUMP/DMO METHOD Composite  AAA        8) Pricing Sources
Maturity   3/ 7/2012 Series   ISSUE SIZE             9) Prospectus Request
NORMAL                         Amt Issued            10) Related Securities
Coupon        5       FIXED    GBP  13,346,466  (M)
S/A           ACT/ACT          Amt Outstanding
Announcement Dt  5/15/01       GBP  13,346,466  (M)
Int. Accrual Dt  5/25/01       Min Piece/Increment
1st Settle Date  5/25/01            0.01/      0.01
1st Coupon Date  9/ 7/01       Par Amount      100.00
Iss Pr  98.8100               BOOK RUNNER/EXCHANGE
                                                     65) Old DES
HAVE PROSPECTUS               LONDON                 66) Send as Attachment
ORIG £2.525BLN 5/24/01. INC TO £10.98BLN 7/23/01 ON COMPLETION OF CONVERSION
OFFER. ADD'L £2.25 BLN ON 3/28/02. £50MM FOR THE DEBT REDUCTION FUND.
Australia 61 2 9777 8600    Brazil 5511 3048 4500    Europe 44 20 7330 7500    Germany 49 69 920410
Hong Kong 852 2977 6000 Japan 81 3 3201 8900 Singapore 65 6212 1000 U.S. 1 212 318 2000 Copyright 2003 Bloomberg L.P.
                                                            G797-57-0 06-Jun-03 12:34:50
```

Source: © Bloomberg L.P. Used with permission.

MARKET STRUCTURE

The gilt market operates within the overall investment business environment in the United Kingdom. As such wholesale market participants are regulated by the Financial Services Authority (FSA), the central regulatory authority brought into being by the Labour government in 1997. The FSA regulates the conduct of firms undertaking business in the gilt market; it also supervises the exchanges on which trading in gilts and gilt derivatives takes place. The previous regulatory regime in the UK markets, as conducted under the Financial Services Act 1986, consisted of market participants being authorised by self-regulatory organisations such as the Securities and Futures Authority (SFA). The FSA was set up initially through merging all the different self-regulatory bodies. Hence gilt market makers and brokers are authorised by the FSA on behalf of the SFA, while firms domiciled in European Union countries are authorised by their domestic regulatory authority. The full formal powers of the FSA were assumed by that body once the Financial Services and Markets Act 2000 came into being.

The gilts market is an over-the-counter market, meaning that transactions are conducted over the telephone between market participants. However all individual issues are listed on the London Stock Exchange, which as a Recognised Investment Exchange is also supervised by the FSA.

MARKET MAKERS AND BROKERS

Just as in the United States and France for example, there is a registered primary dealer system in operation in the UK government bond market. The present structure dates from "Big Bang" in 1986, the large-scale reform of the London market that resulted in the abolition of the old distinction between *jobbers* and *brokers* and allowed firms to deal in both capacities if they so wished; it also resulted in stock and share trading moving off the floor of the Stock Exchange and into the dealing rooms of banks and securities houses. Firms that wished to provide a two-way dealing service and act on their own account registered as gilt-edged market makers. In 1986 there were 29 companies so registered, most of whom were the gilts trading arms of the large banks. Firms registered as GEMMs with the BoE, and until 1998 there was a requirement for GEMMs to be separately capitalised if they were part of a larger integrated banking group. This requirement has since been removed. In June 2003, there were 16 firms registered as GEMMs, who must now be recognised as such by the DMO. GEMMs are also required to be members of the LSE. The full list is:

ABN Amro Bank NV	Lehman Brothers International
Barclays Capital*	(Europe)*
Credit Suisse First Boston Gilts	Merrill Lynch International*
Limited	Morgan Stanley & Co. International
Deutsche Morgan Grenfell	Limited
Dresdner Kleinwort Benson*	Royal Bank of Canada (Europe) Ltd
Goldman Sachs International Limited	Royal Bank of Scotland*
ited	Salomon Smith Barney
HSBC Greenwell*	UBS Warburg
JP Morgan Chase Bank	Winterflood Securities

* Indicates IG GEMM status.
Source: DMO.

The key obligation of GEMMs is to make two-way prices on demand in all gilts, thereby providing liquidity to the market. Some firms observe this requirement more closely than others! Certain gilts that the DMO has designated as rump stocks do not form part of this requirement. GEMMs also must participate in gilt auctions, the main method through which the DMO issues gilts, making competitive bids in all auction programmes. The third primary requirement of a GEMM is to "provide information to the DMO on market conditions, [its] positions and turnover" (DMO 1999). In return for carrying out its market-making obligations, a GEMM receives certain privileges exclusive to it, which are:

- The right to make competitive telephone bids at gilt auctions and tap issues.
- A reserved amount of stock at each auction, available at noncompetitive bid prices (currently this is 1/2% of the issue for each GEMM, or 10% if an I-L gilt).
- Access to the DMO's gilt dealing screens, through which the GEMM may trade or switch stocks.
- A trading relationship with the DMO whenever it wishes to buy or sell gilts for market management purposes.
- The facility to strip gilts.
- A quarterly consultation meeting with the DMO, which allows the GEMM to provide input on which type of stocks to auction in the next quarter, plus advice on other market issues.
- Access to gilt inter-dealer broker (IDB) screens.

In 1998 the DMO set up a separate category of GEMMs known as index-linked GEMMs (IG GEMMs). A firm could opt for a registration for either or both category. The role of an IG GEMM is the same as that for a conventional GEMM, as applied to index-linked gilts. An IG GEMM has the same obligations as a GEMM with respect to I-L gilts, and an additional requirement that they must seek to maintain a minimum 3% market share of the I-L gilt market. Therefore an IG GEMM must participate actively in auctions for I-L stock. In addition to the privileges listed above, up until November 2001 IG GEMMs could also ask the DMO to bid for stock. This role of the DMO in the IG market was removed as the market matured. In June 2003, eight of the 16 GEMMs were also registered as IG GEMMs. No firm was registered solely as an IG GEMM.

Gilt Market Broker Functions

There are, at the time of writing, four firms that provide an interdealer broker (IDB) service for GEMMs. This is a facility for GEMMs to advertise, via the IDB's screens, anonymous live dealing prices for any gilt, together with the nominal value of the stock that they are prepared to deal in. Only GEMMs have access to IDB screens, which assist in the provision of market liquidity. IDBs are required to be members of the LSE and are recognised by the DMO. They are pure brokers and are prohibited from taking principal positions in any gilt or providing market intelligence outside their customer base.

A separate category of LSE broker is the broker/dealer. These are firms that act both for their own account or as agents for another party. Broker/dealers therefore trade with both market makers and client firms and can deal with clients either as principal or agent. Broker/dealers may also act as wholesale broker/dealers to GEMMs.

The Role of the Bank of England

Although the responsibility for UK government debt management has been transferred to the DMO, the BoE continues to maintain a link with the gilt market. The Bank is also involved in monitoring other sterling markets such as gilt futures and options, swaps, strips, gilt repo and domestic bonds. The Bank's *Quarterly Bulletin* for February 1999 listed its operational role in the gilt market as:

- Calculating and publishing the coupons for index-linked gilts after the publication of each month's inflation data and inflation index.
- Setting and announcing the dividend for floating-rate gilts, which is calculated as a spread under 3-month Libid each quarter.
- Operating the BoE brokerage service, a means by which private investors can buy and sell gilts by post instead of via a stockbroker. This service was previously operated by National Savings, the government's savings bank for private retail customers. Private investors sometimes wish to deal in gilts via the post because usually commission charges are lower and it is a user-friendly service.

This is in addition to the normal daily money market operations, which keep the BoE closely connected to the gilt repo market. The BoE's dealers also carry out orders on behalf of its customers, primarily other central banks.

The BoE has a duty to "protect the interests of index-linked gilt investors" (DMO 1999). This is a responsibility to determine whether any future changes in the composition of the RPI index would be materially harmful to I-L gilt holders and to effect a redemption of any issue, via HM Treasury, if it feels any change had been harmful.

The BoE used to operate the Central Gilts Office (CGO) settlement mechanism on behalf of CRESTCo Limited; the two bodies have now merged with Euroclear, the international clearing system. The BoE also acts as the central registrar for gilts. The settlement process for gilts is reviewed separately.

The Role of the London Stock Exchange

While the gilt market is an OTC market, all gilts are listed instruments on the London Stock Exchange (LSE) and GEMMs and inter-dealer brokers are members of the LSE. A new gilt issue and further issues of an existing stock are always listed on the LSE, usually on the day the auction or the further issue is announced.

Members of the LSE must follow its conduct of business rules. In addition, there are specific rules that apply to GEMMs. These include the requirement to report all gilt trades to the LSE, except gilt repo and stock loan trades. The LSE publishes market trading statistics that include the monthly turnover, by volume, of gilt transactions. It also publishes the Daily Official List, the list of closing prices for all securities listed on the London market.

ISSUING GILTS

Auctions are the primary means of issuance of all gilts, both conventional and index-linked. They are generally for £2–£3 billion of stock on a competitive bid price basis. Auctions of index-linked gilts are for between £0.5 and £1.25 billion. The programme of auctions is occasionally supplemented in between auctions by sales of stock "on tap." This is an issue of a further tranche of stock of a current issue, usually in conditions of temporary excess demand in that stock or that part of the yield curve. That said, only one conventional stock has been tapped since 1996, a £400 million conventional tap in August 1999. The DMO has stated that tap issues of conventional gilts will only take place in exceptional circumstances.

After an auction the authorities generally refrain from issuing stocks of a similar type or maturity for a "reasonable" period. Such stock will only be issued if there is a clear demand. The 1996/97 remit for gilt issuance was accompanied by changes to the structure for gilt auctions. These changes were designed to encourage participation in auctions and to make the process more smooth. The average size of auctions was reduced and a monthly schedule put in place.

Periodic dual auctions were also introduced. Dual auctions allow the issue of two stocks of different maturity in the same month, which moderates the supply of any one maturity and also appeals to a wider range of investors. Market makers (GEMMs) were allowed to telephone bids in up to five minutes before the close of bidding for the auction, which allowed them to accommodate more client demand into their bids. Instituting a preannounced auction schedule at the start of the fiscal year further assists market transparency and predictability in gilt auctions, which reduced market uncertainty. In theory, a reduction in uncertainty should result in lower yields over the long term, which reduce government borrowing costs.

The DMO has a slightly different auction procedure for I-L gilts. Unlike conventional gilts, which are issued through a multiple price auction, I-L gilts are auctioned on a uniform price basis. This reflects the higher risks associated with bidding for I-L stock. In an auction for a conventional gilt, a market maker will be able to use the yields of similar maturity stock currently trading in the market to assist in their bid. In addition a long position in the stock can be hedged using exchange-traded gilt futures contracts. There is also a very liquid secondary market in conventional gilts. For these reasons a market maker will be less concerned about placing a bid in an auction without knowing at what level other GEMMs are bidding for the stock. In an I-L gilt auction there is a less liquid secondary market and it is less straightforward to hedge an I-L gilt position. There are also fewer I-L issues in existence, indeed there may not be another stock anywhere near the maturity spectrum of the gilt being auctioned. The use of a uniform price auction reduces the uncertainty for market makers and encourages them to participate in the auction.

Auction Procedure

As part of its government financing role, HM Treasury issues an auction calendar just before the start of the new financial year in April. The DMO provides further details on each gilt auction at the start of each quarter in the financial year, when it also confirms the auction dates for the quarter and the maturity band that each auction will cover. For example, the quarterly announcement might state that the auction for the next month will see a gilt issued of between four and six years maturity. Announcements are made via Reuters, Telerate, and Bloomberg news screens. Eight days before the auction date the DMO announces the nominal size and the coupon of the stock being auctioned. If it is a further issue of an existing stock, the coupon obviously is already known. After this announcement, the stock is listed on the LSE and market makers engage in "when issued" trading (also known as the *grey market*). When issued trading is buying and selling of stock to the forward settlement date, which is the business day after the auction date. As in the Eurobond market, when issued trading allows market makers to gauge demand for the stock among institutional investors and also helps in setting the price on the auction day.

Conventional Gilts

In conventional gilt auctions bidding is open to all parties (including private individuals). Institutional investors will usually bid via a GEMM. Only GEMMs can bid by telephone directly to the DMO. Other bidders must complete an application form. Forms are made available in the national press, usually the *Financial Times*. Bidding can be competitive or noncompetitive. In a competitive bid, participants bid for one amount at one price, for a minimum nominal value of £500,000. If a bid is successful the bidder will be allotted stock at the price they put in. There is no minimum price. Telephone bidding must be placed by 10:30 A.M. on the morning of the auction and in multiples of £1 million nominal. Bidding is closed at 10:30 A.M. In a noncompetitive bid, GEMMs can bid for up to ½% of the nominal value of the issue size, while others can bid for up to a maximum of £500,000 nominal, with a minimum bid of £1,000. Noncompetitive bids are allotted in full at the weighted-average of the successful competitive bid price. In both cases, non-GEMMs must submit an application form either to the BoE's registrar department or to the DMO, in both cases to arrive no later than 10:30 A.M. on the morning of the auction.

The results of the auction are usually announced by the DMO by 11:10 A.M. The results include the highest, lowest, and average accepted bid prices, the gross redemption yields for these prices, and the value of noncompetitive bids for both GEMMs and non-GEMMs. The DMO also publishes important information on auction performance, which is used by the market to judge how well the auction has been received. This includes the difference between the highest accepted yield and the average yield of all accepted bids, known as the *tail*, and the ratio of bids received to the nominal value of the stock being auctioned, which is known as the *cover*. A well-received auction will have a small tail and will be covered many times, suggesting high demand for the stock. A cover of less than one and a half times is viewed unfavourably in the market and the price of the stock usually falls on receipt of this news. A cover over two times is well received. On rare occasions the cover will be less than one, which is bad news for the sterling bond market as a whole. A delay in the announcement of the auction result is sometimes taken to be as a result of poor demand for the stock.

The DMO reserves the right not to allot the stock on offer, and it is expected that this right might be exercised if the auction was covered at a very low price, considerably discounted to par. The DMO also has the right to allot stock to bidders at its discretion. This right is retained to prevent market distortions from developing, for example if one bidder managed to buy a large proportion of the entire issue. Generally the

DMO seeks to ensure that no one market maker receives more than 25% of the issue being auctioned for its own book.

Index-Linked Gilts

Auction bids for I-L gilts are also competitive and noncompetitive. Only IG GEMMs may make competitive bids, for a minimum of £1 million nominal and in multiples of £1 million. For I-L gilts there is a uniform price format, which means that all successful bidders receive stock at the same price. A bid above the successful price will be allotted in full. Noncompetitive bids must be for a minimum of £100,000, and will be allotted in full at the successful bid price (also known as the "strike" price). IG GEMMs are reserved up to 10% of the issue in the noncompetitive bid facility. Non-IG GEMMs must complete and submit an application form in the same way as for conventional gilt auctions.

The DMO reserves the right not to allot stock, and to allot stock to bidders at its discretion. The maximum holding of one issue that an IG GEMM can expect to receive for its own book is 40% of the issue size.

SECONDARY MARKET TRADING

As part of its role in maintaining an orderly and efficient market the DMO conducts business in the secondary markets in line with specific requirements and demand. This business generally involves trading with GEMMs in response to particular situations, including the following:

- Bidding for rump stock.
- Switches of stock.
- In special situations, bidding for conventional stock.
- Intervening to make stock available for repo in circumstances where a false market has resulted in specific issues being unavailable for borrowing or purchase.
- Sale of stock from official portfolios.

These situations are now considered in this section.

Bidding for Rump Stock

The DMO acts as a buyer of last resort for gilts that have been designated rump stocks, for which GEMMs are not required to quote two-way prices. Although the DMO only deals direct with GEMMs, institutions or private individuals can ask for a bid price via a broker, who will deal with the GEMM.

Switches of Stock

GEMMs may request switches out of or into stocks that are held on official portfolios, which the DMO will carry out amongst stocks of the same type. The terms of any switch are set by the DMO.

Bidding for Conventional Stock

In exceptional circumstances the DMO will announce that it will accept offers of a specific stock, acceptance of which is at the DMO's discretion.

Supplying Stock for Use in Repo

In certain circumstances a specific issue will go "tight" in the repo market, meaning that it is difficult to borrow the stock for delivery into short sales. This is typically reflected in the stock going *special* in the repo market.[5] On rare occasions the stock may become undeliverable, leading to failed transactions and also failure to deliver into the equivalent gilt futures contract. When this happens the DMO may make the stock available for borrowing, out of official portfolios, or issue a small amount of the stock into the market.

Sale of Stock from Official Portfolios

The DMO will acquire amounts of stock as a result of its secondary market operations, and these holdings may be made available for resale into the market. Although it does not actively offer stock to the market, when holdings are made available from its portfolios the DMO will announce via its news screen the stock on offer, and the size available; this is known as the DMO's "shop window." No offer price is indicated, but bids must be at the market level or above; acceptance is at the DMO's discretion. If more than £50 million of one issue is on offer a minitender is held, announced via the DMO's news screens.

Closing Reference Prices

After the close of business each day the DMO publishes reference prices and the equivalent gross redemption yields for each gilt on its news screens. The final reference price is based on closing two-way prices supplied by each GEMM at the end of the day. The prices, previously referred to as "CGO reference prices" but now following the merger of the CGO with CREST, called DMO or gilt reference prices, are frequently used in the calculation of settlement proceeds in repo and stock loan transactions.

---

[5] A *special* repo rate is below the general repo rate. The repo market is described in Chapter 10.

SETTLEMENT

Originally the settlement of gilts was undertaken by the Central Gilts Office (CGO) of the Bank of England. This was the computerised book-entry settlement system for gilts. It was first introduced in 1986. The system was upgraded in 1995 to allow for the introduction of new gilt products, namely gilt repo and strips. CGO provided facilities for gilt investors to hold stock in *dematerialised* form and transfer stock electronically. Transfers were processed by an assured payment system based on the principle of *delivery versus payment* (DVP). Thus the CGO provided a secure system for the electronic holding and transfer of stocks between members without the need for transfer forms and bond certificates.

The service was originally established by the BoE and the LSE to facilitate the settlement of specified securities, essentially gilts and certain sterling bonds such as bulldogs for which the BoE acts as registrar, and was upgraded by the BoE in 1997. This upgrade enhanced the CGO facility to settle gilt repo trading activity, which commenced in January 1996, and to cater for the introduction of the gilt strips facility in December 1997. It also provided a vehicle for the development of real-time DVP through links to the Real Time Gross Settlement System (RTGS) for wholesale payments, which was introduced in 1996.

In May 1999 responsibility for the CGO service was transferred to CRESTCo Limited, the company that operates the CREST settlement system for London market equities. The gilt settlement service is now operated within CREST, with the merger process completed in July 2000.

The basic concept of the CGO within CREST remains the same—that is, the provision of secure settlement for gilt-edged securities through an efficient and reliable system of electronic book-entry transfers in real time against an assured payment. The CGO is a real-time, communication-based system. Settlement on the specified business day ($T + 1$ for normal gilt trades) is dependent on the matching by CGO of correctly input and authenticated instructions by both of the parties and the successful completion of presettlement checks on the parties stock account balances and credit headroom.

The CGO provides facilities for the following:

- Settlement of stock and cash transfers.
- Overnight transfer of collateral, known as Delivery by Value (DBV), to allow CGO members to pass stock against a secured overnight loan.
- Automatic reporting of all transactions to the London Stock Exchange.
- Matching of instructions between counterparties.
- The movement of stock free of payment.
- Processing of stock lending and repo transactions.

In addition the following facilities were added at the upgrade:

- The stripping and reconstitution of gilts, at the request of GEMMs, the DMO, and the BoE.
- Forward-dated input, useful for the input of gilt repo.
- Greater control by settlement banks over the credit risks run on their customers (by means of a debit-capped payment mechanism).
- A flexible membership structure (allowing the names of "sponsored" as well as "direct" members to appear on the register).
- Multiple account designations.

All GEMMs, as well as most banks and large building societies, are members of CREST. Certain institutional investors and brokers are also members. The membership stood at around 300 in 1999, including nominee companies. Over 90% of the total value of gilts was held in dematerialised form in CGO in September 1999. Firms who trade less frequently in gilts often settle through an agent bank. This indirect participation in CREST is usually done via a nominee company, usually a current bank member, or via sponsored membership. In the case of sponsored membership a company opens a CREST account in its name but the sponsor is responsible for conducting the firm's gilt settlement activity.

Part of the reforms in the gilt market through 1998 included a facility for overseas investors to hold gilts in what was then CGO, via either the Euroclear or Clearstream clearing systems. This became possible after both Euroclear and Clearstream opened accounts at CGO. However in September 2002 CREST merged with Euroclear, hence facilitating pan-European and international settlement.

Delivery by Value

Delivery by value (DBV) is a mechanism whereby a CREST member may borrow money from or lend money to another CREST member against overnight gilt collateral. The CREST system automatically selects and delivers securities to a specified aggregate value on the basis of the previous night's CREST Reference Prices; equivalent securities are returned the following business day. The DBV functionality allows the giver and taker of collateral to specify the classes of security to be included within the DBV. The options are: all classes of security held within CREST, including strips and bulldogs; coupon bearing gilts and bulldogs; coupon bearing gilts and strips; and only coupon bearing gilts.

DBV repo is a repo transaction in which the delivery of the securities is by the DBV mechanism in CREST. A series of DBV repos may be constructed to form an "open" or "term" DBV repo. The DBV functionality allows repo interest to be automatically calculated and paid.

EXHIBIT 9.5 Euroclear/CRESTCo settlement details as at December 2001

	CRESTCo	Euroclear
Value of securities	£96,400 billion	£130,000 billion
	£59,900 billion	$91,000 billion
Number of prenetted transactions settled	74 million	161 million
Number of netted transactions settled	74 million	47 million
Securities held in custody	£2,900 billion	£7,900 billion
	£1,800 billion	£4,800 billion
Number of eligible securities	16,000	208,000
Number of domestic market links	3	32
Number of settlement currencies	3	32

Source: Bank of England *Quarterly Bulletin* 42, no. 4 (2002).

Merger of CREST and Euroclear

In 2002 CREST merged with the Euroclear company. The merger was announced by the respective Boards of the two companies in July 2002, for effect from September 2002. From this time CRESTCo became a wholly owned subsidiary of Euroclear plc. CRESTCo shareholders received a 19% stake in the merged body. In 2004 CRESTCo is expected to become part of Euroclear Bank SA/NV.

The merged group provides settlement services for bonds across a number of markets, including Belgian, Dutch, French, and UK securities, as well as international securities issued into the Euromarkets. The merger means that Europe-wide settlement and clearing systems, including those operated by Euroclear and CREST, have been integrated into one operating entity. The clients of the group may choose the jurisdiction under which they clear and hold securities. The administrative burden is reduced for investors who hold bonds across more than one jurisdiction, as they now have one Euroclear account for all Euromarket securities and certain government bonds as noted above.

Exhibit 9.5 shows settlements statistics for the two bodies at the time of the merger.

EXCHANGE-TRADED GILT DERIVATIVES

The gilt market forms the cornerstone of the sterling asset markets. Therefore the exchange-traded market in gilt derivatives is an important feature of the debt capital markets as a whole. In terms of derivatives both the LIFFE and MATIF futures exchanges trade standard futures and option contracts on gilts. This section presents an overview of the main exchange-traded gilt contract, the LIFFE Long Gilt futures contract.

A futures contract is a financial instrument that is a legally binding obligation to make or take delivery of an underlying specified asset at a fixed date in the future, at a price agreed at the time the contract is entered into. The asset can be a tangible one such as wheat or oil or a nontangible one such as an equity index. Futures contracts written on nontangible assets such as financial instruments are known as *financial futures*. Both commodity and financial futures are used for hedging and speculative purposes.

LIFFE Long Gilt Contract

LIFFE's long gilt futures contract was the first government bond futures contract listed in Europe in 1982. One *lot* of the contract represents £100,000 nominal of a gilt of a *notional* 7% coupon and maturing in from 8½ to 13 years. The price quoted is, like cash gilts, in decimal units (£0.01) and the bid-offer spread is usually £0.01. During 1998 the average daily trading volume in the long gilt was 64,000 lots and the number of *open interest* contracts ran at an average level of 164,000 during the year. Open interest represents the number of contracts that are run overnight and not closed out before the end of the trading day; the level of open interest is one reflection of the size of the hedging demand for gilts and other sterling bonds.

In the early 1990s a medium-gilt future was also traded on LIFFE, but was later discontinued due to low trading volumes. In January 1998 the contract was relaunched, with the same terms as the long gilt future but with the underlying gilt specified as one of between 4–7 years maturity. The delivery cycles of both contracts follow market convention for exchange-traded contracts, with expiry dates in March, June, September, and December each year.

There are a range of users of gilt futures contracts. These include:

- GEMMs and market makers of sterling-denominated bonds.
- Market makers in sterling interest rate swaps.
- Institutional investors in the gilt market including fund managers, pension funds, and life companies.
- Issuers of sterling bonds including Eurobonds and bulldogs.
- Speculators and arbitrageurs such as securities houses and hedge funds.

The market participants noted above use gilt futures for a range of purposes. A GEMM will be concerned with hedging its cash gilt book, institutional investors will also be concerned with hedging as well as investing future cash flows, portfolio duration adjustment, portfolio insurance, and income enhancement.[6] Issuers of sterling bonds use futures to hedge their underwriting positions. Finally, traders such as speculators and arbitrageurs will trade futures as part of a directional play on the market, for yield curve trades, and as part of volatility trading.

The delivery process for a futures contract is connected to its pricing, as this provides the link to (and convergence with) the cash market. However only a small percentage of futures contracts traded are actually taken to delivery. It is the party that is the seller of the contract (and who runs the position into the delivery month) that may choose to deliver a gilt from a list of deliverable gilts that meet the contract's specifications. Therefore the buyer of a contract (again, who runs the position into the delivery month) will anticipate receiving the particular gilt that will create the maximum profit or minimum loss for the delivering seller when assessing the fair price of the contract. This bond is known as the *cheapest-to-deliver* (CTD) gilt. To identify the CTD gilt, and therefore the fair price of the futures contract, it is necessary to look at the potential profit or loss from what is known as a *cash-and-carry* arbitrage. This is a position consisting of a long position in the underlying bond and an equivalent short position in the futures contract. Both positions must be put on simultaneously. The cash-and-carry arbitrage profit/loss calculation is given by

Cash inflow – cash outflow = Short futures – Long underlying:
(Future price × Price factor + Accrued interest at delivery + Coupon income)
(– Long gilt clean price + Accrued interest at purchase + Financing cost)

To consider our arbitrage trade then, since an arbitrage gain can be made if the price of the futures contract and the corresponding price of the CTD gilt are out of line, the market forces the price of the futures contract to closely track the price of the underlying gilt that is the CTD gilt at the time. The close relationship between the long gilt futures price and the price of the CTD gilt means that the future contract provides a flexible hedging mechanism for both gilts and other long-dated sterling bonds. The same consideration applies for the medium gilt futures contract and medium-dated gilts and sterling bonds.

LIFFE Gilt Options

The popularity and liquidity of the gilt futures contract led to the listing of gilt options on LIFFE in March 1986. Average daily volume in this contract was more than 16,000 lots during 2002. The contract is an

---

[6] These last two functions actually employ options on gilt futures.

option on the futures contract and not a cash gilt. The options are "American" style options, which means they can be exercised by the long at any time between trade date and expiry date. They are agreements under which the buyer acquires the right (but not the obligation) to take (*call*) or make (*put*) delivery of the underlying futures contract, at the price agreed at the time of dealing.

On LIFFE "serial expiry months" are available for its exchange-traded options; serial options are expiry months other than the traditional quarterly months of March, June, September, and December. gilt option expiry months are listed such that the two nearest serial months and the two nearest quarterly months are always available for trading.

Traditionally gilt futures and options have been traded by open-outcry in designated pits on the floor of the LIFFE exchange building. In April 1999 the exchange launched an electronic dealing platform known as Connect for Futures. The long gilt contract was the first to be traded on it. The system is a screen-based dealing platform that also enables traders to observe the depth of the market, as orders above and below the current bid and offer level are listed on the screen. Although floor trading in individual pits was retained, LIFFE announced in October 1999 that all futures and options trading was to move to an electronic screen-based platform by the end of the year, and trading had moved off the floor by the end of November 1999. All trading is now on LIFFE Connect.

GILT REPO MARKET

The term *repo* comes from the expression "sale and repurchase" agreement. Repo is a short-term money market instrument and is typically a loan secured with bonds as collateral. Although repo is a well-established instrument and has existed in the US Treasury market since 1918, it was introduced only in the gilt market in January 1996. Prior to this there was no facility to borrow gilts via a repo transaction. Gilt-edged market makers were able to borrow stock from designated Stock Exchange Money Brokers (SEMBs) in order to deliver into a short sale. The SEMBs obtained the stock from institutional investors with large holdings of gilts, and stock was lent to GEMMs in return for collateral, usually posted as other gilts or cash. The introduction of an open market in gilt repo enabled any market participant to borrow gilts and also to fund gilt positions at a lower rate (the *repo rate*) than the interbank lending rate. This contributed to improved cash market liquidity. According to the DMO, the market quickly grew to over £50 billion of repo outstanding, developing alongside the existing unsecured sterling money market. Market size stood at over £120 billion by the end of December 2002.

The BoE is involved in the repo market as part of its daily operations in the sterling money markets. From the first quarter of 2000 the DMO also used gilt repo as part of its cash management operations on behalf of the government, which are designed to smooth the net daily cash flows between central government and the private sector.[7]

---

[7] Gilt repo is covered in detail in chapter 6 of Moorad Choudhry, *The Repo Handbook* (Oxford: Butterworth-Heinemann, 2002).

CHAPTER 10

The European Repo Market

Moorad Choudhry
Senior Fellow
Centre for Mathematical Trading and Finance
CASS Business School, London

The European market in repurchase agreements or *repo* is both large and vitally important to the smooth running of the capital markets. The size of the market is always presented as an estimate, but it is safe to say that markets throughout the continent experienced significant growth during the 1990s and continue to expand. Asset classes that can be subject to repo now include corporate bonds and Eurobonds, as well as structured finance bonds such as ABS and CDO note issues. Repo is also common in equity markets. The growth in repo has been attributed to several factors. However, in essence, the simplicity of repo and the ability to adapt it to any market circumstance is key to its attraction to market participants, whether they are central banks, investment banks, borrowers, investors, or fund managers. The use of repo enhances the liquidity of bond and equity markets, which reduces costs for issuers of capital, and allows market makers to hedge positions with greater efficiency. Estimates of the size of the repo market vary. The turnover in Eurozone countries and the United Kingdom was in excess of $25 trillion in 2002.[1] Repo generally carries a lower profile than other sectors of the market, but its size is substantial in comparison to them. For example the turnover through the Euroclear and Clearstream clearing systems alone was put at $13 trillion in 1998.[2] The introduction of a repo market has impact on areas other than the straightforward provi-

---

[1] Source: ISMA, *Repo Market Survey*, March 2003
[2] ISMA, *Repo Market Survey*.

sion of secured lending and borrowing facilities. In the United Kingdom an open market in repo was introduced only in January 1996,[3] and it has been interesting to observe the impact of gilt repo on the unsecured money market and on the liquidity and turnover of the gilt market. For instance, data on the sterling average interbank overnight rate, known as SONIA, indicated a substantial reduction in the volume of unsecured overnight borrowing and lending from around $7 billion at the start of 1996 to under $4 billion at the start of 2000, as participants started to use repo more heavily. Evidence from the Bank of England also suggested that the volatility of overnight interest rates was reduced.[4] These and other issues in the sterling market are investigated in detail in a separate chapter.

Given its size and importance, it is surprising that repo has such a low profile; for example, there is little discussion of it in the financial press. This reflects the simple and straightforward nature of the instrument. Indeed, the fundamental essence of repo is its simplicity; the sale of securities coupled with an agreement to repurchase them at a future date. It is this simplicity and flexibility that has allowed repo to be used for a variety of purposes, or to meet a range of requirements. The determinants of the growth of repo in Europe are considered in more detail later, although one of the main factors was the need for investment banks and bond market makers to secure a lower funding rate for their long positions, and the ability to cover short positions more efficiently. The introduction of the Bund futures contract on London's LIFFE exchange in 1988 also contributed to the growth of Bund repo, as market participants entered into cash-and-carry or basis trading, arbitraging between the cash and futures market. Such trading is not possible without an open repo market. From around the same time the increasing use of derivative instruments such as swaps and bond options also contributed to greater use of repo, as banks often used the repo market to manage their hedge positions.

There is a wide range of uses to which repo might be put. Structured transactions that are very similar to repo include total return swaps, and other structured repo trades include floating-rate repo that contains an option to switch to a fixed rate at a later date. In the equity market repo is often conducted in a basket of stocks, which might be constituent stocks in an index such as the FTSE100 or CAC40 or user-specified bas-

---

[3] This is the open market in gilt repo. A market in equity repo, for instance, had been in operation in the London market from around 1992.

[4] Volume figures from ISMA. Several Bank of England reports have studied the impact of gilt repo, but note particularly the *Quarterly Bulletin* for February 1998, August 1998 and February 1999.

kets. Market makers borrow and lend equities with differing terms to maturity, and generally the credit rating of the institution involved in the repo transaction is of more importance than the quality of the collateral. Central banks' use of repo also reflects its importance; it is a key instrument in the implementation of monetary policy in many countries. Essentially then, repo markets have vital links and relationships with global money markets, bond markets, futures markets, swap markets and over-the-counter (OTC) interest rate derivatives.

In the remainder of this chapter we discuss key features of the repo instrument, and also introduce selected country markets.

KEY FEATURES

Repo is essentially a secured loan. The term comes from "sale and repurchase agreement"; however, this is not necessarily the best way to look at it. Although in a classic repo transaction legal title of an asset is transferred from the "seller" to the "buyer" during the term of the repo, in the author's opinion this detracts from the essence of the instrument: a secured loan of cash. It is therefore a money market instrument. Later we formally define repo and illustrate its use; for the moment we need only to think of it as a secured loan. The interest on this loan is the payment made in the repo.

There are a number of benefits in using repo, which concurrently have been behind its rapid growth. These include the following:

- Market makers generally are able to finance their long bond and equity positions at a lower interest cost if they repo out the assets; equally they are able to cover short positions.
- There is greater liquidity in specific individual bond issues.
- Greater market liquidity lowers the cost of raising funds for capital market borrowers.
- Central banks are able to use repo in their open market operations.
- Repo reduces counterparty risk in money market borrowing and lending, because of the security offered by the collateral given in the loan.
- Investors have an added investment option when placing funds.
- Institutional investors and other long-term holders of securities are able to enhance their returns by making their inventories available for repo trading.

The maturity of the majority of repo transactions are between overnight and three months, although trades of six months and one year are not uncommon. It is possible to transact in longer term repo as well. Because of this, repo is best seen as a money market product.[5] However, because of the nature of the collateral, repo market participants must keep a close eye on the market of the asset collateral, whether this is the government bond market, Eurobonds, equity or other asset.[6] The counterparties to a repo transaction will have different requirements, for instance to "borrow" a particular asset against an interest in lending cash. For this reason it is common to hear participants talk of trades being stock-driven or cash-driven. A corporate treasurer who invests cash while receiving some form of security is driving a cash-driven repo, whereas a market maker that wishes to cover a short position in a particular stock, against which she lends cash, is entering into a stock-driven trade.

There is a close relationship between repo and both the bond and money markets. The use of repo has contributed greatly to the liquidity of government, Eurobond and emerging market bond markets. Although it is a separate and individual market itself, operationally repo is straightforward to handle, in that it generally settles through clearing mechanisms used for bonds. As a money market product, repo reduces the stress placed on the unsecured interbank market, and empirical evidence indicates a reduction in overnight interest-rate volatility.[7]

MARKET PARTICIPANTS

The development and use of repo in each country to an extent dictates the nature and range of market participants. In a mature market repo counterparties include investors and cash-rich institutions, those seeking to finance asset positions and their intermediaries. Some firms will cross over these broad boundaries and engage in all aspects of repo trading. The main market parties are:

---

[5] The textbook definition of a "money market" instrument is of a debt product issued with between one day and one year to maturity, while debt instruments of greater than one year maturity are known as capital market instruments. In practice the money market desks of most banks will trade the yield curve to up to two years maturity, so it makes sense to view a money market instrument as being of up to two years maturity.

[6] This carries on to bank organisation structure. In most banks, the repo desk for bonds is situated in the money markets area, while in others it will be part of the bond division (the author has experience of banks employing each system). Equity repo is often situated as part of the back office settlement or Treasury function.

[7] Bank of England, *Quarterly Bulletin*, February 1997.

▓ Financial institutions: retail and commercial banks, building societies, securities houses and investment banks.
▓ Investors: fund managers, insurance companies and pension funds, investment funds, hedge funds, local authorities and corporate treasuries.
▓ Intermediaries: Interdealer brokers and money brokers. The main brokers are Cantor Fitzgerald, Prebon Yamane, Garban ICAP, Tullet & Tokyo and Tradition.

Financial institutions will engage in both repo and reverse repo trades. Investors also, despite their generic name, will be involved in both repo and reverse repo. Their money market funds will be cash-rich and engage in investment trades; at the same time they will run large fixed interest portfolios, the returns for which can be enhanced through trading in repo. Central banks are major players in repo markets and use repo as part of daily liquidity or open market operations and as a tool of monetary policy.

Repo itself is an over-the-counter market conducted over the telephone, with rates displayed on screens. These screens are supplied by both brokers and market makers themselves. Increasingly, electronic dealing systems are being used, with live dealing rates displayed on screen and trades being conducted at the click of a mouse button.

TYPES OF REPO

There are three main basic types of repo: the classic repo, the sell/buy-back repo, and triparty repo. A sell/buyback, referred to in some markets as a buy-sell, is a spot sale and repurchase of assets transacted simultaneously. It does not require a settlement system that can handle the concept of a classic repo and is often found in emerging markets. A classic repo is economically identical but the repo rate is explicit and the transaction is conducted under a legal agreement that defines the legal transfer of ownership of the asset during the term of the trade. Classic repo, the type of transaction that originated in the United States, is a sale and repurchase of an asset where the repurchase price is unchanged from the "sale" price. Hence the transaction is better viewed as a loan and borrow of cash. In a triparty repo a third party acts as an agent on behalf of both seller and buyer of the asset, but otherwise the instrument is identical to classic repo.

Exhibit 10.1 illustrates the variety of assets used in repo transactions during 2002.

EXHIBIT 10.1   Assets Used in Repo Transactions During 2002

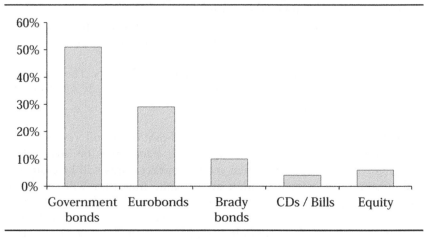

Source: ISMA.

REPO INSTRUMENTS

A repo agreement is a transaction in which one party sells securities to another, and at the same time and as part of the same transaction commits to repurchase identical securities on a specified date at a specified price. The seller delivers securities and receives cash from the buyer. The cash is supplied at a predetermined rate of interest—the repo rate—that remains constant during the term of the trade. On maturity the original seller receives back collateral of equivalent type and quality and returns the cash plus repo interest. One party to the repo requires either the cash or the securities and provides collateral to the other party, as well as some form of compensation for the temporary use of the desired asset. Although legal title to the securities is transferred, the seller retains both the economic benefits and the market risk of owning them. This means that the "seller" will suffer loss if the market value of the collateral drops during the term of the repo, as they still retain beneficial ownership of the collateral. The "buyer" in a repo is not affected in profit/loss account terms if the value of the collateral drops, although as we shall see later, there will be other concerns for the buyer if this happens.

We have given here the legal definition of repo. However, the purpose of the transaction, as we have described above, is to borrow or lend cash, which is why we have used quotation marks when referring to sellers and buyers. The "seller" of stock is really interested in borrowing cash, on which they will pay interest at a specified interest rate. The "buyer" requires security or collateral against the loan they have advanced, and/or the specific security to borrow for a period of time. The first and most important thing to state is that repo is a secured loan of cash and would be categorised as a money market yield instrument.[8]

We now look at the main repo instruments in turn.

THE CLASSIC REPO

The classic repo is the instrument encountered in the United States, United Kingdom, and other markets. In a classic repo one party will enter into a contract to sell securities, simultaneously agreeing to purchase them back at a specified future date and price. The securities can be bonds or equities but also money market instruments such as T-bills. The buyer of the securities is handing over cash, which on the termination of the trade will be returned to them and on which they will receive interest.

The seller in a classic repo is selling or offering stock, and therefore receiving cash, whereas the buyer is buying or bidding for stock, and consequently paying cash. So if the one-week repo interest rate is quoted by a market-making bank as "5½–5¼," this means that the market maker will bid for stock, that is, lend the cash, at 5.50% and offers stock or pays interest on borrowed cash at 5.25%. In some markets the quote is reversed.

Illustration of Classic Repo

There will be two parties to a repo trade, let us say Bank A (the seller of securities) and Bank B (the buyer of securities). On the trade date the two banks enter into an agreement whereby on a set date, the value or settlement date Bank A will sell to Bank B a nominal amount of securities in exchange for cash.[9] The price received for the securities is the market price of the stock on the value date. The agreement also demands that on the termination date Bank B will sell identical stock back to Bank A at the previously agreed price; consequently, Bank B will have its cash returned with interest at the agreed repo rate.

---

[8] That is, a money market product quoted as a yield instrument, similar to a bank deposit or a certificate of deposit. The other class of money market products are discount instruments such as a Treasury bill or commercial paper.

[9] The two terms are not necessarily synonymous. The value date in a trade is the date on which the transaction acquires value; for example, the date from which accrued interest is calculated. As such it may fall on a nonbusiness day such as a weekend or public holiday. The settlement date is the day on which the transaction settles or clears and so can only fall on a business day.

EXHIBIT 10.2 Classic Repo Transaction for 100-Worth of Collateral Stock

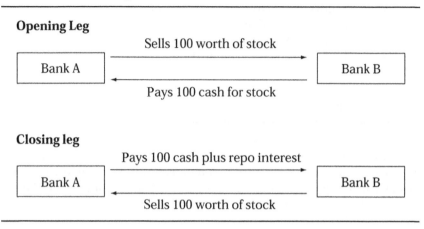

Opening Leg

Bank A → Sells 100 worth of stock → Bank B

Bank A ← Pays 100 cash for stock ← Bank B

Closing leg

Bank A → Pays 100 cash plus repo interest → Bank B

Bank A ← Sells 100 worth of stock ← Bank B

In essence a repo agreement is a secured loan (or collateralised loan) in which the repo rate reflects the interest charged on the cash being lent.

On the value date, stock and cash change hands. This is known as the start date, on-side date, first leg or opening leg, while the termination date is known as the second leg, off-side leg, or closing leg. When the cash is returned to Bank B, it is accompanied by the interest charged on the cash during the term of the trade. This interest is calculated at a specified rate known as the repo rate. It is important to remember that although in legal terms the stock is initially "sold" to Bank B, the economic effects of ownership are retained with Bank A. This means that if the stock falls in price it is Bank A that will suffer a capital loss. Similarly, if the stock involved is a bond, and there is a coupon payment during the term of the trade, this coupon is to the benefit of Bank A, and although Bank B will have received it on the coupon date, it must be handed over on the same day or immediately after to Bank A. This reflects the fact that although legal title to the collateral passes to the repo buyer, economic costs and benefits of the collateral remain with the seller.

A classic repo transaction is subject to a legal contract signed in advance by both parties. A standard document will suffice; it is not necessary to sign a legal agreement prior to each transaction.

Note that although we have called the two parties in this case "Bank A" and "Bank B," it is not only banks that get involved in repo transactions, and we have used these terms for the purposes of illustration only. The basic mechanism is illustrated in Exhibit 10.2.

A seller in a repo transaction is entering into a repo, whereas a buyer is entering into a reverse repo. In Exhibit 10.2 the repo counterparty is Bank A, while Bank B is entering into a reverse repo. That is, a reverse repo is a purchase of securities that are sold back on termination. As is evident from Exhibit 10.2, every repo is a reverse repo, and the name given to a deal is dependent on whose viewpoint one is looking at the transaction.

Examples of Classic Repo

The basic principle is illustrated with the following example. This considers a specific repo, that is, one in which the collateral supplied is specified as a particular stock, as opposed to a general collateral (GC) trade in which a basket of collateral can be supplied, of any particular issue, as long as it is of the required type and credit quality.

We consider first a classic repo in the United Kingdom gilt market between two market counterparties, in the 5.75% Treasury 2009 gilt stock. The terms of the trade are given in Exhibit 10.3 and illustrated in Exhibit 10.4. Note that the terms of a classic repo trade are identical, irrespective of which market the deal is taking place in. So the basic trade, illustrated in Exhibit 10.3, would be recognisable for bond repo in European and Asian markets.

The repo counterparty delivers to the reverse repo counterparty £10 million nominal of the stock, and in return receives the purchase proceeds. The clean market price of the stock is £104.60. In this example no margin has been taken so the start proceeds are equal to the market value of the stock which is £10,505,560.11. It is common for a rounded sum to be transferred on the opening leg. The repo interest is 5.75%, so the repo interest charged for the trade is

$$10,505,360 \times 5.75\% \times 7/365$$

EXHIBIT 10.3 Terms of Classic Repo Trade

Trade date	5 July 2000
Value date	6 July 2000
Repo term	1 week
Termination date	13 July 2000
Collateral (stock)	UKT 5.75% 2009
Nominal amount	£10,000,000
Price	104.60
Accrued interest (29 days)	0.4556011
Dirty price	105.055601
Settlement proceeds (wired amount)	£10,505,560.11
Repo rate	5.75%
Repo interest	£11,584.90
Termination proceeds	£10,517,145.01

EXHIBIT 10.4   Diagram of Classic Repo Trade

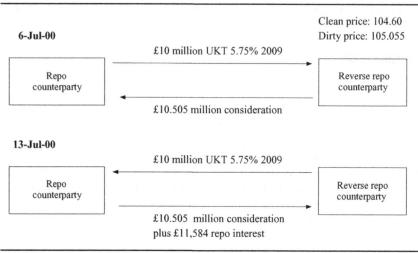

6-Jul-00

Clean price: 104.60
Dirty price: 105.055

£10 million UKT 5.75% 2009

Repo counterparty → Reverse repo counterparty

£10.505 million consideration

13-Jul-00

£10 million UKT 5.75% 2009

Repo counterparty ← Reverse repo counterparty

£10.505 million consideration plus £11,584 repo interest

or £11,584.01. The sterling market day-count basis is actual/365, and the repo interest is based on a seven-day repo rate of 5.75%. Repo rates are agreed at the time of the trade and are quoted, like all interest rates, on an annualised basis. The settlement price (dirty price) is used because it is the market value of the bonds on the particular trade date and therefore indicates the cash value of the gilts. By doing this the cash investor minimises credit exposure by equating the value of the cash and the collateral.

On termination the repo counterparty receives back its stock, for which it hands over the original proceeds plus the repo interest calculated above.

Market participants who are familiar with the Bloomberg trading system will use screen RRRA for a classic repo transaction. For this example the relevant screen entries are shown in Exhibit 10.5. This screen is used in conjunction with a specific stock, so in this case it would be called up by entering

UKT 5.75 09 <GOVT> RRRA <GO>

where "UKT" is the ticker for UK gilts. Note that the date format for Bloomberg screens is the US style, which is mm/dd/yy. The screen inputs are relatively self-explanatory, with the user entering the terms of the trade that are detailed in Exhibit 10.3. There is also a field for calculating margin, labelled "collateral" on the screen. As no margin is involved in this example, it is left at its default value of 100.00%. The bottom of

EXHIBIT 10.5 Bloomberg Screen RRRA for Classic Repo Transaction, Trade Date 5 July 2000

```
<HELP> for explanation.                              DL24 Corp   RRRA
Enter <1><GO> to send screen via <MESSAGE> System.
              REPO/REVERSE  REPO  ANALYSIS
TREASURY      UKT5 ¾ 12/07/09   104.5800/104.6400  (5.13/5.12) BGN  @16:08
            *BOND IS CUM-DIVIDEND AT SETTLEMENT*          CUSIP:  EC0113513
   SETTLEMENT DATE        7/ 6/00     RATE (365)    5.7500%
      <SETTLEMENT PRICE>  <MARKET PRICE>  COLLATERAL: 100.0000% OF MONEY
 PRICE       104.6000000    104.600000   Y/N, HOLD COLLATERAL PERCENT CONSTANT?  Y
 YIELD         5.1275565      5.1275565   Y/N, BUMP ALL DATES FOR WEEKENDS/HOLIDAYS?  Y
 ACCRUED       0.4556011      0.4556011
    FOR  29 DAYS.                         ROUNDING 1  1 = NOT ROUNDED
 TOTAL       105.0556011    105.055601       2 = ROUND TO NEAREST 1/ 8
            *BOND IS CUM-DIVIDEND AT TERMINATION*
   FACE AMT         10000000   <OR>   SETTLEMENT MONEY       10505560.11
 <OR> To solve for PRICE: Enter NUMBER of BONDS, SETTLEMENT MONEY & COLLATERAL
   TERMINATION DATE     7/13/00   <OR>   TERM (IN DAYS)          7
   ACCRUED  0.565574 FOR  36 DAYS.
            MONEY  AT  TERMINATION
 WIRED  AMOUNT                      10,505,560.11
 REPO  INTEREST                         11,584.90
 TERMINATION  MONEY                 10,517,145.01
 NOTES:
```

```
Copyright 2000 BLOOMBERG L.P.  Frankfurt:69-920410  Hong Kong:2-977-6000  London:207-330-7500  New York:212-318-2000
Princeton:609-279-3000  Singapore:226-3000  Sydney:2-9777-8686  Tokyo:3-3201-8900  Sao Paulo:11-3048-4500
                                                             1432-212-0 05-Jul-00 16:13:14
```

Bloomberg

Source: ©Bloomberg L.P. Reproduced with permission.

the screen shows the opening leg cash proceeds or "wired amount," the repo interest and the termination proceeds.

If we wanted to use screen RRRA for other securities we would enter the relevant bond ticker, for example "T" for US Treasuries, "B" for German Bunds and so on. The principles are the same for classic repo trades whatever the jurisdiction, and the screen may be used for all markets that undertake classic repo.

What if a counterparty is interested in investing £10 million against gilt collateral? Let us assume that a corporate treasury function with surplus cash wishes to invest this amount in repo for a one-week term. It invests this cash with a bank that deals in gilt repo. We can use Bloomberg screen RRRA to calculate the nominal amount of collateral required. Exhibit 10.6 shows the screen for this trade, again against the 5.75% Treasury 2009 stock as collateral. We see from Exhibit 10.6 that the terms of the trade are identical to that in Exhibit 10.3, including the bond price and the repo rate; however, the opening leg wired amount is entered as £10 million, which is the cash being invested. Therefore the nominal value of the gilt collateral required will be different, as we now

EXHIBIT 10.6 Bloomberg Screen for the Classic Repo Trade Illustrated in Exhibit 10.7

```
<HELP> for explanation.                              DL24 Corp   RRRA
Enter <1><GO> to send screen via <MESSAGE> System.
                 REPO/REVERSE  REPO  ANALYSIS
TREASURY          UKT5 ³₄ 12/07/09  104.5800/104.6400  (5.13/5.12) BGN  @16:08
             *BOND IS CUM-DIVIDEND AT SETTLEMENT*             CUSIP:  EC0113513
    SETTLEMENT DATE            7/ 6/00    RATE (365)  5.7500%
       <SETTLEMENT PRICE>   <MARKET PRICE>    COLLATERAL: 100.0000% OF MONEY
PRICE        104.6000000     104.600000    Y/N, HOLD COLLATERAL PERCENT CONSTANT?   Y
YIELD          5.1275565       5.1275565    Y/N, BUMP ALL DATES FOR WEEKENDS/HOLIDAYS?  Y
ACCRUED        0.4556011       0.4556011
    FOR  29 DAYS.                           ROUNDING 1  1 = NOT ROUNDED
TOTAL        105.0556011     105.055601                2 = ROUND TO NEAREST 1/ 8
             *BOND IS CUM-DIVIDEND AT TERMINATION*
   FACE AMT            9518769   <OR>   SETTLEMENT MONEY            9999999.99
<OR> To solve for PRICE: Enter NUMBER of BONDS, SETTLEMENT MONEY & COLLATERAL
   TERMINATION DATE     7/13/00   <OR>   TERM (IN DAYS)            7
   ACCRUED  0.565574 FOR  36 DAYS.

                 MONEY  AT  TERMINATION
   WIRED  AMOUNT                      10,000,000.00
   REPO  INTEREST                         11,027.40
   TERMINATION  MONEY                  10,011,027.40
   NOTES:

Copyright 2000 BLOOMBERG L.P.  Frankfurt:69-920410  Hong Kong:2-977-6000  London:207-330-7500  New York:212-318-2000
Princeton:609-279-3000        Singapore:226-3000   Sydney:2-9777-8686   Tokyo:3-3201-8900     Sao Paulo:11-3048-4500
                                                                          1432-212-0 05-Jul-00 16:18:46
Bloomberg
PROFESSIONAL
```

Source: ©Bloomberg L.P. Reproduced with permission.

require a market value of this stock of £10 million. From the screen we see that this is £9,518,769. The cash amount is different from the example in Exhibit 10.5 so of course the repo interest charged is different, and is £11,027 for the seven-day term. The diagram at Exhibit 10.7 illustrates the transaction details.

THE SELL/BUYBACK

We next consider the sell/buyback, which is economically identical to the classic repo but is described under different cash flow terms.

Definition

In addition to classic repo there exists sell/buyback. A sell/buyback is defined as an outright sale of a bond on the value date, and an outright repurchase of that bond for value on a forward date. The cash flows therefore become a sale of the bond at a spot price, followed by repur-

EXHIBIT 10.7   Corporate Treasury Classic Repo

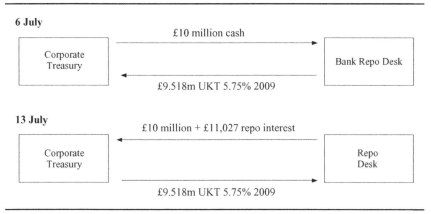

chase of the bond at the forward price. The forward price calculated includes the interest on the repo and is therefore a different price to the spot price.[10] That is, repo interest is realised as the difference between the spot price and forward price of the collateral at the start and termination of the trade. The sell/buyback is entered into for the same reasons as a classic repo, but was developed initially in markets where no legal agreement existed to cover repo transactions, and where the settlement and IT systems of individual counterparties were not equipped to deal with repo. Over time, sell/buybacks have become the convention in certain markets, most notably Italy, and so the mechanism is still used. In many markets therefore, sell/buybacks are not covered by a legal agreement, although the standard legal agreement used in classic repo now includes a section that describes them.[11]

A sell/buyback is a spot sale and forward repurchase of bonds transacted simultaneously, and the repo rate is not explicit, but is implied in the forward price. Any coupon payments during the term are paid to the seller; however, this is done through incorporation into the forward price, so the seller will not receive it immediately, but on termination. This is a disadvantage when compared to classic repo. However there will be compensation payable if a coupon is not handed over straight away, usually at

---

[10] The "forward price" is calculated only for the purpose of incorporating repo interest; it should not be confused with a forward interest rate, which is the interest rate for a term starting in the future and which is calculated from a spot interest rate. Nor should it be taken to be an indication of what the market price of the bond might be at the time of trade termination, the price of which could differ greatly from the sell/buyback forward price.

[11] This is the BMA/ISMA Global Master Repurchase Agreement.

EXHIBIT 10.8   Sell/Buyback Transaction

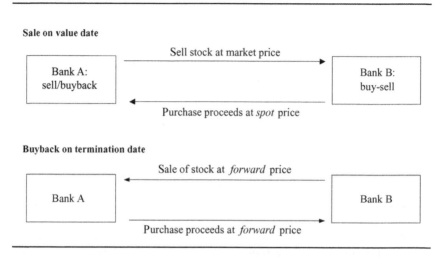

the repo rate used in the sell/buyback. As sell/buybacks are not subject to a legal agreement in most cases, in effect the seller has no legal right to any coupon, and there is no provision for marking-to-market and variation margin. This makes the sell/buyback a higher risk transaction when compared to classic repo, even more so in volatile markets.

Note that in some markets the term "repo" is used to describe what are in fact sell/buybacks. The Italian market is a good example of where this convention is followed.

A general diagram for the sell/buyback is given in Exhibit 10.8.

Examples of Sell/Buyback

We use the same terms of trade given in Exhibit 10.3 earlier but this time the trade is a sell/buyback.[12] In a sell/buyback we require the forward price on termination, and the difference between the spot and forward price incorporates the effects of repo interest. It is important to note that this forward price has nothing to with the actual market price of the collateral at the time of forward trade. It is simply a way of allowing for the repo interest that is the key factor in the trade. Thus in

---

[12] The Bank of England discourages sell/buybacks in gilt repo and it is unusual, if not unheard of, to observe them in this market. However, we use these terms of trade for comparison purposes with the classic repo example given in the previous section. The procedure and the terms of the trade would be identical in other markets such as Italy and Portugal where sell/buyback trades are the norm. In the Italian market for example, sell/buybacks are actually called "repos."

EXHIBIT 10.9   Bloomberg Screen BSR for Sell/Buyback Trade in 5.75% 2009, Trade Date 5 July 2000

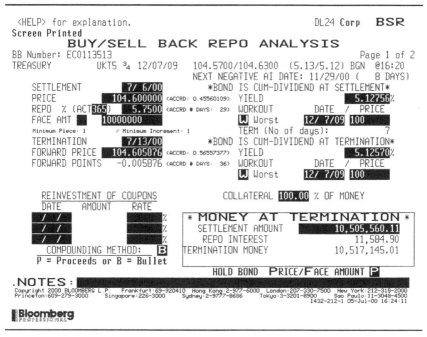

Source: ©Bloomberg L.P. Used with permission.

sell/buyback the repo rate is not explicit (although it is the key consideration in the trade); rather, it is implicit in the forward price.

In this example, one counterparty sells £10 million nominal of the UKT 5.75% 2009 at the spot price of 104.60, this being the market price of the bond at the time. The consideration for this trade is the market value of the stock, which is £10,505,560 as before. Repo interest is calculated on this amount at the rate of 5.75% for one week, and from this the termination proceeds are calculated. The termination proceeds are divided by the nominal amount of stock to obtain the forward dirty price of the bond on the termination date. For various reasons, the main one being that settlement systems deal in clean prices, we require the forward clean price, which is obtained by subtracting from the forward dirty price the accrued interest on the bond on the termination date. At the start of the trade the 5.75% 2009 had 29 days' accrued interest, therefore on termination this figure will be 29 + 7 or 36 days.

Bloomberg users access a different screen for sell/buybacks, which is BSR. This is shown in Exhibit 10.9. Entering in the terms of the trade, we see from Exhibit 10.9 that the forward price is 104.605876. How-

EXHIBIT 10.10   Bloomberg Screen BSR Page 2 for Sell/Buyback Trade in 5.75% 2009 Gilt, Shown at Exhibit 10.9

```
<HELP> for explanation.                              DL24 Corp   BSR
Screen Printed
                 BUY/SELL  BACK  REPO  ANALYSIS
BB Number: EC0113513                                        Page 2 of 2
TREASURY        UKT5 ¾ 12/07/09   104.5700/104.6300  (5.13/5.12) BGN  @16:20

┌─────────────────────────────────┬─────────────────────────────────┐
│        BOND  INCOME             │      FUNDING  COST              │
│                                 │                                 │
│ AT SETTLEMENT DATE:      7/ 6/00│                                 │
│ PRINCIPAL          10,460,000.00│                                 │
│   ACCRUED INTEREST     45,560.11│                                 │
│ TOTAL:             10,505,560.11│ --->      10,505,560.11 @  5.7500│
│                                 │           for   7 day(s)        │
│ AT TERMINATION DATE:     7/13/00│                                 │
│ PRINCIPAL          10,460,000.00│                                 │
│ COUPON(S)                   0.00│                                 │
│   ACCRUED INTEREST     56,557.38│                                 │
│   INTEREST ON CPNS          0.00│                                 │
│ TOTAL:             10,516,557.38│                                 │
│                                 │                                 │
│      NET INCOME:      10,997.27 │  COST:              11,584.90   │
└─────────────────────────────────┴─────────────────────────────────┘

DIFFERENCE            -587.63 TERMINATION
PER  100  NOM:    -0.00587633 AMOUNT                 10,460,587.60
Copyright 2000 BLOOMBERG L.P.   Frankfurt:69-920410  Hong Kong:2-977-6000  London:207-330-7500  New York:212-318-2000
Princeton:609-279-3000   Singapore:226-3000   Sydney:2-9777-8686   Tokyo:3-3201-8900   Sao Paulo:11-3048-4500
                                                                      1432-212-1 05-Jul-00 16:25:39
▌Bloomberg
```

Source: ©Bloomberg L.P. Reproduced with permission.

ever the fundamental nature of this transaction is evident from the bottom part of the screen: the settlement amount ("wired amount"), repo interest and termination amount are identical for the classic repo trade described earlier. This is not surprising; the sell/buyback is a loan of £10.505 million for one week at an interest rate of 5.75%. The mechanics of the trade do not differ on this key point.

Screen BSR on Bloomberg has a second page, which is shown at Exhibit 10.10. This screen summarises the cash proceeds of the trade at start and termination. Note how the repo interest is termed "funding cost." This is because the trade is deemed to have been entered into by a bond trader who is funding his book. This will be considered later, but we can see from the screen details that during the one week of the trade the bond position has accrued interest of £10,997. This compares unfavourably with the repo funding cost of £11,584.

If there is a coupon payment during a sell/buyback trade and it is not paid over to the seller until termination, a compensating amount is also payable on the coupon amount, usually at the trade's repo rate. When calculating the forward price on a sell/buyback where a coupon will be paid during the trade, we must subtract the coupon amount from the forward price. Note also that sell/buybacks are not possible on an open basis, as no forward price can be calculated unless a termination date is known.

COMPARING CLASSIC REPO AND SELL/BUYBACK

Fundamentally both classic repo and sell/buybacks are money market instruments that are a means by which one party may lend cash to another party, secured against collateral in the form of stocks and bonds. Both transactions are a contract for one party to sell securities, with a simultaneous agreement to repurchase them at a specified future. They also involve:

- In economic terms, an exchange of assets, usually bonds but also money market paper or equities as collateral against cash.
- The supplier of cash being compensated through the payment of interest, at an explicit (repo) or implicit (sell/buyback) rate of interest.
- Short-covering of positions by market makers or speculative sellers, when they are stock-driven trades.

In certain respects however, there are significant differences between the two instruments. A classic repo trade is carried out under formal legal documentation, which sets out the formal position of each counterparty in the event of default. Sell/buybacks have traditionally not been covered by this type of documentation, although this is no longer the case as standard documentation now exists to cater for them. There is no provision for marking-to-market and variation margining in sell/buybacks, issues we shall look at shortly.

A summary of the main features of both types of trade is given in Exhibit 10.11.

STOCK LENDING

Stock lending or securities lending is defined as a temporary transfer of securities in exchange for collateral. It is not a repo in the normal sense; there is no sale or repurchase of the securities. The temporary use of the desired asset—the stock that is being borrowed—is reflected in a fixed fee payable by the party temporarily taking the desired asset. In a stock loan, the lender does not monitor interest rates during the term of the trade, but

EXHIBIT 10.11   Summary of Highlights of Classic Repo and Sell/Buyback

Classic Repo	Sell/Buyback
"Sale" and repurchase	Outright sale; forward buyback
Bid at repo rate: bid for stock, lend the cash	Repo rate implicit in forward buyback price
(Offer at repo rate: offer the stock, take the cash)	
Sale and repurchase prices identical	Forward buyback price different
Return to cash lender is repo interest on cash	Return to cash lender is difference between sale price and forward buyback price (the "repo" interest!)
Bond coupon received during trade is returned to seller	Coupon need not be returned to bond seller until termination (albeit with compensation)
Standard legal agreement (BMA/ISMA GMRA)	No standard legal agreement (but may be traded under the GMRA)
Initial margin may be taken	Initial margin may be taken
Variation margin may be called	No variation margin unless transacted under a legal agreement
Specific repo dealing systems required	May be transacted using existing bond and equity dealing systems

instead realises value by receiving this fixed fee during the term of the loan. This makes administration of stock lending transactions less onerous compared to repo. The formal definition of a stock loan is a contract between two parties in which one party lends securities to another for a fixed or open term. The party that borrows must supply collateral to the stock lender, which can be other high quality securities, cash or a letter of credit. This protects against credit risk. In the United States the most common type of collateral is cash; however, in the UK market it is quite common for other securities to be given as collateral, typically gilts. In addition the lender charges a fixed fee, usually quoted as a basis point charge on the market value of the stock being lent, payable by the borrower on termination. The origins and history of the stock-lending market are different from that of the repo market. The range of counterparties is also different, although of course a large number of counterparties are involved in both markets. Most stock loans are on an "open" basis, meaning that they are confirmed (or terminated) each morning, although term loans also occur.

Institutional investors such as pension funds and insurance companies often prefer to enhance the income from their fixed interest portfolios by lending their bonds, for a fee, rather than entering into repo transactions. This obviates the need to set up complex settlement and administration systems, as well as the need to monitor what is, in effect, an interest rate position. Initial margin is given to institutional lenders of stock, usually in the form of a greater value of collateral stock than the market value of the stock being lent.

Basic Concepts

Stock lending transactions are the transfer of a security or basket of securities from a lending counterparty, for a temporary period, in return for a fee payable by the borrowing counterparty. During the term of the loan, the stock is lent out in exchange for collateral, which may be in the form of other securities or cash. If other securities are handed over as collateral, they must be high quality assets such as Treasuries, gilts or other highly-rated paper. Lenders are institutional investors such as pension funds, life assurance companies, local authority treasury offices and other fund managers, and loans of their portfolio holdings are often facilitated via the use of a broking agent, known as a prime broker or a clearing agent custodian such as Euroclear or Clearstream. In addition, banks and securities houses that require stock to cover short positions sometimes have access to their own source of stock lenders; for example, clients of their custody services.

Stock lending is not a sale and repurchase in the conventional sense but is used by banks and securities houses to cover short positions in securities put on as part of market-making or proprietary trading activity. In some markets (for example, the Japanese equity market) regulations require a counterparty to have arranged stock lending before putting on the short trade.

Other reasons why banks may wish to enter into stock loan (or stock borrowing, from their viewpoint) transactions include:

- Where they have effected a purchase, and then sold this security on, and their original purchase has not settled, putting them at risk of failing on their sale.
- As part of disintermediation between the stock loan market and the repo and unsecured money market.

An institution that wishes to borrow stock must pay a fee for the term of the loan. This is usually a basis point charge on the market value of the loan and is payable in arrears on a monthly basis. In the Eurobond market the fee is calculated at the start of the loan, and unless there is a significant change in the market value of the stock, it will be paid at the end of the loan period. In the UK gilt market the basis point fee is calculated on a daily basis on the market value of the stock that has been lent, and so the total charge payable is not known until the loan maturity. This arrangement requires that the stock be marked-to-market at the end of each business day. The fee itself is agreed between the stock borrower and the stock lender at the time of each loan, but this may be a general fee payable for all loans. There may be a different fee payable for specific stocks, so in this case the fee is agreed on a trade-by-trade basis, depending on the stock being lent out. Any fee is usually for the term of the loan, although it is possible in most markets to adjust the rate through negotiation at any time during the loan. The fee charged by the stock lender is a function of supply and demand for the stock in the market. A specific security that is in high demand in the market will be lent out at a higher fee than one that is in lower demand. For this reason it is important for the bank's Treasury desk[13] to be aware of which stocks are in demand, and more importantly to have a reasonable idea of which stocks will be in demand in the near future. Some banks will be in possession of better market intelligence than others. If excessive demand is anticipated, a prospective short seller may borrow stock in advance of entering into the short sale.

The term of a stock loan can be fixed, in which case it is known as a term loan, or it can be open. A term loan is economically similar to a classic repo transactions. An open loan is just that: there is no fixed maturity term, and the borrower will confirm on the telephone at the start of each day whether it wishes to continue with the loan or will be returning the security.

As in a classic repo transaction, coupon or dividend payments that become payable on a security or bond during the term of the loan will be to the benefit of the stock lender. In the standard stock loan legal agreement, known as the OSLA agreement,[14] there is no change of beneficial ownership when a security is lent out. The usual arrangement when a coupon is payable is that the payment is automatically returned to the stock lender via its settlement system. Such a coupon payment is known as a manufactured dividend.

Clients of prime brokers and custodians will inform their agent if they wish their asset holdings to be used for stock-lending purposes. At this point a stock-lending agreement is set up between the holder of the securities and the prime broker or custodian. Borrowers of stock are also required to set up an agreement with brokers and custodians. The return to the broker or custodian is the difference between the fee paid by the stock borrower and that paid to the stock lender. Banks that have

---

[13] Or whichever desk is responsible for covering short positions by borrowing or reverse-repoing stock.

[14] After the trade association overseeing the stock loan market.

their own internal lending lines can access this stock at a lower borrowing rate. If they wish to pursue this source they will set up a stock-lending agreement with institutional investors directly.

Example of Stock Loan

We illustrate a stock loan where the transaction is "stock-driven." Let us assume that a securities house has a requirement to borrow a UK gilt, the 5.75% 2009, for a one-week period. This is the stock from our earlier classic repo and sell/buyback examples. We presume the requirement is to cover a short position in the stock, although there are other reasons why the securities house may wish to borrow the stock. The bond that it is offering as collateral is another gilt, the 6.50% Treasury 2003. The stock lender, who we may assume is an institutional investor such as a pension fund, but may as likely be another securities house or a bank, requires a margin of 5% as well as a fee of 20 basis points. The transaction is summarised in Exhibit 10.12.

Note that in reality, in the gilt market the stock loan fee (here 20 bps) is calculated on the daily mark-to-market stock price, automatically within the gilt settlement mechanism known as CREST–CGO, so the final charge is not known until termination. Within the Eurobond market, for example in Clearstream, the fee on the initial loan value is taken, and adjustments are made only in the case of large movements in stock price.

Note that there is no specialist screen for stock loan transactions on Bloomberg.

EXHIBIT 10.12   Stock Loan Transaction for UK Gilt 5¾% 2009

Value date	6 July 2000
Termination date	13 July 2000
Stock borrowed	5.75% 2009
Nominal borrowed	£10 million
Term	1 week
Loan value	£10,505.560.11
Collateral	6.50%
Clean price	102.1
Accrued interest (29 days)	0.5150273
Dirty price	102.615027
Margin required	5%
Market value of collateral required	
= 10,505,560 × 1.05	£11,030,837.35
Nominal value of collateral	£10,749,729
Stock loan fee (20 bps)	£402.95

COMPARING CLASSIC REPO AND STOCK LENDING

A stock loan transaction in which the collateral is in the form of cash is similar in some ways to a classic repo trade. Here we compare the two transactions. Consider the following situation: ABC is an entity, perhaps a bank or fund manager, that owns government bond G. Bank XYZ is a bank that requires bond G in order to deliver into a short sale that it has transacted in G. To temporarily acquire bond G to cover the short sale Bank XYZ may enter into either a stock loan or a classic repo. Exhibit 10.13 looks at the similarities between the two and the differences.

REPO VARIATIONS

In the earlier section we described the standard classic repo trade, which has a fixed term to maturity and a fixed repo rate. Generally, classic repo trades will range in maturity from overnight to one year, however it is possible to transact longer maturities than this if required. The overwhelming majority of repo trades are between overnight and three months in maturity, although longer-term trades are not uncommon. A fixed-maturity repo is sometimes called a *term repo*. One could call this the plain vanilla repo. It is usually possible to terminate a vanilla repo before its stated maturity date if this is required by one or both of the counterparties.[15]

A repo that does not have a specified fixed maturity date is known as an *open repo*. In an open repo the borrower of cash will confirm each morning that the repo is required for a further overnight term. The interest rate is also fixed at this point. If the borrower no longer requires the cash, or requires the return of his collateral, the trade will be terminated at one day's notice.

In the remainder of this section we present an overview of the most common variations on the vanilla repo transaction that are traded in the markets.

Triparty Repo

The triparty repo mechanism is a relatively recent development and is designed to make the repo arrangement accessible to a wider range of market counterparties. Essentially it introduces a third-party agent in between

---

[15] The term *delivery repo* is sometimes used to refer to a vanilla classic repo transaction where the supplier of cash takes delivery of the collateral, whether in physical form or as a book-entry transfer to its account in the clearing system (or its agent's account).

EXHIBIT 10.13   Comparison of Stock Loan Transaction with Repo

Similarities

ABC transfers bond G to XYZ.

XYZ passes cash to the market value of G to ABC.

At the termination of the transaction, XYZ returns bond G to ABC.

At termination, ABC returns the cash it received at the start of the transaction to XYZ.

Classic repo transaction	Stock loan transaction
ABC is the stock seller. It may be viewed as the borrower of funds, but not in the context of this trade.	ABC is the stock lender.
XYZ is the stock buyer.	XYZ is the stock borrower.
ABC places cash received from XYZ on deposit, or otherwise invests it.	ABC receives cash from XYZ, which is collateral for the loan, and which is placed on deposit. The interest earned is payable to XYZ.
On termination, ABC returns the cash received at the start, together with interest charged at the repo rate.	On termination, ABC returns the cash to XYZ, together with the interest earned on it. XYZ pays over the fee charged by ABC for making the loan.
The net gain to ABC is based on the difference between the repo rate paid to XYZ and the rate earned on the cash placed on deposit.	The gain to ABC is considered as the stock loan fee.
If there is a coupon payment on bond G, this is paid by XYZ to ABC.	If there is a coupon payment on bond G, this is paid by XYZ to ABC.
On termination, ABC "buys back" bond G from XYZ at the repurchase price agreed at the trade start. As this is classic repo, the repurchase price is identical to the sale price, but the cash flow includes repo interest.	On termination, XYZ returns bond G to ABC, who returns the cash collateral it received at the start.

the two repo counterparties, who can fulfil a number of roles from security custodian to cash account manager. The triparty mechanism allows bond and equity dealers full control over their inventory, and incurs minimal settlement cost to the cash investor, but gives the investor independent confirmation that their cash is fully collateralised. Under a triparty agreement, the securities dealer delivers collateral to an independent third-party custodian, such as Euroclear or Clearstream,[16] who will place it into a segregated triparty account. The securities dealer maintains control over which precise securities are in this account (multiple substitutions are permitted) but the custodian undertakes to confirm each day to the investor that their cash remains fully collateralised by securities of suitable quality. A triparty agreement needs to be in place with all three parties before trading can commence. This arrangement reduces the administrative burden for the cash investor, but is not, in theory, as secure as a conventional delivery-versus-payment structure. Consequently the yield on the investor's cash (assuming collateral of identical credit quality) should be slightly higher. The structure is shown in Exhibit 10.14.

The first triparty repo deal took place in 1993 between the European Bank for Reconstruction and Development (EBRD) and Swiss Bank Corporation.[17]

A triparty arrangement is, in theory, more attractive to smaller market participants as it removes the expense of setting up in-house administration facilities that would be required for conventional repo. This is mainly because the delivery and collection of collateral is handled by the triparty agent. Additional benefits to cash-rich investors include:

- No requirement to install repo settlement and monitoring systems.
- No requirement to take delivery of collateral or to maintain an account at the clearing agency.
- Independent monitoring of market movements and margin requirements.
- In the event of default, a third-party agent that can implement default measures.

Set against the benefits is of course the cost of triparty repo, essentially the fee payable to the third-party agent. This fee will include a charge for setting up accounts and arrangements at the triparty agent, and a custodian charge for holding securities in the clearing system.

---

[16] Clearstream was previously known as Cedel Bank. Other triparty providers include JPMorgan Chase Bank of New York.

[17] Stated in Corrigan et al., *Repo: The Ultimate Guide* (London: Pearls of Wisdom Publishing, 1999), p. 27.

EXHIBIT 10.14   Triparty Repo Structure

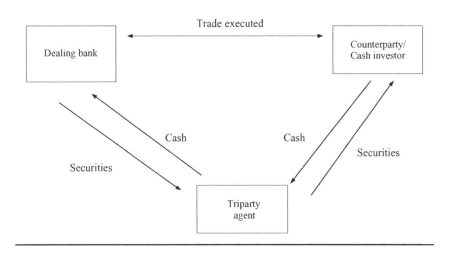

As well as being attractive to smaller banks and cash-rich investors, the larger banks will also use triparty repo, in order to be able to offer it as a service to their smaller-size clients. The usual arrangement is that both dealer and cash investor will pay a fee to the triparty agent based on the range of services that are required, and this will be detailed in the legal agreement in place between the market counterparty and the agent. This agreement will also specify, among other detail, the specific types of security that are acceptable as collateral to the cash lender; the repo rate that is earned by the lender will reflect the nature of collateral that is supplied. In every other respect, however, the triparty mechanism offers the same flexibility of conventional repo, and may be transacted from maturities ranging from overnight to one year.

The triparty agent is an agent to both parties in the repo transaction. It provides a collateral management service overseeing the exchange of securities and cash, and managing collateral during the life of the repo. It also carries out daily marking-to-market, and substitution of collateral as required. The responsibilities of the agent can include:

- The preparation of documentation.
- The setting up of the repo account.
- Monitoring of cash against purchased securities, both at inception and at maturity.
- Initial and ongoing testing of concentration limits.
- The safekeeping of securities handed over as collateral.

■ Managing the substitution of securities, where this is required.
■ Monitoring the market value of the securities against the cash lent out in the repo.
■ Issuing margin calls to the borrower of cash.

The triparty agent will issue close-of-business reports to both parties. The contents of the report can include some or all of the following:

■ Triparty repo cash and securities valuation.
■ Corporate actions.
■ Pre-advice of expected income.
■ Exchange rates.
■ Collateral substitution.

The extent of the duties performed by the triparty agent is dependent of the sophistication of an individual party's operation. Smaller market participants who do not wish to invest in extensive infrastructure may outsource all repo-related functions to the triparty agent.

Triparty repo was originally conceived as a mechanism through which repo would become accessible to smaller banks and nonbank counterparties. It is primarily targeted at cash-rich investors. However users of the instrument range across the spectrum of market participants, and include, on the investing side, cash-rich financial institutions such as banks, fund managers including life companies and pension funds, and savings institutions such as UK building societies. On the borrowing side users include bond and equity market makers, and banks with inventories of high quality assets such as government bonds and highly rated corporate bonds.

Triparty Repo Volumes

The overwhelming volume of repo in the global markets is conducted as bilateral contracts. The use of triparty contracts is growing however, particularly in equity repo. In June 2001 approximately 5.5% of repo business by volume in the Euro markets was transacted via a triparty platform. This figure had risen to 7.3% in December 2002.[18] The figure includes repo and reverse repo; so it can be assumed to include an element of double-counting. Exhibit 10.15 illustrates the growth in triparty repo volumes from June 2001, and it share in the market overall (this is for Euromarket securities).

---

[18] *ISF Magazine* (March 2003). www.ISFMagazine.com

EXHIBIT 10.15   Breakdown of Repo Volumes by Contract Mechanism

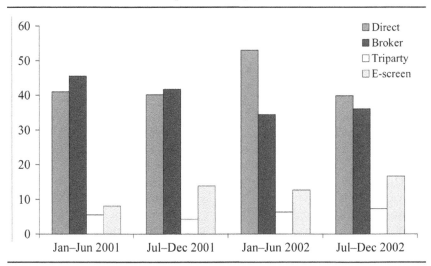

Source: European Repo Market survey, *ISF Magazine*, March 2003. Reproduced with permission.

Hold-in-Custody Repo

This is part of the general collateral (GC) market, and is more common in the United States than elsewhere. Consider the case of a cash-rich institution investing in GC as an alternative to deposits or commercial paper. The better the quality of collateral, the lower the yield the institution can expect, while the mechanics of settlement may also affect the repo rate. The most secure procedure is to take physical possession of the collateral. However, if the dealer needs one or more substitutions during the term of the trade, the settlement costs involved may make the trade unworkable for one or both parties. Therefore, the dealer may offer to hold the securities in his own custody against the investor's cash. This is known as a *hold-in-custody* (HIC) repo. The advantage of this trade is that since securities do not physically move, no settlement charges are incurred. However, this carries some risk for the investor because they only have the dealer's word that their cash is indeed fully collateralised in the event of default. Thus this type of trade is sometime referred to as a *"Trust Me"* repo; it is also referred to as a *due-bill repo* or a *letter repo*.

In the US market there have been cases in which securities houses that went into bankruptcy and defaulted on loans were found to have pledged the same collateral for multiple HIC repo trades. Investors dealing in HIC repo must ensure:

■ They only invest with dealers of good credit quality, since an HIC repo may be perceived as an unsecured transaction.

■ They receive a higher yield on their cash in order to compensate them for the higher credit risk involved.

A safekeeping repo is identical to an HIC repo, whereby the collateral from the repo seller is not delivered to the cash lender but held in "safe keeping" by the seller. This has advantages in that there is no administration and cost associated with the movement of stock. The risk is that the cash lender must entrust the safekeeping of collateral to the counterparty, and has no means of confirming that the security is indeed segregated, and only being used for one transaction.

Due to the counterparty risk inherent in an HIC repo, it is rare to see it transacted either in the US market or elsewhere. Certain securities are not suitable for delivery; for example, the class of mortgage securities known as whole loans in the United States, and these are often funded using HIC repo (termed *whole-loan repo*).

Borrow/Loan versus Cash

This is similar in almost all respects to a classic repo/reverse repo. A legal agreement between the two parties is necessary, and trades generally settle delivery-versus-payment. The key difference is that under a repo agreement legal title over the collateral changes hands. Under a securities lending agreement this is not necessarily the case. The UK standard securities lending agreement does involve transfer of title, but it is possible to construct a securities lending agreement where legal title does not move. This can be an advantage for customers who may have accounting or tax problems in doing a repo trade. Such institutions will opt to transact a loan versus cash. The UK standard lending agreement also covers items such as dividends and voting rights and is, therefore, the preferred transaction structure in the equity repo market.

Bonds Borrowed/Collateral Pledged

In the case of a bonds borrowed/collateral pledged trade the institution lending the bonds does not want or need to receive cash against them, as it is already cash rich and would only have to reinvest any further cash generated. As such this transaction only occurs with special collateral. The dealer borrows the special bonds and pledges securities of similar quality and value (general collateral). The dealer builds in a fee payable to the lending institution as an incentive to do the trade.

To illustrate a bond borrow/collateral pledged trade, suppose ABC Bank plc wishes to borrow DKK 300 million of the Danish government bond 8% 2001. ABC owns the Danish government bond 7% 2007 and is prepared to pay a customer a 40 bp fee in order to borrow the 8% 2001 for one month. The market price of the 8% 2001 (including accrued interest) is 112.70. The total value of DKK 300 million nominal is therefore DKK 338,100,000. The market price of the 7% 2007 (including accrued interest) is 102.55. In order to fully collateralise the customer ABC needs to pledge (338,100,000/1.0255) which is 329,692,832.76; when rounded to the nearest DKK 1 million this becomes DKK 330 million nominal of the 7% 2007. In a bonds borrowed/collateral pledged trade, both securities are delivered free of payment and ABC Bank plc would pay the customer a 40 bp borrowing fee upon termination. In our example the fee payable would be

$$338,100,000 \times (31/360) \times (0.4/100) = DKK\ 112,700$$

Borrow versus Letter of Credit

This instrument is used when an institution lending securities does not require cash, but takes a third-party bank letter of credit as collateral. However, since banks typically charge 25–50 basis points for this facility, transactions of this kind are relatively rare.

Cross-Currency Repo

All of the examples of repo trades discussed so far have used cash and securities denominated in the same currency, for example gilts trading versus sterling cash, and so on. In fact there is no requirement to limit oneself to single-currency transactions. It is possible to trade, say, gilts versus US dollar cash (or any other currency) or pledge Spanish government bonds against borrowing Japanese government bonds. A cross-currency repo is essentially a plain vanilla transaction, but where collateral that is handed over is denominated in a different currency to that of the cash lent against it. Other features of cross-currency repo include:

- Possible significant daylight credit exposure on the transaction if securities cannot settle versus payment.
- A requirement for the transaction to be covered by appropriate legal documentation.
- Fluctuating foreign exchange rates, which mean that it is likely that the transaction will need to be marked-to-market frequently in order to ensure that cash or securities remain fully collateralised.

It is also necessary to take into account the fluctuations in the relevant exchange rate when marking securities used as collateral, which are obviously handed over against cash that is denominated in a different currency.

To illustrate a cross-currency repo, suppose that on 4 January 2000 a hedge fund manager funds a long position in US Treasury securities against sterling, for value the following day. It is offered a bid of 4.90% in the one week, and the market maker also requires a 2% margin. The one-week LIBOR rate is 4.95% and the exchange rate at the time of trade is £1/$1.63. The terms of the trade are given below:

Trade date	4 January 2000
Settlement date	5 January 2000
Stock (collateral)	US Treasury 6.125% 2001
Nominal amount	$100 million
Repo rate	4.90% (sterling)
Term	7 days
Maturity date	12 January 2001
Clean price	99-19
Accrued interest	5 days (0.0841346)
Dirty price	99.6778846
Gross settlement amount	$99,677,884.62
Net settlement amount (after 2% haircut)	$97,723,416.29
Net wired settlement amount in sterling	£59,953,016.13
Repo interest	£56,339.41
Sterling termination money	£60,009,355.54

The repo market has allowed the hedge fund to borrow in sterling at a rate below the cost of unsecured borrowing in the money market (4.95%). The repo market maker is "overcollateralised" by the difference between the value of the bonds (in £) and the loan proceeds (2%). A rise in USD yields or a fall in the USD exchange rate value will adversely affect the value of the bonds, causing the market maker to be undercollateralised.

Repo-to-Maturity

A repo-to-maturity is a classic repo where the termination date on the repo matches the maturity date of the bond in the repo. We can discuss this trade by considering the Bloomberg screen used to analyse repo-to-maturity, which is REM. The screen used to analyse a reverse repo-to-maturity is RRM.

Screen REM is used to analyse the effect of borrowing funds in repo to purchase a bond, where the bond is the collateral security. This is conventional and we considered this earlier. In essence, the screen will compare the financing costs on the borrowed funds to the coupons

EXHIBIT 10.16 Bloomberg Screen REM; Used for Repo-to-Maturity Analysis, for UK Treasury 7% 2001 on 14 August 2001

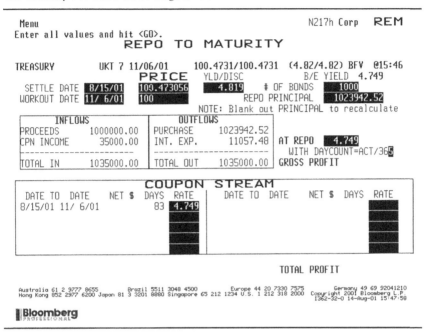

Source: ©Bloomberg L.P. Reproduced with permission.

received on the bond up to and including maturity. The key determining factor is the repo rate used to finance the borrowing. From Exhibit 10.16 we see that the screen calculates the break-even rate, which is the rate at which the financing cost equals the bond return. The screen also works out cash flows at start and termination, and the borrowed amount is labelled as the "repo principal." This is the bond total consideration. Under "outflows" we see the repo interest at the selected repo rate, labelled as "Int. Exp." Gross profit is the total inflow minus total outflow, which in our example is zero because the repo rate entered is the break-even rate. The user will enter the actual repo rate payable to calculate the total profit.

A reverse repo-to-maturity is a reverse repo with matching repo termination and bond expiry dates. This shown at Exhibit 10.17.

Repo-to-maturity is a low-risk trade as the financing profit on the bond position is known with certainty to the bond's maturity. For financial institutions that operate on an accruals basis rather mark-to-market basis, the trade can guarantee a profit and not suffer any losses in the interim while they hold the bond.

EXHIBIT 10.17   Bloomberg Screen RRM, Used for Reverse Repo-to-Maturity Analysis, for UK Treasury 7% 2001 on 14 August 2001

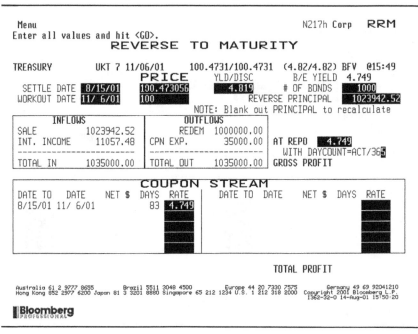

Source: ©Bloomberg L.P. Used with permission.

MARGIN

To reduce the level of risk exposure in a repo transaction, it is common for the lender of cash to ask for a margin, which is where the market value of collateral is higher than the cash value of cash lent out in the repo. This is a form of protection should the cash-borrowing counterparty default on the loan. Another term for margin is overcollateralisation or haircut. There are two types of margin: an initial margin taken at the start of the trade, and variation margin which is called if required during the term of the trade.

Initial Margin

The cash proceeds in a repo are typically no more than the market value of the collateral. This minimises credit exposure by equating the value of the cash to that of the collateral. The market value of the collateral is calculated at its dirty price, not clean price—that is, including accrued interest. This is referred to as *accrual pricing*. To calculate the accrued interest on the (bond) collateral, we require the day-count basis for the particular bond.

The start proceeds of a repo can be less than the market value of the collateral by an agreed amount or percentage. This is known as the *initial margin* or *haircut*. The initial margin protects the buyer against:

- A sudden fall in the market value of the collateral.
- Illiquidity of collateral.
- Other sources of volatility of value (for example, approaching maturity).
- Counterparty risk.

The margin level of repo varies from 0–2% for collateral such as UK gilts or German Bunds, to 5% for cross-currency and equity repo, to 10–35% for emerging market debt repo.

In both classic repo and sell/buyback, any initial margin is given to the supplier of cash in the transaction. This remains true in the case of specific repo. For initial margin the market value of the bond collateral is reduced (or given a "haircut") by the percentage of the initial margin and the nominal value determined from this reduced amount. In a stock loan transaction the lender of stock will ask for margin.

There are two methods for calculating the margin. For a 2% margin this could be one of the following:

- Dirty price of the bonds × 0.98
- Dirty price of the bonds/1.02

The two methods do not give the same value! The RRRA repo page on Bloomberg uses the second method for its calculations and this method is turning into something of a convention.

For a 2% margin level the BMA/ISMA, GMRA defines a "margin ratio" as

$$\frac{\text{Collateral value}}{\text{Cash}} = 102\%$$

The size of margin required in any particular transaction is a function of the following:

- The credit quality of the counterparty supplying the collateral; for example, a central bank counterparty, interbank counterparty and corporate will all suggest different margin levels.

■ The term of the repo; an overnight repo is inherently lower risk than a one-year risk.

■ The duration (price volatility) of the collateral; for example, a T-bill compared to the long bond.

■ The existence or absence of a legal agreement; repo traded under a standard agreement is considered lower risk.

Certain market practitioners, particularly those that work on bond research desks, believe that the level of margin is a function of the volatility of the collateral stock. This may be either, say, one-year historical volatility or the implied volatility given by option prices. Given a volatility level of 10%, suggesting a maximum expected price movement of −10% to +10%, the margin level may be set at 5% to cover expected movement in the market value of the collateral. This approach to setting initial margin is regarded as onerous by most repo traders, given the differing volatility levels of stocks within GC bands. The counterparty credit risk and terms of trade remain the most influential elements in setting margin, followed by quality of collateral.

In the final analysis margin is required to guard against market risk—the risk that the value of collateral will drop during the course of the repo. Therefore the margin call must reflect the risks prevalent in the market at the time; extremely volatile market conditions may call for large increases in initial margin.

Variation Margin

The market value of the collateral is maintained through the use of variation margin. So, if the market value of the collateral falls, the buyer calls for extra cash or collateral. If the market value of the collateral rises, the seller calls for extra cash or collateral. In order to reduce the administrative burden, margin calls can be limited to changes in the market value of the collateral in excess of an agreed amount or percentage, which is called a margin maintenance limit.

The standard market documentation that exists for the three structures covered so far includes clauses that allow parties to a transaction to call for variation margin during the term of a repo. This can be in the form of extra collateral (if the value of the collateral has dropped in relation to the asset exchanged) or a return of collateral, if the value has risen. If the cash-borrowing counterparty is unable to supply more collateral where required, they will have to return a portion of the cash loan. Both parties have an interest in making and meeting margin calls, although there is no obligation. The level at which variation margin is triggered is often agreed beforehand in the legal agreement put in place between individual counter-parties. Although primarily viewed as an

EXHIBIT 10.18   Illustration of Variation Margin

5 January

£1million UKT 5% 2004

Repo seller ⟶ Bank repo desk

£937,708 loan proceeds

A variation margin call is made one month later after the price of the stock has fallen to 92.75

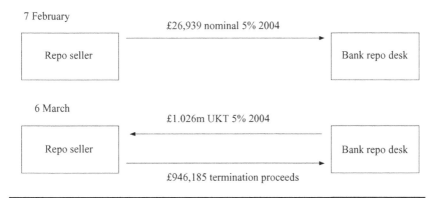

7 February

£26,939 nominal 5% 2004

Repo seller ⟶ Bank repo desk

6 March

£1.026m UKT 5% 2004

Repo seller ⟵ Bank repo desk

£946,185 termination proceeds

instrument used by the supplier of cash against a fall in the value of the collateral, variation margin can of course also be called by the repo seller if the value of the collateral has risen in value.

Let's illustrate variation margin as it is applied to during the term of a trade. Exhibit 10.18 shows a 60-day repo in the 5% Treasury 2004, a UK gilt, where a margin of 2% is taken. The repo rate is 5½%. The start of the trade is 5 January 2000. The clean price of the gilt is 95.25.

Nominal amount	1,000,000.00
Principal	£952,500.00
Accrued interest (29 days)	£3961.75
Total consideration	£956,461.75

The consideration is divided by 1.02, the amount of margin, to give £937,707.60. Assume that this is rounded up to the nearest pound.

Loan amount	£937,708.00
Repo interest at 5½%	£8477.91
Termination proceeds	£946,185.91

Assume that one month later there has been a catastrophic fall in the bond market and the 5% 2004 gilt is trading down at 92.75. Following this drop, the market value of the collateral is now:

Principal	£927,500.00
Accrued interest (59 days)	£8082.19
Market value	£935,582.19

However, the repo desk has lent £937,708 against this security, which exceeds its market value. Under a variation margin arrangement it can call margin from the counterparty in the form of general collateral securities or cash.

The formula used to calculate the amount required to restore the original margin of 2% is given by

Margin adjustment
= [(Original consideration + Repo interest charged to date)
× (1 + Initial margin)]
– (New all-in-one price × Nominal amount)

This becomes

$$[(937,708 + 4,238.96) \times (1 + 0.02)] - (0.93558219 \times 1,000,000)$$
$$= £25,203.71$$

The margin requirement can be taken as additional stock or cash. In practice, margin calls are made on what is known as a portfolio basis, based on the net position resulting from all repos and reverse repos in place between the two counterparties, so that a margin delivery may be made in a general collateral stock rather than more of the original repo stock. The diagrams below show the relevant cash flows at the various dates.

SELECTED COUNTRY REPO MARKETS

There are developed and liquid repo markets throughout the world, in North America, Europe, Asia and Japan. There is a considerable amount of cross-border trading, as well as repo in so-called emerging markets. The size and liquidity of different markets varies but the aggregate whole is considerable, with a large volume of stock being repoed at any one time.

The depth and liquidity of repo markets in Europe varies by each country. Practitioners new to any particular market often contact relevant brokers for specific operating details. Exhibit 10.19 shows the

EXHIBIT 10.19 Approximate Daily Turnover in Selected Country Markets, June 2000

	Daily turnover (€ billion)	Nominal outstanding (€ billion)
Belgium	26.2	86.5
France	42.3	292
Germany	60	137.7
Italy	53	113.3
Spain	21.3	54.4
United States	not available	1,528.9

Source: Euroclear, Clearstream, SICOVAM, Nomura.

approximate daily turnover in selected markets, against the US market for comparison. In this section we introduce selected European repo markets.

France

Development of the repo market in government securities has been actively encouraged by the authorities in France, indeed the Banque de France views the instrument as one method by which bank systemic risk, inherent in unsecured interbank lending, can be reduced. From December 1993 repo has been formally described in legislation that also describes provisions for netting, repo and derivatives, among other areas.[19] Under this legislation repo is defined as a transaction that involves transfer of securities, with both counterparties committed to sell and buyback (or buy and sell, as appropriate) the securities transferred at an agreed price and date. Under this definition the transaction cannot be described as a secured loan. The repo legal agreement in France is the *Pension Livree*, although generally referred to simply as the *Pension*. Repo can be undertaken in the following instruments:

- Securities listed on a French or foreign stock exchange.
- Securities listed on the seconde marché.
- Negotiable debt instruments traded on a French or foreign regulated market, including government paper such as BTANs, OATs, and Treasury bills, as well as CDs and certain other securities.

Other features of the French repo market legal agreement include:

---

[19] See "Repo Market Survey," ISMA (1997).

EXHIBIT 10.20   Breakdown of French Government Bond Repo, 2001

	2001 Q1	2002 Q2
Repo trades		
▪ Value (€ billion)	2.046	1.893
▪ Average size (€ million)	39	37
▪ Outstanding value (€ billion)	184.06	171.17
Collateral		
▪ OAT	54.50%	59%
▪ BTF	13%	9.50%
▪ BTAN	30.50%	29%
▪ Total French government	98%	97.50%
▪ Other securities	2%	2.50%
Repo rate		
▪ Fixed rate	41.50%	39.91%
▪ Floating rate	58.30%	59.91%
▪ Zero	0.20%	0.18%

Source: SICOVAM.

▪ The ability for any corporate, local authority, or financial entity to engage in repo.
▪ A description of margin, without making its use compulsory.
▪ A description of the process followed by the stock buyer in the event of default, including a capability to hold stock sold as collateral.
▪ An allowance for set-off and netting in the event of default and insolvency.

Repo in France is straightforward classic repo and an on-balance-sheet instrument. The market is large and liquid, with daily average turnover of around €40 billion and volume outstanding of approximately €200 billion as at June 2002.[20] The average term of trade is 14 days. Along with countries such as Germany and the Netherlands in the Euro area, French government repo rates invariably trade at a slight premium to the euro GC curve, although as we note later, there is no uniform GC rate due to the perceived credit differences between euro-denominated debt of different sovereign issuers. A BIS study reported that during the first quarter of 2000 French government repo traded approximately 4–5 basis points below the interbank rate in the short dates, that is, overnight to one week, and 8–10 basis points below for one- to three-month maturities.[21] A breakdown of the market is given at Exhibit 10.20.

---
[20] Source is SICOVAM.

EXHIBIT 10.21   Societe Generale French Government Repo Rates on Bloomberg, as at 6 August 2001

```
10                                              DGB 4a Corp    SOCB
Screen Printed

                              SG
                                                    Page 1 of 1
 19:20:22          SOCIETE  GENERALE

              PENSION LIVREE  ON  GOVERNMENT  SECURITIES

      MATURITY    -    ASK    -    BID    -    SIZE
      TN               4.75   -    4.89   -    100 X 100
      1S               4.71   -    4.83   -    100 X 100
      1M               4.77   -    4.89   -    50 X 50
      2M               4.89   -    5.01   -    20 X 20
      3M               4.91   -    5.03   -    20 X 20
      6M               4.96   -    5.08   -    20 X 20
      9M               5.00   -    5.12   -    20 X 20
      12M              5.04   -    5.16   -    20 X 20

           ADJUST        VALUE TOM DOMESTIC CLEARING



Australia 61 2 9777 8655   Brazil 5511 3048 4500   Europe 44 20 7330 7575   Germany 49 69 92041210
Hong Kong 852 2977 6200 Japan 81 3 3201 8880 Singapore 65 212 1234 U.S. 1 212 318 2000 Copyright 2001 Bloomberg L.P.
                                                                           I432-212-0 06-Aug-01 10:50:58
```

Bloomberg

Source: ©Societe Generale, ©Bloomberg L.P. Reproduced with permission.

There are a number of unusual features in the French repo market, in addition to the definition of repo in domestic law. These include a registered market-making system, as one observes in the cash government market, and a significant volume of floating-rate repo. A typical market maker's repo screen is shown at Exhibit 10.21.

Registered Market-Making Structure

As of June 2002 there were 11 firms registered as market makers or primary dealers in French government debt repo. These were originally known as *Spécialistes de la Pension sur Valeurs du Trésor* or SPVTs but are now termed SVTs; they are registered at the French Treasury and are required to make two-way prices in government security repo out to a three-month maturity. The ready dealing size that must be quoted is a maximum of €100 million for overnight trades, decreasing to €20 million for three-month trades. This formal market-making system dates from 1994 and firms that are registered as both cash and repo market

---

[21] Bank for International Settlements, Implications of repo markets for central banks, August 2001.

makers include Societe Generale, BNP Paribas and Credit Commercial de France. These firms post prices on standard vendor services such as Reuters and Bloomberg.

Floating-Rate Repo

An unusual and possibly unique feature of French government repo is the floating-rate repo, which makes up more than half of repo transactions. Before the introduction of the euro, this transaction was based on the French franc interbank unsecured overnight rate known as the *Taux Moyen Pondéré* or TMP. It is now based on the euro overnight rate or EONIA. This rate is the general overnight rate and so practically immune to market manipulation, given the size of the euro interbank market. In a floating-rate repo trade the final rate paid by the stock seller is calculated as the mean of the overnight offer rate applicable each day during the term of the loan. Depending on the credit quality of the stock seller, the actual repo rate may be a spread over or under EONIA.

Settlement

The main securities settlement mechanisms in France is SICOVAM, the central securities depositary system. This body operates a system known as Relit Grand Vitesse or RGV, an integrated real-time settlement mechanism for bonds, money market instruments and equities. It provides real-time matching, settlement and reporting cycles, and operates for 22 hours out of 24. Put simply, the settlement process works as follows:

- SICOVAM continuously calculates each market participant's purchasing power on the basis of cash positions, securities held that can be used as collateral, and collateral and other guarantees held outside the system.
- If a participant has insufficient funds to settle a security transfer during the day, the Banque de France automatically enters into a repo trade with it to guarantee final payment; this eliminates intraday cash shortfall, thus reducing intraday settlement risk.

Repo trades initiated by the Banque de France are settled by close-of-business that day. Thus irrevocable settlement is guaranteed by the Banque de France, and the use of these intraday repos provides liquidity in central bank money to the bank money transfer system, known as TBF.

Spain

The repo market in Spain has a number of distinctive features. One of the most significant of these is that the market trades sell/buybacks rather than classic repo, and by local convention there are two types of transaction: *simultneas* for market professionals and repos traded by other entities such as investment funds and which are also sell/buy-backs. The Bank of Spain defines a sell/buyback as a transfer of owner-ship of stock. The main difference between the two types is that in repos the bonds bought (borrowed) are frozen by the Central de Anotaciones, which is the Bank of Spain book-entry system, until the maturity of the transaction. This feature reduces the inherent credit risk, albeit with the restriction that the bonds are locked away for the term of the trade. In simultneas trades, the bonds are not frozen and so may be sold short. For this reason the majority of domestic professional trading and virtu-ally all nonresident trading are conducted in the form of simultneas, with repos being undertaken by domestic investment funds, retail inves-tors and third parties known as *terceros*. The professional market is dominated by commercial banks. The Spanish market is possibly unique in that domestic savings institutions, known as *Cajas*, market repo as a retail savings product to private customers, who are able to invest in this product at local branches.

The repo market in government securities comprises T-bills known as *Letras*, bonds of between three and five years maturity (*Bonos*) and bonds of 10–15 years maturity (*Obligaciones*). Repo in Letras was introduced first, in 1987. At the start of 2002 there was approximately €251.3 billion nominal of government debt outstanding; repo volume was approximately €141 billion per month.[22]

The money market in Spain, as in other Eurozone markets, is quoted on a 360-day basis. From the start of the euro, as expected Span-ish government collateral trades at a premium to the euro overnight rate (EONIA), although the margin is not great, usually around 5–10 basis points below. Repo in specific issues is on average around 7–9 basis points below Spanish government "GC" rates. There is no real "GC" as such in Euro government repo, as certain collateral trades cheap and others expensive. For instance, German government collateral trades roughly around 5 basis points below others, but for various reasons connected with special status of certain stocks, Spanish collateral also traded through GC. Certain government collateral, for example Italian and Belgian bonds, trade above German, Dutch and Spanish collateral. Generic Euro repo rates are posted on the British Bankers Association page on Bloomberg.

Settlement of Spanish repo is via the Bank of Spain's book entry sys-tem, which allows same-day settlement. For nonresident counterparties settlement is next-day.

---

[22] ISMA (according to trades matched via TRAX).

Spanish government repo rates are posted on numerous vendors including Bloomberg and Reuters; rates can be viewed on Bloomberg page CIMD and Reuters page CIMF among others.

Germany

For Germany we consider briefly the Bund and Pfandbriefe markets.

German Government Repo

The market in German government bonds or Bund market is large and liquid, possibly the most liquid in continental Europe. Sizes of individual issues are at least €10 billion, often larger, and this has allowed Bunds to achieve benchmark status, in a manner similar to US Treasury securities. The Bund repo market reflects the underlying liquidity of cash Bund securities; euro GC prices are those of Bund and French government securities, while remaining Eurozone repo rates are quoted as a spread to these GC rates. The market informally ranks Bund repo as the lowest Euro GC rates, which are rated as equal to French and Dutch government repo for credit quality but considered to be more liquid.

Government bond repo is carried out in the instruments listed in Exhibit 10.22, with ISMA-approved GC securities marked with a *.

Formally repo is described under German commercial law, and classic repo does not require a master agreement in order to be enforceable. The standard legal agreement in any case is the German Master Agreement, applicable to domestic deals. The legal framework is well established. Most market participants use the BMA/ISMA GMRA for international business, although a considerable volume of domestic business is carried out via undocumented sell/buybacks. The GMRA, as applied to repo in Germany, contains an annexe to make it effective under local law, the domestic *Rahmenvertrag für echte Wertpapierpensions-geschäfte*.

EXHIBIT 10.22   German Government Securities Used in Repo

Instrument	Maturity
Treasury bills	1–12 months
Bundesschatzanweisungen	1–2 years
Bundesrepublik (Bundes)*	1–30 years
German Unity Fund*	1–3 years
ERP Sondervermoegen	1–4 years
Bundesobligation (BOBL, OBL)*	1–5 years
Treuhandanstalt*	1–30 years
Treuhand–Obligation (TOBL)*	1–5 years

EXHIBIT 10.23   The Specific Repo Rate Spread to the GC Rate for the DBR 3.75%
January 2009 Bond, 1999–2000

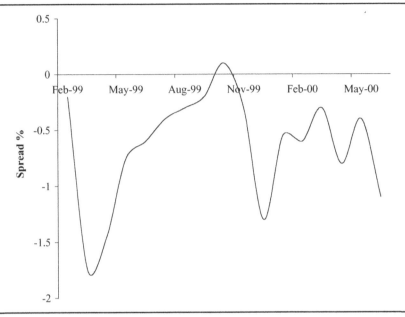

Rates source: Deutsche Bank. Used with permission.

Buy/sellbacks are also common in the German market; the legal
arrangements for them are covered by a buy/sellback annexe of the BMA/
ISMA Global Master Repurchase Agreement. Traditionally, securities
financing has been undertaken using buy/sellbacks; however, this is no
longer the case and today classic repo is more prevalent. The main reason
for the increasing popularity of classic repo was (and is) that unlike buy/
sellback, classic repo was described by the GMRA and allowed margining and repricing of securities.

The market is a traditional OTC one, with trades conducted on the
telephone directly between banking counterparties or via brokers. There
are a number of electronic trading platforms being developed primarily
for the interbank market.

During 2002 Bund GC traded in a range around 2–10 basis points
below EURIBOR in the short dates, while on occasion trading in specials went down to 90 basis points below the GC rate. As in other markets, there are a number of reasons why government stocks become
special in the German market; however, the primary factor is the extent
of its deliverability into the Bund futures contract. For illustration we
show, in Exhibit 10.23, the spread below GC for repo in the DBR

3.75% January 2009 bond, the 10-year benchmark and also the cheapest-to-deliver (CTD) issue for the March 1999 Bund contract. However, it was not the CTD bond after expiry of June 1999 contract, and the extent of specialness declined after this point. Interestingly, this bond remained in the delivery basket for subsequent contracts and its special status fluctuated. Arbitrage traders, who wish to exploit the repo rate differential between benchmark and "off-the-run" issues and GC and special stocks, are active participants in the Bund repo market.

Pfandbriefe Repo

Pfandbriefe are domestic mortgage-backed securities backed with the full faith and credit of the federal government. As such they may be considered to be similar in status to government agency securities in the US dollar market. Large-size issues are known as "Jumbo Pfandbriefe." There is an active market in Pfandbriefe repo, and from January 1999 a market maker facility was introduced, which contributed substantially to liquidity. Essentially, the arrangement is that the underwriting bank (or lead manager) behind the issue of a cash market security also undertakes to make a market in repo in that issue. The only conditions are that the individual stock has a minimum issue size of €1.25 billion and has at least two years to maturity. Market makers are required to quote two-way prices in up to €15 million, with a maximum quote spread of 20 basis points. Exhibits 10.24 and 10.25 show typical brokers screens for government bond repo.

Jumbo issues generally trade with the euro overnight rate (EONIA), although the smaller-sized issues sometimes go special. The offered side in repo is dominated by investment funds and the mortgage bank issuers themselves.

Italy

The Italian repo market dates from 1970 and is the oldest repo market in Europe. It is also the largest European market. Due to historical tax and legal complications with classic repo, trades are actually sell/buybacks, although confusingly they are called "repo."[23] Until recently Italian government bonds paid coupons net of tax, hence this created different opportunities for different users of the repo market. Nonresident institutions were able to reclaim withholding tax via a domestic custodian, while resident institutions accessed the repo market to generate tax cred-

---

[23] Italian repo remains predominantly sell/buyback because of taxation and other issues. These include the retail origination and emphasis of the transaction, and the fact that both legs of a repo may be treated as separate transactions and attract two lots of stamp duty.

EXHIBIT 10.24   German Government Two- and Five-Year Collateral, Repo Rates on Garban ICAP Screen, 9 January 2001

GC	GC	DMK - 10 Year	Germany	Italy	Italy CCT / CTZ	Belgium	UK - Gilts	French	Eurobonds

2 year				Others			
DEC02TRH				9,0JAN01			
TREU 7.125 JAN03				FEB01UNT			
C-20/3	4.62 -	25.0x		OBL 118			
OBL 126				MAR01SCH			
6,75AP03				OBL 119			
APR03TRH				8,37MY01			
OBL 127				JUN01SCH			
JUN03TRH				OBL 120			
				AUG01UNT			
				SEP01SCH			
				8,25SP01			
				OBL 121			
				C-9/2	- 4.70	x100.0	
5 Year				JUN02 SCHATZ			2<
6,50CT05				T-12/1	4.75 -	5.0x	
6,0JAN06				C-7/2	- 4.68	x25.0S	
6,0FEB06				SEP02SCH			
BUND 6.25 APR06			2<	BUND 7.125 DEC02			2<
SN	4.67 -	50.0x		C1M	4.72 - 4.65	25.0x25.0	
C-20/3	4.62 - 4.57	25.0x50.0S		C-20/3	4.50 - 4.40	25.0x50.0S	
				OBL 135			
				S1M	- 4.68	x25.0S	
				6,0JAN07			
				BUND 5.25 JAN08			
				T1W	4.74 -	20.0x	
				BUND 6.25 JAN24			
				S-15/1	4.75 -	14.0x	
				BUND 6.25 JAN30			
				S-17/1	- 4.75	x5.0S	

Source: Garban ICAP. Reproduced with permission.

its which were then used as an offset against income from other sources. From January 1997 bonds paid coupon gross to nonresidents. Repo rates are quoted on both a net and gross basis due to taxable coupon issue, depending on domicile of the investor. Due to the requirement for a domestic custodian all trades are settled onshore. As in the United States the domestic market has a strong retail involvement with interest from savings institutions and fund managers.

The size of the repo market reflects the size of the cash market in government bonds, which is the largest in Europe. The instruments used in the market are listed in Exhibit 10.26. Securities marked with a ~ are listed by ISMA as Euro GC securities. Most transactions are one-week maturity, while, unusually for repo, overnight trades are rarer. This may be because stamp duty is chargeable at a flat rate on domestic deals, and so this is an incentive for market participants to undertake longer-duration repo trades.

Repo settlement is carried out via a domestic custodian bank or via Euroclear or Clear-stream Banking. Generally BTPs, CCTs and BOTs settle domestically while CTEs settle though Euroclear and/or Clear-

EXHIBIT 10.25 German Government 10-Year Collateral, Repo Rates on Garban ICAP Screen, 9 January 2001

| GC | GC | DMK - 10 Year | Germany | Italy | Italy CCT / CTZ | Belgium | UK - Gilts | French | Eurobonds |

10 Year				10 Year		
NEW 7/08				BUND 5.375 JAN10		8<
BUND OLD JUL08				SN	- 4.65	x22.0
SN	- 4.50	x19.0		S1W	4.70 - 4.55	25.0x50.0
BUND 3.75 JAN09			2<	C1W	4.70 - 4.55	25.0x25.0S
T-12/1	4.74 -	5.0x		C2W	4.60 - 4.40	25.0Sx25.0S
S-31/1	4.75 - 4.68	25.0x25.0S		C-20/3	4.50 - 4.42	50.0x25.0
BUND NEW JUL09				C-20/6	4.33 - 4.23	25.0Sx25.0S
TN	4.77 -	70.0x		MARJUN	- 4.15	x25.0
BUND OLD JUL09			2<	C1Y	4.27 - 4.15	25.0x25.0
T1W	4.75 -	25.0x		BUND 5.25 JUL10		6<
S1W	- 4.67	x37.5		C-25/1	4.75 -	22.0x
				C1M	4.73 - 4.65	25.0x25.0S
				C-20/3	4.65 - 4.57	25.0x25.0
				C-20/6	4.55 - 4.35	25.0x25.0
				JUNSEP	4.10 - 3.80	25.0x25.0
				C1Y	4.25 - 4.20	50.0x50.0S
				BUND 5.25 JAN11		5<
				SN	- 4.60	x22.0
				C-14/3	4.65 -	25.0x
				C-20/6	4.50 - 4.35	25.0x25.0
				C-20/9	4.38 - 4.25	25.0x25.0S
				C1Y	4.30 - 4.15	25.0x25.0

Source: Garban ICAP. Reproduced with permission.

EXHIBIT 10.26 Italian Government Securities Used in Repo

Instrument	Maturity
Buoni Ordinari del Tesoro (BOT)~	1–12 months
Buoni Poliennali del Tesoro (BTP)~	2–30 years
Certificati di Credito del Tesoro (CCT)~	2–10 years
Certificati di Credito del Tesoro (ICTZ)~	1–2 years
Credito Tesoro (CTES)	1–2 years

stream. The stock-lending market is virtually nonexistent, as there is no official facility and banks are not keen to enter into a stock loan, as they remain unfamiliar with the concept.

ISMA's Italian regional committee produced an annexe which adapts Annex III of the GMRA (which contains provision for sell/buybacks) for transactions involving an Italian party or Italian securities.

Exhibit 10.27 shows bid-offer repo rates for specific Italian government collateral on a typical broker screen. The dealing size is also indicated, so for instance the December 2001 CCT issue is bid at 4.72% and offered at 4.65%, both up to €25 million. Not all issues have a two-way price posted.

EXHIBIT 10.27 Repo Rates for Specific Italian Government Collateral, Garban ICAP Screen on 9 January 2001

| GC | GC | DMK - 10 Year | Germany | Italy | Italy CCT / CTZ |

		CCT			< >
CCTAPR01					
CCTDEC01					
	C2W	4.72 - 4.65	25.0x25.0		
CCTFEB02					
CCTNOV02					
	C2W	4.75 - 4.65	25.0x25.0		
CCTDEC02					
CCTFEB03					
	C2W	4.74 - 4.69	25.0x25.0		
CCTJUL03					
	C1W	4.70 -	25.0x		
CCTNOV03					2<
	TN	4.65 -	10.0x		
	SN	4.70 -	15.0x		
CCTJAN04					2<
	SN	4.60 -	60.0x		
	C1W	4.60 -	40.0x		
CCTMAR04					
	SN	4.65 - 4.60	7.5x7.5		
CCTSEP04					
	ON	4.65 -	2.5x		
CCTMAY05					
	ON	4.65 -	2.5x		
CCTOCT05					
CCTMAR06					
	C1W	4.72 -	25.0x		
CCTDEC06					2<
	SN	- 4.70	x25.0		
	C1W	4.74 -	25.0x		

Source: Garban ICAP. Reproduced with permission.

CHAPTER 11

European Residential Mortgage-Backed Securities

Phil Adams, Ph.D.
Director
Barclays Capital

esidential mortgages were the first asset class to be securitised in Europe. Although the introduction of new asset classes has reduced the dominance of residential mortgage-backed securities (RMBS), it remains the largest sector today, typically accounting for approximately 35–40% of new issuance. European RMBS have been popular with investors, not least because their performance has been very good. Since the beginning of this market there has never been a default on a European RMBS transaction, very few transactions have been downgraded and none of these downgrades have occurred as a result of a deterioration in the performance of the collateral. These downgrades have all been as a result of the downgrade of third parties supporting the transaction. European ABS are now much less reliant on third-party support, so the level of downgrades experienced between 1991 and 1994 should be less likely to happen again if similar circumstances arose.

The European RMBS market was started in the United Kingdom in 1987 by the centralised lenders that had been set up following the deregulation of the mortgage market in the mid-1980s. The United Kingdom was followed by Spain, which saw its first RMBS issue in 1991. The recession in the early 1990s caused several RMBS issuers in the United Kingdom to withdraw from the market and there was little or no issuance in the United Kingdom or Spain for a few years. The market started to expand again in the mid-1990s (see Exhibit 11.1) and it was around

355

EXHIBIT 11.1   Issuance Volumes of European RMBS (€ billion)

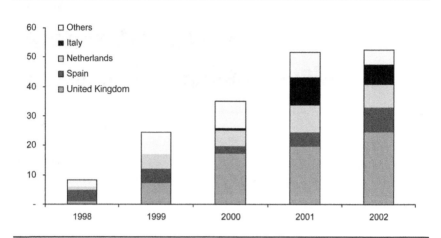

Source: Barclays Capital.

this time that RMBS started to be issued in other European countries. This growth has generally relied on changes to the legal framework within each country and has been driven by a number of factors. For a number of lenders, securitisation provides their primary source of funding. Banks have found that deposits have been switched to other investments and that there has been a need to access new investors as their traditional investors have sought to diversify across other euro assets.

Although we may refer to the European RMBS market as if it is a single entity, in practice it is a collection of diverse markets, with each individual country's issuance reflecting its unique cultural and legal environment. However, there are also considerable similarities between the basic characteristics of European mortgages, and RMBS structures largely follow just a few standard models.

INDUSTRY OVERVIEW

The economy drives the mortgage markets, but governments also play a role. In many countries it has been long-term government policy to promote home ownership, usually through the tax system, and particularly targeting low income households. These schemes have generally been successful but the level of home ownership still varies considerably across Europe (see Exhibit 11.2).

EXHIBIT 11.2   Home Ownership Rates in Europe (%)

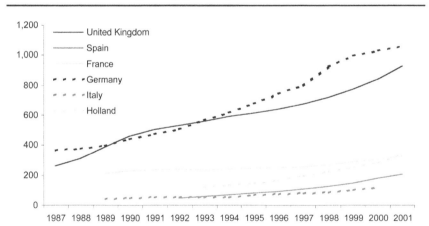

Source: European Mortgage Federation.

EXHIBIT 11.3   Outstanding Mortgage Debt (€ billion)

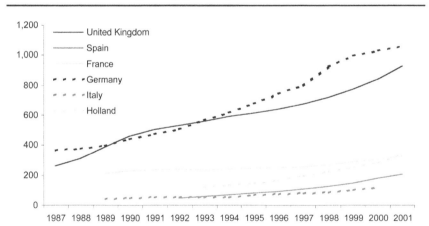

Source: European Mortgage Federation, Bank of England, Bank of Spain, Bundesbank, Datamonitor.

The economic environment has been favourable for the mortgage markets since the recession in the early 1990s in most European countries. Economic growth has been robust, which has brought with it an extended period of real earnings increases and a reduction in unemployment rates. In addition, inflation has been reduced in many countries, allowing interest rates to fall to historically low levels. Against this background, it is not surprising that the mortgage markets have been growing strongly (see Exhibit 11.3).

Strong economic growth with falling unemployment and high consumer confidence has fuelled the demand for housing. Strong real wage growth and falling interest rates improved the affordability of mortgages, and as a result house prices have risen substantially in many countries (although Germany is a notable exception).

This period of strong house price appreciation has followed a period of lacklustre growth or even declines in the early 1990s. The UK housing market was affected particularly severely. Legislative changes in the mid-1980s opened up the UK mortgage market to bank insurance companies and other lenders. Centralised lenders and some foreign lenders entered the UK market and the competition that ensued led to the development of innovative mortgage products, such as self-certified mortgages, 100% loan-to-value loans, and a range of new repayment methods. In addition to the new products, the competitive environment and the favourable economic background caused many lenders to relax their lending criteria. This contributed to the high number of defaults when house prices started to decline in 1989.

During the recession that followed, some lenders withdrew from the market, and those that remained were forced to review their underwriting criteria. As a result, the industry became more risk averse. The recession also left a large number of potential borrowers with adverse credit histories who were then unable to borrow from traditional lenders. This set the stage for the emergence of the nonconforming mortgage sector as the housing market improved. These niche lenders took a risk-based pricing approach to mortgage lending and specifically targeted clients who were unable to borrow from mainstream lenders. These lenders have become significant issuers of mortgage-backed securities.

In addition to the emergence of the nonconforming sector, the United Kingdom has also seen the development of an active "buy-to-let" market, flexible mortgages, and a reverse mortgage market, all of which have been used as collateral for MBS transactions.

Types of Mortgages

There is a considerable variety of mortgages on offer to European consumers, many tailored to the particular circumstances or borrower preferences of a particular country. However, for an investor in an RMBS transaction, these various characteristics can be divided into two largely separate categories: factors affecting the credit quality of the mortgage and those influencing the borrower's payment profile. To a certain extent, the required payment profile on a loan can affect its credit quality so this artificial categorisation is not perfect but it is useful for this discussion. We discuss the factors affecting credit quality later, and the remainder of this section concentrates on the cash flow properties of mortgages.

Interest Rates

The type of interest rate charged on mortgage loans varies between countries. UK mortgages have traditionally charged a variable rate of interest, which has been adjusted at the discretion of the lending institution. However, interest rates that are tied to a particular benchmark interest rate (such as LIBOR or the Bank of England Repo Rate) have become more popular. In Spain, for example, variable rate mortgages must be tied to one of a number of benchmark rates specified by the regulator.

In many other European markets interest rates are normally fixed for a specified number of years agreed at the start of the mortgage. At the end of this period, the borrower may choose to refix the interest rate for a further period at the rates on offer at the time.

Increasing competition has encouraged lenders to offer special incentives to attract new customers. These usually take the form of an initial discounted or a fixed-rate period, which will give the borrower lower payments or certainty over the size of the payments in the first few years of the loan.

Repayment Profile

The repayment profile of a mortgage can take one of two basic forms: (1) a capital repayment loan, where the borrower makes regular payments consisting of the interest due and a portion of the capital outstanding so the loan is repaid in full at maturity, or (2) an interest-only loan, where the capital must be paid in full on the maturity date of the mortgage. Repayment mortgages are often constant payment amortising loans but in certain markets linear amortisation is the norm.

Prepayments

A borrower has the right to repay a mortgage loan (in part or in full) at any time. This can be for a number of reasons, but as interest rates have declined and competition has intensified, reducing margins on mortgage products, the number of borrowers refinancing their mortgages with other lenders has increased. This has been helped in part by the house price increases in many countries.

The borrower may have to pay an early redemption fee. In some markets the rates are tightly regulated but they tend to vary among lenders and mortgage products. These charges can sometimes be high, especially for mortgages with long fixed-rate periods where the prepayment penalty can often largely negate any benefit of refinancing as interest rates decline.

Flexible and Offset Account Mortgages

Flexible mortgages are an increasingly popular innovation. They allow the borrower to make prepayments on a loan at any time without penalty. With most flexible products, the borrower will then be allowed to redraw these prepayments at a later date, either as cash or by taking a payment holiday, provided the original paydown schedule is not exceeded. Offset account mortgages offer the borrower more flexibility by only charging interest on the difference between the outstanding balance of the mortgage and the credit balance on the associated bank account.

COLLATERAL CHARACTERISTICS

RMBS transactions consist of a number of classes of notes that rely on the cash flows generated by an underlying pool of mortgages. The credit assessment of an RMBS transaction can be broken down into two distinct parts: the credit assessment of the collateral and the assessment of the protection provided by the transaction structure. In this section we discuss the key factors to consider when assessing the collateral supporting an RMBS transaction and how these factors can influence performance. Most of these considerations apply to any mortgage irrespective of its origin, although differences between countries make direct comparisons difficult. For example, the tax system in the Netherlands encourages borrowers to take a large mortgage loan, so loan-to-value ratios tend to be significantly higher than in other countries.

Affordability

The key to assessing the probability of borrower default lies in assessing their ability and willingness to pay. Affordability is usually measured either as an income multiple for the loan or the ratio of the borrower's monthly debt obligations to their monthly net income. The higher the level of borrower income is relative to debt obligations, the better the ability of the borrower to absorb any financial shocks.

Loan-to-Value Ratio

The loan-to-value ratio (LTV) gives a measure of the equity a borrower has invested in a property. A large equity stake provides an important motivation to avoid defaulting on a loan. The ability to save a large deposit may indicate a higher level of financial discipline by the borrower, which should also indicate a lower likelihood of default.

The LTV ratio also has an important impact on the extent of any losses sustained in the event that a loan goes into default. A lower LTV loan can absorb a greater decline in the value of a property before losses are realised in the collateral pool. Lenders will often have recourse to other assets belonging to the borrower in addition to the secured property to cover any losses in the event of default, although this is usually ignored in any credit assessment.

When comparing LTVs across countries, it is important to consider the basis for the valuation. Most valuations will be an assessment of the estimated market value of the property provided there is a willing buyer. Valuations that are based on a forced sale assumption (as in the Netherlands) will be lower and therefore the reported LTVs will be correspondingly higher.

Mortgage Type

The type of mortgage can also influence the credit quality of the loan. In summary, mortgage products that exaggerate payment shocks are likely to experience increased levels of defaults, whereas those that provide a degree of stability or payment shock protection are likely to see fewer defaults.

In countries where mortgage interest rates are predominantly variable, an increase in interest rates will immediately feed through to the payments required from mortgage borrowers, so a rapid increase in rates would cause a significant payment shock for borrowers. In countries where mortgages are mostly fixed rate, the rates are not normally fixed for the entire life of the loan but have periodic reset dates. Therefore, short-term changes in interest rates will be less of a concern but payments may change significantly on the interest rate reset date.

Mortgages that offer an initial teaser rate present a payment shock at the end of the discount period that may cause problems for the borrower, so these loans are often penalised in rating agency analysis. Similarly, a loan that charges a fixed rate of interest for an initial period could also create a payment shock when the rate becomes variable but, to a certain extent, this is mitigated by the stability of payments during the early years, protecting the borrower from rate rises when the risk of default is highest.

Interest-only mortgages, where the full balance of the loan has to be repaid at maturity, present a potentially significant payment shock to the borrower. These loans may be linked to a savings or investment product designed to help repay the loan on maturity. Loans without a repayment mechanism rely on the borrower's ability to repay or refinance the loan at the time. These loans are usually penalised in rating agency analysis of the collateral.

Flexible mortgages and current account mortgages have the advantages for the borrower of being able to prepay without penalty and then, at a later date, recover some of these prepayments either through a capital redraw or through a payment holiday. For credit assessment, they are usually treated as a standard interest-only or repayment mortgage.

Buy-to-let mortgages are another type of mortgage product, which started to become popular in the United Kingdom during the late 1990s. It is generally assumed that default probabilities will be higher for a buy-to-let mortgage than one for the borrower's primary residence. However, in the event of default, the lender will have the ability to appoint a receiver of rent to collect rental payments directly from the tenant, and there is a less time-consuming process for gaining vacant possession of the property. These factors should serve to reduce the loss severity.

Seasoning

S&P's analysis of historical data for UK mortgages indicates that a borrower is most likely to default in the first five years of a loan. So a mortgage that has been outstanding for some time and is up to date with its payments should represent a lower risk than a new loan. As earnings and wages tend to rise over the long term, the borrower's ability and incentive to maintain the mortgage payments should increase over time.

Many securitisations by regular issuers of MBS will have a relatively low average seasoning on their collateral pool at launch. Loans that have been originated relatively recently will have had little opportunity to fall behind with their payments so this pool is likely to have low arrears. Experience suggests that arrears tend to increase over the first two years and then stabilise as the collections process and, if necessary, repossessions take effect. Therefore, when comparing the arrears within collateral pools, it is important to also consider the age of the loans in the portfolios.

Loan Purpose

Loans used to purchase or refinance the purchase of the borrower's primary residence are expected to be less likely to default than loans for second homes or investment properties. It is assumed that a borrower with financial problems is most likely to ensure the family home is secure before paying other debts. Remortgages that involve the withdrawal of equity are often used for debt consolidation or to finance spending above the level of available savings. The rating agencies consider loans that release accumulated equity in a property to be higher risk than purchase or simple refinancing loans, and penalise them accordingly.

Borrower Profile

European RMBS are generally supported by mortgages to borrowers with stable earnings and good credit records. Self-employed borrowers are generally considered to present a higher risk of default than those that are paid a salary, although this depends to a large extent on the nature and size of the business.

In the United Kingdom, the specialist nonconforming lenders have built a business from lending to borrowers that would be turned down by mainstream lenders. They will consider lending to borrowers who have had previous credit problems, mortgage arrears, county court judgements against them for not paying debts, or even those who have been declared bankrupt in the past. In addition, they are willing to extend self-certified loans to people who find it difficult to provide sufficient proof of their earnings for the mainstream lenders. These borrowers can have a considerably higher risk of default, depending on the individual. The interest rate these borrowers will be charged will depend on the lender's assessment of this default risk.

Geographic Distribution

European RMBS transactions contain mortgages originated in a single country, so investors wishing to build a diversified European RMBS portfolio will have to invest in a selection of transactions. However, even within a single country property prices can behave differently between regions. So geographic diversity, or at least the absence of a significant regional concentration, is an important characteristic, as it will help mitigate the impact on the transaction of a housing downturn in any one region of the country.

Property Values

Expensive properties tend to experience proportionally greater declines in value in a deteriorating market than homes with an average market price. This greater volatility is due to the limited number of potential purchasers for these properties, causing a lack of liquidity in this market, and less precise pricing information due to the lack of comparable benchmark homes. Very low value properties also tend to realise lower recoveries than average.

Arrears

Arrears on a mortgage loan indicate that the borrower is likely to be suffering some degree of financial stress and, as such, these loans have a higher risk of going into default. The rating agencies usually take the pessimistic assumption that any loan more than 90 days behind with its payments is going to default, and increase the default probability assumptions significantly for loans with less serious arrears. When using arrears as an indicator of the quality of a mortgage pool, it is important to take the seasoning of the pool into account. Arrears levels generally start to stabilise when the average seasoning reaches two to three years. Earlier than this the arrears are likely to be below their long-run sustainable level.

Loss Severities

The severity of losses experienced on enforcement of a loan will depend on the proceeds of the property sale, foreclosure costs, carry costs, the LTV of the loan, and the priority of the charge on the property. In some cases it is possible to recover a proportion of any remaining debt from the borrower after the security has been realised, which would serve to reduce the loss severity. But this cannot be relied on, and so is normally ignored in any credit assessment.

Foreclosure and Carry Costs

The final components of the loss severity are the foreclosure costs and the loss of interest during the foreclosure process. The time it will take to repossess and sell a property will depend largely on the legal process in the relevant country. For example, the time from when the borrower stops paying until sale will typically take 12 months in the Netherlands and the United Kingdom but this process can take several years in Italy. During this period, the transaction will not be receiving interest on the loan, causing a stress on the revenue generated by the collateral pool.

RATING AGENCY ANALYSIS

The rating agencies make an assessment of the overall robustness of the collateral and the transaction structure by applying certain assumptions about how loans will behave in an economic downturn rather than simply looking at the current situation. These assumptions are more pessimistic the higher the rating being considered. As a result, the ratings on RMBS transactions (and other ABS) are resilient to deterioration in the economic outlook.

Each rating agency has its own methodology for assessing the robustness of an RMBS transaction; the details vary from country to country and will be adjusted from time to time but the principles are similar in each case. This section provides an illustration of the rating process based primarily on Fitch's criteria for assessing UK RMBS transactions described in their publication, *UK Residential Mortgage Default Model II*, 13 October 2000.

Default Probability

The first step in the Fitch rating process is to estimate the probability of default for each loan in the collateral pool. This will take into account all the factors discussed in the previous section.

Loan Affordability and LTV

Fitch uses the combination of the LTV and the affordability measure for a loan in order to arrive at a base case default probability for any particular borrower in a particular rating test. In the United Kingdom, the income multiple has traditionally been used as the measure of loan affordability, and Fitch places loans in one of five classifications based on this measure (Exhibit 11.4).

The base case default probability will then depend on the rating being considered and the LTV of the loan. Exhibit 11.5 shows the Fitch default probability assumptions for loans where the income multiple is between 2.75 and 3.00 for various ratings tests.

EXHIBIT 11.4 Fitch Income Multiple Classifications

Income Multiple	From	To
Class 1	0.00	1.99
Class 2	2.00	2.49
Class 3	2.50	2.74
Class 4	2.75	3.00
Class 5	3.01	

Source: Fitch UK Mortgage Default Model.

EXHIBIT 11.5 Fitch Default Probability Assumption for Class 4 Loans (%)

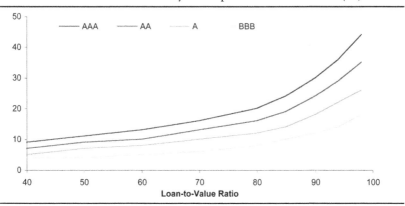

Source: Fitch UK Residential Mortgage Default Model II, October 2000.

Other Factors

The initial default probability assumption is then adjusted (usually increased) to take into account any other important features of the loan. These factors include:

- *Mortgage Type:* Interest-only mortgages that are not linked to a repayment vehicle will have the base case default probability increased by a factor up to 1.33, dependent on the time to maturity of the loan.
- *Equity Withdrawal:* Loans taken out to refinance an existing mortgage will not be penalised unless the borrower uses the opportunity to withdraw equity from the property when the default probability will be increased by 1.10–1.25×.
- *Second Homes:* The assumption is that a borrower in financial difficulties will be more likely to default on a second home than the primary residence (1.10–1.25×).
- *Buy-to-Let Properties:* These loans are assumed to have a higher probability of default as for a second home but the loss severity may be reduced due to an easier repossession process and the ability to appoint a receiver of rent.
- *Borrower Profile:* A number of special factors may arise with nonconforming borrowers. These range from people with court judgements against them for failing to repay a debt or even a previous bankruptcy (1.25–2.50×) to borrowers who cannot provide sufficient proof of income (1.25–1.75×).
- *Servicer Quality:* There is qualitative judgement based on the quality of the underwriting and servicing processes and systems. This can increase or decrease the final default probability assumption.

Property Value Declines

Fitch has carried out an analysis of property price movements by region in the United Kingdom and has used the results to assess the amounts by which property prices might be expected to fall in a time of stress. These assessments become progressively more pessimistic for higher ratings categories, as illustrated in Exhibit 11.6. Fitch has similar tables for other countries.

Fitch will increase the market value decline assumptions for very high or very low value properties or if there are significant regional concentrations in the collateral.

Loss Severities

The expected loss severity for each loan can then be calculated by taking into account the LTV of the loan, market value decline on the property,

EXHIBIT 11.6   Fitch Regional UK Market Value Decline Assumptions (%)

Region	AAA	AA	A	BBB	BB	B
London	48	44	39	35	30	27
Outer Metro	43	39	35	31	27	24
Southeast	42	38	34	30	25	23
N. Ireland	42	38	35	32	29	26
East Anglia	41	36	32	27	22	20
W Midlands	38	34	30	26	22	20
Southwest	37	33	29	25	22	19
E Midlands	37	33	28	25	21	19
Northwest	37	32	28	24	20	18
Yorks./Hum.	30	26	22	17	11	10
North	29	25	22	18	14	12
Wales	27	24	20	18	15	13
Scotland	27	23	19	15	11	10

Source: Fitch UK Residential Mortgage Default Model II, October 2000.

foreclosure and selling costs, and the cost of carry during this process. The default probability and expected loss estimate allow Fitch to calculate an expected loss on the entire transaction for each rating assessment.

Ratings Assessment

The final ratings assessment of the RMBS notes will reflect the ratings scenario under which the notes will continue to receive all amounts due. This assessment will also take into account the potential variations in the timing of the losses and uncertainty in the prepayment rate on the mortgages.

RMBS TRANSACTION STRUCTURES

The challenge facing the designers of RMBS transactions is to provide a structure that will provide an attractive investment while being able to handle the uncertain nature of the cash flows generated by the underlying mortgages. A transaction will usually be structured into several classes of notes with different expected maturities and different risk profiles to appeal to a variety of investors.

EXHIBIT 11.7   A Generic Cash Flow Waterfall

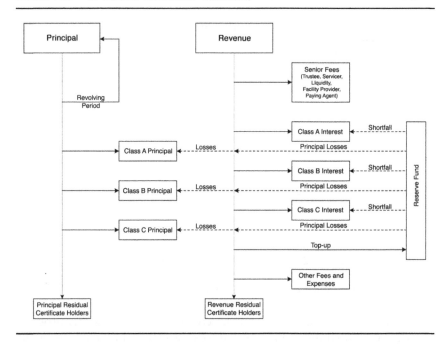

Credit Protection

European RMBS transactions contain a combination of various features designed to protect investors from the impact of defaults on mortgages in the underlying collateral pool, including excess spread, reserve fund, and subordination of any lower priority notes.

Cash Flow Allocation

The heart of the credit protection in a RMBS transaction is governed by rules that determine how the cash flow in the transaction is allocated. Exhibit 11.7 illustrates a generic cash flow allocation scheme (the cash flow waterfall).

Principal and interest are separated and the principal component may be used to redeem notes, to purchase additional collateral or returned to the mortgage originator depending on the type of structure involved. The nonprincipal amount, or revenue component, is used to pay any necessary fees and expenses for the transaction, the interest on the notes, and to cover losses.

Excess Spread

It is normal in European RMBS transactions for the entire revenue component of the receipts from borrowers to flow through the cash flow waterfall. The average interest rate charged on the mortgages will exceed the weighted average rate payable on the notes plus fees and expenses, so there will be excess cash flowing through the waterfall (excess spread). Excess spread will be used first to cover any losses that have been incurred, second to top up the reserve fund to its required balance (if necessary), and finally any remaining amounts are paid back to the originator of the mortgages as its profit.

Principal Deficiency Ledgers

In European RMBS transactions, bonds are not generally written down when losses are incurred in the collateral pool. Instead, the losses are recorded in a principal deficiency ledger, which records the extent to which the balance outstanding on the notes exceeds the remaining assets. Usually, both excess spread and the reserve fund can be used to cover losses and so pay down the principal deficiency ledger. This mechanism is beneficial to holders of the lower-rated notes because the notes do not get written off immediately and any future excess spread will be used to cover the loss.

Reserve Fund

The reserve fund consists of a cash amount that the issuer places on deposit at launch, which is available to cover any shortfalls in income and any principal losses during the life of a transaction. If the reserve fund is used, future excess spread will be retained until it is replenished up to its required balance. The required balance is usually a fixed monetary amount, but some transactions allow the reserve fund to amortise or even require it to increase depending on collateral performance.

Subordination

The cash flow waterfall encapsulates the subordination of the junior classes of notes. As all cash received is used to pay items on the senior notes first, this will inevitably mean that any loss that cannot be covered through trapping excess spread or from the reserve fund will result in a shortfall in the funds available to redeem the most junior class of notes.

Insurance

Many lenders require borrowers taking out high LTV loans to pay for mortgage indemnity guarantee (MIG) to cover the high LTV portion of the loan. If the borrower were to subsequently default, the lender would be able to claim for any additional loss incurred as a result of lending above the standard LTV. This has the advantage for the lender, and consequently the investor, that the loss severity will be reduced. However, it would introduce an element of sensitivity to the financial health of the insurer into the transaction. The conditions and cover provided by MIG insurance vary, but it is usual for the claim to be settled after repossession and sale of the property. This process may take considerable time during which the transaction will need to cover the carry cost for the loan.

Liquidity Facility

Many transactions include a liquidity facility. Although it does not provide protection against losses on the underlying collateral, it is available to cover temporary shortfalls in revenue receipts.

Pass-Through Transactions

Traditionally, European RMBS transactions have been structured as pass-through notes, where the principal received from borrowers is used to repay noteholders. This has the advantage of keeping the outstanding balance of the collateral and the notes in balance, but the disadvantage for noteholders is that the timing of their cash flows is uncertain.

Redemption

In a pass-through transaction, the notes will normally be split into a number of classes that will be redeemed in order of priority. The actual speed at which the notes are redeemed will depend on the underlying repayment schedule of the mortgages in the pool and the rate at which the borrowers prepay their mortgages. (See Exhibit 11.8 for a generic example.)

Transactions may include a substitution period during which the issuer is allowed to use principal receipts to purchase additional mortgages. This, in effect, allows the issuer to prevent the collateral pool (and therefore the notes) paying down, giving noteholders certainty of cash flows during this period. However, at the end of the substitution period, principal payments will be used to redeem notes in the normal manner.

One consequence of the sequential paydown of the notes is that, as the highest rated notes are paid down first, the average cost of the notes increases during the life of the transaction. This will reduce the excess spread and therefore the cash flowing back to the originator. The erosion of excess spread can be reduced by allowing the notes to redeem on a pro rata basis. This will only be allowed after some performance triggers have been met, which usually include the credit enhancement on the senior notes reaching a certain minimum level, the reserve fund being fully funded, and the arrears being below a specified level (see

EXHIBIT 11.8   Example Paydown Profile for a Pass-Through MBS Transaction (15% CPR)

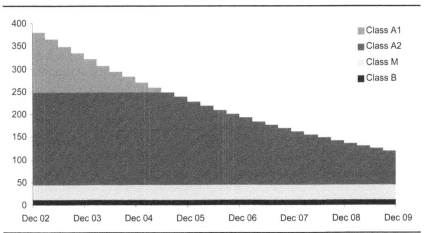

Source: Barclays Capital.

EXHIBIT 11.9   Example Paydown Profile with Switch to Pro Rata Redemptions

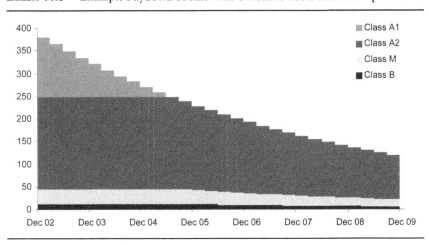

Source: Barclays Capital.

Exhibit 11.9). These transactions normally revert to sequential redemption when the collateral pool reaches a certain minimum size.

The effect of a switch from sequential to pro rata redemption will stop the gradual erosion of excess spread but this will be accompanied by a reduction in the rate of improvement in credit enhancement.

Legal Maturity

The legal final maturity of the notes in a pass-through transaction is normally set to be two years after the maturity date of the longest-dated mortgage. This should allow time for the administrator to repossess and sell the property even if the borrower defaulted on the last mortgage payment. In a few transactions, the fastest paying class of notes may have a shorter legal final maturity if there is a sufficient quantity of mortgages in the pool maturing early enough to guarantee payment by this date, but this is unusual.

Optional Redemption

In a pass-through transaction the issuer normally has the option to call the notes under three specified circumstances:

■ The imposition of withholding tax on noteholder interest payments.
■ The aggregate balance of the mortgage pool falling below a certain percentage (usually 10%) of the initial amount outstanding (a cleanup call).
■ On a specified date, usually five or seven years after launch.

When the issuer has the option to call the notes on a specified date, the interest margin on the notes will usually increase. This gives the originator an additional economic incentive to arrange for the notes to be called. However, in certain jurisdictions this type of call may prevent the off-balance sheet treatment of the securitised loans, so this step and call feature is not found in all transactions.

Prepayments

Prepayments are the most important factor in determining the redemption profile of the notes in a pass-through transaction. The prepayment rate is usually measured as an annualised Conditional Prepayment Rate (CPR), which is defined as the proportion of the outstanding balance of the mortgages that is paid down ahead of schedule during the period. Exhibit 11.10 illustrates the paydown profile for the same example transaction as in Exhibit 11.9, but with an increased prepayment rate of 35% CPR.

The factors driving prepayments will include the path of interest rates, the economic and competitive environment, the type of mortgage, and borrower profile, so they are difficult to predict. Most European RMBS are floating-rate notes and so prepayments will have a limited impact on investors, and with many mortgages being variable rate or having large prepayment penalties, falling interest rates do not necessarily give the borrower the opportunity to refinance at a more competitive

EXHIBIT 11.10   Example Paydown Profile at High Prepayment Speeds

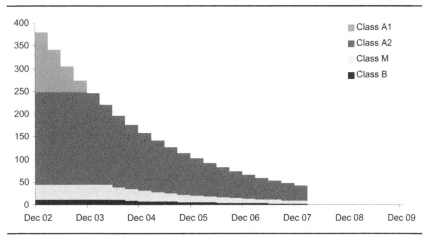

Source: Barclays Capital.

rate. This is in contrast to the United States where both the RMBS and the underlying mortgages are mostly fixed rate. Although European RMBS do not suffer the same degree of negative convexity as their US counterparts, European RMBS are unlikely to trade at a significant premium due to prepayment (and therefore average life) uncertainty.

Credit Enhancement

The credit enhancement for a particular class of notes is the sum of all the credit support provided by the subordinated notes (if any), the reserve fund, and the protection provided by the excess spread. As the collateral is paid down and the notes redeemed, the credit enhancement for all classes of notes will improve. This steady improvement is the main reason behind the ratings upgrades in European RMBS.

Exhibit 11.11 illustrates how the credit enhancement (excluding excess spread) improves during the life of a pass-through transaction. The exhibit corresponds to the generic paydown profile shown in Exhibit 11.9, and illustrates the reduced rate of improvement in credit enhancement once the notes are paying down on a pro rata basis.

Flexible Mortgages

Flexible and offset account mortgages present a significant challenge to pass-through transaction structures. This arises because the borrowers' requests to redraw previous prepayments could in aggregate exceed the principal receipts. The experiences of Australian mortgage lenders,

EXHIBIT 11.11   Example Credit Enhancement Growth (% of subordination)

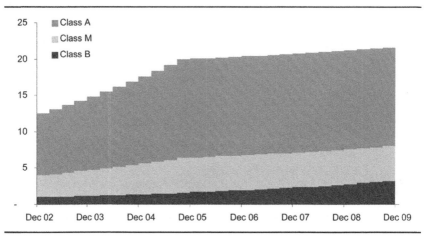

Source: Barclays Capital.

which have considerable experience in originating this type of collateral, suggest this is unlikely to happen. However, the possibility is covered in RMBS transactions by a borrowing facility (redraw facility), which is available to meet the excess redraw requests if the need arises. If this facility had to be exercised, subsequent principal receipts would be used to repay the redraw facility provider before resuming note redemptions.

Reverse Mortgages

Reverse mortgages are designed to allow older customers to borrow some of the accumulated equity in their homes. The borrowers do not make any interest payments on these loans. The return for the mortgage lenders is taken from the sale proceeds when the borrower moves, enters long-term residential care or dies.

There are two main types of reverse mortgage. The shared appreciation mortgage is structured so the mortgage lender receives back the original loan amount and a proportion of the increase in property value. This has certain advantages but does mean that the proceeds are entirely dependent on house prices. The Millshaw SAMS No.1 transaction is backed by this type of mortgage collateral. The notes do not pay interest but pass these cash flows directly on to investors.

The second type of reverse mortgage, securitised in Equity Release Funding (ERF) transactions, accrue interest at a rate set out in the mortgage agreement. The notes in these transactions pay interest, but in the early stages of the transaction these payments are met by borrowing from a large liquidity facility. When the property is eventually sold, there is a risk that the proceeds will not fully cover the debt plus accrued interest. In the ERF transactions, this risk is covered by an insurance policy with Norwich Union, the mortgage originator.

Reverse mortgages differ from standard RMBS transactions by their increased dependence on house-price movements and sensitivity to borrowers' life expectancy and health.

The VPTN Type Structure

The variable pay term note (VPTN) structure was first introduced in automobile transactions in the United States. It was created to mitigate two features of the pass-through structure: the long legal maturity of the notes even if they have a short average life, and the uncertainty in the redemption profile.

Redemption Profile

In the VPTN type structure, an additional class of notes (Class A1R) is issued to a note purchaser. The notes are issued partly paid and the purchaser is obliged to pay the remaining value of the notes on a specified future date. The notes are designed to mirror an existing class of notes. This allows the issuer to use the proceeds from the sale of these notes to redeem the existing outstanding class on the next interest payment date (see Exhibit 11.12). The original notes can then have a short legal maturity, as the redemption depends on the note purchaser and not the collateral.

EXHIBIT 11.12   Note Redemptions in a VPTN Type Structure (RMS 11 Estimate at Launch)

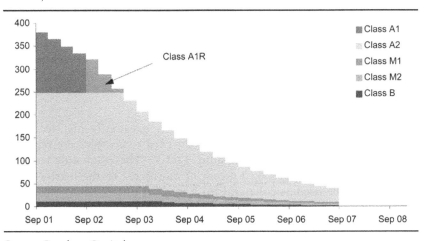

Source: Barclays Capital.

The new note then effectively replaces the old note that has been redeemed, and it will be repaid as in a standard pass-through structure illustrated in Exhibit 11.9.

The combination of this redemption profile with a substitution period and/or a cash accumulation account would allow the creation of bullet securities, although at the time of writing this has not been done for a European issuer. This is not the only way to create notes that expect to have a bullet redemption profile. In the Delphinus 2002-II transaction, the substitution period extended up to the step-and-call date, so the notes are likely to be redeemed on that date. However, if for any reason the issuer is not able or willing to call the notes, they will redeem as in a standard pass-through transaction, and so the legal maturity is dependent on the term of the underlying mortgages.

Master Trust Structures

The master trust represents an alternative method for creating bullet securities from mortgage collateral. This method has the advantage of not relying on any third party for the redemption of the notes on the maturity date. However, in order to be efficient, these master trusts need to be large, and the requirement for a seller's interest in the trust means that it is not possible to fully fund the mortgage operation through this type of securitisation. This makes them most suited to the large prime issuers that have access to alternative sources of funding.

The master trust structure was first introduced in the United States in 1988 for credit card securitisations. This allowed the creation of a series of securitisations by multiple issuers using the same collateral as security. The abolition of MIRAS (tax relief on mortgage interest payments) in the United Kingdom in April 2000 paved the way for the creation of master trust structures based on UK mortgage collateral. To date, five such mortgage master trusts have been created, all by large UK mortgage lenders, and the transactions originated from these programmes account for a significant proportion of European RMBS production.

Structure

The structure of a mortgage master trust is essentially identical to a credit card master trust except that credit card receivables are replaced with mortgage collateral (see Exhibit 11.13). The originator sells an equitable interest in a specified group of mortgages to the master trust. This can then be used as collateral for a number of securitisations. Over time, additional mortgages may be added to the trust, subject to various constraints to protect the quality of the collateral. The same pool of mortgages will support all the series of notes issued by all issuers, with

EXHIBIT 11.13   Master Trust Amortisation Structure

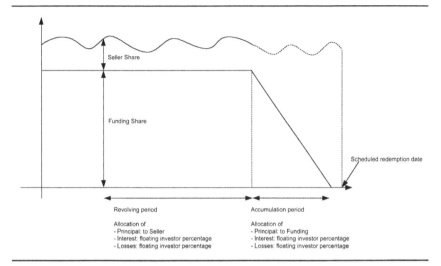

Source: Barclays Capital.

no particular series having rights to specific mortgages within the pool. The master trust may be used to support a new securitisation providing the trust is either large enough to support both, or sufficient additional mortgage collateral is transferred to the trust. In this case, both the existing and the new transaction would be supported by the original and new pool of mortgages.

Mortgage master trusts require the seller to maintain a certain minimum interest in the collateral pool held by the master trust. In credit card transactions this is used to absorb the monthly fluctuations in the balance outstanding on the credit cards and ensure there is always sufficient collateral to support the notes. In RMBS transactions the minimum seller's interest tends to be smaller as the mortgages have a more stable repayment profile, and this is primarily available to cover set-off risk in the event of originator insolvency. In existing transactions it is the minimum trust size rather than the minimum seller's share that has been the key constraint.

Principal Cash Flows Within a Master Trust

The trust will tend to reduce in size as principal payments are received on the mortgages, and this principal can be used in one of three ways. Outside an accumulation period and when there are no amortising notes being redeemed, the principal receipts will be paid to the seller. In an accumulation period for a bullet or scheduled payment, all principal receipts on the entire trust will be collected in the cash accumulation account until the balance is sufficient to meet the required payment. While the junior pass-through notes are redeeming, principal receipts are allocated between the issuer and the seller according to their relative shares in the trust, and issuer's principal receipts are used to redeem the notes.

Redemption Profile

The master trust structure gives originators a high degree of flexibility over the redemption profiles of the notes they can create. The emphasis has understandably been on creating bullet securities in order to attract investors who would prefer to invest in securities with traditional bullet redemption profiles and short legal maturities. There have also been notes with a scheduled redemption profile issued from master trust structures and, in practice, the redemption profiles that can be created will only be limited by the size of the trust, the length of the required accumulation period, and any other note redemptions that are due from the same trust.

The ability to create bullet securities from mortgage collateral is limited by the fact that mortgages are long-term agreements with an uncertain repayment profile (and principal payments are usually small proportion of the regular payment) so the subordinate notes in the master trust transactions have been structured as pass-through notes. The senior notes generally account for more than 90% of the aggregate nominal value of the series. So, when the senior notes have been redeemed, the issuer will be able to call the subordinate notes, and therefore these are also expected to be bullet securities.

Prepayments

The master trust structures we have seen in the United Kingdom so far have been designed to remove, to a large extent, the sensitivity of the senior notes to prepayments on the mortgage collateral. In most cases this is achieved by creating bullet or scheduled amortisation notes, however this is not always the case. For example, the notes secured on the Granite Financing Master Trust, issued by Northern Rock plc, are amortising rather than having scheduled redemption profiles, but the sensitivity of these notes to prepayments is limited by a predetermined maximum amortisation schedule. As mentioned above, the redemption profiles of the subordinated pass-through notes in master trust structures may be dependent on the prepayment rate, but normally the clean-up call allows the issuer to call the notes before they start amortising.

The master trusts have been recording prepayment rates that are higher than on more traditional RMBS transactions. This is because the seller is required to repurchase any mortgage where the borrower wishes to switch product type or where the borrower has been granted a further advance. So these loans have been considered as prepayments in these transactions, even though they would not have been in a traditional MBS transaction. Faster prepayments will help shorten the amortisation periods for scheduled note redemptions and the minimum trust size requirement will protect investors against the erosion of the collateral.

Optional Redemptions

The optional redemption features of the master trust transactions are essentially the same as those for a pass-through transaction. The issuer typically has the option to call the notes for any of the following circumstances:

- Withholding tax being imposed on noteholder interest payments.
- The aggregate balance of the notes within a single series falling to a certain percentage (usually 10%) or less of their initial aggregate size outstanding.
- On or after a specified date.

The interest margin on the notes will usually increase on the date the issuer has the option to call the notes. This gives the originator an additional economic incentive to arrange for the notes to be called.

Performance Triggers

There are a number of performance triggers within the master trust transactions that serve to protect the senior noteholders against certain events. These events can be divided into two categories: asset performance related and nonasset related.

An asset performance trigger event would occur if a principal deficiency is recorded in the Class A Principal Deficiency Ledger. This means that the total balance of realised losses that have not been covered by either the reserve fund or with excess spread exceed the aggregate outstanding amount of the subordinate notes. If this occurs, all receipts on the mortgages will be allocated to the issuers and the seller on a pro rata basis. The notes will start to redeem early with all the Class A notes being redeemed on a pro rata basis. When all the Class A notes have been redeemed in full, the Class B notes would be redeemed, and so on for all other classes of notes until all the notes are redeemed or the trust no longer has any assets.

There are also circumstances where the principal due to Class C noteholders and, if applicable, Class B noteholders may be deferred. These conditions include:

■ A principal deficiency being recorded on the Class C or Class B principal deficiency ledger.

■ The reserve fund being used to cover a principal deficiency and not being replenished.

■ Arrears in excess of three monthly payments are greater than 5% of the mortgage pool.

■ Breach of certain minimum trust size triggers.

The nonasset trigger events relate primarily to the financial health of the originator and servicer, the maintenance of the minimum seller's share, and the minimum trust size. If a nonasset trigger event occurs, all principal payments from the trust (including the seller's share) will be used to redeem the notes. However, in this case the Class A notes will redeem in order of legal final maturity date. When the Class A notes have been redeemed in full, the Class B, Class C, and Class D notes will be redeemed in turn.

Credit Enhancement

The credit enhancement in the master trust transaction is the sum of all the credit support provided by the subordinated notes (if any), the reserve fund, and excess spread.

The calculation of credit enhancement for notes in a master trust transaction seems more complicated than in a traditional pass-through transaction because subordinated notes from an earlier series are expected to be redeemed before the senior notes of later series. However, if the mortgages were to perform poorly, the trigger events ensure that all outstanding junior notes would only be repaid after all the senior notes. So the credit enhancement can be calculated as the aggregate balance of subordinate notes as a proportion of the total notes outstanding.

The notes are expected to redeem a whole series at a time, so the proportions of senior to junior notes will stay approximately the same and there is unlikely to be any upwards ratings drift due to notes being redeemed.

Excess Spread

Excess spread is available to build up the reserve fund to its required level and cover any principal deficiencies. For example, in the Holmes Financing transactions there is a mechanism whereby, if the yield on the mortgages falls below a certain specified level, excess spread will be trapped in a second reserve fund to provide additional credit enhancement as compensation for the reduction in excess spread.

Reserve Fund

To date, the main reserve funds in master trust transactions have been standard fixed cash amounts that are available to the issuer to cover any shortfalls in income or principal losses during the life of the transaction. The reserve funds are built up to their required levels through trapped excess spread.

The Ratings Process

The integrated nature of a master trust transaction means that when a new securitisation is issued that is secured on the same master trust, the rating agencies will have to ensure that the addition of the new transaction still allows all the existing notes from earlier transactions to meet their required payments and does not adversely affect the ratings of any existing notes. In effect, the agencies have to re-run the ratings process for all existing classes of notes every time a new transaction is issued.

Advantages of a Master Trust

A master trust allows an RMBS issuer to establish a sizeable securitisation programme, even with many series of notes secured through multiple SPVs, at a dramatically lower cost than through traditional separate securitisations. The ability to issue notes with a variety of maturities and redemption profiles allows the issuer to expand the available investor base and to tap into specific demand in the market. However, this process does rely on economies of scale and so is probably not the ideal form of securitisation for a smaller lender. Also, the requirement to maintain a minimum seller's share in the trust would make this type of structure less suitable than others for lenders wishing to securitise 100% of their balance sheet.

This type of structure has a number of advantages for investors. The large size of the collateral pool means these transactions have a much greater diversity of assets than a standalone transaction. In a traditional transaction, the diversity declines during its life as mortgages are redeemed, but while the master trusts are increasing in size, so too is the diversity of the collateral. In addition, investors with an interest in several notes secured on the same trust need only track the performance of the underlying master trust rather than each collateral pool separately. The large size of these transactions also leads to better secondary market liquidity for the notes but, most importantly, these structures give investors who require bullet securities and/or short legal life investments the opportunity to invest in RMBS.

COLLATERAL PERFORMANCE

The ultimate aim of any performance analysis is to help form a judgement of the probability that investors in a transaction might not receive the payments they expect at the time they expect them. The differences between the master trust and the pass-through type transactions mean that it is worth considering them separately. It is also useful to look at the performance of the UK nonconforming transactions. The lower quality of borrower in these transactions leads to higher arrears and losses, and the large number of this type of transaction enable us to make some generalisations about the performance of this type of mortgage.

Master Trust Transactions

The master trust transactions are all supported by mortgages to high credit quality (prime) borrowers. These borrowers show very good credit performance and so arrears in these transactions are low and losses are generally negligible. Below the performance of the Holmes Financing Master Trust is used in the illustration. This transaction contains mortgages originated by Abbey National, one of the largest mortgage lenders in the United Kingdom.

Trust Size

Between September 2000 and November 2002, the Holmes Financing trust grew substantially, and there are certain occasions where the changes in the statistics are largely due the inclusion of new collateral. On three occasions during this period, the trust gained a significant quantity of additional mortgages (see Exhibit 11.14).

Arrears

Arrears rates provide an early indication of potential future losses and so are the single most closely followed performance statistic for RMBS transactions. Whether arrears actually result in losses will depend on the property value in relation to the size of the loan, and whether these borrowers are able to recover, or at least make sufficient mortgage payments to allow the lender not to foreclose on the loan.

The level of arrears in a relatively young pool of mortgages is likely to be low initially, particularly if there are restrictions on the selection of arrears loans in the representations and warranties for the RMBS transaction. The level of arrears would then be expected to increase as the loans season. This effect has been observed for the Holmes Financing Master Trust during this period (see Exhibit 11.15), although the general rising trend has been interrupted by the occasional addition of

EXHIBIT 11.14   Holmes Financing Trust Size (£ billion)

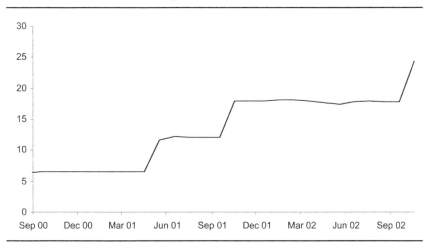

Source: Investor Reports.

EXHIBIT 11.15   Loans More Than Three Months Behind with Payments (% by balance)

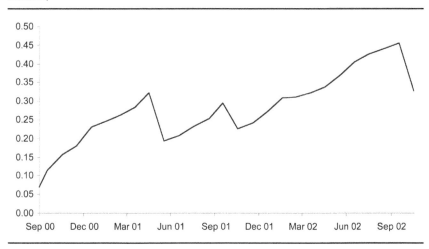

Source: Investor Reports.

new, less seasoned mortgages with lower arrears. This rising trend can be expected to slow as the arrears mortgages that are either recovering or progress through to foreclosure begin to balance the number of new mortgages falling behind with their payments.

EXHIBIT 11.16   Charge-off Rates in Holmes Financing Transaction (%)

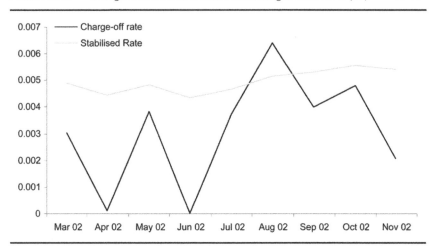

Source: Barclays Capital, Investor Reports.

Losses

Losses in master trust mortgage transactions can be recorded as an annualised charge-off rate in a similar manner to the standard method in credit
card transactions. However, losses on prime mortgages are generally very
small and intermittent so this measure will tend to be relatively volatile.
The results for the Holmes Financing transaction provide a good illustration of this point (see Exhibit 11.16).

Using cumulative loss figures to arrive at an estimate of the average
loss rate on a transaction over its life also presents difficulties when the
trust is changing size significantly. However, taking the ratio of cumulative realised losses to cumulative mortgage redemptions gives an estimate of the stabilised long-run average loss rate on the collateral.

Excess Spread

If any losses are realised on loans in the collateral pool, they will be covered by trapping any excess cash flowing through the cash flow waterfall, so the size of excess spread relative to the losses being incurred is
an important indication of the transaction's financial health. In the
Holmes Financing master trust, excess spread is measured on a quarterly basis. Exhibit 11.17 shows it that has been averaging around 60
bps per year, massively exceeding the 0.5 bp loss rate.

EXHIBIT 11.17   Excess Spread in Holmes Financing Transaction (% pa.)

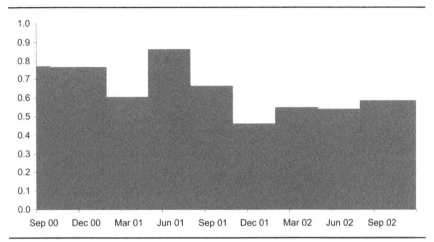

Source: Investor Reports.

Prepayments

The master trust transactions are largely insensitive to prepayment rates. The only requirement is that the principal receipts in the trust are sufficient for it to accumulate the bullet payments to meet the scheduled redemption dates. The principal payment rate, measured as the proportion of collateral redeemed or repurchased, has been running at an average rate of 4% per month.

Exhibit 11.18 shows the principal payment rate is somewhat erratic on a monthly basis but has generally been increasing. However, with a collateral pool of £24 billion and principal collections running at their average rate of 4%, it would take less than one month to accumulate the principal required to redeem the largest outstanding note.

Pass-Through Transactions

The performance analysis of pass-through transactions will be similar in many respects to that described above. However, as the collateral pays down, the credit enhancement in the transaction will improve and therefore these transactions become more financially robust as they age.

In the remainder of this section we discuss the performance of the UK nonconforming mortgage sector. Many of these transactions are backed by collateral that has been originated within a relatively short period of time. These transactions do not have a revolving period, which allows us

EXHIBIT 11.18 Monthly Principal Payment Rate (% of collateral by balance)

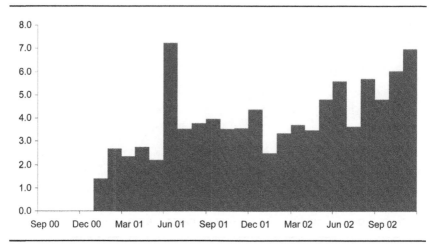

Source: Barclays Capital, Investor Reports.

to track the performance of a fixed set of mortgages over time, giving some additional insight into the behaviour of this type of borrower.

The average seasoning of the loans in collateral pools can vary considerably between different transactions and so a direct comparison may be misleading. For this reason the analysis presented here tracks the performance of the collateral against the estimated average seasoning of the collateral.

In this analysis (see Exhibits 11.19, 11.20, and 11.21), the solid lines indicate the average level of arrears, losses, and prepayments for collateral pools of any given age; the two dashed lines indicate one standard deviation either side of the average. The majority of collateral pools have an estimated average seasoning of 42 months or less and the number of transactions decreases as we look at seasoning beyond this. As the number of transactions decreases, the average will become less smooth. The exhibits only display the average provided it is based on at least four transactions.

Arrears

Exhibit 11.19 shows the average proportion of the collateral that are more than three months behind with their payments, measured against the average age of the mortgages in the pool. As expected, arrears tend to increase during the early stages of a transaction and then stabilise after approximately two years, typically in the 12–14% range. However, there has been considerable variation between issuers.

EXHIBIT 11.19 UK Nonconforming MBS with Arrears Over Three Months (% by balance)

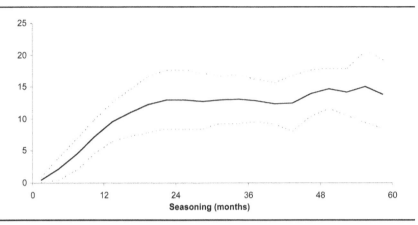

Source: Barclays Capital.

EXHIBIT 11.20 Cumulative Marginal Loss Rates (% of total redemptions by value)

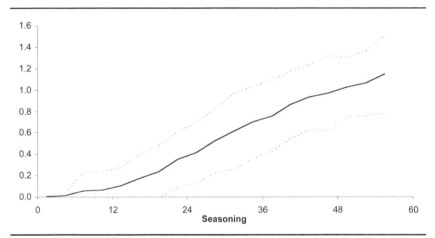

Source: Barclays Capital.

Losses

Similar analysis of the losses within the collateral pools supporting the MBS transactions gives the loss profile shown in Exhibit 11.20. The marginal loss rates used in this analysis are calculated as the total cumulative loss on the transaction as a proportion of the collateral that has been

EXHIBIT 11.21   Prepayment Rates on UK Nonconforming MBS (% CPR)

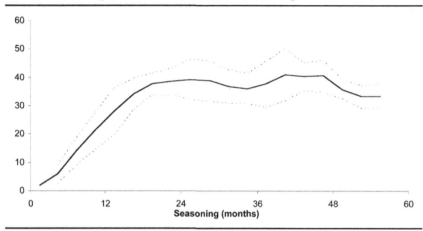

Source: Barclays Capital.

redeemed since launch. (This is essentially the same calculation as the stabilised loss rate for master trust transactions.) This produces a higher figure than the traditional calculation, which compares total losses against the original collateral size, but its advantage is that it should settle down to a more stable value more quickly. While this is evident in this analysis for individual transactions, the average loss rate shows a rising path as a result of the older transactions generally having higher stabilised loss rates than the more recent transactions.

Prepayments

Prepayments have been more consistent across different MBS transactions than either arrears or losses (see Exhibit 11.21). Traditionally, UK nonconforming MBS transactions have been priced using the assumption that the prepayment speed would be at a CPR of 25%. Exhibit 11.21 shows that prepayments have generally started at a much slower rate but then have accelerated up to a CPR of 35% by the time the mortgages are approximately 18 months old. As a result, a 25% CPR assumption is likely to underestimate the average life of a fast-pay security but probably overestimate the average life of a longer-life security.

CONCLUSION

The European RMBS market has grown significantly since its beginnings in the United Kingdom in the 1980s. Although this chapter has concentrated to a large extent on the UK RMBS market because of the additional variety of mortgage types and transaction structures seen in this market, there are well-established RMBS markets in most major European countries.

The performance of this asset class has been very strong. As of early 2003, there have been no defaults, very few downgrades, and a good number of upgrades. This safe-haven status and the increasing variety and liquidity of the transactions should continue to attract investors to this sector.

CHAPTER 12

European Commercial Mortgage-Backed Securities

Phil Adams, Ph.D.
Director
Barclays Capital

Commercial mortgage-backed securities (CMBS) represent an important and growing sector of the European securitisation market. However, in many cases there are significant differences between transactions, even those backed by collateral from the same originator, and it is these differences, in both collateral types and structural features, that make European CMBS such an interesting asset class. This chapter focuses on some of the more important aspects that investors should consider when analysing the collateral supporting these transactions and briefly looks at the key features of the common transaction structures.

CATEGORISATION OF SECURITSATION TRANSACTIONS

There is a wide variety of European securitisation transactions that are backed by one form or another of commercial property. This variety stems from the range of types of commercial property that may be included in the collateral pool, the type of borrower or borrowers, and the level of exposure to any underlying industries or sectors. As a result, it is not always clear where this sector begins or ends, and although it may be tempting to invent new subclassifications for the various fragments of the sector, this is not necessarily particularly helpful for investors or the market in general. To complicate matters further, a number of different structure types are used to create these securities and they are sometimes used as a means of categorising transactions.

Whatever the structure, however, it is the performance of an underlying ring-fenced pool of commercial property backed loans (and therefore the commercial property itself) that will primarily determine the performance of the securitisations, and we believe that it is probably more appropriate, from an investor's perspective, to group transactions according to the type of credit analysis that is most useful for comparing these securities.

Securitised commercial property exposure can be largely broken down into three categories, as described below:

- Large multiborrower deals, where numerous commercial property loans, originated to numerous borrowers and secured on a variety of properties are grouped together into one transaction, in a similar way to a traditional residential mortgage deal. Such a deal may be either a traditional true sale transaction or a synthetic credit-linked structure.
- The securitisation of either a single or limited number of loans secured by a similar number of properties.
- A commercial property based whole business securitisation, where a portfolio of properties generates the principal revenues in support of the business. Deals such as pub or healthcare transactions typically fall into this category. Such deals can range from a single asset to the highly diversified portfolio (by number if not by industry exposure).

While there are other forms of corporate property securitisation transactions (such as sale and lease-back transactions) and there may be some blurring of the distinctions between these categories, the majority of exposures reliant on the performance of the underlying real estate fall largely within the categories identified above.

Large Multiborrower Transactions

The multiborrower securitisations are typically made up of commercial mortgage loans originated by a bank. The ability of the underlying borrowers to service the loan will usually—but not always—be dependent on the ability of the underlying real estate to generate sufficient cash flow. This may be directly linked to the servicing of a lease obligation, for example a tenant of an office building, or may have greater operational dependency as in the case of a loan to a hotel. Importantly, each loan will have undergone separate credit assessment and there will be distinct loan-to-value measurements for each loan facility. The credit assessment for this type of CMBS is usually built around a simulation of the performance of a pool of such loans because statistical techniques become more appropriate the greater the diversification of the borrowers, property types, and regional and industrial dependencies.

Single or Limited Asset Securitisations

For securitisations backed by a limited number of properties, the statistical techniques that can be used in large portfolio transactions become less appropriate, and it is important to undertake more detailed due diligence of the real estate asset or assets and the property company's management.

Property-Based Whole-Business Securitisations

Almost all of the whole-business securitisations derive a significant proportion of their revenues from real estate assets owned or leased by the operating company. As a result, these could be classified as CMBS transactions. However, any credit analysis will need to address not only the operational performance of the company's assets but also the industry in which it operates. The key concern here is the potentially high correlation of overall performance with industry factors and the very high operational gearing of the underlying tenants. As this category extends beyond the CMBS sector, even occasionally without property backing, these transactions are often treated as a separate asset class.

COLLATERAL CHARACTERISTICS

Different techniques are necessary when analysing a large multiborrower CMBS transaction compared to one secured over a single or limited number of assets. This is reflected in the following sections, which briefly describe some of the more important factors in these analyses. In practice, a transaction may include a large number of loans but with significant exposure to a few valuable properties, in which case a combination of techniques will be most appropriate.

Credit Assessment of a Multiborrower Transaction

Where a transaction includes a large number of loans, a property-by-property analysis is unlikely to be justifiable (or even possible) so a higher-level approach will need to be adopted. We believe investors should consider a number of key features in a multiborrower deal:

- Weighted average loan-to-value ratio (LTV).
- Underlying portfolio weighted average debt service cover ratio (DSCR).
- Underlying profile of occupational lease expiry over the term of the transaction.

■ Average tenant quality (if known/available).
■ Weighted average loan seasoning.
■ Industry and geographic concentrations.
■ Significant single loan or property exposures.
■ The quality and ability of the loan origination and servicing process.

Many of these factors, which we discuss in more detail below, also apply to single property analysis.

LTV Ratio

The weighted average LTV ratio provides an overview of the average loan size against the value of the property providing security for the loan on a weighted basis. This provides the investor with a good overall view of the average level of equity the underlying borrowers have in the properties, and as such how far the sale price would have to fall if a borrower defaulted and the property was subsequently enforced before a loss would be incurred.

Although extremely useful, potential limitations should be considered. First, there is the timing and method of the valuations. If the values were obtained at origination, they may be several years old. This raises the question of whether anyone really knows what the value would be in the current market. Also, did the valuers actually visit the properties or were the valuations produced as a "desktop" exercise, which might limit their accuracy?

The profile of the LTVs of individual loans in the portfolio should also be considered. For example, two portfolios, each with a weighted average LTV of 70% may have different profiles. One may have loans evenly spread around the 70% mark, whereas the other may be "bar-belled," with a high number of very low LTV loans compensating for a high number of very high LTV loans. In most circumstances, if defaults were to occur, the loss severity would be higher for the bar-belled portfolio.

It is often widely commentated that LTV is not an indicator of default probability. However, we would argue that a borrower with a 50% equity stake at risk from a potential forced sale of a property would have a greater incentive to maintain debt service payments than if the same borrower had an equity stake of, say, 20%, and so although it may not be the most important influence, the LTV of a loan could be expected to have some influence on the default rate.

Debt Service Cover Ratio

The weighted average debt service cover ratio (DSCR) is an important element in the analysis of commercial property backed loans. It indicates the level of income received by the borrowers from the properties (be it rental receipts or operating profits) compared with the amount of principal and interest due under the loans. This provides an indication of the amount of deterioration in cash flow the borrowers are able to withstand before they are likely to default on their loans. Just as with LTV, investors should consider the profile of DSCR levels, and whether the weighted average is broadly representative of the portfolio, or distorted by very good and very bad DSCR levels.

A low DSCR does not, by itself, imply that the probability of default is necessarily high. It will depend very much on the nature of the underlying loan, the property, and the cash flow derived from it. A property with very stable rents, let to high quality tenants on long leases should be much more able to support high leverage and a consequent low DSCR than a property with volatile cash flows. As such, it is important to consider the nature of the portfolio when reviewing DSCR levels.

Investors should also determine the basis on which the DSCR level has been calculated. For example, does it include principal payments? Where the borrower pays principal from year two, has this been factored in or has the level been calculated using interest payments only? Also, what interest rate has been factored into the calculation: the current floating rate or a more sustainable longer-term interest rate?

Lease Expiry Profile

Where the majority of properties are tenanted via occupational leases, as is common in CMBS deals, it is useful to consider the profile of the expiry of those leases within the term of the transaction. Indeed, where investors rely on a refinance of certain loans in order to repay the principal, the lease profile after the loan maturity may also be important.

Where a significant proportion of the leases expire within the term of the loan, investors will rely on the quality of the property and the ability of the property manager (who may also be the borrower) to relet the underlying properties in a timely manner, at a level sufficient to service the loan. This will tend to increase the investors' exposure to the property fundamentals, while reducing the importance of the quality of the tenants.

Average Tenant Quality

In many instances, and especially in the United Kingdom, the majority of the underlying properties are occupied by a diverse range of tenants on long-term leases (15–25 years), who share the responsibility for maintenance, repair and insurance. In this case, portfolio analysis can sometimes become as much a consideration of the nature and strength of the tenants as a review of the property itself. This is particularly true where the securitisation is significantly shorter in term than the majority of the occupational leases.

However, where the portfolio contains a significant number of multitenanted properties, it is likely that only a few will be credit rated; many could be small regional tenants with neither the need for nor the means of obtaining a credit rating. This will increase the importance of any checks and controls in the origination and underwriting processes.

Seasoning

Loan seasoning is the time since the loan was first originated. Where a loan has existed for a considerable period, comfort can be taken from the fact that the borrower has proved to have a good payment history, and may also have made inroads into loan amortisation.

When loans have been originated against the background of a longstanding relationship between the originating bank and the borrower or borrower sponsors, it may be relevant to consider the length of that relationship. However, when other loans are already in place investors should also consider whether any decisions made in the interests of the originator's overall exposure to the borrower could negatively impact the securitised loan in the event of default.

Industry, Geographic, and Other Concentrations

Where credit exposure is spread across geographic and industry sectors, the risk associated with localised events or problems in any individual sector will be much reduced. Where concentrations do exist, it is important to understand the underlying factors that will affect the performance of those loans.

Taking concentration risks one step further, it is not uncommon for a portfolio to have a single loan that accounts for 10% or more of the overall portfolio. Where this is the case, investors should consider the credit fundamentals of this exposure separately in a manner similar to that used for a single-property transaction.

Origination and Servicing

Investors should review the lender's origination process, the lending criteria for the loans and any warranties for that specific transaction. This review should consider the extent of the origination process, where the lender obtains its business and what resources are available to perform it. Any procedures for assessing the creditworthiness of the borrower will be important, particularly for the smaller borrowers, as well as the valuation process.

Similar considerations apply to the servicing capability. A good servicing operation can limit the instance of loans becoming delinquent and also maximise recoveries should loans default.

Credit Assessment of a Single-Property Transaction

The previous discussion has centred on some of the key credit areas for investors analysing multiborrower CMBS transactions. While much of this also applies to single-property transactions, the analysis necessary for these transactions differs significantly in its detail. Listed below are some of the key additional areas we believe investors should consider when analysing a single-asset deal:

- Cash flow stability and loan leverage
- Property valuation
- Property marketability
- Capital expenditure requirements
- Environmental and planning issues
- Loan structure

These areas are property specific and so an investor will require much more detailed information than would be the case for all but the largest exposures in a multiborrower transaction.

Cash Flow Stability and Loan Leverage

Perhaps the most important aspect of commercial property analysis is the nature and stability of the underlying cash flows. These are usually derived from a large number of tenants occupying a single commercial property. The stability and sustainability of these cash flows are used in part to produce a valuation, and they also determine whether the leverage applied to the property is in itself sustainable.

The review of the cash flows is likely to comprise the following components:

- A review of the tenants and their susceptibility to an economic downturn.
- The nature of the underlying leases, the expiry profile of the leases, and the level of borrower responsibility for items such as capital expenditure and insurance.
- A comparison of the rental level with that in comparable properties in order to assess the sustainability of the rental income.

Having gained an insight into the nature of the cash flow, an investor can then compare it to the anticipated DSCR level to ensure the leverage is appropriate when taking into account the likely volatility and sustainability of the rental income.

Property Valuation

The launch valuation is a useful guide to the refinance value of the property and also as a starting point for estimating the value in a forced sale situation. However, remember that the valuation for a commercial property is directly linked to the amount of income it can generate. As most commercial properties are owned by special purpose companies, with the income from the property used to finance the debt, any difficulty in maintaining the mortgage payments is likely to be a direct result of a reduction in the cash flows from the property. This will reduce the property's value in a forced sale situation.

Property Marketability and Longevity

The key to evaluating the likely future desirability of a property will be the nature of the physical building itself. However, any analysis needs to look at more than just the property. It needs to encompass the surrounding area or sub-market, transportation links, parking facilities, additional infrastructure and the like. An analysis to determine likely future demand for a property should encompass all elements that affect desirability, including possibly the most important factor—competition.

It is important to consider the extent to which new or redeveloped properties may enter the market in the foreseeable future, increasing the level of competition. This will be particularly important when the term of the transaction exceeds a significant level of lease expiries, as this places increased reliance on successfully reletting.

Capital Expenditure Requirements

Different properties require different levels of capital expenditure (capex), depending on a number of factors, including age, construction, and usage. Capex can be broken down into two types—that required for the continual maintenance of the building (maintenance capex) and that required to upgrade or refurbish a building (development capex). Investors should establish who is responsible for each of the above. In the United Kingdom, maintenance capex is usually the tenants' responsibility, but investors should not assume the borrower is immune from capex spend.

On occasion, a borrower is likely to be required to fund general refurbishment to maintain the standard of the property. There may also need to be considerable amounts spent after a major tenant has vacated a property in order to attract a new tenant to that space. Investors should check that a prudent level of capex spend has been factored into the future property cash flow assumptions. In fact, many transactions require a minimum amount to be either spent or reserved for capex each year.

Environmental and Planning Issues

Ideally, the valuation should also identify any environmental or planning issues associated with the building. Environmental issues primarily relate to the land on which the property has been built. Where this is deemed contaminated, the cost of decontamination may well fall with the borrower. Planning issues may also require additional spend during the life of a transaction.

Loan Structure

Loan structure is more than just leverage (an area previously discussed). It includes such elements as the loan amortisation schedule and any performance triggers such as minimum debt service cover ratios. These should also be considered in any credit analysis.

Amortisation is the first consideration. There is a significant difference between a deal that amortises in full over the term of the loan and one that only partly amortises and therefore relies on a refinancing of the property to repay the bonds at maturity. A property is not guaranteed to increase in value over the life of a transaction.

A valuable structural protection for investors is often provided by the use of a DSCR threshold mechanism. Once the ratio reaches a predetermined minimum level, usually some way above what would be needed to meet all the debt service obligations, all free cash will be retained in the structure, for the benefit of the bondholders.

Summary of Collateral Characteristics

Investing in CMBS, whether they are single-asset or multiborrower transactions, requires an appreciation of the nature of the underlying properties and the inherent sensitivities of the cash flows they generate. The type and extent of analysis undertaken should be tailored to reflect the characteristics of the collateral pool and also whether the proposed investment is at a senior or junior level in the capital structure.

In particular, many investors take comfort from a well-diversified multiborrower portfolio and seek to limit the concentration of risks associated with a single-asset transaction. While this approach is understandable and relevant to senior bondholders, this diversification is not necessarily beneficial to junior noteholders who are then exposed to potential losses across the entire portfolio.

CMBS TRANSACTION STRUCTURES

A number of different transaction structures are used in CMBS securitisations. The most appropriate one for any particular case will depend on the nature of the security over the real estate assets, the type of borrower, the number of jurisdictions involved, and any tax implications for the owner of the properties.

Pooled Commercial Mortgage Transactions

There are two basic forms of pooled commercial mortgage transactions: the true sale and the synthetic structures. The true sale mechanism, as its name suggests, involves the sale of assets from the originator's balance sheet to an SPV, which are then used as security for the issue of notes to investors. Synthetic structures, by contrast, involve the creation of a credit derivative linked to the performance of a pool of loans. The loans themselves remain on the balance sheet of the originator but the credit risks associated with these loans are transferred through the credit derivative to investors. Synthetic structures can simplify the issuance process and avoid many of the complexities (and costs) associated with the sale of assets in many jurisdictions.

True Sale Transactions

A typical UK commercial mortgage loan securitisation involves the equitable assignment of a pool of mortgages by the originator of the loans (usually a bank). The loans and all ancillary rights are held in trust for both the originator, who retains the legal title to the properties, and the special purpose vehicle company (SPV). Importantly, a power of attorney is also granted by the originator to the trustee to enforce the loans in the name of the originator and, if necessary, to transfer the originator's legal title to the SPV. This legal structure achieves ring-fencing of the assets such that even in the event of the insolvency of the originator, the cash flows derived from the underlying loans will be available to service the debt issue. This process avoids incurring stamp duty. Monument Securitisation No.1 PLC, comprised by loans originated by Anglo Irish Bank Corporation plc, is an example of this type of structure and is illustrated in Exhibit 12.1.

Synthetic Structures

Synthetic structures can significantly simplify the structuring and issuance process. This advantage is particularly marked when dealing with a portfolio of loans spread across multiple jurisdictions. The difficulties involved in designing a structure for a true sale transaction to cope with different insolvency regimes, unharmonised tax regimes, and vastly dif-

EXHIBIT 12.1 Loan Assignment Structure

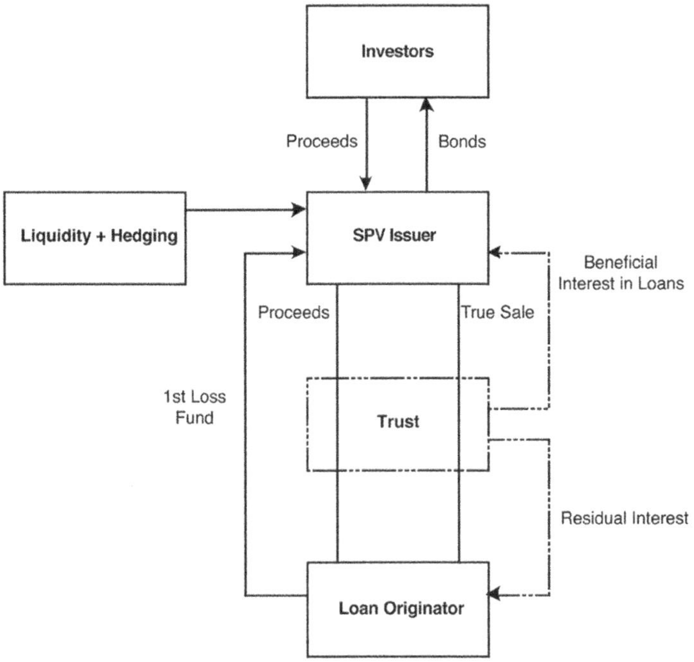

Source: Barclays Capital.

ferent property and foreclosure laws make synthetic structures far more suited to this type of transaction.

In many ways, the synthetic structure is much simpler than one involving an assignment of underlying loans. In these structures, the proceeds of the issue are not used to purchase the reference portfolio of commercial mortgages but instead to purchase other collateral, which might include one or more of the following: Pfandbriefe, notes from the originator, or other securities. This collateral is then used to collateralise the issuer's debt obligations. An example structure for a synthetic transaction is shown in Exhibit 12.2.

Under a guarantee agreement, the originator is able to recover an amount equal to the net realised losses on the reference pool of loans, including the costs incurred in the foreclosure and recovery process, in return for a periodic payment of a guarantee fee. This fee is calculated to make up any shortfall between the interest received on the credit-linked note collateral pool and the expenses and interest costs of the issuing SPV. Realised losses are applied in reverse sequential order to the notes, by can-

EXHIBIT 12.2   Typical Synthetic Structure with a Credit Default Swap

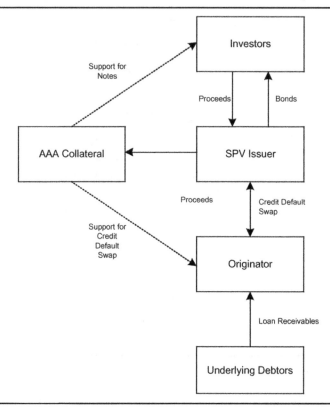

Source: Barclays Capital.

celling a portion of the most junior class outstanding to cover the loss, while amounts equal to the loan redemptions are paid through sequentially.

Double credit risk is a particular feature of such synthetic transaction structures. Not only are investors exposed to the performance of the reference pool of commercial mortgages, but also to the performance of the collateral the issuer is holding. If this includes notes issued by the originator itself then this will also include exposure to the credit rating of the originator.

Secured Loan Structures

A true sale structure, while appropriate for the securitisation of closed-end loans, is likely to have unfortunate tax implications where a property owner wishes to retain overall economic benefit of the asset. This can be overcome through a secured loan structure.

EXHIBIT 12.3   Secured Loan Securitisation Structure

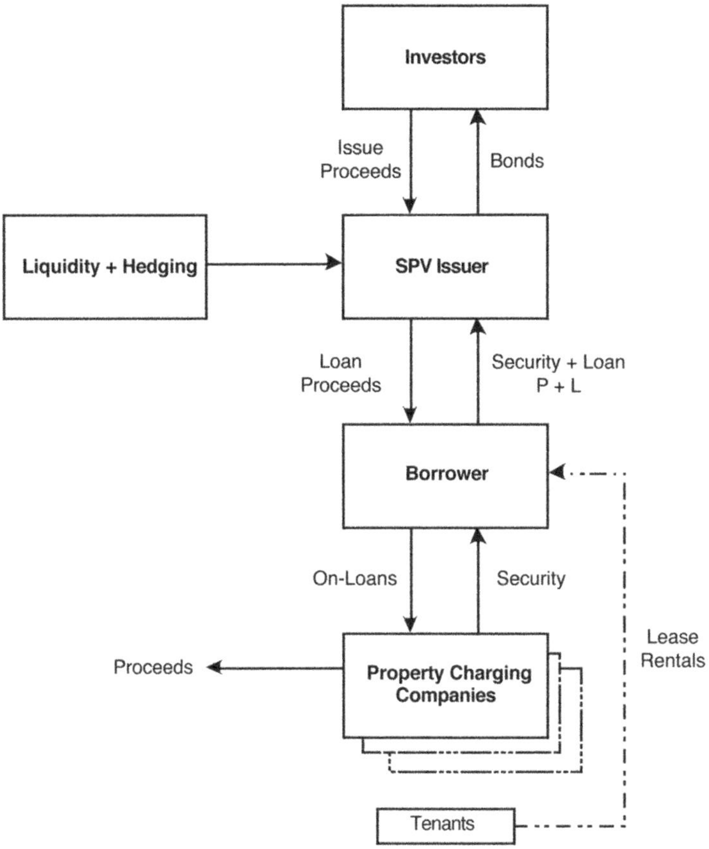

Source: Barclays Capital.

Under this structure, ownership of the assets remains with the borrower, but bondholders have the benefit of a charge over the assets. A bankruptcy remote SPV raises the debt and on-lends the proceeds to a borrower company under a lending arrangement, usually termed the "issuer-borrower" loan. The borrower may then on-lend to one or more property owning companies. A comprehensive security package will include security over all the issuer's assets, first priority fixed charges over the properties charged by the borrower or by the other property companies, and assignment of rental income received from the charged properties in addition to security over other assets such as bank accounts. A typical secured loan structure is illustrated in Exhibit 12.3.

In standard CMBS transactions of this type, rents will be received into a fixed-charge account. This is in contrast to most whole business securitisations in which it is more practical to pass operating income through floating charge accounts.

Under the secured loan structure, the trustee might find it necessary under certain circumstances to enforce the fixed and floating charges. Such circumstances could include unremedied events of default under the issuer-borrower loan, or if third-party creditors were to attempt to put the company into administration. In this case, the trustee would seek to have an administrative receiver appointed on behalf of the secured creditors. However, the process could disrupt the receipt and payment of cash flows. The ratings of the notes are based on timely payment of interest (and sometimes principal) so the transaction will include some form of liquidity support, which is typically sized to enable the issuer to cover one year's debt service.

Sale and Leaseback Structures

The sale and leaseback concept enables a company to retain the operating benefit of the properties while divesting of ownership. The typical structures avoid the adverse tax consequences of a normal sale and can, in comes cases, gain certain tax advantages.

In a securitisation structure, a bankruptcy remote SPV uses the proceeds of the debt issue to acquire the properties. It then leases them back to the seller for a term that will equal or exceed the tenor of the debt issue. Lease payments will service the debt in one of various ways: The debt may be fully amortised over the term (although this gives rise to a significant tax mismatch); the debt may be partially amortised, which requires refinancing or a sale of the property to ensure repayment of the debt at maturity; or the issue size may be increased to fund the purchase of a zero coupon bond to repay the principal at maturity. A typical structure is illustrated in Exhibit 12.4.

CONCLUSION

The European CMBS market presents investors with a wide variety of investment opportunities ranging from short-dated floating-rate notes to long-dated, fixed-rate issues across a rating spectrum from AAA to BB, and so it should appeal to a wide section of the investor community. It is, however, a relatively complex asset class. There are many underlying asset types, which can be spread across more than one country, and there are a number of possible transaction structures. As a result, it is not always easy to compare one transaction against another.

EXHIBIT 12.4   Simplified Sale-and-Lease-Back Structure

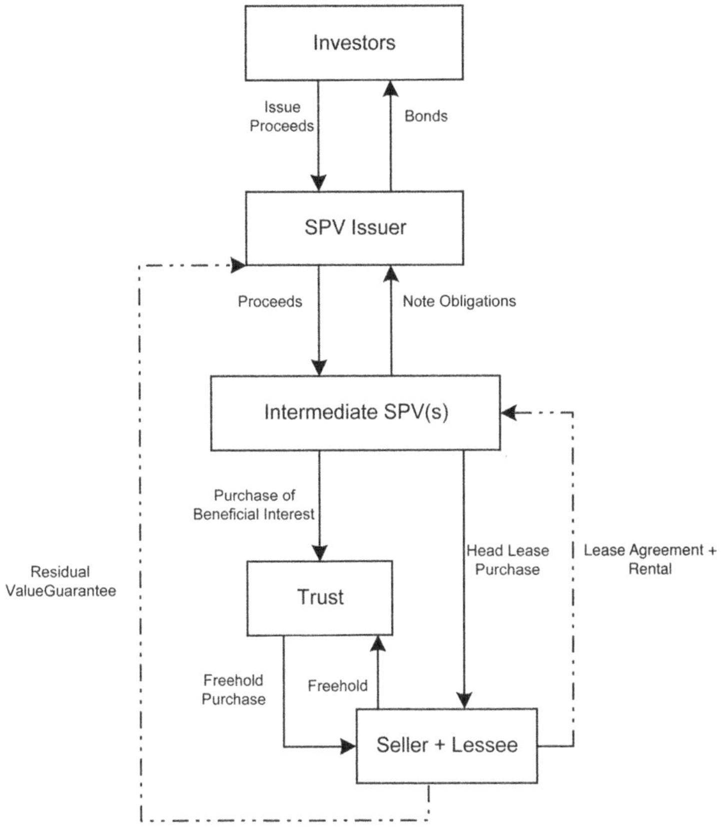

Source: Barclays Capital.

Given the variety and potential volatility of the some of the underlying collateral, different analysis techniques are more appropriate for assessing the various transactions. This is clearly illustrated by the difference between a highly diversified multiborrower pool and a transaction supported by a single prestige property. However, in practice the distinctions are likely to be less clear-cut and a combination of techniques may be more appropriate. Certain key factors underlie all the analysis and these include an assessment of the leverage and cash flow coverage of the debt; the property value; the structure of the loan; any mechanisms designed to protect investors; and an understanding of the sensitivities of the tenants who are ultimately the source of the cash flow within the transaction.

CHAPTER 13

European Credit Card ABS

Markus Niemeier
Manager
Barclays Capital

Credit card ABS (CCABS) constitute one of the most liquid and widely accepted asset classes in Europe and most European ABS investors are likely to hold some credit card securitisations. The purpose of this chapter is to discuss the structural features and investment characteristics of CCABS. The focus is on the UK credit card ABS market because the vast majority of European credit card transactions are backed by sterling-denominated collateral.

CARD TYPES

Usually, credit cards fall into one of two categories: general purpose cards and private label cards. General purpose cards can be further assigned to the categories standard, affinity, and cobranded. Exhibit 13.1 shows the various types of credit cards.

General Purpose

General purpose credit cards are the most widely issued and accepted; the majority are MasterCard and Visa affiliated. Today, most general purpose credit cards are issued in the form of *teaser rate cards*, which offer a very low or even 0% APR to new cardholders for a limited period, usually up to six months. Such offers are aimed at interest-sensitive borrowers, and

---

The views expressed in this chapter are those of the author and not necessarily those of Barclays Capital.

EXHIBIT 13.1   Types of Credit Cards

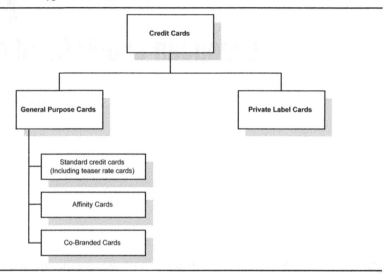

Source: Barclays Capital.

banks have attracted new customers successfully in this way. However, teaser rates on balance transfers (when a customer switches card issuers and transfers the outstanding balance on an existing card to a new card) have encouraged customers to change their card issuers more frequently in order to benefit from the low introductory interest rates. This trend has made it even more important for credit card issuers to build brand awareness and offer additional benefits to keep hold of their customers.

In order to build brand loyalty and increase customer retention, some credit card issuers have started to offer *affinity cards*. In Europe, for example, such cards are issued by MBNA Europe Bank Limited (MBNA EBL), a wholly owned subsidiary of MBNA America Bank, N.A. To be able to issue affinity cards, the company has to identify special interest groups which sign up to an affinity partnership agreement. These could be, for example, associations of medical professionals, fans of auto racing, or college alumni associations. Once an association has established an affinity partnership agreement with a credit card issuer, its members can apply for a credit card, which could have a logo of their association, a picture of their favourite driver, or their school seal. This can build brand loyalty and cardholders are less likely to switch to another credit card issuer. MBNA has traditionally been the largest issuer of affinity credit cards. In the United Kingdom, the company has established partnership agreements with various organisations, including Burberrys Limited, the World Wide Fund for Nature, and Manchester United Football Club.

In the case of *cobranded cards*, the bank allies with a company, such as an automobile manufacturer, and the two companies market the card jointly. Such agreements benefit the bank because it can attract additional customers and increase its receivables under management. It also benefits the company through the promotion of its products. For example, in 1993, HFC Bank PLC, a wholly owned indirect subsidiary of Household, Inc. in the United States, introduced the GM Card in the United Kingdom. It has standard credit card features but customers can also earn reward points for purchases made on the card and redeem them when they buy a new or used Vauxhall car. The agreements for cobranded cards are likely to have different arrangements for sharing expenses and revenues.

Private Label Cards

Private label cards are issued and administered by retailers. Usually, they are given to customers for use in their stores, and their main function is to promote the retailer's products. As a result, credit underwriting may not be as stringent as it is for other types of credit cards. In Europe, as of this writing, there has been only one private label ABS transaction so far. In December 2000, Findomestic Banca S.p.A. securitised credit card borrowings generated through the company's credit card product Carta Aura.

CREDIT CARD PAYMENT CYCLE

Exhibit 13.2 shows a simplified credit card payment cycle. When a customer buys goods and pays with a credit card, the bank which reimburses the shop owner for the purchase does not forward the full amount to the shop owner but deducts a certain fee called *interchange*. This fee is ultimately shared between the bank, the card association (usually Visa or MasterCard), and the original bank that issued the credit card. So the first bank is paid for processing the payment, the card association for providing the payment and clearing network, and the issuing card bank as compensation for assuming credit risk and offering a grace period on finance charge accrual.

THE EUROPEAN CREDIT CARD ABS MARKET

One of the goals in credit card securitisation, as with the securitisation of other assets, is to remove receivables from the issuing card bank's regulatory balance sheet in order to free up capital. Driven by the need of banks to diversify sources of funding and reduce regulatory capital, the first securiti-

EXHIBIT 13.2   Credit Card Payment Cycle

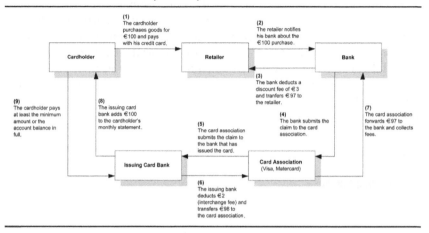

Source: Barclays Capital.

EXHIBIT 13.3   Credit Card Issuance—European Collateral

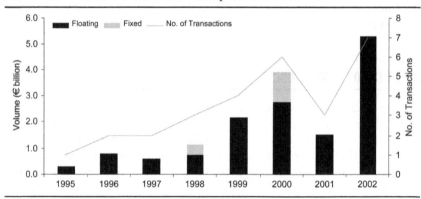

Source: Bloomberg.

sation of credit card receivables was completed in the United States in 1987. Since then, securitisation has become a favourite source of funding for credit card issuers. Following the US success, MBNA EBL completed the first European credit card securitisation[1] in 1995. Exhibit 13.3 shows the issuance of all rated CCABS backed by European collateral from 1995 to 2002.

---

[1] We define European credit card transactions as those transactions that are backed by credit card receivables that originated in Europe. A US dollar-denominated credit card transaction backed by sterling-denominated receivables would therefore count as a European transaction, while a euro-denominated transaction backed by US dollar-denominated receivables would count as a non-European transaction.

EXHIBIT 13.4   European Credit Card ABS Issuers Ranked by Volume
(1995 to 2002)

Rank	Issuer	Originator	Original number of issues	Original size (€ m equiv.)
1	CARDS (MBNA MT 1)	MBNA EBL	12	5,191
2	CARDS (MBNA MT 2)	MBNA EBL	4	2,765
3	ARRAN	The Royal Bank of Scotland	3	2,330
4	Gracechurch	Barclaycard	2	2,026
5	Sherwood Castle Funding	Capital One Bank (Europe)	2	1,321
6	Pillar Funding	Egg Banking	1	793
7	Affinity	HFC Bank	1	633
8	Diners Card Finance	Diners Club Europe (and others)	1	339
	Findomestic	Findomestic Banca	1	311
9	Opus	HFC Bank	1	223
		Total	28	15,598

Source: Bloomberg.

The majority of issues since 1995 have come with floating-rate notes. However, in the latter part of 2000, demand for the asset class was expressed by fixed-rate buyers and MBNA EBL issued two fixed-rate transactions, one euro- and one sterling-denominated. Both issues had 10-year maturities and capitalised on the relatively small supply of consumer asset securitisations available in that sector of the curve. Exhibit 13.4 shows issuers of European CCABS ranked by cumulative issuance.

Since the market's inception in 1995, MBNA EBL has been the dominant issuer of CCABS, both in number of issues completed and total volume of issuance. The company has accessed the securitisation market each year and completed 16 transactions in total. The first 12 transactions, Chester Asset Receivables Dealings (CARDS) 1-12, were issued from the same master trust (MBNA MT 1), which was set up in 1995. In 2001, MBNA EBL created a new master trust "UK Receivables Trust II" (MBNA MT 2) from which four transactions, CARDS 2001-A, CARDS 2001-B, CARDS 2002-A and CARDS 2002-B, were issued in 2001 and 2002.

The second largest issuer of European CCABS, The Royal Bank of Scotland PLC (RBS), has accessed the securitisation market three times in 2000. Every transaction from its ARRAN master trust has been denominated in US dollars and backed by sterling-denominated collateral. Barclaycard, a division of Barclays Bank PLC, has completed two transactions from its Gracechurch master trust. Notes have also been US dollar-denominated and backed by UK credit card receivables. Capital One Bank (Europe) Limited (COBE), a wholly owned indirect subsidiary of Capital One Bank in the United States, has issued two transactions from its Sherwood Castle Receivables Trust. The first issue is sterling-denominated and the second issue is euro-denominated, which has enlarged the company's investor base to include the euro-denominated investor universe. In both cases, the collateral is sterling-denominated. HFC Bank PLC, a wholly owned subsidiary of Household International, Inc., is the fourth largest issuer of European CCABS. In 1997, the company completed its OPUS transaction, followed by the Affinity 2002-A transaction in 2002. In both cases, notes and collateral are denominated in sterling.

Issuance of European CCABS is clearly dominated by repeat issuers, accounting for more than 90% of total issuance volume. Credit card Issuers that have accessed the securitisation market only once include Findomestic Banca S.p.A. (2000), Diners Club Europe S.p.A. (and others) (2001) and Egg Banking PLC (2002).

From the 28 CCABS transactions shown in Exhibit 13.4, 26 are backed by sterling-denominated credit card receivables and two have euro-denominated collateral. In 2000, Findomestic Banca S.p.A. issued €311 million of notes backed by Italian credit card receivables. In 2001, Diners Card Europe S.p.A. (and other European Diners Club operations) completed its first transaction in a euro-denominated issue. The collateral includes receivables in Italy, Germany, the United Kingdom, Ireland, the Netherlands, and Belgium.

Most credit card transactions completed have usually come with three tranches. The Class A Notes, approximately 90% of all European CCABS issued, are usually triple-A rated, the Class B Notes, which account for approximately 5%, are usually single-A rated and the most junior tranche, the Class C Notes, accounts for approximately 5% and is usually rated triple-B. Exhibit 13.5 shows European credit card issuance by rating since the market's inception in 1995.

STRUCTURAL CHARACTERISTICS

In this section the fundamental structural characteristics of European CCABS are presented. Most of the examples included in this section refer to MBNA EBL's CARDS 2002-A, which was completed in June 2002. The transaction is fairly representative of most other European credit card transactions.

EXHIBIT 13.5 European Credit Card Issuance by Rating

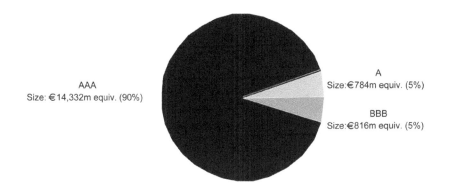

AAA
Size: €14,332m equiv. (90%)

A
Size:€784m equiv. (5%)

BBB
Size:€816m equiv. (5%)

Source: Bloomberg.

Master Trust versus Standalone

In the United States, standalone trusts were the dominant issuance vehicles from 1987 to 1991. An originator designates a specific pool of credit card accounts and sells the receivables and rights to the future receivables arising from those accounts to a discrete trust. The major disadvantage with standalone trusts is that each subsequent securitisation requires the issuer to set up a new trust. This structure was used until 1991 when the master trust became the preferred issuance vehicle.

Master trusts allow issuers to sell multiple securities from a single trust. There is no segregation of any sort between the receivables in the trust and as such, all issues are backed by the same collateral. The master trust structure affords the issuer great flexibility, since the cost and effort associated with issuing a new series from a master trust is lower than for creating a new trust for every issue. For example, an issuer creates a new master trust and sells €100 million in credit card receivables from selected accounts into the master trust and then issues securities backed by these receivables. When more financing is needed, the issuer sells a further €100 million in receivables from more accounts into the same trust and issues more securities. This means that the issuer does not have to set up new master trusts if it wants to securitise new receivables. All securities are issued from the same master trust and backed by the *same collateral.*

A simplified credit card master trust structure is shown in Exhibit 13.6. This particular structure has been developed in the United States and was introduced in Europe with the creation of MBNA's UK Receivables Trust II.

EXHIBIT 13.6   Credit Card Master Trust Structure

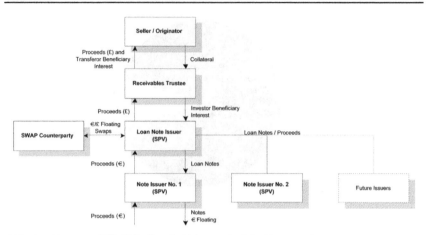

Source: Barclays Capital.

As shown in Exhibit 13.6, the seller or originator transfers receivables from selected accounts to the master trust (Receivables Trustee) and collects the proceeds from the sale. The seller also retains an ownership interest in the trust (Transferor Beneficiary Interest). This participation performs some crucial functions. The transferor interest absorbs seasonal fluctuations in the credit card receivables balance and is allocated all dilutions (balances cancelled due to returned goods) and ineligible receivables (fraudulently generated receivables or receivables that do not comply with stipulated origination standards). The transferor interest also has the function of aligning the originator's interests with the interests of the investors, that is, if the originator retains an interest in the collateral, the company has a certain interest in servicing the portfolio and making sure that it performs as expected.

In Exhibit 13.6, the loan note issuer, a special purpose vehicle (SPV) acquires the investor interest (Investor Beneficiary Interest) in the trust and finances the purchase by issuing loan notes to the issuer of the notes, a second SPV (Note Issuer No. 1). If new financing is required, the originator transfers new receivables into the trust and the loan note issuer creates a new investor interest in the trust, which is financed by the issuance of loan notes to a new notes issuer (Note Issuer No. 2, Note Issuer No. 3, and so on). The note issuer in turn finances the purchase of these loan notes by issuing notes to investors.

Transaction Structure

The typical credit card transaction structure has three different cash flow periods: revolving, accumulation, and early amortisation. Each period performs a distinct function and allocates cash flows differently. Credit card transactions are usually structured as soft bullets in order to mimic a traditional corporate bond, that is, investors receive monthly or quarterly payments of interest with one single payment of principal on the scheduled redemption date.

During the revolving period, all receipts of principal are reinvested in new receivables. It is the ability to revolve the receivables that provides an issuer with tremendous flexibility in choosing a maturity profile for a securitisation, especially as the average life of credit card receivables is a short five to ten months. A simple amortisation structure in which all principal receipts would be passed through to the investor from day one would result in securities with very short average lives and lumpy, unpredictable principal repayments to investors.

Usually 12 to 18 months before the scheduled maturity date, the accumulation period commences. The length of the accumulation period is determined by the rating agencies (for UK banks that are regulated by the FSA, the length of the accumulation period is determined by the rating agencies together with the FSA) and subject to the monthly payment rate of the receivables pool (see below). During this period, principal collections are accumulated in a trust account and invested in short term instruments. On the scheduled maturity date, a bullet payment of principal is made from the trust account to noteholders.

If the portfolio experiences severe asset deterioration, the seller's interest in the collateral falls below a specified level, the notes are not redeemed in full on the scheduled redemption date, or in the case of certain legal problems, the transaction enters into rapid amortisation. During the rapid amortisation period, all principal receipts are, depending on the specific transaction structure, either directly passed through to the investors to amortise the notes or held in a trust account to redeem the notes in full on their scheduled redemption date. Early amortisation triggers are usually found on the trust and series level. If one of the trust's early amortisation triggers is breached, all series issued from the trust enter into early amortisation. If a series early amortisation trigger is breached, only the specific series enters into early amortisation. The following list includes typical trust and series early amortisation triggers:

Trust early amortisation triggers:

▪ Events of default, bankruptcy or insolvency by the seller or servicer.
▪ Seller is unable to transfer receivables to the trust when necessary.
▪ Seller ceases to be resident for tax purposes.

EXHIBIT 13.7   Amortisation Structure

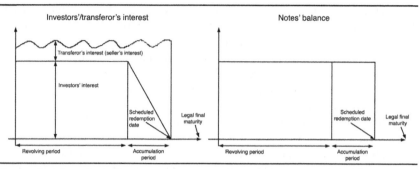

Source: Barclays Capital.

- Change of tax law creating a liability for the trustee, other than for stamp duty.

Series early amortisation triggers:

- Failure to make required deposits or payments.
- False representations or warranties that remain unremedied for a certain number of days.
- Three-month average excess spread falls below zero.
- Seller interest falls below the required level.
- Servicer default that would have a material adverse effect on the issuer of the loan notes.
- The investor interest is not reduced to zero on the scheduled redemption date.
- Early termination of any of the swap agreements if not replaced within a certain number of days.
- Change of tax law creating a liability for the loan note issuer.

All collections arising from the pool of receivables are split into finance charge income and principal receipts. Finance charges include interest on the receivables, annual fees, late payment fees, overlimit charges and interchange and are used every month to pay the coupon on the notes, servicing fees, and other expenses. Finance charges are also used to cover receivables that have been charged off. Finance charge income left over after these deductions is called excess spread and is usually paid to the seller. Principal receipts are reinvested in new receivables during the revolving period and used to amortise the notes during the amortisation period (or invested in short term instruments during the accumulation period). Exhibit 13.7 shows a typical soft bullet structure, in which the transaction enters the revolving period followed by the accumulation period.

As shown on the left side in Exhibit 13.7, the transaction enters the revolving period immediately following the closing date. During the revolving period, the investor interest remains stable and the seller's interest absorbs any fluctuations in the collateral balance. All principal receipts during this period are reinvested in new receivables. Following the end of the revolving period, the transaction enters the accumulation period. As shown on the right side of Exhibit 13.7, the notes' balance remains constant until the scheduled redemption date, when all principal receipts accumulated in a dedicated trust account are used to redeem the notes in full.

The legal final maturity shown in Exhibit 13.7 is different form the scheduled maturity (also called *expected maturity*). The expected maturity is established when a transaction is being structured and is based on the length of the revolving period and the monthly payment rate of the portfolio. The legal final maturity is the date the rating agencies use when assigning their ratings to the notes. This is the date at which if full principal were not paid, the issue would be in default. The legal final is typically two years after the expected maturity date. An issue could extend past its expected maturity date if the monthly payment rate (discussed in the next section) fell dramatically during the accumulation period.

Credit Enhancement

A typical issue will feature a triple-A rated tranche, a single-A rated tranche, a triple-B rated tranche and a dynamic spread account. The subordination structure for a typical credit card issue is shown in Exhibit 13.8. In this example, the class A noteholders benefit from the subordination of the class B and class C notes, which together provide 12% credit enhancement. The class B noteholders benefit from the subordination of the class C notes, which provide 7% credit enhancement. The class C noteholders benefit from a dynamic spread account.

The amount of credit enhancement for a transaction is determined by the rating agencies and varies by issuer depending primarily on the performance of the underlying collateral. Exhibit 13.9 shows total enhancement levels for three recent transactions completed by different issuers.

The class C noteholders benefit from a dynamic spread account. If 3-month average excess spread falls below a predetermined level, the spread account builds from monthly excess spread until the target level is reached. In order to fully understand the protection afforded by the spread account we need to assess the degree to which the spread account traps excess spread. Exhibit 13.10 shows excess spread trigger levels and trapping levels for a typical credit card issue.

EXHIBIT 13.8 A Credit Enhancement Structure

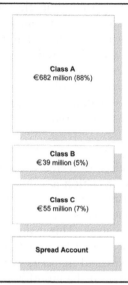

Source: Barclays Capital.

EXHIBIT 13.9 Total Credit Enhancement Levels

Issuer	Class A
CARDS 2002-A	12.0%
Sherwood Castle Funding Series 2002-1	16.0%
Affinity 2002-A	15.5%

Source: Offering circulars.

EXHIBIT 13.10 Trapped Excess Spread Levels

Excess Spread (3-month average)	Excess Spread Trapped Up to
Greater than 5.00%	0.0%
4.01–5.00%	1.5%
3.01–4.0%	3.0%
Less than or equal to 3.0%	5.0%

Source: Barclays Capital.

EXHIBIT 13.11   Trapped Excess Spread (Slowly Deteriorating Environment, %)

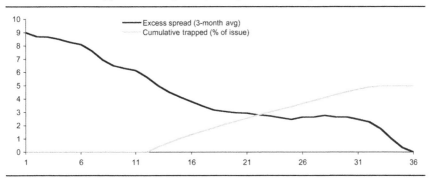

Source: Barclays Capital.

In the following example, the spread account starts to trap excess spread when the 3-month average excess spread level is 5% or lower. As the excess spread level continues to decrease, the level of spread that is trapped increases to a maximum of 5% of the total transaction size.

As the spread account traps excess spread over a period of deteriorating collateral performance, a driving factor in the effectiveness of the spread account is the rate at which the excess spread decreases. If the collateral performance deteriorates slowly, the spread trapping mechanism will most likely be able to trap the maximum amount of spread allowed. However, if there is a rapid deterioration in the collateral performance, the spread trapping mechanism may not be able to trap the maximum allowable amount of spread before the excess spread in the transaction turns negative. Exhibit 13.11 shows a scenario in which excess spread deteriorates from an initial level of 9% to zero over a 36-month period. After 12 months, 3-month average excess spread falls to 5% and excess spread is getting trapped.

In this example, the dynamic spread account builds up to the maximum 5% of the transaction size. The spread account reaches the maximum of 5% in month 33 and then stays at this level. Exhibit 13.12 shows a scenario in which excess spread falls from the initial 9% to zero within 24 months, that is, the same deterioration in excess spread as in the previous example happens over a 2- instead of a 3-year period.

In this example, the dynamic spread account builds up only to approximately 1.6% of the transaction size, which is well below the target level of 5%. These two examples highlight the importance of the originator's ability to service the receivables pool effectively and, as such, avoid a rapid deterioration in the performance of the collateral. An originator that follows strict credit underwriting procedures and has experienced staff servicing accounts that enter a state of delinquency

EXHIBIT 13.12   Trapped Excess Spread—Rapidly Deteriorating Environment (%)

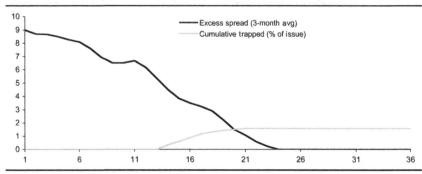

Legend:
— Excess spread (3-month avg)
---- Cumulative trapped (% of issue)

Source: Barclays Capital.

would be in the best position in the event of an economic downturn. The underwriting and servicing abilities of the originator must be analysed and a judgement about its ability to effectively manage any deterioration in the collateral performance must be made to gain comfort with an issuer's class C notes.

COLLATERAL CHARACTERISTICS

Analysing the collateral characteristics of a credit card portfolio is essential because it tells us how the transaction is likely to perform. The major characteristics we focus on are:

- Account balance (distribution across various ranges, weighted average).
- Weighted average credit limit and utilisation.
- Account age (distribution across various ranges, weighted average).
- Geographic distribution of accounts.

The distribution of cardholder balances across various balance ranges and the weighted average account balance are both determinants of how well credit risk in the portfolio is diversified. However, it should be noted that although a portfolio with a lower weighted average account balance across all cardholders is preferable to a portfolio with a higher balance because of the lower loss severity for a single cardholder, lower account balances are generally given to customers with bad credit records. As such, the weighted average account balance of a pool of credit card receivables should always be reviewed in conjunction with the credit card issuer's origination strategy.

EXHIBIT 13.13 Account Age as a Percentage of Total Receivables

	ARRAN 2000-A	Gracechurch No. 1
2 years or less	44.52	12.08
Over 2 to 4 years	37.48	11.90
Over 4 to 8 years	8.00	19.57
Over 8 to 12 years	3.69	12.29
Over 12 to 16 years	3.02	14.12
Over 16 to 20 years	1.42	11.95
Over 20 years	1.87	18.10

Source: Offering circulars.

Furthermore, the weighted average account balance should be analysed in conjunction with the weighted average utilisation of the assigned credit limit. Everything else being equal, we would prefer a portfolio with a lower average utilisation. On average, cardholders with a low credit balance are less likely to default in times of economic downturns than cardholders who have already made full use of the credit given to them.

The composition of a credit card portfolio by account age tells us how the seasoning of the collateral can vary significantly across various portfolios. Exhibit 13.13 shows the initial composition of two credit card portfolios by account age.

The Arran 2000-A portfolio is relatively unseasoned. By the time the transaction was completed, less than 55% of the cardholders in the securitised trust had held a credit card with The Royal Bank of Scotland for more than two years. This is very different from the Gracechurch portfolio where almost 88% of the cardholders in the portfolio had held a card for more than two years by the time the deal was launched.

Advanced seasoning is a positive attribute for a trust as the portfolio is more likely to exhibit stable collateral performance than a relatively unseasoned portfolio. This is because a pool of new receivables usually experiences increasing losses for the first 18 months after which the losses usually decline and then level out. Over time, positive selection occurs as the lower quality and riskier accounts become charged-off and removed from the pool, leaving the higher quality accounts which should demonstrate more stable performance.

Lastly, it is important to analyse the geographic distribution of accounts. A diverse account base is positive for portfolios of loans as it helps mitigate losses caused by an economic downturn in any one region.

COLLATERAL PERFORMANCE

The key performance indicators for analysing credit card portfolios include portfolio yield, monthly payment rate (MPR), delinquencies, charge-offs, and excess spread. For most European credit card ABS, these performance indicators are published on a monthly basis on Bloomberg. The high degree of standardisation in terms of which performance indicators are published and how they are calculated makes the credit card ABS market very transparent. This also allows us to construct meaningful indices which help us track the performance of the whole (or a significant part) of the credit card market.

Barclays Capital has developed an index for the European CCABS market, called the Barclays European Credit Card Indicators (BECCI). BECCI includes approximately €12 billion equivalent in receivables held in publicly rated ABS credit card transactions. It covers approximately 85% of the whole European credit card ABS market. Transactions are not included if their performance data is not or not yet publicly available. The various performance indicators are calculated on a weighted average based on the publicly rated notes outstanding.

We will discuss portfolio yield, monthly payment rate (MPR), delinquencies, charge-offs, and excess spread as well as excess spread efficiency (ESE) and charge-off coverage (COC); the latter two are combinations of the first five performance indicators. The various performance indicators will be shown for European and US credit card collateral. We will use our BECCI for European collateral and Standard & Poor's Credit Card Quality Indexes (S&P Index) for US collateral.

Portfolio Yield

Portfolio yield equals finance charges expressed as a percentage of the portfolio's outstanding receivables balance. Finance charges include interest on the receivables, annual fees, late payment fees, overlimit accounts and interchange. Portfolio yield is also driven by the way customers make use of their credit cards. Usually, revolving accounts generate higher finance charges than accounts held by convenience users, that is, customers who usually pay off their balance by the end of each month. Yield also depends on the seasoning of accounts included in the portfolio. If seasoning is low, a substantial proportion of customers may benefit from teaser rates. This proportion falls as accounts are becoming seasoned, which leads to a rise in yield. Exhibit 13.14 shows historical yields for European and US credit card transactions.

EXHIBIT 13.14 Yield, Annualised (%)

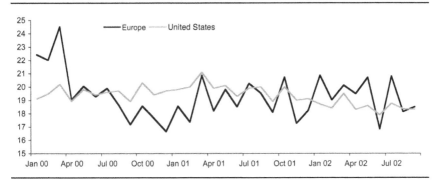

Source: Barclays Capital, Standard & Poor's.

As Exhibit 13.14 shows, yields have fluctuated on a month-on-month basis, both in Europe and in the United States, owing to the different number of days available for collection each month. For example, there was an extra bank holiday in June 2002 in the United Kingdom for the Queen's Jubilee Celebration. As more than 90% of European credit card trusts hold solely UK collateral, the reduced number of collection days in June had a significant impact on our European performance indicators. Cash collections for the master trusts fell by more than a fifth in June with a direct knock-on effect of reducing portfolio yield by almost 20%.

Monthly Payment Rate

The monthly payment rate (MPR) includes monthly collections of principal, finance charges, and fees. It is an important variable because it indicates how quickly the receivables base can be liquidated assuming a static pool. As such, with higher MPRs investors can be paid out more quickly during early amortisation. MPR depends on the proportion of convenience customers and is therefore subject to the originator's customer strategy. A high proportion of convenience users, while depressing yield, can lead to a significant increase in MPR.

There is usually a correlation between the MPR and the credit quality of the cardholder. Convenience users are not overextended, while cardholders who make the monthly minimum payment have less flexibility in their budget should an interruption in their income occur. Exhibit 13.15 shows that while fluctuating on a month-on-month basis, monthly payment rates overall were relatively stable between January 2000 and September 2002.

EXHIBIT 13.15   Monthly Payment Rate (%)

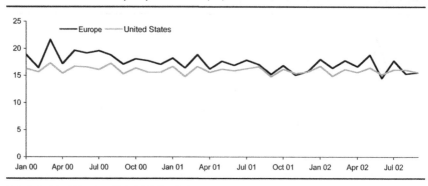

Source: Barclays Capital, Standard & Poor's.

EXHIBIT 13.16   Delinquencies (%)

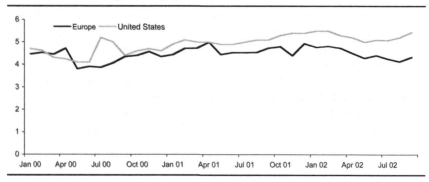

Source: Barclays Capital, Standard & Poor's.

Delinquencies

Delinquencies refer to the number of days that a customer has failed to make payments when due and tends to be a reliable indicator of the (anticipated) trend of charge-offs in a portfolio.

As Exhibit 13.16 shows, delinquencies for European and US credit card collateral basically moved in tandem between April 2001 and September 2002, with figures for Europe consistently lower than those in the United States. In September 2002, the European one-year average stood at 4.53%. This is 76 bp lower than the one-year average for the S&P Index of 5.29%.

When analysing the delinquencies of a particular credit card portfolio, the reported levels should be reviewed on a like-for-like basis, that is, it is important to know about the originator's policies towards delinquencies and charge-offs. Exhibit 13.17 shows receivables that have

EXHIBIT 13.17 30-Day Plus Delinquencies (%)

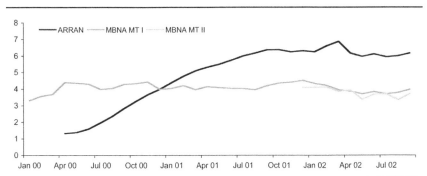

Note: Charge-off policies: ARRAN (365 days), MBNA (180 days).
Source: Bloomberg.

been delinquent for 30 days or more, expressed as a percentage of the total portfolio balance, for three UK credit card master trusts: Arran from RBS and MBNA EBL's two UK master trusts.

At first sight, the Arran portfolio looks inferior to its peers, having experienced a steady increase in delinquencies until October 2001. With more than 6% by the end of September 2002, the Arran portfolio has significantly higher delinquencies than the two MBNA EBL portfolios (below 4%). However, a review of the charge-off policies of the two originators puts this into perspective. MBNA EBL follows the charge-off policy of its parent company, MBNA America, and charges off an account after it becomes 180 days overdue. US companies are required to write off accounts after they have been in arrears for 180 days. There is no policy in the United Kingdom that stipulates writing off debt after a certain time period. Instead, receivables are written off when they are believed to be uncollectable. RBS charges off accounts after 365 days, which is about six months after MBNA EBL's charge-off date. This explains the much higher delinquency ratios revealed by Arran.

Delinquencies are usually reported within delinquency buckets, generally 30–59 days, 60–89 days and 90 days and more. We developed a model that allows us to estimate like-for-like steady state delinquency levels for different portfolios regardless of the originators' charge-off policies. This model allows us to take 30-day-plus delinquencies which are reported by a company that has a charge-off policy of 365 days and restate these figures assuming a 180-day charge-off policy. Exhibit 13.18 shows actual delinquencies for the Arran portfolio together with two dotted horizontal lines, which represent modeled steady state delinquencies.

EXHIBIT 13.18   ARRAN Delinquency Levels for 180-day and 365-day Charge-Off
Policy (%)

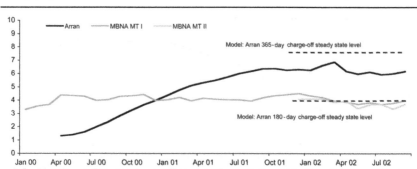

Source: Bloomberg, Barclays Capital.

Assuming a 365-day charge-off policy, *modeled* delinquencies are at
8.91%. Assuming a 180-day charge-off policy, the figure drops to
4.05%. This model does not take recoveries into account and so the difference between *modeled* delinquencies of 8.91% and *actual* delinquencies of 6.06% (average over the six months ending September 2002)
suggests that the collections process is effectively reducing the total
arrears level by approximately 32% (total delinquencies predicted by
the model are 8.91% and actual reported delinquencies are 6.06%. The
difference of 2.85% is likely to be due to recoveries and therefore
2.85%/8.91% = 32%).

Exhibit 13.18 shows that on a like for like basis, delinquencies for
the Arran portfolio are in line with its peers. Again, the model does not
take recoveries into account, and this value may even be considered conservative.

Charge-Offs

Charge-offs are credit losses experienced by the portfolio. Peak losses
for credit card accounts are generally observed at about 18 to 24
months of seasoning. Exhibit 13.19 shows charge-offs for the BECCI
and the S&P Index.

As with delinquencies, charge-offs for Europe and the United States
show similar patterns. However, the significant gap between charge-offs
in Europe and the United States shows the relative attractiveness of
European credit card collateral compared with US collateral, reflecting
the intensity of competition in the US market and the greater tendency
to file for individual bankruptcy.

EXHIBIT 13.19   Charge-Offs, Annualised (%)

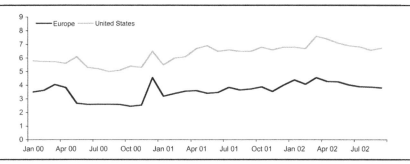

Source: Barclays Capital, Standard & Poor's.

EXHIBIT 13.20   Excess Spread, Annualised

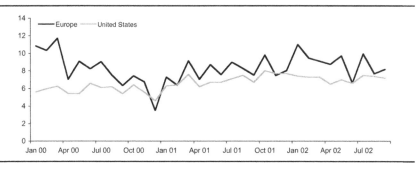

Source: Barclays Capital, Standard & Poor's.

Excess Spread

Excess spread is a particularly important measure of the health of a credit card portfolio and negative excess spread will usually trigger early amortisation. Excess spread is portfolio yield less servicing fees, note coupon, charge-offs, and other costs. Exhibit 13.20 shows 3-month average excess spread for European and US credit card collateral.

Excess spread for European credit card collateral has traditionally been higher than excess spread for US collateral. This is due both to higher portfolio yield and significantly lower charge-offs in Europe.

Excess Spread Efficiency and Charge-off Coverage

Excess spread is important because it is the first line of protection for noteholders in that it absorbs charge-offs. While this is true, two portfolios with similar levels of excess spread can behave very differently in a worsening economic environment. Exhibit 13.21 shows excess spread for two different credit card portfolios.

EXHIBIT 13.21   Performance Statistics

	Portfolio Yield	MPR	Charge-Offs	Excess Spread	Excess Spread Efficiency	Charge-Off Coverage
Issuer 1	16.5%	24.6%	3.5%	5.8%	35.2%	1.66
Issuer 2	24.8%	6.8%	11.2%	5.9%	23.8%	0.53

Source: Barclays Capital.

Although the two portfolios exhibit very similar levels of excess spread, all their other performance indicators are very different. Based on portfolio yield, MPR and charge-offs for the two portfolios, the first portfolio seems to be composed of prime borrowers, while the second portfolio seems to be composed of mid-/subprime borrowers. Whether a portfolio is composed of prime or subprime borrowers impacts the portfolio's performance in a worsening economic environment. Subprime borrowers are usually on a very tight budget with little flexibility for increases in expenses or reductions in income (as expressed in the low monthly payment rate) and as such, a weakening economy could lead to significantly higher delinquencies and charge-offs for the second portfolio. Prime borrowers on the other hand should be in a better position to cope with a worsening economic environment because they often have a higher level of savings. As such, the severity of the change in the performance characteristics of the collateral should be much smaller for the prime portfolio.

However, we are introducing two ratios to help predict the severity of change in collateral performance with a worsening economic environment. The two ratios are excess spread efficiency (ESE) and charge-off coverage (COC).

The ESE ratio is defined as excess spread divided by portfolio yield; it measures the ability of the servicer to turn yield into excess spread. The greater the ratio, the smaller the predicted impact of a slowing economy on the performance of the collateral. As Exhibit 13.21 shows, the prime issuer (issuer 1) has a much higher ESE ratio than the subprime issuer. The September 2002 ratios for European and US credit card portfolios are 44% and 39%, respectively.

The COC ratio is more a measure of security for the investor as it compares the level of excess spread with charge-offs. The higher the ratio, the greater the ability of the trust to weather a slowdown. Again, the prime portfolio (issuer 1) has a much higher COC ratio than the subprime portfolio (issuer 2). For the prime portfolio, the ratio stands at 1.66, meaning that excess spread would be able to absorb an increase in charge-offs of up to 166%. For the subprime portfolio, current losses could increase by only 53%. The September 2002 ratios for European and US credit card portfolios are 2.15% and 1.06%, respectively.

CONCLUSION

The European credit card securitisation market has grown substantially, both in terms of absolute size and in number of issues. Although the market has traditionally been dominated by sterling-denominated collateral, the securitisation environment in various European countries bodes well for credit card securitisations which should attract banks and specialty lenders looking for alternative sources of funding and effective ways to manage their balance sheets.

The CCABS market continues to be a safe haven for European ABS investors. Especially in 2002, when corporate bonds of various sectors showed increased price volatility and the CDO market experienced a significant number of downgrades, credit card ABS transactions continued to show strong and stable performance. In fact, since the market's inception in 1995, no European CCABS have experienced any downgrades. We believe that CCABS are likely to continue to exhibit strong and stable performance and remain one of the core asset classes for European ABS investors.

CHAPTER 14

European Auto and Consumer Loan ABS

Markus Niemeier
Manager
Barclays Capital

T hree types of consumer finance receivables have been securitised in the past: credit card receivables, auto receivables (essentially auto loan and auto lease receivables), and "other" consumer finance receivables, which typically include unsecured personal loans. Credit card receivables are discussed in Chapter 13. The purpose of this chapter is to provide an overview of the European auto and consumer loan ABS markets and review the structural, collateral, and performance characteristics of the two asset classes. We decided to review auto and consumer loan ABS combined in one chapter because of the many similarities between the two asset classes.

THE EUROPEAN AUTO AND CONSUMER LOAN ABS MARKET

Although the first public securitisations of European auto and consumer loan receivables were completed in the early 1990s, issuance in both sectors did not really take off until the mid- to late 1990s. But since then, for lenders of auto and consumer loans alike, securitisation has become one of the favourite sources of funding and an effective way of managing their balance sheets. European auto and consumer loan ABS originators have

---

The views expressed in this article are those of the author and not necessarily those of Barclays Capital.

traditionally been banks and finance companies. In the case of auto loans, finance companies can be further divided into independent finance companies and captive in-house finance companies owned by an automobile manufacturer. Exhibit 14.1 shows the issuance of publicly rated auto and consumer loan ABS backed by European collateral from 1997 to 2002.[1]

EXHIBIT 14.1   European Auto and Consumer Loan ABS Issuance by Year (1997–2002)
Auto ABS

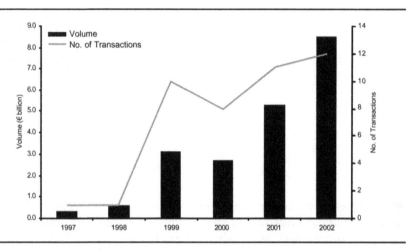

Consumer Loan ABS

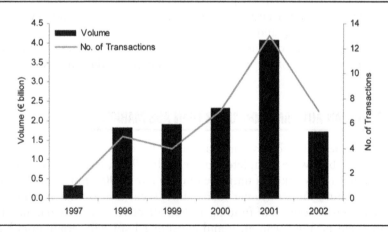

Source: Bloomberg.

---

[1] We define European auto and consumer loan transactions as those transactions that are backed by auto and consumer loan receivables which were originated in Europe.

EXHIBIT 14.2   Top Five European Auto and Consumer Loan ABS Issuers (1997–2002)

Auto ABS

Rank	Seller	Issuer	No. of Transactions	Total Issuance (€ billion)
1	Fiat	FIAT, SIAT, ALFA, EAS	4	3,317
2	Banque PSA Finance	Auto ABS Compartiment	2	2,500
3	FCE Bank	Globaldrive	4	2,434
4	Volkswagen Leasing	VCL	3	2,250
5	RCI Banque/DIAC	Cars Alliance	1	1,400
		Total	14	11,901

Consumer Loan ABS

Rank	Seller	Issuer	No. of Transactions	Total Issuance (€ billion)
1	Cetelem	Noria, MasterNoria	6	2,386
2	ABN Amro	Amstel Consumer Loan Securitisation	2	1,624
3	Paragon Group	Paragon Auto&Secured Fin., Paragon Pers.&Auto Fin.	3	1,107
4	Banco Comercial Portugues	Nova	3	895
5	Banco Espirito Santo, Besleasing Mobiliaria	Lusitano	2	700
		Total	16	6,712

Source: Bloomberg.

Traditionally, the two sectors have been clearly dominated by repeat issuers. For example, in 2002, repeat issuers accounted for approximately 75% of all auto ABS issued and 82% of all consumer loan ABS issued (by issuance volume). Exhibit 14.2 shows the top five European auto and consumer loan ABS issuers ranked by cumulative issuance volume from 1997 to 2002.

Auto ABS—Top Five Issuers

Fiat is the dominant issuer of European auto ABS in terms of total issuance volume. The company has accessed the securitisation market four

times, issuing notes from four special purpose vehicles (SPVs), namely
First Italian Auto Transaction (FIAT 1), Second Italian Auto Transaction (FIAT 2), Absolute Funding (ALFA), and European Auto Securitisation (EAS). In the case of FIAT 1 and FIAT 2, all receivables are
originated in Italy; receivables included in the ALFA portfolio are originated in Germany and those included in the EAS portfolio are originated in France and Spain. For all transactions, notes and collateral are
euro-denominated.

Credipar Group, a wholly owned subsidiary of Banque PSA Finance,
which is the captive in-house financing arm of the French PSA Group, has
completed just two transactions but with relatively large issue sizes of €1
billion and €1.5 billion, respectively. The loans in the Auto ABS Compartiment 2001-1 portfolio are originated by Credipar via Banque SOFI (Citroën outlets) and Banque DIN (Peugeot outlets), two wholly owned
subsidiaries of Credipar. The Auto ABS Compartiment 2002-1 pool also
includes loans originated in Spain by Banque PSA Finance. In both cases,
notes and collateral are euro-denominated.

FCE Bank, the captive financing arm of Ford, has completed four
EAABS transactions since 1997 (Globaldrive B, C, D, and E), issuing
notes under the umbrella of its well-known Globaldrive programme.
(Globaldrive 1, the first transaction completed under the Globaldrive
programme, is backed by US collateral and as such is not included in
Exhibit 14.2.) As one of the earlier and larger auto ABS programmes,
Globaldrive is often viewed as a benchmark in the European auto ABS
market. The Globaldrive transactions are discussed in more detail below.

Volkswagen Leasing has accessed the securitisation market three
times since 1997 under the umbrella of its VCL programme.[2] All transactions are backed by German auto leases and notes and collateral are
Deutschmark/euro-denominated.

RCI Banque, the parent company of DIAC, is a 100%-owned subsidiary of Compagnie Financière Renault, the 100%-owned Renault
subsidiary in charge of finance and cash management. The company has
completed one EAABS transaction, Cars Alliance Funding—Series
2002-1. Notes and collateral are euro-denominated.

Consumer Loan ABS—Top Five Issuers

Among the dominant issuers of European consumer loan ABS is Cetelem, the consumer credit arm of Compagnie Bancaire, which in turn is

---

[2] Two other transaction, VCL No. 1 and VCL No. 2, were completed in 1996 and
are two of the first public European auto ABS issues completed. However, Exhibit
14.2 includes only transactions completed since January 1997, and so shows only
three VCL transactions.

the financial services subsidiary of BNP Paribas. Cetelem has completed six public ABS transactions since 1997, issuing approximately €2.4 billion of notes backed by French unsecured consumer loans. Notes and collateral are French franc-/euro-denominated.

The second largest issuer of European consumer loan ABS is ABN Amro, which has accessed the securitisation market twice since 1997 through its Amstel Consumer Loan Securitisation programme. In each of the two cases the notes are euro-denominated and backed by Dutch consumer loans.

The Paragon Group of Companies has accessed the consumer loan ABS market three times since 1997; once in 2000 under the Paragon Auto & Secured Finance programme and twice in 2001 under the Paragon Personal & Auto Finance programme. In each case, the receivables and notes are sterling-denominated. Although all three pools include some auto receivables, they have been counted as consumer loan ABS for the purpose of this chapter.

Banco Comercial Português has completed three consumer loan ABS transactions since 1997. Nova Finance No. 1, Nova Finance No. 2, and Nova Finance No. 3 were issued in 1998, 2001, and 2002, respectively. Nova Finance No. 1 is Deutschmark-denominated and Nova Finance No. 2 and Nova Finance No. 3 are euro-denominated. All three transactions are backed by Portuguese consumer loans.

Banco Espirito has completed two European consumer loan ABS transactions, Lusitano Finance No. 1 (Portuguese consumer loans) and Lusitano Finance No. 2 (Portuguese consumer loans and leases; the consumer loans are originated by Banco Espirito, the leases are originated by Besleasing Mobiliária). Notes and collateral are euro-denominated.

Issuance by Country

The auto and consumer loan ABS markets are very much pan-European. Exhibit 14.3 shows issuance in 2002 for both markets according to country. Auto receivables have been originated in Austria, Belgium, France, Germany, Italy, Portugal, Spain, and the United Kingdom. Consumer loan ABS have been backed by loans originated in France, Italy, the Netherlands, Portugal, Spain, and the United Kingdom. Exhibit 14.4 shows issuance volume and number of transactions from 1997 to 2002 according to country (transactions are considered to be backed by receivables originated in a particular country if more than 50% of the receivables included in the pool were originated in that country).

Tranching of European auto and consumer loan ABS transactions is much less standardised than, say, European credit card transactions. While most credit card transactions come with three tranches, typically

EXHIBIT 14.3   European Auto and Consumer Loan ABS Issuance by Country (2002)

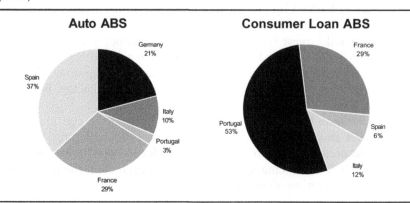

Source: Bloomberg.

EXHIBIT 14.4   European Auto and Consumer Loan ABS Issuance by Country (1997 to 2002)
Auto ABS

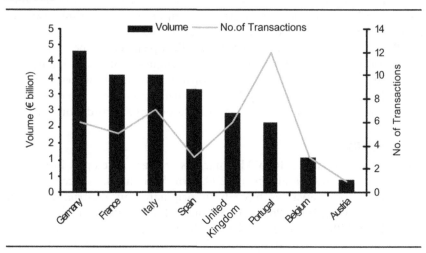

rated triple-A, single-A, and triple-B, respectively, auto and consumer loan ABS transactions have come with one, two, three or even four tranches. The most senior tranche is usually rated triple-A and the most junior tranche is usually rated triple-B. If available, the mezzanine tranche is usually rated single-A and double-A. Exhibit 14.5 shows European auto and consumer loan ABS issuance by rating from 1997 to 2002.

EXHIBIT 14.4 (Continued)
Consumer Loan ABS

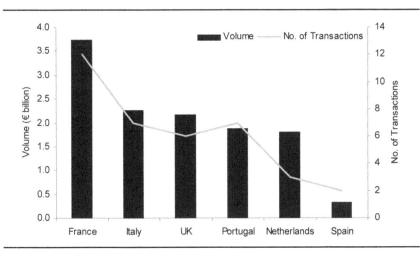

Source: Bloomberg.

EXHIBIT 14.5 European Auto and Consumer Loan ABS Issuance by Rating (1997 to 2002)

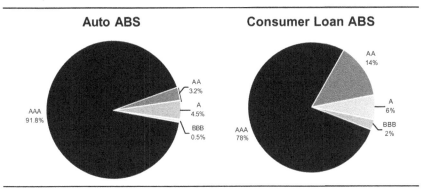

Source: Bloomberg.

STRUCTURAL CHARACTERISTICS

Although auto and consumer loan ABS structures are not very standardised, most transactions have a range of structural features in common. The purpose of this section is to provide an overview of typical auto and consumer loan ABS structures.

EXHIBIT 14.6   Auto/Consumer Loan Transaction Structure

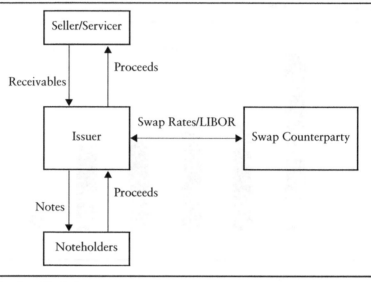

Source: Barclays Capital.

Transaction Structure

Exhibit 14.6 below shows the structural diagram for a typical auto or consumer loan ABS transaction. Although there have been attempts to create a master-trust like structure for consumer loan ABS, we discuss in this chapter the most common structure used for auto and consumer loan ABS issuance.[3]

Using the transaction structure shown in Exhibit 14.6, a portfolio of auto or personal loans are transferred from the originator of the loans to the issuer (an SPV). Usually, the transfer of the assets is conducted in a manner that results in a "true sale," which effectively removes the assets from the bankruptcy or insolvency estate of the originator. This allows the originator to issue notes with a higher rating than itself. If the issuer were not bankruptcy remote, a double-B rated originator would generally not be able to issue notes with an investment-grade rating. However, through asset securitisation, the same originator would

---

[3] For example, the Master Noria transactions are issued from a master-trust type structure. The transactions, backed by unsecured consumer loans, use the concept of an FCC (Fonds Commun de Créances), which may issue different series over time. Master Noria may acquire new eligible loans using both funds from the amortisation of its assets and proceeds from future series issuance.

EXHIBIT 14.7   FIAT 1, Globaldrive B and PPAF 1 Structural Details

	FIAT 1	Globaldrive B	PPAF 1
Issue Size (€ 000 equiv.)	965,000	490,750	279,095
Pricing Date	July 2000	March 1999	Jun 2001
Original Weighted Average Life (Years)	3.8	3.9	5.0
Length of Revolving Period (Years)	3	3	4
Expected Maturity	March 2005	September 2004	September 2008[a]
Legal Maturity	July 2008	June 2008	June 2021

[a] June 2007, if call-option is exercised.
Source: Bloomberg, offering circulars.

be in a position to issue a tranche of triple-A rated notes (assuming an appropriate securitisation structure and sufficient collateral quality).

Exhibit 14.6 also shows a swap agreement between the issuer and a swap counterparty. A swap agreement is not necessary for all transactions but is generally present to mitigate interest rate risk. The vast majority of auto and consumer loan ABS tranches have traditionally come with floating-rate coupons. If the underlying collateral (or a certain proportion of the receivables in the pool) pays fixed-rate interest, the rating agencies usually require the issuer to enter into an interest rate swap agreement in order to mitigate such interest rate risk.

Auto and Consumer Loan ABS Mechanics

In the following review of some of the fundamental auto and consumer loan ABS mechanics, we will use three transactions as practical examples; two auto ABS transactions, FIAT 1 and Globaldrive B, and one consumer loan ABS transaction, Paragon Personal and Auto Finance (No. 1) (PPAF 1). The FIAT 1 transaction was completed by Fiat in July 2000 and at that time it represented the largest European auto transaction completed. Globaldrive B was completed by FCE Bank in March 1999. PPAF 1 was completed in 2001 by Paragon Finance PLC. In Exhibit 14.7 we outline the structural details for the senior notes of FIAT 1, Globaldrive B and PPAF 1.

Issue Size

Many Participants in the European auto and consumer loan ABS markets tend to be buy-and-hold investors, and so offer-side liquidity in the secondary market may be limited for many issues. However, liquidity tends to improve with larger issue sizes because the size of the transaction impacts the number of investors involved. The FIAT transaction ranks among the largest European auto ABS transactions and is roughly twice the size of the Globaldrive B transaction and more than three times the size of the PPAF 1 transaction. It comes as no surprise that since the closing date, it is one of the few auto issues to have an active secondary market presence.

Revolving Period

In most completed European auto ABS transactions, the senior classes have been structured so that the bonds feature an amortising payment structure with an average life of between 3.5 and 4.5 years; consumer loan ABS transactions tend to have slightly longer average lives, often between four and five years.

Usually included in these structures is a revolving or substitution period during which principal received from borrowers is reinvested in new receivables with the interest paid to noteholders. The revolving period usually lasts for between two and three years, allowing the bonds to have a longer average life than if structured as a straight pass-through. Preset criteria are established regarding the purchase of new collateral during the revolving period that protect investors against a deterioration in the underlying pool of assets.

For example, FIAT 1 benefits from four triggers that measure certain characteristics of the collateral. During the three-year revolving period, new receivables can only be purchased if the eligibility criteria shown in Exhibit 14.8 are met.

The revolving period usually ends on a certain date (e.g., in the case of the FIAT 1 transaction the revolving period is scheduled to last for three years, and would therefore end in July 2003) or following the breach of an early amortisation trigger. Exhibit 14.9 shows the three FIAT 1 early amortisation triggers together with the respective maximum trigger levels.

EXHIBIT 14.8 FIAT 1 Collateral Eligibility Criteria

Trigger	Initial Pool	Maximum
Used Vehicles in Portfolio (%)	17.60	20.00
Borrowers located in South Italy (%)	28.80	40.00
Weighted Average Remaining Maturity (months)	23.30	36.00
Weighted Average Interest Rate (%)	5.31	10.00

Source: Offering circular.

EXHIBIT 14.9   FIAT 1 Delinquency and Write-off Triggers

Trigger	Maximum
2–4-month Delinquencies (%, 3-month average)	4.75
5–8-month Delinquencies (%, 3-month average)	1.50
Cumulative Write-offs (%)	Dynamic calculation: (Quarter number + 1)/12 × 4%

Source: Offering circular.

EXHIBIT 14.10   FIAT 1 Amortisation Structure (€ million)

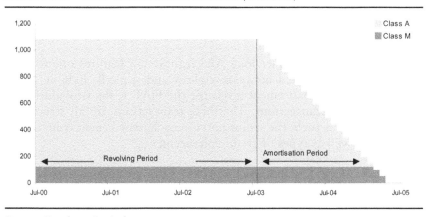

Source: Barclays Capital.

Amortisation Period

Following the substitution period, the transaction typically enters the amortisation period, during which principal collected from receivables is passed through to noteholders. This may lead to a degree of variability in the average life of the security if the borrowers repay their loans more quickly or slowly than the modelled prepayment speed used to price the notes. Exhibit 14.10 shows a simplified paydown structure for the FIAT 1 transaction.

Principal Window

The time period over which principal amortises and is returned to investors is called the *principal window*. The length of the principal window can vary depending on how quickly the collateral is prepaying. As such, cash flows paid to investors during the pass-through period are always subject to a degree of uncertainty. Note also that during this period investors are exposed to reinvestment risk (i.e., the risk that returned principal may have to be reinvested at lower interest rates). The longer the principal window, the greater the investors' exposure to reinvestment risk.

Legal Maturity and Expected Maturity

The legal final maturity is usually different from the expected maturity which is calculated based on the start of the pass-through period and the rate at which the collateral is prepaying. The legal final maturity is the date the rating agencies use in assigning their ratings to the notes. This is the date at which, if sufficient principal were not paid, the issue would be in default. The legal final is typically two to three years after the expected maturity date and depends on assumptions made about the length of repossession or other legal procedures.

Credit Enhancement

A typical auto or consumer loan ABS transaction features one to four tranches, generally rated between triple-A and triple-B. Exhibit 14.11 shows the credit enhancement levels for the FIAT 1, the Globaldrive B, and the PPAF 1 transactions. The three transactions are all structured differently and as such, the senior notes in each issue benefit from different levels as well as types of credit enhancement.

EXHIBIT 14.11   FIAT 1, Globaldrive B and PPAF 1 Credit Enhancement Structures

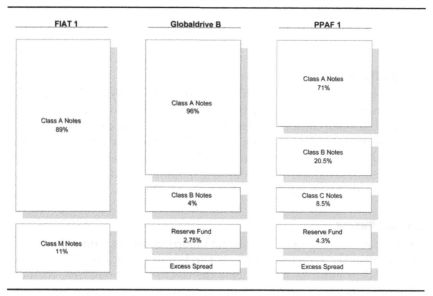

Source: Offering circulars.

The FIAT 1 issue benefits from a credit enhancement level of 11% from subordination of the unrated class M notes. The Globaldrive B issue benefits from 4% credit enhancement of the class B notes and a reserve fund, which builds up from 1.8% at the closing date to 2.75% of the balance of the initial pool. Fully funded, the Globaldrive B class A notes benefit from a total credit enhancement of 6.75%. The PPAF 1 issue benefits from a credit enhancement level of 33.3% from subordination of the class B and the class C notes (20.5% and 8.5%, respectively) and a cash reserve of 4.3% of the initial notes balance.

For both Globaldrive B and PPAF1 the first layer of protection is excess spread in the transaction, which is the difference between (1) the income received from the pool of receivables, and (2) the coupon due under the notes/payments due to the swap counterparty plus a certain servicing fee. Excess spread that is not used to cover losses on the loans within a certain period is returned to the originator (i.e., excess spread benefits the transaction on a "use it or lose it" basis).

Strictly speaking, the FIAT 1 transaction does not generate excess spread. This explains the high level of credit enhancement from the unrated class M notes (usually, unrated tranches are either privately sold or kept as an equity tranche by the originator). On the closing date, an amount of notes was issued which was equal to the net present value of all future cash payments due from the collateral (as opposed to the principal balance of the collateral). The discount rate used was the fixed rate payable to the swap counterparty (swap rate plus coupon on the class A notes and all fees associated with the transaction). Structured this way, the receivables always yield the discount rate, leaving no excess spread in the transaction. However, losses on the FIAT 1 portfolio can be covered to a certain degree from interest collections because the structure provides for delinquent principal and defaults to be covered before interest is paid on the class M notes.

PRODUCT TYPES AND COLLATERAL CHARACTERISTICS

The purpose of this section is to review the most common types of auto and consumer finance products that are offered to customers and that have traditionally been included in ABS transactions. We then describe the fundamental characteristics of auto and consumer loan portfolios and discuss common ways of analysing them.

Product Types

The universe of both auto and consumer loan products offered to customers has become very diverse; products may differ for example in terms of amortisation profile, interest calculation, discounts granted, incentive schemes, or balloon payment terms. The following description of the most common types of auto finance products, namely instalment loans, balloon loans, leases, and long-term rentals shall provide an example.

Instalment Loans

Instalment loans (also called *amortising loans*) are the standard type of auto finance contracts. If customers choose instalment loans, they are required to make the same instalments over the life of the loan, with decreasing interest proportions and increasing principal proportions. Usually, the borrower has to make a certain down payment in the beginning, which is typically about 5–10% of the sales price, but can vary between lenders.

Balloon Loans

Balloon loans allow borrowers to repay the loan in relatively low monthly instalments followed by a single balloon payment at the end (usually up to 60% of the loan). In general, balloon loans are considered more risky than loans with full repayment under equal instalments due to the high residual value (RV) and the possibility that the borrower may not be able to afford to make the final balloon payment. Balloon loans may offer the borrower a set of options before the final payment is due: (1) pay the balloon payment and be released from all future obligations; (2) refinance the final payment by taking on an additional instalment loan; or (3) return the vehicle to the dealer under a repurchase agreement. For example, FIAT 2 is an auto ABS transaction that is partly backed by balloon loans, accounting for approximately 28% of the total initial pool.

Leases

Leases are generally made to commercial parties. Under the lease contract, the lessee makes small monthly payments to the lessor and at the end of the term holds an option to purchase the vehicle for the stated RV. This option is likely to be exercised if the RV is equal to or below the retail value of the car, otherwise the lessee is likely to return the car to the dealer, which can then decide whether or not to take the car. If the dealer also decides not to purchase the car, the lessor takes possession and sells it at its wholesale price. Because of the uncertainty about the realisation of the RV, which can be large relative to the lessee's lease payments, it is important for investors to know if the pool of receivables that backs the transaction comprises only the rental component of the lease contracts or if it also includes the RV component. For example, the five transactions issued under the VCL programme are backed solely by the rental component of the lease contracts.

Long-Term Rentals

Long-term rentals (LTR) have been used only in Portugal. In many aspects, they are similar to lease contracts. A major difference between an LTR and a lease contract is that in the case of the former, borrowers are required to make a cash collateral payment, which may be 30% of the related vehicle value. The cash collateral payment remains untapped over the term of the LTR if the borrower makes timely payments as agreed in the initial contract. In the case of nonpayments, the lender takes possession of the vehicle and the cash collateral payment is used to cover any losses the lender might incur if the price at which the vehicle was sold is below the final contract RV. LTR products have been part of the collateral for the LTR transactions, which were completed in 1999, 2000, 2001, and 2002 by Sofinloc.

Collateral Characteristics

Analysing a portfolio of auto or consumer loan receivables is essential because it tells us how the transaction is likely to perform in the future. The major characteristics we focus on are:

- Term distribution
- Annual percentage rate (APR)
- Geographic distribution
- Seasoning
- Model and make diversification (auto ABS only)
- Proportions of new and used vehicles (auto ABS only)
- Loan-to-value (LTV) (auto ABS only)

Term Distribution

The term of the loan defines the period over which the total amount of principal is repaid. Most auto and consumer loan securitisations allow loans with original terms of 60 months or less. The distribution of loans across the term spectrum is important because losses tend to increase with the term of the loan. For auto loans, this is most likely a result of a slower build up in equity with a longer amortising loan. Exhibit 14.12 shows the amortisation profile for 48-, 60-, and 72-month loans along with a depreciation curve.

The amortisation profiles in this example assume a car sales price of €35,000, a 10% down payment, and an APR of 15%. The most worrying situation is when the amortisation line is greater than the depreciation line; this would imply negative equity in the vehicle and the greatest propensity for default. In this example, the 48-month loan never exhibits negative equity, the 60-month loan experiences some negative equity and the 72-month loan experiences the longest period and the greatest

EXHIBIT 14.12   Generic Principal Amortisation and Depreciation Profiles (auto loans, €000, months)

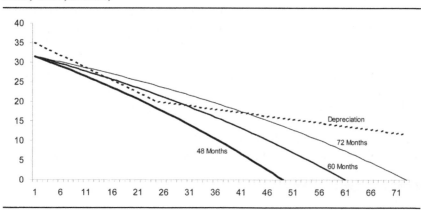

Source: Barclays Capital.

magnitude of negative equity. It is during this period of negative equity that there is the greatest potential for loss on a receivables pool.

Annual Percentage Rate (APR)

Most lenders have models in place that allow them to charge higher interest rates to more risky borrowers. However, it is not appropriate to assess a borrower's credit quality solely based on the weighted average coupon for a pool of collateral. Other considerations include the absolute level of interest rates when the loan was originated and the degree of incentive loans in the pool. Incentive loans carry a below market interest rate, which is typically supported by the manufacturer or the captive finance company in the case of auto loans or the lender or retailer in the case of consumer loans. A pool with a large number of incentive loans may experience a declining amount of interest available as the deal ages. As the borrowers with incentive loans have a below market rate, there is very little reason for them to prepay while those borrowers being charged a higher interest rate may prepay their loans if they have available cash. This lopsided prepayment scenario could leave the pool with a higher percentage of lower yielding loans, and hence lower interest income, as the deal ages.

Geographic Distribution

A pool of collateral should be well diversified geographically to minimise the effect on the pool in the event of a rise in unemployment or recession in any one region. Exhibit 14.13 shows the initial Globaldrive B portfolio, which is geographically well diversified among nine major German regions.

EXHIBIT 14.13   Globaldrive B Geographic Distribution (% of principal balance)

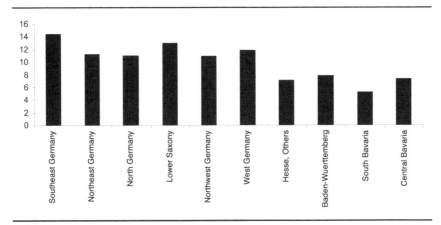

Source: Offering circular.

Seasoning

Advanced seasoning is a positive attribute for a pool of receivables because the portfolio is more likely to exhibit stable performance than a relatively unseasoned portfolio. This is because a pool of new receivables usually experiences increasing losses for the first 18 to 24 months after which the losses are expected to decline and then level out. Over time, positive selection occurs while the lower quality and riskier accounts become charged-off and removed from the pool, leaving the higher quality accounts which should demonstrate more stable performance.

Model and Make Diversification for Auto ABS

When assessing a pool of auto receivables, we usually prefer portfolios that are diversified according to model and make. This is because a concentration in one particular brand can expose investors to additional risk if the manufacturer becomes insolvent. A concentration in a particular type of vehicle or model may have negative consequences if customers' tastes change, problems with the particular model emerge or the manufacturer exits the particular market segment.

Model and make diversification are of particular importance if the loans included in the pool have a high RV component, because problems associated with the manufacturer or the car could then lead to depressed sales prices in the used-car market. This in turn could lead to higher loss levels if customers default due to lower recovery values realised by the originator.

New versus Used for Auto ABS

Everything else being equal, we prefer a portfolio that includes only new car loans to a portfolio that includes some used car loans. This is because used vehicles generally experience higher delinquencies and losses than new vehicle loans. Therefore, it is important to pay close attention to the initial share of used vehicle loans in a portfolio, how this share changes over time, and the maximum number of used vehicle loans that can be added to the pool during the revolving period. As Exhibit 14.8 shows, there is a ceiling on the proportion of used car loans that can be added to the FIAT 1 pool during the revolving period. Other auto ABS transactions have similar collateral eligibility criteria.

Loan-to-Value for Auto ABS

The loan-to-value ratio (LTV) represents the size of the loan relative to the sales price of the vehicle. The lower the LTV, the more equity a borrower has invested in the vehicle. The equity in the vehicle should act as an incentive to keep the borrower from defaulting, and thus losing the invested equity. Over time, the amount of the loan will decrease as principal is repaid by the borrower. However, the value of the vehicle will most likely be decreasing as well, based on the vehicle's depreciation curve. This makes it necessary to analyse the rate at which principal is being repaid (amortisation schedule) against the rate at which the vehicle is depreciating in order to determine the borrower's expected equity in the vehicle (see term distribution above).

COLLATERAL PERFORMANCE

The two key quantitative performance indicators for analysing portfolios of auto and consumer loan receivables are delinquencies and charge-offs.

Delinquencies

The performance of a pool of assets is affected by the borrowers' willingness and ability to repay their debt. A key performance characteristic that measures this is the amount of delinquencies in a pool. Delinquencies refer to the number of days that a borrower has failed to make payments when due and tends to be a reliable indicator of the (anticipated) trend of charge-offs in a portfolio.

Additionally, it is important to understand the company's servicing methods and the effectiveness of such methods. The end result of a successful servicing operation is the ability to bring delinquent accounts current and thus minimise charge-offs. Exhibit 14.14 shows total delin-

EXHIBIT 14.14   Globaldrive D Delinquency Rates (%, annualised)

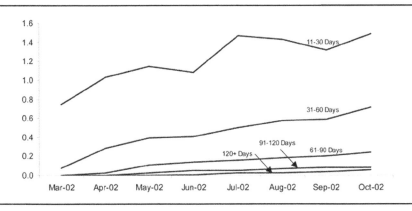

Source: Investor reports.

quencies for the Globaldrive D transaction split up into five delinquency buckets. Globaldrive D was completed by FCE Bank in March 2002.

Delinquencies are usually reported within delinquency buckets and in the case of the Globaldrive transactions, those buckets are 11–30 days, 31–60 days, 61–90 days, 91–120 days, and 120 days and more. The exhibit shows that the figure for 11–30 days delinquencies is significantly higher than the figure for 31–60 days, which, in turn, is higher than the figures for the following three buckets. This result is positive for it shows that FCE Bank is very effective in bringing a proportion of customers in each delinquency bucket current. For example, by the end of September 2002, there were 1,985 loans with a total principal balance of €10,518,858 that fell into the 1–30 days delinquency bucket. By the end of October 2002—30 days later—1,021 loans with a total principal balance of €5,724,505 fell into the 31–60 days delinquency bucket. This means that a significant number of borrowers became current (assuming one loan is made to one borrower). The total number of borrowers who become current is expected to increase further according to the servicer's collection processes, which typically include telephone calls, written reminders, and other measures.

Exhibit 14.14 also shows that delinquencies for each bucket have been rising since the transaction's closing date in March 2002. This trend is entirely expected while the receivables age. By the time the transaction was completed, more than 60% of the receivables (by principal balance) were seasoned for 18 months or less and more than 40% were seasoned for 12 months or less. Therefore, we would expect delinquencies to rise as the receivables age. Exhibit 14.15 shows the same delinquency buckets for the Globaldrive B transaction, which is backed by a much more seasoned pool of auto loan receivables.

EXHIBIT 14.15   Globaldrive B Delinquency Rates (%, annualised)

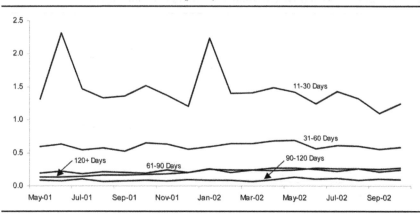

Source: Investor reports.

Delinquencies for each bucket show a high degree of stability (with the exception of the two spikes in the 11–30 days delinquency bucket in June 2001 and January 2002). We generally expect delinquencies to reach steady state levels once a portfolio is fully seasoned, which is usually the case after about 18–24 months. Therefore, we would expect delinquencies for the Globaldrive D portfolio to rise and then plateau after a certain period of time, just as shown in for the more seasoned Globaldrive B portfolio.

Charge-Offs

Another important performance measure is the default rate. The monthly default curve for auto and consumer loan receivables originated by a generic originator is shown in Exhibit 14.16. The curve is built showing monthly defaults from the number of months since origination of the obligation. The loss curve is minimal for the first year after which there is a fairly sharp spike lasting usually 6 to 18 months. Between the 18th and 24th month, the loss curve reaches a peak and declines fairly rapidly for the life of the receivable. This bell-shaped curve is typical for other auto and consumer loan receivables.

Vintage Charge-Offs

Each originator has its own underwriting and servicing standards. These standards ultimately determine the net loss rate in the originated collateral. It is also important to be aware of the overall health of the economy, for this will affect the performance of the collateral. Collateral that has been originated and serviced in a consistent manner can behave

EXHIBIT 14.16   Charge-Offs (month, %)

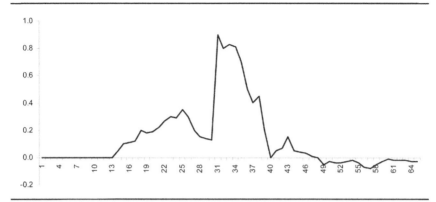

Source: Barclays Capital.

EXHIBIT 14.17   Charge-Offs for Various Quarters of Origination

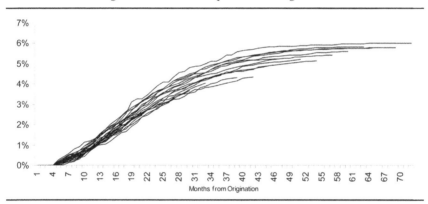

Source: Barclays Capital.

very differently under different economic situations. Changes in underwriting and servicing standards can also result in a change in the performance of the collateral. In Exhibit 14.17 we show a generic vintage
charge-off analysis which helps us to identify the impact of a changing
economic environment and different origination standards on charge-
offs. We have assumed a six-month charge-off policy.

The various lines in Exhibit 14.17 represent charge-offs according
to the month from origination. Each line represents loans that were
originated in a certain quarter, so the shorter the line, the more recently
the loans were originated. For example, for all loans that were originated in January 2001, there would be 18 months of charge-off data

available by the end of 2002 (loans are charged-off after being delinquent for six months and therefore 24 – 6 = 18). For loans originated in January 2002, there would be only six months of charge-off data available, and the line in would be shorter.

The exhibit shows that loans originated more recently tend to have lower charge-offs, which reflects positively on the originator's strategy.

CONCLUSION

There has been solid growth in European auto and consumer loan securitisations traditionally, both in terms of absolute size and in number of issues. Many issuers have come to market with a series of issues, giving them repeat issuer status. This has helped provide liquidity to the asset class while more investors devote time and resources to understanding the asset class and the various issuers. We feel this trend will continue in the future with the vast majority of transactions coming from established programmes.

The securitisation environment in Europe bodes well for auto securitisations which should attract banks and specialist lenders looking for alternative sources of funding and effective ways to manage their balance sheets. Transaction structures continue to improve and we may see some of the largest originators of auto and consumer loan receivables to move from the amortising structure to a bullet-type structure in the future, which should further add interest and liquidity to the asset class.

CHAPTER 15

Structured Credit: Cash Flow and Synthetic CDOs

Oldrich Masek
MD, Global Structured Credit Origination, Repackaging and Solutions
JPMorgan Securities Ltd.

Moorad Choudhry
Senior Fellow
Centre for Mathematical Trading and Finance
CASS Business School, London

The advent of collateralised debt obligations (CDOs) was a natural evolution in the ever-growing and increasingly global securitisation market. A CDO is an area of structured finance whereby a distinct legal entity known as a *special purpose vehicle* issues debt and equity-like instruments secured against a portfolio of assets, or more generally, credit risk. The credit risks behind a CDO can be sourced directly from the marketplace (a key distinction from traditional ABS secutitisation) or identified by reference (that is, transferred from an existing bank, corporate, or other balance sheet). The first CDOs were developed principally as vehicles to accumulate and repackage financial instruments that, when evaluated on an asset by asset basis, were relatively illiquid

The authors would like to thank Tim van den Brande, Dorothee Fuhrmann, Sandra Wong, Vicki Lamb, and Ketul Tanna at JPMorgan, and Edwin Noomen at Robeco for their input and constructive review comments. Any errors remain the responsibility of the authors.

or too complex for some investors to consider (for example, high-yield debt).

With that objective in mind, CDO vehicles were used to selectively aggregate individual credits within an asset class in attempt to construct portfolios with very specific investment themes as well as risk/return profiles. By doing so, structured financiers would seek to make these new asset classes more appealing to investors that could not prudently or practically invest into the asset class directly. Direct investing challenges can arise when an investor is deprived of the necessary credit selection skills in the desired asset class and/or lacks the sufficient risk management or operational infrastructure to surveil the ongoing quality of the asset portfolio. Furthermore, the investor may be unable to satisfactorily diversify its obligor and industry concentration risk due to limited investable funds or the investor is simply precluded by geography (i.e., limited local knowledge or cross-border investing barriers such as tax, regulatory, or legal constraints).

Hence, in very simple terms, the *pooling* concept that a CDO provides can attract scalable liquidity to an asset class that on its own would be limited for the aforementioned reasons. Again, the high-yield market serves as a good example in this regard; without the capacity made available to high-yield issuers through CDOs, the market would not have been able to develop as rapidly as it has in terms of size and breadth. This is best evidence by the fact that today it is estimated that approximately two-thirds of all US high-yield new issuance is intermediated to end investors through CDOs globally. The significance of this should not be understated; the ability to enhance overall market liquidity for an asset class is a key value proposition of CDOs. This feature alone secures CDOs a critical role in the global financial marketplace (if not a major driver of its expansion). With that said, although the market initiated with high-yield debt, the scope of asset classes being repackaged today is extensive both in terms of type and risk characteristics (for instance, hedge funds, credit derivatives, real estate, ABS, and CDOs themselves). Various asset class case studies will be offered for discussion later in this chapter.

Expanding on this theme, the barriers that CDOs help investors overcome are not limited to providing diversified asset class access alone. More fundamentally, they provide a means to diversify into an asset class with the optional benefit of expert advice. Although static portfolios (and more recently indexation-based portfolios) can be constructed, most CDOs formally contract an asset manager with a unique specialization in the targeted asset class to administer the portfolio. In such fiduciary capacity, the asset manager selects the initial portfolio and has an ongoing responsibility to manage and maximize the value of the portfolio for the investor. Given that a CDO's liabilities are directly linked to the cash flows realized by the underlying portfolio, the choice of asset manager can significantly enhance or damage the overall ability of the CDO to repay its debt and equity obligations. Consequently, investors will spend considerable time evaluating an asset manager's capabilities and performance track record before investing. (A CDO is no different from a simple mutual fund in these respects.)

Another service a CDO affords investors is an ability to select the *degree of risk* an investor takes to an asset class (and, if applicable, the asset manager) depending on where in the CDO's capital structure the investor invests. An investor participating at the equity level, for instance, has more exposure to the management and ultimate performance of the asset-side activities of a CDO's balance sheet than a senior debt investor would—in this regard, it is no different than any other financial entity investment. This point is worth expanding upon, by overlaying rating technology to CDO vehicles, investor capacity can now be sourced from across the risk spectrum of investing clients (AAA through equity investors) creating investing options in virtually any asset type. The impacts of combining securitization rating technology with portfolio theory are profound; the ability to tailor risk/return exposure to an asset class radically alters the scope of investible assets an investor has to choose from in order to manage and maximize its broader asset allocation/return objectives.

Consequently, CDOs have developed into sophisticated investment management vehicles in their own right. Therefore it is not surprising that through the 1990s, CDOs were the fastest growing asset class in the asset-backed securities market. The 1990s were a period where the complexity in financial markets increased significantly due to the globalization of investable opportunities. Many credit markets have *come of age* in the last decade: European, Asian, Emerging Markets. Acknowledging the increasing complexities of the collateral markets in light of the industry trends facing the investor and asset manager community, one would expect the CDO market to continue its pace of growth. In many ways, a CDO's value creation is very transparent; this is illustrated in Exhibit 15.1. In a global context, CDO technology has and continues to be a major factor in reducing the global investing barriers between risk originators and risk consumers worldwide. Said differently, the market functions as an efficient conduit between the suppliers of capital and those who require capital acccelerating the flow and recycling of the global money supply.

EXHIBIT 15.1   Illustration of CDO Value Creation

	Asset Managers	Collateral Markets	End Investors
Observations	Looking to establish branding and differentiation Need channels for growth which are scalable	Collateral options expanding in scope and size (Europe, CDS, alternative investments) Complexity naturally follows (practical access, information)	Investible pools growing/ consolidating (fewer players, pension privatisation) Increased focus on return hurdles and form (tax, legal, accounting efficiency)
Implications	Structured asset gathering will continue Structures need to respect, not restrict, management styles	Identifying relative value given choices Portfolio/risk management frameworks needed (diversification/correlation)	Customisable/scalable investing programs Outsourcing expertise

CDO business objective: to create efficient platforms for intermediation that respect these developments

STRUCTURED CREDIT: A TOOL FOR FINANCIAL INTERMEDIATION

As highlighted, the discipline of structured credit in its broadest characterisation is principally focused on creating new approaches to more efficiently intermediate borrowers and savers (i.e., *risk* originators and *risk* consumers). While structured credit had its genesis in the United States, the business has quickly globalised and become an essential component of global financial market development. Much of this growth is attributable to the flexibility and customisation CDOs provide in terms of product offerings. In many ways, financial products are no different than tangible goods; opportunities for market expansion are created by delivering new product options to end users. Equally, like most tangible goods, the ability to tailor CDOs rapidly while maintaining scale economies was only made possible through the advent of computing technology (portfolio analytics, risk frameworks, and so on).

Although the products typically identify with structured credit seem extensive and often confusing, reflecting the numerous underlyings that are possible: bonds, loans, credit default swaps, and so on *versus* CBOs, CLOs, CSOs, and so on. They all achieve a very similar value proposition: they are vehicles to pool and redistribute risk. In many ways, all these products are best classified as derivative instruments given that they employ techniques to either reference, repackage, or reconstitute risks in order to enhance the overall liquidity in the *underlying collateral* markets. It would be incorrect to assume that the concept of risk used here in as limited to credit risk: like the underlying instruments, CDOs can encapsulate many different forms of risk (interest rate, currency, market, and so on) albeit either reduced, enhanced or eliminated through product structuring (*tailoring*). Again, this will be explored further in the case studies.

If we adopt the premise that a CDO is nothing more than a customised intermediary, the easiest way to consider its mechanics is by drawing analogy to existing financial intermediary models. For instance, a CDO can be viewed as a limited purpose *minibank*, albeit more efficient than a bank given its focused nature in terms of the scope of its asset mix and the fact that CDOs have a limited life (they are not ongoing concerns). A CDO's limited purpose aspects makes them much more easier to understand—and value—from an investor point of view. Necessarily, the asset pool securing a bank's liabilities will be very diverse (loans, real estate, private equity, and so on) given the wide variety of customers/constituents a bank serves. CDOs, on the other hand, rarely commingle different asset types. In many ways, the benefit that this creates goes back to basic finance principles. Market efficiency is best achieved when the investor can choose the scope and composition of their asset allocation. Investors can achieve their targeted risk/return goals by investing in a series of different CDOs. For instance, an investor can replicate the types of exposures found in our bank example above, by investing in three different CDOs each uniquely secured by one of the three asset types identified. Interestingly, not only can the investor manage its percentage allocation across the various asset classes, the investor can also increase or decrease the amount of risk taken to each sector depending on where in the CDO capital structure the investor has chosen to participate (i.e., how much *leverage* is taken to the asset class).

The risk and return taken to any asset class will increase as an investor moves lower down the CDO's capital structure. Conversely, as the investor participation moves up the capital structure, its risk/return to the particular asset class decreases (in fact, the risk associated with a senior tranche can be less risky than the underlying asset class itself). This should not be surprising, given that the investor in this case is taking second, third, and so on, loss risk. Said differently, each class of notes benefits from the class of notes subordinated to them. The equity in a CDO, for instance, is in the first loss position, meaning the first unit of realised loss (or gain for that matter) on the underlying portfolio accrues to the equity investors. Relative seniority, in fact, is the basis upon which the credit rating agencies assign their ratings to the various tranches once they have assessed the range of cash flow expectation (assuming various stress scenarios) the underlying portfolio could generate. Not surprisingly, the cash flow outcomes under these different scenarios depend significantly on the type of asset class being considered, the diversity achieved within the asset class portfolio and, of course, the capability of the asset manager.

Coming back to our *minibank* analogy, we have established that investors are best served by constructing/controlling their own portfolio asset allocation. In many ways, direct investing into a series of CDOs affords the investor absolute transparency. Some banks, by virtue of their complexity, are often too opaque for some investors. Forcing them to value the bank based on a lowest common denominator principle. For example, if an investor was adverse to emerging market exposure and a bank had 10% of its assets held in such asset class, the investor would discount the value of any securities issued by such bank relative to one that did not have these types of exposures. Alternatively, the investor may like emerging market risk but feels the bank is not *best-in-class* in terms of originating or managing such risk resulting in a similar dilemma. In the extreme, the investor may never invest, depriving that bank (or more generally, the financial markets) of the liquidity that would otherwise be made available to the other asset pools being originated by the bank. Ultimately, the end result is the same, the velocity of the global money supply is reduced unless the investor can find a bank that meets his or her specific investing needs.

Stepping back, the analogy being drawn here has purposefully been exaggerated—banks have many differentiating features, not to mention the fact that they are ongoing concerns with broader societal importance. Nonetheless, it highlights the point: CDOs can fill the practical gaps that exist between borrowers and savers in the global economy.

Building a CDO: Basic Principles

The best and, perhaps, most durable opportunities for CDO creation arise when investable funds in a particular jurisdiction begin to outgrow the investment options historically available. Under such circumstances, investors begin searching elsewhere to invest their excess liquidity. The skilled structured financier will, in partnership with his or her distribution channels, recognise this liquidity disparity and begin his or her work.

For illustrative purposes, it is worth considering the German experience of the 1990s in conjunction with the high-yield debt example mentioned previously. During this period, German institutional investors were seeking to diversify and increase their overall returns. This need arose due to, among other things, the fact that prior to the advent of the Euro (or more generally, a European credit market), there were limited investing alternatives other than domestic German Pfandbrief (secured AAA bank notes with a commensurate low yield). Simultaneously, the US high-yield market had reached a reasonable critical mass such that itself was looking for new capacity or liquidity. As a result, CDOs became the tool by which these two trends intermediated. The German institutional investor achieved its goals by gaining indirect access to an asset class that for reasons such as geography would have been impractical. For most of the early cross-border participants, direct investing would have been imprudent given the practical inability to select and monitor the individual high-yield issuers from afar, let alone any overall market subtleties. Conversely, the US high-yield market benefited by the fact that this new capacity introduced a broader bid for their issues, which, in turn, afforded high-yield issuers increased market access at acceptable issuance spreads.

Development of the Structured Asset Management Business

With that said, a new group of beneficiaries had been generated as well, the high-yield bond CDO manager or, more generally, the CDO asset management business. The asset management industry was, in many ways, transformed with the advent of structured credit. The *best-in-class* asset managers were afforded a unique opportunity to efficiently expand their asset gathering activities globally. In fact, many specialty asset manager brands have built their businesses almost exclusively through structured asset gathering. For most that participate in this space, their structured asset gathering platforms fit equally among their various other distribution options. The potential for scale economies are significant. Not only do CDOs bring sizable portfolios of assets under management at once with each issue ($300–500 million), they are *locked up* for seven to 12 years (the average maturity of a CDO) as well.

For an asset manager, this compares favourably to having a series of smaller, yet separate discretionary management mandates, each with different strategies and objectives since the requirements for credit infrastructure, systems and, of course, portfolio managers can be prohibitive. Not only are they more expensive to administer, discretionary funds tend to have more flight risk in periods of market volatility. The operational/scale benefits are clear, perhaps less obvious is the efficient global brand recognition it provides the asset manager. For smaller asset management brands, CDOs allow equal visibility in the global investing community with larger, more established global brands. This will certainly bear influence over the structure of the global industry as it continues to consolidate.

Shifting back to building a CDO, we will assume we have identified the existence of the German investor/high-yield bond CDO opportunity and have selected an asset manager that is *best-in-class* in terms of managing and trading high-yield bonds. Equally, we will assume that the portfolio manager is sufficiently exercised in a management style consistent with the constraints set out in the CDOs' management guidelines such that the asset manager is not encumbered in his efforts to maximise the value of the portfolio. A CDO's operating parameters or *by-laws* are imposed jointly by the credit rating agencies, as part of achieving the desired debt rating on the CDO notes and the investors, as investor sophistication has evolved, who have gained more influence over a CDO's operating construction.

Building a Minibank: Illustration of CDO Mechanics

Firstly, we must establish the corporate existence of our new limited purpose *minibank*: CASH CDO I—or *CCDO* I. CCDO I will be the vehicle by which we will attempt to intermediate the US high-yield market with the German institutional investor base. Exhibit 15.2 illustrates the mechanics described in this hypothetical example.

Specifically, we will look to domicile CCDO I in a jurisdiction such as Cayman Islands, Netherlands, and so on that introduces no or limited incremental risks or friction costs to the broader transaction being contemplated. Risks or friction costs would include things such as weakened legal perfection over the underlying assets or double taxation, for instance. Provided that CCDO I is now legally functioning with all

EXHIBIT 15.2 A CDO as a Minibank

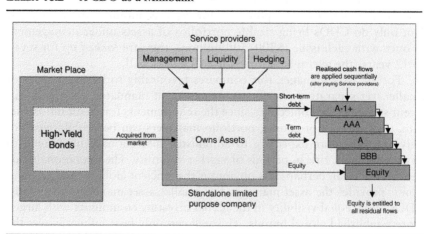

its necessary licensing and regulatory authorisations, CCDO I will next need to engage its service providers in order to begin building its balance sheet as well as developing and implementing its asset/liability management strategy.

Engaging CDO Service Providers

The first, and perhaps most important, service provider that CCDO I will engage is the asset manager, effectively the CDO's management. In our example, a speciality US high-yield manager is contracted to administer CCDO I helping to define and then execute on the investment theme of our CDO. Equally, we will look to outsource the operational/ financial reporting aspects of the CDO vehicle. Other service providers would include third parties such as trustees, custodians, and paying agents. Among other things, they will provide services to CCDO I like validating payment calculations, administering disbursements, affecting underlying collateral sales/transfers, as well as ensuring general compliance with the CDO's management guidelines. In terms of other services sought, CCDO I will engage one or more credit rating agencies to evaluate and pass its credit opinion upon the debt securities that CCDO I plans to issue, thus making them more placeable with investors. At the same time, CCDO I will be considering, to the extent necessary, its various hedging or risk-taking counterparties. These counterparties may provide, for instance, interest rate or currency swaps to CCDO I if its asset and liability strategy warrants such hedging tools. Another form of counterparty CCDO I may employ is a credit enhancement provider— market participants willing to accept a range of different risks in a CDO's complex architecture in exchange for a fee or premium. Often external credit enhancement mechanisms (e.g., bond insurance, letters of credit, liquidity facilities) are sourced when certain risks become too complicated for the rating agencies or investors to comfortably and fairly assess. In such cases, it is often easier to educate and convince one party of a unique risk's particulars than a broad syndicate of investors. Credit enhancement providers are specialised in valuing, pricing and accepting nonstandard or illiquid risks. Consequently, it may simply be that the market price for a particular risk is just more efficiently offered by third parties than born by CCDO I's capital structure directly. CCDO I, by construction, is a rational participant in the financial community and will source comparative advantage from others no differently than any other market participant.

Now that CCDO I has its asset manager employed and its operational infrastructure outsourcing in place, let's assume the following CDO strategy is identified. Firstly, the asset manager (and investor) sees value in the B–BB rated bond sector spread across all industries. Equally, the strategy contemplates significant trading to maximise portfolio value in what are expected to be volatile markets. We begin the practical implementation of the strategy by focusing on the asset accumulation tactics.

Building the Asset Side of the CDO Balance Sheet

The physical activity of purchasing the actual securities underlying a CDO (the *raw material*) is principally about collateral access and market timing. In our example, efficient access to high-yield new issues and the secondary market are important. There are situations when the underlying portfolio for a CDO is accumulated or *warehoused* well in advance of a CDO's debt issuance. Under such arrangements, the collateral is warehoused on a third party's balance sheet until the CDO's liabilities are sold, the proceeds from which are then used to purchase (or *take out*) the warehoused portfolio from the third party. In our case, the high-yield market has a relatively consistent new issuance calendar, and most importantly, a deep secondary market to purchase existing issues. Not only does this permit CCDO I to acquire and finance (i.e., issue the CDO's liabilities) the target portfolio almost simultaneously, it also allows for better blending of assets—seasoned securities will perform differently from new issues in terms of credit performance offering investors diversification by year of origination or *vintage*. Appreciative of the flexibility afforded by the market in terms of rapid collateral access (asset building), CCDO I must still evaluate the timing of its purchase in the context of its overall liability strategy, not to mention its deliverability (i.e., is the market open to financing a CDO with CCDO I's high-yield theme, and if so, at what cost).

Irrespective of collateral availability, the timing of portfolio acquisition is important. As part of its overall portfolio maximisation strategy, the asset manager attempts to accumulate the portfolio (i.e., the asset-side of our *minibank*) when it is *cheap* relative to historical values. The initial purchase price combined with the cash flow (or *revenue*) expectation of the acquired portfolio will determine the amount of debt financing CCDO I's balance sheet can support and, for that matter, the value of any residual or equity interest available in CCDO I. The value of a CDO's equity at any point in time is simply the value of its assets, the portfolio's mark-to-market value after defaults or losses, *less* all its outstanding liabilities: remaining debt obligations, service provider expenses, unreimbursed credit enhancement borrowings.

This general relationship, asset class yield *minus* cost of financing, is what defines the expected equity value (or *enterprise value*) of CCDO I upon its launch. This relationship is dynamic given that value of the portfolio moves overtime, as does the cost and availability of debt financing for particular combinations of asset classes and/or speciality asset managers. This relationship (*market opportunity* measure) is closely monitored by all market participants as a barometer to when a CDO becomes the most efficient tool for leveraging up a particular asset class. (Incidentally, this is why the CDO market demonstrates cyclical issuance patterns around asset class themes.) In practice, when a *market opportunity* is identified, the first parties approached are repeat CDO equity buyers, who themselves are aware of this dynamic relationship.

Building the Liability Side of the CDO Balance Sheet

Accepting that the *market opportunity* for high-yield debt is positive, CCDO I must now shift its focus to the liability structure of our *minibank*. In developing the liability strategy, we must optimize around four influential factors: the asset manager style, cash flow dynamics of high-yield bonds, investor customisation or *repackaging*, and, of course, the credit rating agencies.

In terms of fitting the liability structure around the style of the asset manager in our example, CCDO I will focus on financing mechanics that complement its high turnover trading approach. We have already established that CCDO Is chosen asset manager has a developed, proven track record in generating consistent excess returns (*alpha*) through high-yield trading. It is this unique capability our asset management brand possess that CCDO I will use to attract investors to its note offerings *versus* the invariability of competing CDOs that will follow, each attempting to exploit the same *market opportunity*.

Anticipating the high trading turnover, CCDO I decides to adopt a *market value* operating framework (cash flow *versus* market value operating models are further described later in the chapter). By construction, a market value approach will afford the asset manager the most flexibility with respect to portfolio composition. Counter to the more prevalent cash flow-based structure, investors and rating agencies depend mainly on daily valuation measures as opposed to asset mix constraint when evaluating a CDO's creditworthiness. In exchange for asset mix flexibility, however, the *CDO management team* will be subject to a more dynamic, and hence more complicated, liability structure featuring *less* permanent financing. The notes issued by CCDO I provide permanent financing as long as the current mark-to-market value of the portfolio *less* all outstanding liabilities is above a predetermined cushion. This cushion (*market value trigger*) is analogues to the CDO *enterprise value* concept mentioned earlier. Mechanically, if the value of our high-yield bond portfolio deteriorates, such that the market value trigger is breached, the asset manager is obligated to commence portfolio liquidation in order to raise the proceeds necessary for the orderly repayment of the outstanding debt, which is now manditorily redeemable. This process will continue until the asset/liability relationship is back in compliance with those set out for CCDO I at inception.

Although a CDO's permissible leverage ratio is principally ascribed by the credit rating agencies, CCDO I's asset manager must understand well the circumstances that can drive an unwind of its operations. A CDO's portfolio can deteriorate for many reasons other than poor asset selection or default avoidance. For instance, by employing a market value-based structure, a significant change in asset spreads, or interest rates generally, can reduce the notional value of the portfolio sufficiently to trigger an unanticipated call on its debt financing. The seasoned and prudent asset manger will understand the various sensitivities that impact a CDO's asset/liability flexibility and often operate at leverage ratios safely below those permitted by the rating agencies. This highlights the importance of engaging a CDO asset manager who has developed the skills, infrastructure, as well as general appreciation of managing the liability-side of a CDO balance sheet. Managing the liability side of a CDO warrants the same importance that is placed on managing the asset side. In our *minibank* example, a CDO's asset manager has a fiduciary responsibility similar to a bank's treasurer or CFO in this regard.

There is more that the CDO structure can do to facilitate the needs of the asset manager's trading style and the market value-based, prepayable financing arrangement. For instance, CCDO I could complement its term debt financing strategy with the issuance of short-term liabilities such as rated commercial paper (or *CP*). By staggering the term structure of our CDO's financing, the asset manager can more readily match the market value dynamics of the underlying collateral portfolio. For example, CCDO I can increase its CP issuance as short-term relative value purchase opportunities arise while repaying CP once the trading opportunities are exited or monetized. This approach provides a means to maintain some of the benefits core term funding offers, yet managing the liquidity needs necessary to fund our dynamic asset strategy. That is, short/long liabilities strategies are common for most financial institutions; there is no reason why it should be different for our *minibank*.

Focusing on the specifics of the collateral and it's bearing on the way CCDO I should be administered, another technique our CDO will most likely employ is the use of interest rate swaps. US high-yield bonds almost always carry a fixed-rate coupon. As highlighted earlier, asset-side duration risk does not fit well with our market-value-based structure given the impact it can have over the portfolio value over time. One way to immunize CCDO I against this potential for higher portfolio volatility is by swapping the portfolio's fixed-rate coupon streams in exchange for a coupon benchmarked to a floating-rate index (LIBOR). Not only does this dampen the portfolio's volatility, it also better matches the coupons payable on the CDO's notes; in practice, most of the CDO debt issued is offered with a floating-rate coupon and the CP portion of our financing structure is floating rate, by definition. Hence, another ordinary banking risk management type of activity.

Hopefully, at this point, one has gotten a flavour as to how our *minibank* can be shaped to accommodate the particulars of the underlying collateral and an asset manager's style. We shift our discussion to the investor and rating agencies, each of which also have influence on CCDO I's construction.

Influence of Rating Agencies and the Investor

As a general matter, once the basic aspects of CCDO I's asset and liability strategy is established and the vehicle's existence, domicile, legal form is identified, the credit rating agencies are approached for a debt rating on the notes. They are presented with an information package detailing CCDO I's mission statement, intended operating approach/constraints, as well as supporting analytics. Information around the contemplated asset manager is also provided; in fact, the rating agencies will visit the asset manager's facilities (*due diligence*) in order to gain comfort that the particular asset manager has the sufficient skills and infrastructure to manage the actual CDO on behalf on the investors. The actual analytical process around rating a CDO's liabilities is relatively complicated and probably warrants a chapter onto itself (separately, the rating agencies offer their criteria and rating analytic tools freely to market participants). In our high-yield example, they will assess the cash flow impacts on the portfolio under different patterns of default. In general terms, the path dependency of the default stresses being applied are based on a series of factors such as historical default probabilities on individual assets given their initial rating, pairwise correlation across rating categories and industry sectors, as well as expected recoveries on any defaulted assets once they have been worked-out. More perspective on the roles and areas of focus for rating agencies are offered later in the chapter.

An important constituent that we have not mentioned lately is the German institutional investor. For those that remember, the catalyst behind the overall transaction. Now that we have built the basic product or tool (CCDO I) to help intermediate the high-yield market to the investor, we should explore any tailoring the CDO can provide to the end investor. The vehicle thus far has been customised principally around the collateral and asset manager.

We begin by presenting the German institutional investor the current value of the *market opportunity*, that is, the potential value an equity investment in the CCDO I can yield given current asset yields, expectations around defaults and the cost of financing). Assuming it has remained attractive, despite the time we have used in assessing the feasibility of the CDO, the equity investor either agrees to invest or not. Once sufficient equity interest is *circled*, then the process of sourcing debt investors begins. In practice, the equity investments are typically subject to certain conditionalities. The most obvious condition is that a minimum absolute *market opportunity* threshold must be achieved (so that a minimum yield on the CDO equity can be realized.

Investor-Specific Repackaging

In addition to expected yield thresholds, the investor may seek features that are highly customized around requirements typical to his or her jurisdiction of residence as well as risk/return goals. In our German example, for instance, the investor may appreciate the necessary flexibility a market value-based structure affords the asset manager (i.e., the investor's contracted management team), but not the mark-to-market volatility it introduces to his potential CCDO I equity investment. As a result, we will look to *repackage* the equity in a form that will help immunize the equity investment against certain downside scenarios. Investor *repackaging* is an important and regular element of the CDO intermediation process; repackaging allows customisation for investors outside the CDO without complicating the core operating vehicle. By bifurcating the tailoring in this way, the mechanics required by the asset manager and the collateral can be satisfied at the same time multiple investor customisation can be achieved—that is, introducing scalability to the specialized intermediation being sought. This is illustrated at Exhibit 15.3.

For reference, a repackaging vehicle employs similar techniques to a CDO in terms of establishing its legal and operational existence. However, the assets securing the repackaging vehicle notes tend to be single instruments (CDO equity). This should not be surprising given they tend to be single-investor specific.

In terms of reducing the equity volatility concerning the German investor, we can repackage CCDO I's equity with a zero-coupon government bond in a separate vehicle. Specifically, the investor will invest in the notes of the newly created vehicle, rather than CCDO I directly. In effect, the investor will be purchasing notes secured by a blended portfolio of two investments: one *risky* and one *riskless*. The ratio of risky to riskless—the amount of CCDO I equity purchased relative to the amount of AAA zeros—is determined such that the initial value of the

EXHIBIT 15.3   Illustrating Repackaging

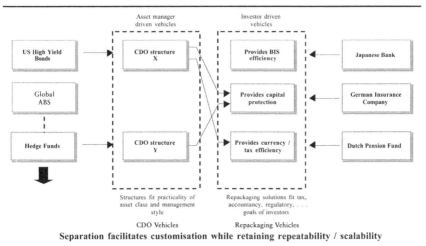

Asset manager driven vehicles — Investor driven vehicles

US High Yield Bonds → CDO structure X → Provides BIS efficiency ← Japanese Bank

Global ABS → Provides capital protection ← German Insurance Company

Hedge Funds → CDO structure Y → Provides currency / tax efficiency ← Dutch Pension Fund

Structures fit practicality of asset class and management style

Repackaging solutions fit tax, accountancy, regulatory, . . . goals of investors

CDO Vehicles   Repackaging Vehicles

Separation facilitates customisation while retaining repeatability / scalability

riskless zero accretes overtime to the investors targeted total initial investment. Given that the maturity value of the riskless zero coupon instrument is equivalent to the initial total investment (i.e., the initial capital), at a minimum; the investors' capital is protected against any loss that may arise on the equity portion of our two-asset portfolio. The investor will at least get his or her principal back.

Under this strategy, it should not go unnoticed that by investing some of his or her initial capital in the AAA zero, the German investor has purposefully diluted some of the absolute yield (and risk) a pure equity investment might return. In fact, the investor will be returned the realized combined weighted average yield of the equity and zero instruments. From the investor's perspective, however, the yield reduction relative to what the *naked* equity investment could yield can be viewed as the necessary premium payable in order to insure against the loss of capital (to buy the AAA zero). In conclusion, the net result of our repackaging is an investment with a payout profile consistent with the German investor's initial intentions: meaningful upside participation in a new, diversifying asset class while maintaining meaningful downside protection (immunizing against high volatility). The German investor's risk/return has been tailored.

With that said, investor-driven repackaging is not limited to risk/ return customisation only. In many cases, the physical form (or *format*) of the repackaged equity is altered. For instance, the aforementioned capital protection structure can be complemented by the fact that the repackaging vehicle can issue a loan rather than a note to the investor.

In Germany, a privately placed loan instrument, a Schuldschein, has much more acceptance than an investment in note format. By structuring a Schuldschein, German insurance companies, for instance, can tap the larger pools for investment available in their general accounts rather than from the more limited funds otherwise available for CDO equity.

In summary, a CDO is a very powerful tool that facilitates the needs of many market constituents. Like all tools, however, they have to be used properly. A CDO structured where the unique particulars of the collateral, the asset manager, and investor are considered, and most importantly balanced, begins to define the minimum standard of excellence that all good structured financiers should respect.

Credit Derivatives: A New CDO Asset Class

The advent of credit derivatives has radically altered the way credit risk is originated, managed, and transferred in the global financial economy. Similar to the way interest rate swaps have decoupled duration risk management from fund raising, credit derivatives have further bifurcated funding into liquidity sourcing and *pure* credit risk management. The impacts are profound; not only have they allowed pure credit risk an ability to trade (efficiently price) independent of the cash market's technical factors (i.e., new issue supply and demand), they have created comparative advantage opportunities between end-credit risk takers and funders. To appreciate such subtlety, one must understand the nature of these instruments.

What Is a Credit Derivative

A credit derivative in many ways is nothing more than an insurance policy on the credit performance of a particular asset. For example, a protection buyer pays a premium in exchange for a contingent payment payable upon an asset-related credit event defined principally around asset default, payment suspension, or restructuring. Credit derivatives on portfolios of credit risk take the analogy one step further in that they often have a deductible (i.e., the first loss or *equity* in the reference portfolio). This means the contingent payment is only triggered once the cumulative notional amount of defaults on a series of individual assets in the reference portfolio exceeds the deductible notional. Consequently, comparative advantage opportunities can arise between end credit risk takers based on their ability to finance or accept credit risk in its newly expanded forms (cash-based or synthetically). For instance, when a cash investor purchases a bond from an issuer, that investor is providing that issuer financing as well as accepting that issuers credit risk, that is, the ability of the issuer to repay on the borrowed funds received from the investor's investment. From an investor's point of view, the *income value* of this cash investment will depend in part on his or her cost of funds to purchase the instrument.

To be specific, assume a bond with a risked-adjusted yield (i.e., the net anticipated yield after default expectations) of LIBOR plus 50 bps; an investor with a cost of funds of LIBOR flat will find more *income value* in the bond than an investor who borrows at LIBOR plus 25 given the different levels of margin that can be secured (i.e., 50 bps in the first instance, 25 bps in the second). However, the investor with the higher cost of funds, now has an alternative in terms of sourcing the credit risk-based investment. He or she can invest in the bond *synthetically* by writing a credit derivative on the bond, becoming a protection seller on the bond. As a general matter, the credit derivative will pay a premium to the investor roughly equivalent to the bond spread (50 bps in our example). In effect, the high-cost-of-funds investor has replicated the margin realizable by the cash-instrument investor. This is made possible by the fact that the investor does not need to raise cash in order to enter into this agreement. The only time the synthetic risk taker will need to borrow cash and trigger his or her funding comparative disadvantage is when a credit event arises, obligating the investor to either take receipt of the underlying (now defaulted) bond or cash settle the difference between the bond's par value and its current distressed value. Hopefully, this example illustrates how comparative advantages in funding impacts the amount of liquidity that can be made available to the cash or synthetic market for credit risk. And more broadly, what credit derivatives have done in terms of increasing the overall opportunity set for credit risk intermediation in the financial marketplace (not to mention, its efficiency).

In-depth coverage of credit derivatives is given in Chapter 21.

The Advent of Synthetic CDOs

It is the afore mentioned features that have made credit derivatives a unique element of the CDO market, making it the fastest growing CDO segment in terms of volume. The category of CDOs utilizing credit derivatives as an underlying have come to be known by practitioners as *synthetic CDOs*. The concept of synthetic CDOs was first pioneered by JPMorgan through its BISTRO program in 1997. As an alternative to the cash securitization approach prevalent at the time—*balance sheet CDOs* further defined later—these programs used portfolio-based credit derivatives as an alternative to transfer credit risk from a bank's balance sheet without the associated asset transfer complications, that is, client relationship management, asset retitling/assignment, altered collections administration/processing. More specifically, these programs were designed to retain the benefits of cash securitizations (credit risk management and capital efficiency) without, however, a securitization's most prohibitive friction: *expensive funding*.

Cash securitizations are premised on the fact that the assets are *sold* to, and in effect financed by, the securitization vehicle. As a consequence, by employing cash securitization methods, a bank is replacing its on-balance sheet cost of financing a portfolio with the funding levels realizable by the securitization vehicle. Not surprisingly, banks generally achieve lower funding costs than structured vehicles can on a ratings equivalent basis. (As in our cash *versus* synthetic bond investor example earlier, the bank has a funding comparative advantage.) Prior to the advent of portfolio-based synthetic risk transfer, this incremental cost was a necessary friction in order to achieve the other benefits already described, and on balance, not sufficiently prohibitive to offset them (economically nor strategically). The use of portfolio credit derivatives have allowed banks or any asset originator for that matter to separate the funding component inherent in administering a credit portfolio from the credit risk component. More specifically, this new technology means a bank can continue financing and servicing its portfolio on balance sheet, effectively monetizing its comparative funding advantage without foregoing the other benefits it may have otherwise been seeking with a more traditional cash securitization approach.

Interestingly, the balance sheet version of synthetic CDOs was embraced mostly by European bank participants; given that their comparative funding advantages have been uniquely more pronounced relative to their global competitors. From a cost of funds perspective, banks in Europe have been more structurally advantaged. They tend to be more highly rated and some of the few remaining beneficiaries of *cheap* retail deposits, each of which are changing given poor performance issues as well as increased self-directed investing by individuals.

Evaluating synthetic CDOs in a broader context, it is worth clarifying a general misconception: Synthetic CDOs are not an asset class onto themselves. A synthetic CDO (or *SCDO*) is no different that any other CDO except for the uniqueness of the underlying collateral: *unfunded credit risk*. It is true that SCDOs can reference all the various asset classes that are offered in cash flow-based CDOs; but the true point of distinction is the fact that their different *forms* of collateral warrant very different liability structures. The contingency of cash flow exchange inherent in the underlying collateral for an SCDO (i.e., credit derivatives) results in radically different cash flow repayment dynamics than those observed with physical securities.

It is worth emphasizing, absent of the building or *structuring* challenges faced on the SCDO's liability-side, all other basic CDO building principles apply. An SCDO, like a traditional CDO, also engages service providers to administer its operational, compliance, and management requirements. Relative to our traditional CDO, however, we are charged with identifying an asset manager that has a combined capability; it is not sufficient to have credit selection, surveillance and trading skills in the underlying reference asset alone. In fact, an SCDO warrants a trading capability in the asset class in credit derivative form as well. Although linked, the two markets—cash versus derivative—will interact differently around certain technical factors warranting cross-market knowledge. In practice, it is difficult to source this combined capability; in part, it is a function of the market's maturity. There are many participants who are skilled in using credit derivatives for hedging purposes (i.e., buying *insurance* on an asset once it has fallen out of favour as an alternative to *selling*), but very few can in fact trade the instrument for value and generate *alpha*. Coming back to our CDO basic building-block analogy, the SCDO will also seek a credit opinion from the rating agencies, provide risk/return customisation through credit tranching, as well as facilitate investor idiosyncratic needs through repackaging. It is the SCDO's liability structure where the similarities fade.

Building a Synthetic CDO's Liability Structure

In order to best understand the appropriate CDO liability structure, one should draw comparison of an SCDO to a *mini-insurance company* (or *mini-inco*). This should not be surprising given the fact that we have already established that a credit derivative is similar in nature to credit insurance. Conceptually, an SCDO's primary purpose is to *write* credit insurance to the financial marketplace, albeit in a much more standard, tradable, and hence, liquid form. Like a *mini-inco* then, an SCDO's liability strategy should not contemplate raising capital to fund or secure 100% of its credit insurance commitments. Specifically, as a seller of protection to the market, an SCDO's needs for cash (amounts and timing) are contingent upon the cumulative number of credit events that can be expected on its designated reference portfolio. In other words, an SCDO must be sufficiently liquid to either fund physical delivery of the underlying asset or cash settle the contract as credit events arise. In fact, as part of its credit assessment, an SCDO's *regulator* (i.e., credit rating agencies) will stress the claims-related liquidity needs of the vehicle under various rates and patterns of credit events. In broader terms, any third party—bank, insurance company, dealer)—that accepts protection from the SCDO will also evaluate its claims paying ability based on its *funded* collateralisation. In other words, the SCDO's counterparty value as a protection seller will depend on the overall quality of the portfolio protection written relative to the total capital (debt and equity) raised to support its performance.

It is worth noting that the capital raised in SCDO is, in some instances, itself an *unfunded* commitment. Meaning, as an alternative to investing in an SCDO note (i.e., raising cash upfront for the vehicle), an investor can *write* protection to the structure in the form of a *portfolio swap*. These swaps are structured to reproduce the same risks and ratings that are offered in funded or note form. For example, the credit risk embedded in a A rated note with a notional of 4% and subordinated equity of 5% can be replicated as a portfolio swap that has a *risk layer* of 4% attaching to the reference portfolio at 5%. As observed in the single-asset credit derivative market, comparative advantage opportunities can also arise between portfolio swap and note investors depending on their cost of funds and their own credit quality, that is the vehicle is taking counterparty credit risk to the investor under the swap format. In the extreme, the entire capital structure can be synthetically sourced. Under those circumstances, the value of the SCDO's claims-paying ability is exclusively dependent on the credit quality of the synthetic investors. Consequently, the value of an investor portfolio swap relative to a funded note (or *cash*) will depend on the credit rating of the investor as well as where in the capital structure the investor is attached. In other words, the *cash value* of a portfolio swap will reflect the joint probability that (1) the investor's risk layer gets called because portfolio credit events have been severe enough to *call* on the investor's protection, and (2) that the investor is still in existence—not in default—to honour the protection payment due at such time.

In practice, an SCDO vehicle will utilize both forms of liability: note and swap. Swaps are typically used higher up in the capital structure reflecting the lower risk and, therefore, reduced dependency upon the counterparty, while notes or *cash* are secured upfront for the riskier portions of the vehicle's risk layers (e.g., BBB–BB mezzanine debt or equity). Another reason why swaps are used at the higher end of the capital structure is that they facilitate efficient risk-adjusted pricing. If we assume the top 80% of a portfolio is tranched and rated AAA (the highest possible rating), as a note or *cash* investor there is no way to distinguish the difference between the first unit of loss on the tranche from the last. (The last 1% of loss on a portfolio is virtually risk free.) Given there is no real concept of AAA+++ rated risk, the investor accepts the average risk/return available across the tranche; in effect, the vehicle is underpaying for the first unit of loss embedded in the AAA tranche and forced to overpay for the last unit of protection. Portfolio swaps can be

EXHIBIT 15.4 Comparing Cash and Synthetic CDOs in Terms of Risk
Intermediation

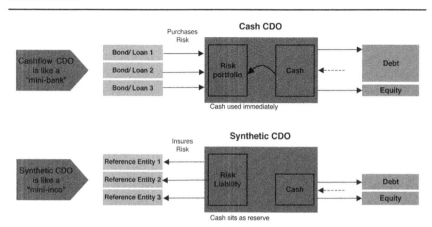

used by investors to further tranche the blended AAA into its true risk
components affording more exact risk-based pricing. For instance, a
blended AAA tranche might pay 50 bps across its entire notional, while
an isolated top 20% tranche may warrant only 3 bps and the bottom
20% perhaps 100 bps (evidencing its increased leverage).

For illustrative purposes, refer to Exhibit 15.4. This diagram demonstrates the conceptual differences of an SCDO *versus* a cash flow-
based CDO under our *mini-inco* and *minibank* model, respectively. Following this framework, the traditional CDO necessarily issues funded
liabilities in order to raise cash from the market such that the target
portfolio can be purchased (i.e., acquire the physical securities). As the
underlying physical assets mature or repay, the cash received is then
used to retire the liabilities outstanding. Conversely, the SCDO issues
liabilities in an amount less than its total insured amount—the notional
amount of credit protection written—yet sufficient enough to satisfy the
requirements of the rating agencies and vehicle's protection buyers. In
this case, the top 90–80% may not need to be hedged by either a note or
swap; in fact, it may be a *naked* exposure that the vehicle's protection
buyers are willing to accept. (The probability of actually exceeding 10–
20% losses in our example is low.) Again, the SCDO's contingent
claims-paying ability will depend on the robustness of its capital base
relative to unanticipated increases in historical loss expectations. It is
worth highlighting, the *naked* exposure an SCDO may be permitted to
run is a significant driver of value for an equity investor in terms of the
cost of leverage he or she is realizing, which is almost free.

Variations on the Synthetic CDO Theme

We have identified that an SCDO's liability structure can adopt two forms: note and/or swap (i.e., cash and/or synthetic risk transfer). Along the same lines, the collateral securing an SCDO can also include cash instrument. As already indicated, an SCDO typically raises cash in order to manage its own credit quality as protection writer; hence, there is no reason why that cash cannot be deployed into physical securities. This makes possible *hybrid* cash/synthetic structures where the asset side of the CDO's balance sheet is mixed across bonds and credit derivatives and the liability side is mixed between note and swap issuance. Of course, a significant aspect of designing this type of CDO rests on building an appropriately matched asset/liability architecture. By construction, these types of CDOs are designed to exploit fully the anomalies that exist between the cash and derivative market for credit, or *basis* trading, as well as the comparative funding advantages that exist among end credit risk takers.

One unique value proposition afforded by credit derivatives that we have not highlighted yet is the ability that they give an asset manager to *short* individual credits. Prior to credit derivatives, short selling as means of generating trading value was, in practice, not executable on illiquid credits given the difficulty that can arise in sourcing the bonds in order to cover. The ability to use cash settlement with credit derivatives has helped to overcome this problem. Consequently, some CDOs have the faculty to use some of their net margin (i.e., net asset yield after liabilities and expenses) to short individual credits as a means to hedge existing bond positions or make *naked* directional bets on a particular credit. CDO vehicles that employ long/short capabilities can be viewed as *minihedge funds* (rounding out and completing our various financial institution analogies: bank, inco, and hedge fund). Under the *minihedge fund* model, an asset manager with the appropriate skills has significant ability to create trading value for the SCDO's equity investors.

CDOS: VARIATIONS AND MORE DETAILS

As already discussed, collateralised debt obligations are a form of security whose interest and principal payments are linked to the performance of a specific pool of assets (sourced either directly or by reference). These underlying assets act as the *collateral* for the issued notes, hence the name. In terms of basic principals, there are many similarities between CDOs and their predecessors: asset-backed securities (ABS) (see Exhibit 15.5). The major difference between CDOs and other ABS securities is

EXHIBIT 15.5   CDOs as ABS Products

The mechanics involved in structuring a cash flow CDO are similar in many respects to more traditional ABS securities. The following areas of commonality have been identified by Satyajit Das:

- The originator of the transaction establishes a bankruptcy-remote legal entity known as a special purpose vehicle (SPV) that is the formal issuer of the notes.
- It is the SPV that formally purchases the assets and their associated cash flows from the originator, thus taking the assets off the latter's balance sheet.
- Funds used to purchase the assets are raised through the issue of bonds into the debt capital market, which may be in more than one *tranche* and include an equity piece that is usually retained by the originator.
- Tranched securities are generally rated by a rating agency, with the rating reflecting both the credit quality of the underlying assets as well as any measures put in place to reduce credit risk, known as *credit enhancement*.
- Investors purchasing the issued notes can expect to receive interest and principal payments as long as the underlying asset pool does not experience default to any significant extent.

Source: Satyajit Das, *Structured Products and Hybrid Securities* (Singapore: John Wiley and Sons, 2001).

that the collateral pool (or reference risk) is principally sourced from the marketplace and managed by an independent asset manager. Like ABS, CDOs feature a multitranche, sequential-pay note reimbursement structure, with most of the notes being rated by one or more of the public credit ratings agencies. The payment priority of the issued securities is commensurate with the credit rating for each note, with the most senior note being the highest rated. The term *waterfall* is used to refer to the order in which cash flow receipts are applied.

In most cases, a CDO's debt securities offer investors a floating-rate coupon indexed to LIBOR (payable on a semi-annual, quarterly or monthly basis) with a broad range of credit qualities (where the senior notes are rated from AAA to A and the junior/mezzanine notes are rated BBB to B). Investors are attracted to the senior notes of a CDO because they allow them to earn relatively higher yields when compared to other similarly rated securities. (Much of the pick-up is a function of their complexity and relative illiquidity.) Other advantages for investors include: exposure to a diversified range of unique credits (often credits that are not easily accessible in public markets); access to the origination, fund management, and credit analysis skills of the portfolio manager; as well as risk/return customisation afforded through credit tranching and repackaging.

In addition to debt, there may be unrated subordinated—or *equity*—interests issued. Although the equity interest in a CDO is structured like a bond, it does represent the residual interest in the CDO vehicle; its return is variable and linked to the residual value of the collateral pool after all debt liabilities have been extinguished. Given that the equity resides in the first loss position, it carries the greatest risk and warrants the highest return—and represents a leveraged exposure to the asset class. More is offered on CDO equity later in this chapter.

CDOs can be broken down into two main categories: *balance sheet* CDOs and *arbitrage* CDOs. Balance sheet CDOs are most akin to a traditional securitisation. They are designed to remove assets from a sponsor's balance sheet (usually a bank) in order to diversify funding sources, manage credit risk and improve regulatory capital efficiency. An arbitrage CDO is created when the sponsor, who may be a bank or as asset manager, in conjunction with the investors wishes to exploit a margin differential that can materialize between the underlying asset yields and a CDO's cost of financing/debt. This differential can be enhanced by active management of the underlying portfolio. Arbitrage CDOs are bifurcated further into *cash flow* and *market value* CDOs. Almost invariably, balance sheet CDOs utilize cash-flow-based technology. As mentioned earlier in the chapter, a cash-flow-based CDO is one where the underlying collateral is expected to generate sufficient cash flow to repay the principal and interest on the notes. In a market value CDO, the collateral manager actively manages the portfolio and, by means of this trading activity, is expected to generate sufficient returns (i.e., increase its value) to repay the CDO obligations. The underlying securities are marked-to-market on a daily basis in a manner similar to a trading book.

Variations on the CDO Theme

As discussed, CDOs are generally categorised as either *balance sheet* CDOs or a*rbitrage* CDOs depending on their intended purpose. In terms of operating mechanics, balance sheet CDOs are almost exclusively cash-flow-based; while, arbitrage CDOs are structured either as cash-flow-based or market-value-based. A later development, *synthetic* CDOs, now account for a growing number of transactions.

Balance Sheet CDOs

As stated, balance sheet CDOs are almost exclusively cash-flow-based, and on that basis, cash flow CDOs are similar in nature to other asset-backed securitisations involving a special purpose vehicle (SPV). Like asset backed securities, assets are pooled together in order to collateralize the liabilities of the SPV. As the underlying assets are sold to the SPV,

EXHIBIT 15.6   Generic Cash Flow CDO

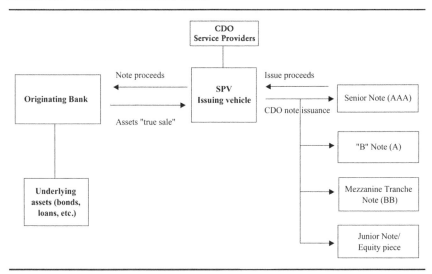

they are removed from the originator's balance sheet; hence, the credit risk associated with these assets is transferred to the holders of the issued notes. The originator also obtains funding by issuing the notes. The generic structure is illustrated with Exhibit 15.6.

Banks and other financial institutions are the primary originators of balance sheet CDOs. Sponsors/originators utilize balance sheet CDOs as a means to pool, repackage, and redistribute their wholesale assets. Historically, the predominate banking assets underlying these securitizations have been commercial loans in the investment grade or subinvestment grade rating categories, hence the nomenclature: CLOs. The main motivations for banks as sponsors of these types of transactions are credit risk management, capital efficiency, and alternative funding capacity.

Investors are often attracted to balance sheet CDOs because they provide investors with a higher return relative to more traditional ABS when compared on a rating equivalency basis, that is, the incremental spread is attributable to the fact that CDOs tend to be less liquid and more complex. Investors also see value in the diversification they offer when included as part of a broader, more traditional structured finance portfolio. For reference, a typical bank balance sheet CLO has the following capital structure characteristics:

- Senior note, AAA rated, and 90–95% of the issue.
- Subordinated note, A rated, 3–5%.

■ Mezzanine note, BBB rated, 1–3%.
■ Equity note, non-rated, 1–2%.

Like ABS, the cash flows realised on the underlying assets are the primary source of funds used to extinguish the CDO's liabilities. These realised collections are applied to each class of notes pursuant to a *priority of payments* that is commensurate with the rating seniority. Pursuant to this payment *waterfall,* the most senior payment obligation must be satisfied in full before the next payment can be addressed, this continues sequentially until the most junior liability is discharged. For the avoidance of doubt, if there are insufficient funds available, the payment obligations of the most junior liabilities will be suspended and payable in the future to the extent subsequent collections become available.

The waterfall process for interest payments is shown at Exhibit 15.7. Before paying the next priority of the waterfall, the vehicle must pass a number of compliance tests designed to measure the overall robustness of cash flow being generated by the collateral portfolio. These metrics include tests such as interest coverage and principal (par) coverage, which is similar in concept to bank loan covenants and explained more fully later.

During the life of a CDO, a portfolio administrator is obliged to produce a periodic report detailing the quality of the collateral pool. This report is known as an Investor (or *Trustee*) Report. This report details the results of the compliance tests and is used by the rating agencies, the CDO's regulator, to monitor the CDO's performance relative to its currently assigned rating.

Arbitrage CDOs

Arbitrage CDOs employ two types of operating models: cash flow and market value. Arbitrage CDOs differ from balance sheet CDOs by virtue of the fact that the assets are generally sourced from third parties or the marketplace. As the name suggests, they are utilized for the sole purpose of taking advantage of *market opportunities* as defined previously that arise between asset yields and the cost of CDO financing the assets (the cost of leverage).

The appropriateness of either model (cash-flow-based *versus* market value-based) will depend on the asset manager's trading style as well as the particulars of the asset class: the asset's market liquidity, duration profile, and credit spread volatility. In terms of mechanics, *cash flow arbitrage* CDOs are no different than balance sheet CDOs, (again, the only difference being their intended purpose and asset sourcing strategy). Consequently, one should see the section on "Balance Sheet CDOs" for further details. Now, we shift the discussion to *market value* CDOs.

EXHIBIT 15.7   Interest Cash Flow Waterfall for Cash-Flow-Based CDO

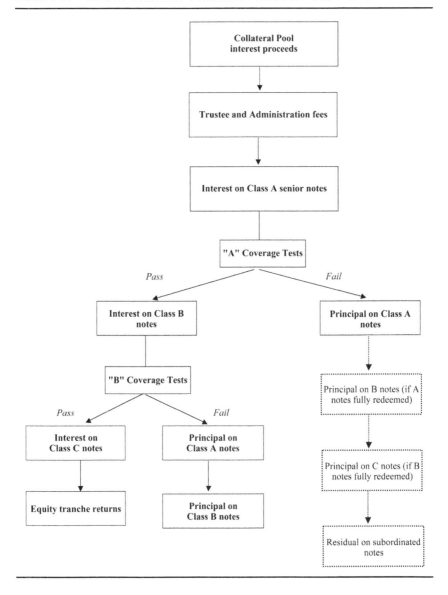

Market Value CDOs

The sponsors of market value CDOs are predominantly asset managers in partnership with investors. By construction, these transactions provide the asset manager with much more freedom to actively trade assets in and out of the collateral portfolio, as well as less restrictive asset eligibility criteria overall. This flexibility, in turn, requires that the assets are marked-to-market by the portfolio administrator on a regular basis (possibly as frequently as daily) in order to ensure the value of the portfolio is at least greater than the CDO liabilities outstanding. Investors are attracted by these types of structures based on a asset manager's trading credentials as well as the trading flexibility the structure provides to better manage losses when the market is experiencing a correction.

Market value transactions aggressively use *ramp-up* periods to acquire assets when accumulating the collateral pool. There is typically a liquidity facility, which is in place prior to the closing of the transaction, to help bridge the acquisition of assets. The principal repayment of liabilities are extinguished when the underlying assets are sold (traded) out of the portfolio, rather than when they mature.

Synthetic CDOs

Synthetic CDO's are a subclass of CDOs where the underlying collateral represents a portfolio of credit derivatives. Compared with conventional balance sheet CDOs, which feature an actual transfer of ownership or *true sale* of the underlying assets to a separately incorporated legal entity, *balance sheet synthetic* CDOs are engineered so that the credit risks of the assets are transferred from the sponsor to the CDO by means of a portfolio credit swap. Therefore, the sponsor is a credit protection buyer and the CDO is a credit protection seller. In some cases, the credit risk may be transferred to investors directly without an intermittent SPV, that is, the investor becomes the credit protection seller in stead of the SPV. By using synthetic risk transfer, the underlying (*reference*) assets are not removed from the sponsor's balance sheet. This technology is employed whenever the primary objective is to achieve risk transfer rather than balance sheet funding.

There are two types of CDO liability structures utilized in synthetic transactions: completely *unfunded* structures that use portfolio swaps exclusively to transfer the entire credit risk of the reference portfolio to investors and *partially funded* structures which transfer only the highest credit risk segment of the portfolio.

The first synthetic deals were observed in the US market, while the first deals in Europe were observed in 1998. Market growth in Europe has been rapid; the total value of cash and synthetic deals in Europe in

2002 approached \$120 billion, and a growing share of this total has been synthetic-based transactions.

The first European synthetic transactions were driven by bank originators with the underlying reference assets being commercial loans on the originator's balance sheet. *Arbitrage synthetic* CDOs have also been sponsored. Within the synthetic market, arbitrage-based transaction were the most frequently issued during 2001.

Arbitrage synthetic CDOs are originated generally by asset managers focusing on increasing their fee income and by investors who wish to exploit the difference between the underlying asset yield and financing cost payable on the CDOs. These structures source their credit risk from the market via single-name credit derivatives or from a third party's balance sheet warehousing (or *financing*) the assets and the risk is transferred subsequently to the SPV using a portfolio specific credit derivative. The second technique is used when certain assets such as ABS are not available in credit derivative form.

Credit Enhancement and Compliance Testing

Common to all the CDO themes are the use of various forms of credit enhancement. In addition to the natural credit enhancement afford through subordination of sequential pay notes, the following methods are also employed:

- **Overcollateralisation:** protection created by the contribution of excess collateral above and beyond the face value of notes; for example, \$250 million nominal of assets are contributed to secure \$170 of CDO liabilities.
- **Cash reserve accounts:** protection in the form of cash providing periodic liquidity and loss reimbursement; the funds can be sourced from the transaction's initial proceeds, and if drawn, replenished overtime with excess spread in order to maintain its requisite balance.
- **Excess spread:** protection afforded intraperiod by the availability of excess interest income on the portfolio after discharging all service provider and interest expenses payable for the period.
- **Insurance wraps:** protection provided by third parties in the form of a insurance policy guarantying the ultimate repayment of the notes pursuant to their stated terms.

As a matter of CDO surveillance, the quality of a CDO's collateral portfolio is monitored regularly and reported on by the portfolio administrator by way of a *Trustee Report*. This report details the results of various *compliance tests*, which are performed on an asset-by-asset level as well as on an aggregate portfolio level. Compliance tests are designed to monitor:

▓ **Weighted average spread** and **weighted average rating:** measures the average interest spread and average credit rating of the assets (i.e., portfolio income and credit quality), which must remain at a specified minimum.

▓ **Concentration:** establishes a set maximum share of assets that can be exposed to any particular asset class, single obligor, industry sector, and so on.

▓ **Diversity score:** a statistical value that is calculated via a formula developed by the rating agencies and designed to measure the level of diversity in the asset portfolio, thus minimizing pairwise correlation in terms of each asset's probability of default.

These tests are calculated on a regular basis as well as each time the composition of the portfolio is altered, that is, each time assets are sold, purchased, or paid off ahead of their legal maturity date. If the test results fall below the required minimum, trading activity is restricted to only those trades that will improve the test results. Certain other compliance tests are viewed as more critical in terms of maintaining note repayment integrity; therefore, if any of them are *failed*, the cash flows will be diverted from the normal priority of payments and begin sequentially paying off the notes based on seniority until the test results improve. These include:

▓ **Overcollateralisation:** the overcollateralisation level vis-à-vis the issued notes must remain above a specified minimum; for instance, it must be at 120% of the nominal value of the senior note.

▓ **Interest coverage:** the level of net interest income on the portfolio (i.e., after defaults) must be sufficient to cover interest due on the liabilities.

Compliance tests are specified as part of the CDO's credit-rating process. The ratings analysis is comprehensive and focuses on the asset type/quality, liability/capital structure, as well as the sponsor's performance track record and reputation.

Analysing the Risks in a CDO's Underlying Portfolio

The risk analysis for CDOs performed by potential investors is necessarily different to that undertaken for other securitised asset classes. For CDOs, the three main factors to consider are default probabilities, default correlations and recovery rates. Analysts make assumptions about each of these with regard to individual reference assets, usually with recourse to historical data. We introduce each factor in turn.

Default Probabilities

The level of default probability will vary with each transaction depending on the underlying asset class. Analysts such as the rating agencies will use a number of methods to estimate default probabilities, such as individual reference credit ratings and historical probability rates. Assuming a statistically significant number of assets, a common approach is to use the average rating of the underlying or reference portfolio.

Correlation

The correlation between assets in a specified portfolio is an important aspect in CDO risk analysis. Challenges exist in terms of determining what precise correlation values to use; these can be correlation between default probabilities, correlation between timing of default, and correlation between spreads. The *diversity score* value of a portfolio attempts to measure and encapsulate these concepts by way of simplification. The higher the score, presumably the less correlated the default likelihood of each asset becomes.

Recovery Rates

Recovery rates for individual obligors differ by issuer and industry classification. Rating agencies publish data on the average prices of all defaulted bonds, and generally analysts will construct a database of recovery rates by industry and credit rating for use in modelling the expected recovery rates of assets in the collateral portfolio.

By using the aforementioned variables, analysts undertake simulation modelling to generate scenarios of portfolio return. For instance ,they may model the number of defaults up to maturity, the recovery rates of these defaults and the timing of defaults. All these variables are viewed as random variables, so they are modelled using a stochastic process.

CDO Equity

Equity is the most junior note in the capital structure of a CDO. For this reason it is also known as the *first-loss* piece of the CDO, carrying the highest risk of payment delays and losses due to credit events or defaults. The equity, which actually takes the legal form of a debt instrument, receives all residual portfolio cash flows after all other liabilities and claims have been paid. In a cash flow structure, the return to the equity holder will be a function of defaults and payment delays of assets in the collateral portfolio; the level of trading or credit rating downgrades do not have an impact on the equity unless they affect the expected cash flows. Although the equity piece receives all residual cash flows generated by the structure, there is a distinction between coupon cash flows and principal cash flows. The residual coupon is paid out as it is received, while the residual principal cash flows are not paid out until all the outstanding notes have been extinguished.

Given all this, we see that CDO equity is a *leveraged* exposure to credit risk, taken on by the equity investor. The holder of CDO equity takes a view that the cash flows generated by the underlying assets are sufficient to bear expected credit losses and provide enough surplus to pay sufficient return on the equity given its risk. This risk/return assessment must take into account the amount of leverage being taken in the structure.

The timing, as well as extent, of defaults is critical to equity return. As a general matter, equity holders receive a significant part of their return early in the life of a transaction. This is because the initial excess spread tends to be highest given that defaults are unlikely to occur until later on in the deal's life. The later in a CDO's life that defaults occur, the less the return to the equity holder will be affected. Examples of equity returns patterns and their sensitivity to default will be demonstrated later in case studies.

CDO equity is not a straightforward instrument and must be assessed carefully by investors due to their complexity and limited liquidity. The asset manager, the quality of the collateral pool and the amount of leverage are very important issues for consideration. In addition, potential investors must consider how the equity investment fits with his or her broader portfolio.

CASE STUDIES

In this section we will attempt to complement the theory and approaches discussed so far with actual transaction examples. Specifically, we will highlight Euro Zing I CDO as a further example of the flexibilities a CDO's liability structure can adopt. Equally, we will explore the use of indexation in CDO structures with the Rosetta CBO I transaction. And finally, Robeco CSO III will be examined as the first fully managed, standalone CDO backed by credit derivatives.

Euro Zing I CDO

Euro Zing I is a cash flow CDO that presents several features of novelty and interest. It is the first true arbitrage CDO of European asset-backed securities in that, 100% of the assets were sourced from the marketplace rather than an existing balance sheet. It is also the first CDO to use a unique, innovative dual-currency liability structure in sterling and euro to access the sterling ABS market in a cost-efficient way as opposed to currency swapping each asset individually to a common currency.

EXHIBIT 15.8 Euro Zing I CBO Structure

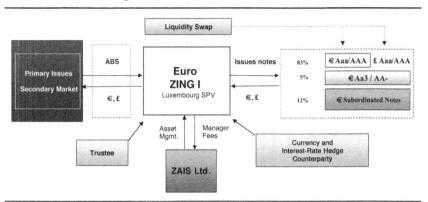

EXHIBIT 15.9 Euro Zing I CBO Tranching

Tranche	Structure	Currency	Sub-ordina-tion	Moody's/ S&P Rating	Spread	Coupon Frequency	WAL/ Maturity
Class A-1	60%	€	29%	Aaa/AAA	E + 50	6 months	8.0/38 yrs
Class A-2[a]	23%	£	17%	Aaa/AAA	L + 55	6 months	8.0/38 yrs
Class B	5%	€	12%	Aa3/AA–[b]	E + 90	6 months	9.5/38 yrs
Sub. Notes	12%	€	N/A	BBB–[c]			NA/38 yrs

[a] Delayed draw-down note.
[b] Fitch Rating.
[c] Principal only (Fitch Rating).

The originator of Euro Zing I CDO is Zais plc. The transaction structure diagram is shown at Exhibit 15.8. The overlying note tranching is shown at Exhibit 15.9.

Investor interest in this deal was spurred by a variety of factors:

▪ **Defensive asset Class:** European ABS securities benefit from embedded structural subordination and credit enhancements, with excellent credit performance and stability in ratings despite a market environment that was volatile at the time of marketing the issue such that a variety of investors sought access to this specialty asset class.
▪ **Portfolio quality and inherent diversification:** The portfolio of European ABS represents credit exposure to different consumer and corporate sectors, across multiple countries and multiple asset managers/ servicers. The portfolio on closing had an average rating of Baa2/BBB.

■ **Conservative structure:** The use of prudent leverage (only 8-times leveraged) and the stability of the asset class allow the subordinated notes to receive an investment-grade rating (BBB– by Fitch). The reduced leverage affords the asset manager greater flexibility to manage the portfolio over time.

Transaction Terms

Name:	Euro Zing CBO I S.A.
Manager:	Zais Group Investment Ltd.
Arranger:	JPMorgan Securities Ltd.
Closing date:	23 August 2002
Legal Maturity:	23 August 2040
Size:	€300 million
Number of Issuers:	70
Portfolio Administrator:	JPMorgan Chase Bank Institutional Trust Services

The expected returns of the subordinated notes are shown at Exhibit 15.10, under specified assumptions.

EXHIBIT 15.10   Euro Zing I CBO Returns

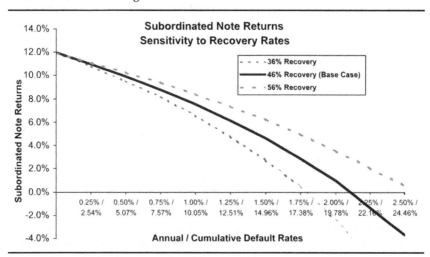

Note: No assurance can be given with respect to the returns. The assumptions underlying the return analysis illustrated above are unlikely to be consistent with actual experience.

EXHIBIT 15.11   Rosetta I CBO Structure

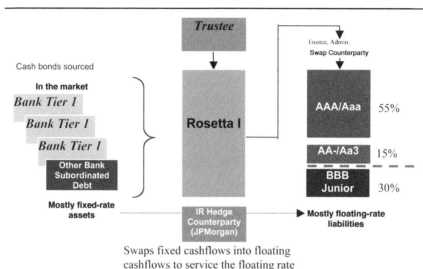

Swaps fixed cashflows into floating
cashflows to service the floating rate

Case Study: Rosetta CBO I

Rosetta CBO I is the first leveraged credit transaction based on an index of European financial institutions subordinated debt[1] (specifically, JPMorgan's SUSI index[2]). Indexation was the asset selection tool of choice as investors were unwilling to pay an asset manager due to quality and stability of the underlying but wanted to ensure a nonbiased selection of the underlying portfolio. Rosetta I's key structural innovation was to transform a portfolio of predominantly perpetual debt into a leveraged instrument with a fixed 10-year maturity. In the case of Rosetta I, assets that extend beyond their call date will generally be sold through an auction procedure. While the first transaction was based on a static portfolio of cash bonds, next generation products are being developed using credit derivatives on subordinated debt as a means to source the risk and are likely to include some substitutability.

The transaction structure is shown at Exhibit 15.11, and overlying note tranching at Exhibit 15.12.

---

[1] Deeply subordinated exposures at the Tier 1 and Upper Tier 2 level.

[2] JPMorgan's SUSI index focuses on the largest (issues size >= €400 million) and most liquid issuances in the European subordinated debt market. The SUSI subindices cover Bank Lower Tier II, Banker Upper Tier II, Bank Tier I, Insurance Subordinated as well as Landesbanks Lower Tier II and Tier I. With the exception of the Landesbanks subindices, all SUSI indices are available in € and £. The composition of each index is revisited every six months.

EXHIBIT 15.12   Rosetta I CBO Tranching

	Notional	Percent	S&P/Moody's Rating	Spread	WAL	Legal Final
Class A	€220,000,000	55%	AAA/Aaa	45 bp	8 yrs	11 yrs
Class B	€60,000,000	15%	AA–/Aa3	80 bp	10 yrs	11 yrs
Junior	€120,000,000	30%	BBB/Baa2		NA	11 yrs
Total		100%				

Investor interest was spurred by a variety of factors:

■ **Asset Class:** Focus on European subordinated debt because of the yield pickup for what is perceived as little incremental risk compared to senior debt.
■ **Portfolio diversification:** Immediate access to most of Europe's highly rated financial institutions; static nature of the portfolio-allowed investors to conduct a name-by-name review.
■ **Structure:** The introduction of moderate leverage allowed junior notes (only 3-times leveraged) to receive enhanced returns while still achieving an investment-grade rating (BBB by S&P; Baa2 by Moody's).

Transaction Terms:

Name:	Rosetta CBO I S.A.
Manager:	N/A, based on JPMorgan's SUSI index
Arrangers:	JPMorgan Securities Ltd.
Closing date:	28 October 2002
Maturity:	28 October 2012
Size:	€153.5 million
Number of Issuers:	27
Number of Issues:	37
Portfolio Administrator:	JPMorgan Chase Bank Institutional Trust Services
Auction Administrator:	JPMorgan Chase Bank Institutional Trust Services

The expected return of the junior note (the shaded piece in Exhibit 15.12) is shown at Exhibit 15.13 as a spread over LIBOR.

EXHIBIT 15.13   Rosetta I CBO Returns

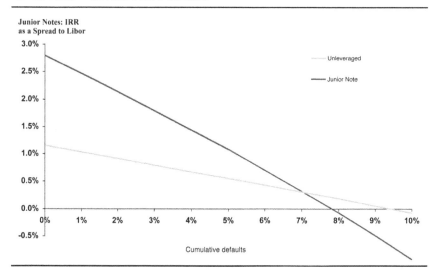

Note: No assurance can be given with respect to the returns. The assumptions underlying the return analysis illustrated above are unlikely to be consistent with actual experience.

Case Study: Robeco CSO III B.V.

Robeco CSO III was the first standalone, managed synthetic CDO and closed in December 2001. Its structure has since been replicated by a number of fund managers and arrangers. The transaction is in the form of a risk intermediation vehicle that transfers exposure to a portfolio of corporate US and European credits from the credit derivatives dealer market into the cash investors market through rated, tradeable cash instruments. Robeco III CSO is innovative in the sense that it brings together for the first time structural and asset management features from the traditional CDO market with risk transfer technology from the credit derivatives market. The transaction has not created a new asset class in its own right. It is still based on the application of portfolio diversification theory to create different layers of risk from a pool of credit risk as any other form of CDO. However, the utilisation of credit derivatives technology has impacted the industry with a few fundamental evolutions:

- **Impacts on the credit derivative market:** Introduction of a new type of risk counterparty in the credit derivatives market that has the capacity to sell protection on large portfolios of risk, increasing the capacity and the efficiency of the credit derivatives market. Along the same lines, it has helped intermediate credit risk away from the bank market into a new investor base, making it an efficient risk spreading tool for credit risk.

- **Impacts on the asset manager community:** Expanded access to credit risk through the utilisation of CDS, rather than the multiple forms of cash instruments available. The asset manager benefits from a broader universe of credits to choose from given that the credit derivatives market has the largest number of different credit entities available. Consequently, the asset manager's ability to perform is enhanced; the scope of credits and their liquidity provide more ability to extract value through trading rather than by up-front credit selection alone. As a general matter, these type of programs offer a new asset management model, as synthetic CDOs allow for rapid and efficient asset accumulation over a short period of time as well as a new flexibility entirely: the ability to short credits (i.e., buying protection on reference names).

Investor interest was spurred by a variety of factors:

- **Access to CDS market dynamics:** The CDS market provides the structure with liquidity and exposures which are not available in either the loan or the bond market, across a diversity of currencies and maturities.
- **Managed transaction:** In case some of the credit quality of some of the exposures in the portfolio change, the manager is able to trade in and out of the exposure.
- **Cheap leverage:** The structure benefits from cheap leverage as it issues only a portion of the CDS portfolio under a funded cash format. The leverage is provided by the CDS counterparties.
- **Portfolio quality and diversification:** The portfolio of CDS represents exposure to a pool of 100 different corporate and financial entities representing over 20 industries across multiple countries. The exposures are principally investment grade, which offers a diversification from cash CDO portfolios.

The structure diagram is shown at Exhibit 15.14. The note tranching is shown at Exhibit 15.15, while the expected return of the subordinated notes is shown at Exhibit 15.16.

Transaction Terms

Name: ROBECO CSO III BV
Manager: Robeco AM

Arrangers: JPMorgan Securities Ltd.
Closing date: 7 December 2001
Maturity: 17 September 2008
Credit Portfolio Size: €1,000,000,000
Notes Issued: €300,000,000
Number Reference Entities: 100
Portfolio Administrator: JPMorgan Chase Bank Institutional Trust Services

EXHIBIT 15.14   Robeco CSO III Structure

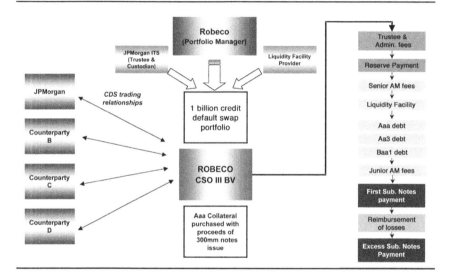

EXHIBIT 15.15   Robeco CSO III Tranching

Tranche	Moody's Rating	Tranche Size ($ million)	Available Subordination (%)	Spread	Final Maturity
A	Aaa	213.0	8.70	55 bp	7 yrs
B	Aa3	15.5	7.15	85 bp	7 yrs
C	Baa1	31.5	4.00	275 bp	7 yrs
Sub	NR	40.0	0.00	NA	7 yrs
P[a]	Baa1[b]	7.5	NA	NA	7 yrs
Total		300			

[a] Combination note.
[b] Principal rating only.

EXHIBIT 15.16   Robeco CSO III Returns

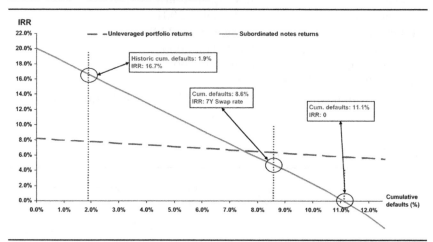

Note: No assurance can be given with respect to the returns. The assumptions underlying the return analysis illustrated above are unlikely to be consistent with actual experience.

Three

Interest Rate and Credit Derivatives

CHAPTER 16

European Interest Rate Futures: Instruments and Applications

Brian A. Eales
Principal Lecturer
London Metropolitan University

The continuing need for governments to issue bonds in order to raise capital to fund medium- and long-term projects taken together with greater interest rate volatility in financial markets has led, over the last three decades of the 20th century, to the development of a mature European bond futures market. This chapter starts by providing a brief historical perspective, tracing the evolution of presentday futures markets in Europe. It touches on the role of government bonds, price/yield behaviour, and portfolio strategies that can be undertaken in the cash market. It goes on to examine the evolution of European bond futures contracts.

Questions such as the uses to which European bond futures can be put, contract specifications and trading volumes are discussed with illustrative examples. Technical issues, which surround the use of bond futures, are also examined and presented with numerical examples. The issues include: the calculation of gross and net basis, identifying the cheapest-to-deliver (CTD) cash market bond, different approaches to measuring relative volatility, calculating hedge ratios, and portfolio duration adjustment. Bloomberg screen output is used to provide a real world flavour to the topics covered.

BRIEF HISTORY OF FUTURES CONTRACTS

The introduction and subsequent evolution of the European Bond Futures Exchanges traces its origin back to Chicago in the 1970s. Although in truth futures markets, albeit in some primitive form, have been in existence from the earliest times in recorded history—for example, the Agora of Athens in ancient Greece and the Fora Vendalia in ancient Rome—it was the establishment of the Chicago Board of Trade (CBOT) in 1848 and its rival, the Chicago Mercantile Exchange (CME), some 50 years later that laid the foundation stone for the establishment of modern derivative exchanges.

In 1970 the collapse of the postwar Bretton Woods system, in which exchange rates were fixed and the price of one ounce of gold was pegged at $35, provided a driving force for change. Recognising the need and seizing the opportunity Leo Melamed, chairman of the CME, established the International Monetary Market (IMM) in 1972. Primarily this new exchange offered futures contracts on exchange rates. The contracts offered by the IMM were financial instruments that would provide market players with the possibility of protecting themselves against adverse movements in exchange rates. A strong supporter of this move towards a free market was Milton Friedman. He recognised that the IMM with its currency futures would be the catalyst for the introduction of other financial futures. His vision proved correct. From a modest, but respectable, beginning a total of more than 144,000 contracts were traded in the first year of the IMM's existence, rising to over 500,000 by the end of 1973.

In 1973, events on the world's political scene led to severe oil shortages. Huge rises in the price of crude oil had knock-on economic effects in the form of rapid inflation and increases in interest rates worldwide. These developments provided a further stimulus to the demand for derivatives to help offset the market's revealed volatility. Market participants, however, would have to wait until late in 1975 for the CBOT to release the Government National Mortgage Association (GNMA or Ginnie Mae) contract. This was followed early in 1976 by the introduction of the 90-day Treasury bill contract by the IMM, and, in August 1977, the CBOT entered the marketplace with the 30-year Treasury Bond futures contract—the long bond.

Perhaps surprisingly, the achievements of the Chicago exchanges did not bring an immediate response in Europe. There was, of course, great interest in the new financial instruments that had been introduced but there was no headlong rush to copy the innovators.

With several hundred years tradition behind them, financial institutions in the City of London slowly realised that the era of silk top hats and bowlers was coming to an end. Slow, steady deliberations and negotiations involving the Bank of England, the Stock Exchange, the International Commodities Clearing House, and representatives from city institutions led to the opening of The London International Futures Exchange (LIFFE) in September 1982.

The opening of LIFFE did not mirror the immediate trading success of the Chicago-based exchanges. Indeed, problems concerning the clarification of the tax position relating to futures and adverse press probably played a key role in the sluggish take up of the contracts on offer. It was not until 1986 that the gilt contract, which was introduced in November 1982, really took off.

The average volume in gilt contracts over the period 1983–1985 was 663,829. In 1986 volume rose to 2.6 million contracts and settled down to an annual average of approximately 5.6 million between 1987–1991. A second surge in interest in the contract saw trading hit a peak of 19.6 million contracts in 1997, however, from 1998 onwards interest in the contract has slumped to late 1980s levels with annual average of 6.8 million contracts between 1998 and 2001.

The success of the gilt contract naturally led to the introduction of more bond contracts. June 1984 saw the introduction of the US Treasury bond future followed in September 1985 by the short gilt contract, in July 1987 by the Japanese government bond, in January 1988 by the medium gilt, in September 1988 by the German government bond (Bund), in March 1989 by the ECU bond, in April 1991 by the new Japanese government bond (JGB), in September 1991 by the Italian government bond (BTP), in January 1993 by the medium-term German government bond (Bobl),[1] and in March 1993 by the Spanish government bond (Bonos). Of course, with such a palette of products it was reasonable to expect that some of the instruments would not excite enough interest to generate trading volumes that warranted their continued existence. Cases in point are the US Treasury bond suspended in June 1993, the short gilt in January 1990, the medium-term gilt in January 1990, the ECU bond in November 1992, the Bobl in 1994, and the Bonos in September 1993.

For other futures, however, the story is one of success. In the late 1980s liquidity in US dollar products stimulated a change in focus. Europe became the centre of attention. The lack of a German government Bond futures contract was an anomaly in the market that needed to be addressed. Senior members of LIFFE sounded out the possibility of introducing such a contract with the German banking authorities. At

---

[1] Bundesobligationen are 5-year, fixed coupon German government bonds with a bullet maturity.

that time the Bundesbank, the large German banks, and the Federation of German stock exchanges were already collaborating to introduce their own derivatives exchange—the German Options and Financial Futures Exchange (GOFFEX)[2]—and there was a natural reluctance to support an external initiative. GOFFEX though would need to have supporting legislation before it could be established and commence operations and, after many discussions and fact-finding sorties into the German banking sector, LIFFE received the sanction to offer the contract.

The Bund[3] future was launched on 29 September 1988. With the introduction of the German government bond futures contract LIFFE was now trading bond contracts in the US Treasury bond, the Japanese government bond, the Italian government bond and UK gilts. It was the first financial futures exchange to have achieved this position. The contract specifications on the UK and European bond futures offered at that time appear in Exhibit 16.1.

Of course, these contracts have evolved to reflect new political and economic regimes. Today the Bund has become the Euro-Bund, denominated in euros, and traded on Eurex and LIFFE CONNECT platform. The UK gilt has been decimalised and the open outcry system of trading has been replaced by LIFFE CONNECT. While the Italian bond, now also quoted in euros, is traded solely on the Italian Exchange.

LIFFE's Bund future was a story of success. Following its release, this contract powered ahead of the volume in gilt trading in its first full year of trading. Exhibit 16.2 illustrates this point and the tremendous interest in the Bund contract compared to the gilt at least up until the end of 1997.

In the late 1980s and early 1990s the French futures exchange, the Marché à Terme Instruments Financières[4] (MATIF) became a serious competitor to LIFFE as did the DTB in Frankfurt and the Swiss Options and Financial Futures Exchange (SOFFEX). Battles have been fought over individual contracts, new contracts have appeared and subsequently been withdrawn; and the issue of open-outcry versus screen-based trading has been resolved and, according to Bloomberg European, derivative exchanges as of September 2002, number 24. Exhibit 16.3 provides a list of the European futures and options exchanges.

---

[2] When the German derivatives exchange finally opened its title was the Deutsche Terminbörse (DTB) and has more recently become Eurex-Deutschland.

[3] Bund refers to long-term bonds issued by the Federal Government of Germany.

[4] This is now the Marché à Terme Internationale de France (MATIF) or Euronext-Paris.

EXHIBIT 16.1 Initial LIFFE Contract Specifications

	UK Gilts	Bunds	JGBs	BTPs
Nominal Contract Value	£50,000	DM250,000	¥100,000,000	ITL200,000,000
Maturity Range of Deliverables	10–15 Years	8.5–10 Years	7–11 Years	8–10.5 Years
Notional Coupon	9%	6%	6%	12%
Quotation	Points and 32nds	Points and 100ths	Points and 100ths	Points and 100ths
Tick Size	1/32nd	0.01	0.01	0.01
Tick Value	£15.625	DM25.00	¥10,000	ITL20,000
Exchange	LIFFE	LIFFE	LIFFE	LIFFE
Trading	Open outcry	Open outcry	Open outcry	Open outcry

EXHIBIT 16.2 Annual Volume Comparison Statistics Bund versus Gilt (1988–1998)

Year	Volume Bund	Volume Gilt
1988	315,224	5,587,199
1989	5,328,570	4,062,467
1990	9,520,794	5,665,734
1991	10,112,305	5,639,081
1992	13,604,639	8,804,639
1993	20,440,442	11,808,998
1994	37,335,437	19,048,097
1995	32,231,210	13,796,555
1996	39,801,928	15,408,010
1997	44,984,029	19,653,565
1998	14,548,537	16,185,316

EXHIBIT 16.3 Futures and Options Exchange Directory

GRAB   Comdty **CEPR**

FUTURES AND OPTIONS   PAGE 2 OF 3
EXCHANGE DIRECTORY

Europe

1) Austrian Futures & Options Exchange   14) International Petroleum Exchange
2) Athens Derivatives Exchange   15) London Intl. Fin. Futures Exch.
3) Bolsa de Derivados do Porto   16) London Metal Exchange
4) Budapest Stock Exchange   17) Meff Renta Fija (Barcelona)
5) Copenhagen Exchange   18) Meff Renta Variable (Madrid)
6) Eurex Deutschland   19) Milan Stock Exchange
7) Eurex Zurich   20) OM Stockholmsborsen
8) Euronext Amsterdam Exchange   21) OML London
9) Euronext Brussels Exchange   22) Oslo Stock Exchange
10) Euronext Paris Exchange-MATIF   23) Warsaw Stock Exchange
11) Euronext Paris Exchange-MONEP   24) WTB-Hannover Comm. Exchange
12) FC&M Valencia
13) Helsinki Exchanges

Australia 61 2 9777 8600   Brazil 5511 3048 4500   Europe 44 20 7330 7500   Germany 49 69 920410
Hong Kong 852 2977 6000 Japan 81 3 3201 8900 Singapore 65 212 1000 U.S. 1 212 318 2000 Copyright 2002 Bloomberg L.P.
G666-32-0 09-Sep-02 13:36:09

Source: Bloomberg Financial Markets.

GOVERNMENT BONDS

In this section we address the following questions regarding government bond futures:

- What futures contracts are available in the European arena and how are the contracts specified?
- Who uses futures contracts on Government bonds?
- How are the contracts used?
- What are their operational characteristics?

To answer these questions it is first necessary to take a step back and ask why are futures contracts on government bonds needed at all and, indeed, why do governments issue bonds in the first place?

In a nutshell government bonds are issued capital markets to enable the funding of medium to long-term projects. A good example of this can be seen in the early 1990s when the reunification of Germany brought about a need for financing on an enormous scale in order to fund the redevelopment initiative, instigated by West Germany's Chancellor, Helmut Kohl. Generally speaking, government issued bonds are of a high credit quality[5] and are highly sort after for inclusion in the portfolio's of institutional and private investors on both a domestic and international level. Much of the increase in the demand for Bund futures illustrated in Exhibit 16.2 can be explained by Germany's need to increase its borrowing requirements to fund the government's fiscal deficits in the early years of the 1990s.

Once issued the yields on government bonds across different maturities provide a benchmark for yields on other less creditworthy bonds.

Given the low risk nature of these government bonds, why are futures contracts required? The answer is quite simple. Interest rates change over time driven by political and economic necessities. Germany's experience in the early part of the 1990s is a case in point. In the initial reunification phase interest rates were relatively low but as, over time, the funding requirement grew and economic pressures forced interest rates to rise. With increased German government paper in circulation a higher coupon was needed to attract more investors when new issues were released. This, of course, means that the yield on "seasoned" bonds would need to change to reflect the higher coupons now available on new issues. Thus changes in interest rate have a knock on effect on bond yields, which in turn change bond prices throughout the market.

---

[5] There are obvious exceptions to this low risk characteristic of government bonds—Russia, Mexico, and more recently Argentina are prime examples.

Bond Price/Yield

It is a fact that bond yields and bond prices possess predictable behaviour patterns. Several well-documented rules have been established that can assist a fixed income security analyst/portfolio manager in deciding which bonds to hold in a portfolio given a future potential interest rate scenario and the goal of the portfolio.

At the lowest level of predictability, there is a fundamental negative relationship between the price of a bond and its yield. As yield rises the bond's price must fall and vice versa. There is, however, much more that can be said about this inverse relationship. To illustrate the price/yield relationship, take the case of a straightforward bond: no options attached, nonconvertible, no warrants associated with the bond, a fixed coupon, nonindex-linked, and a defined redemption date. From this list of restrictive assumptions there are still two features that can be allowed to vary: (1) the bond's coupon and (2) the bond's fixed redemption date. The interplay between these two variables provides a clue to some simple risk management strategies assuming a given background interest rate scenario.

Consider the hypothetical case where a portfolio manager suspects that bond yields are about to rise by as much as 1%. Further assume that currently the portfolio contains only a 20-year, 6% coupon bond priced at £127.18. A general rise in yield from 4% to 5% will, if reflected exactly in the case of this 6% coupon bond, result in a fall in the bond's price to £112.46, a drop of 11.57%. A simple but effective strategy in this case would be to switch the portfolio holding to a bond with both a shorter time to maturity and a higher coupon. If the bond selected for switching purposes were to be the 5-year to maturity bond offering a coupon of 10% then the relative fall in the bond's price would be limited to 3.99%. Exhibit 16.4 portrays the price/yield relationship for 16 hypothetical bonds with coupons of 10%, 8%, 6%, and 0%, maturities of 20, 15, 10, and 5 years, under a 1% rising yield scenario.

In part, the logic behind this outcome is that the higher coupons, which will be paid at regular intervals throughout the bond's life, can now be reinvested at the higher interest rates prevailing in the market place. The higher proceeds from this investment will help to offset the fall in the bond's price brought about by the increase in yield.

On the other hand, if interest rates were expected to fall, switching to long-dated, low coupon bonds—or zero-coupon bonds—would be a way of benefiting most from the rise in the bond's price that must follow.

Exhibit 16.5 shows very clearly the price responses for three 20-year bonds offering 10%, 6% annual coupon, and zero-coupon payments. One feature worth noting is that the curvilinear, price/yield relationship is not constant. It varies at different points on the curve for each type of

EXHIBIT 16.4   Bond Price/Yield Sensitivities

Description of Bond: par 100; coupon 6%; following years to maturity

	20 Years		15 Years		10 Years		5 Years	
Yield	4%	5%	4%	5%	4%	5%	4%	5%
Price	127.18	112.46	122.23	110.38	116.22	107.72	108.90	104.33
% Change in price		−11.57		−9.69		−7.31		−4.20

Description of Bond: par 100; coupon 8%; following years to maturity

	20 Years		15 Years		10 Years		5 Years	
Yield	4%	5%	4%	5%	4%	5%	4%	5%
Price	154.36	137.38	144.47	131.13	132.44	123.16	117.80	112.98
% Change in price		−11.00		−9.23		−7.01		−4.09

Description of Bond: par 100; coupon 10%; following years to maturity

	20 Years		15 Years		10 Years		5 Years	
Yield	4%	5%	4%	5%	4%	5%	4%	5%
Price	181.53	162.31	166.70	151.89	148.65	138.60	126.70	121.64
% Change in price		−10.59		−8.88		−6.76		−3.99

Description of Bond: par 100; coupon 0%; following years to maturity

	20 Years		15 Years		10 Years		5 Years	
Yield	4%	5%	4%	5%	4%	5%	4%	5%
Price	45.64	37.69	55.53	48.10	67.56	61.39	82.19	78.35
% Change in price		−17.42		−13.37		−9.13		−4.67

bond. Exhibit 16.4 also displays the percentage change in a bond's price brought about by the change in yield for each bond. Clearly when interest rates are rising—or are expected to rise—zero-coupon bonds are the bonds to avoid. A 1% rise in yield from 4% to 5% results in a loss of 17.42% of a 20-year, zero-coupon bond's value. Even for much shorter dated bonds the impact on the bond's price will be greater than for same maturity coupon bearing bonds.

EXHIBIT 16.5   Price/Yield Relationship

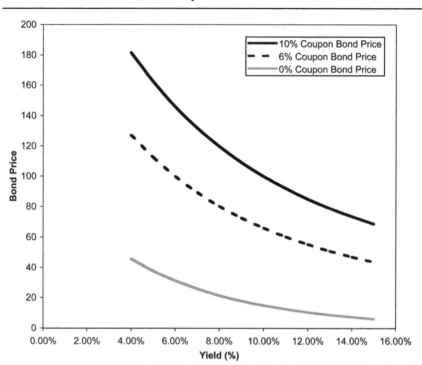

Assume that there is a rising interest rate regime and that a fund manager has little alternative to holding bonds that he or she has under management. A simple and effective strategy, in light of the interest rate uncertainty, would be to cash in the current bond holdings and switch to higher coupon bonds of comparable or shorter-dated maturities to those currently held in the portfolio. In the case of falling interest rates and yields, a reverse strategy would be appropriate. Futures contracts, however, under both rising and falling interest rate regimes would offer a far more efficient and cost effective way of handling the same problem. This will be considered in some examples developed below.

Examples of Price/Yield Behaviour
To develop further the ideas outlined above, there are a number of formal rules that can be defined and which will help establish a more scientific approach to the study of bond price/yield behaviour.

Rule 1: If a bond's market price increases, its yield decreases and vice versa.

A real market example can be found in the UK gilt market. On Thursday, 4 October 1990, the closing price of the 10.25% Exchequer 1995 stood at 93-30 at a quoted 11.91 yield to maturity. (At that time and until close of business on 8 May 1998 UK Government bonds prices were quoted in 32nds, hence a quote of 90-30 is read as 90 30/32 which converts to 90.9375 as a decimal.) At 4:04 P.M. on Friday, 5 October 1990, the Chancellor of the Exchequer announced Britain's entry into the Exchange Rate Mechanism (ERM) and, simultaneously, a 1% cut in interest rates. The theoretical price of this gilt, assuming a 1% drop in yield, would lead to a price of approximately 97-17. The actual price in the market at close on Monday was 96-23, the high for the day was 97-5 with a 11.19% yield to maturity.

Rule 2: As the maturity date of a bond approaches the size of the bond's discount/premium decreases.

Consider the 10.5% UK Treasury 1992. The quoted price for this bond was 97-1 compared to the 10.5% Exchequer 1997 quoted at 93-10.

Rule 3: As the maturity date of a bond approaches the size of its discount/premium will decrease at an increasing rate.

Rule 4: A fall in the bond's yield will raise the bond's price by more than the fall in the bond's price that would result from an equivalent increase in the bond's yield.

Taking as a base the example in Rule 1 above the theoretical increase in the bond's price is approximately 3.8% ($\{[97 - 17/93 - 30] - 1\} \times 100$) assuming a yield to maturity of 10.91%. If, on the other hand, the bond's yield were to rise 100 bps to 12.91%, the accompanying fall in the bond's price would be 3.5%. This is due to the nonlinear relationship that exists between a bond's price and its yield.

Rule 5: For high coupon bonds with a maturity date greater than one year, the percentage change in a price will be smaller than for low coupon bonds with the same maturity.

Treasury 13%, maturing 3 March 2000, was quoted at 104-28 on Friday, 5 October; Monday's close was quoted at 107-31, a rise of 2.9%. The 14 July 2000, 9% Conversion stock had quotes respectively of 84-20 and 87-16, a rise of 3.4%. The implication of this is as discussed above: If interest rates are expected to fall and medium- to long-term bonds are to be the investment instruments held in a portfolio, then lower coupon issues should be used.

Clearly some of these rules can easily be verified by considering the price/yield behaviour of a real or fictitious bond under a variety of maturity and interest rate scenarios as demonstrated above.

MODERN EUROPEAN BOND FUTURES CONTRACTS

Financial markets are well known for the pace at which they develop and respond to market needs. It is not surprising that since the introduction of the euro in January 2002, futures contracts on the bonds of member states within the common currency area have changed.

Probably the most popular euro-denominated contracts available on European bonds are those offered by Eurex Deutschland and, in particular, those on longer-dated bonds issued by the German Federal Government: the Buxl, Bund, and Bobl. Also popular but at the shorter end of the maturity spectrum are short-term notes issued by either the Federal Government or the Treuhandanstalt[6]: the Euro-Schatz notes.

For longer-dated debt instruments investors have the a choice of the very long-term notional 30-year, 6% coupon Euro-Buxl contract which covers cash market bonds with a maturity of between 20 and 30.5 years, or the notional 10-year, 6% coupon Euro-Bund contract which covers the 8.5–10.5 years maturity section of the yield curve. The nominal size for each contract is €100,000; both have a minimum allowable price movement (tick) of 1 basis point, which is valued at €10, and a contract cycle of March, June, September, and December, of which the three nearest-to-delivery, successive contracts will be available for trading.

The medium term, 4.5–5.5 years, is the domain of the Euro-Bobl contract, while the 1.75–2.25 year maturity segment is covered by the Euro-Schatz[7] contract. Both of these futures contracts have basically the same specification as the longer-dated contracts described above. All contracts require the delivery of an acceptable German government bond at settlement.

As a measure of the demand for these instruments, consider the average open-interest figures over the November 2002 period in respect of the December 2002 maturing contract, drawn from Bloomberg:

---

[6] The Treuhandanstalt is a trust establishment that was set up in 1991 by the German Government to oversee the financial affairs of the former German Democratic Republic following reunification.
[7] German Government Treasury Notes.

Instrument	Average Open Interest (1 November 2002–29 November 2002)
Euro-Schatz	565,287
Euro-Bobl	592,053
Euro-Bund	702,273

As an alternative to Eurex's 10-year Euro-Bund future, Euronext LIFFE offers a similar contract again based on a nominal €100,000 contract size, tick value of €10, and the same expiry cycle. The Euro-Schatz counterpart, however, offers a contract size of €200,000. The smallest allowable price movement is one half of a basis point and hence the value of a tick remains at €10.

A variation on these futures contracts based on German Government paper is offered by Euronext Paris—MATIF. Both the Euro Notional Future, which covers the 8.5-10.5 year section of the yield curve and the 30-year E-Bond Future which covers the 25-35 year segment, allow delivery of either French or German Government bonds into the contract on settlement.

Inside the Eurozone, the Spanish exchange MEFF Renta Fija in Barcelona offers a notional 10-year, 4% coupon Spanish government bond future and covers the 7.5–10.5-year cash market bond maturity range. It has a March, June, September, and December expiry cycle, a nominal contract value of €100,000, and a tick size of 1 basis point with a value of €10. The average open interest over the period 1 November 2002–29 November 2002 was relatively small at approximately 1,260.

Outside the Eurozone noneuro-denominated futures contracts on government bonds are offered by Euronext-LIFFE, Eurex-Zurich, and the Stockholm exchange. The contracts available are the long gilt future on LIFFE which allows delivery of UK government bonds with maturities between 8.75 and 13 years, the Swiss federal bond future, and the 10-year Swedish government bond.

The UK gilt contract specifies a notional 10-year, 7% coupon bond. Its contract size is £100,000; the smallest allowable price change is a basis point valued at £10. The cycle of expiry dates is the usual March, June, September, and December. This contract, while not enjoying the same level of international popularity as the German government bond futures, is widely used. The open interest statistics for the December 2002 maturing gilt future, sourced from Bloomberg during the month of November 2002, reveal an average of 74,031 contracts. The maturing December 2002 contract in respect of the Swiss federal bond has an average open interest of some 10,700 contracts, indicating that use of the contract is mainly of domestic interest.

USE OF BOND FUTURES CONTRACTS

Political and economic factors lie behind interest rate fluctuations. These fluctuations provide the data from which statistically measurable volatility of interest rates can be obtained. Remember it was the phenomenon of changing foreign exchange rates and interest rates that led to the introduction of financial futures in the United States. Expectations concerning the magnitude and direction of future movements in interest rates provide the rationale behind a multitude of bond portfolio strategies. Futures contracts enhance greatly the palette of strategies available to portfolio managers.

From the discussion above it is clear that the introduction of futures contracts on government bonds was strongly motivated by the need to hedge against increased market volatility. This remains one of the main functions of these instruments. The existence of bond futures, though, attract other desirable, indeed essential players, into the market place:

- Speculators who help ensure market liquidity and who play a vital role in price discovery.
- Arbitrageurs who monitor the cash and futures markets and trade on pricing anomalies.
- Asset allocators/financial engineers who use futures contracts to manipulate the payoff profiles of bonds or other specially constructed portfolios.

To illustrate how bond futures function and to demonstrate their usefulness to asset allocation mangers consider the following scenario: On 9 September 2002, a bond portfolio manager holds €1,000,000 of the Bund 5%, 4 July 2011 in her portfolio. The price is currently quoted at 104.280, which implies a yield to maturity of 4.401%. The portfolio manager suspects that inflationary pressures may bring about a rise in interest rates in the next few weeks. While in the very short term, the anniversary of 11 September 2001, may see a dip in market prices generally. She decides that a full short hedge of the position is called for and opts for using the futures contract with a December 2002 maturity.

How can this short hedge be achieved?

Calculating the Number of Futures Contracts to Fully Hedge a Portfolio

Assume that the value of the portfolio position in bonds can be expressed as:

$$V_p = V_{\text{CMB}} + (h)(V_F) \qquad (16.1)$$

where

V_p = the current value of the portfolio
V_{CMB} = the current valuation of the bond(s) held in the portfolio
V_F = the value of the futures contract held in the portfolio
h = the number of futures contracts required to achieve a desired portfolio value

Intuitively, if the value of the portfolio is to be hedged against potential adverse market movements, the long position in bonds would need to be set against a short position in the futures contracts. A negative value for h indicates the number of contracts that will need to be shorted.

Any change in the value of the portfolio can be explained by the expression:

$$\Delta V_p = \Delta V_{CMB} + (h)(\Delta V_F) \qquad (16.2)$$

where Δ represents a finite change in the value of a variable.

To maintain a neutral position ΔV_p must equal zero so that any loss on the bond side of the portfolio will be offset by a gain on the futures side of the hedge and vice versa. If that is the case then equation (16.2) can be rewritten as:

$$\Delta V_{CMB} + (h)(\Delta V_F) = 0$$

which in turn implies that:

$$h = (-1)\frac{\Delta V_{CMB}}{\Delta V_F} \qquad (16.3)$$

Note that if only one bond is held in the portfolio, then from the price change formula a very small change in the value of the portfolio (ΔV_{CMB}) can be written as dP while a very small change in the value of the futures position (ΔV_F) can be written as $dPCTD$. If more than one bond is held in the portfolio then, given that dollar duration is additive, dP can be found by adding together the changes in each bond's price, estimated in the same way as for the single bond case but, additionally, taking into account the proportions of each bond's holding in the portfolio. Note that a very small change in the value of the future is still assumed to be given by $dPCTD$.

Relative Volatility

Hedging the underlying portfolio hence requires the relative volatility
that exists between the cash market bond(s) held in the portfolio and
the futures contract. Dollar duration can assist in this search since modified duration can help predict the effect of small changes in yield on the
price of a bond:

$$dP = (-1)(\text{Mod}_{\text{duration}})(P_0)(dr) \qquad (16.4)$$

where

dP = price change
dr = rate change
P_0 = initial price
$\text{Mod}_{\text{duration}}$ = modified duration

So when seeking to put a hedge in place, one way of estimating the
relationship that exists between different instruments would be

$$\text{Relative volatility} = \left[\frac{P_{\text{CMB}}}{P_{\text{CTD}}}\right]\left[\frac{\text{Mod}_{\text{CMB}}}{\text{Mod}_{\text{CTD}}}\right]\left[\frac{\text{ACT}\Delta r_{\text{CMB}}}{\text{ACT}\Delta r_{\text{CTD}}}\right] \qquad (16.5)$$

where

P_{CMB} = price of cash market bond (CMB) to be hedged
P_{CTD} = price of the cheapest-to-deliver instrument
Mod_{CMB} = modified duration of CMB position
Mod_{CTD} = modified duration of CTD instrument
$\text{ACT}\Delta r_{\text{CMB}}$ = actual change in yield of CMB(s) position
$\text{ACT}\Delta r_{\text{CTD}}$ = actual change in yield of CTD instrument

The effect of any change in yield ($\text{ACT}\Delta r_{\text{CMB}}$ and $\text{ACT}\Delta r_{\text{CTD}}$) is
often assumed to be the same for the bond(s) to be hedged and the CTD,
which allows the change in yield terms in the numerator and the denom-
inator to cancel. So, if $\text{ACT}\Delta r_{\text{CMB}}$ and $\text{ACT}\Delta r_{\text{CTD}}$ are assumed to be of
the same order of magnitude then equation (16.5) becomes

$$\text{Relative volatility} = \left[\frac{P_{\text{CMB}}}{P_{\text{CTD}}}\right]\left[\frac{\text{Mod}_{\text{CMB}}}{\text{Mod}_{\text{CTD}}}\right] \qquad (16.6)$$

Other approaches used to measure relative volatility will be considered
later.

The action undertaken by the portfolio manager is then as follows. Assume that the cash market bond held in the portfolio is deliverable into a futures contract and is a natural candidate for hedging using the Euro-Bund futures contract on Eurex-Deutschland. The contract specification appears in Exhibit 16.6.

The contract specification of the Euro-Bund bond future introduces a concept of a notional bond. This is also true for all other bond futures contracts. For example, in the case of the UK gilt, the description of the futures contract bond is a 10-year gilt with a 7% coupon; for the Euro-Bund future it is a 10-year German government bond with a 6% coupon; the Spanish bond (bonos) future is a Spanish Government bond with a 4% coupon, and so on.

In other words the 7% gilt, the 6% Bund, and the 4% bonos around which the futures contracts are constructed do not exist. A cash market bond that can be delivered into the contract on maturity has to be identified and converted to match the futures contract specification. In full exchange-based contract specifications, the list of deliverable cash market bonds are well defined and are restrictive. Deliverable bonds in the case of the Bund future will be bonds issued by the Federal Government of Germany and will have a maturity between 8.5 and 10.5 years. Normally, bonds offering early redemption, floating coupons, or some form of convertibility will not be in the list of deliverables.

Identifying the Cheapest-to-Deliver

It is important to note that the bond that will eventually be delivered into the contract, and the date on which it will be delivered, will be decided by the seller of the futures contract. This flexibility on the part of the seller allows him or her the possibility of selecting a bond that will be the cheapest-to-deliver (CTD).

A rough idea of which bond will be the CTD can be obtained by using the gross or raw basis, that is the current offer price of a bond (S) minus the current futures (F) quotes multiplied by that bond's conversion factor (CF). That is,

$$\text{Gross basis} = S - (F)(\text{CF}) \qquad (16.7)$$

From that set of bonds, which meet the regulations regarding deliverability, the bond which has the smallest value will be the CTD. Three bonds are identified in Exhibit 16.7.

Having established a rule that will facilitate the identification of the CTD, there is one component of the formula that needs to be found, namely CF, the conversion factor. As was mentioned above, the future is based on a fictitious bond but physical delivery will be in the form of a real bond. The real bond, therefore, will have to be converted in order

EXHIBIT 16.6 Euro-Bund Futures Contract

```
GRAB                                                        Comdty DES
Type # <GO> For Related Function
Futures Contract Description                          Page 1/2
Exchange (EUX) Eurex Deutschland (was DTB)     Related Functions
Name          EURO-BUND FUTURE  Dec02           1) CT  Contract Table
Ticker        RXZ2   <CMDTY>                     2) FHG Futures History Graph
Notional      Euro-Bund 10yr 6%                  3) EXS Expiration Schedule
Contract Size  EUR 100,000                       4) DLV Cheapest to Deliver
Value of 1.0 pt EUR 1,000                        5) WECO World Economic Releases
Tick Size       .01                                      Margin Limits
Tick Value     EUR 10                                        Speculator
Current Price  111.22                          Initial          1600
Contract Value EUR 111,220      @ 13:10:32

Cycle --- Mar --- Jun --- Sep --- Dec
                               Long-term notional debt security issued by the
   Trading Hours              German Federal Government with a term of 8.5-10.5
Frankfurt       Local         years. Basis Spreads RXmyDLVA - C Comdty.
08:00-19:00   07:00-18:00     **The Euro Bund contract was listed on October 5th
                              1998 with the March 99 contract.  Prior history is
                              the DEM Bund contract.

First Delivery  Tue Dec 10, 2002   Life High  111.89
Last Delivery   Tue Dec 10, 2002   Life Low   104.16
Last Trade      Fri Dec  6, 2002
First Notice    Fri Dec  6, 2002            Generics Available
First Trade     Fri Mar  8, 2002
                                            RX1 <CMDTY>
                                            RX2 <CMDTY>
                                            RX3 <CMDTY>
Australia 61 2 9777 8600      Brazil 5511 3048 4500    Europe 44 20 7330 7500    Germany 49 69 920410
Hong Kong 852 2977 6000 Japan 81 3 3201 8900 Singapore 65 212 1000 U.S. 1 212 318 2000  Copyright 2002 Bloomberg L.P.
                                                                                       G666-32-0 09-Sep-02 13:25:50
```

Source: Bloomberg Financial Markets.

EXHIBIT 16.7   Identifying the CTD

```
GRAB                                                        Comdty DLV
Hit {NUMBER} <GO> to view Historical Basis/Repo
Cheapest  to  Deliver              Trade 9/ 9/02 Dlv 12/10/02
EURO-BUND FUTURE   Dec02   RXZ2  111.22    Set 9/12/02 Cheapest IRP= 3.22
                                           DECIMAL   89 Days Act/360   DECIMAL
                    (Mid)         Conv.     Gross Implied    Actual   Net
       Order DR re-sort? Y  Price Source Yield C.Factor Basis Repo%   Repo%  Basis
              MASTER                                               3.32
1) DBR 5 07/04/11   104.280 BGN  4.401 .934161 .383  3.22   3.32 .026
2) DBR 5 01/04/12   104.230 BGN  4.433 .931496 .629  2.22   3.32 .292
3) DBR 5 07/04/12   104.320 BGN  4.445 .928434 1.060  .61   3.32 .703
```

Source: Bloomberg Financial Markets.

to meet the contract specification and determine how much will have to be delivered into the contract to satisfy the nominal contract size. In the case of the Euro-Bund, the CF can be thought of as the price of the deliverable bond were it to be priced with a yield to maturity of 6%, the yield specified in the futures contract. The C. Factor column in Exhibit 16.7 presents the conversion factors for each of the three listed bonds.

The conversion factor in respect of the cash market bond in this scenario is 0.934161. Applying this conversion factor in equation (16.7) the gross basis is found to be 0.383, and this appears as the first entry in the gross basis column of Exhibit 16.7, in respect of the 5% Bund maturing on 4 July 2011.

$$\text{Gross basis} = 104.280 - (0.934161)(111.220) = 0.383 \qquad (16.8)$$

There is, of course, a more rigorous way of identifying the CTD bond. The method, which takes into account coupon income, gross basis, and the cost of financing the position over the holding period yields a net or value basis figure and is calculated using

$$\text{Net basis} = \text{Coupon income} - \text{Gross basis} - \text{Financing cost} \qquad (16.9)$$

Calculation of the coupon income is the difference between the accrued interest bought in at the time of purchasing the cash market bond subtracted from the accrued interest received when the bond is sold. Market conventions play an important role here, for example: How many days between trade and settlement? How many days in a month? How many days in a year? In the United Kingdom the market convention is actual number of days in a month and a 365 days in a year. In Germany the convention is actual number of days in month and 360 days in a year.

To illustrate the idea of net basis, consider the 5% Bund maturing on 4 July 2011 examined earlier in the gross basis example illustrated in equation (16.7).

Coupon income is defined as follows. From July 4, 2002, the date of the last coupon payment, until the settlement date, September 12, 2002, there are 71 days of accrued interest. Based on a coupon of 5.00% per annum and a 360-day year this amounts to 0.986.[8]

If the futures contract is held until 10 December 2002, a total of 159 days will have elapsed since the last coupon payment. This period will generate interest to the value of 2.208. The coupon income will be 2.208 − 0.986 = 1.222.

Financing cost is computed as follows. This can be found by calculating the cost of borrowing the funds necessary to purchase the cash market bond. The price of the bond will include any accrued interest up until the settlement date. The cost of these funds over the holding period will be determined by the repo rate. On the Bloomberg CTD Table (Exhibit 16.7) the actual repo rate is given as 3.32%. The financing cost will be $(104.280)(0.0332)(89/360) = €0.864$. The gross basis is already known to be 0.383.

Combining these results as indicated in equation (16.9) yields a net basis of −0.025.[9] Not surprisingly this figure is negative. This is normally the case since the formula given in equation (16.9) is in effect looking at the possibility of making a risk-free profit, and since true arbitrage opportunities in the marketplace are very rare, a negative pay out from the strategy is to be expected. By convention, net basis is reported as a positive result and one way of achieving this is to rewrite equation (16.9) as:

$$\text{Net basis} = \text{Gross basis} - \text{Coupon income} + \text{Financing cost} \qquad (16.10)$$

---

[8] All calculations have been rounded to three decimal places.
[9] The difference between the figure quoted in the Bloomberg Table and the calculation here is due to rounding.

$$0.025 = 0.383 - 1.222 + 0.864$$

It is clear that the bond identified as being the CTD is actually that bond that the portfolio manager wishes to hedge.

The Euro-Bund contract specifies a contract size of €100,000. To establish an appropriate hedge ratio, a natural starting point is to divide the value of the underlying portfolio by the contract size:

$$\text{Number of contracts} = \frac{\text{Portfolio value}}{\text{Contract size}} = \frac{€1,000,000}{€100,000} = 10$$

This, however, is only part of the picture. Even though the bond held in the portfolio is the CTD, the cash market bond's behaviour relative to the notional bond described in the futures contract needs to be taken into account. The following equation illustrates how, in general, the appropriately adjusted hedge ratio can be estimated.

$$h = \left[\frac{\text{Portfolio value}}{\text{Contract size}}\right]\left[\frac{\text{Mod}_{\text{CMB}}}{\text{Mod}_{\text{CTD}}}\right]\left[\frac{P_{\text{CMB}} + \text{AI}_{\text{CMB}}}{P_{\text{CTD}} + \text{AI}_{\text{CTD}}}\right]\text{PF}_{\text{CTD}} \qquad (16.11)$$

where

h = number of contracts required to hedge the position
Mod_{CMB} = modified duration of the cash market bond
Mod_{CTD} = modified duration of the cheapest-to-deliver
P_{CMB} = clean price of the cash market bond
P_{CTD} = clean price of the cheapest to deliver bond
AI = accrued interest for both the CMB and CTD
PF = price factor of the CTD

If it is assumed that, in response to changes in interest rates, the behaviour of the futures price matches that of the CTD exactly, and that the cash market bond held in the portfolio is the CTD bond, then equation (16.11) reduces to

$$h = \left[\frac{\text{Portfolio value}}{\text{Contract size}}\right]\text{PF}_{\text{CTD}} \qquad (16.12)$$

Hence the appropriate number of contracts required to hedge the portfolio will be:

$$h = \left[\frac{€1,000,000}{€100,000}\right]0.934161 = 9.34161$$

So in this case a sound but less than perfect hedge could be achieved by selling or shorting just nine futures contracts.

In the case of a fully hedged portfolio there is, of course, a cost. The fully hedged portfolio is a portfolio whose return over a specific, short period of time has been transformed to be approximately the return on a short-dated instrument. The flexibility afforded by the futures contracts allows the return to be adjusted according to the risk preferences of the fund manager. Risk-averse fund managers will tend to fully hedge their portfolios; risk takers may choose to short fewer contracts and, in effect, use only a partial hedge.

Alternative Measures of Relative Volatility

An alternative way estimating relative volatility between the instruments and hence adjusting the basic number of contracts required to achieve a tighter hedge would be to use the value of a basis point (BPV) of the futures and the BPV of a cash market bond. A basis point value is the price change of a bond brought about by a 1 basis point (0.0001) change in the yield on that instrument. One way in which the BPV can be calculated is to use regression analysis. Specifically,

$$\Delta F_t = \alpha + \beta \Delta r_{CTD_t} + \varepsilon_t \tag{16.13}$$

where

ΔF = changes in the price of the futures contract from one day to the next

Δr_{CTD} = change in yield on the CTD from one day to the next

α and β = unknown intercept and slope coefficients in the regression equation, and the estimate of β will provide the BPV for the futures contract

ε_t = error term

A numerical example will help to clarify the method. The data in Exhibit 16.8 are daily observations, drawn from Bloomberg, on the Euro-Bund Futures quotes and CTD yield-to-maturity over a period of 12 days. Columns (4) and (5) display the changes in futures quotes and yields, respectively, that have taken place from one day to the next. Using the data in columns (4) and (5) equation (16.10) can be estimated using least squares regression.[10]

EXHIBIT 16.8   Data for Regression Analysis

(2)	(3)	(4)	(5)	(6)	
Futures (FQ)	CTD YTM	Price CMB	Changes in FQ	Changes in CTD YTM	Changes in CMB
111.43	4.426	103.766	0.55	−0.047	0.321
110.88	4.473	103.445	−0.35	0.053	−0.425
111.23	4.42	103.87	0.51	−0.059	0.434
110.72	4.479	103.436	0.24	−0.047	0.323
110.48	4.526	103.113	0.43	−0.044	0.329
110.05	4.57	102.784	−0.34	0.044	−0.357
110.39	4.526	103.141	0.51	−0.058	0.412
109.88	4.584	102.729	−0.05	0.035	−0.239
109.93	4.549	102.968	−0.38	0.008	−0.108
110.31	4.541	103.076	0	0.01	−0.077
110.31	4.531	103.153	0.07	−0.013	0.108
110.24	4.544	103.045	−0.07	0.042	−0.317
110.31	4.502	103.362			

The resulting estimated equation is

$$\Delta F_t = 0.04739 - 7.2542\Delta r_{CDT_t}$$

where the estimate of (−7.2542) that a 1 bp change in YTM will bring about an estimated 7.2542 tick change in the futures quote.

The BPV for other bonds can be found following a similar procedure. If, for example, ΔF in equation (16.10) is replaced by ΔP_{CMB} (i.e., price changes in a cash market bond) the resulting estimate of β will provide an estimate of the BPV of the CMB.

$$\Delta P_{CMB_t} = \alpha + \beta\Delta r_{CTD_t} + \varepsilon_t$$

If the data in column (6) of Exhibit 16.8, ΔP_{CMB}, replaces the data in respect of ΔF and a new regression is carried out the BPV of a cash market bond (CMB) can be found.

---

[10] It would also be possible to perform the regression with the constraint imposed that α term is zero. The implication of this constraint is to force β to reflect that changes in the futures quote are driven uniquely by the changes in CTD yield.

$$\Delta P_{\text{CMB}_t} = -0.01345 - 7.4400 \Delta r_{\text{CTD}_t}$$

Here a 1 bp change in the YTM of the CTD will bring about an estimated 7.4400 bp change in the price of the cash market bond.

The hedge adjustment process can then be performed using

$$h = \left[\frac{\text{Portfolio value}}{\text{Contract size}}\right]\left[\frac{\text{BPV}_{\text{CMB}}}{\text{BPV}_F}\right] \tag{16.14}$$

Substituting the estimated BPVs into equation (16.11) provides and an adjust hedge ratio based on the relative volatility estimated to exist between the cash market bond and the futures contract.

$$h = \left[\frac{\text{€}1,000,000}{\text{€}100,000}\right]\left[\frac{-7.4400}{-7.2542}\right] = 10.2561 \text{ contracts} \tag{16.15}$$

There are problems with the regression approach. One is that the CTD does not remain constant throughout the life of the futures contract. In other words, if the CTD changes the left-hand-side variable in the expression, it will also change and the data will be inconsistent. An additional problem is deciding over what time period the relationship should be estimated. The example developed above used 12 observations for T, but the choice of an optimal T is not defined. The minimum requirement would be $T = 2$, but this would be trivial and would ignore longer-term effects. Setting $T = 90$ or $T = 180$ would also be a possibility, but using too many observations will bring in old, stale data, and possibly changes in the CTD bond, which may distort the measure of relative volatility. The choice of T is though of crucial importance; α and β will almost certainly change with the choice of T.

In hedging portfolios of bonds both modified duration and BPV analysis play an important role. From the above it is clear that the Euro-Bund Future can help protect against declining bond prices brought about by rising interest rates. They could, however, also be used to lock-in today's prices should the CTD appear to be cheap and there is an expectation that interest rates are set to fall. So short and long hedges, arbitrage and speculation are facilitated by the existence of a liquid futures market.

This formula is fine if the bond to hedge is the CTD. If, however, the bond(s) is not the CTD then finding a further adjustment factor can help the hedger to establish a more appropriate number of contracts to buy or sell in order to hedge the exposed position. As discussed earlier an adjustment factor can be estimated in a number of ways. Equation (16.5) illustrates how duration may be used to find a value for this term, while equation (16.14) identifies a BPV alternative.

Example: Hedging a Non-CTD bond

Consider the case where the CTD bond is priced at 104.28 and has a modified duration of 6.874 while the bond held in the portfolio is priced at 104.32 and has a modified duration of 7.491. Since bond to be hedged is not the CTD, then an adjustment needs to be made to the number of contracts shorted. This is the case where the relationship between the CTD and the bond to be hedged plays an important role.

From equation (16.6) it is evident that to be able to perform the necessary calculations the modified durations of the two bonds need to be established

$$\text{Relative volatility} = \left[\frac{(104.32)(7.491)}{(104.28)(6.874)}\right] = 1.09101\ldots$$

So a further adjustment to the extent of 1.09101... is required using this duration measure of relative volatility. The number of contracts required will then be

$$\text{Adjusted no. of contracts} = (1.09101)(9.34161) = 10.18329$$

Thus, an extra contract would need to be shorted to improve the effectiveness of the hedge in the case of a bond that is not the CTD.

Example: Adjusting the Duration of a Portfolio

The idea of shortening the maturity of a bond portfolio was discussed above in the context of a rising interest rate scenario. The example assumed a bond yield regime of 4% rising to 5% and a strategy of switching to higher coupon and shorter maturity bonds was advocated. That cash market bond approach, while effective, is expensive. The bonds currently held in the portfolio must be sold and new securities purchased. This strategy implies transactions and institutional costs at the very least. A similar outcome could have been achieved with significantly less disruption to the portfolio composition and at a lower cost by using futures contracts.

Futures contracts are purchased on margin so that only a small fraction of the nominal value of the position needs to be committed and the futures positions can be opened and closed very quickly at low transac-

EXHIBIT 16.9   Initial Margin Requirements

Instrument	Initial Margin
Euro-Buxl	€3,000
Euro-Bund	€1,600
Euro-Bobl	€1,000
Euro-Schatz	€500
Euro notional 10-year	€1,500
Euro notional 5-year	€1,000
Spanish 10-year	€1,650
UK gilt	£1,300
Swiss federal 10-year	Sfr1,600

Source: Bloomberg Financial Markets.

tions cost. An idea of initial margin deposits required for European futures are provided in Exhibit 16.9.

Consider the opposite scenario, bond yields are expected to fall substantially and in the near future. In this case, the fund manager will be seeking to extend the maturity or duration of the bond portfolio. However, instead of adopting a physical bond-switching strategy government bond futures will be used. Here is such a scenario:

	Modified duration of the portfolio	Target duration	Futures quote
Now	7.4908	14.341	110.28

The portfolio is valued at €100,000,000 and has been constructed to track a bond index for which the Euro-Bund Future is a very good hedge instrument. The basis point value (BPV) of the Euro-Bund futures contract is 72.03 and the yield is 5.595% calculated on an annual 360-day year basis. The bond index, which the portfolio has been designed to track, is quoted at 117.80.

The appropriate number of futures contracts needed to achieve the desired lengthening of duration can be found by taking the difference between the BPV of target portfolio duration and the BPV of the current portfolio and dividing that difference by the BPV of the futures contract. As a formula this appears as

BPV of portfolio = (Modified duration)(Portfolio value)(0.0001) (16.16)

$$[7.4908](€100,000,000)(0.0001) = €74,908$$

BPV of target portfolio is

$$[14.341](€100,000,000)(0.0001) = €143,410$$

Number of futures required to adjust the duration:

$$\text{Number of contracts} = \frac{€143,410 - €74,908}{72.03} = 951 \text{ (long)}$$

Therefore, 951 contracts will need to be purchased to achieve the required increased duration effect.

To analyse the outcome of the adjustment assume that some days later the bond index rises to 120.86. The outcome of the strategy will be:

	Cash	Future
Now	€100,000,000	110.28
Horizon	€102,600,000	112.37
Result	€2,600,000	€1,987,590

The strategy of selling the Euro-Bund futures contracts to increase the portfolio's duration has been successful—indeed it has generated a pay out of almost €2,000,000. However, had the fund manager's forecast proved inaccurate and bond yields remained static, the value of the cash market portfolio and the futures position would have remained—at least approximately—at those values prevailing when the strategy was adopted. If the bond index had fallen in value representing a rise rather than a fall in yields, both the cash market and futures position would have registered a loss. Under any scenario, basis plays an important role and, depending on the basis when the strategy was initiated, even under a best-case scenario the futures transaction could well have resulted in a loss.

Example: Adjusting Portfolio Mix

Another way in which futures could be used to advantage would be to modify the mix of bonds and equity in a diversified portfolio.

Consider the following scenario: poor company results, gloomy domestic and international economic prospects, and concern about the impact of global conflicts have combined to severely depress stock markets worldwide over the last few months.

An asset allocation manager, with both bonds and equity in the portfolio for which she is responsible, anticipated the slump in share prices before a large downturn in prices had occurred. She switched out of equity and into bonds so that the weightings in her portfolio are now 75% bonds and 25% equity.

Analysts are now advising that the slump in equity prices has bottomed out, but that further reductions in the rate of interest are a possibility. The fund manager decides to leave the composition of the bond portfolio unchanged, but in view of the likely rise in share prices, decides to realign the portfolio weightings so that a 50/50 bond/equity mix is achieved.

The bond portfolio has the following characteristics: Modified duration is 7.4908 yield is 4.595%, current valuation is €300,000,000. The BPV of the Euro-Bund future is 72.03.

The stock index that the fund is tracking is the Dow Jones EuroSTOXX^{SM} 50 and is quoted at 2,450. The portfolio's beta is 0.98. The sum of €100,000,000 is currently invested in the equity section of the portfolio.

Clearly to rebalance the portfolio and achieve the 50/50 weighting, €100,000,000 bonds need to be sold and the same amount of equity need to be purchased.

The question is: how many bond futures need to be shorted to achieve the desired 25% reduction in weighting? From the previous example, the BPV of the bond portfolio can be found by equation (16.15). In this case the BPV of the desired reduction will be given by

$$7.4908(€100,000,000)(0.0001) = €74,908$$

Dividing this by the BPV of the Euro-Bund future will determine the number of contracts to short:

$$\frac{€74,908}{72.03} = 1,040 \text{ contracts}$$

At the same time the equity weighting needs to be increased and this can be achieved by dividing the notional principal by the value of the Dow Jones EuroSTOXX futures contract and using the result to adjust the portfolio's beta.

$$\frac{\text{Notional principal}}{(\text{Futures quote})(\text{Value of an index point})}\beta = \text{Number of contracts}$$

$$\frac{€100,000,000}{(2,450)(€10)}0.98 = 4,000 \text{ contracts}$$

The arithmetic indicates that a long position of 4,000 contracts is required to give the fund manager the desired exposure to the equity index.

The above examples have focused on the use of the Euro-Bund future as a vehicle for achieving a particular bond portfolio exposure. As indicated earlier, there are several other futures contracts available in the European arena and these could be used in the same way as described above. The futures contracts could also be used to alter the maturity characteristics of the portfolio by using, for example, futures contracts constructed around shorter or longer dated instruments than those currently held in the portfolio. The fact that the contracts can be bought or sold on margin, that the major contracts are liquid and span the European markets, and their flexibility of use make them essential financial market instruments.

CHAPTER 17

Interest Rate Options

Lawrence Galitz, Ph.D.
Director
ACF Consultants Ltd.

This chapter explores *interest rate options*—a vital part of the European fixed income securities market. The first section looks at exchange-traded options, where €20 billion worth of bond options and over €250 billion of options on short-term rates change hands every day. Next, we'll look at the flexible OTC markets for interest rate options, including caps, collars, swaptions, and structured products. Finally, having explained the products themselves, we'll move on to explore how they can be used to hedge interest rate risk.

Before all that, however, we'll start by outlining what interest rate options are, and how they differ from other financial products.

HOW OPTIONS DIFFER FROM OTHER PRODUCTS

An option gives the holder the right to execute a specific transaction. For example, a bond option might allow the holder to buy €100 face value of a particular bond, in three months time, at the fixed price of 98. If the bond price is above 98 three months from now, the owner of the option would be happy to exercise his option, pay over the €98 and receive delivery of the bond, which is worth more than €98.

How does this bond option differ from, say, a bond futures contract bought at 98? The option confers a *right*, but *not an obligation*. This is the key difference between options and most other financial instruments. No one forces the holder of an option to exercise the right. He or

525

EXHIBIT 17.1   Value of Bond Option at Expiry

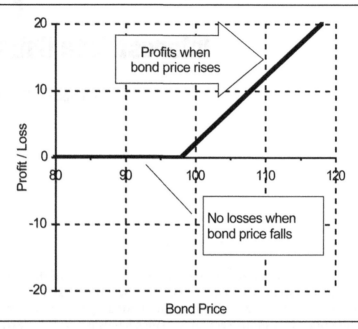

she will do so if it is worthwhile, but can simply let the option expire unexercised if he or she wants. If the bond in the above example were trading at 99, the option holder would exercise the option, saving €1 for every €100 face value of bonds purchased in this way. On the other hand, if the bond were trading at 97, the option holder would simply tear up the contract and, if he or she really needed the underlying bond, could simply buy this in the cash market in the usual way.

The buyer of a bond futures contract at 98 would also save €1 for every €100 face value of bonds, if these bonds eventually traded at 99. However, the buyer would not be able to benefit if the underlying bonds dropped to 97. He or she would still be obliged to buy them at 98. Futures—and similar financial instruments—lock the counterparties into a trade at a specific price. They confer a right, *and* an obligation, which must be honoured, whether or not it is financially advantageous. Options confer a right, but *not* an obligation—that's the key difference.

Because options confer a right, without any offsetting obligation, you are never at a disadvantage if you are given one—you can only gain, not lose. This is illustrated in Exhibit 17.1, which shows the value of the bond option we have been discussing. For every €1 that the underlying bond price exceeds 98 when the option expires, the option is worth €1. So if the bond is trading at 118, the option would be worth €20.

EXHIBIT 17.2   Value Profiles for Option Buyer and Seller

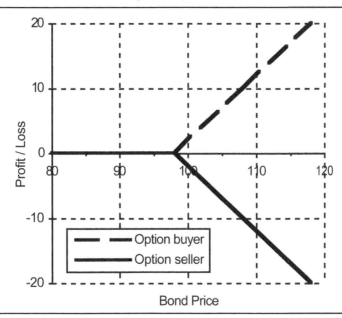

The opposite is true for an option seller, whose value profile is shown in Exhibit 17.2. The option seller can only lose, not gain. No one in their right mind would therefore sell options for free! Instead, the option buyer must pay a *premium* to the option seller to acquire the rights conferred by the option. This is another important distinction between options and other derivatives (like swaps and forward rate agreements) for which no up-front payment is due.

Exhibit 17.3 shows the payoff profiles for the buyer and seller of the bond option, once the option premium—€2 in this example—is taken into account. If the underlying bond is trading below 98, the option will expire worthless, and the option buyer will now be €2 down, as the chart shows. It is this premium income that provides the incentive for option sellers. As Exhibit 17.3 shows, so long as the bond trades at a price of 100 or lower when the option expires, the option seller ends up with a profit.

OPTIONS TERMINOLOGY

In discussing the example of a bond option in the previous section, we introduced a number of terms without actually naming them. Let's now define some of the terminology:

EXHIBIT 17.3   Payoff Profiles for Option Buyer and Seller (with Premiums)

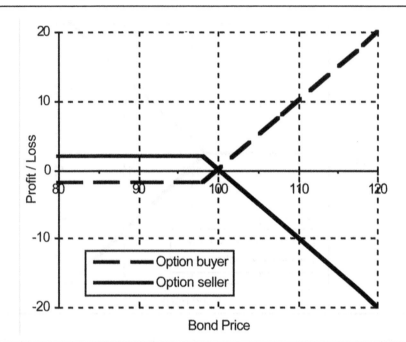

- *Call Option*—This gives the holder the right to *buy* the underlying asset, as in the examples given in the previous section. Call options become more and more valuable as the underlying asset price increases; this is clear from all the charts seen so far.
- *Put Option*—This gives the holder the right to *sell* the underlying asset. Exhibit 17.4 contrasts the payoff profile from a call with that of a put. In both cases, the fixed price at which the bond may be bought (for the call) or sold (for the put) is 98. For illustrative purposes, the call premium is 2, while the put premium is 3.
- *Strike Price* (or *Exercise Price*)—The price, fixed at the outset, at which the underlying asset may be bought (for a call) or sold (for a put). In the previous example, the option was a call struck at 98, giving the holder the right to buy the bond at this price.
- *Expiry Date* (or *Maturity Date*)—All options have a finite life. The last date when the holder can exercise his right is the option's expiry date. In the example given earlier, this was three months from now.
- *European Style*—This is nothing to do with geography! A European style option is one which can only be exercised on the expiry date, not before.

EXHIBIT 17.4 Payoff Profiles for Calls and Puts

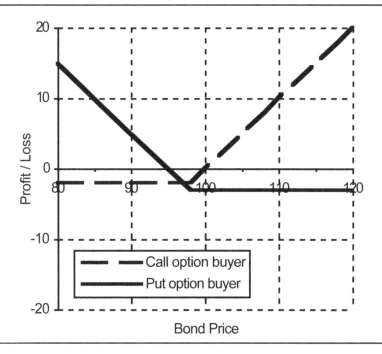

- *American Style*—In contrast, an American Style option can be exercised at any time up to and including the expiry date.
- *Moneyness*—Is the option worth exercising? If so, it is said to be *in-the-money* (ITM). Our call option struck at 98 would be in-the-money if the underlying bond was trading above 98. If the bond were trading below 98, the call would instead be *out-of-the-money* (OTM). Finally, if the current price of the underlying asset was the same as the strike price, 98 in this example, the option would be *at-the-money* (ATM).
- *Premium*—The amount paid by the buyer of an option is called the *premium*. This is normally paid up-front.
- *Intrinsic Value*—This is the value that would be realised if the option were exercised right now at prevailing market prices, provided that exercise was worthwhile. For example, a call option struck at 98 would have an intrinsic value of 3 if the underlying bond were trading at 101. The put option at the same strike price would have an intrinsic value of 0, however, not –3, as it would not be worth exercising.
- *Time Value*—Option premiums normally exceed their intrinsic value. For example, the premium for a call option struck at 98 on a bond trading at 101 might be 4, not 3. The time value of an option is the

amount by which the premium exceeds the intrinsic value of the option. For an out-of-the-money option, the entire premium is time value, because there is no intrinsic value for an OTM option.

EXCHANGE-TRADED OPTIONS

In this section we will explore *exchange-traded* interest rate options— contracts traded on organised exchanges. In contrast, OTC options offered by banks will be examined in the next section.

In Europe, there are two principal exchanges offering interest rate option contracts: Eurex (based in Frankfurt) and Euronext.liffe (based in London). Both exchanges offer option contracts on long-term interest rates and short-term interest rates but, in practice, Eurex dominates the market for the former, while Euronext.liffe handles the latter. We'll start by looking at the bond option contracts offered by Eurex.

Bond Options

Eurex offers three principal bond option contracts, all of these being options on the futures contracts traded on the same exchange. The contracts available are:

- *Options on Euro-BUND futures (OGBL).* The BUND future is a contract on a notional long-term instrument issued by the German Federal Government with a remaining time to maturity between 8.5 and 10.5 years, bearing a 6% coupon.
- *Options on Euro-BOBL futures (OGBM).* The BOBL future is exactly like the BUND, except that the remaining maturity of the German Government bond is between 4.5 and 5.5 years, and is therefore a medium-term contract.
- *Options on Euro-SCHATZ futures (OGBS).* Again this is similar, except that the SCHATZ futures focuses on short-term obligations either of the German Federal Government or the Treuhandanstalt[1] with a remaining maturity between 1.75 and 2.25 years.

Each of these is an option on the underlying futures. If an investor exercises one call option contract, he or she will be assigned a long position of one contract in the underlying future, at the strike price. Equally, after exercising one put option contract, an investor will be assigned a

---

[1] The Federal Agency set up by the German Government in 1990 to handle the reunification process.

short position in one contract of the underlying future, again at the option strike price. Any difference between the strike and the prevailing futures price is credited to the investor's margin account at the exchange.

Although an option into a future sounds somewhat esoteric, each contract is effectively an option on €100,000 of German government bonds carrying a 6% coupon of the appropriate maturity.

Trading in these bond options contracts is extensive across the bond maturity spectrum, averaging at over 200,000 contracts per day during January 2003, as the monthly statistics in Exhibit 17.5 shows. The total open interest in bond options, amounting to around 2 million contracts, represents an underlying position of €200 billion.

The Eurex bond options are all identical, differing only in the underlying futures contract, and therefore the maturity of the underlying bonds. Their common features are summarised in Exhibit 17.6.

EXHIBIT 17.5   Trading Statistics for Eurex Bond Options January 2003

Contract	Trading Volume			End-Month Open Interest		
	Futures	Calls	Puts	Futures	Calls	Puts
Euro-Bund	22,301,183	1,259,790	1,360,482	824,032	358,806	428,561
Euro-Bobl	12,244,884	249,345	209,292	631,615	169,639	161,202
Euro-Schatz	9,262,553	854,764	332,952	680,974	677,065	165,138

Source: Eurex.

EXHIBIT 17.6   Eurex Bond Option Specifications

Underlying	One contract in the underlying future, which in turn represents a bond with €100,000 face value.
Quotation	In percentage points, to two decimal places. So a price of 1.23 means 1.23% of €100,000.
Minimum price movement (tick size and value)	0.01, which is worth €10
Trading hours	8:00 until 19:00 (8:00 A.M. to 7:00 P.M.) CET
Last trading day	Six exchange trading days prior to the first calendar day of the option expiration months.
Expiration months	The next three calendar months, plus the next quarter-end month.
Exercise style	American
Strike prices	In 0.50 steps. Each new contract is introduced with nine strike prices.

Source: Eurex.

EXHIBIT 17.7   Trading Volumes for Eurex Bond Futures and Options on 7 March 2003

		Apr-03	May-03	Jun-03	Sep-03	Dec-03
Bund	Futures			1,038,320	3,873	300
	Calls	40,955	21,731	22,751	110	
	Puts	38,140	34,153	5,837	110	
Bobl	Futures			469,112	400	0
	Calls	13,213	800	0	0	
	Puts	6,300	4,500	3,650	0	
Schatz	Futures			399,891	2,687	0
	Calls	29,250	21,500	46,100	0	
	Puts	17,850	500	750	0	

Source: Eurex.

As an example, in March 2003 bond options expiring in April, May, June, and September were all available. The first three were exercisable into the June futures contracts, while the last one was exercisable into the September futures contract. Although all four expiry dates were theoretically available, only those options exercisable into the *front* futures contract (the next one to mature) were liquid. On 7 March 2003, the front contract was the June 2003 future, and over 99% of all futures trades and 99.9% of bond options trades involved this contract. Exhibit 17.7 provides a breakdown of these figures, showing the total number of contracts traded on that day.

Let's now look at the bond options in more detail. We will focus on the Euro-BUND contracts, as trading in these is greater than the trading volume of the Euro-BOBL and Euro-SCHATZ contracts put together. Exhibit 17.8 shows the closing prices for the three liquid expiry dates for a range of strike prices. Note that the prices are quoted to two decimal places, while the strike prices are 0.50 apart, as in the contract specifications. Also important to know is the closing price for the underlying June 2003 futures contract, which was 116.42. The table highlights the at-the-money options struck at 116.50.

A number of features become apparent after studying these figures:

■ For calls, the lower the strike price, the more expensive the premium. This is because calls confer the right to buy the underlying at the strike price fixed at the outset. The right to buy the June 2003 future at 113.50 is clearly more valuable than the right to buy at 119.50.

EXHIBIT 17.8 Closing Prices for Euro-BUND Options on 7 March 2003

	Calls			Puts		
Strikes	Apr-03	May-03	Jun-03	Apr-03	May-03	Jun-03
113.50	2.93	3.05	3.19	0.01	0.13	0.27
114.00	2.45	2.62	2.79	0.03	0.20	0.37
114.50	1.98	2.21	2.41	0.06	0.29	0.49
115.00	1.53	1.83	2.06	0.11	0.41	0.64
115.50	1.13	1.49	1.73	0.21	0.57	0.81
116.00	0.77	1.18	1.44	0.35	0.76	1.02
116.50	0.51	0.93	1.18	0.59	1.01	1.26
117.00	0.31	0.71	0.96	0.89	1.29	1.54
117.50	0.17	0.52	0.77	1.25	1.60	1.85
118.00	0.09	0.39	0.61	1.67	1.97	2.19
118.50	0.04	0.28	0.48	2.12	2.36	2.56
119.00	0.02	0.19	0.36	2.60	2.77	2.94
119.50	0.01	0.13	0.28	3.09	3.21	3.36

Source: Eurex.

- For puts, the converse is true, with higher strike puts being more valuable. This also follows from the definition of a put option, which confers the right to sell the underlying. In this case, the right to *sell* the June 2003 future at 119.50 is more valuable than the right to sell the future at 113.50.
- The longer the option's time to expiry, the more valuable is the option. In all cases, the options expiring in May are more valuable than those expiring in April with the same strike price and, similarly, June options are more valuable still. This is sensible when one thinks of the risk experienced by the option seller. The further the expiry date, the greater the uncertainty as to where the price of the underlying bond will be in the future, and therefore the more valuable the right to execute a trade in the future at a price fixed at the outset.
- The time value of at-the-money options is the greatest. This is not so apparent from Exhibit 17.8 which shows the total premiums, comprising intrinsic value and time value. Exhibit 17.9 shows the time value component by itself, which makes this feature obvious. With OTM options, the entire premium is time value—this applies to the 117-strike calls and the 116-strike puts, for example. With ITM options, the time value is the total premium less the intrinsic value. For example, the intrinsic value for the April 2003 call option struck at 115 is 1.42 (116.42 less 115). Subtracting this from the total premium of 1.53 gives the time value of 0.11 shown in the table.

EXHIBIT 17.9 Time Values for Euro-BUND Options on 7 March 2003

	Calls			Puts		
Strikes	Apr-03	May-03	Jun-03	Apr-03	May-03	Jun-03
113.50	0.01	0.13	0.27	0.01	0.13	0.27
114.00	0.03	0.20	0.37	0.03	0.20	0.37
114.50	0.06	0.29	0.49	0.06	0.29	0.49
115.00	0.11	0.41	0.64	0.11	0.41	0.64
115.50	0.21	0.57	0.81	0.21	0.57	0.81
116.00	0.25	0.76	1.02	0.35	0.76	1.02
116.50	0.51	0.93	1.18	0.51	0.93	1.19
117.00	0.31	0.71	0.96	0.31	0.71	0.96
117.50	0.17	0.52	0.77	0.17	0.52	0.77
118.00	0.09	0.39	0.61	0.09	0.39	0.61
118.50	0.04	0.28	0.48	0.04	0.28	0.48
119.00	0.02	0.19	0.36	0.02	0.19	0.36
119.50	0.01	0.13	0.28	0.01	0.13	0.28

Why is time value greatest for ATM options? Think first about OTM and ITM options. For deep ITM options, the owner is virtually certain to exercise the option, so the right to tear up the option instead is minimal. In a similar way, the owner of a deep OTM option is virtually certain to let the option expire unexercised, so the right to exercise the option instead is also minimal. For ATM options there is no such certainty; on the contrary, uncertainty is at its greatest, so the right to decide later whether or not to exercise is also highest at this strike level.

Let's now consider what happens when an investor trades one of these contracts. To illustrate this, suppose an investor buys 10 of the June 2003 Euro-BUND call options struck at 116.50 at a price of 1.18.

Trade: BUY 10 Jun 03 Calls Struck at 116.50 at 1.18

If the option is eventually exercised, the investor would be assigned a long position in the underlying June 2003 futures contract at a price of 116.50. If the futures were actually trading at 117 at the time, the position would be worth €5,000:

10 contracts × 50 ticks × €10 tick value = €5,000

This would be realised by crediting the investor's futures margin account with €5,000. This €5,000 can also be thought of as the benefit of buying €1 million of Bunds at a price 0.50% cheaper than the current market price.

The premium of 1.18 per contract works out at €11,800, calculated as

$$10 \text{ contracts} \times 118 \text{ ticks} \times €10 \text{ tick value} = €11,800$$

Unlike the OTC options that we shall be examining later, the premium for these exchange-traded options is not actually paid up-front. Instead, until exercise or expiry, the option buyer and seller are both *margined* in the same way as with futures positions. The premium of €11,800 is only paid—again through the margining system—when the option expires or is exercised.[2]

In a later section we will examine why investors and others might want to use these exchange-traded bond options. Before this, however, we will turn our attention towards the other major exchange-traded interest rate product, short-term interest rate options.

Short-Term Interest Rate Options

While short-term interest-rate (STIR) options are also offered on Eurex, liquidity in the Eurex options is negligible. Instead, Euronext.liffe in London provides the major world market for STIR option contracts in European currencies.

Euronext.liffe creates a market in contracts on 3-month interest rates in three currencies: the euro, the pound sterling, and the Swiss franc, but only contracts in the first two currencies are liquid, as Exhibit 17.10 shows.

EXHIBIT 17.10 Trading Statistics for Euronext.liffe STIR Options Jan *2003*

	Volume		Open Interest	
Contract	Futures	Options	Futures	Options
3m EURIBOR	9,612,443	4,204,637	2,340,059	4,884,679
3m Sterling	2,918,333	1,687,285	937,550	1,816,333
3m Euroswiss	339,432	1,000	185,545	21,500

Source: Euronext.liffe.

---

[2] For a detailed explanation, see: *Eurex Clearing—Risk Based Margining,* Eurex (January 2003), pp. 31–33. (Available for download at http://www.eurexchange.com/clearing/download/rbm_final_en.pdf.)

EXHIBIT 17.11 Euronext.liffe STIR Option Specifications

Underlying	One contract in the underlying future, which in turn represents a 3-month deposit of €1 million at a fixed interest rate.
Quotation	In percentage points. So a price of 1.230 means 1.230% of €1 million over a nominal 90-day period, equivalent to €3,075.
Minimum price movement (tick size and value)	0.005, which is worth €12.50
Trading hours	7:02 until 18:00 (7:02 A.M. to 6:00 P.M. London time)
Last trading day	Two business days prior to the third Wednesday of the expiry month at 10.00am.
Expiration months	The next two calendar (serial) months, plus March, June, September, December, such that: (a) the nearest three expiry months are consecutive, and (b) 10 expiry months are available for trading.
Exercise style	American
Strike prices	In 0.125 steps for the first four quarterly and all serial months; 0.25 steps thereafter. Each new contract is introduced with nine strike prices.

Source: Euronext.liffe.

As with bond options, each of these options contracts are exercisable into one contract in the underlying futures, also traded on the same exchange. The detailed specifications for EURIBOR STIR options are given in Exhibit 17.11, with those for the other currencies being very similar. However, as the EURIBOR contracts are the most liquid, we will concentrate on these for the remainder of this section.

Understanding how a STIR option works can be a little convoluted, so let's start by recapping the definition of the EURIBOR futures contract itself.

The EURIBOR *futures* contract provides the buyer with the theoretical commitment to place €1 million on deposit at a fixed interest rate for a nominal 90-day period starting on the futures expiry date, the third Wednesday of the delivery month. The fixed interest rate is not quoted directly, but is defined as 100 minus the quoted futures price. So if an investor buys a future at a price of 97, he or she is theoretically committed to deposit €1 million at 3% for 90 days. We have twice used the word "theoretically" because, in practice, these futures contracts are always *cash settled*, which means that buyers and sellers effectively pay or receive the difference between:

■ The interest rate originally agreed.
■ The interest rate eventually prevailing.

So if an investor buys one EURIBOR futures contract at 97.000, implying a 3% rate of interest, and the contracts expire at 97.500, implying a 2.5% interest rate, the investor receives

$$0.5\% \times €1,000,000 \times (90/360) = €1,250$$

In STIR futures parlance, the price difference between the buying price of 97.000 and the selling price of 97.500 is 100 ticks, and each tick is worth €12.50, so the profit is simply $100 \times €12.50$ or €1,250, as above.

Now that we understand how the EURIBOR futures contract works, let's think about options on these futures. Suppose an investor buys one STIR call option struck at 97.75 on the June 2003 futures contract, which is trading also at 97.750. The option is quoted at a price (premium) of 0.100. This means:

■ The investor effectively has to pay €250 to buy the option. This is 20 ticks (0.100 price with a 0.005 tick size) at €12.50 per tick.
■ The investor has the right, but not the obligation, to exercise the option at any time until expiry.
■ If the investor exercises the option, he or she will be assigned a long position in the June 2003 futures contract at an effective purchase price of 97.750. Any difference between the prevailing futures price and 97.750 will be credited to the investor's margin account.
■ The STIR option—being a call in this example—will only be worth exercising if the futures price rises above the strike price of 97.750. If, for example, the option is exercised when the June 2003 contract is trading at 98.000, the investor's margin account would be credited with €625 upon exercise.
■ The investor will therefore only exercise the option if there is a *fall* in the June 2003 3-month interest rate.

Buying call STIR options is therefore consistent with a view that forward interest rates will fall, or a need for protection against a fall in rates. Typical call buyers might be investors who would suffer if interest rates fell. Conversely, buying put STIR options is consistent with a view of rising interest rates, or the need to protect against that eventuality. A corporate borrower might therefore buy STIR put options to protect against an unexpected rise in interest rates and fall in futures prices.

EXHIBIT 17.12   Trading Volumes for Euronext.liffe STIR Futures and Options on 7 March 2003

	Mar-03	Apr-03	May-03	Jun-03	Sep-03	Dec-03
Futures	75,673	5,594	0	106,426	107,992	118,385
Calls	177,667	5,600	0	183,803	38,295	26,000
Puts	76,826	7,105	0	32,127	4,995	39,650

	Mar-04	Jun-04	Sep-04	Dec-04	Later dates	Total
Futures	77,815	47,363	24,725	21,870	6,075	591,918
Calls	350	0	1,000	0	0	432,715
Puts	1,400	0	1,040	0	0	163,143

Source: Euronext.liffe.

To provide an idea of which of the EURIBOR contracts are liquid, Exhibit 17.12 shows the trading volumes on 7 March 2003 for the 10 expiry months available on that date. As with the bond options discussed earlier, the March 2003 options are exercisable into the March 2003 futures contract, the April through June 2003 options are exercisable into the June 2003 future, and the remaining options are exercisable into the future expiring in the same month.

It is apparent from these figures that 99% of the trades in these STIR options involves contracts maturing within one year, with almost 80% of this volume coming from trades in the March and June 2003 contracts (there being little liquidity in the serial months). With only 10 days before their expiry on 17 March 2003, the March options do not exhibit much optionlike behaviour, so we will focus instead on the June 2003 contracts, whose settlement prices are shown in Exhibit 17.13.

The exhibit shows the option premiums quoted to the nearest 0.005 and strike prices separated by 0.125 intervals as required by the contract specification. The underlying June 2003 future settled at 97.745 that day (implying a 3-month interest rate in June of 2.255%), so the table highlights the 97.750 ATM options.

As with the Eurex bond options:

■ The most expensive options are the low strike calls and the high strike puts. Remember that the STIR call grants the right to buy the underlying future at a fixed price, which in turn confers the right to invest at a fixed rate of interest. The right to invest at a high interest rate (low strike price) is clearly more valuable than the right to invest at a low

EXHIBIT 17.13 Closing Prices, Volumes, and Open Interest for June 2003 STIR Options on 7 March 2003

Strikes	Settlement Prices		Trading Volume		Open Interest	
	Calls	Puts	Calls	Puts	Calls	Puts
97.000	0.745		2,000	750	66,940	67,474
97.125	0.620		0	0	33,650	78,925
97.250	0.500	0.005	0	2,000	54,960	87,299
97.375	0.380	0.010	150	4,200	54,750	74,515
97.500	0.265	0.020	21,200	17,197	163,154	87,134
97.625	0.170	0.050	1,255	2,070	157,226	27,800
97.750	0.100	0.105	31,337	5,910	140,836	21,815
97.875	0.055	0.185	19,000	0	73,085	3,000
98.000	0.025		66,349	0	234,241	0
98.125	0.010		11,000	0	56,904	0
98.250	0.005		31,512	0	74,943	0
Other			0	0	130,590	174,073
Totals			183,803	32,127	1,241,279	622,035

Source: Euronext.liffe.

    interest rate (high strike price). Similar reasoning applies to the put options.

■ Time value is greatest for the ATM options struck at 97.750, equalling 0.100 for both puts and calls. The 97.875 strike options have a time value of 0.055, while the 97.625 strike options have a time value of only 0.050. As we will see when we examine hedging applications, this makes the *economic cost* of ATM options the highest.

OTC OPTIONS

Until recently, the interest rate options market was dominated by OTC transactions—trades executed directly between professional counterparties like banks, insurers, investment institutions, and corporates. However, as Exhibit 17.14 shows, dramatic growth of the exchange-traded markets in recent years has seen them catch up with the OTC markets in terms of notional amounts outstanding, and the two are now neck-and-neck.

    Despite the recent growth of exchange-traded products, the OTC market is still very much a major feature of the interest rate options

EXHIBIT 17.14   Growth of OTC versus Exchange-Traded Interest Rate Derivatives
Markets

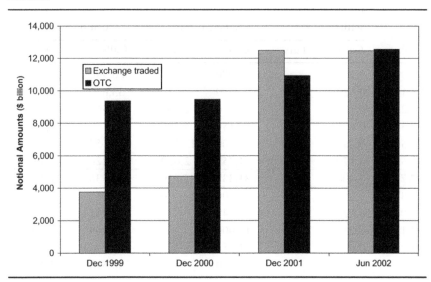

Source: BIS Quarterly Review (March 2003).

markets, offering a range of products and wide flexibility unrivalled by
the exchanges, which are mostly limited to offering standardized contracts with rigid terms.

Statistics on the relative size of the European market for exchange-
traded interest rate options are relatively easy to come by, and the Bank
for International Settlement (BIS) publishes a regular breakdown of geographic activity. This is summarised in Exhibit 17.15, which shows how
notional amounts outstanding on European exchanges have quadrupled
over the 3-year period from 1999 to 2002.

Unfortunately, without a central clearing house to monitor and
record all transactions, it is difficult to obtain reliable statistics for the
OTC interest rate options market. However, the BIS conducts regular sur-
veys of the markets and publishes a breakdown of notional amounts outstanding by currency (but not by country) of all interest rate derivatives
(including swaps, FRAs, futures, as well as options) across all markets
(OTC as well as exchange-traded). A summary of this is shown in Exhibit
17.16, from which it can be seen that the size of the euro-denominated
market now virtually matches that of the US dollar, signalling the increasing importance of the European interest rate derivatives market.

While the exchanges offer standardized interest rate options on
bonds and 3-month interest rates, the OTC market offers products

EXHIBIT 17.15   Geographic Breakdown of Exchange-Traded Interest Rate Options

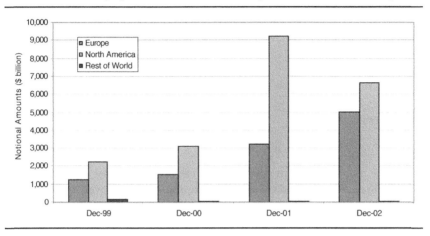

Source: BIS Quarterly Review (March 2003).

EXHIBIT 17.16   Currency Composition of Interest Rate Derivatives

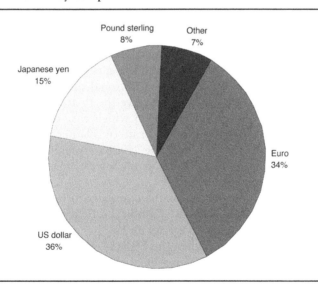

Source: BIS Quarterly Review (December 2002).

which can be tailored to meet clients' individual needs. In the following sections we will review these products, including:

- Caps, floors, and collars
- Swaptions
- Structured products
- Structured interest rate options

Caps, Floors, and Collars

Caps

A cap is an interest rate derivative offering protection against unexpected fluctuations in short-term interest rates, but over an extended period of time. An example will make this clearer.

Suppose a company has arranged to borrow €1 million for five years at six-month EURIBOR plus 100 bp. Let's say that 6-month EURIBOR right now is 2%, so the company will pay 3% for the first six months. In six months time, however, the company's borrowing rate will be reset to 1% above the level of 6-month EURIBOR prevailing at the time. Under this financing arrangement—which is very common—the company is exposed to the risk that interest rates could rise in the future, directly increasing its borrowing costs.

One solution to this problem, of course, is for the company to enter into a 5-year interest rate swap on a notional principal of €1 million, agreeing to pay the fixed rate and receive the floating rate. In our illustration, the fixed rate might be 3%, in which case the company would effectively lock into paying the fixed rate of 3% per annum over the 5-year period. While this protects the company against higher interest rates, the company cannot benefit from lower rates, especially at the outset when rates are just 2%.

An alternative solution is for the company to buy a 5-year *interest rate cap* on 6-month EURIBOR. Exhibit 17.17 illustrates the effect of such a cap if the strike price were set at 3%.

In any 6-month period when the EURIBOR setting is below 3%, the interest rate cap struck at 3% is out-of-the-money and does not affect the borrower, who can benefit from the lower rates, especially at the outset. However, whenever EURIBOR fixes above 3%, the interest rate cap pays the difference between the 3% strike rate and the rate prevailing. For example, if EURIBOR fixed at 4%, the company would receive €5,000 from the cap counterparty (assuming a 180-day period), and this sum would bring the effective EURIBOR down from 4% to 3% for that period.

EXHIBIT 17.17   Illustration of 5-Year Interest Rate Cap

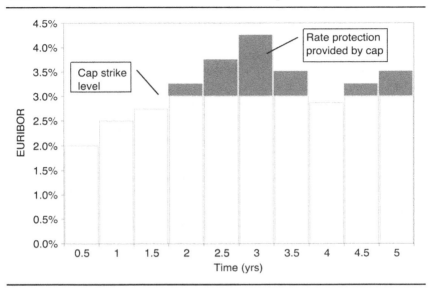

In this way, an interest rate cap allows the borrowing company to benefit when interest rates are low, while protecting the company when interest rates are high. This is marvellous, as it provides the best of both worlds, but such a result does not come free! As with other interest rate options, the company would have to pay an up-front premium to purchase the cap. In the example here, this up-front premium might be around 165 bp of the notional principal, i.e., €16,500, which is equivalent to around 35 bp per annum if this cost were spread over the lifetime of the cap. This caps the effective EURIBOR at around 3.35% rather than 3%. Contrast this with the interest rate swap, which does not involve an up-front payment, but penalizes the company with a higher initial interest rate instead.

By convention, caps are quoted as an up-front premium expressed as a percentage of the notional principal. So in the above example, the cap would be quoted at 1.65% or 165 bp.

Although caps may seem complex products compared to the exchange-traded options seen earlier, they can be deconstructed into a series of single-period interest rate options. Exhibit 17.18 illustrates how the company's 5-year cap actually comprises a strip of nine single-period options. The first such option—called a *caplet*—is a 6-month option into the 6-month rate starting six months from now. The second caplet is a 1-year option into the 6-month rate starting in a year, and the last caplet is a 4.5-year option into the 6-month rate starting in 4.5 years.

EXHIBIT 17.18   Deconstructing an Interest Rate Cap

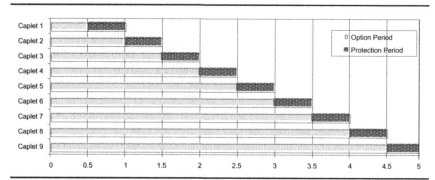

Note that there is no need for a Caplet 0 covering the very first interest period. As the interest rate for the very first interest period is fixed at the outset, and is therefore known, there is no need to have an option. Options are only required to provide protection against the unknown.

The diagram highlights for each caplet the difference between the *option period* and the *protection period*. For example, the last caplet has a 4.5 year *option period* during which interest rates can vary and expose the company to risk. When the caplet expires, the caplet provides compensation over the 6-month *protection period* if the EURIBOR setting at the outset of that period exceeds the strike rate.

You can see why a cap is actually a combination of single-period options by thinking about what happens every six months. In our example, the expiry dates of the nine caplets are set to coincide with the company's EURIBOR setting dates. Six months after the loan commences, the rate for the second interest period will be set by reference to the EURIBOR fixing that day. On the same date, the first caplet expires. If EURIBOR is above the strike rate of 3%, the company will exercise the caplet and receive compensation; if EURIBOR is lower, the company will simply let the caplet expire worthless. The same process will apply six months later, and so on.

An interest cap therefore features *multiple exercise dates*. The holder can decide on each EURIBOR setting date whether or not to exercise the corresponding caplet. Contrast this with the bond and STIR options seen earlier, which have a single exercise date.

Floors

An interest rate cap is effectively a call on interest rates. If interest rates exceed the strike rate, the cap expires in-the-money. Just as a put option is the mirror image of a call, a *floor* is the mirror image of a cap. An interest rate floor expires in-the-money when interest rates are *lower* than the strike rate.

Floors therefore provide protection against lower interest rates, and might be used by investing institutions to protect their returns when rates fall. This is exactly analogous to the way a borrower would use a cap to protect their costs when interest rates rise.

Collars

Caps and floors can be combined to create a third product, the *interest rate collar*. Let's return to the example of our corporate borrower, who is thinking about buying an interest rate cap, but is deterred by the up-front cost of 165 bp. If the company were to buy a cap and, at the same time, *sell* a floor, the premium received by the company from selling the floor will help to offset the cost of buying the cap.

As an example, let's suppose the company bought a 5-year cap with a slightly higher strike rate of 3.50% at an up-front cost of 84 bp, and sold a 2.50% floor to bring in 30bp premium up-front. The premium income from the floor reduces the net cost by 35% to just 54 bp up-front, equivalent to 12 bp per annum if spread over five years.

The result for the company is that EURIBOR will effectively be *collared* in the range 2.50% to 3.50%. If EURIBOR ever rose above 3.50%, the company's costs would be capped at that level. The downside is that whenever the EURIBOR setting was below 2.50%, the company would not pay less. As neither the cap nor the collar include the first interest period, the company in this example is assured of six months borrowing based on a EURIBOR of 2%. Thereafter, even if EURIBOR were to stay low, the company's borrowing would be based on a EURIBOR of at least 2.50%. This may nonetheless still prove less expensive than paying the fixed rate of 3% throughout, which is what the swap would involve.

Swaptions

As the name suggests, a swaption is an option into a swap. The holder of a swaption has the right, but not the obligation, to enter into a swap at the fixed rate defined by the strike rate of the swaption.

Just as there are calls and puts for other options, swaptions also come in two varieties.

- A *payers swaption* grants the holder the right to enter into the underlying swap as the fixed-rate payer.

■ A *receivers swaption* grants the holder the right to receive the fixed rate in the underlying swap.

Practitioners seldom refer to swaptions as calls or puts, because this would be ambiguous. Nonetheless, the payoff profile from a payers swaption can be thought of as analogous to that of a call option, because payers swaptions become more valuable as the underlying swap rate rises. At maturity, a payers swaption is only worth exercising if the underlying swap rate exceeds the swaption strike. Similarly, a receivers swaption can be thought of as being analogous to a put option on swap rates.

An example term sheet for a swaption might have the following specifications:

Product:	1-year payers swaption into a 3-year swap
Trading date:	29 March 20X3
Expiry:	29 March 20X4
Exercise style:	European
Notional amount:	€10 million
Strike rate:	4%
Underlying swap:	3-year IRS fixed at 4% p.a. against 3-month EURIBOR
Effective date:	31 March 20X4
Termination date:	31 March 20X7
Interest calculation basis:	Actual/360

The buyer of this swaption has the right, one year from now, to enter into a 3-year swap as the fixed-rate payer, paying 4% p.a. against receiving 3-month EURIBOR, on a notional principal of €10 million. If 3-year swap rates on 29 March 20X4 were, say, 4.5%, it would be worthwhile for the owner to exercise the swaption, paying a fixed rate of only 4% when the market rate was 4.5%.

In practice, to minimise credit risk problems for the swaption writer, swaptions are usually *cash settled* rather than physically exercised. In the above example, if 3-year rates were 4.5%, the swaption writer would pay the swaption owner around €140,000, being the present value of the 0.5% p.a. on €10 million, rather than entering into the underlying swap for three years.

In addition to the traditional European and American exercise styles, swaptions are also available *Bermudan-style*, which allows the owner to exercise the swaption on a set of prespecified dates. This style is in between American and European style, hence the use of the geographic epithet "Bermudan." Such swaptions are often linked to bonds or swaps, with the permitted exercise dates matched to the coupon dates of the underlying instrument.

Suppose a "one by three-year" Bermudan-style swaption (a 1-year swaption into a 3-year swap) is exercised after six months. What is the maturity of the resulting swap—3 years or 3.5 years? Both possibilities exist:

- With a *variable swaption*, the tenor of the underlying swap is fixed at the outset. If the swaption is exercisable into a 3-year swap, the owner will get a swap with a 3-year tenor dating from the exercise date. This means that the termination date of the underlying swap will depend upon when the swaption is exercised.
- With a *wasting swaption*, the termination date of the underlying swap is fixed at the outset. The later the swaption is exercised, the shorter the remaining tenor of the underlying swap.

Swaptions are very versatile products, and are often used in conjunction with other financial products like bonds and swaps to create structured products like:

- *Cancellable swaps*—which can be cancelled by one party prior to the scheduled termination date. For example, the party with the cancellation right may elect to do so if he or she was the fixed-rate payer and interest rates had fallen substantially.
- *Extendible swaps*—which can be extended by one party beyond the scheduled termination date. In this case, the party with this ability may choose to extend a 3-year swap to five years if they were the fixed-rate payer, and rates had risen substantially.
- *Reversible swaps*—which allow one party to reverse the direction of the swap. For example, the party could switch from being the fixed-rate payer to being the fixed-rate receiver. This might happen if a company was able to repay its borrowing prematurely, was now a net investor, and rates had fallen substantially.

Later in the chapter we will examine some of the ways in which swaptions may be used. Before this, however, let's look at the way in which banks can go beyond the offering of "vanilla" interest rate options, to design and create *structured products*.

Structured Products

One of the ways in which banks can add value is to offer financial products not available elsewhere on the organised markets. Such *structured products* may offer investors:

- Enhanced yield, in return for accepting higher risk.

■ Higher current yield, in return for a potentially lower yield later on.

■ Higher potential yield, in return for a lower yield right now.

■ Exposure to a specific market rate that would not otherwise be attainable.

In nearly all these cases, the structured product can be engineered using a combination of a straightforward fixed-rate bond and one or more interest rate derivatives. Examples follow.

Capped Notes

A capped note is like a regular floating-rate note (FRN), but paying an enhanced return subject to an absolute cap on interest rates. For example, with 6-month EURIBOR currently at 2%, a regular 3-year FRN issued by XYZ Corp might pay 6-month EURIBOR plus 40 bp. A 3-year capped note from XYZ might pay 6-month EURIBOR plus 50 bp, subject to a maximum rate of 3.5%.

Effectively, the investor has sold XYZ a 3-year cap on 6-month EURIBOR struck at 3% for an up-front premium of 33 bp, equivalent to 11 bp p.a. XYZ keeps 1 bp of this annual premium, and uses the other 10 bp to pay the enhanced margin above EURIBOR.

Both XYZ and its investors are happy. Investors receive an enhanced yield, and XYZ has limited its borrowing costs in the event that rates rise.

Floored Notes

A floored note is similar to a capped note, except that the investor is promised a *minimum* interest rate. Continuing the previous example, XYZ might offer its investors a 3-year floored note paying 6-month EURIBOR plus 38 bp, with a guaranteed minimum rate of 2.38%. This promises the investor that the return can never fall below the initial prevailing rate.

In this case the investor has effectively bought from XYZ a 3-year floor on 6-month EURIBOR struck at 2% for an up-front premium of around 2 bp (very cheap), equivalent to less than 1 bp p.a. over three years. XYZ deducts 2 bp from its normal EURIBOR margin to offer investors a slightly lower yield of EURIBOR plus 38 bp right now, in return for guaranteeing that the rate cannot fall any lower. XYZ uses 1 bp of the 2 bp deduction to buy the 3-year floor (perhaps from a bank), and keeps the other 1 bp itself.

Again, this arrangement offers benefits both to investors and to XYZ. XYZ lowers its cost of funding, and investors are guaranteed a minimum return.

Range Floaters

A range floater is a combination of a capped and floored note. The investor receives a floating rate, subject to both a maximum and a minimum rate. Effectively, the investor has sold a cap and bought a floor. The net premium paid or received will either detract or enhance the return from the note in-between the two strike rates.

As an example, XYZ might offer a 5-year note paying 6-month EURIBOR plus 60 bp (the standard margin for XYZ at this tenor), subject to a EURIBOR floor of 2.25% (25 bp higher than the current 6-month rate) and a EURIBOR cap at 4%. This would promise investors an immediately enhanced return starting with the next EURIBOR fixing, and a guaranteed minimum return, with the only proviso being the cap at 4%—but this is at twice the prevailing level of EURIBOR.

Range Accrual Notes

These notes accrue interest daily at an enhanced yield, provided that a particular market rate falls within a specified range. For example, when the 1-year yield on vanilla instruments is 4%, a dollar-denominated, 1-year range accrual note might accrue interest at 6% p.a. on every day that 3-month EURIBOR fixes in the range 2.5% to 3.5%, otherwise it accrues nothing that day.

Such a note offers investors having a particular view—in this case on the stability of European interest rates—a way of monetizing their view with minimal risk. It would be difficult, if not impossible, for an investor to capitalize on this view through other means.

Range accrual notes can be based on almost any quoted market rate. In this example, the return on a dollar-denominated instrument is linked to European short-term interest rates, but it could also be linked to exchange rates, stock or commodity prices. In most cases they are structured using strips of digital options.

Digital Knock-Out Note

This is another short-term note that pays an enhanced rate provided that another market rate meets certain criteria. However, unlike the accrual note, all the accrued interest will be eliminated if the criteria are not met.

For example, a dollar-denominated, 1-year digital knock-out note might pay a 7.5% coupon at the end of the year, provided that 3-month EURIBOR throughout the year stays in the range from 2.25% to 3.75%. If EURIBOR ever fixes outside this range—even for just one day—the knock-out note will pay no interest at all, although the investor's principal will be returned intact at the end of the year.

Leveraged Capped Floaters

By effectively embedding caps and/or floors on a notional principal equal to a multiple of the underlying bond's face value, a company can offer investors significantly higher current yields, but with the risk that future returns could *fall* markedly if rates rose beyond a certain level.

As an example, XYZ could offer investors a 5-year note with the following specification:

Current 6-month EURIBOR:	2%
Coupon on vanilla 5-year FRNs:	EURIBOR plus 50 bp
Coupon on structured note:	The lesser of:
	(a) EURIBOR plus 70 bp
	(b) 23.20% less 4 × EURIBOR, floored
	at 0%

With a little arithmetic, you can see that the coupon on the structured note will be EURIBOR plus 70 bp, so long as rates stay below 4.50%. This is an enhanced return. If rates rise above 4.50%, however, the investor's return falls substantially, reaching 0% if EURIBOR reaches 5.80%. This note would appeal to the investor who thought that rate would rise from their current levels of 2%, but not beyond 4.5%.

The structure is achieved by XYZ effectively buying 5-year caps struck at 4.50% on five times the notional principal of the note issued. For example, if XYZ issued notes with a face value of €10 million, it would effectively buy interest rate caps from investors with a notional principal of €50 million. The up-front premium of 19 bp in this example, therefore, becomes geared up to 95 bp, equivalent to 20 bp p.a. This enables the investor to receive their enhanced coupon, but the geared payment from the caps sold means that investors' return diminishes rapidly in any period where EURIBOR sets above 4.50%.

Structured Interest Rate Options

In addition to using vanilla interest rate options to create the structured products discussed in the previous section, banks can also create structured interest rate derivatives. These can be tailored to meet client needs and include the products discussed in the following paragraphs. In each case, we illustrate the structure by reference to an interest rate cap, but the same principles apply equally well to floors and collars.

Amortising, Accreting, and Rollercoaster Caps

With a vanilla cap, the notional principal remains constant throughout the lifetime of the product. However, a customer might need an interest rate cap linked to a loan which is steadily being paid down over time.

To match the declining principal outstanding on the loan, a bank could create an *amortising cap*, in which the notional principal reduces in line with that of the loan.

If the cap's notional principal increases steadily over time, it is called an *accreting cap*, and if the notional principal increases in some periods and reduces in others, it is called a *rollercoaster cap*. In all cases, however, the schedule of notional principals must be agreed in advance—this cannot be left to the whim of the customer later on.

These products are no more difficult for a bank to price than vanilla caps. The bank has to price each caplet individually anyway, so pricing the strip with different notional principals each period does not complicate the calculation unduly.

Step-Up and Step-Down Caps

The strike rate for a vanilla cap is constant throughout, but with step-up and step-down caps the strike rate can vary according to a predefined schedule. If structured appropriately, this can provide a substantial cost saving for customers buying these products.

Take, for example, a borrower who needs protection against unexpected rises in interest rates over the course of a 5-year loan. EURIBOR might be low right now but, in a rising yield-curve environment, may increase significantly over time. For example, 6-month EURIBOR might currently be 2%, but 6-month forward rates may rise to 5% in the last six months of a 5-year loan. A cap struck at 4% would be well out-of-the-money in early periods, but well in-the-money for later periods.

In such a situation, the company can easily anticipate the forthcoming rise in rates from 2% to 5%, and plan accordingly. What it may require is protection against an *unanticipated* rise in rates. An unexpected 50 bp rise in rates from 2.5% to 3% in the near future might actually be more damaging than an unexpected 25 bp rise from 5% to 5.25% later on.

The solution is a *step-up* cap, where the strike rate might be set at 50 bp above the forward rate for each interest period. The strike rate might be 2.75% in the first period, rising to 5.50% for the final six-month period. The up-front premium for such a cap might be just 49 bp (equivalent to just 11 bp p.a.), half the cost compared to 87 bp up-front (19 bp p.a.) for a vanilla cap struck at a level 4%.

Ratchet Caps

A ratchet cap is one where the strike price increases when interest rates rise. Unlike a step-up cap, however, this is not according to a pre-ordained schedule. Instead, as each caplet expires, the strike price of all the remaining caplets is reset to the greater of:

(a) A spread above the prevailing EURIBOR.

(b) The current strike rate.

For example, suppose the ratchet cap initially had a strike rate of 3%, and a spread of 50 bp. So long as EURIBOR stayed below 3%, the caplets would expire out-of-the-money, and the strike rate would remain at 3%. The first time that EURIBOR sets above 3%, however, the expiring caplet would result in a payment to the owner of the cap, but the strike rates for all the remaining caplets would be reset to 3.5%. The cap would therefore not pay out again until rates rose to this higher level, whereupon the strike rate would be ratcheted up to 4%, and so on.

A ratchet cap therefore provides protection against rapid *rises* in interest rates, rather than interest rates exceeding a particular level.

Barrier Caps

These products include a *knock-out* or *knock-in* feature. In addition to the strike rate, there is a barrier level that, if touched, triggers for:

- A knock-out cap, the extinguishing of the product.
- A knock-in cap, the activation of the product.

This structured derivative is best illustrated by an example. Suppose that, when 6-month EURIBOR was 3%, a borrower purchased a knock-out cap with a strike rate of 5%, and a knock-out rate of 1.75%. This cap would behave normally provided EURIBOR stayed above 1.75%. If, however, EURIBOR traded down to 1.75% or lower, the cap would be permanently knocked out, and would provide no further protection, even if rates subsequently rose above 5%.

The advantage of such a product[3] for the borrower is twofold. First, barrier caps are always cheaper than their vanilla counterparts, because there is always a chance that the cap will not survive, saving the cap seller the cost of future payouts. Second, the event causing the cap to knock out is a benign one—rates have declined—and the borrower can therefore take advantage, perhaps by buying a cheaper cap, or by entering into a swap at the lower rates prevailing.

A knock-in cap works in an analogous way, except that the barrier has to be hit for the cap to be activated. As an example, consider a knock-in version of the 5-year cap struck at 5%, with a knock-in rate of 1.75%. The borrower would pay a reduced premium, but the cap would be ineffective until and unless EURIBOR first fell to 1.75%. Once that happened, the cap would be knocked in, and thereafter would behave

---

[3] Sometimes called a *down-and-out cap*.

like a vanilla cap. However, if rates never sank to that level but rose instead, even beyond the strike rate of 5%, the borrower would receive nothing.

A knock-in cap would therefore be potentially dangerous, because it could leave the borrower unprotected against a possible rise in rates, despite having paid a premium. It would suit a borrower who was sure that rates would first fall, and then rise, and would provide a very low-cost way of obtaining interest rate protection.

Self-Funding Caps

These are an attractive product for the borrower who is required (perhaps by mandate) to obtain protection against higher interest rates, but who doesn't think that such protection is really needed. A self-funding cap has no up-front premium payment. Moreover, if interest rates stay below the strike rate, no premium is payable in arrears, either. Only when rates rise through the strike rate is a premium eventually payable, but this is typically double what the vanilla premium would have been.

Diff or Quanto Caps

These pay if the difference between two interest rates—typically in two different currencies—exceeds a predetermined strike differential. For example, a diff cap might pay out if

6-month US Dollar LIBOR *less* 6-month EURIBOR

exceeded 75bp. Such products are not usually sold in isolation, but are embedded within other structured products.

USING INTEREST RATE OPTIONS

This chapter has so far looked at bond options, STIR options, caps, floors, collars, swaptions, as well as a number of structured products and derivatives, but focusing on the products themselves. In this section we will examine some of the many applications for interest rate options.

Hedging a Bond Portfolio

In the first two examples, we will look at an investor who, on 7 March 2003, is holding €50 million face value of a German government bond paying a 4.5% coupon, maturing on 4 January 2013, priced at 105.69 to yield 3.80%.

EXHIBIT 17.19 Bond Option Prices on 7 March 2003 for June 2003 Euro-BUND Options

Strikes	Calls	Puts
115.00	2.06	0.64
115.50	1.73	0.81
116.00	1.44	1.02
116.50	1.18	1.26
117.00	0.96	1.54
117.50	0.77	1.85
118.00	0.61	2.19

Source: Eurex.

At the time, the June 2003 Euro-BUND future is trading at 116.42, and the cheapest-to-deliver (CTD) bond for the June 2003 futures contract is the 5% bond maturing on 4 January 2012, and having a conversion factor of 0.9341. The PVBP (or DV01) for the CTD bond is 0.0788, while that for the bond actually held is 0.0840. The hedge ratio for the bond portfolio is therefore

$$\frac{50}{0.1} \times 0.9341 \times \frac{0.0840}{0.0788} = 498 \text{ contracts}$$

The investor fears that increased government borrowing will push up long-term interest rates, and wishes to hedge against this eventuality. We will examine two alternative strategies designed to achieve this aim, using the bond option quotations shown in Exhibit 17.19.

Basic Hedging—Buy Put Options

The simplest hedge against a drop in bond prices is to buy put options on the bond. Let's first consider using the June 2003 put option struck at 116.50, which are priced at 1.26, or €627,480 for 498 contracts. Exhibit 17.20 shows the payoff profile for the bond, the put option, and the combination. The kink in the option payoff profile at an option strike price of 116.50 corresponds to a price of around 105.75 in the bond being hedged.

Unhedged, the bond portfolio will lose €500,000 for every 1% fall in the bond price. The ATM put hedges this loss, while allowing the bond portfolio to profit if bond prices rise. However, the up-front cost of €627,480 may seem onerous.

EXHIBIT 17.20   Hedging with ATM Put Options

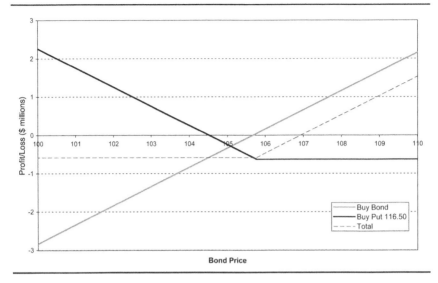

An alternative is to hedge with cheaper OTM puts, for example, the 115 puts priced at only 0.64, costing €318,720—half the price of the ATM options. As the revised payoff diagram of Exhibit 17.21 shows, however, while the investor benefits more when bond prices rise (because the premium wasted is smaller), the maximum loss is greater when bond prices fall. This is because the bond portfolio remains unhedged while bond prices fall 1.42%, until the put strike is reached, losing around €700,000. Together with the premium of around €300,000, the investor could lose more than €1 million, as the chart shows.

Hedging with a Price Collar

A slightly more sophisticated strategy is to combine buying OTM puts with selling OTM calls to create a *collar*. The premium collected from selling the calls can offset, either partially or completely, the premium cost of the puts purchased.

Exhibit 17.22 shows the payoff profile from the combination of:

▨ Buying the 115 puts at 0.64.
▨ Selling the 118 calls at 0.61.

The net premium in this case is negligible, just 0.03, or €14,940 for the 498 contracts needed.

EXHIBIT 17.21   Hedging with OTM Put Options

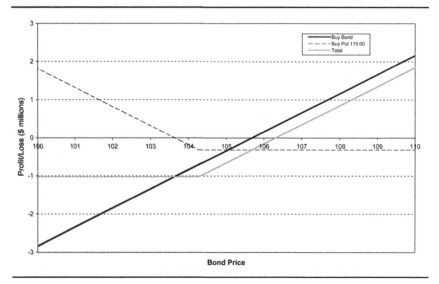

EXHIBIT 17.22   Hedging with a Price Collar

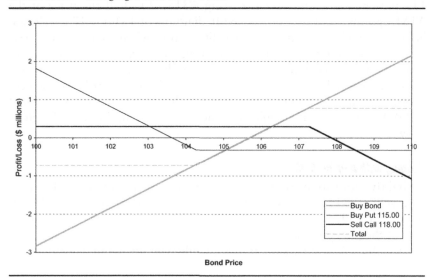

EXHIBIT 17.23   Buying ATM Calls to Speculate

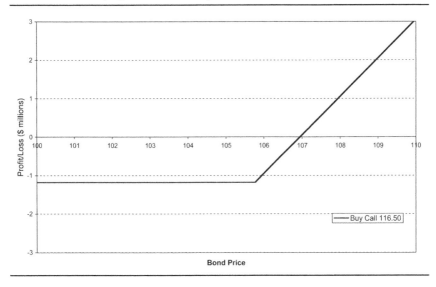

Bond Price

Maximum losses are floored at around €700,000, similar to those with the ATM options, but the up-front premium cost is almost zero, comparing very favourably with the cost of the ATM options in excess of €600,000. If the investor is wrong, and bond prices continue to rise, the investor can still enjoy the benefit of a rise in bond prices of more than 1.50% before the calls sold cap the investor's profits at around €800,000. For many investors in this position, the price collar is an excellent strategy.

Speculating with Bond Options
Bond options can also be used to speculate on anticipated movements in bond prices or volatility. In this section we will explore both possibilities.

Speculating on a Rise in Bond Prices
The simplest way to speculate is simply to buy bond call options. The ATM calls struck at 116.50 are priced at 1.18, so buying these options on a notional bond face value of €100 million would involve buying 996 contracts, and would cost €1.18 million. Exhibit 17.23 illustrates the resulting payoff profile.

If bond prices rise, profits would rise without limit. A 50 bp drop in yields would push the 10-year bund seen earlier up from 105.69 to 110, and the call option strategy would deliver net profits of more than €3 million, as the chart clearly demonstrates.

EXHIBIT 17.24   Creating a Bull Call Spread to Speculate on a Rise in Bond Prices

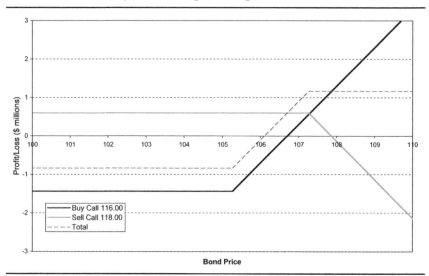

Although this strategy creates the potential for an investor to treble his money for a 50 bp drop in bond yields, the investor would lose everything if bond prices stay the same or fall. An alternative strategy is to create a *bull call spread* by:

- Buying an ATM or ITM call option.
- Selling an OTM call option.

The premium income from the call option sold offsets to some extent the premium cost of the call purchased. Exhibit 17.24 shows the result achieved by:

- Buying the 116.00 strike call at 1.44, costing €1.43 million for 996 contracts.
- Selling the 118.00 strike call at 0.61, bringing in €0.61 million for 996 contracts.

The net cost of this strategy is €0.82 million, which is the maximum amount the investor can lose if he or she is wrong and bond prices fall. If bond prices stay the same, the net loss is only €0.34 million, as the option bought is in-the-money, and will expire with some intrinsic value that will be returned to the investor. If bond prices rise up to 1.50%, the investor can enjoy the benefit until the 118.00 strike is reached and profits are capped at around €1.2 million.

Although the maximum benefits are limited, the cost of the bull call spread pictured here is 30% cheaper than buying the ATM call, so maximum losses are also 30% lower. Moreover, if bond prices remain the same, the net loss of €0.34 million from the bull call spread is less than 30% of the loss realised from the ATM call. Finally, if bond prices rise 1.50%, the bull call spread makes a €1.2 million profit, or almost 150% of the premium invested, while the ATM call only makes a €0.32 million profit, or just 27% of the premium invested.

For these and other reasons, many investors prefer the option spread strategies like the one illustrated here in preference to the simpler strategy of buying calls.

Speculating on an Increase in Volatility

In addition to speculating on bond prices themselves, bond options also allow professional investors to speculate on anticipated changes in *volatility*. Volatility in this context is not necessarily the actual fluctuations in bond prices, but the fluctuations that option traders anticipate will happen in the future, and which are constantly being factored into bond option prices.

The most commonly used volatility strategy is to buy a *straddle*, which involves buying both a call and a put option at the same strike price. At maturity, this will give a V-shaped profile. However, straddles are normally short-term strategies, and are seldom held until maturity. For this reason, it is more relevant to look at the straddle profile in the short-term, well before the maturity of the options. Exhibit 17.25 shows the curved profiles of the straddle components—long a call and long a put option—when the straddle is created. The combination of the two gives the straddle a U-shaped profile at the outset as the chart illustrates.

When volatility rises, it is because option writers are more uncertain about the future, and increase their quotations for option premiums. Buyers of straddles—holding both puts and calls—will therefore benefit, as Exhibit 17.26 shows. Here we chart the payoff profile of the original straddle, and compare this with the profile after volatility has risen by 1%. The gap between these lines is around €400,000—the profit generated by the straddle from a 1% increase in volatility.

Hedging Interest Rate Risk

Let's now turn our attention to look at situations where interest rate options are used to hedge against changes in interest rates. To illustrate this, we will consider the case of a company that is borrowing €10 million at 6-month EURIBOR plus 1% for a 5-year period, with the interest rate reset every six months. The floating rate for the first period has just

EXHIBIT 17.25 Creating a Straddle

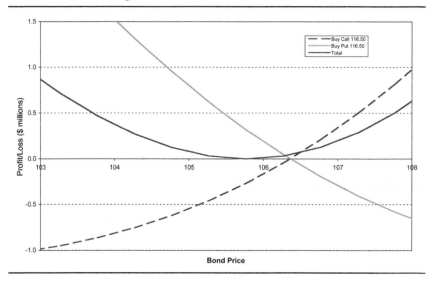

EXHIBIT 17.26 Straddle Payoff Following a 1% Rise in Volatility

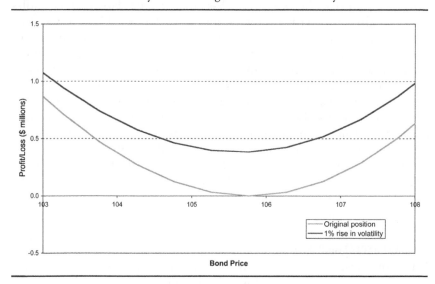

EXHIBIT 17.27 Quotations for 5-Year Cap Premiums

Strike	Cap Premium	Strike	Floor Premium
3.0%	1.63%	2.00%	0.02%
3.5%	0.84%	2.25%	0.10%
4.0%	0.41%	2.50%	0.30%
4.5%	0.19%	2.75%	0.64%

been fixed at 2%, but the company is concerned that interest rates may rise substantially over the next five years, rather more than the market's expectation that, in 4.5-years' time, 6-month rates will reach 4%.

Creating a Zero-Cost Collar

The company obtains the quotations shown in Exhibit 17.27 for 5-year cap and floor premiums, each one expressed as an up-front percentage of the notional principal.

The company chooses the 4% strike cap is being the best compromise between up-front cost and level of protection. It then asks its bank to find the floor strike such that the floor premium is also 41 bp, matching the premium for the 5-year cap. From Exhibit 17.27 it is apparent that the floor strike must lie between 2.50% and 2.75%, and the exact figure turns out to be 2.59%.

By buying the 4% strike cap and selling the 2.59% floor, the company would have a *zero-cost collar*, an interest rate collar structured so that there is no net premium paid.

The payoff profile from this zero-cost collar is shown in Exhibit 17.28, which contrasts the company's borrowing cost when unhedged with the collared rate.

As the chart shows, the company's unhedged cost is simply 1% over EURIBOR, reflecting the company's 1% credit margin. With the collar in place, the company's borrowing costs are unaffected when EURIBOR resets in-between the strike rates of 2.59% and 4%. This is because the collar has a zero cost, and neither the cap nor the floor are exercised when EURIBOR stays within this range. If, however, EURIBOR exceeds 4%, the cap compensates the company for the excess interest paid, capping the effective cost at 5%. Similarly, if EURIBOR fixes below 2.59%, the company's borrowing costs are floored at 3.59%.

Although the 2.59% floor may be slightly above the prevailing EURIBOR rate of 2% at the outset, the company may be quite prepared to hedge at this level, expecting as it does that rates will rise substantially.

EXHIBIT 17.28   Effective Borrowing Cost for Zero-Cost Collar

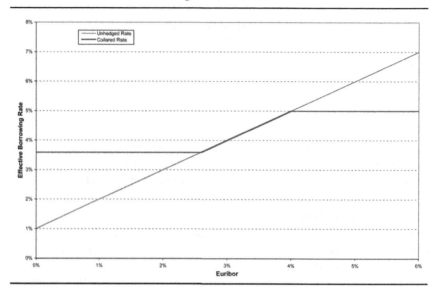

Creating a Participating Cap

Many option packages—like the zero-cost collar just describe—involve customers buying interest rate options to hedge an adverse market exposure, and then selling other options to offset or eliminate the cost.

As an alternative to the zero-cost collar, some borrowers prefer a *participating cap*. This involves the company:

- Buying a cap to hedge against rates higher than the strike rate
- Selling a floor *at the same strike rate* but for a lower notional principal, to match the cap premium exactly.

To illustrate this, suppose that the company now wants to cap its borrowing costs at 3.5%. From Exhibit 17.27 we can see that the up-front premium for a 5-year cap struck at 3.5% is 84 bp. A floor struck at the same rate would be priced at 2.40%, almost three times as expensive.

Given these quotations, suppose the company:

- Buys a 5-year cap struck at 3.5% on €10 million, priced at 84 bp, therefore paying an up-front premium of €84,000.
- Sells a 5-year floor struck at 3.5% on only €3.5 million, priced at 240 bp, therefore receiving an up-front payment of €84,000.

EXHIBIT 17.29   Effective Borrowing Cost for Participating Cap

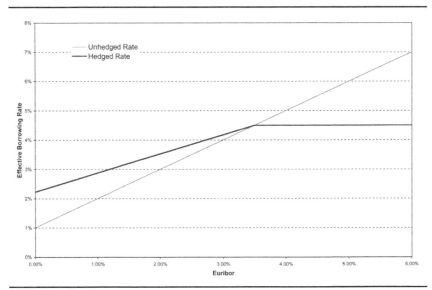

The net premium for this structure would therefore be zero, just like that of the zero-cost collar. This is a participating cap, and the payoff profile is illustrated in Exhibit 17.29.

If EURIBOR sets above the strike rate of 3.5%, the cap purchased by the company limits the effective borrowing cost to 4.5%, 1% above the cap strike, while the floor for that period expires out-of-the-money. The company's maximum borrowing rate is therefore capped, in the same way as with a zero-cost collar.

If EURIBOR sets below 3.5%, however, the story is a little different. The floor which the company has sold will be exercised, forcing the company to borrow at 1% above the floor rate of 3.5%, or 4.5%. However, this rate will only apply to the €3.5 million principal covered by the floor. The remaining €6.5 million can be financed at the company's usual 1% margin above prevailing rates. If EURIBOR sets at 2%, for example, the company's effective borrowing cost will be 3.53%, comprising the weighted average of:

▧ €3.5 million borrowed at 4.5%.
▧ €6.5 million borrowed at 3.0%.

The company is therefore protected against EURIBOR rising above 3.5%, and can also participate in 65% of the benefit from EURIBOR lower than 3.5%. When EURIBOR fixes at 2%, as in the above example, the company can save 65% of the 150 bp interest saving, shaving 97 bp off the 3.5% rate to give an effective EURIBOR of 2.53%, and an all-in borrowing cost of 3.53% with the company's margin, as we have just seen. This ability to participate from a beneficial movement in rates is why this structure is called a participating cap.

Zero-cost collars and participating caps are both attractive hedges against higher interest rates. Both are zero-cost products, providing companies with "free" protection against higher interest rates. The zero-cost collar allows the company to benefit fully from interest rates lower than the cap rate, until the floor is reached, beyond which there are no more savings. The participating cap allows the company to participate in part of the savings from rates lower than the cap rate, but this saving is without a lower limit; the lower rates go, the more the borrower can save.

Creating a Cancellable Swap

Suppose an investor has purchased a 5-year note paying 6-month EUR-IBOR plus 50 bp, with 6-month EURIBOR initially set at 2%. Interest rates are currently very low, so the investor is thinking about using a 5-year swap to boost the return. With 5-year swaps quoted at 3%, against EURIBOR flat, the investor could switch from 6-month EURIBOR plus 50 bp to an effective yield of 3.5%, enjoying an immediate 100 bp improvement in yield. This structure is pictured in Exhibit 17.30.

The only problem with this strategy is that the investor cannot gain from any subsequent increase in EURIBOR. The swap freezes the yield to 3.5% for five years, regardless of what happens to EURIBOR in the future.

One answer to this problem is for the investor to use a cancellable swap instead of a vanilla swap. Suppose that the investor is interested in a 5-year swap, cancellable by the investor after three years. This can be structured by combining:

- A vanilla 5-year swap where the investor receives fixed and pays floating.
- A 3-year European-style payer's swaption into a 2-year swap, struck at the fixed rate of the vanilla swap.

EXHIBIT 17.30   FRN with Vanilla 5-Year Swap

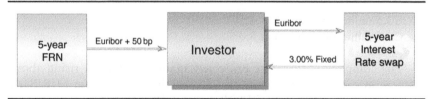

EXHIBIT 17.31   Creating a Cancellable Swap—Stage 1

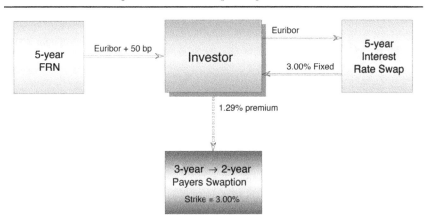

If 2-year rates rise sufficiently in 3-years' time, the swaption will expire in-the-money, and the investor can exercise the payer's swaption, entering into a second swap as the fixed-rate payer at exactly the same rate as the original swap, for which the investor is the fixed-rate receiver. This second swap exactly offsets the first swap, effectively cancelling the original swap for the last two years of its life.

This arrangement could be structured as in Exhibit 17.31. This shows the vanilla 5-year swap coupled with the payer's swaption. Unfortunately, the need for the investor to make an up-front payment of 1.29% to acquire the payer's swaption makes the arrangement somewhat untidy.

A neat way round this problem is to reduce the fixed rate of the swap below the market's fair rate of 3.00%, and have the swap counterparty make an up-front payment to the investor to restore parity. Reducing the swap rate also means that the strike rate of the payer's swaption must also be reduced in line, which increases the up-front premium payable.

Using trial-and-error, we can find the correct fixed rate for the off-market swap such that the up-front payment from the swap counterparty exactly matches the up-front payment to the swaption writer. In this example, this works out as 2.60%, as shown in Exhibit 17.32.

The combination of the below-market swap and the payer's swaption therefore creates a cancellable swap. From the investor's viewpoint, he or she can now compare:

- A vanilla swap paying 3.00% fixed for five years.
- A cancellable swap paying 2.60% fixed for five years, but giving the investor the "free" right to cancel the swap after three years if he or she chooses.

EXHIBIT 17.32   Creating a Cancellable Swap—Stage 2

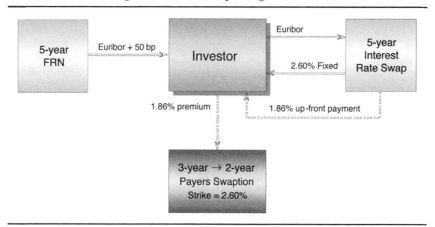

If 2-year swap rates are higher than 2.60% in three years time, the investor would cancel the original swap, and either enter into another swap at a better rate, or enjoy the higher floating rate from the FRN.

Using a Structured Product

Suppose that another investor believes that European interest rates over the next year are likely to remain relatively stable, and wishes to take advantage of this view. He or she suggests this view to an investment bank, which creates the following 1-year structured product:

- If daily fixings of 3-month EURIBOR over the next year stay in the range 2.00% to 3.50%, the investor will receive an enhanced yield of 6.75% p.a. on a structured note, this coupon being paid as a single annual payment on the maturity of the note. This compares well with the 4.50% one year rate currently available on vanilla notes of similar credit quality.
- If on any day over the next year 3-month EURIBOR fixes below 2.00% or above 3.50%, the investor will receive no coupon at maturity, just the return of principal.

Such a structured note can be created by combining:

- A vanilla 1-year note paying a fixed rate of 4.50%.
- Selling a *double no touch* (DNT) digital option.

This structure is pictured in Exhibit 17.33.

EXHIBIT 17.33   Creating a Digital Knock-Out Note

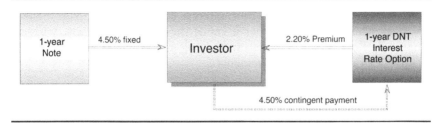

A DNT option is a *path-dependent digital option*. The digital charac-teristic means that payment at maturity is not dependent on how much the option is in-the-money; instead, the payout, if made, is fixed at the outset. The path-dependent characteristic means that market rates throughout the lifetime of the option are monitored, not just on the matu-rity date. If, at any time, the underlying market rate "touches" (trades at or through) the barrier levels, this triggers the payout at maturity.

In the example the DNT is structured with:

- Barriers at 3-month EURIBOR rates of 2.00% and 3.50%.
- An initial up-front premium of 2.20%. With interest, this is equivalent to 2.25% at the expiry of the option at the end of the year.
- A payout at maturity of 6.75% if either (or both) the barriers are touched during the year.

If 3-month EURIBOR stays within range, as the investor expects, he or she will keep the premium from the DNT option, which is equivalent to 2.25% of the notional principal. Together with the 4.50% income from the vanilla note, the investor receives the enhanced yield of 6.75%.

If, on the other hand, 3-month EURIBOR trades outside the range—even on a single day—this will trigger the payout from the DNT option. The investor will then have to pay out 6.75% of the notional principal, which exactly wipes out the income from the vanilla bond plus the option, leaving him with zero income, but the principal intact.

In practice, the investment bank creating this structured note would offer the vanilla note and DNT option together as a complete package. All the investor would see is the coupon at maturity of either 6.75% or 0%, depending upon what 3-month EURIBOR did during the year, rather than being concerned with the separate components.

SUMMARY

In this chapter we have seen how interest rate options provide banks, investors, companies, and other users of the financial markets, with an immensely flexible set of tools for hedging against or taking advantage of European interest rate movements.

CHAPTER 18

Pricing Options on Interest Rate Instruments

Brian A. Eales
Principal Lecturer
London Metropolitan University

Radu Tunaru, Ph.D.
Senior Lecturer
London Metropolitan University

This chapter briefly describes the range of interest rate and bond options available on two of the major European derivative exchanges. It then moves on to establish a framework for option pricing by presenting some important theoretical models of the term structure of interest rates. The chapter then focuses on bond option pricing and discusses some of the main pricing theories, highlighting their assumptions and weaknesses. Some illustrative numerical examples are included in the text at appropriate junctures.

DERIVATIVE EXCHANGE-BASED OPTIONS

The two major European derivatives exchanges, Euronext-LIFFE and their German-Swiss competitors Eurex, offer options on interest rate futures that cover a wide spectrum of maturities. Eurex and Euronext-LIFFE both offer options on their money market futures, 3-month EURI-BOR contracts. Contracts which have the European Interbank Offered

Rate for 3-month time deposits as their underlying instrument. Euronext-LIFFE also has options on 3-month sterling LIBOR and 3-month Euro-Swiss futures contracts at the short end of the maturity curve.

There are also several important government bond option contracts on offer through Euronext-LIFFE and Eurex. The most important of these is the option contract offered by Eurex on the Euro-Bund Future. As an example of its popularity on 2 May 2003, there were 114,827 trades in calls and puts on the Euro-Bund Future across the spectrum of June, July, August, and September expiration months. The bulk of this volume was in respect of the nearby June contract with over 44,000 calls and over 50,000 puts being transacted. There are, however, other exchange-based contracts available. Eurex covers the 1.75- to 2.25-year maturity with its Euro-Schatz contract and the 4.5- to 5.5-year maturity with its Euro-Bobl. While Euronext-LIFFE offers its own version of the Euro-Bund futures option and also an option contract on the UK government bond future.[1] Exhibit 18.1 gives an example of a typical contract specification as presented by Bloomberg.

EXHIBIT 18.1   Euro-Bund Option Contract Specification

```
GRAB                                                         Comdty OTD
            Option Ticker Description          Page 2/2
       Sample Option              Underlying Security      Strikes
Ticker   RXM3C   115.00 <CMDTY>  Ticker   RXM3   <CMDTY>     111.00
Name     Call on RXM3            Name     Call on RXM3       111.50
Price    .49                     Price    114.80             112.00
Contract on 1 RXM3 Future       Contract Size EUR 100,000    112.50
Market Value   € 490.00         Contract Value € 114,800.00  113.00
First Trade  Mon Nov 25, 2002   First Delivery Tue Jun 10, 2003  113.50
Last Trade   Fri May 23, 2003   Last Trade   Fri Jun 6, 2003  114.00
Expiration   Fri May 23, 2003   Last Delivery Tue Jun 10, 2003  114.50
Exercise Type  AMERICAN                                      115.00
Cycle  --- --- Mar --- --- Jun --- --- Sep --- --- Dec + serial  115.50
Exchange Data (EUX) Eurex Deutschland (was DTB)   Volatility  116.00
Frankfurt     08:00-19:00                         Analysis    116.50
Frankfurt     08:00-19:00                                     117.00
                 Option         Future      Historical Volatility  117.50
Value of 1 pt   € 1,000        € 1,000     30 Day HVT   6.74   118.00
Tick Size        .01            .01        60 Day HVT   6.49
Tick Value      € 10           € 10        90 Day HVT   6.01

                                            Implied      5.19
            Related Functions               Delta      0.44852
1)OMON Option Bid/Ask Monitor 2)HIVG Implied Vol Graph 3)GIP Intraday Price Chart  Gamma  0.26911
4)GPO Daily Bar Chart  5)OV Option Valuation
Australia 61 2 9777 8600    Brazil 5511 3048 4500    Europe 44 20 7330 7500    Germany 49 69 920410
Hong Kong 852 2977 6000 Japan 81 3 3201 8900 Singapore 65 6212 1000 U.S. 1 212 318 2000 Copyright 2003 Bloomberg L.P.
                                                                    G700-32-0 01-May-03 14:24:50
```

Source: Bloomberg Financial Markets with permission.

---

[1] These futures contracts are described in Chapter 16.

The content of the Bloomberg page provides information on the underlying security in the form of a Ticker (RXM3), the current price of a sample call option (0.49 = 49 ticks), the market value of the option on one Euro-Bund contract €490 (49 ticks multiplied by €10), the current quote for the underlying future (114.80) information on trading dates for both the option and the underlying future, and style of exercise (American). A similar layout structure is used for other options on government bond futures.

Although the sample option price is easy to read and interpret in respect of this screen, there is a mass of academic and practitioner research literature that provides a platform from which bond option prices in general can be calculated with integrity. The literature on modelling interest rate derivatives in this arena is frequently divided into one-, two-factor, or multifactor, models.

When calculating option prices in a one-factor model, a frequently made assumption is that the process is driven by the short rate often with a mean reversion feature linked to the short rate. There are several popular models which fall into this category, for example, the Vasicek model,[2] and the Cox, Ingersoll, and Ross model[3] both of which will be discussed in more detail later. Calculating option prices in a two-factor model involves both the short- and long-term rates linked by a mean reversion process.

The problem with some of the models just discussed is that they generate their own term structures that, in the absence of adjustment, do not match the term structure observed in the market. A category of arbitrage-free models proposed by Ho and Lee,[4] Hull and White,[5] and Black, Derman, and Toy[6] seek to eliminate this problem. For example, the Black, Derman and Toy model enjoys a degree of popularity among market practitioners because (1) it takes account of and matches the term structure observed in the market, (2) it eliminates the possibility of

---

[2] Oldrich Vasicek, "An Equilibrium Characterization of the Term Structure," *Journal of Financial Economics*, 5 (1977), pp. 177–188.

[3] John C. Cox, Jonathan E. Ingersoll, and Stephen A. Ross, "An Analysis of Variable Rate Loan Contracts," *Journal of Finance* (1980), pp. 389–403; and John C. Cox, Jonathan E. Ingersoll, and Stephen A. Ross, "A Theory of the Term Structure of Interest Rates," *Econometrica* no. 2 (1985), pp. 385–407.

[4] Thomas Ho and San Bing Lee, "Term Structure Movements and Pricing Interest Rates Contingent Claims," *Journal of Finance* 41 (1986), pp. 1011–1029.

[5] John C. Hull and Alan White, "Pricing Interest Rate Derivative Securities," *Review of Financial Studies* 3, no. 5 (1990), pp. 573–592.

[6] Fisher Black, Emmanuel Derman, and William Toy, "A One-Factor Model of Interest Rate and its Application to Treasury Bond Options," *Financial Analysts Journal* (1990), pp. 33–39.

generating negative interest rates; and (3) it models the observed interest rate volatility. These models together with other propositions will be discussed in more detail below.

In order to examine some of the major developments in option/derivative pricing in the interest rate field it is appropriate at this point to establish a working framework.

MODELLING THE TERM STRUCTURE AND BOND PRICES

Let $(\Omega, \Sigma, \{F_t\}_{t \geq 0}, Q)$ be a filtered probability space modelling a financial market, where the filtration $F = \{F_t\}_{t \geq 0}$ describes the flux of information and the probability measure Q denotes the risk-neutral measure. The starting point in modelling bond prices is the assumption that there is a bank account $B = \{B(t)\}_{t \geq 0}$ that is linked to the bank instantaneous interest rate (also called *shortrate spot rate*) process $r = \{r(t)\}_{t \geq 0}$ through

$$dB(t) = r(t)B(t)dt$$
$$\text{or}$$
$$B(t) = B(0)\exp\left[\int_0^t r(s)ds\right] \tag{18.1}$$

From a practical point of view, we can safely assume that the majority of stochastic processes representing prices of traded financial assets are adapted to the filtration F and that the short rate process $r = \{r(t)\}_{t \geq 0}$ is a predictable process, meaning that $r(t)$ is F_{t-1} measurable. This implies that $B(t)$ is also F_{t-1} measurable and this condition is automatically satisfied for continuous or left-continuous processes.

In this chapter we consider only default-free securities. We use interchangeably the notation $E_t(\cdot) \equiv E^Q(\cdot | F_t)$. We shall denote by $p(t,T)$ the price at time t of a pure discount bond with maturity T and obviously $p(t,t) = p(T,T) = 1$.

The following relationships are well-known in the fixed income area

$$0 < p(t, T) \leq 1,$$
$$r(t) = \left.\frac{\partial \ln p(t, T)}{\partial t}\right|_{T = t} = -\left.\frac{\partial \ln p(t, T)}{\partial T}\right|_{T = t} \tag{18.2}$$
$$\text{for any } t < T$$

Let $f(t,s)$ be the forward rate at time $s > 0$ calculated at time $t < s$. The instantaneous forward rate at time t to borrow at time T can be calculated from the bond prices using

$$f(t, T) = -\frac{\partial \ln p(t, T)}{\partial T} \tag{18.3}$$

The reverse works as well: if forward rates are known then bond prices can be calculated via

$$p(t, T) = e^{-\int_t^T f(t, s)\,ds}$$

The short rate is intrinsically related to the forward rates because $r(t) \equiv f(t,t)$.

Short Rate Models

Many models proposed for the short rate process $r = \{r(t)\}_{t \geq 0}$ are particular cases of the general diffusion equation

$$dr(t) = a[t, r(t)]dt + b[t, r(t)]dW(t) \tag{18.4}$$

where $W = \{W(t)\}_{t \geq 0}$ is a standard Wiener process defined on $(\Omega, \Sigma, \{F_t\}_{t \geq 0}, Q)$. The following list of models describes a chronological evolution without claiming that it is an exhaustive list.

The Merton model is[7]

$$dr(t) = \alpha r(t) + \sigma dW(t) \tag{18.5}$$

The Vasicek model is

$$dr(t) = [\alpha - \beta r(t)]dt + \sigma dW(t) \tag{18.6}$$

One advantage of this model is that the conditional distribution of r at any future time, given the current interest rates at time t, is normally distributed. The main moments are

---

[7] Robert C. Merton, "Theory of Rational Option Pricing," *Bell Journal of Economics and Management Science*, no. 4 (Spring 1973), pp. 141–183.

$$E_t[r(s)] = \frac{\alpha}{\beta} + \left[r(t) - \frac{\alpha}{\beta}\right]e^{-\beta(s-t)}, t \leq s$$

$$\text{var}_t[r(s)] = \frac{\sigma^2}{2\beta}[1 - e^{-2\beta(s-t)}], t \leq s \tag{18.7}$$

$$\text{cov}_t[r(u), r(s)] = \frac{\sigma^2}{2\beta}e^{-\beta(s+u-2t)}(e^{2\beta(u-t)} - 1), t \leq u \leq s$$

Another advantage is that this model can be also derived within a general equilibrium framework as illustrated by Campbell.[8]

One disadvantage that is often discussed in the interest rate modelling literature is that there is a long-run possibility of negative interest rates. However, Rabinovitch[9] proved that when the initial interest rate $r(0)$ is positive and the parameter estimates have reasonable values, the expected first-passage time of the process through the origin is longer than nine months. This result supports the use of Vasicek model in practice since the majority of options traded on the organized exchanges expire in less than nine months.

The Dothan model is[10]

$$dr(t) = \alpha r(t)dt + \sigma r(t)dW(t) \tag{18.8}$$

This is the same model as that proposed by Rendleman and Bartter.[11] This model is the only log-normal, single-factor model that leads to closed formulae for pure discount bonds. Nonetheless there is no closed formula for a European option on a pure discount bond.

The Cox-Ingersoll-Ross (CIR) models are

$$dr(t) = \beta[r(t)]^{3/2}dW(t)$$
$$dr(t) = [\alpha - \beta r(t)]dt + \sigma[r(t)]^{1/2}dW(t) \tag{18.9}$$

CIR wrote arguably the first of several papers developing one-factor models of the term structure of interest rates. Other papers which were

---

[8] John Campbell, "A Defence of Traditional Hypotheses about the Term Structure of Interest Rates," *Journal of Finance* (March 1986), pp. 183–194.

[9] Ramon Rabinovitch, "Pricing Stock and Bond Options when the Default-Free Rate is Stochastic," *Journal of Financial and Quantitative Analysis* 24, no. 4 (1989), pp. 447–457.

[10] Michael U. Dothan, "On the Term Structure of Interest Rates," *Journal of Financial Economics* 6 (1978), pp. 59–69.

[11] Richard J. Rendleman and Brit J. Bartter, "The Pricing of Options on Debt Securities," *Journal of Financial and Quantitative Analysis* 15 (1980), pp. 11–24.

published around the same time and which propose models in the same spirit as CIR include Vasicek, Dothan, Courtadon[12] and Brennan and Schwartz.[13] The movements of longer maturity instruments are perfectly correlated with the instantaneous short-term rates.

The Ho-Lee model is

$$dr(t) = \alpha(t)dt + \sigma dW(t) \tag{18.10}$$

This is the continuous version of the original model that was probably the first model designed to match exactly the observable term structure of interest rates.

The Black-Derman-Toy (BDT) model is

$$dr(t) = \alpha(t)r(t)dt + \sigma(t)dW(t) \tag{18.11}$$

The Hull-White (HW) models are[14]

$$
\begin{aligned}
dr(t) &= [\alpha(t) - \beta(t)r(t)]dt + \sigma(t)dW(t) \\
dr(t) &= [\alpha(t) - \beta(t)r(t)]dt + \sigma(t)[r(t)]^{1/2}dW(t)
\end{aligned} \tag{18.12}
$$

These models are two more general families of models incorporating Vasicek model and CIR model, respectively. The first one is used more often as it can be calibrated to the observable term structure of interest rates and the volatility term structure of spot or forward rates. However, its implied volatility structures may be unrealistic. Hence, it may be wise to use a constant coefficient $\beta(t) = \beta$ and a constant volatility parameter $\sigma(t) = \sigma$ and then calibrate the model using only the term structure of market interest rates. It is still theoretically possible that the short rate r may go negative. The risk-neutral probability for the occurrence of such an event is

$$Q[r(t) < 0] = N\left(-\frac{\tilde{f}(0, t) + \dfrac{\sigma^2}{2\beta^2}(1 - e^{\beta t})^2}{\sqrt{\dfrac{\sigma^2}{2\beta^2}(1 - e^{2\beta t})}} \right) \tag{18.13}$$

---

[12] George Courtadon, "The Pricing of Default-Free Bonds," *Journal of Financial and Quantitative Analysis* 17 (March 1982), pp. 75–100.
[13] Michael J. Brennan and Eduardo Schwartz, "A Continuous Time Approach to the Pricing of Bonds," *Journal of Banking and Finance* 3 (1979), pp. 133–155.
[14] Hull and White, "Pricing Interest Rate Derivative Securities."

where $\tilde{f}(0, t)$ is the market instantaneous forward rate. In practice this probability seems to be rather small as empirical evidence illustrated by Brigo and Mercurio[15] shows. However, the probability is not zero and this may bother some analysts.

An example will provide an idea of how a variation of one of the models proposed by Hull and White described above by the first of equation (18.12) models can be used to price an option on a zero-coupon bond. If the assumptions are made that both β, the reversion rate, and σ, the volatility, are constant then the model can be restated as

$$dr(t) = [\alpha(t) - \beta r(t)]dt + \sigma dW(t) \tag{18.14}$$

and the function $\alpha(t)$ can be calculated from a given term structure using

$$\alpha(t) = f_t(0, t) + \beta f F(0, t) + \frac{\sigma^2}{2\beta}(1 - e^{-2\beta t}) \tag{18.15}$$

The future market price of a zero-coupon bond in this framework can be found by defining the reversion rate, β, the volatility, and the time period involved.

$$p(T_0, T) = A(T_0, T)e^{-B(T_0, T)r(T)} \tag{18.16}$$

where T_0 represents the forward date at which the bond is to be priced, T represents the bond's maturity date, t is a time period index typically taken to be equal to zero (i.e. representing the current point in time)

$$B(T_0, T) = \frac{1}{\beta}(1 - e^{-\beta(T - T_0)}) \tag{18.17}$$

$$\ln A(T_0, T) = \ln\left[\frac{p(t, T)}{p(t, T_0)}\right] - B(T_0, T)\frac{\partial \ln p(t, T_0)}{\partial T} -$$
$$- \frac{1}{4\beta^3}\sigma^2(e^{-\beta(T-t)} - e^{-\beta(T_0-t)})^2(e^{2\beta(T_0-t)} - 1) \tag{18.18}$$

and $r(T)$ is the prevailing short rate at the forward date.

[15] Damiano Brigo and Fabio Mercurio, *Interest Rate Models: Theory and Practice* (Berlin: Springer, 2001).

To illustrate how this works, consider the case where we wish to find the 1-year forward price of a bond with four years remaining to maturity. Assume that the yield curve offers 4.00% continuously compounded for all maturities, volatility is 2.00%, and the reversion rate is 0.1. In this example T is 4 and T_0 is 1. The price of the bond can be found using $p(1,4) = A(1,4)e^{-B(1,4)(0.04)}$. Clearly $A(1,4)$ and $B(1,4)$ must be evaluated. Starting with $B(1,4)$ we have

$$B(1, 4) = \frac{1}{0.1}[1 - e^{-0.1(4-1)}] = 2.5918$$

The next step requires the evaluation of $A(1,4)$ and the expression for $\ln A(1,4)$ can be broken down into a series of relatively straightforward calculations:

$$\ln\left[\frac{p(t, T)}{p(t, T_0)}\right] = \ln\left[\frac{p(0, 4)}{p(0, 1)}\right] = \ln\left[\frac{e^{-(4)(0.04)}}{e^{-(1)(0.04)}}\right] = \ln\left[\frac{0.8521}{0.9607}\right] = -0.12$$

$B(1, 4)$ has already been calculate and is equal to 2.5918. Moreover,

$$\frac{\partial \ln p(t, T_0)}{\partial T_0}$$

can be approximated by

$$\frac{\ln p(t, T_0 + \Delta t) - \ln p(t, T_0 - \Delta t)}{2\Delta t}$$

which, if a time interval, Δt, is assumed to be 0.1 years, yields

$$\frac{\ln p(0, 1 + 0.1) - \ln p(0, 1 - 0.1)}{2(0.1)} = -0.04$$

This leaves the expression

$$\frac{1}{4\beta^3}\sigma^2[e^{-\beta(T-t)}-e^{-\beta(T_0-t)}]^2[e^{2\beta(T_0-t)}-1]$$

$$=\frac{1}{4(0.1)^3}0.02^2[e^{-(0.1)(4)}-e^{-(0.1)(1)}]^2[e^{2(0.1)(1)}-1]=0.001217$$

Combining all the above calculations we find $\ln A(1,4)=-0.01754$ and then the 1-year forward bond price is $p(1,4)=e^{-0.01754...}e^{-2.5918...(0.04)}$ $=0.8854$ or 88.54%.

The Black-Karasinski (BK) model is[16]

$$dr(t)=r(t)[\alpha(t)-\beta(t)\ln r(t)]dt+\sigma(t)r(t)dW(t) \qquad (18.19)$$

BDT, HW, and BK models extended the Ho-Lee model to match a term structure volatility curve (for example the cap prices) *in addition* to the term structure. The BK model is a generalization of the BDT model and it overcomes the problem of negative interest rates assuming that the short rate r is the exponential of an Ornstein-Uhlenbeck process having time-dependent coefficients. It is popular with practitioners because it fits the swaption volatility surface well. Nevertheless, it does not have closed formulae for bonds or options on bonds.

The Sandmann-Sondermann model is[17]

$$r(t)=\ln(1+\eta(t))$$
$$d\eta(t)=\eta(t)[\alpha(t)dt+\sigma(t)dW(t)] \qquad (18.20)$$

Dothan model, Black-Karasinski model, and the Exponential Vasicek model given below imply that r is log-normally distributed. While this finding may seem reasonable it is the cause for the explosion of the bank account, that is from a single unit of money one may be able to make, in an infinitesimal interval of time, and infinite amount of money. Sandmann and Sondermann model overcomes this problem by modelling the short rates as above.

The Chen model is[18]

---

[16] Fisher Black and Piotr Karasinski, "Bond and Option Pricing When Short Rates Are Lognormal," *Financial Analysts Journal* (May-June 1991), pp. 52–59.

[17] Klaus Sandmann and Dieter Sondermann, "A Term Structure Model and the Pricing of Interest Rate Derivatives," *Review of Futures Markets* 12, no. 2 (1993), pp. 391–423.

[18] Lin Chen, *A Three-Factor Model of the Term Structure of Interest Rates*, preprint (Washington: Federal Reserve Board, July 1995).

$$dr(t) = [\alpha(t) - r(t)]dt + [\sigma(t)r(t)]^{1/2}dW^1(t)$$
$$d\alpha(t) = [\alpha - \alpha(t)]dt + [\alpha(t)]^{1/2}dW^2(t) \qquad (18.21)$$
$$d\sigma(t) = [\gamma - \sigma(t)]dt + [\sigma(t)]^{1/2}dW^3(t)$$

where α and γ are constants and W^1, W^2, and W^3 are independent Wiener processes. This is an example of a three-factor model.

The Schmidt model is[19]

$$r(t) = H[f(t) + g(t)W(T(t))] \qquad (18.22)$$

where $T = T(t)$ and $H = H(x)$ are continuous nonnegative strictly increasing functions of $t \geq 0$ and real x, while $f = f(t)$ and $g = g(t) > 0$ are continuous functions.

The Exponential Vasicek model (Brigo and Mercurio) is

$$dr(t) = r(t)[\eta - a\ \ln r(t)]dt + \sigma r(t)dW(t) \qquad (18.23)$$

This model is similar to Dothan model being a log-normal short rate model. This model, however, does not lead to explicit formulae for pure discount bonds or for options contingent on them. In addition this is an example of a non-affine term-structure model.

The Mercurio-Moraleda model is[20]

$$dr(t) = r(t)\left[\eta(t) - \left(\lambda - \frac{\gamma}{1 + \gamma t}\right)\ln r(t)\right]dt + \sigma r(t)dW(t) \qquad (18.24)$$

The CIR++ model (Brigo and Mercurio) is

$$r(t) = x(t) + \varphi(t)$$
$$dx(t) = k[\theta - x(t)]dt + \sigma\sqrt{x(t)}dW(t) \qquad (18.25)$$

The Extended Exponential Vasicek model (Brigo and Mercurio) is

$$r(t) = x(t) + \varphi(t)$$
$$dx(t) = x(t)[\eta - \lambda\ln x(t)]dt + \sigma x(t)dW(t) \qquad (18.26)$$

[19] Wolfgang M. Schmidt, "On a General Class of One-Factor Models for the Term Structure of Interest Rates," *Finance and Stochastics* 1 (1997), pp. 3–24.
[20] Fabio Mercurio and Juan M. Moraleda, "An Analytically Tractable Interest Rate Model with Humped Volatility," *European Journal of Operational Research* 120 (2000), pp. 205–214.

EXHIBIT 18.2 Market Spot and Forward Rates

Time (months)	Spot Rates	Forward Rates
6	4.000	4.000
12	4.126	4.253
18	4.254	4.508
24	4.382	4.767
30	4.511	5.031
36	4.642	5.298

Two-factor models were based on a second source of random shocks. Two factor models were developed by Brennan and Schwartz,[21] Fong and Vasicek,[22] and Longstaff and Schwartz.[23] However, Hogan[24] proved that the solution to the Brennan and Schwartz model explodes, that is reaches infinity in a finite amount of time with positive probability. The Brennan and Schwartz model shows that adding more factors may cause unseen problems. More complex multifactor models are described by Rebonato, and by Brigo and Mercurio.

Modelling in Practice

One popular way of turning theory into practice is to use a "tree" approach to modelling. The tree can be either binomial or trinomial in its construction. To illustrate the idea consider first the binomial approach. The tree could be set up to reflect observed or estimated market short rates and the data provided in Exhibit 18.2 will help to demonstrate this idea.

The process starts from the first 6-month period where the rate is known to be 4.000%. At the end of the 6-month period the following 6-month forward rates are treated as being the short rates and are split

---

[21] Michael J. Brennan and Eduardo Schwartz, "An Equilibrium Model of Bond Prices and a Test of Market Efficiency," *Journal of Financial and Quantitative Analysis* 17 (1982), pp. 301–329.

[22] H. Gifford Fong and Oldrich A. Vasicek, Interest Rate Volatility and a Stochastic Factor, Gifford Fong Associates, working paper (1992).

[23] Francis A. Longstaff and Eduardo Schwartz, "Interest Rate Volatility and the Term Structure: A Two-Factor General Equilibrium Model," *Journal of Finance* 47 (1992), pp. 1259–1282; and Fletcher A. Longstaff and Eduardo Schwartz, "A Two-Factor Interest Rate Model and Contingent Claim Valuation," *Journal of Fixed Income* 3 (1992), pp. 16–23.

[24] Michael Hogan, "Problems in Certain Two-Factor Term Structure Models," *The Annals of Applied Probability* 3, no. 2 (1993), pp. 576–581.

EXHIBIT 18.3   Term Structure Evolution: Binomial Tree

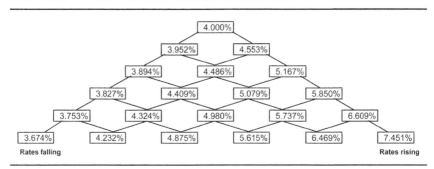

allowing interest rates to rise with a probability of 0.5 or fall with a probability of 0.5 but also taking into account the short rate volatility.[25] Exhibit 18.3 shows how the rates would appear in a binomial tree once the procedure has been performed.

When the rates have been established they must then be calibrated. The calibration procedure is achieved using the observed market price of a bullet government bond and pricing the bond using the "tree" calculated rates to obtain the appropriate discount factors. As an example, consider a government bond trading at par and offering a coupon of 4.625% paid semi-annually. On maturity the bond will be redeemed for 102.3125, which is made up of the bond's face value, say 100, and one half of the annual coupon, 2.3125.

Exhibit 18.4 illustrates how, moving back through the tree, the discounting process of the terminal payment taken together with the discounted interim coupons generate a bond price of 100.009. Given that the observed bond price is 100, the rates in the tree will need to be adjusted to ensure that the backward calculated price agrees with the market price of the bond. In this example the adjustment factor is 0.4 basis points and this will be added to every node in the tree with the exception of the starting value. The resulting rates will then be as displayed in Exhibit 18.5.

The calibrated tree can now be used to calculate corporate bond spreads as well as bond options. The outlined procedure is close to that advanced by Black, Derman, and Toy in that the process fits observed market rates and short rate volatility. There is, however, a danger that interest rates could go negative in this procedure.

---

[25] For a description of how this is achieved see Brian A. Eales, *Financial Engineering* (Basingstoke: Palgrave, 2000).

EXHIBIT 18.4 Calibration

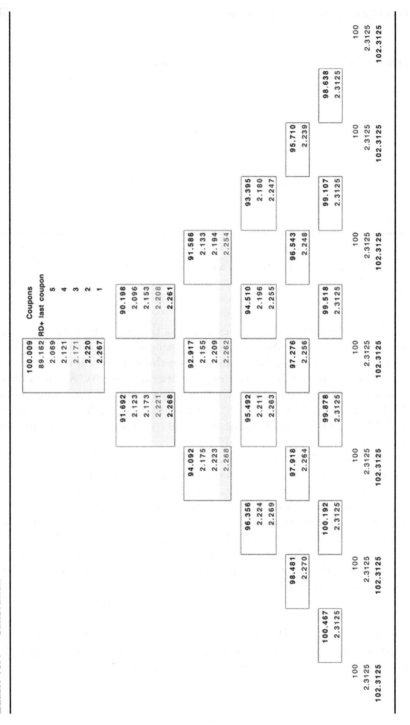

EXHIBIT 18.5   Calibrated Rates

As an alternative to this binomial approach, Hull and White[26] have suggested a two-stage methodology that uses a mean-reverting process with the short rate as the source of uncertainty and calculated in a trinomial tree framework.

The first stage in the approach ignores the observed market rates and centres the evolution of rates around zero and identifies the point at which the mean-reversion process takes effect. The second stage introduces the observed market rates into the framework established in stage one. The trinomial approach gives the tree a great deal more flexibility over its binomial counterpart, not least in relaxing the assumption that rates can either rise or fall with probability 0.5.

HEATH-JARROW-MORTON METHODOLOGY

Heath, Jarrow, and Morton (HJM)[27] derived one-factor and multifactor models for movements of the forward rates of interest. The models were complex enough to match the current observable term structure of forward rate and by equivalence the spot rates. Ritchken and Sankarasubramanian[28] provide necessary and sufficient conditions for the HJM models with one source of error and two-state variables such that the *ex post* forward premium and the integrated variance factor are sufficient

---

[26] John C. Hull and Alan White, "Numerical Procedures for Implementing Term Structure Models I: Single-Factor Models," *Journal of Derivatives* 2, no. 1 (1994), pp. 7–16.

[27] David Heath, Robert Jarrow, and Andrew Morton, "Bond Pricing and the Term Structure of Interest Rates: A Discrete Time Approximation," *Journal of Financial and Quantitative Analysis* 25 (1990), pp. 419–440; "Contingent Claim Valuation with a Random Evolution of Interest Rates," *Review of Futures Markets* 9 (1990), pp. 54–76; "Bond Pricing and the Term Structure of Interest Rates," *Econometrica* 60, no. 1 (1992), pp. 77–105.

statistics for the construction of the entire term structure at any future point in time.

Under this methodology the bond dynamics are described by an Ito process

$$dp(t, T) = r(t)p(t, T)dt + \sigma(t, T)p(t, T)dW(t) \qquad (18.27)$$

Then

$$d \ln p(t, T) = \left[r(t) - \frac{1}{2}\sigma^2(t, T) \right]dt + \sigma(t, T)dW(t) \qquad (18.28)$$

The equation for the forward rate can be derived now

$$
\begin{aligned}
df(t, T) &= -d\left[\frac{\partial}{\partial T} \ln p(t, T) \right] \\
&= -\left[\frac{\partial}{\partial T}d \ln p(t, T) \right] \\
&= -\frac{\partial}{\partial T}\left\{ \left[r(t) - \frac{1}{2}\sigma^2(t, T) \right]dt + \sigma(t, T)dW(t) \right\} \\
&= \sigma(t, T)\frac{\partial\sigma(t, T)}{\partial T}dt - \frac{\partial\sigma(t, T)}{\partial T}dW(t)
\end{aligned}
\qquad (18.29)
$$

The Wiener process $W = \{W(t)\}$ is symmetric and, therefore, we can safely replace W with $-W$, so

$$df(t, T) = \sigma(t, T)\frac{\partial\sigma(t, T)}{\partial T}dt - \frac{\partial\sigma(t, T)}{\partial T}dW(t) \qquad (18.30)$$

Applying the fundamental theorem of calculus for $\partial\sigma(t, T)/(\partial T)$ leads to

$$\sigma(t, T) - \sigma(t, t) = \int_t^T \frac{\partial\sigma(t, s)}{\partial s}ds \qquad (18.31)$$

---

[28] Peter Ritchken and L. Sankarasubramanian, "Volatility Structures of Forward Rates and the Dynamics of the Term Structure," *Mathematical Finance* 5 (1995), pp. 55–72.

It is obvious that $\sigma(t,t) = 0$ and therefore the volatility of the forward rate determines the drift as well. In other words all that is needed for the HJM methodology is the volatility of the bond prices. The short rates are easily calculated from the forward rates. Once a model for short rates is determined under the risk-neutral measure Q the bond prices are calculated from

$$p(t, T) = E^Q\left[e^{-\int_t^T r(s)ds}\middle| F_t\right] \tag{18.32}$$

Using equation (18.3) it follows that

$$\int_t^T f(t, s)ds = -\ln p(t, T) = g[r(t), t, T]$$

where

$$g(x, t, T) = -\ln E^Q\left[e^{-\int_t^T r(s)ds}\middle| r(t) = x\right] \tag{18.33}$$

The continuous variant of the Ho-Lee model can be obtained for

$$g(x, t, T) = x(T-t) - \frac{1}{6}\sigma^2(T-t)^3 + \int_t^T (T-s)\alpha(s)ds \tag{18.34}$$

where $\sigma(t,T) = \sigma(T - t)$, which implies that

$$\frac{\partial f(t, T)}{\partial t} = \sigma^2(T-t)dt + \sigma dW(t)$$

so the initial forward curve is

$$f(0, T) = \frac{\partial g(r(0), 0, T)}{\partial T} = r(0) - \frac{1}{2}\sigma^2 T^2 + \int_0^T \alpha(s)ds \tag{18.35}$$

The short rate is given by

$$r(t) = f(0, t) + \sigma^2 \frac{t^2}{2} + \sigma W(t) \tag{18.36}$$

and the price of the pure discount bond with maturity T is

$$p(t, T) = \exp\left[-\int_t^T f(t, s)ds - \sigma^2 t \int_t^T \left(s - \frac{t}{2} \right)ds - \sigma(T - t)W(t) \right] \tag{18.37}$$

Similarly, the Vasicek model is recovered for

$$\sigma(t, T) = \sigma e^{-\beta(T-t)}$$

and

$$f(0, t) = \frac{\alpha}{\beta} + e^{-\beta T}\left[r(0) - \frac{\alpha}{\beta} \right] - \frac{\sigma^2}{2\beta^2}(1 - e^{-\beta T})^2 \tag{18.38}$$

and this leads to

$$r(t) = \frac{\alpha}{\beta} + e^{-\beta T}\left[r(0) - \frac{\alpha}{\beta} \right] + \sigma e^{-\beta t}\int_0^t e^{\beta s}dW(s) \tag{18.39}$$

BOND OPTION PRICING

Formulas for bond options were found by Cox, Ingersoll, and Ross using the CIR model (square root process) for short rates, and by Jamshidian,[29] Rabinovitch,[30] and by Chaplin[31] using the Vasicek model for the short rate process.

---

[29] Farshid Jamshidian, "An Exact Bond Option Formula," *Journal of Finance* 44, no. 1 (1989), pp. 205–209.

[30] Ramon Rabinovitch, "Pricing Stock and Bond Options when the Default-Free Rate is Stochastic."

[31] Geoff Chaplin, "A Formula for Bond Option Values under an Ornstein-Uhlenbeck Model for the Spot," Actuarial Science Working Paper No. 87-16, University of Waterloo (1987).

Rabinovitch advocated the idea that the bond follows a log-normal process (similar to equity prices). Chen[32] pointed out that this assumption is grossly misleading since the bond price is a contingent claim on the same interest rate. As a result the bond option pricing model cannot be a two-factor model as proposed by Rabinovitch rather it collapses to a one-factor model, in which case the formulae are the same with those proved respectively by Chaplin and by Jamshidian.

Bonds are traded generally over the counter. Futures contracts on bonds may be more liquid and may remove some of the modelling difficulties generated by the known value at maturity of the bonds. Hedging may be more efficient in this context using the futures contracts on pure discount bonds (provided they are liquid) rather than the bonds themselves. Chen[33] provides closed-form solutions for futures and European futures options on pure discount bonds, under the Vasicek model.

Hull and White used a two-factor version of the Vasicek model to price discount bond options. Turnbull and Milne[34] proposed a general equilibrium model outside the HJM framework. They provide analytical solutions for European options on Treasury bills, interest-rate forward and futures contracts and Treasury bonds. In addition a closed-form solution is identified for a call option written on an interest-rate cap. A two-factor model is also investigated and closed-form solutions are provided for a European call on a Treasury bill. Chen and Scott[35] use a two-factor CIR model that is essentially the same as the model analysed by Longstaff and Schwartz, and derive solutions for bond and interest rate options. The two-factor model is used with the first factor having a strong mean reversion, explaining the variation in short-term rates, while the second factor has a very slow mean reversion, modelling long-term rates. The model is also used for calculating premium for caps on floating interest rates and for European options on discount bonds, coupon bonds, coupon bond futures, and Eurodollar futures. These are not closed-form solutions but they are expressed as multivariate integrals. However, the calculus can be reduced to univariate numerical integrations.

---

[32] Ren-Raw Chen, "Pricing Stock and Bond Options when the Default-Free Rate is Stochastic: A Comment," *Journal of Financial and Quantitative Analysis* 26, no. 3 (1991), pp. 433–434.

[33] Ren-Raw Chen, "Exact Solutions for Futures and European Futures Options on Pure Discount Bonds," *Journal of Financial and Quantitative Analysis* 27, no. 1 (March 1992), pp. 97–107.

[34] Stuart M. Turnbull and Frank Milne, "A Simple Approach to Interest-Rate Option Pricing," *The Review of Financial Studies*, 4, no. 1 (1991), pp. 87–120.

[35] Ren-Raw Chen and Louis Scott, "Pricing Interest Rate Options in a Two-Factor Cox-Ingersoll-Ross Model of the Term Structure," *The Review of Financial Studies* 5, no. 4 (1992), pp. 613–636.

European Options on the Money Fund

In this section we consider the pricing of a European option on the money fund. (This is the same as a bank account when the initial value $B(0) = 1$.) Thus, the payoff of a European call option with exercise price K is $\max[B(T) - K, 0]$. The continuous version of the Ho-Lee model is assumed for the short interest rate process. The risk-neutral valuation methodology provides the solution as[36]

$$
\begin{aligned}
c_{B(0),\, T,\, K} &= E^{Q}\!\left[e^{-\int_0^T r(u)\,du} \max[B(T) - K, 0] \,|\, F_0 \right] \\
&= B(0)N(d_+) - p(0, T)KN(d_-)
\end{aligned}
\tag{18.40}
$$

where

$$
d_+ = \frac{\ln\!\left[\dfrac{B(0)}{p(0,\, T)K}\right] + \sigma^2 \dfrac{T^3}{6}}{\sigma \sqrt{\dfrac{T^3}{3}}}
$$

and

$$
d_- = \frac{\ln\!\left[\dfrac{B(0)}{p(0,\, T)K}\right] - \sigma^2 \dfrac{T^3}{6}}{\sigma \sqrt{\dfrac{T^3}{3}}} = d_+ - \sigma \sqrt{\dfrac{T^3}{3}}
$$

Options on Discount Bonds

Discount bond options are not very liquid, but they form an elementary component for pricing other options. For example, a floating-rate cap can be decomposed into a portfolio of European puts on discount bonds. Similarly with the European option contingent on the bank account we can price European options contingent to discount bonds.

When the short rate process $r = \{r(t)\}$ follows the continuous time version of the Ho-Lee model given by equation (18.10), the price at time

---

[36] A proof of this formula is described in T. Wake Epps, *Pricing Derivative Securities* (Singapore: World Scientific, 2000).

0 of a European call option with maturity T_0 with exercise price K on a discount bond maturing at $T(T_0 < T)$ is[37]

$$c_{p(0,\,T);T;K} = E^Q\!\left[e^{-\int_0^T r(u)\,du} \max[p(T_0, T) - K, 0]\,\big|\,F_0\right]$$

$$= p(0, T)\frac{p(0, T)}{p(0, T_0)}N(d_+) - p(0, T_0)KN(d_-) \qquad (18.41)$$

where

$$d_+ = \frac{\ln\!\left[\dfrac{p(0, T)}{p(0, T_0)K}\right] + \sigma^2\dfrac{(T - T_0)T_0}{2}}{\sigma\sqrt{(T - T_0)T_0}}$$

and

$$d_- = d_+ - \sigma\sqrt{(T - T_0)T_0}$$

There is a similar put-call parity for European options contingent on a discount bond. If $p_{p(0,\,T);T_0;K}$ is the price at $t = 0$ of a European put option on the discount bond with maturity T, then for $B(0) = 1$,

$$c_{p(0,\,T);T_0;K} - p_{p(0,\,T);T_0;K}$$

$$= E^Q\!\left[e^{-\int_0^{T_0} r(s)\,ds}(\max[p(T_0, T) - K, 0] - \max[K - p(T_0, T), 0]\,|\,F_0)\right]$$

$$= E^Q\!\left[e^{-\int_0^{T_0} r(s)\,ds}[p(T_0, T) - K]\,|\,F_0\right] = E^Q\!\left[e^{-\int_0^{T} r(s)\,ds}\,\Big|\,F_0\right] - p(0, T_0)K$$

$$= p(0, T) - p(0, T_0)K$$

Put-call parity can be used to derive the price of a European put option

$$p_{p(0,\,T);T_0;K} = p(0, T_0)KN(-d_-) - p(0, T_0)\frac{p(0, T)}{p(0, T_0)}N(-d_+) \qquad (18.42)$$

---

[37] A proof of this result is provided in Epps, *Pricing Derivative Securities*.

Initially the first formulas on pricing options on pure discount bonds used the Vasicek model for the term structure of interest rates. Thus, given that r follows equation (18.6), the price of a European call option with maturity T_0 with exercise price K on a discount bond maturing at $T(T_0 < T)$ is

$$c_{p(0,\,T);T_0;K} = p(0,\,T)N(d_+) - Kp(0,\,T_0)N(d_-) \qquad (18.43)$$

where

$$d_+ = \frac{\ln\left[\dfrac{p(0,\,T)}{Kp(0,\,T_0)}\right] + \eta^2/2}{\eta}$$

and

$$d_- = d_+ - \eta$$

with

$$\eta = \frac{\sigma(1 - e^{-\beta(T - T_0)})}{\beta}\sqrt{\frac{1 - e^{-2\beta-T_0}}{2\beta}}$$

The put price can be obtained from put-call parity as

$$p_{p(0,\,T);T_0;K} = Kp(0,\,T_0)N(-d_-) - p(0,\,T)N(d_+) \qquad (18.44)$$

Example of a Zero-Coupon Bond Call Option with Vasicek

We will use the Vasicek model for pricing a 3-year European call option on a 10-year zero-coupon bond with face value $1 and exercise price K equal to $0.5. As in Jackson and Staunton,[38] we use for the parameters of this model the values estimated by Chan, Karolyi, Longstaff, and Sanders[39] for US 1-month Treasury bill yield from 1964 to 1989. Thus α = 0.0154, β = 0.1779, and σ = 2%. In addition, the value of the short

---

[38] Mary Jackson and Mike Staunton, *Advanced Modelling in Finance Using Excel and VBA* (Chichester: John Wiley and Sons, Inc., 2001).

[39] Kalok Chan, G. Andrew Karolyi, Francis A. Longstaff, and Anthony B. Sanders, "An Empirical Comparison of Alternative Models of the Short-Term Interest Rate," *Journal of Finance* 47 (1992), pp. 1209–1227.

EXHIBIT 18.6 Calculations of Elements for Pricing an European Call Option on a Zero-Coupon Bond when Short Rates are Following the Vasicek Model

$p(0,T_0)$	$p(0,T)$	d_+	d_-	$N(d_+)$	$N(d_-)$
0.8655	0.5406	2.1013	1.9926	0.9822	0.9767

rate r at time $t = 0$ is needed, so we take $r_0 = 3.75\%$. Feeding this information into equations 18.41–18.44 we get the output in Exhibit 18.6.

Thus the value of the European call option is

$$c_{p(0,\,T);T_0;K} = 0.5406 \times 0.9822 - 0.5 \times 0.8655 \times 0.9767 \cong 0.108$$

A more general case is discussed by Shiryaev[40] for single-factor Gaussian models modelling the short interest rate. These are single-factor affine models where the short rate r is also a Gauss-Markov process. The equation for this short rate process is

$$dr(t) = [\alpha(t) - \beta(t)r(t)]dt + \sigma(t)dW(t) \qquad (18.45)$$

and we can easily recognize the first Hull-White model. The price of a European call option is also

$$c_{p(0,\,T);T_0;K} = p(0,T)N(d_+) - Kp(0,T_0)N(d_-) \qquad (18.46)$$

but where

$$d_+ = \frac{\ln\left[\dfrac{p(0,T)}{Kp(0,T_0)}\right] + \dfrac{1}{2}\eta^2(T_0,T)B^2(T_0,T)}{\eta(T_0,T)B(T_0,T)}$$

and

$$d_- = d_+ - \eta$$

with

---

[40] Albert N. Shiryaev, *Essentials of Stochastic Finance: Facts, Models, Theory* (Singapore: World Scientific, 1999).

$$B(T_0, T) = \int_{T_0}^{T} \frac{\varphi(s)}{\varphi(T_0)} ds$$

and

$$\varphi(s) = e^{-\int_0^s \beta(u)\,du}$$

The price of the European put bond options is obviously again

$$P_{p(0,\,T);T_0;K} = Kp(0, T_0)N(-d_-) - p(0, T)N(d_+)$$

Example Zero-Coupon Bond Call Option with Hull-White

When considering the pricing of a forward pure discount bond earlier in this chapter we used a numerical example. That example can now be expanded to demonstrate how in practice European calls and puts can be estimated in a Hull-White framework. Explicitly the illustration will demonstrate the pricing of a 1-year European call option on a 4-year to maturity discount bond with a strike price set equal to the forward price of the bond (0.8854).

Breaking down (d_+) into its component parts and evaluating each individually yields:

$$\ln \frac{p(0, T)}{K[p(0, T_0)]} = \ln \left[\frac{0.8521}{(0.8858)(0.9607)} \right] = 0, B(T_0, T) = 2.5918$$

$$\eta = \frac{\sigma(1 - e^{-\beta(T - T_0)})}{\beta} \sqrt{\frac{1 - e^{-2\beta T_0}}{2\beta}}$$

$$= \left(\frac{0.02(1 - e^{-0.1(3)})}{0.1} \sqrt{\frac{1 - e^{-2(0.1)(1)}}{2(0.1)}} = 0.0493 \right)$$

The expression for (d_+) reduces to

$$\frac{\eta(T_0, T)B(T_0, T)}{2} = \frac{(0.0493)(2.5918)}{2} = 0.6395$$

The expression for d_- is $(d_-) = (d_+) - \eta = 0.6395 - 0.0493 = 0.0146$. $N(d_+)$ is found to be 0.5255 and $N(d_-) = 0.5058$. Substituting these results into the call option formula given by equation (18.46) gives a premium of:

$$c_{p(0, T); T_0; K} = (0.8521)(0.5255) - (0.8858)(0.9608)(0.5058) = 0.01730$$

or 1.73%.

One notable exception from this general class is the CIR model. There is a closed-formula for this case too. Following Clewlow and Strickland[41] the price at time 0 of a European pure discount bond option is

$$c_{p(0, T); T_0; K} = p(0, T)\chi^2\left\{2\delta[\phi + \psi + B(T_0, T)]; 2\omega, \frac{2\phi^2 r(0)e^{\theta T_0}}{\phi + \psi + B(T_0, T)}\right\}$$

$$- Kp(0, T_0)\chi^2\left\{2\delta[\phi + \psi]; 2\omega, \frac{2\phi^2 r(0)e^{\theta T_0}}{\phi + \psi}\right\} \tag{18.47}$$

where

$$\theta = \sqrt{\beta^2 + 2\sigma^2}$$

$$\phi = \frac{2\theta}{\sigma^2(e^{-\theta T} - 1)}$$

$$\psi = \frac{\beta + \theta}{\sigma^2}$$

$$\lambda = \frac{\beta + \theta}{2}$$

$$\omega = \frac{2\beta}{\sigma^2}$$

---

[41] Les Clewlow and Chris Strickland, *Implementing Derivatives Models* (Chichester: John Wiley and Sons, Inc., 1998).

$$B(t, s) = \frac{e^{\theta(s-t)} - 1}{\lambda(e^{\theta(s-t)} - 1) + \theta}$$

$$\delta = \frac{\omega\{\lambda T + \ln \theta - \ln [\lambda(e^{\theta T} - 1) + \theta]\} - \ln (K)}{B(T_0, T)}$$

and $\chi^2(.;a,b)$ is the noncentral chi-squared density with a degrees of freedom and noncentrality parameter b.

Example Zero-Coupon Bond Call Option with CIR

Taking the same example as that developed to demonstrate the Vasicek model earlier, we now price the 3-year European call option on a 10-year pure discount bond using the CIR model for the short interest rates. Recall that face value is \$1 and exercise price K is equal to \$0.5. As in the example with the Vasicek model, we consider that $\sigma = 2\%$ and $r_0 = 3.75\%$. The CIR model overcomes the problem of negative interest rates (acknowledged as a problem for the Vasicek model) as long as $2\alpha \geq \sigma^2$. This is true, for example, if we take $\alpha = 0.0189$ and $\beta = 0.24$. Feeding this information into the above formulae is relatively tedious. A spreadsheet application is provided by Jackson and Staunton. After some work we get that the price of the call is

$$c_{p(0, T);T_0;K} = 0.5324 \times 1 - 0.5 \times 0.8624 \times 1 \cong 0.1012$$

OPTIONS ON COUPON-PAYING BONDS

When short rates are modelled with single-factor models, Jamshidian[42] proved that an option on a coupon bond can be priced by valuing a portfolio of options on discount bonds. This approach does not work in multifactor models as proved by El Karoui and Rochet.[43]

Consider a bond paying a periodic cash payment ρ at times $T_1, T_2, \ldots, T_m$, and the principal at maturity $T = T_m$. A coupon bond can be mapped into a portfolio of discount bonds with corresponding maturities (under one source of uncertainty, that is one factor model). The value of a coupon bearing bond at time $t < T_m$ is

---

[42] Jamshidian, "An Exact Bond Option Formula."
[43] Nicole El Karoui and Jean-Charles Rochet, "A Price Formula for Options on Coupon Bonds," SEEDS Discussion Series, Instituto de Economica Publica, Spain (1995).

$$p(t, T_1, ..., T_m; \rho) = \rho \sum_{i = i[t]}^{m} p(t, T_i) + p(t, T_m) \qquad (18.48)$$

where $i[t] = \min\{j: t < T_j\}$.

Under the one-factor HJM model corresponding to the Ho-Lee model, a European option on a coupon bond can be valued as a portfolio of options contingent on zero discount bonds with maturities $T_1, T_2, ..., T_m$. Let T_0 be the maturity of such a European option. Epps[44] shows that

$$p(T_0, T_i) = \frac{p(0, T_i)}{p(0, T_0)} e^{\left\{ -\sigma^2 \frac{(T_i - T_0)^2 T_0}{2} - (T_i - T_0)[r(T_0) - f(0, T_0)] \right\}} \qquad (18.49)$$

For any strike price K, there is a value r_K of $r(T_0)$ such that when replaced in equation (18.48) with $t = T_0$, implies $p(T_0, T_1, ..., T_m) = K$. If we denote by K the value of $p(T_0, T_i)$ as calculated from equation (18.49) with r_K instead of $r(T_0)$. Then

$$\rho \sum_{i = i[T_0]}^{m} K_i + K_m = K \qquad (18.50)$$

Hence, the value at time 0 of a European call option with maturity T_0 and strike price K on the coupon bearing bond, under the one-factor HJM model described above, is given by

$$
\begin{aligned}
c_{p(0, T_1, ..., T_m; \rho)} &= E^Q \left\{ e^{-\int_0^{T_0} r(s)ds} \max[p(T_0, T_1, ..., T_m; \rho) - K, 0] \right\} \\
&= \rho \sum_{i = i[T_0]}^{K} E^Q \left\{ e^{-\int_0^{T_0} r(s)ds} \max[p(T_0, T_i) - K_i, 0] \right\} \\
&\quad + E^Q \left\{ e^{-\int_0^{T_0} r(s)ds} \max[p(T_0, T_m) - K_m, 0] \right\} \\
&= \rho \sum_{i = i[T_0]}^{m} c_{p(0, T_i); T_0; K_i} - c_{p(0, T_m); T_0; K_m}
\end{aligned}
\qquad (18.51)
$$

---

[44] Epps, *Pricing Derivative Securities*.

EXHIBIT 18.7 Calculations Using Vasicek Model for Separate Zero-Coupon European Call Options; the Bond Prices Shown are Calculated with the Estimated r_K

Year	$p(T_0,T_i) \mid r_K$	Face Value	ρK_i	Call Option
4.0	0.8094	0.05	0.0405	0.006
5.0	0.6688	0.05	0.0334	0.009
6.0	0.5624	0.05	0.0281	0.012
7.0	0.4800	0.05	0.0240	0.013
8.0	0.4148	0.05	0.0207	0.013
9.0	0.3622	0.05	0.0181	0.013
10.0	0.3192	1.05	0.3351	0.278

Example Coupon-Bond Call Option with Vasicek

We now revisit the earlier Vasicek example for short interest rates to consider the case where the underlying bond pays an annual coupon at a 5% rate ($\rho = 0.05$), all the other characteristics remain as before. In order to calculate the call price of the coupon-bond European option first we need to calculate the interest rate r_K such that the present value at the maturity of the option of all later cash flows on the bond equals the strike price. This is done by trial and error using equation (18.48) and the value we get here is $r_K = 22.30\%$. Next, we map the strike price into a series of strike prices via equation (18.50) that are then associated with coupon payments considered as zero-coupon bonds and calculate the value of the European call options contingent on those zero-coupon bonds as in the above example. The calculations are described in Exhibit 18.7.

Because we started with a one-factor model for the short interest rates we can use the decomposition property emphasized by Jamshidian and calculate the required coupon-bond European call price as the sum of all the elements in the last column in Exhibit 18.7, which include the coupon rate factor ρ. Thus, the value of this option is 0.344.

Example Coupon-Bond Call Option with CIR

We shall repeat the calculation of the coupon-bond call option when the CIR model is employed for the short rates. The procedure is the same as in the case discussed above for the Vasicek model. First we calculate the interest rate r_K such that the present value at the maturity of the option of all later cash flows on the bond equals the strike price. This value is here $r_K = 25.05\%$. Next, we map the strike price into a series of strike prices via equation (18.50) that are then associated with coupon pay-

EXHIBIT 18.8   Calculations Using CIR Model for Separate Zero-Coupon European Call Options; the Bond Prices Shown are Calculated with the Estimated r_K

Year	$p(T_0,T_i) \mid r_K$	Face Value	ρK_I	Call Option
4.0	0.7934	0.05	0.0397	0.006
5.0	0.6503	0.05	0.0325	0.010
6.0	0.5470	0.05	0.0273	0.012
7.0	0.4694	0.05	0.0235	0.013
8.0	0.4094	0.05	0.0205	0.013
9.0	0.3615	0.05	0.0181	0.013
10.0	0.3223	1.05	0.3385	0.267

ments considered as zero-coupon bonds and calculate the value of the European call options contingent on those zero-coupon bonds. The calculations are described in Exhibit 18.8.

The value of the call option is 0.335 that is the sum of all zero-coupon bond call option prices in the last column.

SWAPTIONS

Swaptions are options that allow the buyer to obtain at a future time one position in a swap contract. It is quite elementary that an interest rate swap, fixed for floating, can be understood as a portfolio of bonds.[45] To consider this assume that the notional principal is 1. Then the claim on the fixed payments is the same as a bond paying coupons with the rate ρ and no principal. Let τ be the time when the swap is conceived. The claim on the fixed income stream is worth, at time τ,

$$\rho \sum_{i=1}^{m} p(\tau, T_i)$$

The floating income stream is made up of cash returns on holding, over the period $[T_{i-1}, T_i]$ a discount bond with maturity T_i, which is worth

$$\frac{p(T_i, T_i)}{p(T_{i-1}, T_i)} - 1$$

---

[45] John C. Hull, *Options, Futures, and Other Derivatives* (Upper Saddle River, NJ: Prentice Hall, 2003).

Thus, the value of the whole floating stream at time $t = \tau$ is

$$E_\tau \left(\sum_{i=1}^{m} e^{-\int_\tau^{T_i} r(s)ds} \frac{1 - p(T_{i-1}, T_i)}{p(T_{i-1}, T_i)} \right)$$

$$= E_\tau \left(\sum_{i=1}^{m} e^{-\int_\tau^{T_{i-1}} r(s)ds} \sum_{i=1}^{m} e^{-\int_{T_{i-1}}^{T_i} r(s)ds} \frac{1 - p(T_{i-1}, T_i)}{p(T_{i-1}, T_i)} \right)$$

(18.52)

Applying the properties of conditional expectations it follows that the above is equal to

$$E_\tau \left\{ \sum_{i=1}^{m} e^{-\int_\tau^{T_{i-1}} r(s)ds} E_{T_{i-1}} e^{-\int_{T_{i-1}}^{T_i} r(s)ds} \left[\frac{1 - p(T_{i-1}, T_i)}{p(T_{i-1}, T_i)} \right] \right\}$$

$$= E_\tau \left\{ \sum_{i=1}^{m} e^{-\int_\tau^{T_{i-1}} r(s)ds} [1 - p(T_{i-1}, T_i)] \right\}$$

(18.53)

$$= \sum_{i=1}^{m} [p(\tau, T_{i-1}) - p(\tau, T_i)] = 1 - p(\tau, T_m)$$

Imposing the condition that the two streams have equal initial value leads to

$$\rho \sum_{i=1}^{m} p(\tau, T_i) = 1 - p(\tau, T_m)$$

which is equivalent to

$$\rho \sum_{i=1}^{m} p(\tau, T_i) + p(\tau, T_m) - 1 = 0$$

It follows then that the value of the swap at initialisation is $p(\tau, T_1, ..., T_m) - 1$. Thus, the option to get a long position in the fixed leg of the swap, with a fixed payment rate ρ, is worth at time 0

$$E_0\left\{e^{-\int_0^\tau r(s)ds}\max[p(\tau, T_1, ..., T_m) - 1, 0]\right\}\qquad(18.54)$$

It is clear now that this is the same as a European call option on a coupon-bearing bond when the exercise price is equal to 1.

PRACTICAL CONSIDERATIONS

As mentioned in the introduction of this chapter, the option on the Euro-Bund futures is an extremely popular contract. Exhibit 18.1 presented an example of the contract specification drawn from a Bloomberg screen. Exercise of these options entails taking a position in an underlying Euro-Bund Futures contract which will involve taking or making delivery of a physical bond should the futures contract be held until maturity.

Euronext-LIFFE's 3-month EURIBOR futures option, traded on the Chicago Mercantile Exchange, is an actively traded short-term interest rate option that enjoys high trading volume. If these options are exercised, the buyer and the seller of the option take positions in an underlying 3-month EURIBOR futures contract. The futures contract is cash-settled and the final price at delivery is equal to 100 minus the 3-month LIBOR.

Another liquid interest rate derivative market is the OTC market in floating-rate caps. The majority of caps are contingent on LIBOR (but can be also on a Treasury rate) and discounted payments are made at beginning of each tenor. The payments can be made either at the beginning or the end of each reset period and the life of a cap may be only few months or as long as 10 years. The starting point in pricing these European options is a model for future changes in LIBOR.

Hull and White[46] showed that the cap can be priced as a portfolio of European puts on discount bonds.

CONCLUSION

In this chapter we investigated some of the main issues in bond option pricing. The accuracy of option pricing with bonds as the underlying security depends on the precision of the modelling of interest rates. It is

---

[46] Hull and White, "Pricing Interest Rate Derivative Securities."

a fact that there is no model claiming supremacy, and this is reflected in the relentless search for better models (one-factor and multifactor) over the last 25 years. The models presented here have become in a sense standard for many practitioners. Market LIBOR models[47] are not discussed here due to space limitations. This is a new emerging class of models of interest rates that seems to be more flexible in explaining many facets of the data.

---

[47] A very good introduction and description of practical implementation issues is Riccardo Rebonato, *Interest-Rate Option Models*, 2nd ed. (Chichester: John Wiley and Sons, Inc., 1998).

CHAPTER 19

Interest Rate Swaps

Frank J. Fabozzi, Ph.D., CFA
Frederick Frank Adjunct Professor of Finance
School of Management
Yale University

Steven V. Mann, Ph.D.
Professor of Finance
Moore School of Business
University of South Carolina

An interest rate swap contract provides a vehicle for market participants to transform the nature of cash flows and the interest rate
exposure of a portfolio or balance sheet. In this chapter we explain how
to analyze interest rate swaps. We will describe a generic interest rate
swap, the parties to a swap, the risk and return of a swap, and the economic interpretation of a swap. Then we look at how to compute the
floating-rate payments and calculate the present value of these payments. Next we will see how to calculate the fixed-rate payments given
the swap rate. Before we look at how to calculate the value of a swap,
we will see how to calculate the swap rate. Given the swap rate, we will
then see how the value of swap is determined after the inception of a
swap. In Europe, there is a well-developed interest rate swap market in
the following currencies—euros, Swiss francs and pound sterling. The
euro interest rate swap market is the largest of the three so these contracts will be used to illustrate the principles presented in this chapter.
However, we want to emphasize that the same principles hold with
equal force regardless of the currency of the swap's cash flows.

DESCRIPTION OF AN INTEREST RATE SWAP

In an *interest rate swap*, two parties (called *counterparties*) agree to exchange periodic interest payments. The euro amount of the interest payments exchanged is based on some predetermined euro principal, which is called the *notional amount*. The euro amount each counterparty pays to the other is the agreed-upon periodic interest rate times the notional amount. The only cash flows that are exchanged between the parties are the interest payments, not the notional amount. Accordingly, the notional principal serves only as a scale factor to translate an interest rate into a cash flow. In the most common type of swap, one party agrees to pay the other party fixed interest payments at designated dates for the life of the contract. This party is referred to as the *fixed-rate payer*. The other party, who agrees to make interest rate payments that float with some reference rate, is referred to as the *floating-rate payer*.

The reference rates that have been used for the floating rate in an interest rate swap are various money market rates. The most common in Europe is EURIBOR. EURIBOR is the rate at which prime banks offer to pay on euro deposits available to other prime banks for a given maturity. There is not just one rate but a rate for different maturities. For example, there is a 1-month EURIBOR, 3-month EURIBOR, and 6-month EURIBOR.

To illustrate an interest rate swap, suppose that for the next five years party X agrees to pay party Y 10% per year, while party Y agrees to pay party X 6-month EURIBOR (the reference rate). Party X is a fixed-rate payer/floating-rate receiver, while party Y is a floating-rate payer/fixed-rate receiver. Assume that the notional amount is €50 million, and that payments are exchanged every six months for the next five years. This means that every six months, party X (the fixed-rate payer/floating-rate receiver) will pay party Y €2.5 million (10% times €50 million divided by 2). The amount that party Y (the floating-rate payer/fixed-rate receiver) will pay party X will be 6-month EURIBOR times €50 million divided by 2. If 6-month EURIBOR is 7%, party Y will pay party X €1.75 million (7% times €50 million divided by 2). Note that we divide by two because one-half year's interest is being paid.

Interest rate swaps are over-the-counter instruments. This means that they are not traded on an exchange. An institutional investor wishing to enter into a swap transaction can do so through either a securities firm or a commercial bank that transacts in swaps.[1] These entities can do one of the following. First, they can arrange or broker a swap between two parties that want to enter into an interest rate swap. In this case, the securities firm or commercial bank is acting in a brokerage capacity.

The second way in which a securities firm or commercial bank can get an institutional investor into a swap position is by taking the other side of the swap. This means that the securities firm or the commercial bank is a dealer rather than a broker in the transaction. Acting as a dealer, the securities firm or the commercial bank must hedge its swap position in the same way that it hedges its position in other securities. Also it means that the swap dealer is the counterparty to the transaction.

The risks that the two parties take on when they enter into a swap is that the other party will fail to fulfill its obligations as set forth in the swap agreement. That is, each party faces default risk. The default risk in a swap agreement is called *counterparty risk*. In any agreement between two parties that must perform according to the terms of a contract, counterparty risk is the risk that the other party will default. With futures and exchange-traded options the counterparty risk is the risk that the clearinghouse establishes to guarantee performance of the contracts will default. Market participants view this risk as small. In contrast, counterparty risk in a swap can be significant.

Because of counterparty risk, not all securities firms and commercial banks can be swap dealers. Several securities firms have established subsidiaries that are separately capitalized so that they have a high credit rating which permit them to enter into swap transactions as a dealer.

Thus, it is imperative to keep in mind that any party who enters into a swap is subject to counterparty risk.

INTERPRETING A SWAP POSITION

There are two ways that a swap position can be interpreted: (1) a package of forward/futures contracts and (2) a package of cash flows from buying and selling cash market instruments.

Package of Forward Contracts

Consider the hypothetical interest rate swap used earlier to illustrate a swap. Let's look at party X's position. Party X has agreed to pay 10% and receive 6-month EURIBOR. More specifically, assuming a €50 million notional amount, X has agreed to buy a commodity called "6-month EURIBOR" for €2.5 million. This is effectively a 6-month forward contract where X agrees to pay €2.5 million in exchange for deliv-

---

[1] Don't get confused here about the role of commercial banks. A bank can use a swap in its asset/liability management. Or, a bank can transact (buy and sell) swaps to clients to generate fee income. It is in the latter sense that we are discussing the role of a commercial bank in the swap market here.

ery of 6-month EURIBOR. The fixed-rate payer is effectively long a 6-month forward contract on 6-month EURIBOR. The floating-rate payer is effectively short a 6-month forward contract on 6-month EURIBOR. There is therefore an implicit forward contract corresponding to each exchange date.

Consequently, interest rate swaps can be viewed as a package of more basic interest rate derivative instruments—forwards. The pricing of an interest rate swap will then depend on the price of a package of forward contracts with the same settlement dates in which the underlying for the forward contract is the same reference rate.

While an interest rate swap may be nothing more than a package of forward contracts, it is not a redundant contract for several reasons. First, maturities for forward or futures contracts do not extend out as far as those of an interest rate swap; an interest rate swap with a term of 15 years or longer can be obtained. Second, an interest rate swap is a more transactionally efficient instrument. By this we mean that in one transaction an entity can effectively establish a payoff equivalent to a package of forward contracts. The forward contracts would each have to be negotiated separately. Third, the interest rate swap market has grown in liquidity since its establishment in 1981; interest rate swaps now provide more liquidity than forward contracts, particularly long-dated (i.e., long-term) forward contracts.

Package of Cash Market Instruments

To understand why a swap can also be interpreted as a package of cash market instruments, consider an investor who enters into the transaction below:

- Buy €50 million par value of a 5-year floating-rate bond that pays 6-month EURIBOR every six months.
- Finance the purchase by borrowing €50 million for five years at a 10% annual interest rate paid every six months.

The cash flows for this transaction are set forth in Exhibit 19.1. The second column of the exhibit shows the cash flows from purchasing the 5-year floating-rate bond. There is a €50 million cash outlay and then 10 cash inflows. The amount of the cash inflows is uncertain because they depend on future levels of 6-month EURIBOR. The next column shows the cash flows from borrowing €50 million on a fixed-rate basis. The last column shows the net cash flows from the entire transaction. As the last column indicates, there is no initial cash flow (no cash inflow or cash outlay). In all 10 6-month periods, the net position results in a cash

EXHIBIT 19.1 Cash Flows for the Purchase of a 5-Year Floating-Rate Bond Financed by Borrowing on a Fixed-Rate Basis
Transaction:
  • Purchase for €50 million a 5-year floating-rate bond:
    floating rate = EURIBOR, semiannual pay
  • Borrow €50 million for five years:
    fixed rate = 10%, semiannual payments

| 6-Month Period | Cash Flow (in millions of euros) from: | | |
	Floating-Rate Bond[a]	Borrowing Cost	Net
0	$-€50$	$+€50.0$ €0	
1	$+ (EURIBOR_1/2) \times 50$	-2.5	$+ (EURIBOR_1/2) \times 50 - 2.5$
2	$+ (EURIBOR_2/2) \times 50$	-2.5	$+ (EURIBOR_2/2) \times 50 - 2.5$
3	$+ (EURIBOR_3/2) \times 50$	-2.5	$+ (EURIBOR_3/2) \times 50 - 2.5$
4	$+ (EURIBOR_4/2) \times 50$	-2.5	$+ (EURIBOR_4/2) \times 50 - 2.5$
5	$+ (EURIBOR_5/2) \times 50$	-2.5	$+ (EURIBOR_5/2) \times 50 - 2.5$
6	$+ (EURIBOR_6/2) \times 50$	-2.5	$+ (EURIBOR_6/2) \times 50 - 2.5$
7	$+ (EURIBOR_7/2) \times 50$	-2.5	$+ (EURIBOR_7/2) \times 50 - 2.5$
8	$+ (EURIBOR_8/2) \times 50$	-2.5	$+ (EURIBOR_8/2) \times 50 - 2.5$
9	$+ (EURIBOR_9/2) \times 50$	-2.5	$+ (EURIBOR_9/2) \times 50 - 2.5$
10	$+ (EURIBOR_{10}/2) \times 50 + 50$	-52.5	$+ (EURIBOR_{10}/2) \times 50 - 2.5$

[a] The subscript for EURIBOR indicates the 6-month EURIBOR as per the terms of the floating-rate bond at time t.

inflow of EURIBOR and a cash outlay of €2.5 million. This net position, however, is identical to the position of a fixed-rate payer/floating-rate receiver.

It can be seen from the net cash flow in Exhibit 19.1 that a fixed-rate payer has a cash market position that is equivalent to a long position in a floating-rate bond and a short position in a fixed-rate bond—the short position being the equivalent of borrowing by issuing a fixed-rate bond.

What about the position of a floating-rate payer? It can be easily demonstrated that the position of a floating-rate payer is equivalent to purchasing a fixed-rate bond and financing that purchase at a floating rate, where the floating rate is the reference rate for the swap. That is, the position of a floating-rate payer is equivalent to a long position in a fixed-rate bond and a short position in a floating-rate bond.

TERMINOLOGY, CONVENTIONS, AND MARKET QUOTES

Here we review some of the terminology used in the swaps market and explain how swaps are quoted. The date that the counterparties commit to the swap is called the *trade date*. The date that the swap begins accruing interest is called the *effective date*, while the date that the swap stops accruing interest is called the *maturity date*. How often the floating rate is changed is called the *reset frequency*.

While our illustrations assume that the timing of the cash flows for both the fixed-rate payer and floating-rate payer will be the same, this is rarely the case in a swap. An agreement may call for the fixed-rate payer to make payments annually but the floating-rate payer to make payments more frequently (semi-annually or quarterly). Also, the way in which interest accrues on each leg of the transaction differs, because there are several day count conventions in the fixed-income markets as discussed in Chapter 3.

Normally, the fixed interest payments are paid on the basis of a 30/360 day count; floating-rate payments are paid on the basis of an actual/360 day count. Accordingly, the fixed interest payments will differ slightly owing to the differences in the lengths of successive coupon periods. The floating payments will differ owing to day counts as well as movements in the reference rate.

The terminology used to describe the position of a party in the swap markets combines cash market jargon and futures market jargon, given that a swap position can be interpreted as a position in a package of cash market instruments or a package of futures/forward positions. As we have said, the counterparty to an interest rate swap is either a fixed-rate payer or floating-rate payer. Exhibit 19.2 describes these positions in several ways.

The first two expressions in Exhibit 19.2 to describe the position of a fixed-rate payer and floating-rate payer are self-explanatory. To understand why the fixed-rate payer is viewed as short the bond market, and the floating-rate payer is viewed as long the bond market, consider what happens when interest rates change. Those who borrow on a fixed-rate basis will benefit if interest rates rise because they have locked in a lower interest rate. But those who have a short bond position will also benefit if interest rates rise. Thus, a fixed-rate payer can be said to be short the bond market. A floating-rate payer benefits if interest rates fall. A long position in a bond also benefits if interest rates fall, so terminology describing a floating-rate payer as long the bond market is not surprising. From our discussion of the interpretation of a swap as a package of cash market instruments, describing a swap in terms of the sensitivities of long and short cash positions follows naturally.

EXHIBIT 19.2 Describing the Counterparties to a Swap

Fixed-Rate Payer	Floating-Rate Payer
• Pays fixed rate in the swap	• Pays floating rate in the swap
• Receives floating in the swap	• Receives fixed in the swap
• Is short the bond market	• Is long the bond market
• Has bought a swap	• Has sold a swap
• Is long a swap	• Is short a swap
• Has established the price sensitivities of a longer-term liability and a floating-rate asset	• Has established the price sensitivities of a longer-term asset and a floating-rate liability

Source: Robert F. Kopprasch, John Macfarlane, Daniel R. Ross, and Janet Showers, "The Interest Rate Swap Market: Yield Mathematics, Terminology, and Conventions," Chapter 58 in Frank J. Fabozzi and Irving M. Pollack (eds.), *The Handbook of Fixed Income Securities* (Homewood, IL: Dow Jones-Irwin, 1987).

The convention that has evolved for quoting swaps levels is that a swap dealer sets the floating rate equal to the reference rate and then quotes the fixed rate that will apply. To illustrate this convention, consider the following 10-year swap terms available from a dealer:

◼ *Floating-rate payer:*
Pay floating rate of 3-month EURIBOR quarterly.
Receive fixed rate of 8.75% semi-annually.
◼ *Fixed-rate payer:*
Pay fixed rate of 8.85% semi-annually
Receive floating rate of 3-month EURIBOR quarterly.

The offer price that the dealer would quote the fixed-rate payer would be to pay 8.85% and receive EURIBOR "flat." (The word flat means with no spread.) The bid price that the dealer would quote the floating-rate payer would be to pay EURIBOR flat and receive 8.75%. The bid-offer spread is 10 basis points.

In order to solidify our intuition, it is useful to think of the swap market as a market where two counterparties trade the floating reference rate in a series of exchanges for a fixed price. In effect, the swap market is a market to buy and sell EURIBOR. So, buying a swap (pay fixed/receive floating) can be thought of as buying EURIBOR on each reset date for the fixed rate agreed to on the trade date. Conversely, selling a swap (receive fixed/pay floating) is effectively selling EURIBOR on each reset date for a fixed rate agreed to on the trade date. In this framework, a dealer's bid offer spread can be easily interpreted. Using the numbers presented above, the bid price of 8.75% is the price the dealer will pay to the counterparty to receive 3-month EURIBOR. In other words, buy EURIBOR at the bid. Similarly, the offer price of 8.85% is the price the dealer receives from the counterparty in exchange for 3-month EURIBOR. In other words, sell EURIBOR at the offer.

The fixed rate is some spread above the benchmark yield curve with the same term to maturity as the swap. In our illustration, suppose that the 10-year benchmark yield is 8.35%. Then the offer price that the dealer would quote to the fixed-rate payer is the 10-year benchmark rate plus 50 basis points versus receiving EURIBOR flat. For the floating-rate payer, the bid price quoted would be EURIBOR flat versus the 10-year benchmark rate plus 40 basis points. The dealer would quote such a swap as 40-50, meaning that the dealer is willing to enter into a swap to receive EURIBOR and pay a fixed rate equal to the 10-year benchmark rate plus 40 basis points; and it would be willing to enter into a swap to pay EURIBOR and receive a fixed rate equal to the 10-year benchmark rate plus 50 basis points.

VALUING INTEREST RATE SWAPS

In an interest rate swap, the counterparties agree to exchange periodic interest payments. The euro amount of the interest payments exchanged is based on the notional principal. In the most common type of swap, there is a fixed-rate payer and a fixed-rate receiver. The convention for quoting swap rates is that a swap dealer sets the floating rate equal to the reference rate and then quotes the fixed rate that will apply.

Computing the Payments for a Swap

In the previous section we described in general terms the payments by the fixed-rate payer and fixed-rate receiver but we did not give any details. That is, we explained that if the swap rate is 6% and the notional amount is €100 million, then the fixed-rate payment will be €6 million for the year and the payment is then adjusted based on the frequency of settlement. So, if settlement is semiannual, the payment is €3 million. If it is quarterly, it is €1.5 million. Similarly, the floating-rate payment would be found by multiplying the reference rate by the notional amount and then scaled based on the frequency of settlement.

It was useful to show the basic features of an interest rate swap using quick calculations for the payments such as described above and then explaining how the parties to a swap either benefit or hurt when interest rates changes. However, we will show how to value a swap in this section. To value a swap it is necessary to determine the present value of the fixed-rate payments and the present value of the floating-rate payments. The difference between these two present values is the value of a swap. As will be explained below, whether the value is positive (an asset) or negative (a liability) will depend on the party.

At the inception of the swap, the terms of the swap will be such that the present value of the floating-rate payments is equal to the present value of the fixed-rate payments. That is, the value of the swap is equal to zero at its inception. This is the fundamental principle in determining the swap rate (i.e., the fixed rate that the fixed-rate payer will make).

Here is a roadmap of the presentation. First we will look at how to compute the floating-rate payments. We will see how the future values of the reference rate are determined to obtain the floating rate for the period. From the future values of the reference rate we will then see how to compute the floating-rate payments taking into account the number of days in the payment period. Next we will see how to calculate the fixed-rate payments given the swap rate. Before we look at how to calculate the value of a swap, we will see how to calculate the swap rate. This will require an explanation of how the present value of any cash flow in an interest rate swap is computed. Given the floating-rate payments and the present value of the floating-rate payments, the swap rate can be determined by using the principle that the swap rate is the fixed rate that will make the present value of the fixed-rate payments equal to the present value of the floating-rate payments. Finally, we will see how the value of swap is determined after the inception of a swap.

Calculating the Floating-Rate Payments

For the first floating-rate payment, the amount is known. For all subsequent payments, the floating-rate payment depends on the value of the reference rate when the floating rate is determined. To illustrate the issues associated with calculating the floating-rate payment, we will assume that

- A swap starts today, January 1 of year 1 (swap settlement date).
- The floating-rate payments are made quarterly based on "actual/360."
- The reference rate is 3-month EURIBOR.
- The notional amount of the swap is €100 million.
- The term of the swap is three years.

The quarterly floating-rate payments are based on an "actual/360" day count convention. Recall that this convention means that 360 days are assumed in a year and that in computing the interest for the quarter the actual number of days in the quarter are used. The floating-rate payment is set at the beginning of the quarter, but paid at the end of the quarter—that is, the floating-rate payments are made in arrears.

Suppose that today 3-month EURIBOR is 4.05%. Let's look at what the fixed-rate payer will receive on 31 March of year 1—the date when the first quarterly swap payment is made. There is no uncertainty about what the floating-rate payment will be. In general, the floating-rate payment is determined as follows:

$$\text{Notional amount} \times (\text{3-month Euribor}) \times \frac{\text{No. of days in period}}{360}$$

In our illustration, assuming a nonleap year, the number of days from 1 January of year 1 to 31 March of year 1 (the first quarter) is 90. If 3-month EURIBOR is 4.05%, then the fixed-rate payer will receive a floating-rate payment on March 31 of year 1 equal to

$$€100,000,000 \times 0.0405 \times \frac{90}{360} = €1,012,500$$

Now the difficulty is in determining the floating-rate payment after the first quarterly payment. That is, for the 3-year swap there will be 12 quarterly floating-rate payments. So, while the first quarterly payment is known, the next 11 are not. However, there is a way to hedge the next 11 floating-rate payments by using a futures contract. Specifically, the futures contract used to hedge the future floating-rate payments in a swap whose reference rate is 3-month EURIBOR is the EURIBOR futures contract. We will digress to discuss this contract.

The EURIBOR Futures Contract

As explained earlier in this chapter, a swap position can be interpreted as a package of forward/futures contracts or a package of cash flows from buying and selling cash market instruments. It is the former interpretation that will be used as the basis for valuing a swap. In the case of a EURIBOR-based swap, the appropriate futures contract is the 3-month EURIBOR futures contract. For this reason, we will briefly describe this important contract.

The EURIBOR futures contract trades on LIFFE. Each contract has a €1,000,000 notional value and is traded on an index price basis. The index price basis in which the contract is quoted is equal to 100 minus the annualized EURIBOR futures rate. For example, a EURIBOR futures price of 98.00 means a 3-month EURIBOR futures rate of 2% (100 − 98).

The EURIBOR futures contract is a cash settlement contract and trades with expiration months of March, June, September, and December, up to five years in the future. In addition, the four nearest serial contract months are listed. For example, on 30 June 2003, there were 24 listed EURIBOR futures contracts listed. For the year 2003, the contract expiration months included July, August, September, October, November, and December. In the years 2004–2007, the expiration months were March, June, September, and December. Finally, the expiration months listed for 2008 were March and June.

The EURIBOR futures contract allows a market participant to lock in a 3-month rate on an investment or a 3-month borrowing rate. The 3-month rate begins in the month that the contract settles. For example, an investor on 30 June 2003 purchased a contract that settles on 15 September 2003 and the EURIBOR futures rate is 1.3%, the investor has locked in the rate of 1.3% on a 3-month investment beginning 15 September 2003.

Determining Future Floating-Rate Payments

Now let's return to our objective of determining the future floating-rate payments. These payments can be locked in over the life of the swap using the EURIBOR futures contract. We will show how these floating-rate payments are computed using this contract.

We will begin with the next quarterly payment—from 1 April of year 1 to 30 June of year 1. This quarter has 91 days. The floating-rate payment will be determined by 3-month EURIBOR on 1 April of year 1 and paid on 30 June of year 1. Where might the fixed-rate payer look to today (1 January of year 1) to project what 3-month EURIBOR will be on 1 April of year 1? One possibility is the EURIBOR futures market. There is a 3-month EURIBOR futures contract for settlement on 30 June of year 1. That futures contract will have the market's expectation of what 3-month EURIBOR on 1 April of year 1 is. For example, if the futures price for the 3-month EURIBOR futures contract that settles on 30 June of year 1 is 95.85, then as explained above, the 3-month EURIBOR futures rate is 4.15%. We will refer to that rate for 3-month EURIBOR as the "forward rate." Therefore, if the fixed-rate payer bought 100 of these 3-month EURIBOR futures contract on 1 January of year 1 (the inception of the swap) that settles on 30 June of year 1, then the payment that will be locked in for the quarter (1 April to 30 June of year 1) is

$$€100,000,000 \times 0.0415 \times \frac{91}{360} = €1,049,028$$

(Note that each futures contract is for €1 million and hence 100 contracts have a notional amount of €100 million.) Similarly, the EURIBOR futures contract can be used to lock in a floating-rate payment for each of the next 10 quarters. Once again, it is important to emphasize that the reference rate at the beginning of period t determines the floating rate that will be paid for the period. However, the floating-rate payment is not made until the end of period t.

Exhibit 19.3 shows this for the 3-year swap. Shown in Column (1) is when the quarter begins and in Column (2) when the quarter ends. The payment will be received at the end of the first quarter (March 31 of year 1) and is €1,012,500. That is the known floating-rate payment as explained earlier. It is the only payment that is known. The information used to compute the first payment is in Column (4) which shows the current 3-month EURIBOR (4.05%). The payment is shown in the last column, Column (8).

Notice that Column (7) numbers the quarters from 1 through 12. Look at the heading for Column (7). It identifies each quarter in terms of the end of the quarter. This is important because we will eventually be discounting the payments (cash flows). We must take care to understand when each payment is to be exchanged in order to properly discount. So, for the first payment of €1,012,500 it is going to be received at the end of quarter 1. When we refer to the time period for any payment, the reference is to the end of quarter. So, the fifth payment of €1,225,000 would be identified as the payment for period 5, where period 5 means that it will be exchanged at the end of the fifth quarter.

Calculating the Fixed-Rate Payments

The swap will specify the frequency of settlement for the fixed-rate payments. The frequency need not be the same as the floating-rate payments. For example, in the 3-year swap we have been using to illustrate the calculation of the floating-rate payments, the frequency is quarterly. The frequency of the fixed-rate payments could be semiannual rather than quarterly.

In our illustration we will assume that the frequency of settlement is quarterly for the fixed-rate payments, the same as with the floating-rate payments. The day count convention is the same as for the floating-rate payment, "actual/360." The equation for determining the euro amount of the fixed-rate payment for the period is

$$\text{Notional amount} \times (\text{Swap rate}) \times \frac{\text{No. of days in period}}{360}$$

EXHIBIT 19.3 Floating-Rate Payments Based on Initial EURIBOR and EURIBOR Futures

(1) Quarter Starts	(2) Quarter Ends	(3) Number of Days in Quarter	(4) Current 3-Month EURIBOR	(5) EURIBOR CD Futures Price	(6) Forward Rate	(7) Period = End of Quarter	(8) Floating-Rate Payment at End of Quarter
Jan 1 year 1	Mar 31 year 1	90	4.05%		—	1	1,012,500
Apr 1 year 1	June 30 year 1	91		95.85	4.15%	2	1,049,028
July 1 year 1	Sept 30 year 1	92		95.45	4.55%	3	1,162,778
Oct 1 year 1	Dec 31 year 1	92		95.28	4.72%	4	1,206,222
Jan 1 year 2	Mar 31 year 2	90		95.10	4.90%	5	1,225,000
Apr 1 year 2	June 30 year 2	91		94.97	5.03%	6	1,271,472
July 1 year 2	Sept 30 year 2	92		94.85	5.15%	7	1,316,111
Oct 1 year 2	Dec 31 year 2	92		94.75	5.25%	8	1,341,667
Jan 1 year 3	Mar 31 year 3	90		94.60	5.40%	9	1,350,000
Apr 1 year 3	June 30 year 3	91		94.50	5.50%	10	1,390,278
July 1 year 3	Sept 30 year 3	92		94.35	5.65%	11	1,443,889
Oct 1 year 3	Dec 31 year 3	92		94.24	5.76%	12	1,472,000

It is the same equation as for determining the floating-rate payment except that the swap rate is used instead of the reference rate (3-month EURIBOR in our illustration).

For example, suppose that the swap rate is 4.98% and the quarter has 90 days. Then the fixed-rate payment for the quarter is

$$€100,000,000 \times 0.0498 \times \frac{90}{360} = €1,245,000$$

If there are 92 days in a quarter, the fixed-rate payment for the quarter is

$$€100,000,000 \times 0.0498 \times \frac{92}{360} = €1,272,667$$

Note that the rate is fixed for each quarter but the euro amount of the payment depends on the number of days in the period.

Exhibit 19.4 shows the fixed-rate payments based on different assumed values for the swap rate. The first three columns of the exhibit show the same information as in Exhibit 19.3—the beginning and end of the quarter and the number of days in the quarter. Column (4) simply uses the notation for the period. That is, period 1 means the end of the first quarter, period 2 means the end of the second quarter, and so on. The other columns of the exhibit show the payments for each assumed swap rate.

Calculation of the Swap Rate

Now that we know how to calculate the payments for the fixed rate and floating-rate sides of a swap, where the reference rate is 3-month EURIBOR given (1) the current value for 3-month EURIBOR; (2) the expected 3-month EURIBOR from the EURIBOR futures contract; and (3) the assumed swap rate, we can demonstrate how to compute the swap rate.

At the initiation of an interest rate swap, the counterparties are agreeing to exchange future payments and no upfront payments by either party are made. This means that the swap terms must be such that the present value of the payments to be made by the counterparties must be at least equal to the present value of the payments that will be received. In fact, to eliminate arbitrage opportunities, the present value of the payments made by a party will be equal to the present value of the payments received by that same party. *The equivalence (or no arbitrage) of the present value of the payments is the key principle in calculating the swap rate.*

Since we will have to calculate the present value of the payments, let's show how this is done.

EXHIBIT 19.4 Fixed-Rate Payments for Several Assumed Swap Rates

(1)	(2)	(3)	(4)	(5)	(6)	(7)	(8)	(9)
Quarter Starts	Quarter Ends	Number of Days in Quarter	Period = End of Quarter	Fixed-Rate Payment If Swap Rate Is Assumed to Be				
				4.9800%	4.9873%	4.9874%	4.9875%	4.9880%
Jan 1 year 1	Mar 31 year 1	90	1	1,245,000	1,246,825	1,246,850	1,246,875	1,247,000
Apr 1 year 1	June 30 year 1	91	2	1,258,833	1,260,679	1,260,704	1,260,729	1,260,856
July 1 year 1	Sept 30 year 1	92	3	1,272,667	1,274,532	1,274,558	1,274,583	1,274,711
Oct 1 year 1	Dec 31 year 1	92	4	1,272,667	1,274,532	1,274,558	1,274,583	1,274,711
Jan 1 year 2	Mar 31 year 2	90	5	1,245,000	1,246,825	1,246,850	1,246,875	1,247,000
Apr 1 year 2	June 30 year 2	91	6	1,258,833	1,260,679	1,260,704	1,260,729	1,260,856
July 1 year 2	Sept 30 year 2	92	7	1,272,667	1,274,532	1,274,558	1,274,583	1,274,711
Oct 1 year 2	Dec 31 year 2	92	8	1,272,667	1,274,532	1,274,558	1,274,583	1,274,711
Jan 1 year 3	Mar 31 year 3	90	9	1,245,000	1,246,825	1,246,850	1,246,875	1,247,000
Apr 1 year 3	June 30 year 3	91	10	1,258,833	1,260,679	1,260,704	1,260,729	1,260,856
July 1 year 3	Sept 30 year 3	92	11	1,272,667	1,274,532	1,274,558	1,274,583	1,274,711
Oct 1 year 3	Dec 31 year 3	92	12	1,272,667	1,274,532	1,274,558	1,274,583	1,274,711

Calculating the Present Value of the Floating-Rate Payments

As explained earlier, we must be careful about how we compute the present value of payments. In particular, we must carefully specify (1) the timing of the payment and (2) the interest rates that should be used to discount the payments. We have already addressed the first issue. In constructing the exhibit for the payments, we indicated that the payments are at the end of the quarter. So, we denoted the time periods with respect to the end of the quarter.

Now let's turn to the interest rates that should be used for discounting. In Chapter 3, we emphasized two things. First, every cash flow should be discounted at its own discount rate using a spot rate. So, if we discounted a cash flow of €1 using the spot rate for period t, the present value would be

$$\text{Present value of €1 to be received in period } t = \frac{€1}{(1 + \text{Spot rate for period } t)^t}$$

The second thing we emphasized is that forward rates are derived from spot rates so that if we discounted a cash flow using forward rates rather than a spot rate, we would come up with the same value. That is, the present value of €1 to be received in period t can be rewritten as

$$\text{Present value of €1 to be received in period } t$$
$$= \frac{€1}{\left(1 + \frac{\text{Forward rate}}{\text{for period 1}}\right)\left(1 + \frac{\text{Forward rate}}{\text{for period 2}}\right)\cdots\left(1 + \frac{\text{Forward rate}}{\text{for period } t}\right)}$$

We will refer to the present value of €1 to be received in period t as the *forward discount factor*. In our calculations involving swaps, we will compute the forward discount factor for a period using the forward rates. These are the same forward rates that are used to compute the floating-rate payments—those obtained from the EURIBOR futures contract. We must make just one more adjustment. We must adjust the forward rates used in the formula for the number of days in the period (i.e., the quarter in our illustrations) in the same way that we made this adjustment to obtain the payments. Specifically, the forward rate for a period, which we will refer to as the period forward rate, is computed using the following equation:

$$\text{Period forward rate} = \text{Annual forward rate} \times \left(\frac{\text{Days in period}}{360}\right)$$

For example, look at Exhibit 19.3. The annual forward rate for period 4 is 4.72%. The period forward rate for period 4 is

$$\text{Period forward rate} = 4.72\% \times \left(\frac{92}{360}\right) = 1.2062\%$$

Column (5) in Exhibit 19.5 shows the annual forward rate for all 12 periods (reproduced from Exhibit 19.3) and Column (6) shows the period forward rate for all 12 periods. Note that the period forward rate for period 1 is 4.05%, the known rate for 3-month EURIBOR.

Also shown in Exhibit 19.5 is the forward discount factor for all 12 periods. These values are shown in the last column. Let's show how the forward discount factor is computed for periods 1, 2, and 3. For period 1, the forward discount factor is

$$\text{Forward discount factor} = \frac{\text{€}1}{(1.010125)} = 0.98997649$$

For period 2,

$$\text{Forward discount factor} = \frac{\text{€}1}{(1.010125)(1.010490)} = 0.97969917$$

For period 3,

$$\text{Forward discount factor} = \frac{\text{€}1}{(1.010125)(1.010490)(1.011628)}$$
$$= 0.96843839$$

Given the floating-rate payment for a period and the forward discount factor for the period, the present value of the payment can be computed. For example, from Exhibit 19.3 we see that the floating-rate payment for period 4 is €1,206,222. From Exhibit 19.5, the forward discount factor for period 4 is 0.95689609. Therefore, the present value of the payment is

$$\text{Present value of period 4 payment} = \text{€}1,206,222 \times 0.95689609$$
$$= \text{€}1,154,229$$

Exhibit 19.6 shows the present value for each payment. The total present value of the 12 floating-rate payments is €14,052,917. Thus, the present value of the payments that the fixed-rate payer will receive is €14,052,917 and the present value of the payments that the fixed-rate receiver will make is €14,052,917.

EXHIBIT 19.5 Calculating the Forward Discount Factor

(1) Quarter Starts	(2) Quarter Ends	(3) Number of Days in Quarter	(4) Period = End of Quarter	(5) Forward Rate	(6) Period Forward Rate	(7) Forward Discount Factor
Jan 1 year 1	Mar 31 year 1	90	1	4.05%	1.0125%	0.98997649
Apr 1 year 1	June 30 year 1	91	2	4.15%	1.0490%	0.97969917
July 1 year 1	Sept 30 year 1	92	3	4.55%	1.1628%	0.96843839
Oct 1 year 1	Dec 31 year 1	92	4	4.72%	1.2062%	0.95689609
Jan 1 year 2	Mar 31 year 2	90	5	4.90%	1.2250%	0.94531597
Apr 1 year 2	June 30 year 2	91	6	5.03%	1.2715%	0.93344745
July 1 year 2	Sept 30 year 2	92	7	5.15%	1.3161%	0.92132183
Oct 1 year 2	Dec 31 year 2	92	8	5.25%	1.3417%	0.90912441
Jan 1 year 3	Mar 31 year 3	90	9	5.40%	1.3500%	0.89701471
Apr 1 year 3	June 30 year 3	91	10	5.50%	1.3903%	0.88471472
July 1 year 3	Sept 30 year 3	92	11	5.65%	1.4439%	0.87212224
Oct 1 year 3	Dec 31 year 3	92	12	5.76%	1.4720%	0.85947083

EXHIBIT 19.6 Present Value of the Floating-Rate Payments

(1) Quarter Starts	(2) Quarter Ends	(3) Period = End of Quarter	(4) Forward Discount Factor	(5) Floating-Rate Payment at End of Quarter	(6) PV of Floating-Rate Payment
Jan 1 year 1	Mar 31 year 1	1	0.9897649	1,012,500	1,002,351
Apr 1 year 1	June 30 year 1	2	0.97969917	1,049,028	1,027,732
July 1 year 1	Sept 30 year 1	3	0.96843839	1,162,778	1,126,079
Oct 1 year 1	Dec 31 year 1	4	0.95689609	1,206,222	1,154,229
Jan 1 year 2	Mar 31 year 2	5	0.94531597	1,225,000	1,158,012
Apr 1 year 2	June 30 year 2	6	0.93344745	1,271,472	1,186,852
July 1 year 2	Sept 30 year 2	7	0.92132183	1,316,111	1,212,562
Oct 1 year 2	Dec 31 year 2	8	0.90912441	1,341,667	1,219,742
Jan 1 year 3	Mar 31 year 3	9	0.89701471	1,350,000	1,210,970
Apr 1 year 3	June 30 year 3	10	0.88471472	1,390,278	1,229,999
July 1 year 3	Sept 30 year 3	11	0.87212224	1,443,889	1,259,248
Oct 1 year 3	Dec 31 year 3	12	0.85947083	1,472,000	1,265,141
				Total	14,052,917

Determination of the Swap Rate

The fixed-rate payer will require that the present value of the fixed-rate payments that must be made based on the swap rate not exceed the €14,052,917 payments to be received from the floating-rate payments. The fixed-rate receiver will require that the present value of the fixed-rate payments to be received is at least as great as the €14,052,917 that must be paid. This means that both parties will require a present value for the fixed-rate payments to be €14,052,917. If that is the case, the present value of the fixed-rate payments is equal to the present value of the floating-rate payments and therefore the value of the swap is zero for both parties at the inception of the swap. The interest rates that should be used to compute the present value of the fixed-rate payments are the same interest rates as those used to discount the floating-rate payments.

To show how to compute the swap rate, we begin with the basic relationship for no arbitrage to exist:

$$\text{PV of floating-rate payments} = \text{PV of fixed-rate payments}$$

We know the value for the left-hand side of the equation.

If we let

$$SR = \text{Swap rate}$$

and

$$\text{Days}_t = \text{Number of days in the payment period } t$$

then the fixed-rate payment for period t is equal to

$$\text{Notional amount} \times SR \times \frac{\text{Days}_t}{360}$$

The present value of the fixed-rate payment for period t is found by multiplying the previous expression by the forward discount factor. If we let FDF_t denote the forward discount factor for period t, then the present value of the fixed-rate payment for period t is equal to

$$\text{Notional amount} \times SR \times \frac{\text{Days}_t}{360} \times FDF_t$$

We can now sum up the present value of the fixed-rate payment for each period to get the present value of the floating-rate payments. Using the Greek symbol sigma, Σ, to denote summation and letting N be the number of periods in the swap, then the present value of the fixed-rate payments can be expressed as

$$\sum_{t=1}^{N} \text{Notional amount} \times SR \times \frac{\text{Days}_t}{360} \times \text{FDF}_t$$

This can also be expressed as

$$SR \sum_{t=1}^{N} \text{Notional amount} \times \frac{\text{Days}_t}{360} \times \text{FDF}_t$$

The condition for no arbitrage is that the present value of the fixed-rate payments as given by the expression above is equal to the present value of the floating-rate payments. That is,

$$SR \sum_{t=1}^{N} \text{notional amount} \times \frac{\text{Days}_t}{360} \times \text{FDF}_t = PV \text{ of floating rate payments}$$

Solving for the swap rate

$$SR = \frac{PV \text{ of floating rate payments}}{\sum_{t=1}^{N} \text{notional amount} \times \frac{\text{Days}_t}{360} \times \text{FDF}_t}$$

All of the values to compute the swap rate are known.

Let's apply the formula to determine the swap rate for our 3-year swap. Exhibit 19.7 shows the calculation of the denominator of the formula. The forward discount factor for each period shown in Column (5) is obtained from Column (4) of Exhibit 19.6. The sum of the last column in Exhibit 19.7 shows that the denominator of the swap rate formula is €281,764,282. We know from Exhibit 19.6 that the present value of the floating-rate payments is €14,052,917. Therefore, the swap rate is

$$SR = \frac{€14,052,917}{€281,764,282} = 0.049875 = 4.9875\%$$

EXHIBIT 19.7 Calculating the Denominator for the Swap Rate Formula

(1) Quarter Starts	(2) Quarter Ends	(3) Number of Days in Quarter	(4) Period = End of Quarter	(5) Forward Discount Factor	(6) Days/360	(7) Forward Discount Factor × Days/360 × Notional
Jan 1 year 1	Mar 31 year 1	90	1	0.98997649	0.25000000	24,749,412
Apr 1 year 1	June 30 year 1	91	2	0.97969917	0.25277778	24,764,618
July 1 year 1	Sept 30 year 1	92	3	0.96843839	0.25555556	24,748,981
Oct 1 year 1	Dec 31 year 1	92	4	0.95689609	0.25555556	24,454,011
Jan 1 year 2	Mar 31 year 2	90	5	0.94531597	0.25000000	23,632,899
Apr 1 year 2	June 30 year 2	91	6	0.93344745	0.25277778	23,595,477
July 1 year 2	Sept 30 year 2	92	7	0.92132183	0.25555556	23,544,891
Oct 1 year 2	Dec 31 year 2	92	8	0.90912441	0.25555556	23,233,179
Jan 1 year 3	Mar 31 year 3	90	9	0.89701471	0.25000000	22,425,368
Apr 1 year 3	June 30 year 3	91	10	0.88471472	0.25277778	22,363,622
July 1 year 3	Sept 30 year 3	92	11	0.87212224	0.25555556	22,287,568
Oct 1 year 3	Dec 31 year 3	92	12	0.85947083	0.25555556	21,964,255
					Total	281,764,282

Given the swap rate, the *swap spread* can be determined. For example, since this is a 3-year swap, the convention is to use the 3-year rate on the euro benchmark yield curve. If the yield on that issue is 4.5875%, the swap spread is 40 basis points (4.9875% − 4.5875%).

The calculation of the swap rate for all swaps follows the same principle: equating the present value of the fixed-rate payments to that of the floating-rate payments.

Valuing a Swap

Once the swap transaction is completed, changes in market interest rates will change the payments of the floating-rate side of the swap. The value of an interest rate swap is the difference between the present value of the payments of the two sides of the swap. The 3-month EURIBOR forward rates from the current EURIBOR futures contracts are used to (1) calculate the floating-rate payments and (2) determine the discount factors at which to calculate the present value of the payments.

To illustrate this, consider the 3-year swap used to demonstrate how to calculate the swap rate. Suppose that one year later, interest rates change as shown in Columns (4) and (6) in Exhibit 19.8. In Column (4) shows the current 3-month EURIBOR. In Column (5) are the EURIBOR futures price for each period. These rates are used to compute the forward rates in Column (6). Note that the interest rates have increased one year later since the rates in Exhibit 19.8 are greater than those in Exhibit 19.3. As in Exhibit 19.3, the current 3-month EURIBOR and the forward rates are used to compute the floating-rate payments. These payments are shown in Column (8) of Exhibit 19.8.

In Exhibit 19.9, the forward discount factor is computed for each period. The calculation is the same as in Exhibit 19.5 to obtain the forward discount factor for each period. The forward discount factor for each period is shown in the last column of Exhibit 19.9.

In Exhibit 19.10 the forward discount factor (from Exhibit 19.9) and the floating-rate payments (from Exhibit 19.8) are shown. The fixed-rate payments need not be recomputed. They are the payments shown in Column (8) of Exhibit 19.4. This is the fixed-rate payments for the swap rate of 4.9875% and is reproduced in Exhibit 19.10. Now the two payment streams must be discounted using the new forward discount factors. As shown at the bottom of Exhibit 19.10, the two present values are as follows:

Present value of floating-rate payments   €11,459,495
Present value of fixed-rate payments   €9,473,390

EXHIBIT 19.8 Rates and Floating-Rate Payments One Year Later if Rates Increase

(1)	(2)	(3)	(4)	(5)	(6)	(7)	(8)
Quarter Starts	Quarter Ends	Number of Days in Quarter	Current 3-Month EURIBOR	EURIBOR Futures Price	Forward Rate	Period = End of Quarter	Floating-Rate Payments at End of Quarter
Jan 1 year 2	Mar 31 year 2	90	5.25%			1	1,312,500
Apr 1 year 2	June 30 year 2	91		94.27	5.73%	2	1,448,417
July 1 year 2	Sept 30 year 2	92		94.22	5.78%	3	1,477,111
Oct 1 year 2	Dec 31 year 2	92		94.00	6.00%	4	1,533,333
Jan 1 year 3	Mar 31 year 3	90		93.85	6.15%	5	1,537,500
Apr 1 year 3	June 30 year 3	91		93.75	6.25%	6	1,579,861
July 1 year 3	Sept 30 year 3	92		93.54	6.46%	7	1,650,889
Oct 1 year 3	Dec 31 year 3	92		93.25	6.75%	8	1,725,000

EXHIBIT 19.9 Period Forward Rates and Forward Discount Factors One Year Later if Rates Increase

(1)	(2)	(3)	(4)	(5)	(6)	(7)
Quarter Starts	Quarter Ends	Number of Days in Quarter	Period = End of Quarter	Forward Rate	Period Forward Rate	Forward Discount Factor
Jan 1 year 2	Mar 31 year 2	90	1	5.25%	1.3125%	0.98704503
Apr 1 year 2	June 30 year 2	91	2	5.73%	1.4484%	0.97295263
July 1 year 2	Sept 30 year 2	92	3	5.78%	1.4771%	0.95879023
Oct 1 year 2	Dec 31 year 2	92	4	6.00%	1.5333%	0.94431080
Jan 1 year 3	Mar 31 year 3	90	5	6.15%	1.5375%	0.93001186
Apr 1 year 3	June 30 year 3	91	6	6.25%	1.5799%	0.91554749
July 1 year 3	Sept 30 year 3	92	7	6.46%	1.6509%	0.90067829
Oct 1 year 3	Dec 31 year 3	92	8	6.75%	1.7250%	0.88540505

EXHIBIT 19.10 Valuing the Swap One Year Later if Rates Increase

(1)	(2)	(3)	(4)	(5)	(6)	(7)
Quarter Starts	Quarter Ends	Forward Discount Factor	Floating Cash Flow at End of Quarter	PV of Floating Cash Flow	Fixed Cash Flow at End of Quarter	PV of Fixed Cash Flow
Jan 1 year 2	Mar 31 year 2	0.98704503	1,312,500	1,295,497	1,246,875	1,230,722
Apr 1 year 2	June 30 year 2	0.97295263	1,448,417	1,409,241	1,260,729	1,226,630
July 1 year 2	Sept 30 year 2	0.95879023	1,477,111	1,416,240	1,274,583	1,222,058
Oct 1 year 2	Dec 31 year 2	0.94431080	1,533,333	1,447,943	1,274,583	1,203,603
Jan 1 year 3	Mar 31 year 3	0.93001186	1,537,500	1,429,893	1,246,875	1,159,609
Apr 1 year 3	June 30 year 3	0.91554749	1,579,861	1,446,438	1,260,729	1,154,257
July 1 year 3	Sept 30 year 3	0.90067829	1,650,889	1,486,920	1,274,583	1,147,990
Oct 1 year 3	Dec 31 year 3	0.88540505	1,725,000	1,527,324	1,274,583	1,128,523
			Total	11,459,495		9,473,390

Summary	Fixed-Rate Payer	Fixed-Rate Receiver
PV of payments received	11,459,495	9,473,390
PV of payments made	9,473,390	11,459,495
Value of swap	1,986,105	-1,986,105

The two present values are not equal and therefore for one party the value of the swap increased and for the other party the value of the swap decreased. Let's look at which party gained and which party lost.

The fixed-rate payer will receive the floating-rate payments. And these payments have a present value of €11,459,495. The present value of the payments that must be made by the fixed-rate payer is €9,473,390. Thus, the swap has a positive value for the fixed-rate payer equal to the difference in the two present values of €1,986,105. This is the value of the swap to the fixed-rate payer. Notice, when interest rates increase (as they did in the illustration analyzed), the fixed-rate payer benefits because the value of the swap increases.

In contrast, the fixed-rate receiver must make payments with a present value of €11,459,495, but will only receive fixed-rate payments with a present value equal to €9,473,390. Thus, the value of the swap for the fixed-rate receiver is −€1,986,105. Again, as explained earlier, the fixed-rate receiver is adversely affected by a rise in interest rates because it results in a decline in the value of a swap.

The same valuation principle applies to more complicated swaps. For example, there are swaps whose notional amount changes in a pre-determined way over the life of the swap. These include amortizing swaps, accreting swaps, and roller coaster swaps. Once the payments are specified, the present value is calculated as described above by simply adjusting the payment amounts by the changing notional amounts—the methodology does *not* change.

PRIMARY DETERMINANTS OF SWAP SPREADS

As we have seen, interest rate swaps are valued using no-arbitrage relationships relative to instruments (funding or investment vehicles) that produce the same cash flows under the same circumstances. Earlier we provided two interpretations of a swap: (1) a package of futures/forward contracts and (2) a package of cash market instruments. The swap spread is defined as the difference between the swap's fixed rate and the rate on the Euro Benchmark Yield curve whose maturity matches the swap's tenor.

Exhibit 19.11 presents Bloomberg's World Swap screen which presents swap spreads for various countries around the world for June 27, 2003. In this screen, the tenor of the swaps in this screen is five years as can be seen in the box labeled "Maturity" in the upper left-hand corner. Among the other choices available, a user can choose to display swap rates rather than spreads. Exhibit 19.12 is a time series plot obtained from Bloomberg for daily values of the 5-year euro swap spread (in basis points) for the period June 27, 2002 to June 27, 2003.

EXHIBIT 19.11   Swap Rates and Spreads for Various Maturities

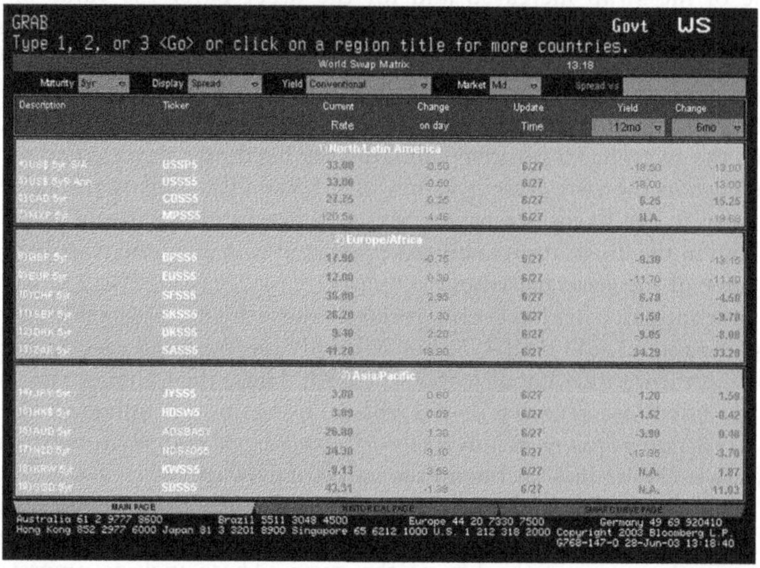

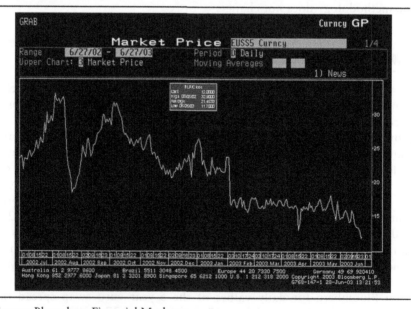

Source: Bloomberg Financial Markets.

EXHIBIT 19.12   Time Series of the 5-Year Swap Spread

Source: Bloomberg Financial Markets.

The swap spread is determined by the same factors that drive the spread over benchmark government on instruments that replicate a swap's cash flows, that is, produce a similar return or funding profile. As discussed below, the swap spread's key determinant for swaps with tenors (maturities) of five years or less is the cost of hedging in the EURIBOR futures market.[2] For longer tenor swaps, the swap spread is largely driven by credit spreads in the corporate bond market.[3] Specifically, longer-dated swaps are priced relative to rates paid by investment-grade credits in traditional fixed- and floating-rate markets.

---

[2] Naturally, this presupposes the reference rate used for the floating-rate cash flows is EURIBOR. Furthermore, part of swap spread is attributable simply to the fact that EURIBOR for a given maturity is higher than the rate on a comparable maturity benchmark government.

[3] The default risk component of a swap spread will be smaller than for a comparable bond credit spread. The reasons are straightforward. First, since only net interest payments are exchanged rather than both principal and coupon interest payments, the total cash flow at risk is lower. Second, the probability of default depends jointly on the probability of the counterparty defaulting and whether or not the swap has a positive value. See John C. Hull, *Introduction to Futures and Options Markets, Third Edition* (Upper Saddle River, NJ: Prentice Hall, 1998).

CHAPTER 20

A Practical Guide to Swap Curve Construction

Uri Ron, CFA
Senior Trader
Bank of Canada

Swaps are increasingly used by banks, corporations, insurance companies, governments, government-sponsored enterprises, hedge funds, pension plans, mutual funds, investment dealers, and institutional money managers for hedging and speculation. Swaps are also used as benchmarks for evaluating the performance of other fixed-income markets, and as reference rates for forecasting.

Swaps offer an operationally efficient and flexible means of transforming cash flow streams. The swap market has little or no government regulation, and provides a high degree of privacy. The swap market's liquidity, depth, and high correlation with fixed-income products, other than plain vanilla government bonds, render its derived term structure a fundamental pricing mechanism for these products and a relevant benchmark for measuring the relative value of different fixed-income products.[1]

The role of the swap term structure as a relevant benchmark for pricing and hedging purposes is expected to increase as government fiscal situations improve. An improved fiscal situation reduces the size of government debt programs, in effect decreasing the liquidity and effi-

---

[1] For correlations of swap rates and other fixed-income rates for the US market, see M. Fleming, "The Benchmark U.S. Treasury Market: Recent Performance and Possible Alternatives," *FRBNY Economic Policy Review* (April 2000).

ciency of government debt markets. Furthermore, the financial markets crisis in the fall of 1998 reinforced the "flight to quality" phenomenon, where spreads between governments' issues and other fixed-income securities widened substantially under adverse market conditions, thereby calling into question the role of the government market as a relevant benchmark for nongovernment issues. The swap term structure again emerges as a potential substitute.

With the increased importance of the swap market, practitioners recognize the importance of a consistent and computationally efficient swap term structure for marking to market financial transactions; marking to market is the practice of valuing an instrument to reflect current market conditions. While the general framework for the construction of the swap term structure is widely known, the derivation details are vague and not well documented. This chapter attempts to bridge this gap by carefully covering all angles of the swap term-structure derivation procedure while leaving enough flexibility to adjust the constructed term structure to the specific microrequirements and constraints of each primary swap market.

Marking to market fixed-income portfolios is instrumental for trading, accounting, performance valuation, risk management, and satisfying interinstitution collateralization requirements. The current methodology in capital markets for marking to market fixed-income securities is to estimate and discount future cash flows using rates derived from the appropriate term structure. The swap term structure is increasingly used as the foundation for deriving relative term structures and as a benchmark for pricing and hedging.

The first section describes the motivation for using the swap term structure as a benchmark for pricing and hedging fixed-income securities. The second section examines the factors that affect swap spreads and swap market flows. The third section describes a swap term structure derivation technique designed to mark to market fixed-income products. Finally, different aspects of the derived term structure are discussed.

THE SWAP CURVE ADVANTAGE

The swap market offers a variety of advantages. It has almost no government regulations, making it more comparable across different markets; some sovereign issues offer a variety of tax benefits to domestic and/or foreign investors, making government curve comparative analysis across countries latently inconsistent. The swap market is an increasingly liquid market, with narrow bid-ask spreads and a wide spectrum of maturities. The supply of swaps is solely dependent on the number of counterparties wishing to transact at any given time. No position in an underlying asset is required, avoiding any potential repo "specials" effects.[2] Given the liquidity and large size of the swap market, new swaps with standard maturities are issued daily, keeping a constant forecast horizon, mitigating any potential coupon effects; bonds with high coupons tend to have lower yields to maturity than bonds with low coupons.[3] The fungibility of swaps also prevents swaps with similar cash flows from trading at substantially different rates, contributing to market efficiency.

Swaps have similar credit risk properties across countries, making them more comparable than the government term structure. Government debt is considered risk-free; however, governments entail different credit risk qualities across countries. Credit risk is embedded in the swap curve as swaps are based on the balance sheet of the banking sector (see Exhibit 20.1 for inputs). In addition, swap rates are highly correlated with yields on other fixed-income securities, even under adverse market conditions, making swaps latently a better hedging vehicle than government issues. Other fixed-income securities include agency debt, corporate debt, and securitized paper.

Swap rates are frequently quoted as a spread over government issues, therefore serving as a rough indicator of credit risk of the banking sector. A swap spread is the difference between the fixed rate on an interest rate swap contract and the yield on a government bond with an equivalent tenor. The fixed swap rate is the rate that equates the present value of the swap to zero. Quoting the swap curve as a spread over the government curve can be unreliable, as there is a maturity mismatch and coupon effect between the different quoted government notes and their corresponding swap issues. Swap rates should be quoted directly off the swap market. Quoting the swap rate as a spread over government issues is common mainly in Anglo-Saxon swap markets.

The most prominent impediment to swap market liquidity is swap counterparty credit exposure, which is balance-sheet intensive, in that it is a bilateral contract. The risk is the potential loss to a counterparty of the present value of a swap position if a swap party defaults. Therefore, parties to a swap transaction must be confident in the credit quality of

---

[2] A repo transaction is the borrowing of money by selling securities to a counterparty and buying them back at a later date at a preagreed price. The repo rate is the interest rate embedded in a repurchase agreement. Repo "specials" carry different rates, thereby introducing inconsistencies to the derived term structure, such as the government term structure.

[3] A.M. Malz, "Interbank Interest Rates as Term Structure Indicators," Federal Reserve Bank of New York (March 1998).

EXHIBIT 20.1   Swap Inputs

European Dollar (EUR)

- Interbank overnight financing rate
- Interbank deposit rates out to three months
- LIFFE 3-month EURIBOR futures out to three years
- Swap rates

United Kingdom Sterling (GBP)

- Interbank overnight financing rate
- Interbank deposit rates out to three months
- LIFFE 3-month sterling LIBOR futures out to two years
- Swap rates

Canadian Dollar (CAD)

- Interbank overnight financing rate
- Banker's acceptance out to three months
- BAX futures out to two years
- Swap rates

Japanese Yen (JPY)

- Interbank overnight financing rate
- Interbank deposit rates out to three months
- CME 3-month Yen LIBOR futures out to two years
- Swap rates

US Dollar (USD)

- Interbank overnight financing rate
- LIBOR fixings out to three months
- Eurodollar futures or FRAs out to five years
- Swap rates (frequently quoted as government bond yield for a chosen
  benchmark adjusted for swap spreads)

their swap counterparty. A variety of credit enhancement mechanisms have been developed to reduce this potential credit exposure. Some of the mechanisms include the use of credit-enhanced subsidiaries, credit derivatives, netting, posting of collateral, recouponing, and an automatic swap unwind clause triggered by a credit event.

In summary, the swap term structure offers several advantages over government curves, and is a robust tool for pricing and hedging fixed-income products. Correlations among governments and other fixed-income products have declined, making the swap term structure a more efficient hedging and pricing vehicle.[4] With the supply of government issues declining and high correlations of credit spreads to swap spreads, the swap term structure is a potential alternative to the government term structure as a benchmark for measuring the relative value of different debt classes.

THE DETERMINANTS OF SWAP SPREADS/RATES

Theoretically, swap markets depend on the relationship between the yield on government issues, implied rates on futures contracts, and prevailing swap spreads over government issues. Traders speculate on swap spread movements by trading the underlying government issues and corresponding futures contracts. This type of activity has greatly increased the liquidity and efficiency of futures markets and swap markets.

The relationship is reduced as maturity is increased because of the low liquidity of futures markets beyond two to five years, increased futures execution risk, and increased interest rate volatility. The convexity problem when using futures contracts (nonconvex instruments) to hedge interest rate swap positions (convex instruments) is more pronounced for long-term transactions, resulting in reduced hedge efficiency. The convexity issue is addressed in detail later in this chapter.

Empirically, there are several factors that affect swap spreads. These factors drive swap flows, pricing, and hedging methods of swap markets. The main factors and their impact on swap spreads are described below.

Government Supply

The level of a government's budget surpluses or deficits influences swap spreads. During periods of increased budget surpluses, the reduction in government supply increases the attractiveness of government issues, develops a scarcity premium, and widens swap spreads. Budget deficits have the opposite effect and result in narrower swap spreads.

---

[4] D. Theobald and G. Singh, "The Outlook for Swaps as a Hedge Vehicle," JP Morgan (2000).

Corporate Supply

Corporations, because of their lower credit ratings, generally have a comparative advantage in short-term financing, but their fundamental need is for long-term funding. Corporations therefore usually issue short-term debt and swap it into long-term debt, exerting upward pressure on swap spreads. In recent years, owing to credit concerns, corporations have sought to lock in relatively expensive long-term financing to avoid the possibility of having to refinance their debt under adverse credit market conditions. Corporations issue long-term debt and swap it into floating-rate liability using interest rate swaps to benefit from recent steep upward-sloping yield curves. In this case, corporations are fixed-rate receivers exerting downward pressure on swap spreads. Therefore, corporate supply can have varying effects on swap spreads.

High Grade Credit Issuance

High grade credit issuance tends to narrow swap spreads. This group of issuers includes supranationals and government agencies. These issuers are either development banks or credit export banks that have a comparative advantage at issuing fixed-rate bonds while their balance sheet needs floating-rate funding. Therefore, they would issue fixed-rate bonds and swap the liability into floating-rate funding, exerting downward pressure on swap spreads. They are fixed-rate receivers.

Mortgage Hedging

A decline in absolute interest rates tends to trigger mortgage refinancing, which accentuates the negative convexity of Mortgage Backed Securities (MBS) portfolios. Interest rate swaps are often used to extend the shrinking duration of MBS portfolios by receiving fixed rates on swaps. The need of MBS portfolios to receive fixed rates in swap markets has a narrowing effect on swap spreads.

Economic Growth

Swap spreads tend to narrow with slower economic growth, reflecting reduced corporate issuance and steady or increased high grade credit issuance. A good proxy for economic growth is capacity utilization.

Equity Markets

Declines in equity market values tend to place upward pressure on swap spreads. A decline in equity market values deteriorates the overall credit health of the banking sector, because it reduces collateral value in the entire system.

Change of Government Benchmark

Swap spreads are quoted off specific government benchmarks. When a benchmark issue is replaced, it can have a technical effect on swap spreads. Swap spreads can either narrow or widen, depending on the new benchmark issue used and the shape of the yield curve. The change is only technical, however, and absolute swap rate levels remain unchanged.

There are a large number of other factors that can have an impact on swap spreads. Each factor can have varying effects on swap spreads over time. Institutional investors and hedge funds continuously develop forward-looking models that incorporate different factors in an attempt to predict swap spread movements for speculation purposes.

SWAP CURVE CONSTRUCTION

The swap curve depicts the relationship between the term structure and swap rates. The swap curve consists of observed market interest rates, derived from market instruments that represent the most liquid and dominant instruments for their respective time horizons, bootstrapped and combined using an interpolation algorithm. This section describes a complete methodology for the construction of the swap term structure.

Curve Inputs

In deriving the swap curve, the inputs should cover the complete term structure (i.e., short-, middle-, and long-term parts). The inputs should be observable, liquid, and with similar credit properties. Using an interpolation methodology, the inputs should form a complete, consistent, and smooth yield curve that closely tracks observed market data. Once the complete swap term structure is derived, an instrument is marked to market by extracting the appropriate rates off the derived curve.

The technique for constructing the swap term structure, as constructed by market participants for marking to market purposes, divides the curve into three term buckets. The short end of the swap term structure is derived using interbank deposit rates. The middle area of the swap curve is derived from either forward rate agreements (FRAs) or interest rate futures contracts. The latter requires a convexity adjustment to render it equivalent to FRAs.[5] The long end of the term structure is constructed using swap par rates derived from the swap market.

A combination of the different interest rates forms the basis for the swap curve term structure. For currencies where the future or forward

---

[5] The adjustment required to convert a futures interest rate to a forward interest rate.

EXHIBIT 20.2   Yield Calculation Conventions by Currency

Currency/Rate	Payment Freq.	Compounding Freq.	Day Count Convention
EUR cash rates			ACT/360
EUR swap rates	A	A	30/360
GBP cash rates			ACT/365
GBP swap rates	S/A	S/A	ACT/365
CAD cash rates			ACT/365
CAD swap rates	S/A	S/A	ACT/365
JPY cash rates			ACT/360
JPY swap rates	S/A	S/A	ACT/365
USD cash rates			ACT/360
USD swap rates	S/A	S/A	30/360

market is illiquid, inefficient, or nonexistent for certain tenors,[6] it is customary to use longer-term interbank deposit rates and rely more heavily on interpolation. On the other hand, for currencies such as the European dollar, where an efficient liquid futures market exists, for longer-term maturities it is customary to use futures contracts with longer maturities (i.e., beyond two years out to four years).

The inputs used to construct the term structure are currency dependent. Some currencies offer more liquid and deeper markets than others (see Exhibit 20.1). A swap term structure should be constructed given these micro constraints.

Deriving the Swap Curve

To derive the swap term structure, observed market interest rates combined with interpolation techniques are used; also, dates are constructed using the applicable business-day convention. Swaps are frequently constructed using the modified following business-day convention, where the cash flow occurs on the next business day unless that day falls in a different month. In that case, the cash flow occurs on the immediately preceding business day to keep payment dates in the same month.[7] The swap curve yield calculation convention frequently differs by currency. Exhibit 20.2 lists the different payment frequencies, compounding frequencies, and day count conventions, as applicable to each currency-specific interest rate type.

---

[6] Time to maturity of financial instrument.
[7] ISDA Credit Derivatives Definitions. International Swaps and Derivatives Association (ISDA) (1999).

The Short End of the Swap Curve

The short end of the swap curve, out to three months, is based on the overnight, 1-month, 2-month, and 3-month deposit rates. The short-end deposit rates are inherently zero-coupon rates and need only be converted to the base currency swap rate compounding frequency and day count convention. The following equation is solved to compute the continuously compounded zero-swap rate (r_c):

$$
r_c = \frac{t_y}{t_m} \times \ln\left(1 + \frac{r_d}{\frac{t_y}{t_m}} \right) \tag{20.1}
$$

where r_d represents the observed market deposit rate, t_m represents the number of days to maturity, and t_y represents the number of days in a year as specified according to the day count convention used. Continuously compounded interest rates are used for consistency with other parts of this chapter.

The Middle Area of the Swap Curve

The middle area of the swap curve up to two years is derived from either FRA rates or interest rate futures contracts. FRAs are preferable, as they carry a fixed time horizon to settlement and settle at maturity, whereas futures contracts have a fixed settlement date and are marked to market daily. FRAs for most currencies, however, are not observable or suffer from lack of liquidity. On the other hand, futures contracts are exchange traded, rendering them more uniform, liquid, and transparent. Extracting forward rates from futures rates requires a convexity adjustment. It is an adjustment for the difference in convexity characteristics of futures contracts and forward rates. Interest rate futures have zero convexity, a fixed payoff per basis point change, regardless of the level of underlying interest rates, whereas FRAs are convex instruments. The convexity bias is positively correlated to the futures contract maturity, and is of the magnitude of one to two basis points for maturities around one year, gradually increasing with term to maturity.

A long position in FRAs or swaps and a short position in futures has net positive convexity. The short futures position has a positive payoff when interest rates rise and lower losses when interest rates fall, as they can be refinanced at a lower rate. This mark to market positive effect of futures contracts creates a bias in favor of short sellers of futures contracts. This bias must be removed from futures contracts prices to derive an unbiased estimator of the equivalent forward rates.

Convexity Adjustment Estimation   Estimating the convexity adjustment requires an estimation of the future path of interest rates up to the maturity of the futures contract. Convexity adjustments for several futures markets are provided by brokers or from market data vendors. An alternative methodology is to use the Hull-White term structure model to estimate the convexity bias.[8] In the Hull-White model, the continuously compounded forward rate, lasting between times t_1 and t_2 (denominated in years from current date), equals the continuously compounded futures rate less the following convexity adjustment:

$$\left(\frac{1-e^{-a(t_2-t_1)}}{a}\right)\left[\left(\frac{1-e^{-a(t_2-t_1)}}{a}\right)(1-e^{-2at_1})+2a\frac{1-e^{-a(t_1)}}{a}\right]\frac{\sigma^2}{4a} \quad (20.2)$$

where σ is the standard deviation of the change in short-term interest rates expressed annually, and a is the mean reversion rate.

Mean Reversion Rate Estimation   Convexity bias estimation requires an estimate of the mean reversion rate (a) and the standard deviation (σ) of the change in short-term interest rates. There are several alternative methodologies for estimating a and σ. The first methodology uses historical data to estimate the parameters.

We assume that the short-term interest rates follow the following Vasicek discount bond prices stochastic process:[9]

$$dr_t = a(\theta - r_t)dt + \sigma dz_t \quad (20.3)$$

where r_t is the short-term interest rate at time t, and dz_t is the increment of a standard Wiener process. Parameter θ specifies the long run value of r_t.

To estimate the Vasicek continuous stochastic time model, the model must be discretized. We discretized and estimated the continuous time model as follows:

[8] J.C. Hull and A. White, "Pricing Interest Rate Derivative Securities," *The Review of Financial Studies* 3 (1990).
[9] O. Vasicek, "An Equilibrium Characterization of the Term Structure," *Journal of Financial Economics* 5 (1977).

$$\Delta r_t = \varphi + \delta r_{t-1} + \varepsilon_t \tag{20.4}$$

where

$$\varepsilon_t | I_{t-1} \sim N(0, \sigma_t^2) \tag{20.5}$$

The parameter δ is used to estimate the negative of the mean reversion rate, $-a$, where I_{t-1} is the information set at time $t-1$.

Estimating σ flows from the mean reversion estimation process. It estimates the conditional standard deviation of short-term interest rates using the $GARCH(1, 1)$ model:

$$\sigma_t^2 = \alpha + \beta \varepsilon_{t-1}^2 + \gamma \sigma_{t-1}^2 \tag{20.6}$$

The conditional density of Δr_t is

$$f(r_t | I_{t-1}) = \frac{1}{\sqrt{2\pi\sigma_t^2}} \exp\left(\frac{-\varepsilon_t^2}{2\sigma_t^2}\right) \tag{20.7}$$

The log-likelihood function, where N represents the total number of observations,

$$L = \sum_{t=1}^{N} \log f(r_t | I_{t-1}) \tag{20.8}$$

is then maximized numerically with respect to the population parameters. Maximizing the log-likelihood function gives estimates of α, β, and γ. The annualized standard deviation equals $\sigma_t\sqrt{252}$, assuming there are 252 trading days in a year.

The second methodology uses market data on actively traded interest rate caps to form an estimate of a and σ. An interest rate cap comprises q caplets, where q is the number of reset dates. Each caplet corresponds to the rate at time t_k and provides payoff at time t_{k+1}. An interest rate cap provides insurance against adverse upward movements in floating-rate obligations during a future period. An interest rate caplet provides the cap holder with the following payoff:

$$n\delta_k \max(R_k - R_x, 0) \tag{20.9}$$

where n denotes the caplet notional, R_x denotes the cap rate, R_k is the reset rate at time t, and $\delta_k = t_{k+1} - t_k$. As the implied volatility of an interest-rate cap is observable, assuming R_k is lognormal, with volatility σ_k the price of the caplet can be computed using the following extension to the Black-Scholes model:[10]

$$n\delta_k P(0, t_{k+1})[F_k N(d_1) - R_x N(d_2)] \qquad (20.10)$$

where

$$d_1 = \frac{\ln(F_k/R_x) + \sigma_k^2 t_k/2}{\sigma_k \sqrt{t_k}}$$

$$d_2 = d_1 - \sigma_k \sqrt{t_k}$$

$P(0, t_{k+1})$ is the spot price of a zero-coupon bond paying \$1 at time t_{k+1}. F_k denotes the forward rate for the period between t_k and t_{k+1}. $N(x)$ is the cumulative probability distribution function, where $x \sim N(0, 1)$. The caplet price is solved for the period between t_k and t_{k+1}.

Cap prices can also be valued analytically using the Hull-White model. The cap prices calculated using the implied volatilities of interest rate caps and the Black-Scholes model serve as the calibrating instruments. After the Hull-White model has been calibrated, the parameters a and σ that minimize a goodness-of-fit measure can be used to solve for the convexity bias.

A third methodology uses a simplified approach to get an approximation of the convexity bias. The mean reversion rate, a, typically varies from 0.001 for negligible effects to 0.1 for high mean reversion. For example, Bloomberg assumes a constant mean reversion rate of 0.03. Observed volatilities of interest rate caps are multiplied by their corresponding swap rates to get an estimate of σ.

The estimated or assumed values of the parameters a and σ can be used in combination with the Hull-White convexity adjustment term to estimate the convexity bias embedded in futures rates.

Futures rates with maturities from the 6-month to the 2-year time horizon are frequently used. For currencies with highly liquid interest rate futures markets, interest rate futures could be used out to five years. Market volatilities of interest rate caps are available for most currencies with maturities out to 10 years.

---

[10] J.C. Hull, *Options Futures and Other Derivatives*, 4th ed. (Upper Saddle River, NJ: Prentice-Hall, Inc., 1999).

Futures Prices   Futures prices are quoted as (100 – Futures interest rate ×
100). The quarterly compounded futures interest rates adjusted for convexity are converted to continuously compounded zero rates, as follows.

Convert the quarterly compounded futures rate to the continuously
compounded futures rate using equation (20.1), where t_m equals the
futures contract accrual period (the difference in days between two consecutive futures contracts).

The continuously compounded futures rate is then converted to a
continuously compounded zero rate using the following transformation:

$$r_2 = \frac{r_f(t_2 - t_1) + r_1 t_1}{t_2} \tag{20.11}$$

where r_f is the continuously compounded futures rate for the period
between t_1 and t_2, and r_1 and r_2 are the continuously compounded zero
rates for maturities t_1 and t_2, respectively.

The Long End of the Swap Curve

The long end of the swap curve is derived directly from observable coupon swap rates. These are generic plain vanilla interest rate swaps with
fixed rates exchanged for floating interest rates. The fixed swap rates are
quoted as par rates and are usually compounded semiannually (see
Exhibit 20.2). The bootstrap method is used to derive zero-coupon
interest rates from the swap par rates. Starting from the first swap rate,
given all the continuously compounded zero rates for the coupon cash
flows prior to maturity, the continuously compounded zero rate for the
term of the swap is bootstrapped as follows:

$$r_T = -\frac{\ln\left[\dfrac{100 - \displaystyle\sum_{i=1/m}^{T-1/m}\left(\dfrac{c}{m}e^{-r_i \times i}\right)}{100 + \dfrac{c}{m}}\right]}{T} \tag{20.12}$$

where m is the swap payment frequency per annum, c is the coupon per
annum, which is equal to the observed swap rate times the swap
notional, and r_i represents the continuously compounded zero rate for
time i. The bootstrapped interest rate, r_T, is the continuously compounded zero rate for time T. The formula summation uses increments
of $1/m$.

Progressing recursively along the observed swap rates interpolating between market observations as required forms the complete long end of the swap curve.

Interpolation Algorithm

There is no single correct way to link deposit, futures, and swap interest rates to construct the complete swap term structure; however, several fundamental characteristics and conventions should be followed, to ensure yield curve validity. The derived yield curve should be consistent and smooth and should closely track observed market data points. However, oversmoothing the yield curve might cause the elimination of valuable market pricing information. This is the main criticism against the use of more advanced interpolation yield-curve-modeling techniques for pricing derivatives, such as the Nelson and Siegel[11] and Svensson[12] functions. These functions fit the market data very loosely, which is appropriate for extracting expectations or comparative analysis across countries, but is not appropriate for market pricing. The market convention has been to use several interpolation techniques to generate a complete term structure that closely mimics the observed market data for the purpose of marking to market. The most prevalent algorithms of interpolation used in practice to create a swap term structure include linear interpolation and cubic splines.[13]

Piecewise Linear Interpolation

All observed market data points are connected by a straight line to form a complete term structure. The value of a new data point is assigned according to its position along a straight line between observed market data points. Linear interpolation is simple to implement and closely tracks observed market interest rates. However, it tends to produce kinks around transition areas where the yield curve is changing slope. Therefore, linear interpolation is inappropriate for modeling yield curves that change slope frequently and exhibit significant term structure curvature. As illustrated in Exhibits 20.3 through 20.7, the swap term structure is not characterized by a continuously changing slope nor does it exhibit significant curvature.

---

[11] C.R. Nelson and A.F. Siegel, "Parsimonious Modelling of Yield Curves," *Journal of Business* 60 (1987).

[12] L.E. Svensson, "Estimating and Interpreting Forward Interest Rates: Sweden 1992–94," CEPR Discussion Paper 1051 (October 1994).

[13] For other nonlinear curve modelling techniques see D. Satyajit, *Risk Management and Financial Derivatives,* (New York: McGraw-Hill, Inc., 1998).

EXHIBIT 20.3   EUR Swap Zero Curve (Continuously Compounded) as of
14 April 2000

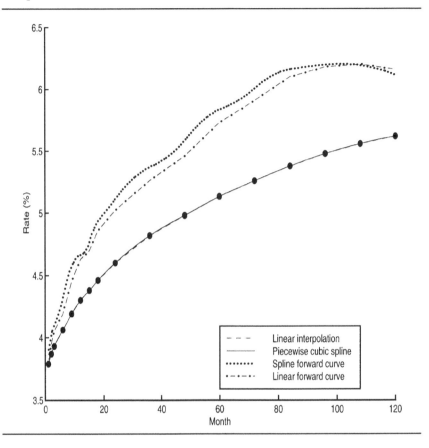

Constructing Piecewise Linear Interpolation   Piecewise linear interpolation can
be presented in a closed form, which simplifies the interpolation process.

$$R(t) = R(t_i) + \left[\frac{(t - t_i)}{(t_{i+1} - t_i)}\right] \times [R(t_{i+1}) - R(t_i)] \qquad (20.13)$$

Here, i is the market observation index with time to maturity of t_i, and $R(t)$
represents the interest rate corresponding to maturity t, where $t_i \leq t \leq$
t_{i+1}. The formula can be used to derive any swap rate between two
market observations $R(t_i)$ and $R(t_{i+1})$.

EXHIBIT 20.4   USD Swap Zero Curve (Continuously Compounded) as of
14 April 2000

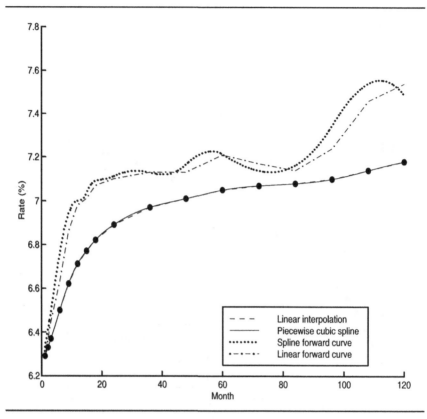

Piecewise Cubic Spline Interpolation

Use of polynomial functions that pass through the observed market data
points create a fitted smooth yield curve that does not oscillate wildly
between observations. It is possible to either use a single, high order
polynomial of degree $n - 1$ (n is the number of observations) or to piece
together low order polynomials (e.g., quadratic, cubic). The advantage
of using a number of lower order polynomials (splines) is that the extra
degrees of freedom can be used to impose additional constraints to
ensure smoothness and prevent wild oscillatory patterns between observations. The piecewise cubic spline technique goes through all observed
data points and creates by definition the smoothest curve that fits the
observations and avoids kinks.

EXHIBIT 20.5 JPY Swap Zero Curve (Continuously Compounded) as of 14 April 2000

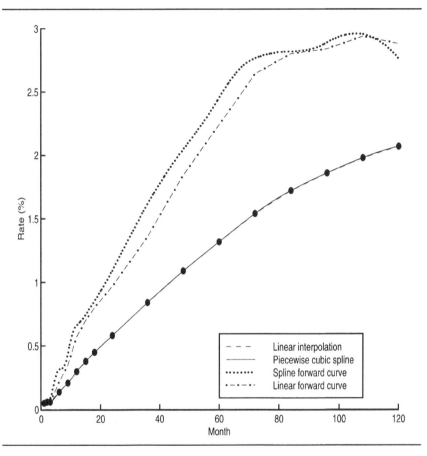

Constructing a Piecewise Cubic Spline To construct a set of cubic splines, let the function $R_i(t)$ denote the cubic polynomial associated with the t segment $[t_i, t_{i+1}]$:

$$R_i(t) = a_i(t - t_i)^3 + b_i(t - t_i)^2 + c_i(t - t_i) + r_i \qquad (20.14)$$

where n is the number of market observations, r_i represents market observation (knot point) i, and t_i represents the time to maturity of market observation i.

There are n market observations, $n - 1$ splines, and three coefficients per spline. Overall, there are $3n - 3$ unknown coefficients. The

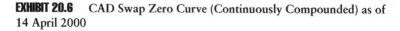

EXHIBIT 20.6   CAD Swap Zero Curve (Continuously Compounded) as of 14 April 2000

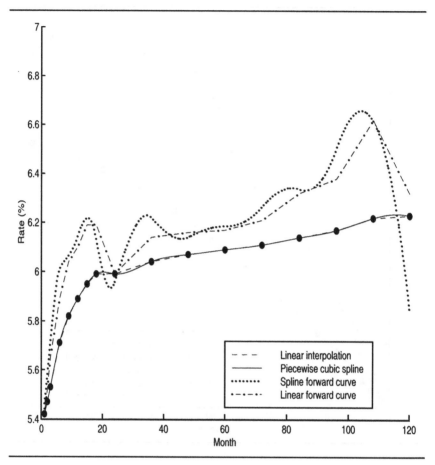

coefficients of the cubic spline function defined over the interval $[t, T]$ can be obtained by imposing the following constraints:

$$a_i(t_{i+1} - t_i)^3 + b_i(t_{i+1} - t_i)^2 + c_i(t_{i+1} - t_i) = r_{i+1} - r_i$$

$$3a_{i-1}(t_i - t_{i-1})^2 + 2b_{i-1}(t_i - t_{i-1}) + c_{i-1} - c_i = 0$$

$$6a_{i-1}(t_i - t_{i-1}) + 2b_{i-1} - 2b_i = 0$$

EXHIBIT 20.7A Linear Interpolation: Swap Zero Curve by Currency (continuously compounded)

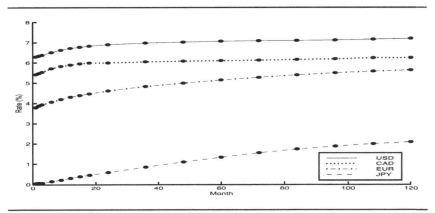

EXHIBIT 20.7B Piecewise Cubic Spline: Swap Zero Curve by Currency (continuously compounded)

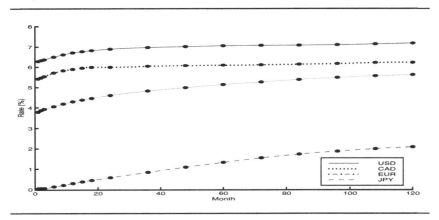

$$b_1 = 0$$

$$6a_{n-1}(t_n - t_{n-1}) + 2b_{n-1} = 0$$

The first set of $n - 1$ constraints require that the spline function join perfectly at the knot points. The second and third set of $2n - 2$ constraints require that first and second derivative constraints match adjacent splines. Finally, the last two constraints are end-point constraints that set the derivative equal to zero at both ends.

The linear algebraic system consists of $3n - 3$ equations and $3n - 3$ unknowns that can be solved to produce the optimal piecewise cubic spline. Press, Teukolsky, Vetterling, and Flannery describe a routine for cubic spline interpolation.[14]

Consolidation

The complete term structure is formed by joining together the different parts of the swap term structure using the chosen interpolation methodology. The result is a complete swap term structure that is a fundamental tool in marking to market fixed-income securities.

The construction of the swap term structure is not a uniform practice. The substitutable inputs, overlapping instrument maturity dates, inconsistencies between different inputs, different alternatives for transition points between different sections of the term structure, and variety of instruments and derivation techniques all combine to form a number of plausible swap term structures. The most prominent problems arise around the transition areas between inputs, as shown in Exhibit 20.6. The transition areas, especially around the 2-year mark, lack smoothness, and an oscillatory pattern is observable. Several possible solutions include using different term structures for different applications and adjustments to the set of rates utilized. In general, institutions tend to adopt their own approaches to these issues. However, overadjustment and oversmoothing of the term structure can be counterproductive. By eliminating variation, valuable pricing information embedded in the term structure might be "smoothed" away.

The swap term structures for major currencies are shown in Exhibits 20.3 through 20.7. In general, both linear interpolation and piecewise cubic spline derivation techniques generate similar zero and forward swap term structures. However, after zooming in on relatively unstable areas of the term structure, one can detect the better fit of piecewise cubic spline over linear interpolation in preserving a term structure curvature and smoothness. Nevertheless, cubic splines may produce inconsistent or implausible forward term structures, as shown at the long end of Exhibit 20.6. Because these are estimates of the swap term structure, it is impossible to determine precisely which estimate serves as a better benchmark. The swap zero and forward term structures for major currencies are much smoother and consistent than those for the less-prevalent currencies. This attribute characterizes more liquid, developed, and deeper markets.

---

[14] W. Press, S. Teukolsky, W. Vetterling, and B. Flannery, *Numerical Recipes in C,* 2nd ed. (New York: Cambridge University Press, 1998). See also Chapter 22 in this book.

CONCLUSIONS

The swap term structure is a pivotal element in pricing fixed-income products, measuring the relative value of debt classes, and measuring interest rate expectations. The swap term structure also offers many advantages over the government term structure. This chapter has outlined a methodology for deriving the swap term structure. The derived zero term structure is used to mark to market financial instruments by estimating and discounting their future cash flows to derive their present value. The different time buckets of the swap term structure are extracted from different market rates and instruments. The variety of plausible extraction and interpolation techniques and data availability problems prevent the derivation of a completely uniform, efficient yield curve.

The outlined model carefully preserves variations in market observations, thereby maintaining important pricing information. However, linear interpolation can introduce inaccuracies when there is significant curvature in the term structure, or sparse or noisy data. Cubic spline interpolation, on the other hand, may produce inconsistent or implausible forward term structures.

The most problematic area of the term structure tends to be the transition area between time buckets. Nevertheless, linear interpolation and cubic splines are the most prevalent yield curve generation techniques used in the marketplace for marking to market purposes. To get mark-to-market prices that are consistent with the marketplace, institutions use the specified inputs and derivation techniques. However, an institution may develop more robust term structure derivation techniques for identifying mispriced securities, such as a multiple-factor model.

CHAPTER 21

Credit Derivatives

Richard Pereira
Credit Derivatives and Securitization
Dresdner Kleinwort Wasserstein, London

Rod Pienaar
Corporate and Investment Banking
Deutsche Bank AG, London

Moorad Choudhry
Senior Fellow
Centre for Mathematical Trading and Finance
CASS Business School, London

Credit Derivatives are a relatively recent addition to the range of financial instruments used by banks and financial institutions. However, there has been strong growth in this innovative area of the capital markets. The British Bankers' Association (BBA) estimates that at the end of 2001 the global market (excluding asset swaps) accounted for over $1 trillion. The projected growth rate for the global credit derivatives market is predicted to reach a $4.8 trillion by 2004.

The views, thoughts and opinions expressed in this chapter represent those of the authors in their individual private capacities and should not be taken to be representative of their respective employing institutions or affiliated entities.

The authors would like to thank Andrey Chirihin, Matteo Mazzocchi, Yunkang Liu, Ganesh Ramchandran, Tim Histed, Mathias Schneider, Jim Wang, Rob Wolff, Kevin Stocklin, Darren Smith, Gregory Lieb, Paul Kozary, Jeremy Vice, Punit Khare, Anthony Brown, Evgeny Stott, Peter Howard, Tarek Hard, George Panayiotou, Anthony Knobel, and Sergio Solorzano for their interesting and useful comments when reviewing this chapter and their insights in this subject.

The rapid rise in use of credit derivatives has contributed to the liquidity and depth of this market worldwide. It has also fostered the adoption of standardized terms and definitions. Terminology and definitions in credit derivative contracts have been developed and harmonized in recent years and assisted in the takeup of these products by a variety of financial and nonfinancial institutions. The need for appropriate "credit derivatives definitions" have been considered by the International Swaps and Derivatives Association (ISDA). ISDA's definitions and terms are used in the confirmations and termsheets for most credit derivative transactions.

In this chapter we introduce the main types of credit derivatives, and describe their uses and applications. We also introduce concepts in pricing and valuation of these instruments.

CREDIT DERIVATIVE INSTRUMENTS

The most common credit derivatives include:

- Credit default swaps
- Total return swaps
- Credit spread derivatives
- Asset swaps
- Credit-linked notes

Credit derivative products are defined by reference to underlying reference entities, and reference obligations, which include corporate bonds, bank loans, sovereign debt, Brady bonds, and Eurobonds. Credit derivatives are now used increasingly in structured transactions. For example synthetic collateralised loan obligations (see Chapter 15) often use credit default swaps to transfer credit risk from the originator to the special purpose vehicle (SPV). Currently, the most common products are credit default products and total return swaps.

Credit derivative transactions involve both a protection buyer and protection seller. Banks currently act as either buyers or sellers of credit protection in a transaction. Insurance companies are also active in the credit derivatives market as sellers of credit protection.

We now consider each of these instruments in turn.

Credit Default Swap

Credit default swaps involve the exchange of periodic payments (usually expressed as basis points multiplied by the notional amount of the swap) paid by the protection buyer for a contingent payment from the protection seller for losses (e.g., par minus recovery rate(R)) on a reference obligation following a credit event in the case of cash settlement or in the case of physical settlement the ability of the protection buyer to deliver a deliverable reference obligation for a payment of par. As a result, the credit default swap is a contract that allows the protection buyer to buy "cover" for losses occurring following a credit event from the protection seller.

The cash flows of a typical credit default swap are set out in Exhibit 21.1. Exhibit 21.2 shows the Bloomberg screen CDS for credit default swap prices.

The payout to the protection buyer is zero if there is no credit event, or in the event of a credit event such as bankruptcy, par value less the recovery rate.

EXHIBIT 21.1 Credit Default Swap

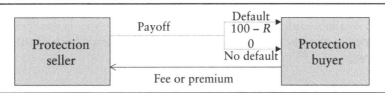

EXHIBIT 21.2 Credit Default Swap Bloomberg Price Screen

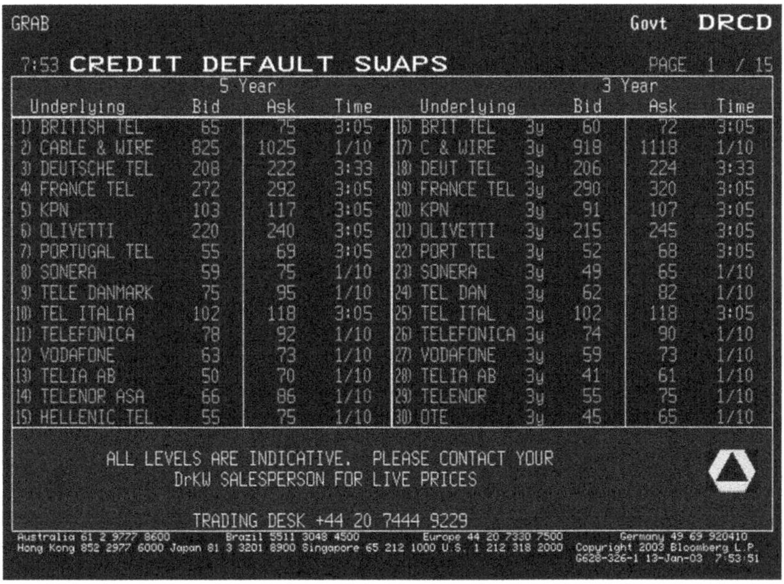

GRAB Govt DRCD

7:53 CREDIT DEFAULT SWAPS PAGE 1 / 15

5 Year				3 Year			
Underlying	Bid	Ask	Time	Underlying	Bid	Ask	Time
1) BRITISH TEL	65	75	3:05	16) BRIT TEL 3y	60	72	3:05
2) CABLE & WIRE	825	1025	1/10	17) C & WIRE 3y	918	1118	1/10
3) DEUTSCHE TEL	208	222	3:33	18) DEUT TEL 3y	206	224	3:33
4) FRANCE TEL	272	292	3:05	19) FRANCE TEL 3y	290	320	3:05
5) KPN	103	117	3:05	20) KPN 3y	91	107	3:05
6) OLIVETTI	220	240	3:05	21) OLIVETTI 3y	215	245	3:05
7) PORTUGAL TEL	55	69	3:05	22) PORT TEL 3y	52	68	3:05
8) SONERA	59	75	1/10	23) SONERA 3y	49	65	1/10
9) TELE DANMARK	75	95	1/10	24) TEL DAN 3y	62	82	1/10
10) TEL ITALIA	102	118	3:05	25) TEL ITAL 3y	102	118	3:05
11) TELEFONICA	78	92	1/10	26) TELEFONICA 3y	74	90	1/10
12) VODAFONE	63	73	1/10	27) VODAFONE 3y	59	73	1/10
13) TELIA AB	50	70	1/10	28) TELIA AB 3y	41	61	1/10
14) TELENOR ASA	66	86	1/10	29) TELENOR 3y	55	75	1/10
15) HELLENIC TEL	55	75	1/10	30) OTE 3y	45	65	1/10

ALL LEVELS ARE INDICATIVE. PLEASE CONTACT YOUR DrKW SALESPERSON FOR LIVE PRICES

TRADING DESK +44 20 7444 9229

Australia 61 2 9777 8600 Brazil 5511 3048 4500 Europe 44 20 7330 7500 Germany 49 69 920410
Hong Kong 852 2977 6000 Japan 81 3 3201 8900 Singapore 65 212 1000 U.S. 1 212 318 2000 Copyright 2003 Bloomberg L.P.
G628-326-1 13-Jan-03 7:53:51

Source: ©Bloomberg L.P. Reproduced with permission.

The market for single-name credit default swaps has rapidly developed in volume over the past few years and represents the highest proportion of the global credit derivatives market by notional value. The credit default swap is linked to the reference entity and its obligations.

Within the credit derivative market, a common tenor for transactions is the 5-year maturity. Credit default swaps have most liquidity at the 3-year and 5-year maturity/tenor. As a result, we often see that 5-year credit default swaps are used in structured credit transactions, such as collateralised synthetic obligations (CSOs) for this reason. Credit derivatives with a long maturity (over five years or with a short maturity (under one year) are less common.

The cover is effective from trade date plus one day (this is not confined to business days). This is referred to as $T + 1$.

Credit default swaps are triggered by the occurrence of *credit events*. If a counterparty provides a Credit Event Notice than this indicates that a credit event has occurred, this is usually accompanied by Public Available Information.

Upon a credit event the settlement of CDSs may be performed in two ways:

- Physical settlement
- Cash settlement

The most common form of settlement chosen is physical settlement, in this situation the buyer of protection will deliver the defaulted asset or other assets that are *pari passu* with the reference obligation—effectively the asset delivered is "covered" by the credit default swap contract—to the seller of protection for par value (in cash).

Cash settlement represents another method of settling credit derivative transactions. In cash settlement, the protection buyer will receive an amount based on the difference between par and the valuation of the reference asset at a given valuation date, as agreed in the credit default swap contract.

Experience during 2001 and 2002 has shown an increase in credit events which trigger payments on credit derivatives. Examples of high-profile credit events included Swiss Air (Bankruptcy), Railtrack (Bankruptcy), and Enron (Bankruptcy).

The legal department of most firms that buy or sell credit derivative instruments carefully monitor the terms of the transaction and in particular will focus on any nonstandard terms. In most cases the market will trade on standard ISDA documentation (terms and definitions). Sources of dispute, which are rare, may arise on the actual contract terms the nature of credit events, the obligation selected by the protection buyer for delivery.

EXHIBIT 21.3   First to Default Basket

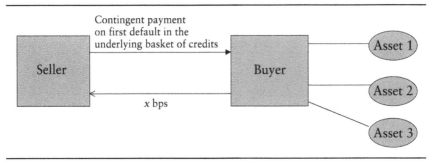

An interesting development in the credit default swap market is the response of protection sellers to credit events, the impact is ultimately reflected in the price of credit default swaps, as reflected by the credit default swap spread. Credit derivative markets have experienced spread widening at times of bad credit related news, in effect this reflects the protection sellers pricing the risk of the additional probability of a credit event into the protection they sell.

Since credit default swaps are written on the reference entities, their pricing provide information on the default probabilities of the issuer and are not subject to liquidity premia that can be present in the credit spreads of the credit risky bonds. Therefore, the term structure of credit default swap spreads for a particular issuer is used to determine the cumulative default probability of the issuer.

Credit default counterparties require absolute clarity on the terms of the CDS at the time they enter into transactions; for example, the reference entity, reference obligation characteristics and deliverable obligation characteristics, credit events, and valuation process are key discussion points.

Another adaptation of the credit default swap is the digital CDS in which a defined cash flow on the contingent leg takes place when a credit event occurs.

More complex default swap products can also be structured, for example, a *first to default basket swap*. In this product the buyer makes periodic payments for a contingent default payment on the first default of a group of securities. A diagrammatic representation is shown at Exhibit 21.3.

Total Return Swaps

A *total return swap* (TRS) is a derivative instrument that allows the protection buyer to swap the total economic return of an asset (e.g., loans or securities) for fixed or floating interest payments.

A typical TRS may have the following cash flows:

EXHIBIT 21.4   Total Return Swap

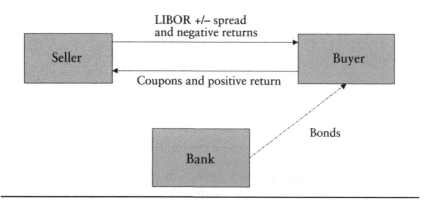

Protection buyer payout:

- Coupons on the bond
- Positive return to the protection seller

Protection seller payout:

- LIBOR +/– spread
- Negative return to the protection buyer

In the event of default the protection buyer would be compensated for any loss in value as a result of a credit event affecting the market value of the reference asset.

In some versions of a TRS the actual underlying asset is actually sold to the counterparty, with a corresponding swap transaction agreed alongside; in this type of TRS, the protection seller will make an upfront payment for the market value of the reference asset to the protection buyer. Yet another variation involves no change in physical ownership but still involves an upfront payment of the market value of the reference asset; an example of this kind of TRS is described in Exhibit 21.4. On occurrence of a credit event the TRS will be terminated using physical settlement, so that the reference asset is delivered to the protection seller.

In other versions of the TRS there is no physical change of ownership of the underlying asset. The TRS trade itself can be to any maturity term, that is, it need not match the maturity of the underlying security. In a TRS the total return from the underlying asset is paid over to the counterparty in return for a fixed or floating cash flow. This makes it slightly different to other credit derivatives, as the payments between counterparties to a

TRS are connected to changes in the market value of the underlying asset, as well as changes resulting from the occurrence of a credit event.

Exhibit 21.4 illustrates a generic TR swap. The protection buyer has contracted to pay the "total return" on a specified reference asset, while simultaneously receiving a LIBOR-based return from the protection seller. The reference or underlying asset can be a bank loan such as a corporate loan or a sovereign or corporate bond. The total return payments include the interest payments on the underlying loan as well as any appreciation in the market value of the asset. The protection seller will pay the LIBOR-based return; it will also pay any difference if there is a depreciation in the price of the asset. The economic effect is as if this entity owned the underlying asset, as such TR swaps are synthetic loans or securities.

The total return on the underlying asset is the interest payments and any change in the market value if there is capital appreciation. The value of an appreciation may be cash settled, or alternatively there may be physical delivery of the reference asset on maturity of the swap in return for a payment of the initial asset value by the total return "receiver." The maturity of the TR swap need not be identical to that of the reference asset and, in fact, it is rare for it to do so.

The swap element of the trade will usually pay on a quarterly or semi-annual basis, with the underlying asset being revalued or *marked-to-market* on the refixing dates. The asset price is usually obtained from an independent third party source such as Bloomberg or Reuters, or as the average of a range of market quotes. If the *obligor* of the reference asset defaults, the swap may be terminated immediately, with a net present value payment changing hands according to what this value is, or it may be continued with each party making appreciation or depreciation payments as appropriate. This second option is only available if there is a market for the asset, which is unlikely in the case of a bank loan. If the swap is terminated, each counterparty is liable to the other for accrued interest plus any appreciation or depreciation of the asset. Commonly, under the terms of the trade, the guarantor bank has the option to purchase the underlying asset from the beneficiary bank and then dealing directly with loan defaulter. Exhibit 21.5 gives an example of a TR swap and sets out typical cash flow calculations.

The Total Return Swap and the Synthetic CDO

A variation on the generic TRS has been used in structured credit products such as synthetic collateralised debt obligations (CDO).[1] An example of this is the Jazz I CDO B.V., which is a vehicle that can trade in

---

[1] See Moorad Choudhry et al., *An Introduction to Credit Derivatives* (working paper, Department of Management, Birkbeck College, University of London, 2002).

EXHIBIT 21.5 Total Return Swap Terms

An investor enters into a TRS to obtain economic exposure to a 5-year Baa1 rated corporate bond. The terms of the TRS are:

Reference asset:	$200 million nominal value of 7% Baa1 corporate bond
Term of TRS:	six months
TRS payer:	Bank
Floating payer:	Investor
6 month LIBOR fixing:	6%
Spread:	30 bps
Clean bond price at inception of contract:	105
Clean bond price at termination of contract:	108

What are the cash flows of the TRS?

Coupon:	$200 million × 0.07/2 = $7 million
Capital movement:	(Price at termination – Price at inception) × nominal value = (108 – 105)/100 × $200 million = $6 million
Floating interest payment:	Nominal × (LIBOR +spread) × Fraction of year = $200 million × (0.06 + 0.003) × 1/2= $6.3 million

Therefore the net cash flow to investor is:

$7 million + $6 million – $6.3 million or $6.7 million

Note: We note that the return to the investor is influenced by the return on the underlying reference asset.

cash bonds as well as credit default swaps and total return swaps. It has been called a hybrid CDO for this reason. In the Jazz structure, the TRS is a funded credit derivative because the market price of the reference asset is paid up-front by the Jazz vehicle to the swap counterparty. In return the swap counterparty pays the principal and interest on the reference asset to Jazz CDO. The Jazz CDO has therefore purchased the reference asset synthetically. On occurrence of a credit event, the swap counterparty delivers the asset to the CDO and the TRS is terminated. Because these are funded credit derivatives, a liquidity facility is needed by the vehicle, which it will draw on whenever it purchases a TRS. This facility is provided by the arranging bank to the structure.

The TRS arrangement in the Jazz structure is shown at Exhibit 21.6.

Credit Spread Derivatives

Credit spread derivatives are forwards and options that reflect views on the credit spread movements of underlying credit assets. Therefore,

EXHIBIT 21.6   Total Return Swap as Used in Jazz I CDO BV

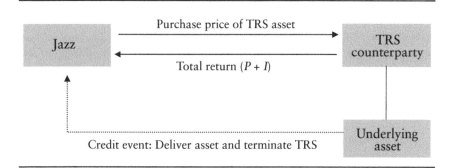

EXHIBIT 21.7   Credit Spread Forward

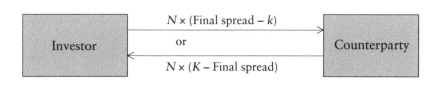

Note: The investor receives a payment if the spread narrows and alternatively makes a payment if the spread widens where N = nominal and K = strike spread.

credit spread derivatives may be used to isolate the credit spread risk of reference assets.

Forward Credit Spread

Forward credit spreads are based on the risky forward rate less the risk-free forward rate. The forward credit spread can be estimated as the difference between the forward yield for a benchmark bond and the yield on the reference credit asset.

Spread forwards may be used by investors who wish to implement an investment strategy based on its view on movements in spreads. Exhibit 21.7 shows the cash flows under a credit spread forward. Exhibit 21.8 illustrates the use of a credit spread forward contract.

Credit Spread Options

Credit spread options are options whose payout is linked to the credit spread of the reference credit. This product can be used to manage the credit risk on corporate bond and corporate bond option positions. It isolates credit spread risk, which is an important factor in the underling

EXHIBIT 21.8   Illustration of Forward Credit Spread

An investor has the view that credit spread on the corporate issue ABC plc maturing in 2008 will narrow from today's level of 80 bps in six months. Therefore the investor enters into a 6-month credit spread forward with the counterparty (for example a bank) with strike level at the 80 bps level. The payout of the contract is structured so that as:

- The spread narrows the counterparty pays the investor nominal multiplied by (strike spread less final spread).
- The spread widens the investor pays the counterparty nominal multiplied by (final spread less strike).

EXHIBIT 21.9   Credit Spread Option

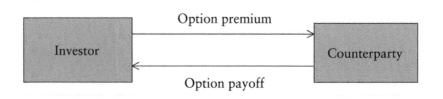

Note: Option payoff (which cannot be less than zero):
(1) Credit spread put = Nominal × (Final credit spread − Strike credit spread)
(2) Credit spread call = Nominal × (Strike credit spread − Final credit spread)

corporate bond pricing. Exhibit 21.9 shows the cash flows under a credit spread option.

Call Options

The buyer has the right to buy the spread and benefits from the spread decreasing in value. The payoff has the form max (strike − spread, 0). This option pays out if the spread tightens below the strike level, a tightening spread would result in an increasing bond price. Therefore the credit spread call option provides a payout should the underlying bond position increase in value.

Put Options

The buyer has the right to sell the spread and benefits from the spread increasing in value. The payoff has the form max (spread − strike, 0). This option pays out if the spread widens above the strike level, a widening spread would result in a decreasing bond price. Therefore, the

EXHIBIT 21.10   Illustration of Investor Strategy

An investor follows a strategy that involves going long of a Latin American sovereign bond. The bond is currently yielding 350 bp over the benchmark US Treasury bond. If the sovereign bond falls in price then the investor will purchase it. The investor expects that the target price for the purchase should be when the spread is 400 bp.

In this case let us assume that the premium for a credit spread put option is 30 bp. The credit spread put option will be sold by the investor to the counterparty (for example a bank) with a strike level of 370 bp. The option will provide the following payout:

- If the spread rises above 370 bp then the bank can put the bond to the investor at the strike level of 370 bp. The investor will pay out under the option in this case. For example if the spread is 450 bp, then the payout under the option is 80 bp. Therefore the total cost is: −80 + 30 bp = −50 bp. The cost of the bond position is therefore 50 bp. The effect in bps is the same as if the investor bought the bond at 400 bp and the price had moved to 450 bp. Alternatively the investor may be able to purchase the bond of the counterparty at the strike rate;
- If the spread is below 370 bp then the option expires. The investor has earned a premium of 30 bp multiplied by the nominal value of the contract; this can be used to buy the bond at a price below market value.

credit spread put option provides a payout should the underlying bond position decrease in value.

The payoffs may be multiplied by a leverage or duration factor to relate the spread changes to price changes of the underlying instrument. However, in our examples, we have ignored this factor. Exhibit 21.10 illustrates how an investor may use a credit spread put option as part of an investment strategy.

Asset Swaps

Asset swaps predate the introduction of the other instruments we discuss in this chapter and strictly speaking are not credit derivatives. However, they are used for similar purposes and there is considerable interplay between the cash and synthetic markets using asset swaps, hence the need to discuss them here.

Asset swaps are used to alter the cash flow profile of a bond. The asset swap market is an important segment of the credit derivatives market since it explicitly sets out the price of credit as a spread over LIBOR. Pricing a bond by reference to LIBOR is commonly used and the spread over LIBOR is a measure of credit risk in the cash flow of the underlying

EXHIBIT 21.11   Asset Swap

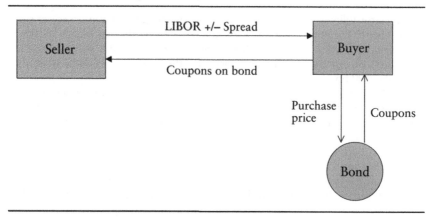

bond. Asset swaps can be used to transform the cash flow characteristics of reference assets, so that investors can hedge the currency, credit, and interest rate risks to create investments with more suitable cash flow characteristics. An asset swap package involves transactions in which the investor acquires a bond position and then enters into an interest rate swap with the bank that sold him the bond. The investor pays fixed and receives floating. This transforms the fixed coupon of the bond into a LIBOR-based floating coupon.

An example would be that a protection buyer holding a fixed-rate risky bond and wishes to hedge the credit risk of this position via a credit default swap. However, by means of an asset swap the protection seller (e.g., a bank) will agree to pay the protection buyer LIBOR +/– spread in return for the cash flows of the risky bond. In this way the protection buyer (investor) may be able to explicitly finance the credit default swap premium from the asset swap spread income if there is a negative basis between them. If the asset swap was terminated, it is common for the buyer of the asset swap package to take the "unwind" cost of the interest rate swap.

The generic structure is shown at Exhibit 21.11.

Credit-Linked Notes

A *credit-linked note* (CLN) is a structured note that combines both a debt instrument and a credit derivative. The structured note includes an embedded credit derivative that isolates the credit risk of the reference asset; in this way an investor in this type of structured note may be able to transform its credit risk exposure. The investor in this note makes a cash investment in a bondlike instrument and receives a return that is

EXHIBIT 21.12   Credit-Linked Note

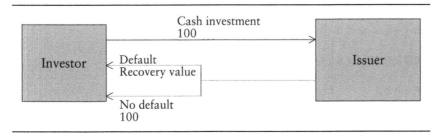

related to the payout from the embedded derivative. Therefore, the return from this cash investment in a CLN is dependent on the credit performance of an underlying reference asset. CLNs may be structured for investors who wish to gain exposure to various credit risks.

CLNs allow investors to take a view on credit without directly buying or selling derivatives and without purchasing the underlying credits.

A variety of credit-linked structures may be created to suit the various risk/reward profiles of investors. For example, some CLNs may protect the principal amount; and credit events may only affect the interest cash flow from the CLN; whereas others may link the redemption of principal to the performance of reference credit instruments.

For example, if we have a CLN that pays out a reduced amount on the event of default of a reference asset, then this CLN may be similar to a straight forward cash investment plus the sale of a credit default swap (CDS).

Then the return to this CLN investor may be:

- 100 if there is no default.
- Recovery rate (R) of the reference asset on default (i.e., 100 received and (100 − R) paid).

In this way the investor in this CLN receives a credit-linked return and is compensated for the credit risk it has assumed by the increased returns from the CLN (i.e., the embedded CDS premium that is paid to the investor in the CLN).

During the life of this type of CLN, the investor would receive LIBOR + spread on the notional outstanding. The spread level would be related to the credit risk in the CLN and the costs of issuing the CLN.

Exhibit 21.12 illustrates the generic credit-linked note.

SUMMARY

We present a summary of the main characteristics of credit derivative swap products in Exhibit 21.13.

EXHIBIT 21.13 Characteristics of Credit Derivative Products

Advantages	Asset Swap	TRS	CDS
(i)	Allows the repackaging of bonds into par bonds.	Manage credit risk without selling the bond. This may be useful in managing economic and regulatory capital.	Manage credit risk and both economic and regulatory capital.
(ii)	Creating synthetic exposure for time periods that are not present in the market.	Gain economic returns without directly holding the security.	Reduce exposure to default risks in a portfolio.
(iii)	Transfer exposure to the credit risk of the underlying asset without sale of the bond.	Provide access to credits that cannot be efficiently (e.g., tax reasons/regulatory) held by the investor.	Used in structured products to synthetically transfer credit risk to an special purpose vehicle or counterparty.
(iv)	Flexible instruments that transform the nature of cash flows of an underlying credit.	Reference asset may include bonds, loans, or a basket of bonds or loans.	Reference asset may be selected from a range of securities (e.g., bonds and loans).
(v)	Clearly prices credit as a spread over LIBOR. In this way links the bond market to the swap market.	Hedge the risk of assets which the investor does not wish to sell for tax reasons.	Hedge the risk of assets that the investor does not wish to sell for tax or commercial reasons (for example, the client relationship).
Disadvantages			
(i)	Exposure to the credit risk of the underlying bond and the swap counterparty.	Illiquidity of the TRS. The liquidity is related to the liquidity of the underlying reference asset.	Illiquidity of the CDS. The liquidity is related to the liquidity of the underlying reference asset.
(ii)	Pricing can be complicated by the existence of illiquid markets for the reference credit.	Development of an appropriate pricing model to capture the risks of the product and provide a fair value.	Development of an appropriate pricing model to provide the fair value for the credit default swap.
(iii)	Documentation must be carefully prepared. It should be clear and consistent with ISDA recommendations.	Documentation must be carefully prepared. It should be clear and consistent with ISDA recommendations.	Documentation must be carefully prepared. It should be clear and consistent with ISDA recommendations.

CREDIT EVENTS

The 1999 ISDA Credit Derivatives Definitions[2] listed six credit events that could be incorporated into credit default swaps. These are

- Bankruptcy
- Failure to pay
- Restructuring
- Repudiation/moratorium
- Obligation default
- Obligation acceleration

Since the 1999 definitions were published, market participants and ISDA have worked to refine these definitions and to express the market view.

Credit events for corporate entities usually conform to ISDA credit derivative definitions and supplements. The events currently commonly used in most CDS confirmations are:

- Bankruptcy
- Failure to pay
- Restructuring/modified restructuring

In Europe and Asia, the standard credit default swap contract used the *restructuring* definition (sometimes referred to as "old restructuring"), whereas in the North American markets the standard credit default swap contracts refer to *modified restructuring*. The 1999 ISDA Credit Derivative Definitions would have been effective until early 2003. The 2003 ISDA Credit Derivative Definitions, which were in place in early 2003 (implementation in May 2003), have implemented some key amendments to the 1999 definitions, some of which were previously included in supplements issued by ISDA.

There have been interesting developments concerning the Restructuring credit event. The restructuring credit event has been considered in the light of market experience involving the actual credit events, for example the Conseco case.

In the Conseco restructuring, this reference entity had restructured bank debt in August/September 2000 as a result of a short-term liquidity issue, therefore it changed the bank loan's maturity by a few months, how-

---

[2] The 2003 ISDA Credit Derivative Definitions expand and revise the 1999 ISDA Credit Definitions and Supplements. The 2003 ISDA Credit Derivative definitions took effect in early 2003.

ever, as a result, it would compensate for this deferral by an increase in the interest rate on the loan. In effect many of the rating agencies did not consider this change to be a "distressed exchange"[3] default. But under the 1999 ISDA credit event definition for restructuring the maturity extension was considered to be a credit event. As a result protection buyers delivered long-dated senior bonds that traded below par at around 68 cents on the dollar, and received a payment under the terms of the credit default swap.

The ISDA Restructuring supplement (also referred to as modified restructuring) was issued in May 2001. The supplement attempts to impose limitations on deliverable obligations, including, for example, restrictions as on maturity. The aim is to ensure that losses incurred by protection sellers are similar to the investors in the actual debt that is restructured. Modified restructuring is the credit event used in the North American markets. However, in Europe the ISDA Credit Derivatives Market Practice group has worked to determine the most appropriate definition for restructuring in the Europe. The main areas of consideration relate to the construction of an appropriate definition relating to deliverable obligations and the maturity limitation of the underlying deliverable obligations. In Europe, this so called "modified modified restructuring" is set to be standard in credit default swap confirmations.

In October 2001, Railtrack Plc had a credit event that was triggered as a result of bankruptcy. This credit event raised an issue over whether the delivery of convertible bonds by protection buyers to protection sellers could take place under credit default swap contracts. The bankruptcy credit event was triggered by the appointment of an administrator by the UK government. ISDA clarified the market view by the publication of the 1999 ISDA Credit Derivatives Definitions Relating to Convertible, Exchangeable or Accreting Obligations on November 9, 2001. As a result of the supplement, the market standard approach in the United States, Asia, and Europe is that most types of convertibles are deliverable obligations, unless they have been specified in the confirmation as excluded deliverable obligations.

The Supplement Relating to Successor and Credit Events to the 1999 ISDA Credit Derivatives Definitions was introduced on 28 November 2001 to clarify the treatment of reference entities which may be affected by a *succession event* (for example: mergers, demergers, or corporate reorganisations). The *successor* is determined by considering

---

[3] In a distressed exchange (i) the borrower offers lenders/debtholders a new security or package of securities that amount to a diminished financial obligation (e.g., preferred or common stock or debt with a lower coupon or par amount) or (ii) the exchange has the purpose of allowing the borrower to avoid default.

how the *reference obligations* are allocated to the entities involved, and by considering which entity will assume the obligations. We may end with a situation in which either the *reference entity* stays the same, a new *successor reference entity* is appointed, or the credit default swap is split evenly amongst a number of *successor reference entities.*

PRICING OF CREDIT DERIVATIVES

The pricing of credit derivatives should aim to provide a "fair value" for the credit derivative instrument. In the sections below we discuss and provide a brief overview of the pricing models currently proposed by the industry. The effective use of pricing models requires an understanding of the models assumptions, the key pricing parameters, and a clear understanding of the limitations of a pricing model. The pricing of credit derivatives has become more sophisticated and the developments in pricing of credit derivatives over the last few years have been significant.

Issues to consider when carrying out credit derivative pricing include:

- Implementation and selection of appropriate modeling techniques.
- Parameter estimation.
- Quality and quantity of data to support parameters and calibration.
- Calibration to market instruments for risky debt.

For credit derivative contracts in which the payout is on credit events other than default, the modeling of the credit evolutionary path is critical. If, however, a credit derivative contract does not payout on intermediate stages between the current state and default then the important factor is the probability of default from the current state.

Pricing Models

Pricing models for credit derivatives fall into two classes:

- Structural models
- Reduced form models

We discuss these models below.

Structural Models

Structural models are characterized by modeling the firm's value in order to provide the probability of a firm default. The Black-Scholes-Merton option pricing framework is the foundation of the structural model approach. The default event is assumed to occur when the firm's assets fall below the book value of the debt.

Merton applied option pricing techniques to the valuation of corporate debt.[4] By extension the pricing of credit derivatives based on corporate debt may in some circumstances be treated as an option on debt, which is therefore analogous to an option on an option model.

Merton models have the following features:

- Default events occur predictably when a firm has insufficient assets to pay its debt.
- Firm's assets evolve randomly. The probability of a firm default is determined using the Black Scholes Merton option pricing theory.

Some practitioners argue that Merton models are more appropriate than reduced form models when pricing default swaps on high-yield bonds, due to the higher correlation of high-yield bonds with the underlying equity of the issuer firm.

The constraint of structural models is that the behaviour of the value of assets and the parameters used to describe the process for the value of the firm's assets are not directly observable and the method does not consider the underlying market information for credit instruments.

Reduced Form Models

Reduced form models are a form of no-arbitrage model. These models can be fitted to the current term structure of risky bonds to generate no arbitrage prices. In this way the pricing of credit derivatives using these models will be consistent with the market data on the credit risky bonds traded in the market. These models allow the default process to be separated from the asset value and are more commonly used to price credit derivatives.

Some key features of reduced form models include the following:

- Complete and arbitrage-free credit market conditions are assumed.
- Recovery rate is an input into the pricing model.
- Use of credit spread data to estimate the risk-neutral probabilities.
- Use of transition probabilities from credit agencies can be accommodated in some of these models. The formation of the risk-neutral transition matrix from the historical transition matrix is a key step.
- Default can take place randomly over time, and the default probability can be determined using the risk-neutral transition matrix.

---

[4] Robert C. Merton, "On the Pricing of Corporate Debt: The Risk Structure of Interest Rates," *Journal of Finance*, 1974, pp. 449–470

When implementing reduced form models, it is necessary to consider issues such as the illiquidity of underlying credit risky assets. Liquidity is often assumed to be present when we develop pricing models. However, in practice, there may be problems when calibrating a model to illiquid positions, and in such cases the resulting pricing framework may be unstable and provide the user with spurious results. Another issue is the relevance of using historical credit transition data, used to project future credit migration probabilities. In practice it is worthwhile reviewing the sensitivity of price to the historical credit transition data when using the model.

Markov Chain and Reduced-Form Models

The predecessors of the reduced-form models are full Markov chain models including those presented by Jarrow, Lando, and Turnbull,[5] Das and Tufano[6] and Duffie and Singleton.[7] We consider these models in this section.

Jarrow, Lando, and Turnbull (JLT) Model

This model focuses on modeling default and credit migration. Its data and assumptions include the use of:

- A statistical rating transition matrix that is based on historic data.
- Risky bond prices from the market used in the calibration process.
- A constant recovery rate assumption. The recovery amount is assumed to be received at the maturity of the bond.
- A credit spread assumption for each rating level.

It also assumes no correlation between interest rates and credit-rating migration.

The statistical transition matrix is adjusted by calibrating the expected risky bond values to the market values for risky bonds. The adjusted matrix is referred to as the risk-neutral transition matrix. The risk-neutral transition matrix is key to the pricing of several credit derivatives.

The JLT model allows the pricing of default swaps, as the risk neutral transition matrix can be used to determine the probability of

---

[5] Robert Jarrow and David Lando, "A Markov Model for the Term Structure of Credit Spreads," *Review of Financial Studies* 10 (1997), pp. 481–523

[6] Darrell Duffie and Kenneth Singleton, "Modelling Term Structures of Defaultable Bonds," *Review of Financial Studies* (1997).

[7] Sanjiv Das and Peter Tufano, "Pricing Credit Sensitive Debt when Interest Rate, Credit Ratings and Credit Spreads Are Stochastic," *Journal of Financial Engineering* (1996).

default. The JLT model is sensitive to the level of the recovery rate assumption and the statistical rating matrix. It has a number of advantages; as the model is based on credit migration, it allows the pricing of derivatives for which the payout depends on such credit migration. In addition, the default probability can be explicitly determined and may be used in the pricing of credit default swaps.

The disadvantages of the model include the fact that it depends on the selected historical transition matrix. The applicability of this matrix to future periods needs to be considered carefully, whether, for example, it adequately describes future credit migration patterns. In addition it assumes all securities with the same credit rating have the same spread, which is restrictive. For this reason the spread levels chosen in the model are a key assumption in the pricing model. Finally, the constant recovery rate is another practical constraint; as in practice, the level of recovery will vary.

The Das-Tufano Model

The Das-Tufano (DT) model is an extension of the JLT model. The model aims to produce the risk-neutral transition matrix in a similar way to the JLT model; however, this model uses stochastic recovery rates. The final risk neutral transition matrix should be computed from the observable term structures. The stochastic recovery rates introduce more variability in the spread volatility. Spreads are a function of factors that may not only be dependent on the rating level of the credit; as in practice, credit spreads may change even though credit ratings have not changed. Therefore, to some extent, the DT model introduces this additional variability into the risk-neutral transition matrix.

Various credit derivatives may be priced using this model; for example, credit default swaps, total return swaps, and credit spread options. The pricing of these products requires the generation of the appropriate credit dependent cash flows at each node on a lattice of possible outcomes. The fair value may be determined by discounting the probability-weighted cash flows. The probability of the outcomes would be determined by reference to the risk neutral transition matrix.

The Duffie-Singleton Model

The Duffie-Singleton modeling approach considers the three components of risk for a credit risky product, namely the risk-free rate, the hazard rate, and the recovery rate.

The *hazard rate* characterizes the instantaneous probability of default of the credit risky underlying exposure. As each of the components above may not be static over time and a pricing model may assume a process for each of these components of risk. The process may be implemented using a lattice approach for each component. The constraint on the lattice formation is that this lattice framework should agree to the market pricing of credit risky debt.

Here we demonstrate that the credit spread is related to risk of default (as represented by the hazard rate) and the level of recovery of the bond. We assume that a zero-coupon risky bond maturing in a small time element Δt where:

λ = annualized hazard rate
φ = recovery value
r = risk-free rate
s = credit spread

and where its price P is given by

$$P = e^{-r\Delta t}[(1 - \lambda\Delta t) + (\lambda\Delta t)\varphi] \qquad (21.1)$$

Alternatively P may be expressed as

$$P \cong e^{-\Delta t(r + \lambda(1 - \varphi))} \qquad (21.2)$$

However, as the usual form for a risky zero-coupon bond is

$$P = e^{-\Delta t(r + s)} \qquad (21.3)$$

Therefore we have shown that

$$s \cong \lambda(1 - \varphi) \qquad (21.4)$$

This would imply that the credit spread is closely related to the hazard rate (i.e., the likelihood of default) and the recovery rate.

This relationship between the credit spread, the hazard rate, and recovery rate is intuitively appealing. The credit spread is perceived to be the extra yield (or return) the investor requires for credit risk assumed. For example:

■ As the hazard rate (or instantaneous probability of default) rises then the credit spread increases.
■ As the recovery rate decreases the credit spread increases.

A "hazard rate" function may be determined from the term structure of credit. The hazard rate function has its foundation in statistics and may be linked to the instantaneous default probability.

The hazard rate function $(\lambda(s))$ can then be used to derive a probability function for the survival function $S(t)$:

$$S(t) = \exp{-\int_0^t \lambda(s)ds} \qquad (21.5)$$

The hazard rate function may be determined by using the prices of risky bonds. The lattice for the evolution of the hazard rate should be consistent with the hazard rate function implied from market data. An issue when performing this calibration is the volume of relevant data available for the credit.

Recovery Rates

The recovery rate usually takes the form of the percentage of the par value of the security recovered by the investor.

The key elements of the recovery rate include:

- Level of the recovery rate.
- Uncertainty of the recovery rate based on current conditions specific to the reference credit.
- Time interval between default and the recovery value being realized.

Generally, recovery rates are related to the seniority of the debt. Therefore if the seniority of debt changes then the recovery value of the debt may change. Also recovery rates exhibit significant volatility.

CREDIT SPREAD MODELING

Although spreads may be viewed as a function of default risk and recovery risk, spread models do not attempt to break down the spread into its default risk and recovery risk components.

The pricing of credit derivatives that pay out according to the level of the credit spread would require that the credit spread process is adequately modeled. In order to achieve this, a stochastic process for the distribution of outcomes for the credit spread is an important consideration.

An example of the stochastic process for modeling credit spreads, which may be assumed, includes a mean reverting process such as

$$ds = k(\mu - s)dt + \sigma s dw \qquad (21.6)$$

where

ds = change in the value of the spread over an element of time (dt)
dt = element of time over which the change in spread is modeled
s = credit spread
k = rate of mean reversion
μ = mean level of the spread
dw = Wiener increment
σ = volatility of the credit spread

In this model when s rises above a mean level of the spread, the drift term $(\mu - s)$ will become negative and the spread process will drift towards (revert) to the mean level. The rate of this drift towards the mean is dependent on k the rate of mean reversion.

The pricing of a European spread option requires the distribution of the credit spread at the maturity (T) of the option. The choice of model affects the probability assigned to each outcome. The mean reversion factor reflects the historic economic features overtime of credit spreads, to revert to the average spreads after larger than expected movements away from the average spread.

Therefore, the European option price may be reflected as

$$\text{Option price} = E\{e^{-rT}[\text{Payoff}(s, X)]\} = e^{-rT}\int_{0}^{\infty} f(s, X)p(s)ds \qquad (21.7)$$

where

X = strike price of the spread option
$p(s)$ = probability function of the credit spread
$E[\ ]$ = expected value
$f(s,X)$ = payoff function at maturity of the credit spread

More complex models for the credit spread process may take into account factors such as the term structure of credit and possible correlation between the spread process and the interest process.

The pricing of a spread option is dependent on the underlying process. As an example we compare the pricing results for a spread option model, including mean reversion to the pricing results from a standard Black-Scholes model in Exhibit 21.14 and Exhibit 21.15.

Exhibit 21.14 and Exhibit 21.15 show the sensitivity on the pricing of a spread option to changes to the underlying process. Comparing these

EXHIBIT 21.14 Spread Option Pricing Analysis—6-Months' Expiry

Expiry in Six Months Risk-free rate = 10% Strike = 70 bps Credit spread = 60 bps Volatility = 20%	Mean Reversion Model Price	Standard Black Scholes Price	Difference Between Standard Black Scholes and Mean Reversion Model Price
Mean level = 50 bps K = 0.2			
Put	0.4696	0.5524	17.63%
Call	10.9355	9.7663	11.97%
Mean level = 50 bps K = 0.3			
Put	0.3510	0.5524	57.79%
Call	11.2031	9.7663	14.12%
Mean level = 80 bps K = 0.2			
Put	0.8729	0.5524	58.02%
Call	8.4907	9.7663	15.02%
Mean level = 80 bps K = 0.3			
Put	0.8887	0.5524	60.87%
Call	7.5411	9.7663	29.51%

exhibits shows the impact of time to expiry increasing by six months. In a mean reversion model, the mean level and the rate of mean reversion are important parameters that may significantly affect the probability distribution of outcomes for the credit spread, and hence the price.

PRICING CREDIT DEFAULT SWAPS

The pricing of credit default swaps is determined in the credit default swap market by traders who determine the credit default swap spread through their assessment of the default risk of the reference obligations. This spread information can give valuable information about the key pricing components of the reference credit: implied probability of default of the reference credit and recovery assumptions. These price

EXHIBIT 21.15 Spread Option Pricing Analysis—One-Year Expiry

Expiry in 12 Months Risk-free rate = 10% Strike = 70 bps Credit spread = 60 bps Volatility = 20%	Mean Reversion Model Price	Standard Black Scholes Price	Difference Between Standard Black Scholes and Mean Reversion Model Price
Mean level = 50 bps K = 0.2			
Put	0.8501	1.4331	68.58%
Call	11.2952	10.4040	8.56%
Mean level = 50 bps K=.3			
Put	0.7624	1.4331	87.97%
Call	12.0504	10.4040	15.82%
Mean level = 80 bps K=.2			
Put	1.9876	1.4331	38.69%
Call	7.6776	10.4040	35.51%
Mean level = 80 bps K=.3			
Put	2.4198	1.4331	68.85%
Call	6.7290	10.4040	54.61%

components are used in the pricing of more exotic instruments, such as first to default credit default swaps.

If the time of default for a reference credit is τ, then let us denote the cumulative (risk neutral) default probabilities for the reference credit as

$$P(t) = P(\tau < t) \qquad (21.8)$$

A credit default swap has two valuation legs, the fee leg and the contingent leg. We can develop an equation of value which describes the valuation of the credit default swap (assuming a deterministic recovery rate) as

$$s(T_m)\sum_{1}^{m}\Delta_k DF(T_k)[1 - P(T_k)] = (1-R)\int_{0}^{T_m} DF(u)P(du) \qquad (21.9)$$

where

s	=	quoted credit default swap spread for maturity T_m
Δ_k	=	accrual period from time t_{k-1} to t_k
$DF(T_k)$	=	discount factor at time T_k
$[1 - P(T_k)]$	=	probability that there is no default at time T_k
R	=	recovery value of the reference credit
$P(du)$	=	probability of default at time u
m	=	number of discrete time intervals

In equation (21.9) the fee leg is set to be equal to the contingent leg of the CDS, since this is by definition the condition for the credit default swap spread.

From these equations, the market implied risk-neutral default curve could be constructed from quoted market spreads.

For ease of interpretation, the equation (21.9) may be expressed in a discrete form in the equations below.

$$\text{PV of Fee leg} + \text{PV of Default accrual}$$
$$= \text{PV of the Contingent leg} \qquad (21.10)$$

The components of equation (21.10) can be expressed as follows:

$$\text{PV of Fee leg} = s \times \text{Fee annuity} = s \sum_{1}^{M} DF_k \Delta_k (1 - P_k) \qquad (21.11)$$

where $(1 - P_k)$ is the probability that there has been no default up to time period k.

$$\text{PV of Default accrual} = s \sum_{1}^{M} DF_k \frac{\Delta_k}{2}(P_k - P_{k-1}) \qquad (21.12)$$

where $(P_k - P_{k-1})$ is the probability of a credit event in time interval Δ_k.

$$\text{PV of Contingent Leg} = (1 - R) \sum_{1}^{M} DF_k (P_k - P_{k-1}) \qquad (21.13)$$

Using these discrete results we could express the *credit default swap spread* as follows:

$$s = \frac{(1-R)\sum_{1}^{M}DF_k(P_k - P_{k-1})}{\sum_{1}^{M}DF_k\Delta_k(1-P_k) + \sum_{1}^{M}DF_k\frac{\Delta_k}{2}(P_k - P_{k-1})} \quad (21.14)$$

This last equation shows the direct relationship between the probability of default and the market credit default swap quotes. Therefore, using equation (21.14) and the term structure of credit, we may be able to "boot-strap" the market implied probability of default from the credit curves, which are in effect the range of credit default swap quotes by maturity. Equation (21.14) is only approximate because in practice we would need to ensure that the timing of projected cash flows are accurately reflected in the pricing model. For example, the actual payment on the contingent leg may depend on the settlement date for the swap.

In practice, the spread information from the CDS market is used to imply the probability of default and the hazard rate for the underlying reference entity. The recovery rate is an input when the calculation of implied probabilities takes place. It is common to assume a recovery rate that reflects the rate on the "cheapest to deliver" deliverable obligation. Credit derivative traders will monitor the prices of the cheapest to deliver bonds (i.e., deliverable obligations with the lowest recovery), when constructing hedges.

Recovery rates on bonds vary by the position in the reference entity's capital structure and the level of security offered to the bond holders. Determining the appropriate recovery rate is not a trivial process and requires careful analysis into the traded prices of deliverable obligations for the reference credit. In practice there is limited historical information on the recovery rates experienced for credit default swaps.

CREDIT SPREAD PRODUCTS

Credit spread products are a rapidly growing class of credit derivative. The spread in the following sections relate to a credit spread over a benchmark security. However, the traded credit spread could also refer to the CDS spread.

The Forward Credit Spread

The forward credit spread can be determined by considering the spot prices for the risky security and risk-free benchmark security, while the

EXHIBIT 21.16   Data for the Forward Credit Spread Illustration

Current date	1/2/98
Forward date	1/8/98
Maturity	1/8/06
Time period from current date to maturity:	8 years and 6 months
Time period from current date to forward date:	6 months
Yield to forward date	
Risk-free security	6.25%
Risky security	6.50%
Yield to maturity	
Risk-free security	7.80%
Risky security	8.20%
Forward yields	
Risk-free security	7.8976%
Risky security	8.3071%

forward yield can be derived from the forward price of these securities. The forward credit spread is the difference between the forward risky security yield and the forward yield on a risk-free security. The forward credit spread is calculated by using yields to the forward date and the yield to the maturity of the risky assets.

The details of the calculation of forward rates for a risk-free security are

$$(1.0780)^{8^{6/12}} = (1.0625)^{6/12} \times (1 + rf_{\text{risk-free}})^8$$

where $rf_{\text{risk-free}}$ is the forward risk-free rate implied by the yields on a risk-free security. This equation implies that $rf_{\text{risk-free}}$ is 7.8976%.

Similarly for the risky security we have

$$(1.082)^{8^{6/12}} = (1.065)^{6/12} \times (1 + rf_{\text{risky}})^8$$

where rf_{risky} is the forward risky rate implied by the yields on a risky security. This equation implies that rf_{risky} is 8.3071%. Exhibit 21.16 summarizes the results derived above.

Therefore, the forward credit spread is the difference between the forward rate implied by the risky security less the forward rate implied by the yields on a risk-free security. In the example above this is rf_{risky} − $rf_{risk-free}$ = 8.3071 − 7.8976 = 0.4095%

The current spread is equal to 8.20 − 7.80 = 0.40% = 40 bps.

The difference between the forward credit spread and the current spread is 0.4095 − 0.40 = 0.0095% = 0.95 basis points.

The calculation of the forward credit spread is critical to the valuation of credit spread products the payoff of spread forwards is highly sensitive to the implied forward credit spread.

Credit Spread Options

First generation pricing models for credit spread options may use models as described in the section on spread models. The key market parameters in a spread option model include the forward credit spread and the volatility of the credit spread.

The volatility of the credit spread is a difficult parameter to determine. It may be approached in different ways including:

- The historical volatility of the difference between the reference asset yield and the yield on a risk-free benchmark.
- Estimation of the historical volatility by considering the components: historic volatility of the reference asset yield, historic volatility of the benchmark yield, correlation of the returns between the reference asset yield and the benchmark yield.
- The estimate of the volatility of the spread by using the implied volatility of the reference asset yield, implied volatility of the benchmark yield and a suitable forward looking estimate of the correlation between the returns on the reference asset yield and benchmark asset yield.

If the model incorporates mean reversion then other key inputs will include the mean reversion level and the rate of mean reversion. These inputs cannot be observed directly and the choice should be supported by the model developers and constantly reviewed to ensure that they remain relevant. Other inputs include:

- Strike price
- Time to expiry
- Risk-free rate for discounting

A key issue with credit spread options is ensuring that the pricing models used will calibrate to the market prices of credit risky reference assets. The recovery of forward prices of the reference asset would be a constraint to the evolution of the credit spread. More complex spread models may allow for the correlation between the level of the credit spread and the interest rate level. The reduced form models described earlier models are a new generation of credit derivative pricing models that are now increasingly being used to price spread options.

Asset Swaps

Assume that an investor holds a bond and enters into an asset swap with a bank. Then the value of an asset swap is the spread the bank pays over or under LIBOR. This is based on the following components:

1. Value of the coupons of the underlying asset compared to the market swap rate.
2. The accrued interest and the clean price premium or discount compared to par value. Thus when pricing the asset swap it is necessary to compare the par value and to the underlying bond price.

The spread above or below LIBOR reflects the credit spread difference between the bond and the swap rate.

The Bloomberg asset swap calculator pricing screen at Exhibit 21.17 shows these components in the analysis of the swapped spread details. Exhibit 21.18 shows an example of an asset swap calculation.

EXHIBIT 21.17   Bloomberg Example of Asset Swap Calculator Screen

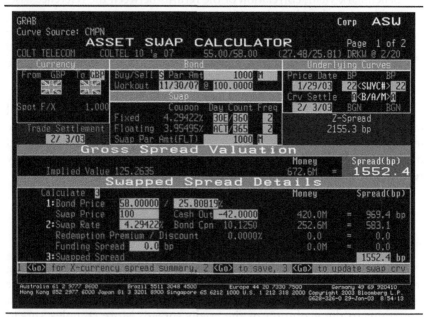

Source: ©Bloomberg L.P. Reproduced with permission.

EXHIBIT 21.18   Asset Swap Calculation

Let us assume that we have a credit risky bond with the following details:

Currency:	Euro
Issue date:	31 March 2000
Maturity:	31 March 2007
Coupon:	5.5% per annum
Price (dirty):	105.3%
Price (clean):	101.2%
Yield:	5%
Accrued interest:	4.1%
Rating:	A1

To buy this bond the investor would pay 105.3% of par value. The investor would receive the fixed coupons of 5.5% of par value. Let us assume that the swap rate is 5%. If the investor in this bond enters into an asset swap with a bank in which the investor pays the fixed coupon and receives LIBOR +/− spread.

The asset swap price (i.e., spread) on this bond has the following components:

  (i) The value of the excess value of the fixed coupons over the market swap rate is paid to the investor. Let us assume that in this case that this is approximately 0.5% when spread into payments over the life of the asset swap.
 (ii) The difference between the bond price and par value is another factor in the pricing of an asset swap. In this case the price premium that is expressed in present value terms should be spread over the term of the swap and treated as a payment by the investor to the bank. (If a dirty price is at a discount to the par value, then the payment is made from the bank to the investor.) For example, in this case let us assume that this results in a payment from the investor to the bank of approximately 0.23% when spread over the term of the swap.

These two elements result in a net spread of 0.5% − 0.23% = 0.27%. Therefore the asset swap would be quoted as LIBOR + 0.27% (or LIBOR plus 27 bps).

Total Return Swap (TRS) Pricing

The present value of the two legs of the TRS should be equivalent. This would imply that the level of the spread is therefore dependent on the following factors:

- Credit quality of the underlying asset.
- Credit quality of the TRS counter-party.
- Capital costs and target profit margins.
- Funding costs of the TRS provider as they will hedge the swap by holding the position in the underlying asset.

The fair value for the TRS will be the value of the spread for which the present value of the LIBOR +/– spread leg equals the present value of the returns on the underlying reference asset. The present value of the returns on the underlying reference asset may be determined by evolving the underlying reference asset. The expected value of the TRS payoff at maturity should be discounted to the valuation date.

The reduced form models described earlier models are a new generation of credit derivative pricing models, which are now increasingly being used to price total return swaps.

CREDIT CURVES

The credit curves (or default swap curves) reflect the term structure of spreads by maturity (or tenor) in the credit default swap markets. The shape of the credit curves are influenced by the demand and supply for credit protection in the credit default swaps market and reflect the credit quality of the reference entities (both specific and systematic risk). The changing levels of credit curves provide traders and arbitragers with the opportunity to measure relative value and establish credit positions.

In this way, any changes of shape and perceptions of the premium for CDS protection are reflected in the spreads observed in the market. In periods of extreme price volatility, as seen in the middle of 2002, the curves may invert to reflect the fact that the cost of protection for shorter-dated protection trades at wider levels than the longer-dated protection. This is consistent with the pricing theory for credit default swaps.

The probability of survival for a credit may be viewed as a decreasing function against time. The survival probabilities for each traded reference credit can be derived from it's credit curve. The survival probability is a decreasing function because it reflects the fact that the probability of survival for a credit reduces over time. For example, the probability of survival to year 3 is higher than the probability of survival to year 5.

Under nonvolatile market conditions, the shape of the survival probability and the resulting credit curve will take a different form to the shape implied in volatile market conditions; the graphs may change to reflect the higher perceived likelihood of default. For example, the shape of the survival probability may take the form as shown in Exhibit 21.19.

The corresponding credit curves, which are consistent with these survival probabilities, take the form shown in Exhibit 21.20. This shows that the credit curve inversion is consistent with the changes in the survival probability functions.

EXHIBIT 21.19   Probability of Survival

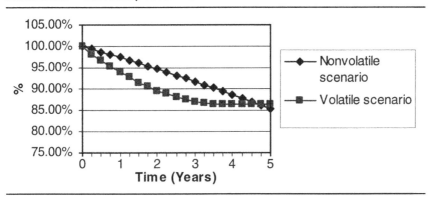

EXHIBIT 21.20   Credit Curves

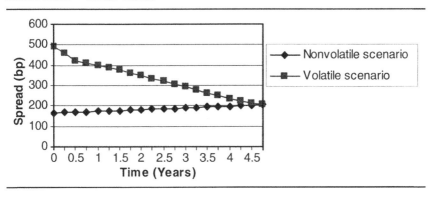

In this analysis, we assume that the assumed recovery rate for the "cheapest to deliver" bond remains the same at 35% of notional value.

CREDIT DERIVATIVES AND RELATIVE VALUE

CDS prices are often compared to bond asset swap levels in order to gain an initial comparison of the credit quality implied by the market. In fact, differences do exist between the CDS spread and the *asset swap* spread,[8] even though both spreads may be viewed as compensating the

---

[8] See Moorad Choudhry, "Issues in the Asset Swap Pricing of Credit Default Swaps," in Frank J. Fabozzi (editor), *Professional Perspectives on Fixed Income Portfolio Management: Volume 4* (Hoboken, NJ: John Wiley & Sons, Inc., 2003).

investor for credit risk, each has important factors that contribute to the difference observed in the market.

For example, let us assume that we have a 5-year credit default swap spread on a corporate credit which is 60 bps p.a.

Assume the reference entity also has an issued bond (which we can assume is eligible for delivery under the credit default swap contract). However, if the asset swap level of this bond is $ LIBOR plus 55 bps p.a. and an investor funds at $ LIBOR plus 5 bps p.a., the investor in the bond would pick up 50 bps p.a. holding the bond. However, this return would be less than the credit default swap premium on the same bond. The investor could generate more value from this *positive basis*, then asset swapping and holding the bond.

This situation may arise in the markets if:

- In the situation where the risk of a *technical default* risk is higher for credit default swaps than cash bonds. This results in protection sellers demanding a higher premium. For example, default swaps may be triggered by events that do not constitute a full default on the corresponding cash asset.
- In a credit default swap, the protection buyer is effectively long a *delivery option*. This delivery option gives the protection buyer the opportunity to deliver the "cheapest to deliver asset" to the protection seller.
- Demand for credit default swap protection (i.e., effectively shorting a credit) may be more attractive than shorting a cash instrument. This demand for protection may cause swap spreads to trade wider than the cash instrument.

However, it is also possible that an investor may find that there is a *negative basis*. For example, the credit default swap spread is less than the asset swap level for a cash instrument issued by the same reference entity.

This situation may arise in the markets:

- If an investor's *funding cost* is above LIBOR, then selling protection would appear more attractive than carrying a cash position and experiencing a reduced "carry" on the bond returns due to the funding cost. Many players in the credit default swap markets fund above LIBOR; and it would seem that selling protection may cause default swap spreads to narrow.
- If standard 3- and 5-year credit default swaps are often more liquid than the cash market for similar tenors. Therefore, the *liquidity premium* to the cash investor in this situation would be included within the asset swap.

■ If the investor is exposed to the *unwind cost* of the interest rate swap in a standard asset swap package in the event of default. This risk may cause investors to require a higher asset swap spread level to compensate them for this risk.

Terminology

The following terminology may be used to describe the credit risk in bond positions ("cash instruments") and credit default swaps positions ("credit derivative instruments"):

Sell credit protection:	Long credit risk (i.e., long the bond risk)
Buy credit protection:	Short credit risk (i.e., short the bond risk)
Positive basis:	CDS spread is higher than the asset swap level
Negative basis:	CDS spread is lower than the asset swap level
Long-basis trade:	Long asset and long protection
Short-basis trade:	Short asset and short protection
Buy bond:	Long-credit risk
Short bond:	Short-credit risk

CREDIT DEFAULT SWAP BASIS MEASURES

Credit default swap positions may be compared to bond positions when examining relative value of between the cash markets and the derivative markets. It is most common to compare the CDS with the bond on one of the following bases:

■ *Asset Swap Basis:* The *asset swap basis* is the spread on the CDS minus the spread on a par asset swap of a bond with a similar average life. A positive basis exists when this difference is positive.
■ *Simple Basis:* The *simple basis* is effectively the spread on the CDS minus the Z-spread[9] of the bond based on the current market price.
■ *Repo Basis:* The *repo basis* is equivalent to the difference between the yield of the deliverable bond priced off the CDS curve, that is, using the same probability of default as implied by the CDS curve, and the actual yield of the bond. Ignoring any delivery options, repo effects, and any liquidity premium the repo basis should be close to zero.

---

[9] Z-spread is the spread over the zero-swap curve by which the bond cash flows can be discounted to get the current market price

CREDIT DEFAULT SWAP HEDGE POSITIONS

Types of hedges in the CDS market include the following.

DV01 Hedge Ratio

The main issue with this hedge ratio is to hedge the position for small movements in the CDS curve. The hedge ratio is such that there is no profit or loss for a small parallel shift in the CDS curve.

For example, the change in profit and loss as a result of "bumping" the credit curve by 1 bp, assuming we have a short credit (i.e., bought credit protection) that is

$$\Delta(P\&L) = [PVCL_1 - PVFL_1] - [PVCL'_1 - PVFL'_1] \qquad (21.15)$$

where

PVCL = present value of the contingent leg payments discounted at the original credit curve

PVFL = present value of the fixed leg payments discounted at the original credit curve

PVCL′ = present value of the contingent leg payments discounted based on the "bumped" credit curve (i.e., original credit curve plus 1 bp)

PVFL′ = present value of the contingent leg payments discounted based on the "bumped" credit curve (i.e., original credit curve plus 1 bp)

Therefore, to hedge against profit and loss (P&L) movements for small changes in the credit curve, we would use the following hedge ratio.

$$\text{Hedge ratio} = \frac{\Delta(P\&L)}{[PVCL'_2 - PVFL'_2]} \qquad (21.16)$$

where

$PVCL'_2$ = present value of the hedging contingent leg payments discounted based on the "bumped" credit curve (i.e., original credit curve plus 1 bp)

$PVFL'_2$ = present value of the hedging fixed leg payments discounted based on the "bumped" credit curve (i.e., original credit curve plus 1 bp)

Therefore, this hedge is such that there is no profit or loss for a small parallel shift in the CDS curve. The P&L generated on the original short credit position is offset by the P&L generated on the long credit hedge position (hedge ratio *multiplied by* the hedge CDS) for a 1 bps shift in the credit default swap curve.

Default Neutral Hedge Ratio

This hedge ratio may be defined as follows:

$$\text{Default neutral hedge ratio} = \frac{P_{bond} - R_{bond}}{1 - R_{CDS}} \tag{21.17}$$

The rationale is to provide a hedge to an investor to protect from loss in the event of default.

For example, let us assume that an investor holds a bond with a price, P_{bond} and that the recovery on this bond in the event of default is R_{bond}. The loss to the investor is ($P_{bond} - R_{bond}$) as a result of the default. However, the investor can hedge the bond position by buying CDS protection, for an amount equal to the *default neutral hedge ratio* multiplied by the standard CDS contract.

The payoff from the standard CDS contract is $(1 - R_{CDS})$ and the *default neutral hedge ratio multiplied by* $(1 - R_{CDS})$ would provide the hedging cash flow to offset the loss on the bond position.

For bond positions hedged via CDSs in a default neutral hedge ratio, the profit and loss generated will depend on the recovery values actually obtained for the bond and the CDS contract. The assumptions regarding recovery are crucial for hedge effectiveness.

Cash Hedge Ratio

The notional value of the CDS protection is equal to the market price of the bond. This is effectively the same as the default neutral hedge ratio with the recovery equal to zero.

CHAPTER 22

The Pricing of Credit Default Swaps and Synthetic Collateralized Debt Obligations

Greg Gentile
Vice-President
Lehman Brothers

David Jefferds
Structured Products Group
CREDITEX, Inc.

Warren Saft
Structured Products Group
CREDITEX, Inc.

In recent years, the valuation of certain synthetic instruments, such as credit default swaps (CDS), has become a routine task in financial markets. Meanwhile, variations on the core CDS product are emerging, and more complex instruments, such as synthetic collateralized debt obligations (CDOs), that use CDSs as building blocks for larger transactions continue to see analytic evolution. This chapter provides an introduction to the basics of pricing and explores some of the tools available to those involved in the synthetics market.

CREDIT DEFAULT SWAPS

While it is not uncommon for active market makers and end users to utilize their own, customized set of tools for credit default swap valuation, many, if not all of these methodologies arise from the same general framework and ask the same two questions: "What is the probability that a particular issuer will default?" and, "Upon the occurrence of a default event, what does one expect to recover from an issuer?"

While the answers to these questions are not always readily apparent in the market, there exist many methods for their computation. Some are relatively simple while others are complex, but the valuation of a default swap is most easily understood if approached backwards, such that we assume the answers to these questions are already known. Once the reader has an understanding of the valuation theory it will be easier to approach these fundamental questions head on.

The Binomial Tree

To begin the valuation of a set of cash flows that are subject to an issuer's credit risk, we can define a fictitious issuer ABC, and a cash flow C that is linked to the performance of issuer ABC. If ABC defaults on or prior to the date on which the cash flow C is due to be paid, no cash will be paid at all. It is commonly said that this cash flow is "risky" since it is subject to the credit risk of issuer ABC.

A simple example involves an investor who is due to receive a single cash flow C at a certain time T, in the future. It is also known that the probability of a default by ABC at any time between today and time T is 5.00%, denoted as p_d. There are only two possible outcomes in this scenario, illustrated from the investor's perspective by the following binomial tree:

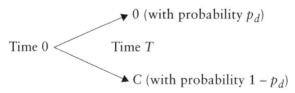

In one outcome the investor receives the cash flow C provided that ABC does not default, but the other outcome receives zero in the case of an ABC default. The amount the investor should be willing to pay today, for the cash flow C, is equal to the expected value of C, or more simply the probability weighted value of all possible outcomes, discounted back to today:

$$E[C] = p_d \cdot 0 + (1 - p_d)C \tag{22.1}$$

Simplified, and in present value terms with a risk-free rate r:

$$PV(C) = (1 - p_d)Ce^{-rT} \tag{22.2}$$

This principle can be easily extrapolated such that the value of any risky cash flow is the present value of that cash flow multiplied by the quantity $(1 - p_d)$, also known as the *probability of survival*, where p_d is specific to the point in time at which the cash flow occurs. Probabilities of default are often quoted in annual terms such that when one states, "The four-year probability of ABC defaulting is 5.00%," it is often meant that ABC has a 5.00% chance of defaulting *per annum* for the 4-year period.

If the binomial example above is expanded to many periods the tree looks like the following:

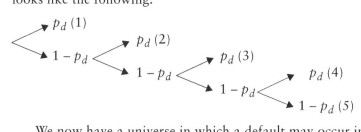

We now have a universe in which a default may occur in any one of four periods—or no default may occur at all. If we take our cash flow C from the previous example and alter the problem such that the investor will receive C in four years, only if there is no event of default during any of the four periods, then what is the present value of C?

Moving forward to the end of the 4-year period and looking backwards, there exist only five possible descriptions of what may have happened over the 4-year period. Four of the possible outcomes are default events (one possible occurrence for each period), and the fifth is a survival for the full four periods. The probability for each outcome can be obtained by following the tree to each of its endpoints, denoted numerically in parentheses in the above tree. The five outcomes are:

Outcome	Probability
1	p_d
2	$(1 - p_d)p_d$
3	$(1 - p_d)^2 p_d$
4	$(1 - p_d)^3 p_d$
5	$(1 - p_d)^4$

Since the investor will only receive the cash flow C if the universe progresses along the bottom of the tree, that is, each period witnesses a survival, then the probability of surviving four periods is $(1 - p_d)^4$. The present value of C is therefore

$$PV(C) = (1 - p_d)^4 C e^{-4r} \qquad (22.3)$$

Further, if the universe is changed such that a default may occur at any time, not necessarily in four incremental periods, it becomes useful to think in continuous time. Assuming a constant probability of default, p_d, over 1 unit of time t, then for an n-period tree contained in time t the survival probability as a function of t is

$$p_s(t) = \left(1 - \frac{p_d}{n}\right)^{nt} \qquad (22.4)$$

This is quite similar to the familiar compound rate function where the rate being compounded is $-p_d$, and, as the compounding frequency n goes to infinity, the function becomes in continuous time

$$p_s(t) = e^{-p_d t} \qquad (22.5)$$

Oversimplified in the above example, the occurrence of a default is actually a Poisson process, with the occurrence of a default in time interval u governed by hazard function $\lambda(u)$, which defines the instantaneous default rate at any point in time du. The probability of survival to time t, according to the Poisson distribution, is

$$p_s(t) = e^{-\int_0^t \lambda(u)\,du} \qquad (22.6)$$

If the hazard rate is assumed to be constant (the resulting process is referred to as a homogeneous Poisson Process), then $\lambda(u) = \lambda$, and equation (22.6) is easy to reduce. Any constant λ integrated from 0 to t is simply λt, and the probability of survival function becomes

$$p_s(t) = e^{-\lambda t} \qquad (22.7)$$

Valuing the Credit Default Swap

Credit default swaps are complex instruments and unfortunately cannot be valued by taking the present value of a single cash flow, or even a

EXHIBIT 22.1   Hypothetical Credit Default Swap

Effective date:	17 March 2003
Termination date:	17 March 2005
Premium (P):	4.00%
Frequency (n):	4 (times/year)
Premium convention:	Actual/360
Assumed recovery value (R):	20%
Hazard rate (λ):	5.00%
Notional (N):	$10,000,000
Risk-free rate (r):	3.00%

series of cash flows, and multiplying by their respective survival probabilities. Although that particular technique is instrumental in the valuation process, there are several components to the credit default swap, and each deserves discussion.

For the purposes of illustration we will examine a credit default swap with the terms shown in Exhibit 22.1.

The Periodic Premium

The buyer of protection pays to the seller a periodic premium, often quarterly, and expressed on a per annum basis. The actual cash amounts of all future premium payments are always known, since the terms of the default swap are set on the trade date. Therefore, we can think of these payments as a series of cash flows and value them according to the method above. We define d to be a function representing the number of calendar days since the inception of the default swap. We then define an integer variable j to represent each premium payment date, such that d is a function of j, $d(j)$. Time is also a function of j, and that is simply the number of years from $t = 0$ until $t = j$.[1] For our sample 2-year credit default swap, the dates are shown in Exhibit 22.2.

The function $d(j)$ comes in handy as the premium payments for the credit default swap are calculated using the Actual/360 convention, therefore it is necessary to know the number of calendar days in each period. The present value of the series of premium payments is therefore:

$$PV(\text{premium}) = \sum_{j=1}^{8} N \times P \times \frac{d(j) - d(j-1)}{360} \times (e^{-rt}e^{-\lambda t}) \qquad (22.8)$$

---

[1] For the sake of choosing a convention, we define 1 unit of t to be exactly 365 days. As a result, since our sample default swap witnesses the leap year date on 29 February 2004, the maturity of the swap occurs in 2.003 years instead of an even 2.000.

EXHIBIT 22.2   Calculation of Calendar Days and t for Each Payment Date

j	Calendar Date	$d(j)$	t
0	17 March 2003	0	0.000
1	17 June 2003	92	0.252
2	17 September 2003	184	0.504
3	17 December 2003	275	0.753
4	17 March 2004	366	1.003
5	17 June 2004	458	1.255
6	17 September 2004	550	1.507
7	17 December 2004	641	1.756
8	17 March 2005	731	2.003

EXHIBIT 22.3   Calculation of Each Premium and Their Sum

t	Calendar Date	Days in Period	Premium Payment	Discount Factor	Survival Probability	Present Value
0.000	17 March 2003					
0.252	17 June 2003	92	102,222.22	0.9925	0.9875	100,182
0.504	17 September 2003	92	102,222.22	0.9850	0.9751	98,182
0.753	17 December 2003	91	101,111.11	0.9777	0.9630	95,197
1.003	17 March 2004	91	101,111.11	0.9704	0.9511	93,317
1.255	17 June 2004	92	102,222.22	0.9631	0.9392	92,459
1.507	17 September 2004	92	102,222.22	0.9558	0.9274	90,613
1.756	17 December 2004	91	101,111.11	0.9487	0.9159	87,858
2.003	17 March 2005	90	100,000.00	0.9417	0.9047	85,195

Total Premium Value: 743,003

Here each premium P is calculated on the notional amount and multiplied by its appropriate daycount fraction. The resulting cash flow is then discounted at the risk-free rate and finally multiplied by its survival probability, that is, the probability that the relevant premium payment will actually take place, since in the event of a default all future premium payments will be cancelled.

For our 2-year default swap example, Exhibit 22.3 displays the calculation of the value of each premium payment and their sum.

The Default Payout

Perhaps the most important part of the default swap is the payment the buyer of protection will receive if a default occurs during the life of the swap. After all, this is precisely the "protection" the buyer is paying for. Upon a default, the buyer of protection will receive the notional amount of the swap after delivering to the seller-defaulted assets of the issuer. We define *recovery value*, or more briefly *R*, to be the value of these defaulted assets immediately following the credit event, so it can be more easily stated that upon a default the buyer of protection will receive 100% − R.

Since a default may occur on any particular day of the transaction, there is a small chance, on each day, that the buyer will be entitled to receive 100% − R; this is what is referred to as the "value of the protection." On any given day the probability of default can be thought of as the probability of *not* surviving on that particular day. Since the probabilities of every possible path for a transaction must add to one, the probability of default for any given day is the probability of survival for the previous day *less* the probability of survival for the current day. As seen in the multiperiod binomial tree, the survival probability decreases with each passing period. This difference in survival probabilities is the probability that was *transferred* from the survival side of the tree to the default side—in other words the decrease in the survival probability from day to day represents the incremental daily probability of default. Mathematically this is equivalent to saying that the probability of default for a small time dt is equal to the rate at which the survival probability *decreases,* or simply $-dp_s$. Differentiating $p_s(t)$, from equation 22.7, gives

$$-dp_s = \lambda e^{-\lambda t} dt \qquad (22.9)$$

For each moment in the life of the default swap we can sum up all of the instantaneous chances of actually receiving a default payout of $1 - R$ by integrating the above equation from time 0 to the maturity date, T. However, we need to make one adjustment, and that is to weight each chance of default by its present value. It is only appropriate that receiving a payout of $1 - R$ is worth more if that payout occurs tomorrow rather than next year, so after weighting each potential payout by its appropriate discount factor the value of the default protection becomes

$$(1 - R)\int_0^T \lambda e^{-\lambda t} e^{-rt} dt \qquad \text{or} \qquad (1 - R)\int_0^T \lambda e^{-t(r + \lambda)} dt \qquad (22.10)$$

After integrating equation (22.10) the present value of the default protection is calculated to be

$$PV(\text{protection}) = (1 - R) \times \frac{\lambda}{r + \lambda} \times (1 - e^{-T(r + \lambda)}) \qquad (22.11)$$

Using the values of $\lambda = 5.00\%$, $r = 3.00\%$, $T = 2.003$, and $R = 20\%$ for our fictitious 2-year swap, the value of the default protection is equal to $740,215.

Accrued Interest Upon Default

The final component of the default swap is the accrued premium that may be payable by the buyer to the seller. If a default occurs somewhere in between two premium payment dates, which is likely considering there are only four payment dates a year on a quarterly default swap, then it is standard market practice for the buyer of protection to pay the accrued premium from the most recent premium payment date to and including the date of default. The value of this "accrued on default" is calculated in a similar manner to the value of the default protection above. However, instead of receiving $1 - R$ upon a default, the buyer will be paying a certain amount of accrued interest.

Since the premium accrues linearly with the passing of each day, on an actual/360 convention, we can define the formula for accrued interest as a function of time:

$$AI(t) = P \times N \times \frac{365}{360} \times (t - a) \qquad (22.12)$$

where a represents the most recent premium payment date in units of t. The function AI is a step function, since at every premium payment date the accrued interest immediately steps down to zero, and begins accruing all over again. Thus for an 8-period default swap, there will be eight functions AI, each with a different value for a corresponding to the beginning of each period. To find out the expected accrued interest payment upon a default, all possible values of accrued interest during the swap must be weighted by their appropriate probabilities of default and discount factors, and then summed. For each period j beginning at time a and ending at time b, the summation can be performed as follows:

$$\sum_{j=1}^{8} \int_{a}^{b} P \times N \times \frac{365}{360} \times (t - a) \times \lambda e^{-t(r + \lambda)} dt \qquad (22.13)$$

After integrating, the value of the expected amount of accrued interest payable upon a default is determined to be for each period j:

$$\lambda \times P \times N \times \frac{365}{360} \times \left[\frac{e^{-a(r+\lambda)}}{(r+\lambda)^2} - \frac{e^{-b(r+\lambda)}}{(r+\lambda)} \left(b - \left(a + \frac{1}{r+\lambda} \right) \right) \right] \qquad (22.14)$$

Substituting in the numbers for each of the eight periods in our sample default swaps yields a table of expected accrued on default (aod) values for each period:

j	t	aod
1	0.252	635.55
2	0.504	622.86
3	0.753	597.31
4	1.003	585.52
5	1.255	586.55
6	1.507	574.85
7	1.756	551.27
8	2.003	528.65
		4,682.56

And finally, the total value of our default swap is merely the sum of its components:

Component	Present Value
Premium payable:	(743,003)
Default protection:	740,215
Accrued on default:	(4,683)
	(7,471)

The reader may notice that the value of the example default swap is close to zero; this is not coincidental and does warrant some explanation. It is often heard in the market that default swap spreads are representative of default probabilities—it is clear from our example that the hazard rate, λ, equals 5.00%, but the premium of the default swap is only 4.00%. The reason for this discrepancy is not complex and results directly from our assumption of the recovery value, $R = 20\%$.

Take for example a single lottery ticket with a face value of \$100. If the probability of winning the lottery is exactly 5.00%, then a rational investor should be willing to pay $5 for this ticket (a 5.00% chance of receiving $100, plus a 95% chance of receiving nothing at all). If however, the lottery winner were required to pay, say, a 20% "shipping and handling" fee to claim the $100 prize, a rational investor would no longer be willing to pay $5 for this ticket. Instead the correct price would be the sum of a 5.00% chance of winning only 80%, after expenses, and a 95% chance of receiving nothing at all, for a total of $4.

The default swap market is not unlike the lottery ticket. What if the "shipping and handling" fee for the winning ticket was unknown or turned out to be zero? In that case, if an investor observed these lottery tickets trading at a price of $4, it may appear that the probability of winning was simply 4.00%. In the case of a default swap this is what is referred to as the *risk-neutral probability of default*. The risk-neutral probability of our default swap is approximately equal to the premium of 4.00%. By applying the lottery ticket example to our default swap, it is easy to see how the hazard rate is dependent on both the risk-neutral probability as well as the recovery value assumption, and thus can be approximated[2] by $\lambda = P/(1 - R)$.

Estimating Default Probabilities

Although the pricing of a credit default swap can be numerically reduced to a model, the inputs to that model still remain subjective. How can one calculate an exact value for R, the recovery value of an issuer's assets post-default? Or, more importantly, how can one calculate the hazard rate λ for an issuer? What is the probability that a particular issuer will default in five years? Determining the true credit risk of an issuer has been a topic of intense focus in recent years and, as a result, quite a variety of methods and models have surfaced.

Default Swaps

Given the lengthy discussion devoted to valuing the credit default swap, it makes perfect sense to be able to solve backwards for λ, given observable data in the market. If the default swap market is active for a particular issuer, a trader can observe the premium being paid for default protection directly in the market. With a known value for the premium P, and an assumption for R, the hazard rate λ can be extracted. Since there is no initial exchange of cash when a default swap is executed, it

---

[2] The word *approximately* is used several times in this example because we are using a real-world scenario—one where premium is not paid in continuous time but instead on a quarterly actual/360 basis. This example combines the best of both worlds by using continuous time probability theory but applying it to the real-word conventions and idiosyncrasies of credit default swaps.

must be the case that the value of this default swap is zero at the moment the trade is observed in the market. In other words, the buyer and seller both agree that the value of the premium leg and the expected accrued interest payment upon default exactly offset the value of the protection; thus, the value of the components sum to zero. It is easy to see how a market participant could set up a spreadsheet incorporating the formulas above and, with P as an observed input and by making an assumption for R, solve backwards for λ.

This approach is circular and only works well in cases where liquid credit default markets already exist for an issuer. This is not always the case and was definitely not the case when default swaps were first introduced. Nonetheless, it still requires a highly subjective recovery value assumption.

A Note on Recovery Values

The hazard rate estimation techniques described thus far hinge on an assumption for R, the recovery rate of an issuer's asset upon a default. Many market participants estimate R by studying historical defaults of similar issuers to see, in general, where assets have traded postdefault. This is obviously not an exact science, so in recent years traders have taken a more proactive approach to hedging their guesses for recovery value. Although it is impossible to tell what future asset prices will be after a default event, it is possible for a trader to "lock-in" a value for R ensuring that any profit or loss resulting from a deviation in the realized recovery value will be exactly offset.

The first of these "recovery value" products is the digital default swap. The mechanics of the digital default swap are identical to that of a regular default swap, except for the delivery of assets pursuant to a credit event. If a default occurs, the buyer of protection is not obligated to deliver anything at all, and the seller is obligated to pay 100% of the notional amount to the seller. To price the value of the default protection on a digital, equation (22.11) is again used, but since there is no delivery of recovered assets the term $(1 - R)$ may be replaced with simply 1.

Since no assumption of R needs to be made to price the digital default swap if trading levels are observed in the market, then the implied hazard rate can be deduced exactly—without having to guess a recovery value. Similarly, if a conventional default swap is observed in the market with the same maturity as the digital, using the hazard rate obtained from the digital default swap and the premium payment P for the conventional default swap, R can be solved for directly. Thus given a conventional and a digital default swap both R and λ are exactly known!

Another, and one of the latest products to emerge in the credit markets, is the *recovery swap*. The recovery swap is more or less a default contingent forward, whereby the buyer of recovery agrees to purchase a notional amount of an issuer's assets, immediately after a default, for a preagreed price. This swap is documented exactly like a default swap, except for two small differences: (i) There is no period premium paid by either party; and (ii) upon a credit event, instead of exchanging defaulted assets for par, or 100%, defaulted assets are exchanged for a preagreed recovery price—perhaps 25% or 35%, and so on. The recovery price is set on the trade date, enabling two parties to lock in a recovery value for a class of an issuer's assets.

Debt Prices

Arguably the most widely used technique for extracting the hazard rate is the observation of an issuer's debt prices. Since a bond or a loan is subject to the credit risk of its issuer, these instruments, and the prices at which they trade, may be used to determine λ.

Take for example an issuer's new five-year bond that just hit the market today. This bond pays a 5.00% annual coupon and returns its entire principal amount at maturity. Since each of the five annual cash flows of the bond are subject to the issuer's credit risk they must be multiplied by their respective survival probabilities and discount factors or more exactly $e^{-t(r+\lambda)}$.

In the event of a default, there will be no payment of accrued interest by the issuer since generally coupons are not recoverable, so we can ignore that aspect of the valuation. The only component left to the bond is its value upon a default or its recovery value. If a default occurs, the bondholder will lose all future cash flows of the instrument (i.e., they are at risk), but will be left with a nonperforming asset worth R. The same technique is used here as in the default swap—except this time the payout is R rather than $1 - R$ upon default. Conveniently, this formula is identical to equation (22.11), except that the term $(1 - R)$ is replaced by R.

$$PV(\text{recovery}) = R \times \frac{\lambda}{r + \lambda} \times (1 - e^{-t(r+\lambda)}) \qquad (22.15)$$

The last data point needed is the price of the bond, inclusive of all accrued interest (its dirty price). Since the bond was just issued, it has no accrued interest, and the price observed in the market is 100%. Using the assumptions $r = 3.00\%$ and $R = 20\%$, λ is found by solving backwards such that the value of the bond's cash flows plus its recovery upon default equal 100% of par. In this example λ is found to be approximately 4.09% as illustrated in Exhibit 22.4.

EXHIBIT 22.4 Solving Backwards for the Probability of Default

t	Cash Flow	Discount Factor	$p_s(t)$ with $\lambda = 4.09\%$	Present Value
0				
1	650,000	0.9704	0.9599	605,509
2	650,000	0.9418	0.9214	564,063
3	650,000	0.9139	0.8845	525,453
4	650,000	0.8869	0.8491	489,487
5	10,650,000	0.8607	0.8150	7,471,098

Present value cash flows:	9,655,610
Present value recovery:	344,390
Total value:	10,000,000

Further, if there were a variety of bonds of a particular issuer outstanding, with different maturities, a term structure of hazard rates could be constructed—which in turn could be used to price default swaps of any maturity. By reducing everything to the hazard rate λ, we are able to calculate correctly the prices of different instruments regardless of their interest or premium payment frequencies and daycount conventions. Similarly each instrument's mechanics are stripped away (e.g., a default swap versus a bond) to reveal the true hazard rate.

Finally, apart from these methods using direct market inputs to calculate hazard rates, a variety of analytics firms attempt to predict default probabilities by examining the fundamentals of a company. We will return to this topic in the last section of this chapter.

SYNTHETIC CDOs

A very different set of pricing issues faces the synthetic CDO as opposed to the single name CDS. Whereas the primary issue in pricing a CDS relates to predicting its cash flows given a probability of default, multiobligor structures implicate the additional issue of correlation (of both spread and default) among assets in the pool. Unfortunately, correlations are problematic from a modeling perspective since they can be unstable over time. Certain simplifying assumptions have been utilized in standard analytics to make a start at addressing this problem, and they suggest the likely areas for continuing innovation.

EXHIBIT 22.5   Synthetic CDO Capital

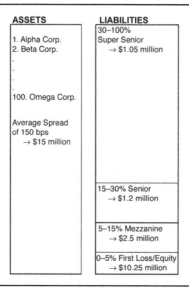

Capital Structure and Spreads

The starting point in analyzing a synthetic CDO is to determine the collateral pool making up the assets and to determine the tranching of the liabilities. Our synthetic CDO will have a pool of 100 corporate CDSs on the asset side, each representing $10 million of risk. We will also assume that the average credit default spread of the underlying pool is 150 bps. In the aggregate this pool will provide $15 million of potential cash flows to fund the liabilities as shown in Exhibit 22.5.

On the liability side, the structure will have tranches whose allocations of income and loss are predefined. From most junior to most senior, the tranches include *equity, mezzanine, senior,* and *super-senior.* Equity, or first loss, is analogous to the equity in a company's balance sheet, and represents the residual interest remaining after other liabilities are paid off. The mezzanine, or middle tier of risk, typically represents low-rated tranches all the way up to AA risk. Senior usually refers to AA and AAA risk. Super-senior represents a level of risk that is deeply subordinated (usually by at least 10%) to AAA, and as its name implies is regarded as extremely safe. In a structure that is not uncommon, we will assume all of the liability tranches are unfunded except for the equity.[3]

---

[3] Just as structures are termed synthetic if the *assets* are CDSs instead of cash instruments, so they are "unfunded" if the *liabilities* are swaps but "funded" to the extent the liabilities are in note form.

EXHIBIT 22.6 Static, No-Loss Return to CDO Tranches

Tranche	Notional	Attach at	Up to	Required Spread	Annual Premium
Super-senior/fourth loss	700,000,000	30%	100%	0.15%	1,050,000
Senior/third loss	150,000,000	15%	30%	0.80%	1,200,000
Mezzanine/second loss	100,000,000	5%	15%	2.50%	2,500,000
Equity/first loss	50,000,000	0%	5%	20.50%	10,250,000

The static, no-loss return of the various tranches in this case might have the profile shown in Exhibit 22.6. Here the equity tranche constitutes the first $50 million of risk, and is compensated for its position in the capital structure with a very high notional spread of 20.5%, or $10.25 million per year on $50 million notional. This spread represents the annual return to the equity holder in the scenario where no losses are incurred. Conversely, the most senior tranche of risk receives only $1.05 million per year on a notional position of $700 million. The low spread return of only 15 bps ($1.05 million/$700 million) underscores the perceived safety of the super-senior tranche.

Of the total spread of the assets available to fund the tranches of liabilities in this example, fully 68.33% goes to the first loss piece even though this piece only represents 5% of the total potential loss. Meanwhile, a mere 7% of the available $15 million asset spread accrues to the most senior 70% of the capital structure. As with all CDOs, in this synthetic deal the senior tranches are providing leverage to the junior tranches in exchange for safety.

In fact, the position of the 5% funded equity holder is exactly equivalent to an investor that has purchased $1 billion of assets with 20 times the nonrecourse leverage. The implied borrowing rate of such leverage is equivalent to the blended spread of the tranches that are senior to the equity. In our case the premiums due to the three tranches above the equity total $4.75 million, and the total tranches of risk that they represent equal $950 million. The annual spread due is 0.50% of the notional on these "liability" tranches and, thus, in this case the equity holder has "borrowed" $950 million at a blended borrowing cost of 50 bps.

With this analysis, the synthetic CDO looks much like any operating company, as shown in Exhibit 22.7. The equity holders have purchased assets of $1 billion. Those assets are predicted to generate a return of $15 million (the "asset spread"). To purchase those assets, the equity holders have put up $50 million, and borrowed $950 million. They must pay $4.75 million per year in aggregate (the "liability spread") to service their "debt," and if it all goes bad they will not lose any more than the $50 million that has been put up. Any losses in excess of this amount will begin to accrue to other tranches according to predetermined rules, which are discussed below.

EXHIBIT 22.7   Equity Coupon and Implied Borrowing Rate

Total assets	$1,000,000,000	Asset spread	$15,000,000	Asset yield	1.50%
Amount "borrowed"	$950,000,000	Liability spread	$4,750,000	Implied lending rate	0.50%
Equity tranche	$50,000,000	Residual spread	$10,250,000	Equity coupon	20.5%

Economic Benefits

Constructing deals synthetically and in unfunded form can provide benefits on both the asset and liability side that explain the recent popularity of synthetic CDOs and their likely continued success. It is worthwhile to take a moment to examine these benefits in the context of pricing our hypothetical portfolio.

On the asset side, the flexibility of CDS assets instead of bonds means that a wider range of credits can be included. Regulatory, geographic, liquidity, and other limitations on particular assets are often made irrelevent by the use of CDSs referencing desired credits. More choices are available. For this reason, a greater spread can usually be achieved for a comparable amount of desired risk through name substitution. In a 100-name portfolio, for example, if 10 names with similar risks could be substituted with an incremental spread of 20 bps per name, this option would be worth 2 bps to the average spread of the portfolio.

Moreover, the ability to rapidly source, or ramp up, collateral for deals means that investors can sometimes avoid the costly but usually unquantified cost of holding commitments firm until closing. If a deal is held firm at agreed levels for several weeks or months until the required cash collateral has been sourced, the short option granted by the investor is significant. In contrast, the ramp-up for a pool of synthetic CDS can happen very quickly in some cases in a single afternoon. For this, the overall value to the portfolio of the ramp-up benefit would depend heavily on the volatility of the underlying assets.

Finally, on the asset side, CDS frequently trade wider than cash bonds for the same credit, and the ability for investors to access this "basis" adds significant potential spread to any deal. We argue this positive basis available on the *same* credit is a benefit distinct from the flexibility of choosing *new* assets, which is described above. For particular wide-trading credits, the basis might easily exceed 50 bps, or in other cases go negative. Because investors will naturally select credits with favorable basis, the benefit also has significant potential value.[4]

---

[4] However, for a variety of technical reasons investors may prefer bond positions rather than CDS. These include a voice in bankruptcy proceedings, liquidity, internal funding costs, recovery assumptions, and others.

EXHIBIT 22.8 Synthetic CDO Economic Benefits

Potential Effect	Benefit Assumption
Flexibility, ramp-up, basis	10 bp
Super senior	40 bp
Super senior tranche	70%
Super-senior net savings	28 bp
Total	38 bp
PVBP of 5-year deal	4.5 bp
Deal size	$1,000,000,000
Total savings	$17,100,000

On the liability side, the primary benefit occurs at the super-senior level. In cash-funded instruments, the level of funding for AAA risk is typically in the range of 40–70 bps. By contrast, super-senior implied funding of the top 70–90% of a synthetic deal usually can be achieved at a level of 7 to 17 bps via swap. The probabilistic view that this risk is safer than AAA is usually lost where notes must be issued. This benefit can often be worth 40 bps across 70% of the capital structure.

The cumulative benefits to synthetic CDO structures versus cash structures, if they are all in play, amount to dramatically improved economics. For instance, if all of the asset side (flexibility, ramp-up, basis) benefits sum to only 10 bps, and the liability benefit is 40 bps on 70% of the capital structure, the savings would amount to 38 bps (= $40 \times 0.7 + 10$) on a $1 billion transaction. For a 5-year synthetic CDO, the PV of those 38 bps amounts to over $17 million. In a leveraged structure, of course, these benefits will primarily accrue to the equity and their impact will be magnified as shown in Exhibit 22.8.[5] Clearly, the synthetic CDO may be an efficient vehicle for investors to use in accessing diversified tranches of risk.

Allocation of Losses and Waterfalls

Having examined a snapshot of the no-loss potential return to investors as well as the potential execution benefits of synthetic CDO structures, the next question becomes the potential for loss. The allocation of gains and losses, and their order of priority (the "waterfall"), is negotiated and governed by the language of the synthetic CDO. In a typical syn-

---

[5] This value proposition may be conservative. CSFB assigns 15 bps of value to the basis alone, and 40 bps of value to 87% of the capital structure on the liability side. Neil McPherson, Helen Remeza, and David Kung, *Synthetic CDOs and Credit Default Swaps*, CSFB (November 2002).

EXHIBIT 22.9   Traditional Impact of Loss on Tranche Notional

Assumed recovery	30%
Defaults	1
Notional equity tranche, preloss	$50,000,000
Cash payment by equity holder	–$10,000,000
Recovered asset payment to equity holder	+$3,000,000
Remaining equity tranche, post-loss	$43,000,000
Coupon spread (unchanged)	20.50%

thetic CDO built on the collateral of CDSs, each default of a credit in the collateral pool will result in normal CDS payments (as described above in the pricing of single-name CDSs) up to the limit of the tranche. The equity holder in our example will be required to make payments of up to $50 million of actual losses, but no more. For this reason the most important features of a waterfall are the attachment points determining the maximum possible loss for the various tranches of risk.

However, the very flexibility of synthetics mean that there are a variety of other important decisions to be made regarding the allocation of cash flows. For example, in a "traditional" structure, the equity holder in our deal would undergo what is shown in Exhibit 22.9 upon the experience of a loss. The tranche size is reduced by the amount of the loss. The coupon will remain at the same spread, but the spread will be paid only on the reduced notional amount.

Logical as this rule of allocating gains and loss appears, it is not the only possible waterfall. In fact, a variety of cash flow structures are in use that appear superficially similar but that can have significantly different impacts on investors. Starting with the same tranche size and targeted equity coupon spread, many rules in theory could be applied to losses. Exhibit 22.10 illustrates the variety of changes in coupon an investor might experience in several common structures, given different rules for the same notional $10 million loss.

In comparison with the "traditional" structure mentioned above, a "residual" structure would retain a significantly better coupon upon experiencing a loss. In the residual case, the notional amount upon which coupons would be paid would remain unchanged, but the coupon spread would be reduced by the spread of the defaulted credit. If the defaulted credit entered the portfolio contributing a spread of 1,000 bps (a very risky credit), its default would dramatically reduce the coupon paid, but the investor would still be better off than in the "traditional" case. The total impact on the coupon for a similar loss in the two scenarios would differ by approximately $400,000 per annum (rows 2 and

EXHIBIT 22.10   Changes in Calculating Coupons upon Default

New Reference Amount	Example	New Nominal Spread	Example	New Net Coupon
Reduced by notional default	40,000,000	Unchanged	20.50%	8,200,000
Reduced by actual loss	43,000,000	Unchanged	20.50%	8,815,000
Unchanged	50,000,000	Reduced by defaulted credit spread (e.g., 1000)	18.50%	9,250,000
Unchanged	50,000,000	Reduced by average spread (e.g., 150)	20.20%	10,100,000
Unchanged	50,000,000	Unchanged	20.50%	10,250,000

3 in Exhibit 22.10). Obviously, at inception the pricing for these two types of structures (as with the others) would differ accordingly.

For the balance of the discussion we will assume a traditional type of structure, but it is worth noting that, in lengthy bilateral contracts, issues far removed from attachment points and spread can have large impacts on pricing.[6] The very flexibility available to investors in synthetic CDO structures means that additional attention is required to evaluate transactions.

Probabilities and Ratings

Having examined several possible impacts on cash flows where there is a loss, the next issue to address is the probability of suffering losses. While the pricing of an individual credit, as discussed above, is a function of that particular credit's probability of default, the key issue for a portfolio of credits is the correlation among all possible defaults.

Simply analyzing the individual credits and averaging their individual probabilities of loss is likely to understate the actual losses that will occur across the portfolio because certain factors, whether macroeconomic, sector-specific, or otherwise, are likely to impact more than one credit simultaneously. A variety of institutions use proprietary analytic methods (i.e., Monte Carlo based simulation techniques) to explore correlation assumptions in light of these factors.

Models that make simplifying assumptions about correlations are also commonly used industry-wide, and despite their limitations have

---

[6] These can include trapping and diversions of cash flows from some tranches to others in certain scenarios (e.g., breach of over-collateralization tests). We note but do not explore these issues.

provided a *lingua franca* for discussing potential transactions. Perhaps the most commonly used of these models has been the Moody's Binomial Expansion Technique model. Before working through an example and exploring the pricing of a hypothetical synthetic CDO, we outline the basic steps of the approach:

> *Step 1: Select Portfolio.* Select a target portfolio of assets that meet defined criteria for spread, and weighted average rating factor (WARF).

> *Step 2: Estimate Average Portfolio Loss.* Using the rating of each asset and the tenor of the transaction as inputs, estimate the expected average loss over the period of the deal by reviewing the Moody's table of "Idealized" Cumulative Loss Rates.

> *Step 3: Calculate Diversity Score.* Calculate a diversity score for the portfolio based on the Moody's industry groupings assigned to each asset. The diversity score will provide the important simplifying assumption driving correlation analysis of the portfolio.

> *Step 4: Calculate Tranche Loss Scenarios.* Calculate the probability of each loss scenario for each tranche using a binomial distribution. Calculate the amount of loss for each tranche in each scenario.

> *Step 5: Rate and Price Tranches.* Evaluate the probability-weighted losses in each scenario to generate an overall expected loss for each tranche, and from this expected loss calculate an implied rating for the tranche. Price the tranche based on spreads for comparably rated investments. Having determined the cost of each ratable liability tranche, estimate the available excess spread applicable to the (unrated) equity tranche.

Hypothetical Transaction
We will demonstrate the model with a hypothetical transaction.

Step 1: Select Portfolio
In constructing our hypothetical portfolio of corporate credits, we first identify a suitably diversified list of names that meet our rating and spread requirements.

The portfolio generates a set of aggregate statistics we will utilize as we work through the valuation (see Exhibit 22.11). Starting with the most straightforward statistic, the weighted average spread will simply be the average of all the credit spreads weighted by their notional amounts in

EXHIBIT 22.11   Hypothetical Portfolio Summary Statistics

Statistics

Deal term (years)	5	WARF	271.72
Number of credits	100	Average rating	Baa2
Diversity	49.24	Average spread	150
Expected average loss	0.677%		

Portfolio

#	Name	Spread	Rating	Industry	Industry Code
1	Alpha Corp.	174	Baa1	Printing, publishing, and broadcasting	26
2	Beta Corp.	74	A1	Automobile	2
3	Delta Corp.	47	A2	Containers, packaging and glass	7
...	....	...	...	...	...
100	Omega Corp.	100	A1	Insurance	20

the portfolio. For ease of analysis, we assume an equal-weighting for each of the 100 names. This assumption is also important because it allows us to use the binomial distribution in our analysis later.

The weighted average rating factor of the portfolio is the weighted average of numeric values assigned to each rating by Moody's. The rating factor reflects Moody's assessment of the 10-year probability of default associated with a particular rating level.

For our portfolio of 100 credits, the WARF is 271 (see Exhibit 22.12), which rounds down to an implied portfolio rating of Baa2, which is a first-cut assessment of the risk of the portfolio.

Step 2: Calculate Expected Loss

However, to create a more accurate assessment of the portfolio risk and to estimate the average expected loss for the portfolio, each individual credit must be found in a table of Moody's Idealized Cumulative Loss Rates according to its tenor and rating. The values in our hypothetical portfolio would all be found in the 5-year column of such a table for credits that are Baa3 or better. The weighted average of these loss rates in our hypothetical case results in an aggregate expected loss of slightly less than 0.68% for the entire hypthetical portfolio.

We know from the discussion above that adjusting this loss estimate by a recovery assumption will leave us with a probability of default. Since

$$E(\text{loss})_i = P_i(1 - R_i) \qquad (22.16)$$

EXHIBIT 22.12   Hypothetical Portfolio WARF Calculation

Rating Factors		Hypothetical Portfolio	
Rating	Value	# Credits	Contribution
Aaa	1	2	2
Aa1	10	0	0
Aa2	20	2	40
Aa3	40	7	280
A1	70	9	630
A2	120	14	1680
A3	180	9	1620
Baa1	260	21	5460
Baa2	360	18	6480
Baa3	610	18	10980
Ba1	940	0	0
Ba2	1350	0	0
Ba3	1766	0	0
B1	2220	0	0
B2	2720	0	0
B3	3490	0	0
		Sum	27172
		Average	271.72

Source: For the list of rating factor values by rating, see, e.g., Natasha Chen, Stephen Lioce, and Lisa Washburn, *Approach to Rating US Municipal Cash-Flow CDOs,* Moody's (November 26, 2002).

we can make an assumption of 30% recovery and know that the average probability of default is $0.68/(1 - 0.3) = 0.97\%$. If we assumed a recovery of 20% as we did earlier in the valuation of a single-name CDS, the implied default probability would be correspondingly lower. We will assume a 30% recovery, and it is this average expected probability of default for each of the credits in the portfolio that we will use going forward.

Calculate Diversity Score

It is important to note that this expected default probability does not say anything about potential correlations among the 100 credits. It is still merely a starting point for assessing the overall risk of the portfolio. Other inputs are required to reach our goal—including the principal correlation proxy for this model: *diversity score.*

The diversity score takes a pool of different assets which have some actual correlation and reduces them to a smaller pool of assets that are assumed to be homogeneous and uncorrelated. It is hoped that the mean and standard deviation of this model portfolio's performance will match the actual performance of the collateral.

Effectively, in calculating the diversity score, credits within the same industry are assumed to have some correlation, whereas credits in different industries are assumed to be completely uncorrelated. Each additional member of the portfolio adds to the diversity score, but members that are within the same industry add less and less as the industry concentration grows. For example, 20 assets in 20 different industries might add 20 to the diversity score; 20 assets within the same industry, however, might only add 5 to the diversity score.

Our portfolio, which we assume to be relatively clumped within a few industries, has a diversity score of 49. It is expected to behave as if it were composed of 49 equal-weighted, uncorrelated assets, each of which has the same expected default probability of approximately 0.97%. When defaults occur, we will assume each increment of default is 1/49 of the portfolio rather than 1/100.

Calculate Tranche Loss Scenarios

We now have sufficient information to calculate the probability that a certain number of defaults will occur portfolio-wide and to estimate the depth of those losses as they impact individual tranches.

Generally, to calculate the probability of a certain number of successes in a series of trials, where the probability of success is constant, and where the trials are independent, it is appropriate to use the binomial probability mass function:

$$B(x;n,p) = \binom{n}{x} p^x (1-p)^{(n-x)} \tag{22.17}$$

Given n (or 49 in our case) trials, each of which has a probability p (or 0.97%) of occurring, we will evaluate the probability of experiencing each x total number of defaults (that is, test "successes"). Having determined the likelihood of all scenarios, our waterfall rules will then dictate the cash flow magnitude of losses in each one.

For our portfolio, the analysis of expected losses to the first loss equity tranche might look like that shown in Exhibit 22.13. Our binomial distribution indicates that there is a 29.7% chance of 1 default occuring. This default would generate a 70% loss (30% recovery) on $\frac{1}{49}$ of the portfolio, or about 1.43% of the total notional amount. How-

EXHIBIT 22.13   Calculating Expected Loss to the Tranche

Average default probability	0.97%
Number of independent assets	49
Tranche attachment start	0%
Tranche attachment end	5.0%
Stress factor	1

Defaults	Probability	Losses	Expected Loss
0	62.1%	0%	0.00%
1	29.7	29	8.49
2	7.0	57	3.98
3	1.1	86	0.91
4	0.1	100	0.12
5	0.0	100	0.01
6	0.0	100	0.00
7	0.0	100	0.00
8	0.0	100	0.00
	Expected loss to tranche		13.51%

ever, this loss of 1.43% is nearly ⅓ of the 5% equity tranche. In fact, summing all of the probability-weighted losses shows that the total expected loss as a percentage of the equity is 13.51%, a significant crimp on returns!

Note that for safer tranches, the probability of default will be grossed up by a "stress factor" to more accurately reflect tail risk. The stress factor corrects for the fact that the model assumes constant default rates, whereas actual default rates are stochastic. Using constant, long-term average rates of default tends to understate the possibility of severe, multiple-default scenarios. Therefore, to account for this tail risk the constant default rates are "stressed" upward. The stress increases for higher-rated tranches since losses in higher tranches will necessarily be farther out on the tail.

Rate and Price Tranches

Having calculated the expected loss to each tranche, we can return to the Idealized Cumulative Default table to generate a rating for them. In our hypothetical portfolio, we find implied ratings of Aa3 for the second loss tranche because of its expected loss of 0.039%, and Aaa for the third loss tranche, where the probability of loss is negligible. The most

EXHIBIT 22.14   Possible Mezzanine Tranches and Ratings

Attach	Layer					
	5%	7%	8%	10%	15%	20%
5%	Aa3	Aa3	Aa3	Aa3	Aa2	Aa2
6%	Aa1	Aa1	Aa1	Aa1	Aa1	Aa1
6.50%	Aa1	Aa1	Aa1	Aa1	Aa1	Aa1
7%	Aa1	Aa1	Aa1	Aaa	Aaa	Aaa
8%	Aaa	Aaa	Aaa	Aaa	Aaa	Aaa
9%	Aaa	Aaa	Aaa	Aaa	Aaa	Aaa

senior piece, attaching more than 10% beyond the start of a Aaa tranche, we evaluate as *super senior.*

At this point, a structurer would normally look at the spreads of similarly rated credits to price each tranche, then fine-tune and modify the attachment points until he could place them all to complete the transaction. In doing so, he might evaluate many possibilities for tranching the same underlying portfolio as shown in Exhibit 22.14.

Limitations and Guideposts

This example of one ratings-based model, and the useful simplifying assumptions it makes, provide some guideposts as to where we find continuing innovation in the CDO-pricing field. Many models, as mentioned, use Monte Carlo analysis to evaluate various parameters stochastically rather than with fixed values. Other models make simplifying assumptions that are static, but which differ from this discussion. In contrast to what we have shown with this example, other models may make very different assumptions with regard to the following issues:

- Stochastic assumptions of recovery.
- Stochastic assumptions of default.
- Stochastic assumptions of correlation.
- Correlations that vary by industry (or other parameters).
- Correlations of default with recovery.
- Homogeneity of collateral pools.
- Accounting for barbelling and distribution of spreads.

As the sophistication of participants in the market increases with these and other modeling improvements, demand for better pricing and analysis tools also will necessarily increase.

Fortunately, the market is meeting this demand with an encouraging array of useful products.

DATA AND ANALYTICS PROVIDERS

This section examines a few commercially available software packages and analytic tools designed to mitigate risk in the increasingly innovative credit derivative market. It reviews CDS data providers, examines analytic programs designed to provide expected default probabilities and theoretical prices, and highlights applications intended to simplify CDO investments.[7]

Credit Default Swap Data Providers

Access to live CDS prices is critical for evaluating synthetic CDOs, monitoring hazards in the equity markets, performing capital structure relative value analysis, considering targeted risk assumption within an existing portfolio, and analyzing the diversification benefits of changes to an existing portfolio. In fact, most of the products and services mentioned in the remainder of this section rely on CDS prices as an input to their models.

Interdealer brokers such as GFI, Credit*ex*, and CreditTrade are in a unique position to collect unbiased information on the CDS market. Our discussion will examine a service from Credit*ex*: PriceTracker, which is similar to products offered by the other firms.

Creditex PriceTracker

Credit*ex*, a market-supported interdealer credit derivative broker, offers PriceTracker as a tool for accessing and monitoring CDS prices. Users have complete access to all of the live prices collected through the interdealer brokerage business.

PriceTracker allows users to find the latest default swap price on a single company or particular sector, customize graphs, view market movements with "big mover" and "rating deviation" reports, and create personalized portfolios. The main search screen is show in Exhibit 22.15. The current and historical prices for Deutsche Telekom AG, as well as a time series graph, are displayed on the screen. The graph also displays the average spread of companies with the same rating as the ref-

---

[7] The authors are not endorsing any of the companies mentioned or their products; rather, this section is intended to provide an overview of the types of services available in the market.

EXHIBIT 22.15 Creditex Pricetracker Search Screen

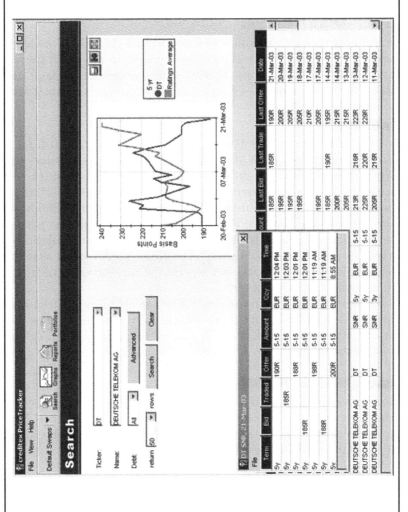

717

erence entity retrieved. This allows users to determine if a credit is "rich" or "cheap" compared to other credits sharing its rating. In this particular example, Deutsche Telekom AG is trading approximately 50 basis points below the rating average spread.

Analytics—Default Probabilities

We will now turn our attention to sophisticated risk management tools. These tools are critical for companies involved in the credit derivative market. The following products are designed to produce default probabilities, the fundamental building block for effective risk management.

Moody's KMV

Moody's KMV (formerly KMV) has been focused on credit risk for over a decade. In general, the KMV model is considered a structural model, relying on equity prices as the input. The KMV model attempts to determine when a company's assets will drop below the value of its liabilities. A more pertinent piece of information is to focus on the default point. They "have found that the *default point*, the asset value at which the firm will default, generally lies somewhere between total liabilities and current, or short-term, liabilities." The KMV model states that a firm will default when its market net worth, the market value of its assets minus the default point, is zero.[8]

Their tool used for measuring a firm's probability of default is an Expected Default Frequency (EDF^{TM}). The EDF is designed to be consistent over time. As a result, the EDF is an actual probability of default. It is not a ranking.

Kamakura KRIS-Credit Risk (KRIS-cr)

Kamakura's KRIS-cr platform is a risk management system specially focused on ensuring that companies are compliant with the new Basel II Capital Accord. KRIS-cr relies on multiple models to provide daily output of default probabilities. Their current models include:

- *Structural*: The structural models are based on Robert Merton's approach, utilizing accounting information.[9]
- *Reduced Form*: Kamakura implements reduced form models from the Robert Jarrow family, such as the Jarrow-Chava version. These models use equity, debt, and credit derivative prices.

---

[8] Peter J. Crosbie and Jeffrey R. Bohn, "Modeling Default Risk," *Moody's KMV White Paper* (January 14, 2002).

[9] Robert Merton, "On the Pricing of Corporate Debt: The Risk Structure of Interest Rates," *Journal of Finance* 29, no. 2 (1974), pp. 449–470.

■ *Hybrid Reduced Form and Structural*: These models combine the Merton structural approach with Jarrow's variables.[10]

Kamakura utilizes an ROC Accuracy Ratio to evaluate the performance of models. This ratio is designed to determine which family of models is "best" by determining if a model correctly identifies defaults and nondefaults in a sample of historical observations. A score of 100 would be a perfect score. According to Kamakura's analysis, the Jarrow-Chava reduced form model received a score of 92.74. This compares to scores in the 80's for various Merton models.[11]

In addition, Kamakura's research has shown that reduced form models utilizing credit derivatives prices are the most effective default predictor:

> "Our results indicate that reduced form models based on credit derivatives prices and bond prices have the best performance from both a statistical and a practical point of view," said Professor Jarrow.[12]

NumeriX NX CR Engine

The NX CR Engine is a pricing and risk management tool that allows users to model a wide range of credit derivative products. It produces theoretical prices for single-name credit default swaps, baskets and CDOs. In addition, NumeriX's software produces survival probabilities, recovery rates and correlations.

The NX CR Engine also relies on multiple models, depending on the type of product being modeled. For example, it utilizes 1-dimensional models for valuing callable credit default swaps and uses more complicated models (such as quasi-multiperiod, diffusion multiperiod (Hull-White), Copula function, etc.) for baskets and CDOs.

Analytics—CDO Management Solutions

As the CDO market continues to grow, evaluation and monitoring tools become more essential. The products discussed in this section allow investors to make educated investment decisions and monitor their existing investments.

---

[10] Robert Jarrow and Stuart Turnbull, "Pricing Derivatives on Financial Securities Subject to Default Risk," *Journal of Finance* 50, no. 1 (1995), pp. 53–86.
[11] Kamakura Risk Information Services: Credit Risk Overview
[12] Kamakura's Press Release, *Kamakura Launches Basel II Default Probability Service and Announces First Client*, October 31, 2002.

DM Partners CDO Investor™

CDO Investor combines analytic tools with a historical database of publicly available CDO transactions. Investors can analyze their existing investments, as well as perform relative value analysis between different transactions. CDO Investor allows users to model projected cash flows, find current and historical ratings on CDO tranches, review details on underlying collateral, and make internal rate of return (IRR) projections.

RiskMetrics Group: CDOManager™

RiskMetrics Group CDOManager is designed to analyze cash and synthetic CDO structures. It helps assess the risk associated with a CDO and calculate prices. CDOManager produces expected cash flow from the assets and feeds them into a waterfall to determine the cash flow to the notes. Exhibit 22.16 provides a screenshot from CDOManager.

In order to model the asset's cash flow, it uses a Monte Carlo simulation to generate expected default times for each piece of collateral and utilizes Copula functions and equity indexes to estimate correlation in the default times. The default times allow CDOManager to determine the cash flow expected from each asset over the life of a transaction. Summing up the cash flow from all of the assets generates a picture of the expected future cash flow from the CDO collateral pool.

Once the asset's future cash flows are estimated, it is necessary to model the liability structure. CDOManager allows users to model various waterfall structures to accommodate for reinvestment into new collateral, payments of interest, reserve accounts, fee accounts, etc.

SUMMARY

All in all, the proliferation of publicly available toolkits such as these, as well as the continued evolution of modeling techniques built on the basics we have outlined in this chapter, suggest a promising and interesting future for the growth of the synthetics market in years to come.

EXHIBIT 22.16 Riskmetrics Group CDOManager

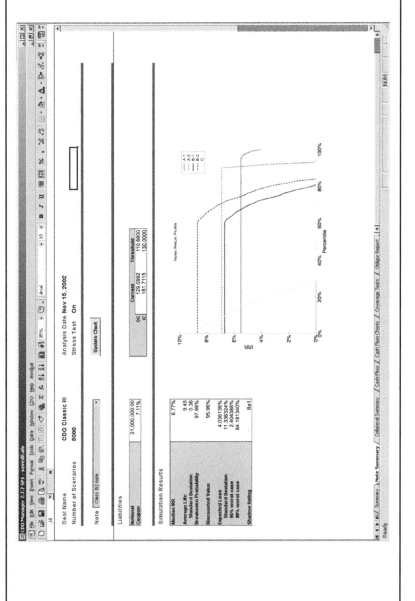

Portfolio Management

Four

CHAPTER 23

Fixed Income Risk Modeling for Portfolio Managers

Ludovic Breger, Ph.D.
Manager
Fixed Income Research
Barra, Inc.

The European credit market, consisting mainly of euro- and sterling-denominated debt, is second only to the US domestic market in terms of size, influence, and liquidity. Not surprisingly, European securities are becoming common in global portfolios. The recent turmoil in credit markets has shown once again that understanding risk is or should be a critical aspect of portfolio management. However, as the European credit market is a mosaic of widely different instruments, issuers, and currencies, identifying and forecasting the risk of European fixed income securities is not a simple task.

This chapter will take the reader through the process of building a European risk model and discuss the important sources of risk in generic fixed income portfolios. Our intention is not to cover the whole spectrum of securities, but to address some typical modeling challenges such as accommodating different benchmarks and securities and providing a wide coverage without compromising accuracy. With a general framework in place, the model can be easily extended to cover more markets or bond types.

The author thanks Jean-Martin Aussant, Oren Cheyette, and Darren Stovel for insightful comments and suggestions on how to improve this chapter.

A FRAMEWORK FOR UNDERSTANDING AND MODELING RISK

This discussion covers the main factors affecting bond returns in the European fixed income market, namely, the random fluctuations of interest rates and bond yield spreads, the risk of an obligor defaulting on its debt, or issuer-specific risk, and currency risk. There are also other, more subtle sources of risk. Some bonds such as mortgage-backed and asset-backed securities are exposed to prepayment risk, but such instruments still represent a small fraction of the total outstanding European debt. Bonds with embedded options are exposed to volatility risk. However, it is not apparent that this risk is significant outside derivatives markets.

A detailed understanding of correlations between asset returns is required to accurately estimate the risk of a portfolio. Unfortunately, estimating correlations directly is in practice impossible as unknowns severely outnumber observations even in relatively small portfolios. The standard solution is to decompose the portfolio's vector of asset returns using marketwide common factors:[1]

$$r_{\text{excess}} = X \times f + r_{\text{specific}} \tag{23.1}$$

where

X = matrix of asset exposures
f = vector of factor returns
r_{specific} = vector of asset residual returns not explained by factors or specific returns idiosyncratic to individual assets

Decomposing returns is a key step in identifying, understanding, and modeling the sources of risk that are at work in the market. It is also crucial in understanding risk exposures.

We begin our analysis by writing the excess returns of assets in a portfolio as

$$r_{\text{excess}} = (r_{\text{IR}} + r_{\text{curr}} + r_{\text{spread factor}} + r_{\text{specific}}) \tag{23.2}$$

where

r_{IR} = vector of returns due to changes in interest rates

---

[1] For more information on factor models, see for instance Richard C. Grinold and Ronald N. Kahn, "Multiple Factor Models for Portfolio Risk," John W. Peavey III (ed) *A practitioner's Guide to Factor Models* (Charlottesville, VA: AIMR, 1994).

r_{curr} = vector of returns due to changes in currency exchange rates

$r_{\text{spread factor}}$ = vector of returns due to sectorwide changes in yields or credit spreads

r_{specific} = vector of specific returns not explained by common factors

Note that the decomposition implicitly ignores the predictable component of return that is irrelevant for risk modeling purposes.[2] The return common horizon will be one month in most cases. Although daily or even weekly returns would provide a much larger data set, they are also on average much more sensitive to noise in bond data.[3] We will also see in what follows that it is sometimes possible to use returns over a shorter time horizon.

If the return factor model adequately accounts for common factors, then the specific returns are uncorrelated and we can write portfolio risk as

$$\sigma^2 = {}^Th \times \Sigma \times h \qquad (23.3)$$

with

$$\Sigma = {}^TX \times \Phi \times X + \Delta \qquad (23.4)$$

where

h = vector of portfolio holdings
Σ = covariance matrix of asset returns
Φ = covariance matrix of factor returns
Δ = diagonal matrix of specific variances

Equation (23.4) will yield active risk forecasts when h is a vector of active holdings.

The data that can go into computing factor returns will of course depend on what the factors are. It can include bond and index level data as well as currency exchange rates. Assume that we have the factor return series. To construct covariances, we could postulate that the underlying random processes are time stationary and compute covariances using equally weighted factor returns. We actually know that mar-

---

[2] Some market idiosyncrasies such as settlement conventions are an important part of a valuation model but irrelevant to a risk model.

[3] For instance, short horizons spread returns observed for high grade corporate bonds are small and are typically very noisy.

kets change over time and that recent data are more representative of current market conditions than are older data. A simple method for accommodating this fact consists in exponentially weighting factor returns to calculate the covariance matrix. The relative weight of returns from time τ in the past relative to the most recent returns is $e^{-t/\tau}$, where τ is a time-decay constant.[4] The optimal time constant τ can be obtained empirically using, for instance, a maximum-likelihood estimator. However, series that are particularly volatile may require a different treatment (see for instance Currency Returns discussed later).

Much of the art of constructing a model goes in choosing relevant factors. Note that factors are descriptive and not explanatory. In other words, they allow for forecasting risk without necessarily being linked to the forces that *really* drive interest rates or returns. Let's now proceed with a discussion of several classes of factors.

INTEREST RATE RISK

Interest rate or term structure risk stems from movements in the benchmark interest rate curve. Excluding exchange rate risk, it is the main source of risk for most investment-grade bonds. Any reasonable model will include markets that are stable and actively traded. A typical coverage, taken from JP Morgan GBI Broad Index, is shown in Exhibit 23.1. Note the presence of two emerging markets.

Building a term-structure risk model for the European market involves choosing several benchmarks—at least one for each currency. A recent complication is that domestic government yields are no longer the universal choice. The LIBOR/swap curve has recently emerged as the Eurozone's preferred benchmark due to the absence of a natural sovereign yield curve and the growing liquidity and transparency of swap

EXHIBIT 23.1 European Markets in JP Morgan GBI Broad Index as of 1 January 2003

Austria	Greece	Portugal
Belgium	Hungary	Spain
Czech Republic	Ireland	Sweden
Denmark	Italy	Switzerland
Finland	Netherlands	United Kingdom
France	Norway	
Germany	Poland	

---

[4] The half-life is $\tau \ln 2$.

curves. However, many markets continue to trade primarily with respect to the government benchmark. In some emerging markets, the absence of a liquid market for sovereign debt makes the LIBOR/swap curve the only available benchmark. A simple approach used at Barra and which permits alternative views is to use the sovereign term structure as the local benchmark whenever possible and include a swap spread "intermediate" factor that can be added to the sovereign-based interest rate factors to allow interest rate to be expressed with respect with the swap curve. This swap spread factor will be described in more detail in the next section. In markets where the benchmark is already the LIBOR/swap curve, there is obviously no need for a swap factor.

The existence of a Eurozone born from the union of several legacy markets introduces an additional modeling challenge. More than one domestic government is issuing euro-denominated debt, and although yields have converged, some differences clearly remain that suggest building a set of factors for each legacy market. (See Exhibit 23.2 for some examples of sovereign term structures within the Eurozone.) Some bonds also need to be analyzed almost completely independently of other assets. This is the case for Inflation Protected Bonds (IPBs) denominated in euro or sterling, which offer investors a "real" inflation-adjusted yield. Such securities are weakly correlated with other asset classes and are exposed to a set of IPB-specific interest risk factors simi-

EXHIBIT 23.2   Examples of Sovereign Term Structures within the Eurozone on 31 July 2002

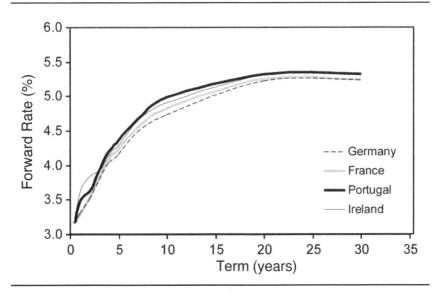

lar in nature to the conventional interest rate factors but derived from IPB data and real yields.

What should the interest rate factors be? Key rate durations, which are rate changes at the term structure vertices, seem a natural and somewhat appealing choice. However, because rates for different maturities are highly correlated, using so many factors is unnecessary, and causes difficulty with spurious correlations. Anywhere from 90% to 98% of term structure risk can in fact be modeled using only three principal components commonly referred to as *shift, twist,* and *butterfly*. The principal component analysis is now a fairly standard approach that we describe in more details in the Appendix to this chapter. Exhibit 23.3 shows examples of factor shapes. Note how principal components derived from Portuguese sovereign euro-denominated debt are very different from the German shapes. Such large differences within the Eurozone confirm the need for a different set of factors in each legacy market.

Shift, twist, and butterfly volatilities are shown in Exhibit 23.4. Quasi-parallel shifts in the term structure are the dominant source of risk in all cases with volatilities ranging from 35 to 200 basis points per year. In spite of these large differences, term structure risk is relatively homogeneous across most markets and in particular within the Eurozone. Note,

EXHIBIT 23.3 Examples of Shift, Twist and Butterfly Interest Risk Factors Shapes (top) and Return Volatilities (bottom) on 31 July 2002

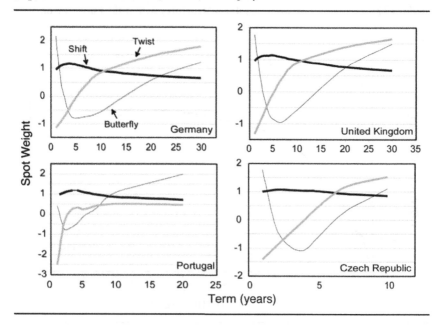

again, that the differences in factor volatilities are sufficiently large to justify building separate legacy factors.[5] As expected, the largest volatilities are observed for emerging market benchmarks, Czech Republic being the riskiest market. And not surprisingly, real yields appear to be more stable than their noninflation protected sovereign counterparts.

EXHIBIT 23.4   Interest Rate Factor Volatilities on 31 July 2002

---

[5] An alternative but less accurate approach would be to build a unique set of EMU interest rate factors and capture each legacy market idiosyncrasies with a spread factor.

EXHIBIT 23.5   Examples of Interest Rate Risk Breakdown

	Exposure			Risk (bp/yr)			
	Shift	Twist	Butterfly	Shift	Twist	Butterfly	Total
Federal Republic of Germany 8.5% 07/16/07	4.9	–0.3	–2.9	310	8	35	312
Federal Republic of Germany 4.75% 07/04/28	10.8	18.7	10.6	680	490	130	850
Czech Republic 6.95% 01/26/16	10.2	15.0	10.3	1,900	2,700	500	3,300

The interest rate risk of any given bond will depend on the bond's exposures to the factors and on correlations between factors. Exhibit 23.5 gives detailed risk decompositions for three sovereign bonds. The typical annualized risk of a straight bond issued by the Federal Republic of Germany varies from about 200 to 300 bp to over 800 bp, depending on its duration. At the other end of the spectrum, the interest rate risk of a bond issued by the Czech Republic can reach as much as 3,000 bp,[6] which exceeds the risk of most speculative corporate issues in developed markets. Clearly, such extreme cases will require special attention when controlling risk.

Spread Risk

Until fairly recently, outside the United States, United Kingdom, and Japan, there were relatively few tradable nongovernment bonds. The recent explosion of the global corporate credit market now provides asset managers with new opportunities for higher returns and diversification. Unlike domestic government debt, however, corporate debt is exposed to spread risk, which arises from unexpected yield spread changes. For modeling purposes, such changes can again be decomposed into a systematic component that describes, for instance, a marketwide jump in the spread of A-rated utility debt and can be captured by common spread factors, and an issuer or bond-specific component. This section discusses model market-wide spread risk, while the next section will address issuer specific spread risk and default risk.

Data considerations are crucial in choosing factors. The choice of factors will be somewhat limited in markets with little corporate debt. Spread factors should increase the investor's insight and be easy to interpret. Meaningful factors will in practice be somewhat connected to the portfolio assets and construction process and allow a detailed analysis of market risk without threatening parsimony.

---

[6] Note here how twistlike movements of the Tchek benchmark account for more risk than the shift distortions themselves. A simpler, duration-based model would severely underforecast risk.

Swap Spread Factors

First, as mentioned earlier, there is usually no universal benchmark in a given market. Again, a possible approach, used in Barra's models, is to introduce a swap spread factor that describes the average spread between sovereign and swap rates and can conveniently allow spread risk to be expressed with respect to the LIBOR/swap curve when interest rate risk factors are originally based on the sovereign yield curve.

This same factor can also be used to compute spread risk in markets where there is not enough data to build a detailed credit block. It can also be used in markets where more detailed credit factors are available, but when there is not enough information to expose a bond to the appropriate credit factor. As we will see in what follows, this will be the case when a euro- or sterling-denominated corporate bond is not rated. Based on the observation that bonds with larger spreads are on average more risky, Barra's model assumes the following exposure to the swap factor:

$$x = D_{\text{eff}} + (\alpha - 1) \times D_{\text{spr}}$$
$$\text{with } \alpha = \max\left[1, \left(\frac{\text{OAS}}{S}\right)^{\gamma}\right] \qquad (23.5)$$

where

D_{eff}	= bond effective duration
D_{spread}	= bond spread duration
OAS	= bond spread
S	= swap spread
γ	= a scaling exponent determined empirically and equal to 0.6

At the time of this writing, corporate bonds denominated in currencies others than euro and sterling are only exposed to the local interest factors and if it exists, the swap factor. This swap factor is roughly equivalent to a financial AA spread factor, as the bulk of organizations that engage in swaps are AA-rated financial institutions. The swap model is coarser than the two local credit models discussed in the next section, but it performs adequately because spread changes are highly correlated within markets.

Swap spread volatilities for several currencies are shown in Exhibit 23.6, with values that vary from about 15 bp/year to 40 bp/year. Also shown are the resulting spread risks in the euro and sterling markets for several rating categories. We will see further below that the swap model predicts reasonably accurately both the absolute magnitude of the spread risk in each market and their relative values.

EXHIBIT 23.6 Swap Spreads

Panel A: Swap Spread Annualized Volatility for Markets Covered in the Model

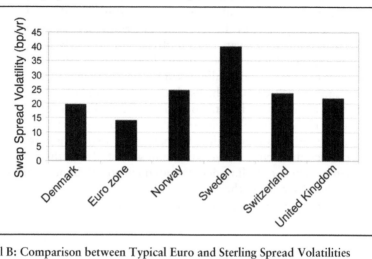

Panel B: Comparison between Typical Euro and Sterling Spread Volatilities
Computed Using the Swap Factor for Different Rating Categories

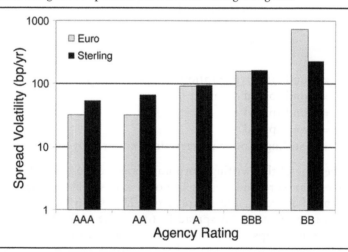

Credit Spread Factors

The euro and sterling markets are broad and liquid markets. Accurately modeling spread risk in these two markets requires market-dependent, "credit blocks."

Various considerations drive the choice of spread factors. Factors built on little data can end up capturing a large amount of idiosyncratic risk and be representative of a few issuers rather than the market. A cor-

EXHIBIT 23.7   Example of Sector and Rating Breakdown in the Euro Market*

Euro	
Sectors	Ratings
Agency	AAA
Financial	AA
Foreign sovereign	A
Energy	BBB
Industrial	
Pfandbrief	
Supranational	
Telecom	
Utility	
	BB
	B
	CCC

*A nondomestic sovereign bond is exposed to the factor corresponding to its sector and rating. Due to the limited number of high-yield bonds outstanding, non-investment grade factors are only broken down by ratings.

ollary is that it is often wiser to avoid building separate factors for thin industries. Spread factors should be meaningful for the investor and somehow be related to the process of constructing a portfolio.

An obvious and natural approach is to capture fluctuations in the average spread of bonds with the same sector and rating. As the size of the high-yield European bond market is still modest, there is unfortunately not enough data to construct sector-by-rating factors for speculative ratings. The simplest alternative is then to construct rating-based factors. A typical sector and rating breakdown for the euro market is given in Exhibit 23.7.

Note that using market-adjusted ratings as opposed to conventional agency ratings can increase the explanatory power of sector-by-rating spread factors. The idea is to adjust the rating of bonds with a spread that is not too different from the average spread observed within their rating category. For instance, a AA rated euro-denominated bond with a spread equal to 200 bps would be reclassified into a BBB rated bond.[7]

Credit spreads are computed with respect to the local swap curve to accommodate for the swap spread factor.

---

[7] See Ludovic Breger, Lisa Goldberg, and Oren Cheyette, OAS implied ratings, *Barra Research Insight*, 2002.

EXHIBIT 23.8   Euro and Sterling Spread Factor Volatilities as of 30 November 2002

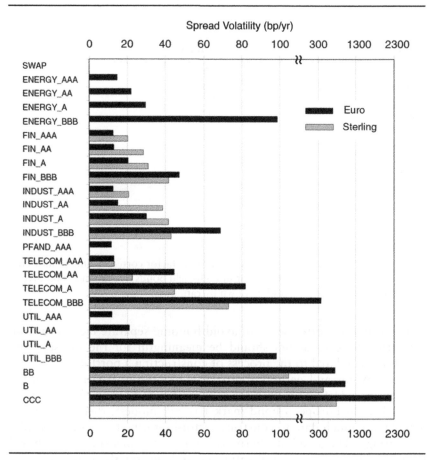

Note that arbitrage considerations imply that the spread risk of issues from the same obligor should be independent of the market. Why then do we need two sets of credit factors? After all, a model with only one set would be more parsimonious. Empirical evidence simply shows that spread risk is indeed currency dependent, at least for higher credit quality issuers.[8]

Volatilities for selected factors are displayed in Exhibit 23.8. Spread risk in the euro and sterling markets is, on average, comparable. Looking now in more details, sterling factors tend to be more volatile than

[8] Alec Kercheval, Lisa Goldberg, and Ludovic Breger, "Modeling Credit Risk: Currency Dependence in Global Credit Markets," *Journal of Portfolio Management* (Winter 2003), pp. 90–100.

euro factors for AAA, AA, and A ratings, and less volatile for lower ratings. This is a trend already seen in Exhibit 23.6 that confirms that the swap factor would be a simpler but meaningful alternative. Significant differences exist for individual factors that illustrate the need for currency dependent factors (see for instance the Telecom A and BBB factors). Also note how the high volatilities of the energy, utility, and especially telecom factors reflect the recent problems in these industries.

Each corporate bond will only be exposed to one of these factors, with an exposure that will typically increase with the bond's maturity. A rule of thumb is that it will be comparable to the bond's exposure to the shift factor. The spread risk of almost all AAA, AA, and A rated bonds will be less than their interest rate risk, and it is only for BBB rated bonds and in some very specific market sectors such as Energy and Telecoms that spread risk starts exceeding benchmark risk. Spread risk is by far the dominant source of systematic risk for high-yield instruments.

Emerging Markets Spread Factors

Emerging debt can be issued either in the local currency or in any other external currencies (i.e., Mexico issuing in euro or sterling). These two types of debt do not carry the same risk,[9] and need to be modeled independently. "Internal" risk was discussed in the interest risk section and we will now address external risk.

A rather natural approach is to expose emerging market bonds to a spread factor. The sovereign spread factor turns out to be a poor candidate as the risk of emerging market debt strongly depends on the country of issue. Exhibit 23.9 shows average Argentinean monthly spread returns from June 30, 1999 to June 30, 2002 for US dollar-denominated debt. The collapse of the peso, the illiquidity of the financial system, and the brutal decline in the economic activity are all reflected in Argentinean returns. Chilean spreads remained virtually unaffected despite a strong economic link between the two countries. As a result, any accurate model will need at least one factor per country of issue.

The amount of data available for building emerging market spread factors is unfortunately scarce. First, there are often at best only a few bonds issued by sovereign issuers in emerging markets. The second problem is that there are mostly US dollar-denominated. Even when some bonds denominated in, say, euro are available, there is generally little returns history. In some cases, we will seek risk forecasts for an

---

[9] External debt is more risky than internal debt. If needed, sovereign governments can generally raise taxes or print money to service their internal debt. A shortage of external currencies can be more dramatic. This can be seen in the credit ratings delivered by agencies.

EXHIBIT 23.9   Examples of Spread Returns for Two Emerging Markets

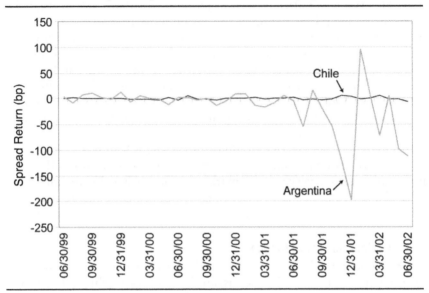

issuer with no history of issuance in a specific currency. Since the risk of an emerging market bond is directly related to the creditworthiness of the sovereign issuer, which is independent of the currency of denomination, we can actually borrow from the history of US dollar-denominated emerging market returns to forecast spread volatilities in other currencies. Spread return data can be obtained from an index such as JP Morgan Emerging Markets Bond Index Global (EMBIG).

Strictly speaking, these factors are applicable only to sovereign and sovereign agency issuers, based on the inclusion criteria for, say, EMBIG if we happen to use this particular index to estimate emerging markets spread factors. However, many issuers of external debt domiciled in these markets carry a risk that is comparable to the corresponding sovereign issuers, so that it is reasonable to use the sovereign factor as a proxy for corporate issuers.

Emerging market spread volatilities are shown in Exhibit 23.10. The spread risk of Latin American obligors tend to be above average, currently largest for Argentinean and Brazilian markets that have a spread risk comparable to a B to CCC rated euro corporate. The risk of Asian issuers is on the other hand below average and comparable to the interest rate observed in developed markets. We clearly observe a wide spectrum of risk characteristics that confirms the need to build a separate factor for each market.

EXHIBIT 23.10   Emerging Market Spread Volatilities as of 30 November 2002

SPECIFIC RISK

Specific returns are residual returns not explained by common factors. Common factors returns are typically larger than specific returns for higher quality investment-grade instruments; this is no longer the case in the lower portion of the investment grade segment and for high-yield instruments.

One option is to use a CreditMetrics-like model based on transition probabilities reported by rating agencies. The model assumes that specific return variance of any bond can be written as

$$\sigma_{\text{spec}}^2 = \sum_j p_{i \to j}[D(s_j - s_i) - r_m]^2 + p_{i \to d}(1 - R - r_m)^2 \tag{23.6}$$

with

$p_{i \to j}$ = one-month probability of transitioning from rating i to j
D = bond spread duration
s_i = average spread level observed among bonds with rating i
R = recovery rate

$$r_m = \left[\sum_j p_{i \to j} D(s_i - s_j) \right] + p_{i \to j}(1 - R) = \text{Average expected return}$$

Transition probabilities are a crucial ingredient to this formula, and more generally, to any credit portfolio model based on ratings. Although agencies such as Standard and Poor's do report European-specific rates, they are based on a small number of credit events, particularly for low quality ratings, yielding poorly constrained values. Global transition rates are statistically more robust because they are derived from a dataset that covers far more obligors and a longer time period.

The model uses average spread levels observed within each rating category. Since these levels are market-dependent, so is specific risk. Another consequence is that this approach can only be implemented in highly liquid markets, where there are enough bonds to robustly estimate average spread levels—in practice, markets for which we can construct sector-by-rating credit factors.

In markets where there is not enough data to construct a detailed model, a simple solution is to write the specific risk forecast as:

$$\sigma_{\text{spec}} = (a + b \times s)D \qquad (23.7)$$

where

s = bond spread
D = bond duration

The two constants a and b are fitted in each market using observed residual returns. Typical values for Swiss francs-denominated bonds are on the order of 5×10^{-4} bp/year and 5×10^{-6} bp/year, respectively, if spreads are expressed in basis points.

CURRENCY RISK

Currency risk is potentially a large source of risk for global investors that can be handled with a multifactor model with one factor per currency. Yet, special attention has to be paid in forecasting the variances and covariances of currency factors due to their high volatility and rapidly changing risk characteristics. The goal is to obtain a model that quickly adjusts to new risk regimes and responds to new data.

Various forms of General Auto-Regressive Conditional Heteroskedastic (GARCH) models have been used to estimate return volatility. Such models express current volatility as a function of previous returns and forecasts. For instance, the GARCH(1,1) model takes the form:

$$\sigma_t^2 = \omega^2 + \beta(\sigma_{t-1}^2 - \omega^2) + \gamma(r_{t-1}^2 - \omega^2) \qquad (23.8)$$

where

σ_t^2 = conditional variance forecast at time t

ω^2 = unconditional variance forecast

β = persistence

γ = sensitivity to new events

r_{t-1} = observed return from $t-1$ to t

The constants β and γ must be positive to insure a positive variance, even if large events occur. For the same reason, the condition $\beta + \gamma < 1$ must hold. The higher the sensitivity, the more responsive the model is. The weight given to past forecasts increase with the persistence constant.

Using daily exchange rates as opposed to weekly or monthly exchange rates ensures the convergence of GARCH parameters and minimizes standard errors.[10] The aggregation formula for monthly GARCH forecasts is:

$$\sigma_{t,n}^2 = n\omega^2 + \frac{1 - (\beta + \gamma)^n}{1 - (\beta + \gamma)}(\sigma_t^2 - \omega^2) \qquad (23.9)$$

where n is the number of business days in a month, typically 20 or 21.

Exhibit 23.11 shows US dollar versus euro returns from 1994 to 2000. Note how volatility forecasts (gray lines) quickly adjust to periods of small or large returns. The overall currency risk is large compared to interest rate risk. Consider a German government bond with a duration equal to five years. A US investor holding this asset is facing an additional currency risk of at least 8% per year in addition to an interest risk of roughly 70 bps × 5 = 3.5%.[11] The volatilities of several European currencies are plotted in Exhibit 23.12, and typically range from roughly 6.5% to 10% per year.

---

[10] This is because daily exchange rate returns represent a much larger dataset than weekly and monthly returns.

[11] 70 bps is the German shift volatility reported in Exhibit 23.4.

EXHIBIT 23.11   US Dollar Against Euro Currency Returns and Volatility

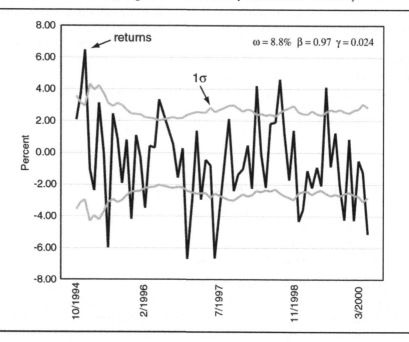

EXHIBIT 23.12   Examples of European Currency Volatilities

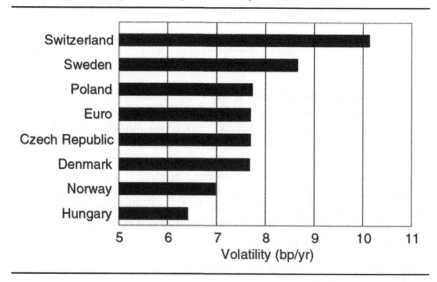

GARCH volatilities can be combined with correlations computed independently, for instance from weekly returns, to produce the covariance matrix of currency factors. This approach has the advantage of combining accurate and highly responsive estimates of exchange rate volatilities with correlations computed over a longer time horizon and which are typically more robust.

PUTTING IT TOGETHER

Common factors, returns, exposures, and a specific risk model—everything is there except for one last critical ingredient: the covariance matrix. Building a sensible covariance matrix for more than a few factors is a complicated task that involves solving several problems.

Coping with Incomplete Return Series

Factor return series often have different lengths, some series starting earlier than others. Return series can also have holes. As a result, what works well for two factors is here useless. That is, filling the factor covariance matrix row i and column j using the usual formula[12] produces a non-positive definite matrix. A statistical approach known as the EM algorithm is the conventional workaround. Details on the algorithm can be found in Dempster, Laird, and Rubin,[13] and for the purpose of this discussion, we only need to know that there exists a tool that can use incomplete series to produce an optimal estimate of the true covariance matrix.

Global Integration

With a model that has on the order of 180 factors, we need to solve for over 16,000 covariances. Factor returns series include, in many cases, less than 30 to 40 periods. With such a small sample size compared to the number of factors, we have a severely underdetermined problem and are virtually assured that the covariance forecasts will show a large degree of spurious linear dependence among the factors. One consequence is that it becomes possible to create portfolios with artificially low risk forecasts.[14] The structure of these portfolios would be pecu-

---

[12] $\mathrm{Cov}(i,j) = \sum \dfrac{(r_i - \bar{r}_i)(r_j - \bar{r}_j)}{(N-1)}$

[13] A. P. Dempster, N.M. Laird, and D. B. Rubin, "Maximum likelihood from incomplete data using the EM algorithm," *Journal of the Royal Statistical Society* 39 (1977), pp. l–38.

[14] For example, by use of an optimizer.

liar—for example, they might be overweight UK AA financials, apparently hedged by an underweight in Euro industrial and telecom.

Reducing the number of factors would compromise the accuracy of our risk analysis at the local level. However, we have seen for instance that the euro and sterling credit markets are to a large extent independent so that we do not need $34 \times 16/2 = 272$ covariances to describe the coupling between these two markets. Using our knowledge of the market in a more systematic fashion could go a long way in reducing the spurious correlations amongst factors.

The structured approach presented in Stefek provides a solution to this problem.[15] In this method, factor returns are decomposed into a global component and a purely local component, exactly as we already decomposed asset returns into systematic and nonsystematic returns. For instance, in the sterling market we can write

$$f_{UK} = X_{f_{UK}} \times g_{UK} + \varepsilon_{f_{UK}} \tag{23.10}$$

where

f_{UK} = vector of factor returns for the sterling market
g_{UK} = vector of global factor returns for the sterling market
X_{UK} = exposure matrix of the local factors to the global factors
ε_{UK} = vector of residual factor returns not explained by global factors or purely local returns.

Local factors in each market include the shift, twist, butterfly, and spread factors. Currency and emerging market factors form two independent sets of local factors. The choice of global factors is based on econometric considerations. To a large degree, sterling credit factors behave independently of factors in other markets. As a result, we know *a priori* that we will gain very little by choosing more than one or two sterling global credit factors. Once the global factors are chosen, exposures are determined and also based on structural arguments.

Equation (23.9) can then be easily extended to all the original factors in the model. Assuming now that purely local returns are uncorrelated across markets and uncorrelated with global returns, the covariance matrix can be written as:

$$F = XG^TX + \Lambda \tag{23.11}$$

where

[15] D. Stefek, "The Barra Integrated Model," *Barra Research Insight*, 2002.

G = covariance matrix of global factors
X = exposure matrix of the local factor to the global factors
Λ = covariance matrix of local factors

Global factors could typically include:

■ Shift, twist, and butterfly factors (including ipb) except in euro legacy markets.
■ Swap spread factors.
■ An average credit spread factor in the euro and sterling market.
■ An average emerging market spread.
■ Currency factors.

Far less unknowns than before now separate us from the covariance matrix. For one, there are much fewer global factors than local factors (33 against 160 if we except currencies). The local covariance matrix Λ is also block diagonal, with only on the order of 10,000 nonzero entries.

Unfortunately, we cannot stop there and use equation (23.11). The benefit of using global factors is that they help compute cross-market terms and constitute the skeleton of the matrix. The drawback is a loss of resolution at the local level. A solution to this problem is to replace local blocks by a local covariance matrix computed using the full set of original local factors. Off-diagonal blocks need to be adjusted in the process to insure that the final matrix is positive definite. A more detailed discussion of how the local covariance blocks are replaced can be found in Stefek.[16] Local covariance blocks can be computed individually for each market, but also for emerging markets spread factors and currency factors. As a result, shorter half-life can be used for return series that are typically more volatile, such as currency and emerging market returns.

At this point, we have a method for building a model that reconciles two conflicting goals, that is, provide a wide coverage of markets and securities while permitting an accurate and insightful analysis, particularly at the local level.

In Exhibit 23.13, we compare correlations obtained using the standard and structured integration methods. As expected, running the EM algorithm on over 180 factors produces a large number of spurious correlations, notably between emerging market and euro spread factors. These artifacts disappear in the structured integration. Most of the cross-market coupling happens at the interest rate level—and not for all markets. For instance, Czech and German Treasury yields vary in concert, but rather independently of Swiss yields. All other factors are clearly currency or market-dependent.

---

[16] Stefek and al., "The Barra Integrated Model," *Barra Research Insight*, 2002.

EXHIBIT 23.13   Examples of Factor Correlations in the Standard and Structured Integrations

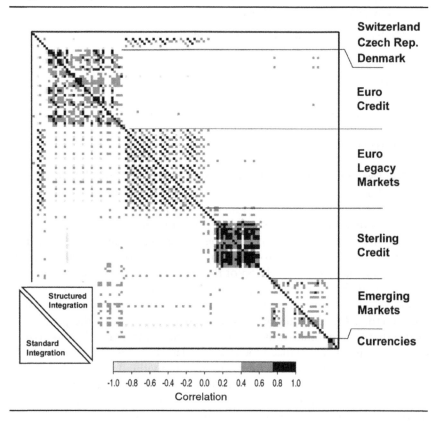

THE MODEL IN ACTION

European fixed income portfolios are now often managed against a broad index. The risk characteristics of an index like the Merrill Lynch EMU Corporate Large Cap are presented in Exhibit 23.14. This index tracks the performance of large investment grade corporate issues denominated in euro and is balanced to reflect the contributions of each market sector to the total outstanding corporate debt. Fluctuations in the euro exchange rate constitute the dominant source of risk and would amount to about 8% per year for a US-based investor. This risk disappears for investors based in the Eurozone. Local market risk originates for the most part from interest rate risk with spread risk only

EXHIBIT 23.14   Merrill Lynch EMU Large Cap Risk Decomposition as of
30 November 2002

Risk Source	Exposure	Return Volatility (%/yr)
Interest rate		
Shift	4.1	2.9
Twist	0.35	0.09
Butterfly	−1.9	0.22
Total		2.9
Spread	4.3	0.9
Specific		0.1
Currency	1	8.1
Total		8.5

responsible for about 90 bps per year. Specific risk is small because all assets in the index are rated BBB or above.

Hedging currency and interest rate risk is relatively straightforward. This is not the case for spread risk so that understanding exposures to spread factors is a critical aspect of risk control. In Exhibit 23.15, we show a "risk map" of the Merrill Lynch EMU Corporate Large Cap index. Each row i column j entry represents the fraction of the total index return variance due to covariance between factor i and factor j. Credit factors are ordered by market sector and ratings. Lines indicate entries corresponding to negative covariances. This representation takes into account factor volatilities and correlations, the assets exposures to each factor as well as the index weight in each sector and rating category.

Because sector-by-rating spreads are relative to swaps, all assets are exposed to the swap factor, yielding a large swap risk. This risk would be transferred to the other credit factors in a model where spreads are computed relative to Treasury. The negative covariances between corporate spread returns and both the shift and swap factors can be interpreted as follows. Inspection of the correlation matrix in Exhibit 23.13 shows that correlations between credit factors and the shift factor are negative with a magnitude that tends to be small for AAA and AA like factors, but can reach large values for A and BBB like factors. Swap spreads move nearly independently of corporate spreads to government. As a result, swap spreads and corporate spreads to swap are negatively correlated.

EXHIBIT 23.15   Risk Map of the Euro Component of the Merrill Lynch Large Cap
Index as of 30 November 2002

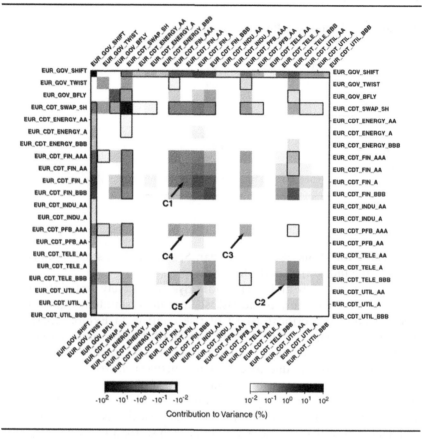

Contribution to Variance (%)

Most of the remaining credit risk originates from five clusters (C1 to
C5 in Exhibit 23.15):

- A large contribution from Financial securities, which represent over
  65% of the portfolio (C1).
- An unusually large contribution of Telecom assets, considering their
  weight in the index (~7%), that is due to very high Telecom volatilities
  (C2).
- A Pfandbrief "hotspot," due to a high Pfandbrief portfolio weight of
  about 8% (C3).
- Two clusters of high covariances created by high Financial/Pfandbrief,
  Financial/Telecom and Financial/Utility cross-sector correlations (C4,
  C5).

Such an analysis clearly identifies risk clusters and provides important clues on how to further diversify the portfolio.

COMPARISON WITH OTHER MARKETS

In today's asset management industry, organizations' operations often extend beyond the European fixed income market. Controlling risk firm wide therefore calls for a detailed understanding of what the levels of risk in each market are and how markets interact with each other. The purpose of this last section is to provide a few elements of comparison between the euro and US dollar fixed income markets.

We compare in Exhibit 23.16 the volatilities of a few selected euro and US dollar factors. The common denominator is that euro volatilities are less than their US dollar counterparts. This is true for all factors if we ignore the volatility bursts sometimes observed over a few months for some factors (for instance the Industrial A factor in Exhibit 23.16). The average level of systematic risk observed amongst euro-denominated fixed income instruments is more generally low compared to other markets. Exhibit 23.16 shows one case where euro volatilities seem to be catching up with US levels. A more systematic analysis of how euro volatilities have recently evolved since 2002 would show that this is an exception. On average, euro volatilities have remained low with respect to US ones. Note that this is consistent first with the predictions of the swap factor model, euro spread levels and swap volatility being low compared to other markets.

Examples of correlations between shift, twist, and butterfly factors in selected markets are given in Exhibit 23.16. Not surprisingly, changes in

EXHIBIT 23.16   Selected Interest Rate Factor Correlations

	Germany			
	Shift		Twist	
	30/11/1999	30/11/2002	30/11/1999	30/11/2002
Australia	0.4	0.65	0.6	0.5
Canada	0.4	0.65	0.6	0.5
Japan	0.3	0.1	0.064	0.02
New Zealand	0.4	0.5	0.2	0.15
South Africa	−0.04	0.25	0.25	0.08
United States	0.6	0.8	0.6	0.5

European sovereign rates are generally comparable with those in other developed markets and especially the United States. In 2001 and 2002, correlations have been particularly high due to the global decrease in interest rates stemming from a general economic slowdown. Exceptions correspond to emerging markets such as South Africa, and markets where the economic cycle is at a different phase, such as Japan. Conversely, high-grade credit spreads show on average very little correlation across markets. High correlations do appear, but temporarily, and for market sectors that are globally experiencing distress such as Telecommunications companies.

SUMMARY

In a complex European market, adequately measuring risk requires sophisticated methods and considerable care. A good risk model should provide a broad coverage without sacrificing accuracy, retain details but remain parsimonious, be responsive to ever-changing conditions, and so on. Certainly, there is no shortage of challenges.

The typical euro investment grade corporate index is perhaps halfway between the conservative and speculative ends of the risk spectrum. We have seen that it has very specific credit risk characteristics, such as being heavily exposed to financials and telecommunications. European fixed-income instruments are on average less risky than their US dollar equivalent, which by no means implies that a sound risk management is less relevant. Building a reasonable risk model is fortunately not an elusive task as long as we know how to design or where to find the right tools.

APPENDIX—PRINCIPAL COMPONENT ANALYSIS

Factor Shapes

Changes in benchmark yields[17] for different terms are highly correlated regardless of the market, which constitutes a strong incentive to step away from a key rate model in which the factors are rate changes at the term structure vertices. The principal component analysis consists in extracting a set of linear combinations of key rate changes that capture

---

[17] For sovereign benchmarks, domestic government bond returns are used to compute term structures and key rate returns. For LIBOR/swap benchmarks, key rate returns can be computed directly from market yields.

most of the variations in a market's benchmark. This is done mathematically by diagonalizing[18] the key rate covariance matrix, each eigenvalue being a measure of how much of the benchmark variance is explained by the corresponding shape or eigenvector. The covariance matrices of principal components and key rates returns are such that

$$C_{PC} = {}^{T}\Pi C_{KR}\Pi$$

where the columns of matrix Π are the principal components, and the covariance matrix C_{PC} is diagonal.

In most markets, over 95% of changes in term structures can be captured with only three principal components usually called *shift*, *twist*, and *butterfly*, to reflect how term structures actually change. Interest rates tend to increase or increase simultaneously, which can be described as a shift of the term structure. The second most important effect is a twist that alters the slope of the term structure. The third factor is a butterfly that reflects a change in the term structure's curvature.

Factor Returns

Factor returns, hereafter called *STB returns*, are computed by regressing government bond's returns or LIBOR/swap key rate returns onto the shift, twist, and butterfly principal components. STB returns and other factor returns then go into the computation of the covariance matrix of all common factors. The shift, twist, and butterfly shapes are stable over time and only need to be reestimated periodically.

---

[18] The diagonalization is always possible because the KR covariance matrix is symmetric.

CHAPTER 24

An Empirical Analysis of the Domestic and Euro Yield Curve Dynamics

Lionel Martellini, Ph.D.
Assistant Professor in Finance
Marshall School of Business—University of Southern California
and
Research Associate
EDHEC Risk and Asset Management Research Center

Philippe Priaulet, Ph.D.
Fixed Income Strategist
Treasury and Capital Markets Department
HSBC-CCF
and
Associate Professor
Department of Mathematics—University of Evry Val d'Essonne

Stéphane Priaulet
Senior Index Portfolio Manager
Structured Asset Management Department
AXA Investment Managers

The term structure of interest rates is defined as the graph mapping interest rates corresponding to their respective maturity. The term structure of interest rates can take at any point in time various shapes and the key question from a risk management perspective is to understand how the term structure of interest rates evolves over time.

In this chapter, we perform a factor analysis of the zero-coupon euro interbank yield curve, and also of zero-coupon Treasury yield curves from five individual countries, France, Germany, Italy, Spain, and the Netherlands, so as to isolate the key aspects of the dynamics of term structures of interest rates in the Eurozone.

Using a principal components analysis (PCA) has become a popular way to study movements of the term structure because it allows one to aggregate the risks in a nonarbitrary way.[1] The concepts behind this powerful statistical technique are fairly straightforward:

- Different interest rates for different maturities are highly correlated variables. A limited set of common economic, monetary, and financial factors affect money bond markets of different maturities. As a result, interest rates for various maturities tend to move in the same direction.[2]
- Highly correlated variables provide redundant information one with respect to another. As a consequence, it is tempting to try and identify a set of independent factors that would account for most of the information contained in the time series of interest rate variations. This is exactly what a PCA does.

THE DATA

We now apply the PCA methodology both to the zero-coupon euro interbank yield curve, and to zero-coupon Treasury yield curves from five individual countries—France, Germany, Italy, Spain, and the Netherlands.

Deriving the Treasury Yield Curves

We derive daily zero-coupon yield curves from five countries of the Eurozone (France, Germany, Italy, Spain, and the Netherlands) during the period from 2 January 2001 to 21 August 2002, using zero-coupon rates with 26 different maturities ranging from one month to 30 years.[3] The yield curves are extracted from daily Treasury bond market prices by using a standard cubic B-splines method. Our input baskets are composed of

---

[1] We summarize in Appendix A of this chapter the results of some of the most popular studies on that matter.

[2] Even though they are highly correlated, interest rates of different maturities are not perfectly correlated, as can be inferred from the occurrence of nonparallel shifts of the yield curve.

▓ EURIBOR rates with maturities between one month and one year.
▓ Homogeneously liquid bonds with maturities exceeding one year.

We use Bloomberg Generic closing prices (BGN prices) for bonds.[4] The inputs of the model are market gross prices of all instruments in the basket. The model we use falls into the category of discount function fitting models.[5]

Deriving the Euro Interbank Yield Curve

We compute PCA with the zero-coupon euro interbank yield curve for the period from 2 January 2001 to 21 August 2002. We use zero-coupon rates with 17 different maturities from one month to ten years.[6]

The basket of inputs contains three kinds of instruments: money market rates, futures contracts, and swaps.

▓ We consider EURIBOR rates with maturities ranging from one day to one year. These rates, expressed on an actual/360 basis, are first converted into equivalent zero-coupon rates on an Actual/365 basis. For example, on 1 January 1999, the 1-month EURIBOR rate was equal to 2.5%. Using the Actual/365 basis, the equivalent zero-coupon rate (denoted by $R(0,1/12)$) is given by

$$R(0, 1/12) = \left(1 + \frac{31}{360} \times 2.5\%\right)^{\frac{365}{31}} - 1$$

▓ We consider futures 3-month EURIBOR futures contracts and find zero-coupon rates from raw data. The price of a 3-month LIBOR contract is given by 100 minus the underlying 3-month forward rate. For example, on 15 March 1999, the 3-month LIBOR rate was 3%, and

---

[3] Maturities are 1 to 6 months, 9 months, 1 to 12, and 15, 18, 20, 22, 25, 27, and 30 years. For more details, see Lionel Martellini, Phillippe Priaulet, and Stéphane Priaulet, "The Euro Benchmark Yield Curve: Principal Component Analysis of Yield Curve Dynamics," in Frank J. Fabozzi (ed.), *Professional Perspectives on Fixed Income Portfolio Management: Volume 4* (Hoboken, NJ: John Wiley & Sons, Inc., 2003).

[4] BGN (Bloomberg Generic Price) is Bloomberg's market consensus price for government bonds.

[5] For more details, see Lionel Martellini, Stéphane Priaulet, and Philippe Priaulet, *Fixed-Income Securities: Valuation, Risk Management and Portfolio Strategies* (Hoboken, NJ: John Wiley & Sons, Inc., 2003).

[6] Maturities are 1 to 6 months, 9 months, and 1 to 10 years.

the 3-month LIBOR contract with maturity date June 1999 had a price equal to 96.5. Hence on March 15, 1999, the 3-month forward rate, starting on June 15, 1999 is 3.5%. The 6-month spot rate (denoted by $R(0,6/12)$) is obtained as follows:

$$R(0, 6/12) = \left[\left(1 + \frac{92}{360} \times 3\%\right)\left(1 + \frac{92}{360} \times 3.5\%\right)\right]^{\frac{365}{184}} - 1$$

■ We consider three-or-six-month EURIBOR swap yields with maturities ranging from one year to 10 years and find recursively equivalent zero-coupon rates. Swap yields are par yields; so the zero-coupon rate with maturity two years $R(0,2)$ is obtained as the solution to the following equation:

$$\frac{SR(2)}{1 + R(0, 1)} + \frac{1 + SR(2)}{[1 + R(0, 2)]^2} = 1$$

where $SR(2)$ is the 2-year swap yield, and $R(0,1)$ is equal to $SR(1)$. Spot rates $R(0,3)$, ..., $R(0,10)$ are obtained recursively in a similar fashion.

Least-squared methods used to derive the current interbank curve are very similar to those used to derive the current nondefault Treasury curve. After converting market data into equivalent zero-coupon rates, the zero-coupon yield curve is derived using a two-stage process, first writing zero-coupon rates as a B-spline function, and then fitting them through an ordinary least-squared method.

PCA OF THE TREASURY AND EURO INTERBANK YIELD CURVES IN THE EUROZONE

We now apply the methodology just described to study the dynamics of the Treasury yield curve for selected individual countries from the Euro-zone, as well as the dynamics of the Euro Interbank yield curve.

Percentage of Explanation by the Factors

We first discuss the percentage of explanation power on the whole period and then analyze the breakdown on different subperiods.

EXHIBIT 24.1 Global Percentage of Explanation by the Five First Factors—2001–2002

France	Factor 1	Factor 2	Factor 3	Factor 4	Factor 5
Eigenvalue	16.228	5.685	1.758	1.422	0.577
% Explained	62.42%	21.87%	6.76%	5.47%	2.22%
% Cumulative	62.42%	84.29%	91.05%	96.52%	98.74%

Germany	Factor 1	Factor 2	Factor 3	Factor 4	Factor 5
Eigenvalue	17.386	5.796	2.057	0.373	0.232
% Explained	66.87%	22.29%	7.91%	1.44%	0.89%
% Cumulative	66.87%	89.16%	97.07%	98.51%	99.40%

Italy	Factor 1	Factor 2	Factor 3	Factor 4	Factor 5
Eigenvalue	17.191	5.842	2.154	0.439	0.187
% Explained	66.12%	22.47%	8.28%	1.69%	0.72%
% Cumulative	66.12%	88.59%	96.87%	98.56%	99.28%

The Netherlands	Factor 1	Factor 2	Factor 3	Factor 4	Factor 5
Eigenvalue	16.909	5.797	1.933	0.734	0.388
% Explained	65.03%	22.30%	7.44%	2.82%	1.49%
% Cumulative	65.03%	87.33%	94.77%	97.59%	99.08%

Spain	Factor 1	Factor 2	Factor 3	Factor 4	Factor 5
Eigenvalue	16.176	5.879	2.496	0.732	0.402
% Explained	62.22%	22.61%	9.60%	2.82%	1.55%
% Cumulative	62.22%	84.83%	94.43%	97.25%	98.80%

Euro Interbank	Factor 1	Factor 2	Factor 3	Factor 4	Factor 5
Eigenvalue	8.082	4.357	1.854	0.986	0.589
% Explained	47.54%	25.63%	10.91%	5.80%	3.46%
% Cumulative	47.54%	73.17%	84.08%	89.88%	93.34%

Percentage of Explanation by the Factors on the Entire Period

We first consider the global fraction of the total variance of the zero-coupon yield curve changes that is accounted for by the five first factors (see Exhibit 24.1).

- *PCA of the Treasury yield curves.* The first five factors account for 98.74% to 99.40% of interest rate changes for the examined period (see Exhibit 24.1) depending on the country we consider. The first three factors, typically interpreted as level, slope, and curvature factors, account for 91.05% to 97.07%. The results are very homogeneous from one country to another, since the explanation power from the first factor ranges from 62.22% to 66.87%, while it ranges from 21.87% to 22.61% for the second factor and from 6.76% to 9.60% for the third factor. The nontrivial weights on factors four and five signals the presence of nonnegligible residuals. For the period under consideration, these two factors account sometimes for more than 5% of the interest rate changes (in particular 7.69% for France).
- *PCA of the Interbank yield curve.* Because they do not apply to the same variables, it should be expected that results obtained with the Interbank yield curve be different from results obtained with Treasury yield curves. This is confirmed by the numbers in Exhibit 24.1. The first factor only accounts for 47.54% of the interest rate changes, while the second factor explains 25.63%. The inferior percentage of explanation by the first factor can be related to the fact that eight out of the 17 variables we use relate to the short-term segment of the curve. The three first factors account for 84.08% of the yield curve deformations while the first five factors account for 93.34%, which means that residuals are not negligible.

Percentage of Explanation by the Factors on Selected Periods

We provide in Exhibit 24.2 the percentage of explanation by the factors for the years 2001 and 2002.

- *PCA of the Treasury yield curves.* The percentage of explanation for each factor can vary substantially with the selected period (see Exhibit 24.2). The first factor is predominant in 2002 while its weight declines in 2001 (below 60% in 2001). Of course, such variations can be explained not only by changes in the dynamic behavior of term structures but also by sample fluctuations. In 2001, Treasury yield curves were more affected by steepening and flattening moves than in 2002. That is why the second factor is less than 19.2% in 2002 while it is higher than 22% in 2001, whatever the country. The presence of non-negligible residuals is particularly obvious in France in 2001, where the weight of residuals are higher than 10%. We note that these residuals are not homogeneous from one country to another and from one period of time to another.

EXHIBIT 24.2   Global Percentage of Explanation by the First Three Factors Depending on the Selected Period

Curve	Factor	2001	2002	Curve	Factor	2001	2002
	Factor 1	59.06%	73.59%		Factor 1	62.26%	73.16%
France	Factor 2	22.37%	18.09%	The Netherlands	Factor 2	23.37%	16.50%
	Factor 3	7.82%	5.34%		Factor 3	8.97%	5.82%
	Total	89.25%	97.02%		Total	94.60%	95.48%
	Factor 1	64.05%	74.35%		Factor 1	59.93%	69.80%
Germany	Factor 2	23.47%	16.66%	Spain	Factor 2	23.38%	19.17%
	Factor 3	9.29%	6.44%		Factor 3	11.06%	6.49%
	Total	96.81%	97.45%		Total	94.37%	95.46%
	Factor 1	66.12%	73.83%		Factor 1	59.09%	42.70%
Italy	Factor 2	22.47%	16.75%	Euro Interbank	Factor 2	27.16%	25.49%
	Factor 3	8.28%	6.53%		Factor 3	6.43%	13.70%
	Total	96.87%	97.11%		Total	92.68%	81.89%

■ *PCA of the Interbank yield curve.* The percentage of explanation by the first factor is relatively low and even gets lower than 50% in 2002 to reach 42.70%. The residuals account for a fairly significant fraction (almost 20%) of the total variation in interest rates in 2002. This suggests that a strategy intended at immunizing the value of a bond portfolio with respect to small changes in the level, slope, and curvature of the term structure would have failed to properly hedge the portfolio.

Percentage of Explanation by the Factors for Each Maturity

For France, we summarize in Exhibit 24.3 the extent to which the ith factor explains the variance of the kth variable. We provide the same table for the other countries in Appendix B of this chapter.

The first factor is more significant (greater than 70%) for maturities between 2 years and 20 years and very significant (greater than 84%) for the maturities ranging from 4 years to 12 years. The short rates (with maturities ranging from one to six months) are significantly affected by the second factor (greater than 60%), while that factor is virtually negligible for medium-term maturities from two years to eight years. That the medium-term segment of the yield curve remains stable under changes in the second factor suggests that it can be interpreted as a slope factor. The curvature effect, related to the third factor, traditionally opposes end segments of the curve to the medium-term segment.

EXHIBIT 24.3 Percentage of Explanation by the Factors for Each Maturity—France (01/02/2001–08/21/2002)

Maturity	Factor 1	Factor 2	Factor 3	Factor 4	Factor 5	Factor 6–26
1M	6.15%	70.11%	11.31%	0.00%	12.04%	0.39%
2M	11.14%	76.33%	7.43%	0.00%	4.98%	0.12%
3M	17.12%	78.00%	3.94%	0.01%	0.92%	0.01%
4M	23.27%	75.16%	1.46%	0.02%	0.05%	0.03%
5M	28.94%	69.11%	0.21%	0.03%	1.57%	0.14%
6M	33.85%	34.52%	0.05%	0.03%	4.29%	0.26%
9M	45.14%	39.62%	3.29%	0.00%	11.50%	0.44%
1Y	66.12%	12.49%	13.89%	0.56%	6.11%	0.83%
2Y	72.44%	0.11%	19.76%	2.56%	0.85%	4.29%
3Y	75.55%	0.36%	16.87%	1.50%	2.85%	2.87%
4Y	84.62%	0.22%	12.32%	0.23%	1.19%	1.43%
5Y	90.25%	0.10%	7.40%	0.01%	0.17%	2.08%
6Y	93.52%	0.30%	3.79%	0.01%	0.04%	2.34%
7Y	95.48%	1.09%	1.51%	0.02%	0.09%	1.80%
8Y	95.18%	2.62%	0.34%	0.19%	0.30%	1.38%
9Y	93.01%	4.55%	0.00%	0.37%	0.62%	1.46%
10Y	90.59%	6.31%	0.18%	0.29%	0.85%	1.78%
11Y	88.65%	7.72%	0.60%	0.07%	0.94%	2.02%
12Y	87.10%	8.78%	1.13%	0.03%	0.89%	2.07%
15Y	81.94%	9.85%	2.86%	3.89%	0.29%	1.16%
18Y	73.33%	8.55%	4.53%	13.42%	0.03%	0.32%
20Y	68.33%	7.47%	6.00%	17.10%	0.47%	0.63%
22Y	67.07%	7.03%	8.62%	14.27%	1.43%	1.58%
25Y	69.19%	8.07%	16.60%	0.24%	3.12%	2.77%
27Y	42.44%	7.41%	18.47%	29.25%	1.71%	0.73%
30Y	22.40%	5.64%	13.30%	58.23%	0.39%	0.04%
Mean	62.42%	21.87%	6.76%	5.47%	2.22%	1.27%

Factors 4 and 5 are not negligible. Factor 4 has only an effect on the very long-term segment (longer than 15 years) whereas factor 5 is a kind of curvature factor affecting more the short-term and the long-term ends of the curve. These results illustrate once more that:[7]

---

[7] See Lardic, Priaulet, and Priaulet, "PCA of the Yield Curve Dynamics: Questions of Methodologies."

▨ The second factor explains most of the short-term segment.
▨ The long-term segment is explained much more by the first factor, but it is the medium segment with maturities between 1 year and 10 years, which is best explained by the first factor.
▨ The third factor seems to have a major impact first on the short-term segment and then on the long-term segment; when we eliminate the short-term and long-term segments, its percentage of variance explained decreases dramatically.

Note finally that the mean of R_{ik}^2 with respect to maturity k gives the percentage of variance explained by the ith factor (see Exhibit 24.3), and that results are homogeneous from one country to another (see Appendix B of this chapter).

Factors Correlation

We now compute the correlation between factor 1 (as obtained from PCA) of the different Treasury yield curves and the Interbank yield curve. We do the same for factor 2 and factor 3. Results are first detailed for the whole period, and then on each year (see Appendix C of this chapter).

Generally speaking, the five Treasury yield curves prove to be very correlated with each other. This evidence is consistent with the fact that there is uniqueness of monetary policy (same short-term rate for all countries); and that selected countries are fairly homogeneous in terms of credit quality and liquidity.

These correlations have strengthened from 2001 to 2002, which supports the notion of increased financial integration in the Eurozone. The core countries seem to be France, Germany, the Netherlands, and Italy. Indeed, France, Germany, and the Netherlands have the same credit quality, namely AAA; French, German, and, especially, Italian Treasury bonds are very liquid. Italy has now the highest weight in the Euro area. To some extent, Spain seems to be slightly less correlated with the other countries (presumably because of the liquidity premium).

The swap yield curve is correlated with the Treasury yield curves, but this correlation has decreased from 2001 to 2002. This may be explained by the increase in the investors' risk aversion as continuing poor performance of equity markets in 2002 has triggered a search for liquidity and quality. The correlation with the Treasury yield curves is high for the first factor (see Exhibit 24.4), but weak for the second and third factors (see Exhibits 24.5 and 24.6).

EXHIBIT 24.4 Correlation Matrix between the PCA Factor 1 of the Different Treasury Curves and the Interbank Curve: 2001–2002

	France	Germany	Italy	The Netherlands	Spain	Euro Interbank
France	1	0.9929	0.9831	0.9940	0.9796	0.8511
Germany		1	0.9891	0.9906	0.9865	0.8542
Italy			1	0.9825	0.9843	0.8431
The Netherlands				1	0.9830	0.8445
Spain					1	0.8411
Euro Interbank						1

EXHIBIT 24.5 Correlation Matrix between the PCA Factor 2 of the Different Treasury Curves and the Interbank Curve: 2001–2002

	France	Germany	Italy	The Netherlands	Spain	Euro Interbank
France	1	0.9669	0.9641	0.9932	0.5733	0.2164
Germany		1	0.9892	0.9725	0.6031	0.2047
Italy			1	0.9698	0.5931	0.1949
The Netherlands				1	0.5687	0.2245
Spain					1	0.0898
Euro Interbank						1

EXHIBIT 24.6 Correlation Matrix between the PCA Factor 3 of the Different Treasury Curves and the Interbank Curve: 2001–2002

	France	Germany	Italy	The Netherlands	Spain	Euro Interbank
France	1	0.9027	0.9066	0.9372	0.6491	0.1363
Germany		1	0.9428	0.8904	0.7063	0.1743
Italy			1	0.9156	0.6639	0.1779
The Netherlands				1	0.6484	0.1411
Spain					1	0.0785
Euro Interbank						1

EXHIBIT 24.7   Sensitivity of Zero-Coupon Rate Changes with Respect to Factor 1

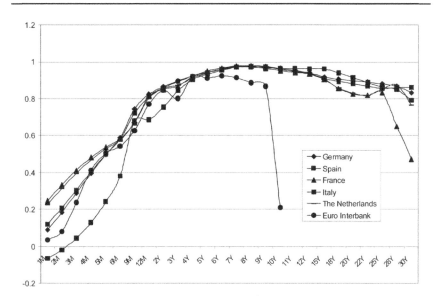

SENSITIVITIES OF THE ZERO-COUPON RATES

Exhibits 24.7–24.9 display the sensitivities s_{ik} as functions of the interest rate maturities k for factors 1, 2, and 3. We can see that the sensitivities are fairly similar whatever the country under consideration.

For the period as a whole, the first factor (see Exhibit 24.7) may actually be regarded as a level factor since it affects similarly all zero-coupon rates, except for the portion (1 month–1 year), which moves differently. Displaying the sensitivity of interest rates with respect to the second factor, Exhibit 24.8 shows a decreasing shape, first positive for short-term maturities then negative beyond. Hence, the second factor may be regarded as a rotation factor around a medium maturity between two and four years depending on the country we consider. The third factor (see Exhibit 24.9) has different effects on intermediate maturities as opposed to extreme maturities (short and long). Hence, it may be interpreted as a curvature factor.

EXHIBIT 24.8 Sensitivity of Zero-Coupon Rate Changes with Respect to Factor 2

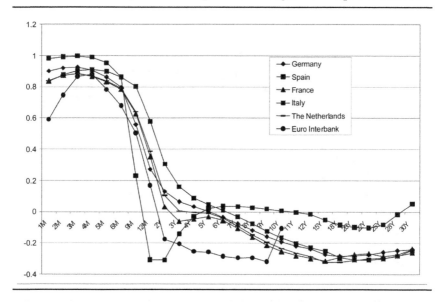

EXHIBIT 24.9 Sensitivity of Zero-Coupon Rate Changes with Respect to Factor 3

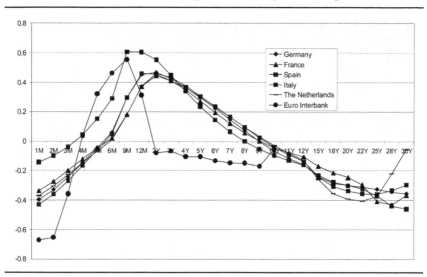

CONCLUSION

In this article we present an empirical analysis of the term structure dynamics in the Eurozone, based on daily data over the period 2 January 2001 to 21 August 2002. We study both the zero-coupon Euro Interbank yield curve, and zero-coupon Treasury yield curves from five individual countries, France, Germany, Italy, Spain, and the Netherlands. Using principal components analysis, we find that three main factors typically explain more than 90% of the changes in the yield curve, whatever the country and the period under consideration. These factors can be interpreted as changes in the level, the slope, and the curvature of the term structure. We also find strong evidence of homogeneity in the dynamics of the yield curve for different countries in the Eurozone, signaling an increasing financial integration.

APPENDIX A

In the past few years there have been several many studies on the topic of PCA of interest rate curves by both academics and practitioners. Exhibit A1 summarizes the main results of these studies.

EXHIBIT A1 Results of Some Popular Studies on PCA of the Yield Curve Dynamics

Authors	Country (Period)—Kind of Rates	Range	Factors	% of Explanation
Robert Litterman and José Scheinkman, "Common Factors Affecting Bond Returns," *Journal of Fixed Income* (June 1991), pp. 54–61.	US (1984–88)—Spot Zero-Coupon (ZC)	6M–18Y	3	88.04/8.38/1.97
C. Kanony and M. Mokrane, "Reconstitution de la courbe des taux, analyse des facteurs d'évolution et couverture factorielle," *Cahiers de la Caisse Autonome de Refinancement* 1 (June 1992).	France (1989–90)—Spot ZC	1Y–25Y	2	93.7/6.1
R.L. D'Ecclesia and S.A. Zenios, "Risk Factor Analysis and Portfolio Immunization in the Italian Bond Market," *Journal of Fixed Income* 4, no. 2 (September 1994), pp. 51–58.	Italy (1988–92)—Spot ZC	6M–7Y	3	93.91/5.49/0.42
J. Kärki and C. Reyes, "Model Relationship," *Risk* 7, no. 12 (December 1994), pp. 32–35.	Germ./Switz./USA (1990–94)—Spot ZC	3M–10Y	3	Total: 97/98/98
J.R. Barber and M.L. Copper, "Immunization Using Principal Component Analysis," *Journal of Portfolio Management* (Fall 1996), pp. 99–105.	US (1985–91)—Spot ZC	1M–20Y	3	80.93/11.85/4.36
A. Bühler and H. Zimmerman, "A Statistical Analysis of the Term Structure of Interest Rates in Switzerland and Germany," *Journal of Fixed Income* 6, no. 3 (December 1996), pp. 55–67.	Germany (1988–96)—Spot ZC Switzerland	1M–10Y	3	71/18/4 75/16/3
Golub, B. W., and L. M. Tilman, "Measuring Yield Curve Risk Using Principal Components Analysis, Value at Risk, and Key Rate Durations," *Journal of Portfolio Management* (Summer 1997), pp. 72–84.	RiskMetrics–09/30/96—Spot ZC	3M–30Y	3	92.8/4.8/1.27
I. Lekkos, "A Critique of Factor Analysis of Interest Rates," *Journal of Derivatives* (Fall 2000), pp. 72–83.	US (1984–95) Germany (1987–95) 1 Year Forward UK (1987–95) Japan (1987–95)	1Y–9Y	5	56.5/17.4/9.86/8.12/4.3 50.6/17.3/13.5/8.8/5.8 63.5/6.3/7.5/8.1/5.3 42.8/25.5/17.1/6/4.9
L. Martellini and P. Priaulet, *Fixed-Income Securities: Dynamic Methods for Interest Rate Risk Pricing and Hedging* (New York: John Wiley & Sons, 2000).	France (1995–98)—Spot ZC	1M–10Y	3	66.64/20.52/6.96

Note: M stands for month and Y for year. For example, "88.04/8.38/1.97" means that the first factor explains 883.04% of the yield curve deformations, the second 8.38%, and the third 1.97%. Sometimes, we also provide the total amount by adding up these terms.

APPENDIX B

The exhibits in this appendix provide the percentage of explanation by the factors for each maturity for Germany, Italy, the Netherlands, Spain, and the Euro Interbank for during the period from 2/1/01 to 21/8/02.

EXHIBIT B1   Percentage of Explanation by the Factors for Each Maturity: Germany (1/2/01–21/8/02)

Maturity	Factor 1	Factor 2	Factor 3	Factor 4	Factor 5	Factor 6–26
1M	0.82%	81.05%	15.64%	1.42%	0.64%	0.44%
2M	3.41%	84.69%	10.73%	0.70%	0.28%	0.19%
3M	8.36%	85.42%	5.95%	0.19%	0.05%	0.03%
4M	15.78%	82.05%	2.15%	0.00%	0.01%	0.01%
5M	24.97%	74.36%	0.18%	0.20%	0.18%	0.11%
6M	34.57%	63.55%	0.36%	0.71%	0.50%	0.30%
9M	55.34%	31.24%	8.66%	2.54%	1.47%	0.76%
1Y	67.96%	7.46%	20.60%	2.45%	1.13%	0.40%
2Y	74.82%	1.72%	21.95%	0.57%	0.06%	0.88%
3Y	80.28%	0.43%	18.20%	0.03%	0.25%	0.82%
4Y	84.90%	0.11%	13.45%	0.03%	0.89%	0.61%
5Y	88.80%	0.00%	8.86%	0.23%	1.31%	0.80%
6Y	92.36%	0.11%	5.03%	0.59%	1.19%	0.71%
7Y	95.03%	0.56%	2.20%	1.11%	0.73%	0.37%
8Y	96.01%	1.38%	0.51%	1.70%	0.27%	0.14%
9Y	95.12%	2.46%	0.00%	2.21%	0.02%	0.19%
10Y	92.95%	3.63%	0.42%	2.50%	0.05%	0.45%
11Y	90.52%	4.69%	1.35%	2.51%	0.27%	0.66%
12Y	88.35%	5.59%	2.47%	2.29%	0.60%	0.70%
15Y	84.19%	7.38%	5.73%	0.92%	1.55%	0.22%
18Y	81.99%	7.98%	8.02%	0.01%	1.85%	0.15%
20Y	80.63%	7.84%	8.96%	0.35%	1.49%	0.73%
22Y	79.23%	7.42%	9.59%	1.57%	0.78%	1.41%
25Y	77.57%	6.65%	10.45%	4.15%	0.00%	1.18%
27Y	75.25%	6.08%	11.74%	5.00%	1.88%	0.04%
30Y	69.42%	5.72%	12.51%	3.35%	5.71%	3.29%
Mean	66.87%	22.29%	7.91%	1.44%	0.89%	0.60%

EXHIBIT B2   Percentage of Explanation by the Factors for Each Maturity:
Italy (2/1/01–21/8/02)

Maturity	Factor 1	Factor 2	Factor 3	Factor 4	Factor 5	Factor 6–26
1M	1.47%	76.94%	18.49%	1.60%	0.94%	0.55%
2M	4.39%	81.33%	12.84%	0.80%	0.43%	0.21%
3M	9.41%	82.98%	7.27%	0.22%	0.09%	0.02%
4M	16.54%	80.65%	2.79%	0.00%	0.01%	0.02%
5M	25.04%	74.02%	0.32%	0.20%	0.22%	0.19%
6M	33.70%	64.20%	0.26%	0.73%	0.66%	0.45%
9M	52.16%	33.53%	8.82%	2.59%	2.04%	0.86%
1Y	65.57%	9.38%	21.03%	2.20%	1.73%	0.08%
2Y	73.99%	2.61%	20.66%	0.27%	0.14%	2.35%
3Y	79.93%	0.78%	16.91%	0.01%	0.26%	2.12%
4Y	85.00%	0.23%	13.10%	0.00%	1.11%	0.56%
5Y	88.72%	0.01%	9.18%	0.02%	1.69%	0.38%
6Y	91.98%	0.10%	5.63%	0.17%	1.50%	0.61%
7Y	94.52%	0.59%	2.79%	0.63%	0.88%	0.60%
8Y	95.46%	1.49%	0.90%	1.42%	0.29%	0.44%
9Y	94.54%	2.70%	0.06%	2.36%	0.01%	0.33%
10Y	92.31%	3.99%	0.15%	3.15%	0.08%	0.32%
11Y	89.78%	5.19%	0.85%	3.51%	0.34%	0.33%
12Y	87.49%	6.23%	1.88%	3.46%	0.64%	0.30%
15Y	82.74%	8.44%	5.72%	1.78%	1.20%	0.11%
18Y	79.69%	9.41%	9.42%	0.12%	1.03%	0.33%
20Y	77.61%	9.41%	11.31%	0.21%	0.64%	0.82%
22Y	75.44%	8.97%	12.48%	1.63%	0.22%	1.26%
25Y	73.26%	7.91%	12.73%	5.21%	0.03%	0.86%
27Y	74.17%	6.88%	11.10%	6.93%	0.79%	0.14%
30Y	74.23%	6.22%	8.69%	4.66%	1.74%	4.46%
Mean	66.12%	22.47%	8.28%	1.69%	0.72%	0.72%

EXHIBIT B3 Percentage of Explanation by the Factors for Each Maturity:
The Netherlands (2/1/01–21/8/02)

Maturity	Factor 1	Factor 2	Factor 3	Factor 4	Factor 5	Factor 6–26
1M	5.21%	70.25%	13.69%	5.69%	4.96%	0.20%
2M	9.91%	76.31%	9.26%	2.50%	1.96%	0.06%
3M	15.77%	78.19%	5.17%	0.55%	0.31%	0.01%
4M	22.04%	75.75%	2.12%	0.00%	0.06%	0.02%
5M	27.99%	70.07%	0.43%	0.56%	0.87%	0.08%
6M	33.21%	62.72%	0.01%	1.74%	2.18%	0.15%
9M	44.95%	41.04%	3.21%	5.15%	5.42%	0.23%
1Y	64.46%	15.02%	14.12%	3.33%	2.38%	0.69%
2Y	73.31%	1.14%	21.20%	0.03%	0.89%	3.44%
3Y	76.32%	0.00%	18.87%	0.25%	2.61%	1.95%
4Y	83.35%	0.00%	14.36%	0.00%	1.59%	0.70%
5Y	88.48%	0.01%	9.41%	0.13%	0.56%	1.42%
6Y	92.26%	0.16%	5.49%	0.06%	0.19%	1.83%
7Y	94.93%	0.81%	2.69%	0.02%	0.09%	1.46%
8Y	95.51%	2.11%	0.92%	0.35%	0.07%	1.05%
9Y	94.16%	3.79%	0.10%	0.87%	0.08%	1.00%
10Y	92.09%	5.44%	0.07%	1.11%	0.10%	1.18%
11Y	90.00%	6.89%	0.65%	0.97%	0.13%	1.36%
12Y	88.01%	8.11%	1.69%	0.60%	0.17%	1.42%
15Y	81.65%	10.27%	6.72%	0.15%	0.31%	0.89%
18Y	73.61%	10.32%	12.47%	3.09%	0.32%	0.19%
20Y	68.88%	9.65%	15.23%	5.84%	0.18%	0.22%
22Y	66.97%	8.96%	16.41%	6.91%	0.02%	0.73%
25Y	72.67%	8.64%	13.96%	2.36%	0.56%	1.82%
27Y	76.33%	8.10%	4.79%	4.74%	4.62%	1.42%
30Y	58.79%	5.92%	0.31%	26.41%	8.17%	0.40%
Mean	65.03%	22.30%	7.44%	2.82%	1.49%	0.92%

EXHIBIT B4   Percentage of Explanation by the Factors for Each Maturity:
Spain (1/2/01–21/8/02)

Maturity	Factor 1	Factor 2	Factor 3	Factor 4	Factor 5	Factor 6–26
1M	0.42%	96.40%	2.03%	0.18%	0.75%	0.22%
2M	0.03%	98.36%	0.96%	0.06%	0.45%	0.14%
3M	0.20%	99.42%	0.15%	0.00%	0.17%	0.06%
4M	1.69%	97.99%	0.19%	0.12%	0.00%	0.02%
5M	5.91%	90.95%	2.35%	0.60%	0.15%	0.04%
6M	14.60%	74.23%	8.41%	1.69%	0.87%	0.20%
9M	46.52%	5.30%	36.93%	5.77%	4.66%	0.83%
1Y	47.16%	9.39%	36.50%	4.30%	2.50%	0.15%
2Y	56.87%	9.46%	30.50%	1.88%	0.00%	1.28%
3Y	71.36%	1.95%	20.19%	0.12%	3.24%	3.14%
4Y	81.80%	0.08%	11.62%	0.25%	5.05%	1.21%
5Y	86.82%	0.05%	5.57%	1.35%	3.20%	3.02%
6Y	91.26%	0.14%	2.08%	2.97%	0.90%	2.65%
7Y	94.13%	0.12%	0.42%	4.53%	0.01%	0.79%
8Y	94.31%	0.08%	0.00%	5.30%	0.25%	0.06%
9Y	93.60%	0.03%	0.27%	5.27%	0.71%	0.11%
10Y	92.95%	0.01%	0.89%	4.68%	1.00%	0.47%
11Y	92.62%	0.00%	1.68%	3.76%	1.03%	0.91%
12Y	92.57%	0.02%	2.56%	2.68%	0.86%	1.32%
15Y	92.28%	0.26%	5.27%	0.17%	0.06%	1.96%
18Y	88.42%	0.70%	7.65%	1.07%	0.48%	1.68%
20Y	83.72%	0.95%	9.00%	3.67%	1.49%	1.17%
22Y	78.91%	1.03%	10.42%	6.79%	2.26%	0.59%
25Y	74.69%	0.67%	13.68%	9.44%	1.31%	0.21%
27Y	72.13%	0.03%	19.09%	5.70%	0.53%	2.52%
30Y	62.67%	0.27%	21.16%	0.90%	8.26%	6.73%
Mean	62.22%	22.61%	9.60%	2.82%	1.55%	1.21%

EXHIBIT B5 Percentage of Explanation by the Factors for Each Maturity: Euro Interbank (1/2/01–21/8/02)

Maturity	Factor 1	Factor 2	Factor 3	Factor 4	Factor 5	Factor 6–26
1M	0.12%	35.12%	45.17%	0.10%	2.33%	17.16%
2M	0.66%	55.74%	42.62%	0.02%	0.05%	0.90%
3M	5.72%	74.93%	12.79%	0.02%	0.49%	6.05%
4M	17.11%	77.60%	0.14%	0.12%	0.95%	4.08%
5M	25.63%	61.25%	10.38%	0.17%	0.60%	1.97%
6M	29.49%	46.04%	21.39%	0.15%	0.22%	2.70%
9M	39.38%	25.52%	30.76%	0.02%	0.12%	4.20%
1Y	59.24%	2.88%	9.71%	0.61%	4.24%	23.31%
2Y	71.54%	3.05%	0.62%	3.29%	11.36%	10.13%
3Y	64.31%	4.19%	0.42%	3.16%	15.97%	11.95%
4Y	84.72%	6.35%	1.08%	0.04%	0.11%	7.69%
5Y	83.15%	6.59%	1.09%	0.00%	0.03%	9.13%
6Y	85.52%	8.08%	1.73%	0.02%	1.32%	3.33%
7Y	83.42%	8.61%	2.13%	0.58%	3.07%	2.20%
8Y	78.53%	8.55%	2.23%	0.00%	6.24%	4.45%
9Y	75.14%	10.07%	2.87%	0.37%	7.69%	3.86%
10Y	4.50%	1.11%	0.28%	89.96%	4.05%	0.10%
Mean	47.54%	25.63%	10.91%	5.80%	3.46%	6.66%

APPENDIX C

The exhibits in this appendix show the factors correlations for the periods identified.

EXHIBIT C1 Correlation Matrix between the PCA Factor 1 of the Different Treasury Curves and the Interbank Curve—2001

	France	Germany	Italy	The Netherlands	Spain	Euro Interbank
France	1	0.9901	0.9776	0.9919	0.9755	0.8738
Germany		1	0.9865	0.9854	0.9836	0.8786
Italy			1	0.9754	0.9806	0.8718
The Netherlands				1	0.9792	0.8625
Spain					1	0.8591
Euro Interbank						1

EXHIBIT C2 Correlation Matrix between the PCA Factor 2 of the Different Treasury Curves and the Interbank Curve—2001

	France	Germany	Italy	The Netherlands	Spain	Euro Interbank
France	1	0.9688	0.9676	0.9953	0.5668	0.2707
Germany		1	0.9918	0.9738	0.5937	0.2590
Italy			1	0.9716	0.5852	0.2572
The Netherlands				1	0.5654	0.2767
Spain					1	0.1219
Euro Interbank						1

EXHIBIT C3 Correlation Matrix between the PCA Factor 3 of the Different Treasury Curves and the Interbank Curve—2001

	France	Germany	Italy	The Netherlands	Spain	Euro Interbank
France	1	0.8864	0.9022	0.9282	0.5854	0.1837
Germany		1	0.9434	0.8700	0.6549	0.2201
Italy			1	0.9130	0.6092	0.2209
The Netherlands				1	0.5868	0.1801
Spain					1	0.1268
Euro Interbank						1

EXHIBIT C4 Correlation Matrix between the PCA Factor 1 of the Different Treasury Curves and the Interbank Curve—2002

	France	Germany	Italy	The Netherlands	Spain	Euro Interbank
France	1	0.9974	0.9918	0.9974	0.9867	0.7975
Germany		1	0.9929	0.9981	0.9908	0.7967
Italy			1	0.9927	0.9897	0.7735
The Netherlands				1	0.9886	0.8028
Spain					1	0.7998
Euro Interbank						1

EXHIBIT C5   Correlation Matrix between the PCA Factor 2 of the Different Treasury Curves and the Interbank Curve—2002

	France	Germany	Italy	The Netherlands	Spain	Euro Interbank
France	1	0.9587	0.9404	0.9789	0.7354	0.0297
Germany		1	0.9654	0.9616	0.7791	0.0034
Italy			1	0.9533	0.7502	−0.0394
The Netherlands				1	0.6702	0.0469
Spain					1	−0.0763
Euro Interbank						1

EXHIBIT C6   Correlation Matrix between the PCA Factor 3 of the Different Treasury Curves and the Interbank Curve—2002

	France	Germany	Italy	The Netherlands	Spain	Euro Interbank
France	1	0.9684	0.9255	0.9744	0.9130	0.0761
Germany		1	0.9414	0.9680	0.9030	0.1273
Italy			1	0.9261	0.8786	0.1359
The Netherlands				1	0.8954	0.0998
Spain					1	0.0054
Euro Interbank						1

CHAPTER 25

Tracking Error

William T. Lloyd
Managing Director
Barclays Capital

Bharath K. Manium
Associate Director
Barclays Capital

Mats Gustavsson
Associate
Barclays Capital

A growing number of money managers in Europe have adopted a "beat the benchmark" approach to measure the performance of their fixed-income portfolios. This approach has been given a further boost by the rapid acceptance of the iBoxx indices by European investors. Increasingly, managers are compensated based on the performance of their funds relative to a benchmark, so straightforward risk measures are required to ensure they do not take on excessive risk. Many ways of measuring portfolio risk have been brought into the fixed-income market despite questions about their accuracy and suitability.

We believe there is no one magical number that can capture the entire risk profile of the portfolio, and investors should not place too

---

We would like to specifically thank Ashok Varikooty and Naum Krochik for their contributions to this research. This chapter would not have been possible without their efforts.

much faith on measures that claim to do so. We would instead advocate the use of more in-depth and forward-looking analyses that lay the foundations of understanding portfolio risk.

In this chapter, we examine several techniques used in the market for estimating relative risk in a portfolio, their assumptions, advantages and pitfalls. We also look at what we believe are the more accurate procedures for understanding and estimating this risk, and the tools that allow managers to do so quickly and easily.

TRACKING ERROR—THE FUNDAMENTALS

Tracking error is the standard deviation of the difference in returns between a portfolio and a selected benchmark, which is usually a suitable bond index. Assuming a normal distribution of returns, a portfolio manager can expect to deviate by no more than the tracking error amount for 68% of the time during a selected period.

Tracking error calculations have a relatively long history in the equity markets of measuring the relative risk of a portfolio against an index. The popularity of this methodology in equities has led many fixed-income managers to adopt the same approach, but we believe it is not as appropriate for the fixed-income markets.

The following are some of the fundamental assumptions common to all tracking error calculations:

1. *A static portfolio and index:* We know that indices are not static and composition changes (especially for the Euro market) can lead to significant changes in duration and other factors. In the following section, we illustrate how index characteristics in various markets have been far from static in the past, and we believe they will continue to vary.

2. *Rely on historical data:* As the standard disclaimer states, we know that past performance does not guarantee future results. While history can be a useful guide, the importance of historical data is often overemphasised. For example, the correlations on which these models depend tend to break down during periods of high volatility. Historical data largely ignore the current economic and political realities and can exclude shocks that have not occurred during the observed period, but are very likely to occur at some point (e.g., convergence of interest rates prior to the introduction of the euro).

3. *A normal distribution of returns:* This point is more amenable to mathematical testing. Most common tracking error models assume a

multivariate normal distribution of returns.[1] The long and short of all the fancy footwork is that bond returns tend not to be normally distributed. In this chapter, further references to normal distribution should be interpreted as multivariate normal distribution unless otherwise stated.

CHANGING MARKETS

The belief that markets will change in structure and composition over time is almost axiomatic among market participants. These changes are often more pronounced in fixed-income market than in the equities market, primarily due to the fact that the number of securities in fixed income is much larger, and the churn associated with new issues and bonds maturing is significant.

Duration

Unlike bonds, equities do not mature. Equity portfolios and their benchmarks have the same expected duration (i.e., that of a perpetual security) at the end of a certain period as they did at the beginning. The duration of a fixed-income portfolio comes down over time through a process known as *duration drift*, which does not occur in equities. Duration drift is an important consideration when looking at a portfolio over a 1-year horizon given that returns are predominantly duration-driven in fixed income markets.

For example, on 31 January 2002, the average modified duration of the iBoxx Euro Index was 4.81. Assuming there was no change in interest rates, its duration (holding the constituents constant) would have been 4.41 in 12 months. In reality, the constituents of the index do change, and they change every month. In fact, the average modified duration of the index was 4.95 on 31 January 2003. So it is unrealistic to assume that the duration of a portfolio and its benchmark index will change at the same rate.

Exhibits 25.1 and 25.2 show how the iBoxx indices have evolved during 2002. Notice the rebalancing spikes at the turn of each month, caused by bonds falling under a year to maturity, the addition of new, longer-dated issues and the removal of cash.

---

[1] For empirical evidence on the nonnormality of bond returns, see the appendix to William Lloyd, Bharath Manium, and Mats Gustavsson, "Tracking Error," in Frank J. Fabozzi (ed.), *Professional Perspectives on Fixed Income Portfolio Management: Volume 4* (Hoboken, NJ: John Wiley & Sons, 2003).

EXHIBIT 25.1   iBoxx Euro Index—Modified Duration 31 January 2002 to
January 31, 2003

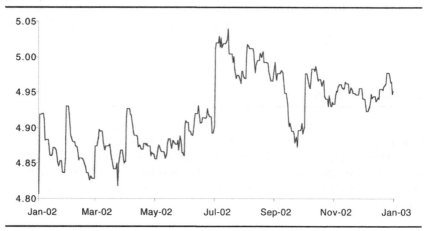

Source: Barclays Capital, iBoxx.

EXHIBIT 25.2   iBoxx GBP Index—Modified Duration 31 January 2002 to
31 January 2003

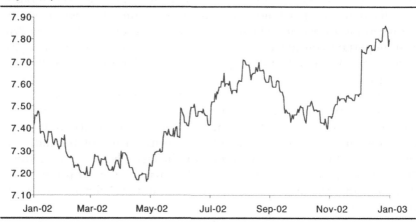

Source: Barclays Capital.

HISTORICAL VIEW OF DURATION

Exhibit 25.3 shows the average duration of bonds in the sterling market
from December 1990 to January 2003, we find that it has increased

EXHIBIT 25.3   Barclays Sterling Bond Index Duration

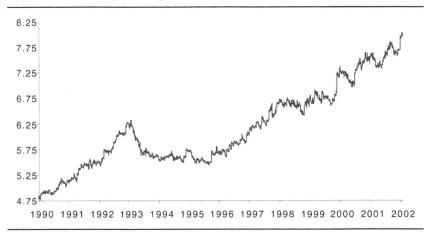

Source: Barclays Capital, iBoxx.

EXHIBIT 25.4   Market Value of Long-dated Sterling Issuance 1991–2002
(£ million)

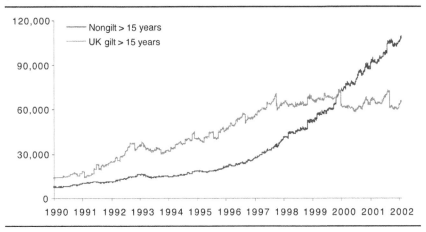

Source: Barclays Capital.

from 4.8 to 8.0. This increase represents more than a 60% extension of duration. Average life increased from 9.1 to 12.7 over the same period.

The main driver of the increase in duration until 1998 was the falling interest rate environment. During this period the yield on the index fell from 11.4% to 6.6%. This fall in interest rates resulted in an increase in supply of longer-dated nongilts (see Exhibit 25.4). During this period the yield on the longest gilt fell from 10.1% to 4.4%.

Due to the youth of the Euro credit market, an accurate comparison with the sterling market is difficult to make, but we can still observe an increased issuance of longer-dated bonds.

Sectors and Ratings

As we have already discussed, the constituents of an index usually change every month, but the impact is not limited to duration. The sector weightings and credit ratings of an index can change dramatically as well. This is especially true in markets where corporate bond issuance is rapidly expanding, such as Europe. Given the number of issues in the broad indices, it is necessary to categorize them by rating, sector, and maturity.

In 2002 credit quality deteriorated, reflected in the increased share of lower-rated bonds in the indices (see Exhibits 25.5 and 25.6). In particular, we note that the proportion of triple-B rated bonds in the iBoxx Euro

EXHIBIT 25.5   iBoxx Euro Index from 31 January 2002 to 31 January 2003

	MV (%)		Duration Contribution (%)	
iBoxx Euro Index	31/1/02	31/1/03	31/1/02	31/1/03
Sovs.	72.2	69.1	75.1	74.5
Subsovs.	6.6	7.9	6.3	7.0
Collateralized	10.8	10.9	9.2	8.6
Corp.	10.4	12.1	9.3	9.9
Total	100.0	100.0	100.0	100.0
Corp. triple-B	3.7	4.9	2.8	3.3

Source: Barclays Capital, iBoxx.

EXHIBIT 25.6   iBoxx GBP Index from 31 January 2002 to 31 January 2003

	MV (%)		Duration Contribution (%)	
iBoxx GBP Index	31/1/02	31/1/03	31/1/02	31/1/03
Gilts	48.0	46.5	46.9	44.7
Sovs and subsovs.	19.5	18.3	20.4	19.7
Collateralized	4.5	5.4	6.0	6.9
Corp.	28.0	29.9	26.7	28.7
Total	100.0	100.0	100.0	100.0
Corp. triple-B	7.2	7.4	6.1	6.1

Source: Barclays Capital, iBoxx.

Index has risen from 2.8% to 3.3% by duration contribution. This change in itself would have made a tracking error calculated at the beginning of the period a poor predictor of relative performance throughout the year. Even the more developed sterling market can be subject to substantial movements, and indeed we see the same pattern as in the Euro market, albeit a less dramatic increase in triple-B rated credit.

The data support the argument that sector and rating characteristics of markets and indices change significantly over time. This could lead to larger actual performance differences between a portfolio and an index than would be expected from a tracking error estimate at the beginning of that period.

DIFFERENT WAYS TO LOOK AT TRACKING ERROR

An increasing number of institutional investors are measuring their fixed-income managers' performance relative to major indices. At the same time, these institutions want to be sure that their managers are not taking excessive risks that could ultimately be hazardous to their clients and shareholders. Consequently, many managers are now required to regularly report a tracking error figure. However, there is still some uncertainty over the best way to calculate tracking error.

There are three commonly used methods for calculating tracking error: (1) variance-covariance model, (2) historical simulation value at risk, and (3) Monte Carlo simulations. We discuss each model in this chapter. Before we proceed, a distinction should be made between *ex post* and *ex ante* tracking error. *Ex ante tracking error* is the expected difference over a given future time period, whereas *ex post tracking error* is the actual difference measured between the portfolio and benchmark, or in other words, the divergence that actually occurred. The absolute value of the *ex post* tracking error should be less than or equal to the *ex ante* tracking error approximately 68% of the time.

THE VARIANCE-COVARIANCE MODEL

The variance-covariance model approach extracts volatility information from historical returns and builds a model intended to predict divergence in performance. For this type of model, the underlying data are typically a time series of yields, spreads or returns. The model relies heavily on historical data and assumes both stable correlations and a normal distribution of returns.

Full Covariance Method

The first and most straightforward way to calculate tracking error is by using the full covariance model. This method depends heavily on past data for every single instrument in the index and portfolio. Using matrix algebra, the covariance of daily total returns between every pair of assets in the index can be calculated, as well as the variance of total returns for every single asset in the index. A variance-covariance matrix of the bond returns is then constructed based on these calculations. The variance-covariance matrix is then multiplied by the exposures' vector, as shown in the equation below:

$$\sigma^2 = \Phi^T \times V \times \Phi \qquad (25.1)$$

σ = tracking error
Φ = exposures vector (Φ^T = transposed exposures vector)
V = variance-covariance matrix

The exposure vector is the difference in the weight vector of the portfolio and the index. The weight vector is simply the percentage weight of each instrument in the index or the portfolio. Naturally, the sum of the weights in each vector equals one and the sum of the exposure vector is zero. The tracking error can then be calculated by multiplying the transposed exposures vector by the variance-covariance matrix, and then by the exposures vector, as shown in equation (25.1).

As an example with

$$\Phi^T = \begin{bmatrix} p1 & p2 & p3 \end{bmatrix}$$

$$V = \begin{bmatrix} v11 & v12 & v13 \\ v21 & v22 & v23 \\ v31 & v32 & v33 \end{bmatrix}$$

σ is calculated as

$$\sigma^2 = \Phi^T \times V \times \Phi = \begin{bmatrix} p1 & p2 & p3 \end{bmatrix} \begin{bmatrix} v11 & v12 & v13 \\ v21 & v22 & v23 \\ v31 & v32 & v33 \end{bmatrix} \begin{bmatrix} p_1 \\ p_2 \\ p_3 \end{bmatrix}$$

Building and Testing the Model

In the following example, we illustrate how a full covariance model (FCM) can be constructed, and its performance measured during a one-year verification period using corporate bonds.

We selected a universe of corporate bonds with maturities (on 31 May 2001) between two and six years from the iBoxx Euro Corporate Nonfinancial Index. We chose a cut-off at two years to ensure the bonds would still be in the index at the end of the 1-year test period. This produced 97 nonfinancial corporate bonds, which we aggregated into their own index.

By using a random number generator to assign varying bond weights, we then constructed 1,500 different test portfolios from these 97 instruments, thereby creating a large number of different exposure vectors. We then calculated the *ex ante* tracking errors for each portfolio as at 31 May 2002.

We verified the accuracy of the predicted tracking error by comparing *ex post* daily tracking errors with *ex ante* daily tracking errors for the months of June and July 2002. The *ex post* exceeded the *ex ante* tracking error for 39.8% of the time, which is significantly higher than the expected 32% for a normal distribution.

The results of these comparisons indicate that the method is not accurate in this example (remember we expect the deviation to exceed the tracking error no more than 100% − 68% = 32% of the time), and this technique is often criticized in practice.

Construction of the variance-covariance matrix can be extremely burdensome and requires large amounts of data. A covariance matrix for n instruments must have $n \times n$ elements. For an index with 1,000 instruments, the corresponding variance-covariance matrix would contain 1,000,000 cells. This would make it less suitable for an automatic portfolio optimizer as the computational difficulty of inverting such a large matrix is great and prone to numerical errors.

Furthermore, if a security is issued during the time period for which the matrix is constructed, then it may be difficult to calculate accurate covariances for that security. One possible solution would be to use the total returns of a proxy bond in terms of sector, maturity and rating on the trading days for which there is no available data for the newer bond.

Multifactor Model

Another form of the variance-covariance model incorporates a multifactor approach. Instead of looking at covariances between individual bonds the multifactor model aggregates information into *common factors*. These so-called *principal factors* can be obtained either by regression or by a market participant using qualitative modelling. In our model, we use the latter approach.

The multifactor model (MFM) stipulates that a portfolio's return is a function of a number of factors, and its exposures to those factors. The factors are designed to extrapolate information regarding past movements of the yield curve and selected spread factors relating to rating bands and sector classifications. Effectively, the factors are grouped into those related to yield curve movements or credit spreads, and allow the portfolio manager to distinguish between the tracking error generated by each factor (though it is not possible to add these two figures together because the factors may be correlated).

While this also uses a variance-covariance matrix much like the full covariance method, the actual matrix is much more condensed. As an example, the matrix used in a 20-factor model would have a size of (20 × 20) 400 cells, which is moderate compared with the one-million-cell matrix mentioned previously for the full variance-covariance model. The advantages of using a multifactor model are that it easily allows for mapping a new issue into past data for similar bonds by looking at its descriptive characteristics, and it can be inverted for use in a portfolio optimizer without too much effort. The multifactor model is also more tolerant to pricing errors in individual securities since prices are averaged within each factor bucket.

An "m"-factor returns model takes the following form:

$$R_i = \beta_{i1}F_1 + \beta_{i2}F_2 + \dots + \beta_{im}F_m + \varepsilon_i \qquad (25.2)$$

where

R_i = return on security i
β_{im} = sensitivity of security i to factor m
F_m = value of factor m
ε_i = residual error of security i

The returns model stipulates that return is function of m-factors. Splitting up return into several factors allows us to approach the model in the following way:

$$\sigma_p^2 = \sum_{k=1}^{m} \sum_{l=1}^{m} \alpha_k \alpha_l \sigma_{kl}^2 + \sum_{i=1}^{n} \varepsilon_i^2 w_{ip}^2 \qquad (25.3)$$

where

σ_p^2 = variance of portfolio p

$$\alpha_k = \sum_{i=1}^{n} \beta_{ik} w_i = \text{portfolio } p\text{'s sensitivity to factor } k$$

σ_{kl}^2 = covariance between factors k and l
ε_i = residual error of security i
w_{ip} = weight of security i in portfolio p
β_{ik} = sensitivity of security i to factor k
n = number of securities in the portfolio
m = number of factors in the model

Using the MFM described in equation (25.3) to model, expected tracking error takes the following form:

$$\sigma_{TE} = \sqrt{\sum_{k=1}^{m} \sum_{l=1}^{m} \gamma_k \gamma_l \sigma_{kl}^2 + \sum_{i=1}^{n} \varepsilon_i^2 (w_{ip} - w_{ib})^2} \qquad (25.4)$$

where

σ_{TE} = tracking error of portfolio p with respect to benchmark b

$$\gamma_k = \sum_{i=1}^{n} \beta_{ik} w_{ip} - \sum_{j=0}^{o} \beta_{jk} w_{jb} = \text{the net (portfolio – benchmark) sensitivity to factor } k$$

σ_{kl}^2 = covariance between factors k and l
ε_i = residual error of security i
w_{ip} = weight of security i in portfolio p
w_{ib} = weight of security i in benchmark b
β_{ik} = sensitivity of security i to factor k
n = number of securities in the portfolio
o = number of securities in the benchmark
m = number of factors in the model

An Illustrative Example: The Sterling Multifactor Model

For the following example, we utilize the Barclays Capital Portfolio Analytics System XQA, which incorporates the aforementioned multifactor model. Again, this model incorporates factors that include points on the yield curve as well as factors related to credit spreads. We took the yield curve data in the sterling model from gilts and for the euro model from Bunds. The credit spread factors consist of "buckets" by sector and rating, among other factors.

Our sterling multifactor model consists of 32 factors reflecting changes in yield curve and credit spreads. We obtained historical monthly data on the above factors in order to create a variance-covariance matrix for the monthly changes in the various factors. We refer to this as the "Static VcV Matrix." The exposures vector for the portfolio and index consist of the duration contributions of bonds that fall into the various buckets. For instance, if a portfolio contains a triple-A rated/Financial zero-coupon bond with a duration of 10, and the bond's contribution to the portfolio's market value is 20%, the bond will be reflected in the exposure vector by placing 2.0 (20% × 10) into the 10-year interest rate bucket, and 2.0 into the triple-A rated/Financial bucket. However, for a bond that makes coupon payments, each individual cash flow must be placed into the appropriate interest rate bucket based on its own contribution to duration. The difference in the exposures vectors between the index and portfolio is used for calculating the tracking error.

We created a random portfolio with a duration of 8.05 containing 50 corporate bonds for evaluating the sterling model, and selected the Barclays Nongilt All Maturities Index of duration 7.33 as a benchmark. We calculated the daily *ex ante* tracking error at the beginning of each month, and then compared it with the daily *ex post* tracking error for each day of that particular month, for 12 consecutive months until 31 July 2002. An analysis of the results indicates that the absolute value of the difference in price returns between the index and portfolio (*ex post* tracking error) exceeded the *ex ante* tracking error on 36.3% (91/251) of the trading days.

Based on the aforementioned test, this method produced results relatively close to the expected 32% for this trial. We recalculated the exposure vectors at the beginning of each month to reflect any changes in the portfolio and index holdings.

We ran identical tests for the same portfolios and index using a monthly updated variance-covariance matrix. We refer to this as the "Monthly Updated VcV Matrix." This means that the matrix used for each month includes new data that did not exist at the beginning of the previous month. An analysis of the results indicates that the absolute value of the difference in price returns between the index and portfolio exceeded the tracking error on 36.7% (92/251) of the days. The effect of updating the covariance matrix on a monthly basis had little or no effect on the model's accuracy in this particular case. However, looking at a longer time period, it is important to update the matrix regularly in order to get an adequate representation of changing markets.

We ran the previous tests using simply weighted variance-covariance matrices. This means that each piece of data was equally weighted when constructing the matrix. For instance, we gave the 1-year gilt rate on 31 January 2001 the same consideration as the one on 30 April 2002. In order to compensate for recent changes in volatility of the various factors, it is possible to construct an exponentially weighted variance-covariance matrix. Under this technique, recent data is more heavily weighted than older data. Basically, weights are assigned to observations, based on their order of occurrence, using an exponential formula.

Assuming the weighting factor to be used is 0.99, the calculation works as follows:

Let N = the total number of observations. The nth observation is therefore assigned a weight of $0.99^{(N-n)}$. The Nth (final) observation is assigned a weight of 1 (0.99^0). The sixth out of 10 observations would be assigned a weight of 0.99^4.

Selecting a weighting factor can be somewhat arbitrary. A "forgetting factor" of 0.99 implies that an earlier value is 1% less important than its successor. The value chosen is usually between 0.96 and 0.99. When dealing with daily data, we would normally expect a higher weighting factor than when dealing with monthly data, which in turn would have a larger factor than quarterly data. This is because data that are closer in time by nature are more closely related.

Once the weights are calculated, it is possible to construct a diagonal matrix, whereby the upper left-hand corner contains the weight that was assigned to the earliest observation, and the lower right-hand corner represents the weight assigned to the most recent observation.

The simple covariance matrix is constructed using the following formula:

$$V = \frac{Y^T \times Y}{n - k}$$

where

Y = value of each observation minus the average value for that particular column. Each column represents a different factor. (T = matrix transpose)

n = number of observations

k = number of factors (number of columns)

An example of a covariance matrix containing three factors (in this case, yield curve movements for three different tenors):

Tenor	1 Year	2 Year	3 Year
1 Year	0.049898774	0.040937125	0.039697223
2 Year	0.040937125	0.046663569	0.046349494
3 Year	0.039697223	0.046349494	0.052633651

(% returns exceed daily TE)

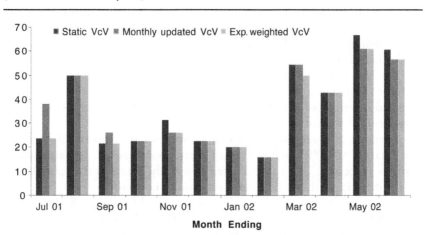

Source: Barclays Capital.

Calculating the exponentially weighted covariance matrix is done by

$$V = \frac{Y^T \times W \times Y}{(n-k)\sum_i w_i}$$

where

W = matrix containing weight factors on diagonal (as described above)
w_i = individual weight factors from matrix above

We again calculated *ex ante* daily tracking error at the beginning of each month, and then compared it with *ex post* daily tracking error for each trading day of the same month. The results were better than those produced by the simply weighted covariance matrix—*ex post* tracking error exceeded *ex ante* for 34.7% of the days observed using exponential weighting (recall that the result for the unweighted covariance matrix was 36.7%). Therefore, exponentially weighting the matrix marginally improved the accuracy of the calculated tracking error.

Exhibit 25.7 shows the percentage of times return exceeded the daily tracking error for different month ending using the Static VcV Matrix, Monthly Updated VcV Matrix, and Exponentially Weighted VcV Matrix.

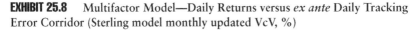

EXHIBIT 25.8   Multifactor Model—Daily Returns versus *ex ante* Daily Tracking
Error Corridor (Sterling model monthly updated VcV, %)

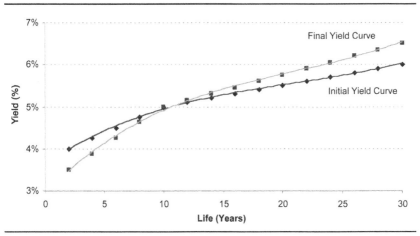

Source: Barclays Capital.

Size of Maximum Deviations

As previously mentioned, one of the assumptions made for calculating
tracking error is that of normally distributed returns. However, return
distributions in reality show "fat tails," which means that there are
more extreme (large positive or negative) events occurring than would
be expected from a normal distribution. Furthermore, even though the
occurrence of deviations larger than one standard deviation (i.e., the
tracking error) is in line with predictions, the size of these deviations is
of great interest. If these over- or undershoots are excessively large, then
the portfolio's performance is still subject to a large amount of risk.

To illustrate this point, we plotted the daily price returns during a
one-year period with the tracking error (see Exhibit 25.8). Notably, the
tracking error that was updated monthly stays constant through one-
month periods. In the exhibit we see that tracking error is shown as a
corridor bounded by the positive and negative tracking error values calculated monthly. The scatter plot shows that many data points lie far
away (several tracking errors) from the predicted tracking errors. This
highlights the fact that large deviations could occur even though your
portfolio's performance against the index is adhering to the prescribed
tracking error limits. Therefore, in order to overcome this weakness of
the tracking error model, practitioners turn to historical simulations,
which we look at in the next section.

Advantages of the Variance-Covariance Method

The advantages of using the variance-covariance method are:

- The factor models allow for analysis of risk due to distinguishable factors (e.g., yield and spread curve movements).
- New issues can be mapped into an existing framework using descriptive characteristics.
- The least computationally intensive of the three methods considered.

Disadvantages of the Variance-Covariance Method

The disadvantages of using the variance-covariance method are:

- A normal distribution of returns has to be assumed.
- Future correlations are assumed to be equal to historical correlations.
- The size of deviations larger than the tracking error is not considered.
- The variance-covariance is not suitable for options.

HISTORICAL SIMULATION

Historical simulation and value at risk (VaR) emerged in the 1980s as large derivatives houses sought an innovative method for measuring and controlling their risk positions. The need for change came about due to the increased complexity in their books during this decade of growth. These firms were looking for a measure that was accurate, and at the same time could be easily communicated within the organization. Therefore, by applying past market movements to their positions to simulate current risk, the value at risk methodology was born.

Definition of VaR

The historical simulation approach uses the historical distribution of returns from the instruments in a portfolio to simulate the portfolio's VaR. VaR is always defined for a certain probability α and time horizon h. Alternatively, we could refer to the $1 - \alpha$ quantile (or confidence level) of the loss distribution. For instance, we could say that for a particular portfolio the one-day (time period) 5% (α) probability VaR is \$100,000, or that the one-day 95% ($1 - \alpha$) confidence level VaR is \$100,000, which would mean that there is a 5% chance that the portfolio will lose \$100,000 in one day.

For calculating tracking error, historical simulations can be used by considering a position of being long the portfolio and short the index. Therefore, the difference in returns between the portfolio and the index is the variable for which the VaR is calculated. To get a tracking error

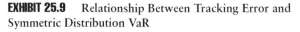

EXHIBIT 25.9 Relationship Between Tracking Error and
Symmetric Distribution VaR

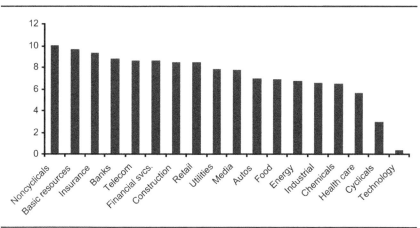

Source: Barclays Capital.

measure using this methodology we have to calculate the 16% VaR as
illustrated in Exhibit 25.9).

It is worth noting that the VaR refers only to the potential loss,
whereas the tracking error refers to the absolute value deviation between
portfolio and benchmark. Also note that in order to calculate this conversion into tracking error, the underlying assumption is that of a symmetric
distribution of bond returns.

Observation Period and Histogram

The first step in trying to perform a historical simulation analysis is to
select an observation period (e.g., 250 trading days). The observation
period should be selected carefully; a longer period could be detrimental
because it might include older and less appropriate information in the
simulation whereas too short an observation period would limit the
data. A good example of too long an observation period is the case of
telecom bonds in Europe. In early 1999, most incumbent telecom operators in Europe were rated high double-A and have steadily migrated
downward to triple-B by 2002.

The daily changes in the yield curve and credit spreads are re-
enacted during this 250-day period. The portfolio would then be revalued under each of these 250 scenarios, thereby producing a daily profit
and loss for each scenario. This profit and loss figure can be easily con-

EXHIBIT 25.10   Daily Return for a Portfolio Holding versus a Benchmark (%)

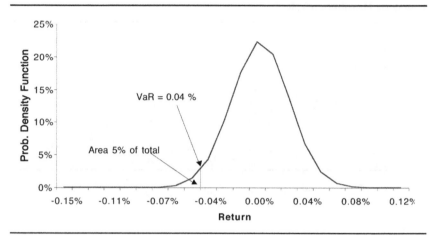

Source: Barclays Capital.

verted to a daily percentage profit and loss. The same process is then used for the benchmark index.

We can calculate the daily differences in percentage profit and losses between the portfolio and the index by subtracting one from the other. We can then create a histogram for the daily differences in profit and loss. The VaR can be determined by looking at the histogram (for instance, the value representing the second percentile would be the 2% VaR).

In the example shown in Exhibit 25.10, 5% (the area to the left of the vertical line) of the expected variations would cause a daily loss of more than 0.04%. This is referred to as the "95% confidence level VaR."

When the $x\%$ probability VaR (portfolio versus index) is calculated for the desired confidence level, the portfolio's daily return should not lag that of the index by that amount on more than $x\%$ of trading days. For instance, if the 5% daily VaR equals 0.04%, the portfolio's daily return should lag the index's daily return by 0.04% or more on approximately 5% of the future trading days.

Advantages of Historical Simulation

The advantages of using the historical simulation method are:

- Returns do not need to have any particular distribution (e.g., normally distributed); it is a nonparametric approach so it is possible to use skewed distributions. However, to get a tracking error number that is symmetric, we need to assume a symmetric distribution.

- Higher confidence intervals can easily be calculated; the only limitation is the number of historical observations available.
- Easy to understand; the risk can be expressed as a loss amount or a loss percentage.
- Unlike the variance-covariance model, it is suitable for options and other derivatives.
- Can be used on a single universe with short/long positions as well as in the relative approach of being long a portfolio and short an index.
- Crisis periods can be used for incorporating known extreme events.

Disadvantages of Historical Simulation

The disadvantages of using the historical simulation method are:

- Assumption that distribution of spreads and market correlations remain the same in the future implies that volatility stays the same, too. (We address this issue in the following section.)
- Problem of data quality. Since tails are the primary focus of interest, and they are represented by very few samples, it might be difficult to get an accurate estimate of the loss figure.
- Data that go back several years are of limited value.
- Limitations in analyzing complex products such as baskets of credit default swaps as the availability of historical data is limited.

Further Developments of the VaR Methodology

The standard VaR approach assumes that the volatility of the markets today is the same as it is during the period under consideration. Therefore, if the current market were more volatile than the previous one, this model would underestimate risk; conversely, if markets experienced a peak in volatility recently, the model would overestimate risk. There are several methods of weighting VaR calculations to rebalance the calculations.

Overweighting Current Values

A simple solution to the problem of not reflecting current market conditions consists of trying to assign more weight to recent observations. This could be thought of as ordering the profit-and-loss series chronologically and then artificially increasing the frequency of the recent observations at the expense of the older values.

Volatility Update

A more widely used approach first normalizes all historical returns with respect to the corresponding historical volatilities and then calculates return projections by multiplying the standardized returns by the current volatility.

The advantage of using this method is that the original correlation structure is left intact while at the same time reflecting changing market conditions in the results. Disadvantages are that we have to assume linearity in the profit and loss values, which means it cannot be applied to portfolios containing options.

To conclude, historical simulation with all its variants is another method that relies on past data to predict the future. It has problems coping with complex instruments, instruments with no history, and where the number of observations is limited. We look at a method that uses numerous computer simulations to overcome this, the Monte Carlo simulation, in the next section.

MONTE CARLO SIMULATION

Monte Carlo simulations are an alternative to parametric and historical approaches to risk measurements. They approximate the behavior of financial prices by using computer-generated simulations of price paths. The underlying idea is that bond prices are determined by factors that each have a specific distribution. As soon as these distributions (e.g., normal distributions) have been selected, a sequence of values for these factors can be generated. By using these values to calculate bond prices (and thus portfolio returns), the method creates a set of simulation outcomes that can be used for estimating value at risk.

The approach is similar to the historical simulation method, except that it creates the hypothetical changes in prices by random draws from a stochastic process. It consists of simulating various outcomes of a state variable (or more than one in case of multifactor models), whose distribution has to be assumed, and pricing the portfolio with each of the results. A state variable is the factor underlying the price of the asset that we want to estimate. It could be specified as a macroeconomic variable, the short-term interest rate or the stock price, depending on the economic problem.

For fixed-income portfolios, this method theoretically represents an improvement because it takes into account all the factors affecting bond prices (and could also include pull-to-par) and it is a very powerful method for calculating VaR.

Calculation Framework

The simulation involves the following steps:

1. For each state variable choose a stochastic process and corresponding parameters.
2. Generate a sequence of values $e_1, e_2, ..., e_n$, from which prices are computed $S_{t+1}, S_{t+2}, ..., S_{t+n}$
   In multifactor models, it is also important that the random variables generated have the desired correlation.[2]
3. Calculate F_T, the value of the asset (the portfolio) under this particular sequence of prices at the target horizon.
4. Repeat steps 2 and 3 as many times as necessary, say 10,000, to obtain a distribution of values, $F_T^1, ... F_T^{10,000}$, from which the VaR can be generated. At the selected confidence level c, the VaR is the portfolio value exceeded in level $c \times 10,000$ replications.

The number of iterations should reflect the usual trade-off between accuracy and computation cost. However, there are other techniques to increase the speed of convergence. There is always some error in the simulation estimate due to sample variability. As the number of replications increases, the estimate converges to the true value at a speed proportional to the square root of the number of replications. More replications bring about more precise estimates but take longer to estimate. In fast-moving markets, or with complex securities, speed may be more important than accuracy.

If the underlying process is normal, the simulated distribution must converge to a normal distribution. In this situation, Monte Carlo analysis theoretically should yield exactly the same result as the multifactor variance-covariance method. The VaR estimated from the sample quantile must (not considering sampling variation) converge to the value of $\alpha\sigma$, where

α = quantile corresponding to the desired level of confidence (e.g., 1.96 for 95%)

σ = standard deviation of the distribution

Examples of Simulation Models

In order to illustrate the application of Monte Carlo simulation, we present two methods in detail below. The first considers price movements, and the second, which also handles pull-to-par, is a short-term interest rate model.

---

[2] This is achieved through Cholesky factorization, which is a method to simulate multivariate normal returns, based on the assumption that the covariance matrix is symmetric and positive-definite. It is used to ensure the simulated series have a certain desired correlation.

Model I: Small Price Movements

Geometric Brownian motion is a commonly used model, which assumes that changes in asset prices are uncorrelated over time and that small movements in prices can be described by

$$dS_t = \mu_t S_t dt + \sigma_t S_t dz$$

where

S_t = asset price

dS_t = change in asset price

dz = a random variable distributed normally with mean zero and variance dt; this variable drives the random shocks to the price and does not depend on past information

μ = parameter representing the instantaneous drift at time t

σ = parameter representing the instantaneous volatility at time t

In practice, the process with an infinitesimally small increment dt is approximated by discrete moves of size Δt. Integrating dS/S over a finite interval, we have approximately

$$\Delta S_t = S_{t-1}(\mu_t \Delta t + \sigma_t \Delta t \sqrt{\Delta t})$$

where ε = a standard normal random variable (mean zero, unit variance).

Using this linearization, it is possible to simulate the price path for S, starting from S_t and generating a sequence of ε to calculate S_{t+1}, S_{t+2}, ..., S_{t+n}.

The Monte Carlo method, however, is prone to model risk. If the stochastic process chosen for the underlying variable is unrealistic, so will be the estimate of VaR. This is why the choice of the underlying model is particularly important. The geometric Brownian motion model described above adequately describes the behavior of some financial variables, but certainly not that of short-term fixed-income securities. In the Brownian motion, shocks on prices are never reversed. This does not represent the price process for default-free bonds, which must converge to their face value at expiration.

Model II: Dynamics of Interest Rates

Another approach, which was used by Cox, Ingersoll, and Ross to model the term structure in a general equilibrium environment, consists of a model of the dynamics of interest rates.[3] This process provides a

---

[3] John Cox, Jonathan E. Ingersoll Jr., and Stephen A. Ross, "A Theory of the Term Structure of Interest Rates," *Econometrica* (March 1985), pp. 385–498.

simple description of the stochastic nature of interest rates that is consistent with the empirical observation that interest rates tend to be mean reverting.

It is a one-factor model of interest rates, which is driven by movements in the short-term rates dr_t. In this model, movements in longer-term interest rates are perfectly correlated with movements in the short-term rate through dz.

$$dr_t = \kappa(\theta - r_t)dt + \sigma\sqrt{r_t}dz$$

where $\kappa < 1$ defines the speed of mean reversion towards the long-run value q. Situations where the current interest rates are high, such as $r_t >$ θ, imply a negative drift $\kappa(\theta - r_t)$ until the rates reverts to θ and vice versa for $r_t < \theta$.

Also, r can never fall below 0 because while it decreases its variance $\sigma\sqrt{r_t}$ also decreases, and as the limit of r_t goes to zero, the variance goes to zero.

The Monte Carlo experiment consists of first simulating movements in short-term interest rates, then using the simulated term structure to price the securities at the target rate.

This interest rate process can be extended to a multicurrency environment, incorporating correlations across interest rates and exchange rates. For currencies, the drift can be based on short-term uncovered interest parity, which defines the expected return as the difference between the domestic and foreign interest rates. This creates a large system with interactions that provide realistic modelling of global fixed-income portfolios. For more precision, additional factors can be added. Longstaff and Schwartz extend the Cox-Ingersoll-Ross model to a two-factor model, using the short-term rate and its variance as variables.[4]

Advantages of Monte Carlo Simulation

The advantages of the Monte Carlo simulation method are the following:

- It overcomes the problems encountered when measuring the risk of a portfolio comprised of instruments nonlinearly dependent on the underlying factors (e.g., baskets of credit default swaps).
- It can be used for pricing some types of path-dependent instruments, such as barrier options or other exotic derivatives.

---

[4] Francis Longstaff and Eduardo S. Schwartz, "Interest Rate Volatility and the Term Structure: A Two-Factor General Equilibrium Model," *Journal of Finance* (September 1992), pp. 1259–1282.

Disadvantages of Monte Carlo Simulation

The disadvantages of the Monte Carlo simulation method are the folowing:

- Because the method is based on the same kind of assumptions on the behavior of financial prices made in the variance-covariance method, it is prone to model risk. If the stochastic process chosen for the underlying variables is unrealistic, the estimate of tracking error will be incorrect.
- If corporate bonds were to be included in the analysis, a model for the credit factors (sector, issuer, rating) would have to be developed to take into account credit risk and default probability.
- It is computationally intensive, although there are methods to increase the speed of convergence to the solution.

SCENARIO ANALYSIS

Fortunately for the investment community, there are alternatives to calculating tracking error that give an accurate idea of where a portfolio's risks lie. These methods start with understanding the exposures of a portfolio relative to its benchmark, along several dimensions such as duration, term structure, rating, sector, and issuer. They then create interest rate and credit spread scenarios for different future time periods and perform a "what-if" analysis on the portfolio and the benchmark for these scenarios. These scenarios should encompass both expected and extreme conditions (best and worst case) in order to generate a return profile, both absolute and relative to the index, as well as to identify key thresholds.

We have discussed the weaknesses of the tracking error calculations in previous sections, but there is an alternative way to estimate risk in a portfolio: scenario analysis.

We explain the method in detail below. It is imperative to fully understand the following parts of the contribution to risk in terms of: (1) portfolio composition and (2) index composition.

To better understand the future relative performance, we should carry out extensive stress tests on user-defined assumptions. A portfolio can be stress-tested by analyzing the performance under different scenarios comprising various interest rate and credit curve assumptions.

A scenario analysis should be conducted using the following steps:

1. Start by identifying the composition of an index and portfolio in terms of sectors, duration, rating, and so on.
2. Determine the time period over which a risk estimate is desired (e.g., one year, three months, or instantaneous shocks).

EXHIBIT 25.11 XQA Scenario Analysis—Yield Curve Forecasting
Choose any horizon yield

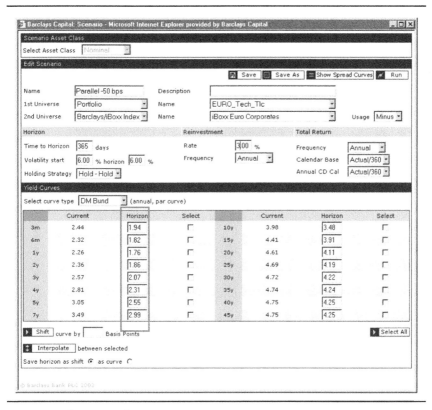

Source: Barclays Capital.

3. Choose a select number of interest curve scenarios in terms of shifts and twists.
4. Take a credit view (widening or narrowing of credit spreads during the selected period). For this purpose views could be taken by sector, rating (e.g., A, triple-B) or even on issue level.
5. Run the scenarios and calculate horizon returns.
6. Interpret the results, change the bets, and by iteration come up with a portfolio that meets your requirements (or simply identify a range of performance figures for your portfolio against the benchmark under the chosen conditions).

Scenario analysis is illustrated in Exhibits 25.11, 25.12, 25.13, and 25.14 using Barclays Capital Portfolio Analytics System XQA.

EXHIBIT 25.12 XQA Scenario Analysis—Credit Spread Forecasting by Rating (Change credit spread by rating or sector . . .)

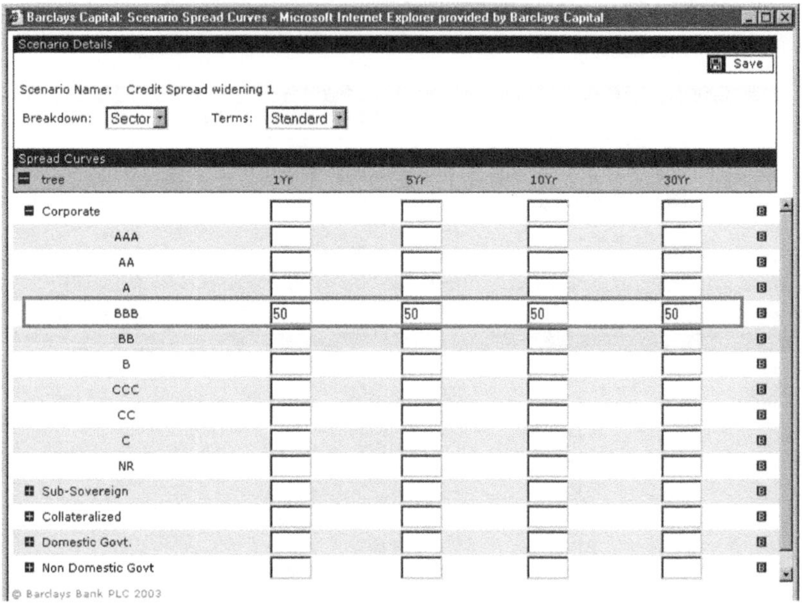

Source: Barclays Capital.

EXHIBIT 25.13 XQA Scenario Analysis—Credit Spread Forecasting by Issue and Sector (. . . or by issuer to identify fallen angel risk)

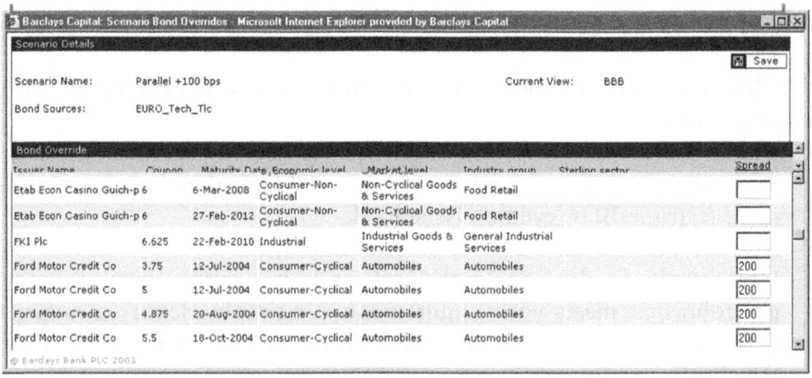

Source: Barclays Capital.

EXHIBIT 25.14   XQA Scenario Analysis—Interpreting the Results
(Analyze results at the portfolio and the individual bond level)

Barclays Capital: Scenario Analysis - Microsoft Internet Explorer provided by Barcl...	_ □ X
Scenario - Parallel +100 bps	Trade date: Thursday 6 March 2003

	Portfolio - EURO Tech Tlc	Barclays/iBoxx Index - iBoxx Euro Corporates
Semi Annual Yield	5.56	5.27
Annual Yield	5.64	5.34
Semi Annual Mod. Duration	2.85	3.49
Annual Mod. Duration	2.77	3.40
Duration	2.93	3.58
Market Value (millions)	99	475,326
Holding Period Return	2.10	1.39
Coupon Return	5.61	5.12
Principal Return	0.00	0.00
Price Return	-3.64	-3.83
Reinvestment Return	0.13	0.10
Total Return	2.10	1.39
Annualized CD Return	2.10	1.39
Bond Failures	0	0

▼ Download

Source: Barclays Capital.

The beauty of the scenario analysis method is that the fund manager has full control of the process in which the estimates are produced. The effect of changing the individual variables can be seen on relative performance. It requires more articulate views on possible scenarios than a tracking error number but the results are traceable, which leads to a more straightforward way of identifying the weak points and take appropriate countermeasures based on them.

CONCLUSION

After reviewing the various methodologies that can be used to calculate tracking error, it is apparent that such a measure is incomplete for assessing portfolio risk. The root causes of this interpretation lie in the underlying assumptions used across all the methodologies.

Major banks have traditionally used historical simulations to assess firmwide portfolio risk, and relied heavily on empirical data and historical distributions. Monte Carlo simulations, despite being computationally intensive, work well for instruments that have little or no history, and for more exotic derivative instruments.

However, both methods suffer from the same assumption: whether you utilize a historical return distribution (historical simulation) or choose to model an arbitrary distribution (Monte Carlo), the dependence on such a distribution prevailing in the future can be dangerous, if not disastrous. (WorldCom, Enron, need we go on?) The resolution lies in analytics that make no such assumptions, and are flexible in modelling various scenarios or outcomes.

We believe that scenario analysis offers such a solution by providing fund managers with a more comprehensive picture of the risk in their portfolios against a benchmark. Whereas tracking error provides just one number, scenario analysis generates several different return outcomes, including anything from recent trends to extreme price changes. It also allows fund managers to test their market forecasts, which is a necessity for any market participant.

CHAPTER 26

Portfolio Strategies for Outperforming a Benchmark

William T. Lloyd
Managing Director
Barclays Capital

Bharath K. Manium
Associate Director
Barclays Capital

The introduction of an index approach to portfolio management has marked a fundamental shift in the way fixed income portfolios are managed in Europe. Increasingly, fund managers and, more importantly, chief investment officers are looking to measure the performance of portfolios and portfolio managers in an objective fashion. We believe that the best way to approach the problem is to adopt a "beat the benchmark" approach.

The first question that this approach raises is: "What is an appropriate benchmark?" We address this in this chapter where we discuss six widely recognised academic principles of a good index. A good index should be:

- Relevant to the investor.
- Representative of the market.
- Transparent in rules with consistent constituents.
- Investible and replicable.
- Based on high data quality.
- Independent.

The second question that we address in this chapter follows naturally from the first, which is: "how does one beat a benchmark?" There are countless strategies that can be employed to outperform a benchmark. In this chapter we focus on nine important strategies that can be employed to achieve this goal. These strategies involve taking views on:

- Duration
- Convexity
- Yield curve
- Industry sector
- Credit quality
- Name selection
- Issue selection
- Financing and leverage
- Off-index instruments

SELECT THE RIGHT BENCHMARK

Having identified the market to invest in, a portfolio manager is faced with the choice of choosing the right benchmark with which to measure that market. In the current environment there are myriad index providers, each with a different set of qualifying criteria defining the market. Index selection is important, as it is used to measure performance and ascertain if a manager is doing a good job relative to others. The European Federation of Financial Analyst Societies (EFFAS) has developed a series of standardised rules for calculating bond indices that have a wide acceptance in the market and provide consistency of calculation across index providers.

In addition, there are some widely recognised academic principles of what constitutes a good index. The six major principles are discussed in the following sections.

Principle 1: Relevant to the Investor

Any index chosen as a benchmark must be relevant for the investor to invest in. One of the most common examples of relevance is the quest to avoid "natural concentration" between the business risk of the sponsoring entity and the invested portfolio. For example, a defence contractor would like to benchmark its pension fund to an index that has a low concentration of defence-related businesses. For this purpose many investors use custom indices, excluding specific industries, which cause natural concentration, while creating their benchmark.

Principle 2: Representative of the Market

A good benchmark should provide an accurate picture of the market it claims to represent. For example, if in a market most of the issues of a particular rating or industry sector are below the index-size threshold, the performance of the index will be very different from the performance of the market. Hence two indices with different minimum thresholds could exhibit vastly different industry and/or ratings distribution and consequently a vastly different risk/return profile.

Principle 3: Transparent Rules and Consistent Constituents

One of the definitions of a bond index is that it is a "rules-based collection of bonds." It is therefore imperative that the rules defining the index are transparent and are applied objectively and in a consistent fashion. It is often tempting to bend the rules to accommodate particular market situations such as avoiding undue concentrations of a particular issuer or industry. For example, the downgrade of KPN in September 2001 has left it teetering on the edge of the investment grade threshold. This has raised concerns among some high-yield fund managers that KPN will account for over a quarter of the Euro high-yield universe were it to make the transition into high yield. These investors have sought changes in the index in the form of sector and issuer caps to address this particular situation. If such caps are implemented, it would violate the principles that define a "good" index.

The treatment of unrated paper for investment grade indices falls under this category. Many index providers include unrated paper in investment grade indices on the premise that if these instruments were to be rated they would end up in the investment grade. The other area where many index providers often vary from each other is the treatment of split-rated bonds, both for the rating tier they represent, as well as to determine whether they form part of the investment grade universe or not.

Principle 4: Investible and Replicable

An investor should be able to replicate the index and its performance with a small number of instruments as well as with relatively low transaction costs and without moving the market too much. For this reason the index constituents should be a set of bonds that have standard features, are liquid, and trade actively in the secondary market. The ability to invest in the index through derivative instruments such as futures and total return swaps is an added attraction of an index.

Indices with higher threshold levels typically contain fewer illiquid instruments and are thus easy to replicate for obvious reasons, and very often easy to beat as well. The reason for the latter is explained by the presence of a "liquidity premium." Everything else being the same (*ceteris paribus* for the Latin buffs) bonds which are more liquid tend to trade at tighter levels than bonds which are less liquid, and the difference is known as the liquidity premium.

Indices that have more liquid bonds have lower yields than those with less liquid bonds, and consequently generate lower returns, which in turn implies that they are easier to outperform.

Principle 5: High Quality Data

It goes without saying that an index is only as good as the data—both prices and static information—that is used to calculate it. Even a well-constituted and well-calculated index is unlikely to represent the moves of the market if it uses distorted prices. Unlike the equity market, where price transparency is high, there have historically been major impediments for getting true market prices for bonds and other OTC instruments.

Most bond indices are proprietary indices that use in-house pricing, and are, for that reason, highly susceptible to be distorted by the presence/absence of long/short positions on the trading book. Often bonds, for which the trader has no position, are not marked actively and reflect an "indicative" price and thus produce erroneous results for return and other calculations. To avoid these pitfalls, it is therefore important to ensure that index pricing is from an accurate and reliable source.

Principle 6: Independence

One of the reasons equity indices are so popular is that the prices used to calculate them are from an independent and a quasi-regulatory source. Independent indices also make index and bond level data available from multiple sources. This encourages the development of after-index products including derivatives, as there are multiple dealers active in the market and the resulting competition is good for all participants.

Striking a Balance

As many market participants observe, the above-mentioned principles are not entirely compatible, and thus create the need to strike the right balance. For example, in the quest to be representative of the market one could sacrifice liquidity of the instruments constituting the index. However, when striking the "balance" one has to consider that for an index to be used as a benchmark, the ability to buy the constituent instruments is paramount. Hence, we argue that principle 4 is more important than principle 2.

Unlike in the equity market, where there are several widely accepted benchmarks, the European credit market does not yet possess a benchmark that has gained broad market acceptance. The iBoxx family of indices is poised to be the "killer-index" for this market in particular and is rapidly gaining acceptance among the investor community. We believe that iBoxx offers a good combination of independence as well as high quality pricing, while at the same time being based on sound academic principles and calculated to EFFAS standards.

OUTPERFORM YOUR BENCHMARK

The first step towards beating a benchmark is to intimately know both the portfolio and the index, both on a standalone basis and relative to each other. The first level of understanding of one's portfolio and benchmark relates to the awareness of the average statistics of duration, yield, and the like. This enables the portfolio manager to take an overall duration view, and raises interesting questions about the portfolio, which will require further investigation. Most portfolio managers possess this level of understanding, and are also aware that averages do not convey the entire picture and, indeed, are often misleading.

The second level of understanding involves knowing the rules that define the indices; the distribution of issuance by maturity and duration buckets, rating tiers, and industry sectors. This level of knowledge will enable managers to take a curve view, as well as views on credit quality and industry sectors. Knowledge of the rules also enables a manager to forecast the changes to the index and manage accordingly. Most active portfolio managers constantly make asset allocation decisions based on credit quality and industry.

The third level is to know the individual issuers and issues in the portfolio, and focus specifically on characteristics such as covenants, step-up clauses, and call features. It is important to be aware of these features, primarily to stop making the wrong decisions while buying/selling bonds. Issuer level knowledge could have helped investors avoid blowouts such as Enron, WorldCom, and Marconi. However, issue level knowledge would lead to investors making the distinction between bonds with and without coupon step-up provisions. For example, with the September 2001 France Telecom downgrade to BBB, coupon step-ups in some of its bonds were triggered, and those bonds outperformed their nonstep-up counterparts by a significant margin. Subsequent downgrades boosted the difference in value further. The case with Stagecoach, which had covenants in the UK pound-denominated bond that let investors put the bond in the event of a restructuring proved valuable, as the investors in the euro-denominated bonds realised to their detriment.

A good understanding of what makes up the portfolio and the benchmark will give an insight into how they will perform under different market scenarios and help the manager achieve their investment objectives.

DURATION

Chapter 4 provides a comprehensive discussion of duration. *Duration* is the change in the price of a bond as a result of a very small shift in its yield. In other words, duration measures the sensitivity of the price of a bond to changes in its yield. An increasingly common measure of duration is *effective duration*, which is the measure of price sensitivity due to a small parallel shift in the spot curve. One would immediately realise that these two definitions of duration would give identical results for zero-coupon bonds and different results for most other instruments.

Most market participants are familiar with the concept of duration and its effect on the returns from fixed income instruments. However, the difference in the calculations of duration of a bond and a portfolio is worth noting. Most index and analytics providers (including Barclays Capital) calculate index and portfolio duration as the market value weighted duration of individual bonds that constitute the index or portfolio. The other measure, known as *cash flow duration*, calculates the duration based on the cash flow of the entire portfolio, using the internal rate of return (IRR) of those cash flows and then measuring the sensitivity of portfolio value to change in that IRR.

The former approach, even though an approximation, has been deemed desirable by EFFAS in the face of the enormity of the task of calculating duration based on the individual cash flows of the constituent bonds. In the trivial case where all the bonds have exactly same yield, the average duration is the same as the "true" duration of the portfolio or the index. That is,

$$\text{Duration}_{\text{portfolio}} = \frac{\sum_{i} \text{Duration}_i \times \text{Market value}_i}{\sum_{i} \text{Market value}_i}$$

Duration is the single most important factor that can generate or destroy returns in any portfolio. While the major effects of duration are well known, all of the effects are not particularly obvious. The attributes provided by portfolio reports (as shown in Exhibit 26.1) can often be misleading, as they represent average statistics for the entire portfolio. It

EXHIBIT 26.1 Summary of Average Portfolio Statistics

	Edit Portfolio								
							🔲 Save	🔲 Save As	▼ Download
Name	Corporate iBoxx Proxy			Description	Corporate iBoxx Proxy				Nominal
Instrument name			▶ Select		Show	⦿ Instruments			
ISIN			▶ Select			○ Embedded portfolios			
									✏ Update

ISIN	Issuer Name ↓	Currency	Coupon	Maturity	Par Amount	Price (%) 1 Oct 2002	Price (%) 30 Sep 2002	🗑
NL0000122588	Abn Amro Bank Nv	EUR	5.375	8-Sep-2009	1,250	104.7650	104.9470	☐
XS0112351662	Ahold Finance Usa Inc	EUR	6.375	8-Jun-2005	1,500	104.2050	104.3790	☐
FR0000487647	Alcatel Alsthom	EUR	7.000	7-Dec-2006	1,200	67.2500	67.2500	☐
DE0002306008	Allianz Finance Bv	EUR	5.000	25-Mar-2008	1,632	101.9840	102.1410	☐
XS0139186356	At&t Corp	EUR	6.000	21-Nov-2006	2,000	93.9825	93.9925	☐
XS0127769858	Aventis SA	EUR	5.000	18-Apr-2006	1,250	103.5150	103.5760	☐

Portfolio Details					● Annual ◉ Semi-Annual		
# of Instruments	95	Yield to Worst	5.21	Mod Dur. to Worst	4.16		
Spread	164	Time to maturity	5.01	YTW DurWeighted	5.26		
Price	101.35	Portfolio Par Amount	152,804	Coupon Return	0.01		
Coupon	5.608	Market Value	159,109	Price Return	-0.16		
Average S&P Rating	BBB+	Average Index Rating	A	Total Return	-0.15		
		Average Moody Rating	Baa1				

Source: Barclays Capital.

EXHIBIT 26.2 Market Value Distribution by Maturity Buckets

Comparison Report Result							
						🖹 Download Printable	

Comparison:Rating by Maturity Portfolio:Corporate iBoxx Proxy					Trade date: Tuesday 1 October 2002		
Life to Maturity	Index Rating	AAA	AA	A	BBB	All others	Total
<=3.00	Market Value (Percent)	2.94	4.51	6.52	11.38	0.00	25.35
3.00 5.00	Market Value (Percent)	0.00	3.82	7.56	14.11	1.50	26.98
5.00 10.00	Market Value (Percent)	2.79	9.97	20.05	11.31	0.00	44.12
10.00 15.00	Market Value (Percent)	0.00	1.83	1.73	0.00	0.00	3.55
>15.00	Market Value (Percent)	0.00	0.00	0.00	0.00	0.00	0.00
Total	Market Value (Percent)	5.73	20.13	35.85	36.80	1.50	100.00

Source: Barclays Capital.

is important to understand the distribution of issuance across the maturity spectrum to better manage duration. Mismatch in allocation across the maturity spectrum leads to an inadvertent yield-curve mismatch (discussed in detail later) and can lead to a mismatch in performance between the portfolio and the index. Exhibit 26.2 shows an analysis of the distribution of market value by maturity buckets.

EXHIBIT 26.3   Duration Contribution in Rating and Sector Buckets

Comparison Report Result							
							Download Printable
Comparison:Rating by Maturity Portfolio:Corporate iBoxx Proxy						Trade date: Tuesday 1 October 2002	
Life to Maturity	Index Rating	AAA	AA	A	BBB	All others	Total
<=3.00	Mod. Duration to Worst annual (Contribution Percent)	1.55	2.33	2.72	4.66	0.00	11.26
3.00 5.00	Mod. Duration to Worst annual (Contribution Percent)	0.00	3.20	6.60	11.06	1.01	21.87
5.00 10.00	Mod. Duration to Worst annual (Contribution Percent)	3.40	14.12	27.57	14.68	0.00	59.77
10.00 15.00	Mod. Duration to Worst annual (Contribution Percent)	0.00	3.83	3.27	0.00	0.00	7.10
>15.00	Mod. Duration to Worst annual (Contribution Percent)	0.00	0.00	0.00	0.00	0.00	0.00
Total	Mod. Duration to Worst annual (Contribution Percent)	4.95	23.48	40.16	30.40	1.01	100.00

Source: Barclays Capital.

Associated with duration is the concept of *dollar duration*. Dollar duration is invaluable for portfolio managers when analysing the concentration of the portfolio in different buckets adjusted for duration. Mathematically, it is the product of the dollar value of the bond and its duration. For the purpose of portfolio analysis duration contribution (the product of duration and market value percentage) is used. Exhibit 26.3 shows the concentration of a portfolio in duration contribution terms.

As a result of the powerful effect of duration on a portfolio's performance, we recommend that most managers dealing with credit product prefer to stay duration neutral in their portfolios. This approach allows us to focus on the credit component to generate excess returns rather than taking on a duration view.

The effect of duration on a portfolio is shown in Exhibit 26.4. The result shown in the exhibit is the effect of a parallel upward shift in the bund curve of 100 bp. As a result, the portfolio with higher duration (on the right hand side) has underperformed in this scenario, as one would have expected. What is more interesting, however, is that the extent of underperformance is different from the (100 bp × difference in duration) one would initially expect. This difference is due to a host of factors, some of which will be explored in greater detail in subsequent sections.

Duration Drift

When it comes to matching duration, once is not enough. With the passage of time, the duration of the portfolio changes in a process known as *duration drift*. This is because bonds automatically drop out of indices when life to maturity is less than a specified threshold, typically one year for most broad indices, and new bonds constantly enter the index. However,

EXHIBIT 26.4   Effect of a Parallel Shift on Two Portfolios of Different Duration

Scenario - EUR parallel shift	Trade date: Tuesday 1 October 2002	
	Portfolio - Corporate iBoxx Proxy	Index - iBoxx Corporate 7+
Semi Annual Yield	5.65	5.83
Annual Yield	5.74	5.92
Semi Annual Mod. Duration	3.40	6.38
Annual Mod. Duration	3.31	6.20
Duration	3.49	6.57
Market Value (millions)	156	99,055
Holding Period Return	4.12	3.12
Coupon Return	5.47	5.59
Principal Return	0.00	0.00
Price Return	-1.49	-2.61
Reinvestment Return	0.14	0.14
Total Return	4.12	3.12
Annualized CD Return	4.12	3.12
Bond Failures	0	0

▼ Download

Source: Barclays Capital.

in the case of the portfolio, none of that happens, and unless actively managed the duration mismatch will grow bigger with time. Duration is also affected over time with the distribution of market value across the curve as shown in Exhibit 26.4. For example, if the issuance is concentrated in the short and long part of the curve in the index, it will drift lower much quicker than if it were concentrated in the middle of the curve.

Duration is an important tool for expressing views on the likely outcome of interest rates in a market. Everything else remaining constant, investors who expect interest rates to fall tend to be overweight duration (duration of portfolio greater than that of the index), and vice versa.

Bond Futures and Interest Rate Swaps: Tools to Manage Duration

As explained in Chapters 19 and 16, swaps and futures contracts represent one of the easiest and most effective methods of managing a portfolio's duration exposure. Government bond futures is a frequently traded and extremely liquid contract in Europe, and investors can buy futures to increase duration, and sell futures to reduce the duration of their portfolio incurring minimal transaction costs.

Investors can also use interest rate swaps for a similar purpose. These contracts exchange fixed-rate cash flows for floating-rate cash flows based on LIBOR/EURIBOR. Investors on the paying (fixed) leg of the swap reduce the duration of their portfolio, while those on the receiving (fixed) leg increase the duration of the portfolio. Since interest rate swaps are extremely liquid contracts, they are an efficient way of expressing a short-term view on interest rates.

CONVEXITY

Convexity is a measure of curvature of a bond's price-yield function. One can also think of convexity as the rate of change of duration with respect to yield. Convexity is discussed in more detail in Chapter 4.

Convexity is a positive number for most normal bonds. However, for bonds with embedded call options such as mortgage-backed securities, it is always negative. Intuitively, it is obvious that if interest rates fall, the bond prices rise and the option to call the bond turns in the money and is often exercised, which shortens the duration of the bond and hence the rate of change of duration with respect to change in yields is negative.

We calculate the convexity of the portfolio in the same way as the duration, by averaging the convexities of the constituent bonds weighted by their market values as recommended by EFFAS and shown below:

$$\text{Convexity}_{\text{portfolio}} = \frac{\sum_i \text{Convexity}_i \times \text{Market value}_i}{\sum_i \text{Market value}_i}$$

Convexity comes into play when yield curve changes are moderate to large and serves to increase the value of the bond irrespective of whether the yield rises or falls. In other words, if yields rise, then bonds with positive convexity fall less than expected from duration alone, and when yields fall, bond prices rise more than expected. To put it bluntly, "convexity is good" for a bond portfolio, but it is exceptionally hard to actively manage a credit portfolio and maximise convexity at the same time.

Portfolio convexity depends on the distribution of cash flows in the portfolio. A portfolio with an even distribution of cash flows has higher convexity than one where cash flows are concentrated in a particular maturity bucket, assuming equal duration and no optionality. By extension, considering a bond to be a portfolio of cash flows, the obvious conclusion is that bonds with higher coupons have higher convexity than bonds with low or zero coupons.

EXHIBIT 26.5   The Effect of Coupon on Convexity of Similar Duration Bonds

	Bond 1	Bond 2	Bond 3
Coupon	0%	5%	10%
Maturity Date	9 October 2007	1 October 2008	13 September 2009
Settlement Date	1 October 2001	1 October 2001	1 October 2001
Duration	5.652	5.658	5.658
Convexity	18.63	20.16	21.51

Source: Barclays Capital.

EXHIBIT 26.6   Effect of Changes in Yield to Returns in Two Portfolios with Identical Duration

Scenario - EUR parallel shift		Trade date: Tuesday 1 October 2002
	Portfolio - Convexity effect	Index - iBoxx Corporate
Semi Annual Yield	5.71	5.58
Annual Yield	5.80	5.66
Semi Annual Mod. Duration	3.49	3.49
Annual Mod. Duration	3.39	3.39
Duration	3.59	3.58
Market Value (millions)	328,381	445,610
Holding Period Return	4.17	3.93
Coupon Return	5.67	5.36
Principal Return	0.00	0.00
Price Return	-1.64	-1.55
Reinvestment Return	0.13	0.13
Total Return	4.17	3.93
Annualized CD Return	4.17	3.93
Bond Failures	0	0

▼ Download

Source: Barclays Capital.

The effect of coupon on the convexity of bonds is illustrated by the example in Exhibit 26.5.

Convexity is one of the reasons why parallel shifts do not result in price changes in the way we would expect. Exhibit 26.6 shows an example that demonstrates the effect on total returns of a parallel shift in the underlying bund curve of +50 bp. As we would now expect, the difference in the returns between the two portfolios (8 bp) cannot be explained by the difference in yields (5 bp) despite identical duration.

As we mentioned earlier, it is difficult for credit portfolio managers (where the market is overwhelmingly noncallable) to actively manage convexity of their holdings. However, preferring higher coupon instruments and premium bonds over lower coupon and discount bonds tends to increase the convexity of the portfolio and in turn increases its total return.

YIELD CURVE

Duration and convexity help explain the change in portfolio value with parallel shifts in the yield curve. However, most yield curve shifts are not parallel, and involve some measure of steepening, flattening, and butterfly shifts, or some combination of the three.

The relative position along the yield curve affects performance in nonparallel yield curve movements and is known as *curve positioning*. Dividing the portfolio into maturity buckets and measuring the duration contribution in each of those buckets can identify curve positions. The narrower these buckets are defined the better will be the understanding of positions along the yield curve. Even though it is difficult to envisage a change in slope of the curve decoupled from other movements such as parallel shifts, it is useful to examine the effects of these movements separately.

Curve positions typically take the form of *bullets* and *barbells*. The former implies the middle of the curve is overweight as opposed to the very short and very long end, and outperforms in a curve-steepening environment. The latter implies the very short and very long end of the curve is overweight as opposed to the middle part and results in outperformance during a flattening environment. It is worth noting that while discussing curve positions the reference is always relative to the benchmark and not in an absolute sense. Quite often bullets and barbells implemented in an absolute sense give results to the contrary of what one would expect.

Exhibit 26.7 is an illustration of a bulleted exposure relative to the benchmark crafted on a duration-neutral basis. Exhibit 26.8 illustrates the effect of a curve steepening on a two-bond portfolio (barbell) to a one-bond portfolio (bullet) with identical dollar durations. As can be observed from the exhibit, the 2–30 part of the curve has steepened by 100 bp, with the two year yields falling 50 bp, 10 year yields rising 50 bp, and the 5-year yields unchanged. In the example, such a scenario would cause the barbell portfolio to underperform the bulleted one by 1.07%

EXHIBIT 26.7   Distribution of Issuance Across the Yield Curve

Comparison Report Result						
						🖹 Download Printable
Comparison:Rating by Maturity Portfolio:Curve effect Index:iBoxx Corporate				Trade date: Tuesday 1 October 2002		
Life to Maturity	Index Rating	AAA	AA	A	BBB	Total
<=3.00	Market Value (Percent)	0.67	3.13	2.97	9.51	16.29
		2.02	3.63	5.69	12.90	24.24
3.00 5.00	Market Value (Percent)	0.69	3.63	11.75	19.87	35.94
		1.14	5.30	9.59	14.01	30.05
5.00 10.00	Market Value (Percent)	0.89	9.76	20.57	16.55	47.77
		1.42	9.27	19.17	12.59	42.45
10.00 15.00	Market Value (Percent)	0.00	0.00	0.00	0.00	0.00
		0.21	1.02	1.66	0.00	2.89
>15.00	Market Value (Percent)	0.00	0.00	0.00	0.00	0.00
		0.00	0.37	0.00	0.00	0.37
Total	Market Value (Percent)	2.25	16.53	35.29	45.93	100.00
		4.79	19.60	36.11	39.50	100.00

Source: Barclays Capital.

EXHIBIT 26.8   Price Effect of Curve Steepening on Portfolios with Identical Duration

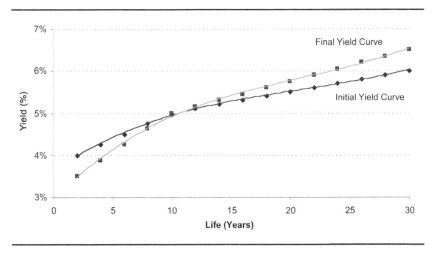

EXHIBIT 26.8   (Continued)

One-Bond Portfolio

Coupon	5.00%
Settlement date	30 November 2001
Maturity date	30 November 2011
Yield	5.00%
Final yield	5.00%
Mod. duration	7.72
Price return due to curve steepening	0.00%

Two-Bond Portfolio	Bond 1	Bond 2	Portfolio Avg.
Coupon	4.50%	5.50%	4.50%
Settlement date	30 November 2001	30 November 2001	
Maturity date	30 November 2003	30 November 2031	
Final yield	4.50%	5.50%	4.96%
Yield	4.00%	6.00%	4.92%
Mod. duration	1.88	13.99	7.48
Percent of portfolio	53.80%	46.20%	100%
Price return due to curve steepening	0.94%	–6.88%	–2.67%

Source: Barclays Capital.

It is important to identify curve positions isolated from the duration view; therefore many investors implement curve views on a duration neutral basis (as shown in Exhibit 26.8). The methodology for doing it is to divide the curve into duration buckets and then adjust the weightings of each bucket in such a way as not to alter the overall duration of the portfolio.

INDUSTRY SECTOR

As "credit" becomes the new buzzword in Europe, portfolio managers have to pay attention to the "spread" or risk premium that they receive as compensation for taking on increased default risk.

There are several different measures of spread; the two most common ones are "spread to benchmark" and "asset swap spread/margin" (ASM). The former is the difference in the yields of a bond and its corresponding benchmark treasury. The latter is the spread over LIBOR that one receives if one were to perform a par-par asset swap on the bond. With the relative lack of issuance in the government bond market and the resultant distortions, market participants are choosing ASM as a better indicator of the risk premium. The development of the credit derivative market and the increase in instruments such as credit-linked notes, has increased the market's focus on ASM.

Why is Sector Rotation Important?

Sector rotation is the process of being able to take overweight and underweight positions based on the credit view of various sectors in the market. This has been a nascent process in Europe, but one that is picking up rapidly. There have been three key drivers to the process of sector rotation. Firstly, the available universe of credit names has grown tremendously in Europe. The process of bank disintermediation has made corporations look to the capital markets for funding their balance sheets, and has created many a big group of first-time borrowers, increasing investor choice in the process. The second driver has been the growth in liquidity in the market. Liquidity has increased, measured both as rising average issue sizes as well as narrowing bid-offer spreads. Finally, sector rotation has been made imperative by the massive differential in excess returns generated by the various sectors. Investors positioned in the "wrong" sectors can experience significant underperformance.

Sector rotation is not only possible but also imperative as can be seen in Exhibit 26.9, which shows the total returns of the sectors in the index.

What Drives Sector Performance?

Sector performance is influenced by a large number of factors, the most important of which are described below.

Business Cycle

The business cycle is perhaps the single most important factor driving sector spread performance. Some sectors such as autos and capital goods are more influenced by business cycles than others such as tobacco and utilities. Therefore, the position in, and direction of, the business cycle will be an important input in portfolio allocation by industry sector.

Swap Spreads

Swap spread correlation with credit spreads has been a topic of discussion ever since the credit market took off in Europe. Of late, this correlation

EXHIBIT 26.9   YTD Returns by Industry Sector in the iBoxx Euro Corporate Index

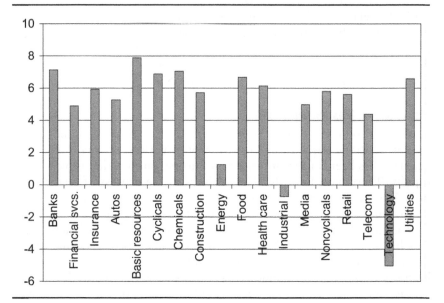

Source: Barclays Capital, Iboxx. Data as of 30 November 2001.

has been breaking down for the market as a whole. However, it remains strong in the higher quality (triple-A and double-A rated) sectors such as supranational, agency, subsovereign and higher-rated financials (double-A rated banks) where credit spreads are highly correlated to swap spreads. Investors using LIBOR targets (typically banks) cause changes in demand for credit with changes in swap spreads as do trading desks and hedge funds that use interest rate swaps to hedge the interest rate risk. Hence, one should bear in mind that making an allocation decision in any of these sectors is in a large sense taking a view on swap spreads.

Supply

There are events which cause an industry-wide build up of supply—typical examples have been the "UMTS financing" deals from telecom operators which started in the middle of last year, and the spate of "CP refinancing" transactions hitting the market this year from auto companies. Issuance of fresh securities can influence spread performance in three ways.

First, the event of new supply may be symptomatic of deterioration in credit quality of the issuing company and/or sector (as in the case of the telecom and auto sectors). Second, some investors have a sector and name limits, hampering demand, resulting in wider spreads. Third, new issues tend to be priced at a discount to elicit demand and effectively lead to a repricing in the secondary market.

Event Risk and External Factors

In today's market, factors extraneous to industry fundamentals have been exerting increasing influence on sector performance. The term "event risk" has traditionally been used to refer to merger and acquisition (M&A) activity, and has been more issuer-specific than affecting the entire sector. However, we take a broad definition of event risk to encompass other external risks, including litigation risk, technological risk, and the like.

A significant form of event risk is litigation risk. Once considered to be confined to the tobacco sector, litigation risk is now threatening industrial goods firms (asbestos liability) to auto manufacturers (Firestone tyre recall). In the current environment, no sector looks immune from these types of external shocks. Technological risk affects businesses that carry a substantial exposure to the future direction of technology development. The sectors that are affected consist predominantly of telecom operators and OEM.

Regulatory Risk

A large section of European corporate bond issuance is generated by sectors that are currently, or until recently, tightly regulated. These include sectors such as telecoms and utilities. Past and expected regulatory changes affect the entire sector and should be kept in mind. An example of an expected shift in the regulatory environment that should be considered is the upcoming review of "block exemption" given to automakers in Europe.

Commodity Prices

Prices of commodities such as oil and metals influence the profitability and demand for several major industries. Oil prices have the most far-reaching effect on spread performance, affecting in particular industries such as oil and gas, utilities, airlines, chemicals and autos.

Measuring Sector Concentration by Duration Contribution

Having considered the many factors affecting sector performance, we now focus our attention on how to measure sector concentration. Several market participants analyse sector concentration by measuring the percentage of market value accounted for in a particular sector. We believe that for investment grade portfolios the correct method is to focus on the duration contribution of bonds in each of the sectors. This is because the primary credit risk facing investors in this asset class is negative ratings migration (and the accompanying spread widening) rather than that of an outright default. Widening spreads cause a bigger price effect on a bond with longer duration. In a more generic spread-widening environment, the effect of duration is magnified due to the associated (in most cases) steepening in the term structure of credit spreads. Exhibit 26.10 presents the duration contribution by industry sector and maturity bucket.

Credit Quality

Having made the case for sector rotation, making one for asset allocation by rating seems rather trivial. After all, one could argue that given the fewer number of rating tiers, making investment decisions would be that much easier. As Exhibit 26.11 shows, the range of performance by credit tier is substantial enough to justify such a stance.

However, there is a more fundamental question that needs to be addressed here: How does one measure credit quality? Traditionally, investors have looked at the rating spectrum to represent credit quality,

EXHIBIT 26.10   Distribution of Duration Contribution by Industry Sector

Comparison Report Result

Download Printable

Comparison:Sector by Maturity
Portfolio:Corporate iBoxx Proxy   Trade date: Tuesday 1 October 2002
Index:iBoxx Corporate

Sector: Market Level	Life to Maturity	<=3.00	3.00 5.00	5.00 7.00	7.00 10.00	All others	Total
Banks Financial Services Insurance	Mod. Duration to Worst annual (Contribution Percent)	2.67	3.16	11.68	11.03	7.10	35.65
		2.70	4.79	9.07	14.23	6.15	36.93
Automobiles	Mod. Duration to Worst annual (Contribution Percent)	2.20	4.39	0.87	3.99	0.00	11.46
		2.67	4.25	1.88	2.21	0.00	11.00
Basic Resources Chemicals Construction Cyclical Goods & Services Industrial Goods & Services	Mod. Duration to Worst annual (Contribution Percent)	1.06	3.80	3.61	0.00	0.00	8.48
		0.78	3.83	3.52	1.63	0.00	9.76
Food & Beverage Healthcare Non-Cyclical Goods & Services Retail	Mod. Duration to Worst annual (Contribution Percent)	1.86	1.21	1.62	1.01	0.00	5.71
		1.36	2.91	2.62	1.01	0.00	7.90
Media Telecommunications	Mod. Duration to Worst annual (Contribution Percent)	2.26	7.60	6.85	5.91	0.00	22.62
		2.55	5.96	4.47	5.83	0.00	18.81
Technology	Mod. Duration to Worst annual (Contribution Percent)	0.37	1.01	0.00	2.22	0.00	3.61
		0.13	0.72	0.00	0.76	0.00	1.61
Energy Utilities	Mod. Duration to Worst annual (Contribution Percent)	0.83	0.69	6.55	4.41	0.00	12.48
		0.58	2.18	6.08	3.56	1.59	13.98
Total	Mod. Duration to Worst annual (Contribution Percent)	11.26	21.87	31.20	28.58	7.10	100.00
		10.76	24.64	27.64	29.22	7.74	100.00

Source: Barclays Capital.

EXHIBIT 26.11 Distribution of YTD Total Return (%) by Ratings in iBoxx Euro Corporate Index

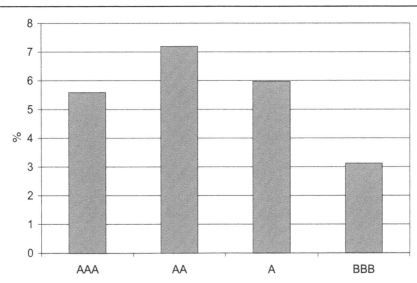

Source: Barclays Capital, iBoxx. Data as of 30 November 2001.

but that does not always convey the complete picture. Although one is tempted to think that the ratings represent a linear scale of credit quality, default probabilities associated with different rating tiers convey a different impression (see Exhibit 26.12). We therefore need to look at the average default probabilities, and then impute the average rating, as shown by the following process:

1. Segregate the portfolio into rating buckets.
2. Calculate weighted average default probability of the portfolio from the individual rating tiers.
3. Impute the rating of the portfolio from its average default probability.

Looking at the distribution of ratings (as shown in Exhibit 26.13) provides a good handle on identifying the "credit exposure" present in the portfolio. Again, since we are dealing with predominantly investment grade portfolios, it is important that we use duration contribution as a measure of portfolio concentration rather than market value percentage. Exhibit 26.13 illustrates the measurement of credit exposure in a portfolio.

EXHIBIT 26.12   Average Cumulative 5-Year Default Rates (%) for Various Rating
Tiers (logarithmic scale), 1970–2000

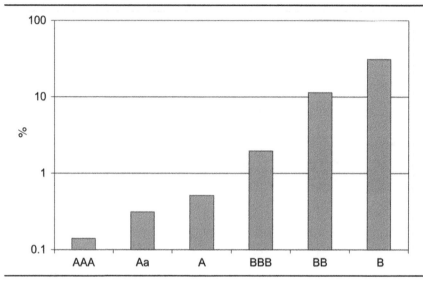

Source: Barclays Capital, Moody's.

EXHIBIT 26.13   Distribution of Issuance by Rating Tier

Comparison Report Result							
							🖺 Download Printable
Comparison:Rating by Maturity Portfolio:Corporate iBoxx Proxy					Trade date: Tuesday 1 October 2002		
Life to Maturity	Index Rating		AAA	AA	A	BBB	All others	Total
<=3.00	Mod. Duration to Worst annual (Contribution Percent)	1.55	2.33	2.72	4.66	0.00	11.26
3.00 5.00	Mod. Duration to Worst annual (Contribution Percent)	0.00	3.20	6.60	11.06	1.01	21.87
5.00 10.00	Mod. Duration to Worst annual (Contribution Percent)	3.40	14.12	27.57	14.68	0.00	59.77
10.00 15.00	Mod. Duration to Worst annual (Contribution Percent)	0.00	3.83	3.27	0.00	0.00	7.10
>15.00	Mod. Duration to Worst annual (Contribution Percent)	0.00	0.00	0.00	0.00	0.00	0.00
Total	Mod. Duration to Worst annual (Contribution Percent)	4.95	23.48	40.16	30.40	1.01	100.00

Source: Barclays Capital.

With the introduction of the credit element, a new dimension is
added to the concept of the yield curve. It becomes imperative to look at
the credit spread curve, that is, the spreads offered by instruments in
various credit quality buckets over the maturity continuum on the horizontal axis with the associated spread associated with those ratings on
the vertical axis, as shown in Exhibit 26.14.

EXHIBIT 26.14   Credit Spread Curves by Rating Tier

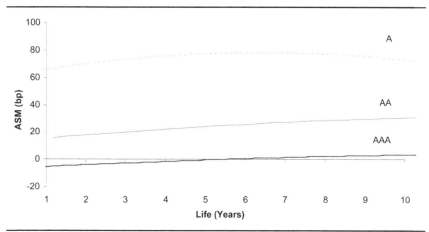

Source: Barclays Capital. Data as of 30 November 2001.

Asset allocation decisions by credit quality are similar to those for the yield curve but with an added dimension. When spreads widen, typically the lowest rated credits widen the most, and the spread differential between the triple-A and triple-B rated bonds increase, the opposite happens in cases where spreads tighten. Therefore, a portfolio with lower credit risk will generally outperform in a spread widening environment and vice versa.

Introducing credit quality generates interesting possibilities for implementing portfolio strategies. For example, a credit barbell might be implemented by going long triple-B rated paper at the front end of the curve, and match it with a long triple-A position in the longer end.

Portfolio allocations by credit quality need to be taken in conjunction with that by industry sector. This is due to the concentration of names in the industry in a particular rating tier; for example, in Europe most major telecom operators are now in the single-A category, while banks constitute a large chunk of double-A rated bonds. It would therefore be virtually impossible to construct a portfolio that is overweight Banks and simultaneously underweight double-A credit.

NAME SELECTION

The importance of name selection in portfolio construction is growing rapidly. It has been propelled primarily by two factors. First, there has been an increase in the number of borrowers, which has led to better and more diversified sector population. Second, the process of bank dis-

EXHIBIT 26.15 Number of Issuers in iBoxx Euro Corporate Index

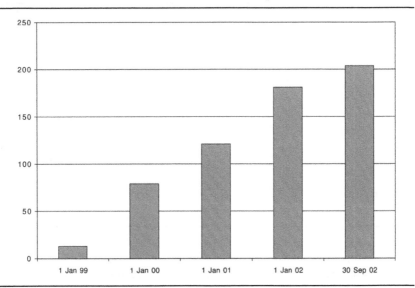

Source: Barclays Capital, iBoxx.

intermediation is driving several fundamental changes in the European economy; one of which is the creation of a number of "debut" bond issuers in the Euro market, giving the investors the ability to choose between multiple issuers in the same sector. Exhibit 26.15 shows the growing diversity in the European credit market. The rapid growth of the credit derivative market has provided an excellent benchmark to perform intrasector relative value analysis.

The second driving force has been the divergence of returns on names within a sector. While this had always been true for sectors such as industrial and consumer, which were driven more by individual credit fundamentals than any major sector drivers, increasingly it is evident in sectors such as telecom, which had hitherto been driven by industry fundamentals. Investor attention has also been diverted by some of the high profile blowouts witnessed in 2001. Borrowers such as Invensys, Marconi, Enron, and Swissair have investors paying more attention to the process of name selection.

We would like to highlight here that given the asymmetric payoff profile of corporate bonds (limited upside and fairly large downside), the focus of name selection should be on avoiding the dogs rather than picking the stars. This process is far more complicated, requiring a detailed analysis of a company's business and financial profile, and formulating a forward-looking credit view.

EXHIBIT 26.16 Difference in Market Value and Duration Contribution for Top Issuers in the iBoxx Euro Corporate Index

Issuer	Market Value	Issuer	Duration Contribution
Deutsche Telekom	4.43%	Deutsche Telekom	4.53%
Ford	3.93%	ING	3.61%
ING	2.96%	Deutsche Bank	3.12%
France Telecom	2.81%	RWE	2.40%
Daimler Chrysler	2.68%	Ford	2.04%

Source: Barclays Capital. Data as of 30 September 2002.

As with other parameters we have discussed, the name concentration also needs to be measured on a duration contribution basis. There can be substantial differences between duration contribution and percentage of market value of issuers. Exhibit 26.16 highlights the top five issuers by both criteria in the iBoxx Euro Corporate Index.

The divergence of performance is a powerful reason to adopt name selection when constructing portfolios. The increase in credit research capabilities with investors and with the resultant sophistication, it is inevitable that name rotation will become an important input to the portfolio construction and/or management process. As investors become more attuned to individual credit concerns, one can no longer expect bonds in the same sector to move in strict step with each other.

BOND SELECTION

The growth of the market has also led to an increase in the number of issuers with multiple bonds outstanding. There is a growing group of borrowers especially in the nonfinancial universe, with a number of outstanding issues in different maturities enabling the construction of issuer credit curves. The average number of issues per issuer in the iBoxx Euro Corporate Index has grown from less than 1.5 in the beginning of 1999 to nearly 2.2 in October 2002.

In the corporate market some issuers have well-populated credit curves, which enables relative value comparisons for a particular name. Traditionally, European financial institutions have been (and still are) the leading borrowers in the bond market. However, the number of non-financial issuers with well-formed credit curves continues to grow. Exhibit 26.17 lists the top five non-financial borrowers, ranked by the number of

EXHIBIT 26.17   Top Five Nonfinancial Borrowers by Number of Bonds in iBoxx Corporate Index

Issuer Name	Number of Issues
ING	12
Deutsche Telekom	11
Ford	10
Daimler Chrysler	8
Deutsche Bank	7
GM	7
GE	7
FIAT	7
Household Finance	7

Source: Barclays Capital, iBoxx. Data as of 30 September 2002.

EXHIBIT 26.18   Spread Curves of Selected Issuers in the Euro Corporate Market

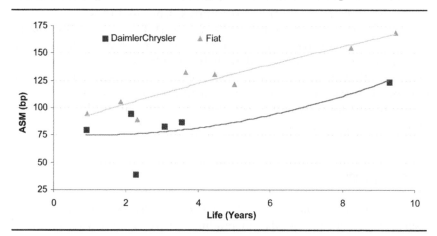

Source: Barclays Capital. Data as of 30 November 2001.

bonds they have outstanding in the iBoxx Euro Corporate Index, and Exhibit 26.18 presents the credit curves for two of those issuers.

The objective for issue level analysis is to identify and capture relative value within a particular name. The features that can distinguish bonds from the same issuer are described below.

Maturity

The simplest form of intraissuer relative value is to make a call on the slope of the curve, and implement flatteners or steepeners. These trades can be done on a duration neutral basis.

Legacy Currency

Despite the euro being launched in January 1999, there is still a significant amount of legacy currency bonds in the market. These bonds tend to trade at a slight discount to their euro-denominated counterparts. This discount normally disappears if the bond is redenominated. Buying legacy currency bonds benefits investors in two ways. Firstly, they get the extra carry, and secondly they benefit from a possible spread tightening in the event of a redenomination; but they also have to be prepared to put up with the relative lack of liquidity in these bonds.

Coupon Step-Ups

Since the middle of 2000, the Euro market has witnessed a deluge of issuance with ratings sensitive coupon language. These bonds pay extra coupon if their ratings are downgraded, and hence are valued differently than existing bonds without such options.[1] The coupon step-up can be valued using the probability of transition from rating migration statistics and calculating the equivalent spread value of the expected cash flows. Most of these bonds are currently in the telecom sector. A good example is France Telecom, where the coupon step-ups were triggered due to the recent downgrade, and bonds that had these features substantially outperformed the ones that did not.

Covenants

Bond covenants offer a useful protection against credit deterioration and event risk by increasing the costs of "bondholder unfriendly" behaviour of the management. Covenants that trigger a put in case of a restructuring or other such credit events are also valuable, as was witnessed in the case of Stagecoach, where an asset sale triggered a put in its GBP denominated bonds and left the USD and EUR bondholders holding a substantially weaker credit. Due to the increase in event risk, one would find that recently issued bonds tend to contain more covenant protection. Coupon step-ups associated to rating changes—discussed above—are another form of covenant protection.

Subordination

An attractive way of getting exposure to higher quality names is through subordinated debt. The most ubiquitous form of subordinated debt in the market is bank capital securities. It needs to be noted that

---

[1] We call them options even though they are not in a strict definitional sense, as like options these covenants generate cash flows contingent on certain events occurring in the future.

these securities carry additional risk not just of subordination, but also extension risk, interest deferral and principal write-down risks, depending on their position in the capital structure.

However, a more common form of subordination that is found in the nonfinancial universe is "structural subordination" and is often dealt with by stealth. This kind of subordination is a result of a holding company structure—or directly as a result of management action such as securitising part of the operational revenue. Structural subordination is common in many industries, especially utilities and now increasingly in telecoms. When buying structurally subordinated paper it is important to analyse the relationship between the operating and holding company as well as the volatility of cash flows at the operating level and management commitment to preserving value for bondholders.

Identifying and capturing intraname relative value is one of the surest ways of beating a benchmark, as there is no additional credit risk involved. The rapid development and growth of the default swap market provides an important reference point for this exercise.

FINANCING AND LEVERAGE

The first picture that comes to mind when someone talks of "leverage" in the bond markets is that of hedge funds and LTCM and all that happened in the summer of 1998. Contrary to popular perceptions, financing and leverage play an important and often positive role in influencing portfolio performance.

Most portfolio managers manage real money, and are often loath to borrow in order to punch beyond their weight. There are, however, two key reasons to look at financing and leverage more closely than before. First is the obvious benefit that leverage provides investors, to increase the magnitude of the payoff on their views. Secondly, leveraged players are the biggest in the market, for example, a €1 billion hedge fund leveraged 10 times (assets to capital ratio), churning its portfolio four times a year generates €40 billion in annual flows, comparable to that generated by the biggest of the world's fixed income asset managers, and their actions affect markets and the portfolios of unleveraged participants.

There are numerous ways of achieving leverage in portfolios, including those discussed below.

Repo

Repo (short for *repurchase agreement*) is the most common method of creating leverage in a transaction. Borrowing in the repo market is often collateralised by the security that is bought. Repo is a very common and popular method of funding long positions in the market, and securities that qualify as general collateral (GC) trade at tighter levels. Quite often some securities trade "special" in the repo market, which means their repo rate is lower than that for GC. "Specialness" in the repo market often results in the bond trading tighter than its peers.

Margin Trading

Transacting on margin is another popular way for creating leverage. In this process the dealer often lends the money required to buy a security after keeping a "haircut" (the margin which needs to be funded out of an investor's own capital). The extent of the haircut depends on the credit quality of the investor and the availability of credit lines with the dealer.

Credit Default Swaps

A much easier method of generating leverage in a credit portfolio is through credit default swaps (CDS). They let investors take on or lay off default risk in an unfunded manner. Selling default protection enables one to receive the premium associated with the additional credit risk without the need to buy a bond of that entity, and in the process creates enormous leverage, especially for higher rated credits. The increased liquidity and the compression of bid/offer spreads have added to the attractiveness of this market.

There are several advantages of using credit derivatives apart from generating leverage. CDS enables investors to assume credit risk in the form and denomination they choose, circumventing to a large extent the constraints on currency and maturity imposed by the bond market. CDS is a cleaner vehicle to take a view on credit without taking interest rate exposure when compared to a traditional asset swap. In the event of default a CDS unlike traditional asset swaps does not leave the investor with residual swap exposure.

Apart from the natural use as a hedge against an existing long and illiquid position, CDS represent one of the cheapest methods of expressing a negative view on a credit. In other words investors can go "short" by buying protection without getting involved in the complexities of the repo and financing issues.

Leveraged Notes

Leveraged notes are notes that are issued by an SPV or an EMTN program and the notional amount of credit risk is larger than the capital commitment. These notes are typically issued as tranches of synthetic securitisation transactions. The collateral pool in these transactions typically involves a combination of CDS and cash instruments.

Subordinated ABS Tranches

Another one of the easier methods of gaining leverage is through the subordinated tranches of ABS transactions with underlying credit collateral. The major drawback of using these instruments is the relative lack of liquidity that can hamper active management of the portfolio's leverage.

Leverage is an important tool in the hands of portfolio managers, helping them magnify specific exposures in their portfolio. These techniques are especially useful to benchmarked investors, as an index cannot create leverage and is at a natural disadvantage. However, leverage is a double-edged sword and can increase the pace of value destruction should a view go wrong, and hence should be used with care.

OFF-INDEX INSTRUMENTS

Adopting an index to measure portfolio performance does not always provide a level playing field. Indices by their very definition have an inherent advantage over portfolios, which include:

- *Transaction costs:* Certain indices ignore bid-offer spreads, which means that bonds get in and out of the index at the same price. Bid-offer spreads and other transaction costs, which affect real portfolios, can cause an index that ignores these to outperform by a significant amount.
- *Price effect of transactions:* Transacting large volumes in any market affects the price of the instruments. This effect is more pronounced in the credit markets and restricts portfolio managers to transact in small market sized blocks.
- *Reinvestment:* Most portfolios carry cash in their portfolio that is invested at the prevailing money market rate, the level of cash varying on the manager's perception of the market and the expected flows from redemptions and coupon payments. Indices on the other hand reinvest the cash generated out of coupon payments and bonds dropping off the index in the index itself, which typically yields higher returns than money market rates.
- *Liquidity premium:* The effect of liquidity premium is more pronounced in indices that have lower thresholds and by extension contain a larger number of illiquid bonds. As discussed earlier, as illiquid bonds have higher yields, and render a natural advantage to the index, as investors are unable to buy them at prices they are quoted in the index.

Despite the advantages enjoyed by the index, being benchmarked to one is not all that depressing. Being a rule-based collection of bonds, an index imposes on itself constraints that lower its performance as well. In other words an index is a "dumb portfolio." "Smart" managers often take advantage of these constraints in achieving their objectives. Owning securities and risk that the index cannot own is one of the most common ways of beating a benchmark.

The major types of off-index instruments that can be employed are discussed below.

Asset-Backed Securities

Asset-backed securities typically trade wider than similarly rated corporate and/or subsovereign bonds, and represent a cheap way of accessing high-quality paper. It is often a good strategy to build the triple-A part of a credit/government bond portfolio around a core of asset-backed paper and some liquid supranational/agency bonds to generate higher returns without sacrificing liquidity.

Credit-Linked Notes

Credit-linked notes (CLNs) are the simplest of all credit derivative instruments. They are funded assets issued by a bank or other entity and have credit risk to a second issuer (the Reference Issuer). These notes pay an enhanced coupon to the investor for taking on the added credit risk. These are typically issued our of repackaging vehicles or EMTN programmes.

CLNs provide an excellent window to create securities bearing the maturity, currency and credit risk one would like to take on, unconstrained by the availability of the bond in the marketplace. For example, in the auto sector one of the stronger names is BMW, but the company does not have many bonds outstanding. However, the name is a very liquid in the default swap market. Therefore, for investors who want exposure to the name would find it easier to gain it by buying a CLN.

Stripped Convertibles

Convertible and exchangeable issuance has risen recently driven by several factors from equity market volatility to German tax reform. Stripped convertibles are convertible bonds where the equity option has been stripped out and represents pure credit, callable after a specified date.

Stripped convertibles offer investors fantastic avenues to access credits at levels significantly cheaper than comparable bullet bonds. Convertibles appeal most to hedge fund investors who are primarily interested in the cheap equity option and don't care about credit. This combined with the lack of interest from the regular fixed income investor base makes stripped convertibles one of the cheapest asset classes in the market.

Loans

Loans have typically been in an unfashionable part of the credit market, conjuring up images of bankers wearing bowler hats and puffing cigars striking deals over a glass of scotch. Recently the combination of loans and securitisation technology allows lenders to parcel off risk to investors willing to take them.

Most loans are floating-rate obligations, and hence bear no interest rate risk. Many are secured, especially in the noninvestment grade credit. Loans also typically are senior to other obligations and provide a higher degree of covenant protection. These characteristics that make loans an interesting vehicle for assuming credit risk. The comparative lack of liquidity is often compensated by higher yields.

Fallen Angels and Rising Stars

Temporary exposure to certain names in the subinvestment grade market allows investors to capture higher yields. However, this strategy should be only employed to take advantage of technical disruptions in the market. These technical disruptions include buying "fallen angels" and "rising stars."

Fallen angels are securities that started out as investment grade bonds and have ended up, or are expected to end up in high-yield territory, such as Marconi and KPN. The former rose substantially before the downgrade to high yield, as it formed a big part of the European high-yield index, and high-yield investors had no choice but to buy the name and bid up the price.

Rising stars on the other hand, are bonds that started out as high-yield names and have subsequently become investment grade companies either through acquisition or through a deleveraging exercise. Rising stars see their spreads tighten dramatically even before they are formally upgraded, and investors can capture considerable upside. Examples of rising stars include Orange, which was bought initially by Mannesmann, later sold to France Telecom, Esat Telecom, which was bought by British Telecom, and Go Outdoor systems, which was bought by Infinity Broadcasting, a subsidiary of CBS/Viacom. All of these issues were subsequently upgraded to investment grade.

Floating-Rate Notes

Floating-rate notes (FRNs) represent an opportunity to buy short duration corporate paper, and are an attractive instrument to manage duration of the portfolio. FRNs however have significant spread duration, and their price is susceptible to changes in credit spreads.

Cross Currency

Several borrowers issue bonds in multiple currencies, which tend to trade at different spreads, even on a fully asset swapped basis. The reasons for this divergence include name recognition, and technical factors such as liquidity and the ability to enter into a repo.

Inflation-Linked Bonds

Inflation-linked bonds enable investors to hedge the effects of inflation. These instruments allow investors to implement their views on the inflation expectations for a particular economy.

New Issues

Indices include new issues typically at the end of the month in which they settle. This gives investors a chance to capture the initial spread tightening before the bond becomes part of the index. Also anticipating index changes ahead of time gives investors a tremendous advantage.

Off index instruments can generate a significant chunk of portfolio alpha and often depends on the skill of the individual portfolio manager. Managers also engage in securities lending in order to earn a steady stream of cash that helps them beat their benchmarks.

CONCLUSIONS

Given the myriad strategies (and their combinations) that can be employed, portfolio managers need to identify those that they think are optimal given their relative effectiveness and the constraints of time, effort, skill and the availability of appropriate tools.

The ability to construct portfolios that concentrate on a couple of key strategies where managers believe their skills lie, while remaining neutral to others is often the key to generating portfolio alpha. "Beat the benchmark" approach aids this process by forcing money managers to ask themselves a simple and important question before every transaction, "Will this trade help me 'beat the benchmark'?"

CHAPTER 27

Credit in Bond Portfolios

Claus Huber, Ph.D.
Corporate Bond Strategist
Private Asset Management
Portfolio Engineering Group
Deutsche Bank

Helmut Kaiser, Ph.D.
Head of Strategic Asset Consulting
Deutsche Bank
Private Banking Investment Strategy

The inauguration of the European single currency led to strong growth in the market of euro-denominated corporate bonds. Thus, one of the largest markets of fixed-income securities issued by industrial corporations second only to the US market came into being. Increasing merger and acquisition activities entailing high funding requirements have given a special impetus to the growth of this market. The significance of corporate bonds will also increase against the background of the rising importance of private pension provisions.

Investment-grade corporate bonds offering higher returns than government bonds at manageable risks are an attractive alternative for investors in search of higher yielding investments. In this chapter we contribute to the discussion whether it makes sense (at all) to add corporate bonds to a fixed-income portfolio. If it does, which bonds of what credit quality and maturity should be selected by an investor taking into account his risk tolerance and investment horizon? After examining the risk/return characteristics of corporate and government bonds we describe a quantitative method which is used to establish optimal portfolios with a view to different risk preferences and investment horizons of an investor. The optimal weighting of government and corporate bonds of various credit categories and maturities is then computed with the help of simulations based on historical data.

RISK-RETURN CHARACTERISTICS OF CORPORATE AND GOVERNMENT BONDS

Corporate bonds can be divided into the two categories of *investment grade* (bonds with a rating of BBB and higher) and *high yield* (rating below BBB). High-yield bonds are not considered in this chapter since this segment of the fixed-income market is not yet fully established in the Eurozone, and the majority of institutional and private investors may only purchase investment-grade bonds due to institutional restrictions and investment policy frameworks.

When determining the allocation to a security or an asset class in the portfolio the most interesting feature is its risk/return ratio in relation to other assets. In this chapter we aim at answering the question how an investor should structure a fixed-income portfolio of government and corporate bonds of different rating categories and maturities from the viewpoint of risk and return. The portfolio optimization approach by Harry Markowitz forms the starting point, which allows determining the allocation to securities in an optimal portfolio under consideration of the investor's risk tolerance.

Government and corporate bonds are regarded as separate security classes here. The two rating categories of AAA and AA are placed in one group because their correlations are very high and the AAA-to-AA yield spread is very low. The further categories of A and BBB each form a group of their own. This leads to three security groups from the investment-grade sector of corporate bonds. Depending on the investor's risk tolerance, he will prefer investing in bonds with short, medium or long maturities. For this reason, bonds are, on the basis of their remaining term to maturity, divided into the four maturity buckets one to three years, three to seven years, seven to 10 years, and over 10 years. This makes a total of 16 security groups (four maturity segments each in the range of AAA/AA,[1] A, BBB, and government bonds) available for empirical analysis.

Ex post simulations are run with historical data in order to determine the optimal portfolio. This allows us to review which portfolio structure would have been optimal with the given data from an *ex post* perspective. Due to the less developed corporate bond market in the

---

[1] The rating segment AAA/AA is denoted AA further on.

Euroland as compared to the United States and the restricted availability of appropriate data, the focus was set on the US financial markets. The US market for government bonds is represented by the Salomon Brothers Treasury indices. We focus on the Salomon Brothers corporate indices as a mirror image of the corporate bond market.

Hence, bonds in contrast to stocks usually have a fixed maturity, their duration decreases with the course of time. Bonds with a shorter duration are less sensitive to changes in the capital markets reflected by interest rate changes. Applying historical bond data in the Markowitz optimization framework thus can lead to biased results. As the indices utilized here have an upper and lower maturity bound for the bonds included, the indexes' durations and maturities are almost constant. Thus, the bias in historical index returns caused by aging securities should be small and can be neglected.

All indices are performance indices and available divided into the four relevant maturity segments. For the simulations, the index figures from January 1980 to November 2002 are used on a monthly basis. The index figures were converted into returns. For reasons of simpler mathematical handling, continuous returns were taken as a basis. After the computation of returns, a total of 275 observation data were available (from February 1980 to November 2002) for every security group.

The risk of an investment in securities is often defined as the volatility of prices or returns. The return is measured here as the sum of coupon income and price gains. From an investor's viewpoint it would be advantageous to hold a portfolio of securities the returns of which correlate as little as possible. In real life investors therefore try to keep correlations between securities in their portfolios as low as possible. Correlations for the database from 6/80 to 11/02 are all positive. They range from 0.66 (Treasury 10 year+ and BBB 1–3 years) to 0.99 (A 3–7 years and AA 3–7 years).[2]

The risk of a security or a portfolio is, in the sense discussed above, usually measured by the volatility or synonymously by the standard deviation of its return. A graphic illustration is useful in an analysis of the risk/return relation. In Exhibit 27.1, the monthly average annualized returns (ordinate) and the corresponding volatilities (*abszissa*) of portfolios are depicted, formed by only one security group each.

Exhibit 27.1 clearly shows that in most cases government bonds earn lower returns with at least the same volatility as corporate bonds from the same maturity segment (e.g., for Treasury 1–3 years).[3] Generally, corporate bonds are thus "dominant" versus government bonds with

---

[2] Due to limitations of space, the correlations are not shown here in detail.

[3] Corporate bonds are less frequently traded than Treasury bonds. Thus stale prices can contribute to the lower volatility of corporates.

EXHIBIT 27.1 Return/Volatility Diagram of Security Groups from 1/80 to 11/02

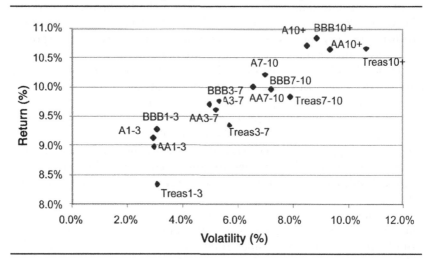

respect to their risk/return ratio. This becomes evident in the exhibit by the position of corporate bonds on the left side above government bonds.

A QUANTITATIVE APPROACH TO DETERMINE OPTIMAL BOND PORTFOLIOS

As a point of reference for the proportions of corporate and government bonds in the portfolio, historical data are analyzed. An *ex post* simulation examines how the risk/return relation of a mixed portfolio would have developed in the past. The (expected) return of a mixed portfolio is made up as follows:

$$r_p = r_1 w_1 + \ldots + r_i w_i + \ldots + r_n w_n$$

where r_i is the return of asset i in the period under review ($i = 1,\ldots,n$, $n =$ number of assets in the portfolio).

The sum of the weights

$$\sum_{i=1}^{n} w_i$$

is always 1.

In his seminal paper published in 1952, Harry Markowitz formulated the framework for portfolio optimization, which helps an investor to maximize his utility depending on expected return and expected risk of the portfolio.[4] The objective is to identify, on the basis of return and variance/covariance estimators, those portfolio weights that maximize the utility of the investor. The solutions for different investors depend on their individual risk preferences. In most cases, an investor achieves maximum utility when the return of his portfolio is maximal:

$$r_P \to \text{Max} \qquad (27.1)$$

When optimizing the return of the portfolio, risk has to be taken into account. Within a shortfall risk approach the portfolio is optimal that falls short of a user specified minimum return (e.g., $r_{min} = 0\%$) with a given shortfall probability p (e.g., 10%).[5] A very risk averse investor requires a higher minimum return and a lower shortfall probability than a less risk averse one.[6] Exhibit 27.2 displays this graphically in the risk/return diagram.

At point Q the capital is completely invested in the risk-free asset. Risk, measured by the standard deviation of expected returns, is 0%. The more risky assets are included in the portfolio, the higher its expected return and risk. This is described by the line QZ.

QS is the shortfall line and depicts expected return of portfolios along the line QZ that are equal or higher than the return of QS in $(1 - p)\%$ of all cases. Portfolio returns fall short of QS in $p\%$ of all cases. Portfolio P (corresponding with point P′ on the shortfall line QS) reaches a return of r_{min} in $(1 - p)\%$ of all cases and thereby complies with the investor's risk aversion. The optimal portfolio P maximizes return taking the investor's risk aversion into account. The following equation formalizes the investor's risk aversion. It is assumed that returns follow a normal distribution.

$$r_P + k \cdot \sigma_P/\sqrt{T} = r_{min} \qquad (27.2)$$

---

[4] Harry M. Markowitz: "Portfolio Selection," *Journal of Finance* 7 (1952), pp. 77–91.
[5] Martin L. Leibowitz and Roy D Henriksson, "Portfolio Optimization with Shortfall Constraints: A Confidence-Limit Approach to Managing Downside Risk," *Financial Analysts' Journal* (March–April 1989), pp. 34–41.
[6] Utilizing the shortfall risk framework an investor's risk aversion can be described more clearly than for example, with a utility function. A common utility function is $U = \lambda \times r_P - \sigma_P^2$ (William F. Sharpe, "A Simplified Model for Portfolio Analysis," *Management Science* 9 (1963), pp. 277–293). Here determination of the parameter λ, which measures the investor's risk aversion, is a problem.

EXHIBIT 27.2   Graphical Display of Shortfall Risk

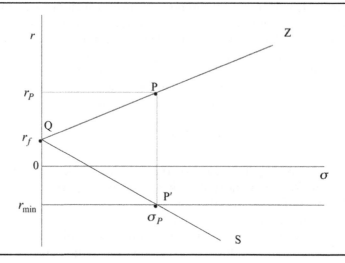

where σ_P is the risk (annualized volatility) of the portfolio, k is the inverse of the standard normal distribution at given shortfall probability p (e.g., $k = -1.28$ when $p = 10\%$), and T is the investment horizon in years.

Equation (27.2) describes a line with slope k starting from point Q in the risk/return diagram (Exhibit 27.2).[7] Maximization of the expected portfolio return in equation (27.1) in compliance with equation (27.2) exactly describes the investor's risk aversion. Additionally, the following collateral conditions are set:

1. $\displaystyle\sum_{i=1}^{n} w_i = 1$

2. $w_i \geq 0$ (no short selling and short positions allowed)

Further collateral conditions such as restrictions of portfolio restructuring may be set but are not considered here.

The minimum return r_{min} was set to 5%. This is approximately the average return on an investment in US bonds from 1871 to 1997.[8] Two different values for the shortfall probability p were investigated to mirror the portfolio compositions of investors with different risk tolerances (Exhibit 27.3).

---

[7] If the portfolio is completely invested in the risk-free asset, its expected return is r_f with an expected volatility of $\sigma_P = \sigma_f = 0$. This defines point Q. If more risk is accepted, the expected return r_P increases along with the expected volatility $\sigma_P > 0$.

[8] Jeremy Siegel, *Stocks for the Long Run* (New York, NY: McGraw Hill, 1998).

EXHIBIT 27.3 Values for the Required Minimum Return Depending on the Investor's Risk Tolerance

Risk Tolerance	p
Averse	1%
Aggressive	10%

A straightforward interpretation of the parameters r_{min} = 5% and p = 10% is that an investor with a moderate risk tolerance and a 10-year horizon, for example, would allow his bond portfolio on average to fall short of 5% in one of 10 years.

In order to answer the question what share should be taken up by corporate bonds in a portfolio, *ex post* simulations were run. The Markowitz approach of portfolio optimization is based on using expected returns. Since the question of determining the optimal fixed income portfolio is to be answered against the background of historical data, the return and variance/covariance estimators are replaced by their historical return means and variances/covariances respectively. These historical data are computed congruently to the relevant investment horizon. For a 3-year investment horizon, the return means and variances/covariances of assets are computed on the basis of 36 monthly returns. The same is, in analogy, done for a 5-year investment horizon on the basis of 60 monthly returns. Investment horizons of three, five, and 10 years are analyzed here. For the investment horizon of, for example, five years, the monthly data in the "time window" from February 1980 to January 1985 are used.

We then determined the "historically optimal" portfolio and the corresponding weights for the period from February 1980 to January 1985. In this way, the optimal portfolio in the sense of the target function described by equation (27.1) restricted by equation (27.2) from the viewpoint of an investor with a 5-year investment horizon is computed *ex post*. This is based on the assumption that the funds are invested in February 1980 according to the optimal portfolio weights to the 16 security groups and remain invested until the end of these five years (buy and hold strategy). At the end of the investment horizon, the portfolio is sold. This meant to represent the behavior of an investor with a 5-year investment horizon. Under risk/return aspects it might make sense to invest, for example, in 10-year paper despite an investment horizon of five years because the bonds will be sold before maturity after the end of the investment horizon has been reached.

After computing the optimal weights, the "time window" was shifted forward by one month and the calculations repeated with the data from March 1980 to February 1985 (so called "rolling approach"). This allows us to check the implications of various investment horizons of investors on the allocation of funds.

The database consists of 275 monthly data sets. For a 5-year investment horizon, 60 data sets are required for every rolling computation of the optimal portfolio. This means that 215 (= 275 − 60) rolling calculations must be run for the 5-year investment horizon (3 year: 239, 10 year: 155). Averaging the weights over all 215 (239, 155) rolling calculations gives an indication of the optimal allocation of funds in a bond portfolio for a 5-year horizon (3-year, 10-year horizon).

EMPIRICAL RESULTS

The weights of the optimal portfolios vary significantly over time due to phases of rising and falling interest rates and periods of rising and decreasing risk aversion (reflected in higher or lower spreads). By investigating a long period of more than 20 years, those effects can be expected to cancel out. As this study aims on giving a coarse guide on bond portfolio construction, averaging the optimal weights should give an indication for setting up a bond portfolio that performs best on average. To implement a bond portfolio, however, current market conditions should be taken into account. In the following, we refer to the average portfolio weights over each investment horizon: for the 5-year horizon, for example, the average weights over the 215 rolling calculations were computed.

Exhibit 27.4 shows the average portfolio weights (in percent) for different investment horizons and risk attitudes, divided into the rating segments AA, A, BBB, and T[9] (columns 2 to 5) or the term structure 1-3 year, 3–7 year, 7–10 year, and 10Y+ (columns 6 to 9). The sum of the weights in columns 2 to 5 is 100%, as well as the sum of columns 6 to 9. Rows 3 and 4 contain the optimal weights for the 3-year horizon, rows 6 and 7 those of the five year, and rows 9 and 10 those of the 10-year horizon.

The risk averse investor with an investment horizon of three years (row 3) allocates his capital according to the weights in 8% corporate bonds with AA rating, 15% in A, 70% in BBB, and 8% in Treasury bonds (columns 2 to 5). His optimal term structure consists of 52% bonds with a 1–3Y maturity, 6% with 3–7 year, 5% with a 7–10 year, and 37% with a 10 year+ maturity (row 3, columns 6 to 9).

---

[9] Treasury bonds are represented by the symbol "T."

EXHIBIT 27.4 Average Weights of the Optimized Portfolios Divided into Rating Segments and Term Structure (%)

	1	2	3	4	5	6	7	8	9
		Rating Segments				Term Structure			
1		AA	A	BBB	T	1–3 Year	3–7 Year	7–10 Year	10 Year+
2	3								
3	Averse	8	15	70	8	52	6	5	37
4	Aggressive	8	13	58	21	26	6	6	62
5	5								
6	Averse	7	14	71	8	38	4	6	52
7	Aggressive	3	9	64	24	6	5	8	81
8	10								
9	Averse	2	4	79	16	3	7	11	78
10	Aggressive	0	0	65	35	0	0	0	100

Surprisingly, the share of Treasury bonds increases with lower risk aversion (column 5). Conversely, corporates make up a higher portion of the portfolio the greater risk aversion is. This is due to the inferior risk/return characteristics of government bonds relative to corporates (Exhibit 27.1). For a 5-year horizon, for example, the risk averse portfolios consist of 71% BBB corporates, whereas this share declines to 64% for the aggressive investor (rows 6 and 7, column 4).

Focusing on the term structure of the optimal portfolios, the portion of longer maturities increases when risk aversion is reduced. The aggressive investor with a 10-year horizon, for example, invests the whole capital in 10-year+ maturities, the averse one only 78% (rows 9 and 10, column 9). According to investment horizon, the 3-year risk averse portfolios consist of 52% short-term maturities in the 1–3-year area (row 3, column 6). The aggressive style, on the other hand, allocates only 26% to this maturity bucket (row 4, column 6).

Exhibit 27.5 shows the average weights of the optimal portfolios in detail depending on both rating segment and term structure for the three investment horizons.

According to Exhibit 27.5, for example, the risk averse investor with a 3-year horizon allocates 4% of his capital to AA1–3-year corporates (row 3, column 2). The 3–7-year segment of this rating category is represented with 2% (row 3, column 3), whereas AA7–10-year is not included (row 3, column 4).

EXHIBIT 27.5 Average Weights of the Optimal Portfolios in Detail Depending on Rating Segment and Term Structure for the Three Investment Horizons (%)

	AA 1–3	AA 3–7	AA 7–10	AA 10+	A 1–3	A 3–5	A 7–10	A 10+	BBB 1–3	BBB 3–7	BBB 7–10	BBB 10+	T 1–3	T 3–7	T 7–10	T 10+
3																
Averse	4	2	0	1	8	0	0	7	39	4	5	22	0	0	0	8
Aggressive	3	4	0	1	5	0	0	8	19	2	6	32	0	0	0	21
5																
Averse	4	2	0	2	10	0	0	4	24	2	6	38	0	0	0	8
Aggressive	0	2	0	1	4	0	0	5	2	3		51	0	0	0	24
10																
Averse	1	0	0	0	2	2	0	0	0	5	11	62	0	0	0	16
Aggressive	0	0	0	0	0	0	0	0	0	0	0	65	0	0	0	35

Up to now, the focus has been set on the optimal allocation of funds and the determination of portfolio weights. An investor is certainly also interested in the economic performance of the optimal portfolios. For this reason, the cumulative returns of optimal portfolios are examined in congruency with the relevant investment horizon. The computation of returns is based on the average weights described above. For every point of time of the rolling procedure, the annualized cumulative returns were calculated with these average optimal weights, neglecting transaction costs. The return of the portfolio at time t is computed as follows:[10]

$$r_{P,t} = \sum_{i=1}^{n} w_i \times r_{i,t}$$

where n is the number of assets, $r_{i,t}$ is monthly return of asset i, and w_i is the average weight of the security group.

The annualized cumulative return (CR) of the portfolio over a period of M months is thus computed:

$$CR = \left[\prod_{t=1}^{M} (1 + r_{P,t}) \right]^{\frac{12}{M}} - 1$$

The upper part (rows 3 to 11) of Exhibit 27.6 displays descriptive statistics of the cumulative return for the three horizons 3, 5, and 10 years. All values are annualized. They can be used to study the performance of a buy-and-hold strategy.

The maximum CR of the aggressive investor with a 3-year horizon, for example, is 21.8% (row 3, column 4). A value of 19.4% in row 6, column 4 (quantile 95% for the aggressive investor) means that only 5% of the optimized portfolios realized a value higher than 19.4% in the 239 rolling calculations of the 3-year horizon. For the 10-year horizon and a risk averse attitude, the minimum CR was 7.2% per annum (row 4, column 7). The average CR for this investment horizon for the risk averse investor was 11.5% (row 9, column 7).

The lower part of Exhibit 27.6 (row 12 to 20) contains the same statistics with respect to the annualized monthly total returns (TR),

---

[10] The optimal portfolios were determined utilizing continuous returns, which were converted to discrete returns: $r_t^{\text{discrete}} = \exp(r_t^{\text{continuous}}) - 1$. Discrete returns are more familiar to investors and thus allow an easier interpretation. All return figures displayed in this chapter are discrete returns.

EXHIBIT 27.6 Descriptive Statistics for the Economic Performance of the Optimized Portfolios

	3 Year		5 Year		10 Year	
	Averse	Aggressive	Averse	Aggressive	Averse	Aggressive
CW						
Max.	20.3%	21.8%	21.0%	23.4%	16.7%	17.2%
Min.	4.8%	4.7%	5.5%	5.5%	7.2%	7.6%
Diff. max – min.	15.5%	17.2%	15.5%	17.9%	9.5%	9.6%
Quantile 95%	18.0%	19.4%	19.1%	20.7%	15.6%	16.0%
Quantile 5%	5.8%	5.5%	6.4%	6.7%	8.2%	8.5%
Diff. quantiles	12.2%	13.9%	12.7%	14.0%	7.4%	7.5%
Mean	10.7%	11.3%	11.0%	11.8%	11.5%	11.8%
Stdev	4.0%	4.4%	3.6%	4.0%	2.4%	2.5%
Mean/Stdev	2.6	2.6	3.0	2.9	4.8	4.8
TR mon.						
Max.	111.8%	132.3%	120.8%	144.5%	144.5%	153.8%
Min.	–47.5%	–69.1%	–60.5%	–85.2%	–86.4%	–92.4%
Diff. max – min.	159.3%	201.4%	181.3%	229.6%	230.9%	246.2%
Quantile 95%	36.1%	48.2%	41.8%	53.7%	50.8%	57.5%
Quantile 5%	–15.8%	–25.9%	–21.0%	–32.0%	–30.6%	–36.8%
Diff. quantiles	51.9%	74.1%	62.8%	85.7%	81.3%	94.2%
Mean	10.0%	10.5%	10.3%	10.9%	10.9%	11.1%
Stdev	5.2%	6.9%	6.1%	8.1%	8.0%	9.0%
Mean/Stdev	1.9	1.5	1.7	1.3	1.4	1.2

which represent the monthly return deviations of the three investment styles. The significant variability between, for example, the differences of the 95% quantile and the 5% quantile of CR and the monthly total returns (row 8 or 17) can be explained by the fact that the CR mirrors a buy-and-hold strategy over the investment horizon under review. High monthly deviations, which can be analyzed in more detail using the lower part of Exhibit 27.6 are equalized over the investment horizon of at least three years. This may be the reason why the relation Mean/Stdev. remains mostly constant for CR independent of the level of risk aversion (row 11). With increasing investment horizon the relation of return to risk for buy-and-hold investors is enhanced and remains mostly constant independent of the level of risk aversion (e.g., columns 7 and 8). The monthly deviations increase significantly for the total returns with decreasing risk aversion (compare the standard deviations of the monthly total returns in row 19, e.g., columns 5 and 6). Thus the relation Mean/Stdev. in the lower part of Exhibit 27.6 declines when risk aversion goes down (row 20).

A noteworthy fact is that fixed-income portfolios in times of economic prosperity in the United States, like at the beginning and mid-1980s, achieved impressive results. Note that all return figures displayed in this chapter are nominal values and apply for the US dollar area. In particular the beginning 1980s were characterized by high inflation rates and nominal yields. In the course of the 1990s, inflation and nominal rates dropped.

SUMMARY

In this chapter we addressed the question of what proportions corporate and government bonds of different credit quality and maturity segments an investor should hold in a fixed-income portfolio. Maximizing the risk/return relation according to the Markowitz approach is the core issue here. Optimal portfolio weights were established in *ex post* simulations.

For an investment horizon of at least three years it pays on average to include risk in the form of corporates in a bond portfolio: the optimized portfolios contained 58% to 79% corporates of the BBB segment. The A category was represented with portions between 0% and 15%, the AA corporates between 0 and 8%. Treasury bonds were weighted between 8% and 35%.

The term structure changed with investment horizon and varying risk attitude: the higher risk aversion, the greater the portion of corporates (due to their superior risk/return characteristics versus Treasuries in the past) and the shorter the maturities in the portfolios. With increasing investment horizon the relation of return to risk for buy and hold investors is enhanced and remains mostly constant independent of the level of risk aversion. Returns vary considerably, but the range of variability of returns decreases with an increasing investment horizon. The risk averse strategy with a 3-year (10-year) horizon, for example, allowed to achieve on average a nominal return of approximately 10.7% (11.5%) p.a. with an annual standard deviation of 4.0% (2.4%). However, these results are to be interpreted against the background of the US data used here and high inflation rates in the United States in the 1980s.

Although all simulations had to be run on the basis of data from the US dollar area due to missing relevant time series for the euro, at least a tendency can be derived for investments in Euro corporate bonds. An immediate implementation of the findings in this analysis does not appear to be reasonable. For example, an investment of 79% in BBB bonds, as suggested by the optimization method, seems to be unrealistic due to investment restrictions and aspects of risk diversification. Here, splitting up investments to other rating categories certainly makes sense. Since corporate bonds are less liquid in relation to government bonds it is advisable to invest always part of the portfolio in government bonds.

CHAPTER 28

Default and Recovery Rates in the Emerging European High-Yield Market

Mariarosa Verde
Managing Director
Fitch Ratings

The European high-yield market's early development will be forever marked by the disastrous aftermath of the new economy issuance boom of the late 1990s. The market's rapid rise and major stumble was deeply linked to aggressive and abundant underwriting in the telecommunication and cable sectors. In record time, the free-wheeling issuance rally produced unprecedented default rates. The meltdown in the telecommunication and cable sectors drove Europe's par-based, high-yield default rate to 8.9% on default volume of $4.2 billion in 2001 and to a gravity defying 24.1% on default volume of $16 billion in the first nine months of 2002 (see Exhibit 28.1). The US market, also severely impacted by the telecommunication debacle and by a deep decline in corporate credit quality, experienced its own difficulties in 2001 and 2002, producing default volume of $169 billion in the span of just 21 months, more than the total volume of defaults from 1980 through 2000.

While defaults reached astonishing new heights in the United States in 2001 and 2002, nonetheless, relative to the fledgling European market, the US market's troubles were preceded by a performance history dating back to the early 1980s. In contrast, the dollar volume of defaults in Europe, a market barely five years in the making, had in 2002

EXHIBIT 28.1 Summary Default Statistics for US and European High-Yield Markets: 2001 and First Nine Months of 2002

2001	United States	Europe
Default Volume (US$ billion)	$78.2	$4.2
Default Rate (%)	12.9%	8.9%
Defaulted Issuers	173	18
Par Weighted Average Recovery Rate (%)*	30	11
January–September 2002		
Default Volume (US$ billion)	$90.5	$16.0
Default Rate (%)	14.3%	24.1%
Defaulted Issuers	136	25
Par Weighted Average Recovery Rate (%)*	23	15

*The US weighted average recovery rate in 2001 excluding fallen angel defaults was 15% of par. For the nine month period ending September 2002, the US weighted average recovery rate excluding fallen angel defaults was 28% of par.

matched the default tally recorded in the United States during the 1990 recession. In 1990, though, the US market was approximately $200 billion in size, nearly four times larger than the 2002 European market and had a fairly established investor and issuer base. Consequently, the US default rate ended 1990 at just shy of 9%. Even lacking this benchmark, clearly the European default rate of 24.1% had reached an extraordinary level in 2002, causing many to question the market's direction and viability. Making matters worse, recovery rates on the first batch of high-yield defaults in Europe were extremely low by US historical standards, further magnifying losses for investors in the nascent market.

Despite this challenging start, by 2002 numerous developments had unfolded in Europe which strongly suggested that the market's long-term growth potential remained in tact notwithstanding the 2001 and 2002 default storm. The most profound changes included the adoption of the euro and the formation of a European central bank. By facilitating the development of a true common market, these developments were expected to promote and accelerate cross-border mergers, acquisitions, and other corporate finance activities aimed at boosting growth and profitability for European corporations. Further, borrowers were beginning to shift the financing of such activities away from banks and toward the capital markets, a sign that capital market instruments would likely flourish in Europe in the next decade.

Given this new landscape, in 2001, Fitch Ratings created a par based default index specific to the European high-yield market. The objective of this chapter is to compare and contrast default and recovery patterns across the two markets in order to give global bond investors and European investors, in particular, historical and current benchmarks for measuring credit risk.

CHARACTERISTICS OF HIGH-YIELD DEFAULTS IN EUROPE 2001–2002

The following characterized high-yield defaults in Europe for 2001 and 2002.

▪ The European market's deep concentration in the struggling telecommunication and cable sectors was the overwhelming catalyst behind the surge in defaults. Telecommunication and cable represented 77% and 91% of default volume in 2001 and 2002, respectively. The two had such a disproportionate impact on default statistics that excluding the two sectors, the default rate would have ended the third quarter of 2002 at just 4.2% compared to the all-in rate of 24.1%.
▪ Due to a combination of aggressive underwriting in the late 1990s, a meltdown in the telecommunication sector, a record number of fallen angel defaults, and a recession in manufacturing, defaults in the United States also soared in 2001 and 2002. The US default rate ended 2001 at 12.9% and the third quarter of 2002 at 14.3%, both unprecedented levels. The average annual default rate in the United States for the period 1980 through 2000 was just 3.4%, with a peak of 8.7% recorded in 1990.
▪ The average time to default in Europe was a very brief 2.1 and 2.5 years in 2001 and 2002, respectively. This statistic was substantially lower than the US average of approximately 3.4 and 4.9 years in 2001 and 2002, excluding fallen angel defaults. Europe's accelerated time to default was a result of the aggressive 1999 and 2000 new issuance rating mix.
▪ Defaults in Europe showed a high degree of correlation to ratings. Approximately 80% of bonds sold in Europe from 1998 through 2000 carried ratings of B or lower.
▪ High-yield defaults in Europe in both 2001 and 2002 produced weighted average recovery rates significantly below US historical averages. Investors recovered just 11% of par value on 2001 defaults and 15% of par on 2002 defaults. In the United States, recovery rates on

defaulted bonds had historically averaged approximately 40% of par but also fell dramatically in 2001 for seasoned high-yield defaults. The US rates rebounded in 2002 while European recovery rates remained low. The default concentration in telecommunication and cable was the key reason for the low recovery rates in Europe.

■ The development of an active secondary market allowed for a mark-to-market analysis of defaults. Similar to the US experience, defaulted issues in Europe were already trading at deep discounts at the beginning of 2002. The average price of 2002 defaulted issues was just 32% of par on December 31, 2001, suggesting that investors absorbed the bulk of par losses on the year's defaults before the year got underway.

■ Following the telecommunication and cable debacles, new issuance fell dramatically in Europe but was more diverse and of better quality. Despite high defaults, the market continued to grow thanks to deteriorating investment-grade credits joining the universe of high-yield bonds.

METHODOLOGY UNDERLYING FITCH'S PAR BASED EUROPEAN HIGH-YIELD DEFAULT INDEX

In 2001, Fitch Ratings launched a default index dedicated to the emerging European high-yield bond market. The index is a par based index and was created using the same methodology Fitch employs for its US high-yield default series (see Exhibit 28.2). In particular, in order to

EXHIBIT 28.2 Parameters of Fitch's European High-Yield Default Index

---

■ Based on noninvestment grade (composite rating of BB+ and below, rated by Fitch or one of the other two major rating agencies), nonconvertible Eurobonds.

■ Eurobonds not denominated in US dollars are converted to their US dollar equivalent using the exchange rate on the day the bonds are priced. Fitch's universe and default calculations are not impacted by exchange rate fluctuations beyond this date.

■ Issuers are considered to have defaulted after passing a 30-day grace period unless there is a bankruptcy filing, in which case defaults are immediate.

■ Defaults include distressed exchanges, where bond investors are offered securities with diminished structural or economic terms compared to existing bonds.

■ Default rates are calculated by dividing the par value of defaulted debt by the average market or sector par value for the period under observation.

Sources: Fitch, Bloomberg, High-Yield Advantage.

compare trends across the two markets, Fitch converts all Eurobond issues regardless of currency to a US dollar equivalent and calculates default rates based on outstanding par or face value. Fitch does not include convertible bonds in its market or default rate series. Defaults are defined as missed interest or principal payments and distressed exchanges. The latter refers to instances where bond investors are offered securities with diminished structural or economic terms compared to existing bonds. Default rates are calculated by dividing the par value of the defaulted bonds by the average par value of the market or specific industry sector for the period under observation. Fitch includes fallen angels (companies downgraded from investment grade to non-investment grade) in its market and default rate calculations. Fitch also includes high-yield Eurobonds sold by companies domiciled outside of Europe. As of September 30, 2002, for example, approximately 17% of the European high-yield market consisted of non-European company bond obligations, with companies domiciled in North America representing 14% of market volume.

THE EUROPEAN HIGH-YIELD MARKET'S EARLY DEVELOPMENT

At $52 billion in size as of September 30, 2002, the European market was just a fraction of the US market ($563 billion), but despite defaults, it had experienced dynamic growth, growing from essentially negligible levels in 1997. New issuance of speculative-grade bonds in Europe began in earnest in 1998, with the bulk, approximately $27 billion, sold in 1999 and 2000. This late 1990s issuance activity was overwhelmingly concentrated in the capital hungry telecommunication and cable sectors, a factor which had huge negative consequences for the market in 2001 and 2002.

The new economy issuance boom was certainly not unique to Europe. In fact, it really took off in the United States beginning in 1997 when the confluence of the deregulation of the telecommunication industry, soaring equity prices, and a permissive debt market allowed telecommunication start-ups to raise over $100 billion in the US high-yield market alone. At its peak, the sector had grown to more than 20% of the US market, an unusually high industry concentration by historical standards. The average credit quality of these deals on both sides of the Atlantic was fairly low. For example, in Europe, where two-thirds of new issuance consisted of telecommunication and cable bonds, approximately 80% of the bonds were initially rated single B or lower. This low quality was really a product of the nature of the businesses being financed—essentially startup ventures predicated on the hopes that the businesses, once operational, would quickly generate enough cash flow to service the piles of debt accumulated to build and expand networks.

Aggressive underwriting in the United States from 1997–1999 permeated nearly all high-yield industries to some degree, but the average quality of bonds sold during the three years was nonetheless higher than that of the collection of bonds sold in Europe. The main reason for this was that telecommunication issuance made up a relatively smaller portion of overall issuance in the more diversified US market. Approximately 60% of bonds sold in the United States from 1997–1999 were rated single B or lower, but within telecommunication, the rating mix more closely resembled the European mix.

In its early development, therefore, the European market really adopted the most aggressive characteristics of the US market—a deep concentration in just two sectors and in the lowest rated and most speculative bonds. As described below, the specific features of 2001 and 2002 defaults, including time to default and average recovery rates, further bear this out. The industry concentration factor is especially worthy of historical comparison. While the US market did have some early industry concentrations in metals and mining, utilities, and energy in the early 1980s, these were mostly due to fallen angels (companies downgraded from investment-grade to noninvestment grade).

By 1990, when the US market had grown from $14 billion at the beginning of the decade to $200 billion, no single industry made up more than 6% of all outstanding volume. (Fitch categorizes the market into 25 sectors.) In fact, other than the early 1980s and late 1990s, no two industries in any year ever made up more than 20% of total outstanding volume in the United States. Therefore, even in the mature US market, the 20% peak concentration in telecommunication in the late 1990s was an unusual occurrence. By 2002, in just less than two years, the near total meltdown in the sector had produced $78 billion in defaults in the United States. As a result, telecommunication's share of the US market had fallen to 14.8% from a high of 20% (see Exhibit 28.3).

The demise of growth expectations in telecommunication and cable not only led to numerous bankruptcies and restructurings, but also resulted in a material slowdown in issuance in the two sectors in 2001 and 2002. In Europe, the two industries dominated new issuance in 1999 and 2000, representing approximately two-thirds of newly minted bonds, but issuance in the two sectors made up just 15% of new bond sales in 2001 and 2002. Overall, lacking a major driver and in the face of a sluggish economy, new issuance fell substantially in Europe in 2001 and 2002 to less than half 1999 and 2000 levels. Nonetheless the high-yield market continued to grow thanks in large part to credit deterioration in the investment-grade sector. Despite a nine month default tally of $16 billion, the market expanded in size as a result of fallen angels such as Alcatel and Ericcson joining the universe of high-yield bonds. Fallen angels had several positive effects on the European market. First, they filled an issuance void and thereby provided badly needed investment product to high-yield investors and secondly, they improved the overall credit quality of the market by boosting the concentration of BB rated bonds.

EXHIBIT 28.3 Industry Mix as of September 2002 in the Two Markets

European High-Yield Market	Par Value Outstanding at 30/9/02	Percent
Telecommunication	19.2	36.8%
Industrial/manufacturing	4.2	8.0%
Utilities	3.3	6.3%
Chemical	3.2	6.2%
Paper and forest products	2.4	4.6%
Cable	2.3	4.3%
Energy	2.0	3.9%
Computers and electronics	2.0	3.9%
Banking and finance	1.9	3.7%
Transportation	1.4	2.7%
Automotive	1.1	2.2%
Food, beverage, and tobacco	1.1	2.1%
Building and materials	1.0	1.9%
Broadcasting and media	0.9	1.7%
Healthcare and pharmaceutical	0.8	1.6%
Insurance	0.8	1.5%
Consumer products	0.5	1.0%
Metals and mining	0.5	0.9%
Retail	0.4	0.8%
Gaming, lodging, and restaurants	0.4	0.8%
Real estate	0.4	0.7%
Textiles and furniture	0.4	0.7%
Supermarkets and drug stores	0.2	0.4%
Other	1.6	3.2%
	52.2	100.0%

EXHIBIT 28.3 (Continued)

US High-Yield Market	Par Value Outstanding at 30/9/02	Percent
Telecommunication	83.6	14.8%
Energy	46.6	8.3%
Utilities	38.6	6.9%
Gaming, lodging, and restaurants	36.3	6.4%
Broadcasting and media	38.9	6.9%
Healthcare and pharmaceutical	24.2	4.3%
Cable	23.3	4.1%
Banking and finance	22.0	3.9%
Chemical	21.8	3.9%
Industrial/manufacturing	21.8	3.9%
Paper and forest products	20.4	3.6%
Retail	19.6	3.5%
Transportation	21.7	3.9%
Computers and electronics	17.9	3.2%
Building and materials	16.7	3.0%
Food, beverage, and tobacco	13.1	2.3%
Automotive	12.6	2.2%
Metals and mining	11.9	2.1%
Leisure and entertainment	8.3	1.5%
Real estate	8.1	1.4%
Consumer products	7.9	1.4%
Textiles and furniture	7.7	1.4%
Supermarkets and drug stores	5.7	1.0%
Other	34.4	6.1%
	563.1	100.0%

Excluding fallen angels, the remainder of new issuance outside of telecommunication and cable was quite diverse and generally of better quality—that is, more highly rated, than past issuance. New bond sales in 2001 and 2002 spanned industrial, financial and consumer related sectors. The ability of European companies in diverse industries to successfully sell high-yield bonds shows that the market had gained a certain measure of acceptance and legitimacy despite the problems plaguing telecommunication and cable. Further, a deeper industry mix had the added benefit of allowing investors to build a more diversified bond portfolio, a necessary feature in terms of minimizing default risk.

The speed and magnitude of defaults in Europe in 2001 and 2002 quickly turned the market's direction to risk aversion but its long-term prospects remained firmly positive. In particular, the need for growth capital by noninvestment grade borrowers, especially in an era of globalization and cross-border transactions, and the desire by European banks to limit exposure to these riskier names all pointed to greater demand for speculative-grade bonds. In fact, similar trends had advanced the US market's growth in the 1980s and 1990s. The adoption of the euro and the formation of a European Central Bank, by creating a true common market and facilitating financial transactions, further enhanced the market's continuity.

Additional developments also suggested that capital market instruments such as high-yield bonds would proliferate in Europe in the coming decade. A potential boon for the speculative-grade bond market included the new framework for assessing bank regulatory capital proposed by the Basel Committee. Under the new accord, banks would be required to set aside significantly higher capital levels for loans to lower rated borrowers. Banks would likely adapt to the new guidelines by either increasing the interest rates they charged these borrowers or by simply reducing concentrations in these credits. In the latter case, the bond market, the closest alternative source of debt financing, would naturally benefit. In fact, even if banks simply raised interest rates to compensate for their higher capital costs, such a move would also make the bond market a relatively more attractive source of capital for borrowers. Additionally, the growing number of institutional investors in Europe seeking a high-yielding investment product was also expected to boost demand for speculative grade bonds.

DEFAULTS BALLOON FOLLOWING SURGE IN LOW QUALITY ISSUANCE

Although the European high-yield market did experience a number of small defaults prior to 2001, 2001, and 2002 proved to be defining years in terms of testing the market's resiliency in the face of such extraordinarily high defaults so soon in its development. After producing a year-end default rate of 8.9%, a level comparable to the previous default peaks in the United States during the recession of 1990–1991, the European high-yield default rate zoomed to 24.1% in the nine months ending 31 September 2002. In fact, the dollar volume of Eurobond defaults through September 2002 of $16 billion nearly matched the US annual default volumes of 1990 and 1991, each year producing approximately $17 billion in defaults. To put the European experience in perspective, annual default volume of $17 billion was considered quite excessive in the early 1990s relative to the then US market's size of

EXHIBIT 28.4   Industry Distribution of European High-Yield Default Volume, 2001 and 2002

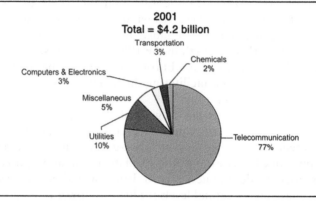

2001
Total = $4.2 billion

Transportation 3%
Chemicals 2%
Computers & Electronics 3%
Miscellaneous 5%
Utilities 10%
Telecommunication 77%

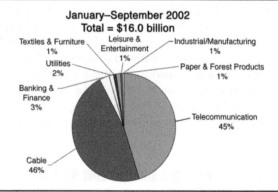

January–September 2002
Total = $16.0 billion

Textiles & Furniture 1%
Leisure & Entertainment 1%
Industrial/Manufacturing 1%
Utilities 2%
Paper & Forest Products 1%
Banking & Finance 3%
Telecommunication 45%
Cable 46%

approximately $200 billion. The US high-yield market was four times larger than the 2002 European market and furthermore had been around for at least a decade before the default storm hit in 1990.

As noted above, the aggressive industry composition and rating mix of deals that made up the European market's early years was the source of its deep troubles in 2001 and 2002. Approximately 77% and 91% of default volume in 2001 and 2002, respectively, came from the telecommunication and cable sectors (see Exhibit 28.4). The two made up such a disproportionate share of defaults, that the default rate through September 2002 would have been 4.2% excluding the two rather than 24.1%. Not to be ignored, defaults in the United States also reached new heights in 2001 and 2002. The US default rate hit 12.9% on default volume of $78.2 billion in 2001, only to be topped in 2002 with a default tally of $90.5 billion and a new record default rate of 14.3% for the first nine months of the year.

Much of what ailed the US market in 2001 and 2002 was also the inevitable outcome of loose credit conditions beginning in 1997 through 1999 and above all, the large exposure to startup telecommunication ventures. New issuance of high-yield bonds exceeded $300 billion during the three-year bull rally in the United States, essentially doubling the market's size but also lowering its overall credit quality since the majority of newly minted bonds carried ratings of single B or lower. Telecommunication issuance was especially robust in the United States, at approximately $100 billion. When the economy and credit conditions began to sour in 2000, and it became apparent that the issuance boom in telecommunication had contributed to overcapacity, many of the companies that had tapped the debt markets so freely in 1997 through 1999 began to experience significant stress. Overcapacity had diminished pricing power and the telecommunication business model could no longer support the excessive debt balances accumulated to build and expand networks. As a result, telecommunication defaults made up a third of total defaults in the United States in 2001 and more than half of defaults through the third quarter of 2002.

A similar situation unfolded in Europe, with overcapacity leading to a collapse in pricing power for the vast majority of highly levered telecommunication and cable startups. The US market was further disrupted in 2001 and 2002 by the domestic recession in manufacturing which led to numerous defaults in basic industries such as metals and mining and chemicals. In addition to this, the US market was hit by a record number of fallen angel defaults, including the now infamous Enron and WorldCom scandals. In fact, as noted in the list of European defaults in Exhibit 28.5, these defaults also affected the European market since the likes of Enron, WorldCom and others raised substantial debt capital in the Eurobond market. In fact, in 2001 and 2002, the default mix in Europe included a number of North American companies such as Winstar, Viatel, PSINet, and 360Networks.

Defaults in 2001 and 2002 both in the United States and in Europe will be remembered not only for the long list of troubled companies but also for the enormous debt balances affected by the defaults. There is little doubt that the two years marked the worst credit environment in the modern history of the corporate bond market, including the early 1990s recession in the United States, simply because the scale of the defaults was unprecedented. In the United States, the volume of defaults in 2001 and through September 2002 reached $169 billion, higher than the entire volume of high-yield defaults from 1980 through 2000 (see Exhibit 28.6). To put the size factor in perspective, in the United States the number of issuer defaults increased 50% in 2001 (from 115 in 2000 to 173), but the volume of debt affected by the defaults nearly tripled from $27.9 billion in 2000 to $78.2 billion in 2001. The trend was further magnified in 2002. The number of

EXHIBIT 28.5 List of All European Defaults 2001 and 2002

2001 Issuer	Par Value Outstanding (US$, 000)	Default Month	Default Source	Fitch Industry
Global Telesystems Inc. (Esprit)	384,585	January/01	Missed Interest Payment	Telecommunication
RSL Communications Plc.	261,488	March/01	File Chapter 11 (Court Protection)	Telecommunication
Winstar Communications	192,900	April/01	File Chapter 11	Telecommunication
Cammell Laird Holdings	108,525	May/01	Missed Interest Payment	Transportation
PSINet Inc.	305,685	May/01	File Chapter 11	Telecommunication
Viatel Inc.	291,523	May/01	File Chapter 11	Telecommunication
360Networks Inc	187,520	June/01	File Chapter 11 (CCAA)	Telecommunication
Derby Cycle Corporation	142	June/01	Missed Interest Payment	Consumer products
Global Telesystems Europe	514,850	June/01	Missed Interest Payment	Telecommunication
Dolphin Telecom Plc.	276,318	July/01	File Chapter 11 (Court Protection)	Telecommunication
Brunner Mond Group Plc.	80,405	August/01	Missed Interest Payment	Chemical
Enitel Asa	234,744	August/01	File Chapter 11 (Court Protection)	Telecommunication
Global Telesystems Europe (Hermes Euro Rail)	93,229	August/01	Missed Interest Payment	Telecommunication
Exodus Communications	182,240	September/01	File Chapter 11	Telecommunication
Atlantic Telecom Grp. Plc.	320,523	October/01	Administration	Telecommunication
Polestar Corp. Plc.	228,410	October/01	Capital Restructuring	Miscellaneous
Brokat AG	121,288	November/01	File Chapter 11 (Court Protection)	Computers & electronics
Enron Corp.	432,320	December/01	File Chapter 11	Utilities
	4,216,694			

860

EXHIBIT 28.5 (Continued)

2002 Issuer	Par Value Outstanding (US$, 000)	Default Month	Default Source	Fitch Industry
Clubhaus Plc.	97,218	January/02	Missed Interest Payment	Leisure & entertainment
Netia Holdings II BV	415,704	January/02	Missed Interest Payment	Telecommunication
Carrier1 Intl. SA	255,897	February/02	File Chapter 11 (Court Protection)	Telecommunication
Citra Marga Finance BV	125,000	March/02	Missed Interest Payment	Banking & finance
United Pan-Europe Communication	4,504,948	March/02	Missed Interest Payment	Cable
Energis Plc.	877,535	April/02	Missed Interest Payment	Telecommunication
Flag Telecom Holding Ltd.	289,320	April/02	Missed Interest Payment	Telecommunication
Grapes Communications NV	177,820	April/02	File Chapter 11	Telecommunication
IFCO Systems NV	192,060	April/02	Missed Interest Payment	Paper & forest products
Telecom Argentina	1,342,761	April/02	Principal Impairment	Telecommunication
Completel Europe NV	116,780	May/02	File Chapter 11 (Court Protection)	Telecommunication
Diamond Holdings Plc.	220,428	May/02	Missed Interest Payment	Cable
Kpnqwest BV	834,258	May/02	File Chapter 11 (Court Protection)	Telecommunication
Metrogas SA	94,556	May/02	Missed Interest Payment	Utilities
Metromedia Fiber Network	257,875	May/02	File Chapter 11	Telecommunication
NTL Communications Corp.	1,641,708	May/02	Missed Interest Payment	Cable
NTL Inc.	2,145	May/02	Missed Interest Payment	Cable
Azurix Corp.	147,870	June/02	Distressed Exchange	Utilities
Versatel Telecom NV	417,684	June/02	File Chapter 11 (Court Protection)	Telecommunication
Callahan Nordrhein	1,196,368	July/02	File Chapter 11 (Insolvency)	Cable
SWT Finance BV	94,320	July/02	Missed Interest Payment	Industrial/manufacturing
Worldcom Inc.	1,816,075	July/02	File Chapter 11	Telecommunication
BCO Hipotecario SA	335,748	September/02	Missed Interest Payment	Banking & finance
Song Networks NV	422,604	September/02	Missed Interest Payment	Telecommunication
Texon International Plc.	136,887	September/02	Missed Interest Payment	Textiles & furniture
	16,013,567			

EXHIBIT 28.6 US High-Yield Default Rates and Volume, 1980–2002

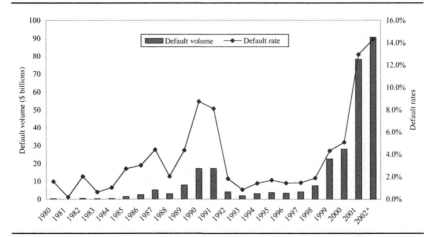

[a] Not annualized, through September. The 2001 default rate excluding fallen angels was 9.7%. The September 2002 year to date default rate excluding fallen angels was 11%.

EXHIBIT 28.7 Issuer and Volume Trends for Europe, 2001–Q3 2002

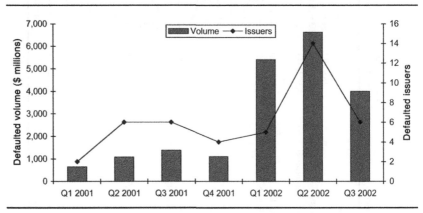

US issuer defaults totaled 136 through the third quarter of 2002, 21% less than the full year 2001 count of 173, but default volume for the nine-month period was 15% higher than full-year 2001 default volume.

In Europe, the number of issuer defaults increased approximately 40% from 18 for full-year 2001 to 25 through the third quarter of 2002, but default volume exploded, quadrupling from $4.2 billion to $16 billion (see Exhibit 28.7). Although the fallen angel phenomenon did have a material influence on the volume tallies, the more significant variable affecting the volume expansion was the role of the telecommunication and cable defaults. In the United States, for example, telecommunication companies carried average bond balances of $640 million upon default, while issuers in other high-yield sectors carried average balances of $216 million upon default. European defaults shared the same pattern. The largest European defaults in 2001 and 2002 included cable operators United Pan Europe Communications and NTL Communications. The two combined represented 40% of the default tally through September 2002. As noted earlier, telecommunication and cable defaults made up 77% and 91% of default volume in Europe in 2001 and 2002 and approximately two thirds of the defaulted issuer counts for the two years.

INDUSTRY DEFAULT RATES MAKE A STRONG CASE FOR DIVERSIFICATION

Cable and telecommunication had such a disproportionate impact on the default statistics in Europe, particularly in 2002, that excluding the two sectors, the default rate for the remainder of the European high-yield market would have been 4.2% through the third quarter of 2002 rather than 24.1%. In fact, the year to date default rate for the two sectors combined was 40% through the third quarter of 2002. Fitch's analysis of industry default rates has revealed that the magnitude of dispersion in default risk across industries is surprisingly high. The data make a strong case for the benefits of diversification which was not truly available to European high-yield investors in the market's early years. For example, from 1980–2000, Fitch calculated an average annual market default rate of 3.4% for the US high-yield market but industry default rates ranged from a high of 8.2% for supermarkets and drug stores to 0.2% for cable (see Exhibit 28.8). Since these are long-term averages, they suggest that some industries are in fact more susceptible to default. While it is true that industries are always evolving, telecommunication being a great example of this, a closer scrutiny of sectors with high historical default rates can provide critical information regarding which variables contributed to high defaults.

In the short-term, industry default rates are also valuable by highlighting pockets of weakness in the broader market. For example, investors with material exposures to the telecommunication sector either in the United States or in Europe experienced severe losses in 2001 and 2002. For the nine-month period ending September 2002, the European telecommunication sector produced a default rate of 30%. The US rate for the sector was 38.5%. Furthermore, the weighted average recovery

EXHIBIT 28.8 Long-Term Industry Default Rates in the United States, 1980–2000

Supermarkets and drug stores	8.2%
Building and materials	7.5
Textiles and furniture	7.1
Retail	6.8
Leisure and entertainment	5.7
Insurance	5.6
Transportation	5.3
Food, beverage, and tobacco	4.2
Banking and finance	4.2
Health care and pharmaceutical	4.1
Energy	4.1
Metals and mining	3.5
Computers and electronics	3.5
Consumer products	3.2
Telecommunications	3.2
Real Estate	3.0
Gaming, lodging, and restaurants	2.9
Miscellaneous	2.9
Industrial/manufacturing	1.7
Chemicals	1.5
Broadcasting and media	1.4
Paper and forest products	1.1
Utilities	1.0
Automobiles	0.9
Cable	0.2
Average annual market default rate	3.4

rates on these defaulted issues on both sides of the Atlantic were clustered in the high-single digits or teens, very low by historical standards. Investors in this sector saw the par value of their bonds evaporate.

AGGRESSIVE RATING MIX EQUALS ACCELERATED TIME TO DEFAULT

In addition to the default rate rising to exceptionally high levels, other characteristics of the first batch of European high-yield defaults reveal the aggressive nature of the market's early years. Fitch observed that the average time to default (length of time in years from issuance to default) in Europe was just 2.1 years in 2001 and 2.5 years in 2002. Exhibit 28.9 shows the distribution of defaulted bonds by issue year. In the United States, this statistic averaged 3.4 years in 2001 and 4.9 years in 2002 (excluding fallen angel defaults). Kmart's heavy issuance in the early 1990s somewhat distorted the 2002 figure. Excluding Kmart's defaulted issues, the September 2002 average time to default in the United States was 4.1 years. The accelerated time to default in Europe is not surprising since the market experienced defaults so soon following record issuance, but what it shows is the vivid contrast to the US experience.

It is only in the late 1990s that time to default contracted to an average of approximately three years in the United States. In the 1980s and up to the mid 1990s, time to default was significantly longer, averaging consistently more than four years. The erosion in this credit statistic in the U.S provides the strongest evidence that the average credit quality of deals brought to market in the United States beginning in 1997, during a time of record issuance and soaring equity prices, was clearly worse than other periods, and the bonds sold in Europe shared this aggressive profile. Of the total par defaults in the United States beginning in 2000 through September 2002, 70% consisted of bonds sold from 1997 through 1999. In fact, Fitch estimated that close to 40% of bonds sold in the US market from 1997 through 1999 had defaulted by September 2002.

EXHIBIT 28.9 Vintage Distribution of Defaulted High-Yield Bonds Excluding Fallen Angel
United States 2001

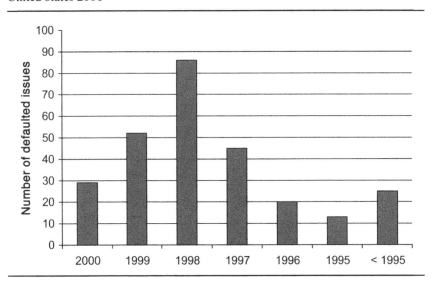

EXHIBIT 28.9 (Continued)
United States, January–September 2002[a]

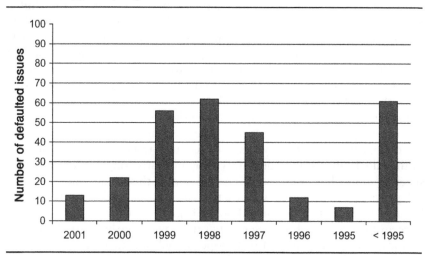

[a] Approximately 60% of defaulted bonds issued prior to 1995 belonged to Kmart

Europe 2001

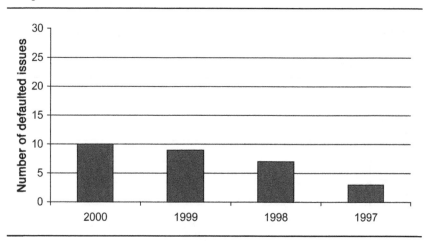

EXHIBIT 28.9   (Continued)
Europe, January–September 2002

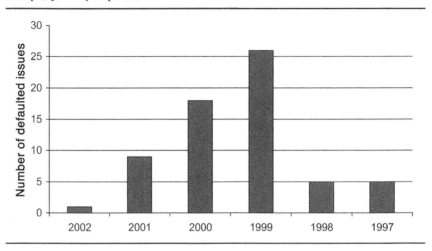

Time-to-default data demonstrate that credit quality at issuance is an important variable, not only in terms of predicting future default activity, but also in terms of anticipating the probable timing of such defaults. It is well known that default probability increases exponentially with each successively lower rating, but the speed at which ratings deteriorate and issuers default also accelerates. For example, Fitch observed that for the batch of 2001 US defaults, the time to default or, as noted above, the number of years from original issuance to default, increased significantly when the defaulted issues were arranged according to their ratings at issuance, from lowest to highest. Bonds originally rated B on average defaulted three years following issuance, compared with four years and seven years for bonds rated BB and BBB, respectively. In other words, the consistent decline in time to default in the United States in the late 1990s was a direct consequence of the aggressive new issuance rating mix. The European market, therefore, with its deeper concentration of credits rated B and below, suffered even faster defaults.

LOW RECOVERY RATES COMPOUND LOSSES IN A HIGH DEFAULT ENVIRONMENT

Obviously the most interesting part of the default equation is the actual dollar losses associated with the defaults. Consistent with all other measures, recovery rates in Europe were also significantly lower than those recorded historically in the United States, although within telecommunication they were essentially the same (see Exhibit 28.10). The concentration of telecommunication and cable defaults in Europe resulted in the market's weighted average recovery rate (weighted by defaulted par amount) to total just 11% of par in 2001 and 15% of par in 2002. This translates into a loss of approximately $17 billion on the aggregate $20.2 billion in par value defaults in Europe over the 21-month period ending

EXHIBIT 28.10   Weighted Average Recovery Rates by Industry

US High-Yield[a]

2001	Percent of Par	January–September 2002	Percent of Par
Cable	53.4%	Paper and forest products	88.2%
Transportation	31.3%	Gaming, lodging, and restaurant	78.8%
Food, beverage, and tobacco	30.9%	Energy	65.0%
Chemical	29.4%	Leisure and entertainment	59.8%
Consumer products	24.7%	Retail	48.5%
Broadcasting and media	22.3%	Cable	41.1%
Supermarkets and drug stores	21.9%	Metals and mining	36.9%
Healthcare and pharmaceutical	18.6%	Broadcasting and media	36.3%
Industrial/manufacturing	16.2%	Industrial/manufacturing	32.0%
Gaming, lodging, and restaurant	15.8%	Transportation	31.3%
Computers and electronics	13.5%	Food, beverage, and tobacco	29.8%
Automotive	12.0%	Textiles and furniture	27.6%
Metals and mining	11.6%	Automotive	22.1%
Telecommunication	11.5%	Chemical	19.0%
Textiles and furniture	11.3%	Building and materials	15.3%
Leisure and entertainment	11.0%	Computers and electronics	14.5%
Building and materials	10.7%	Telecommunication	13.7%
Retail	7.4%	Consumer products	13.3%

Europe High-Yield[a]

2001	Percent of Par	January–September 2002	Percent of Par
Telecommunication	7.7%	Cable	15.2%
Other sectors	16.0%	Telecommunication	11.9%
		Other sectors	42.9%

[a] Excludes fallen angel defaults. Based on bond prices one month following default. Prices provided by High-Yield Advantage.

September 2002. Hence, investors lost approximately 86% of par value on 2001 and 2002 defaults. In the United States, the weighted average recovery rates were 30% of par in 2001 and 23% of par in 2002. Excluding fallen angel defaults though, which in 2001 boosted average recovery rates and in 2002 depressed recovery rates, US recovery rates were just 15% of par in 2001 and had improved to 28% of par in 2002.

What is noteworthy is that the recovery rates for telecommunication defaults were nearly parallel in the two markets. They averaged 11.5% and 13.7% of par in the United States in 2001 and 2002, respectively, and 8% and 12% of par in Europe. Since the cable sector in Europe shared many of the same characteristics of the beleaguered telecommunication sector, the average recovery rate on defaulted cable bonds in Europe was also low at 15% of par. (In contrast, recovery rates on cable bonds in the United States were 53% and 41% in 2001 and 2002, respectively.) Considering that the overwhelming volume of defaults in Europe came from the two sectors, it is therefore apparent that the primary reason for the low recovery rates in Europe was this industry concentration.

An additional disclaimer with regard to the low recovery rates in Europe also had to do once again with bad timing. As illustrated by the US 15% recovery rate on 2001 original issue high-yield defaults, an unfortunate combination during periods of severe credit stress is that not only do defaults balloon but recovery rates typically plummet. In essence, investors are hit with a one-two punch. The reason for the low recovery rates in periods of high defaults has to do with both fundamental and technical factors. First, all the variables that drive up default rates such as lower demand for goods and services, shrinking margins, a difficult funding environment, and the like also depress company valuations thereby driving down the recoverable value of company debt. (This was especially the case in this latest round of defaults since companies took on excessive debt balances in the late 1990s based on overly optimistic revenue projections.) In addition to this, periods of high defaults also create an oversupply of distressed paper and, until distressed investors actively seek out opportunities to buy the debt, recovery rates generally languish at low levels.

Fitch used the market prices of defaulted bonds one month after default as a proxy for recovery value. The growth of a secondary market for European high-yield bonds made this analysis possible but ultimately the various bankruptcy jurisdictions in Europe will determine how bondholders will fare. The outcome of these filings will be very meaningful for the development of the market going forward because each country has its own bankruptcy laws and not all are favorable to bondholders. Some jurisdictions, such as France for example, strongly favor the borrower over creditors. Others, such as the United Kingdom, heavily support the rights of senior-secured lenders over unsecured bondholders. Uncertainty regarding bankruptcy outcomes is further exacerbated by the fact that in most cases high-yield bonds in Europe are not only contractually but structurally subordinate to senior secured loans, meaning they are typically issued by a holding company, while bank loans are held at the asset-rich, operating company level. In the United States, high-yield bonds and senior secured loans are generally issued by the same entity in the corporate structure.

There is a legitimate concern over whether structural subordination, which has the effect of further removing bondholders from the operating assets and cash flows of the company, would have a detrimental effect on postbankruptcy recovery rates. In 2001 and 2002, the European market was just beginning to develop the infrastructure needed to analyze the legal aspects of debt workouts. Clearly, some concessions needed to be made by both issuers and the bankruptcy courts in order to preserve the market's appeal for underwriters and investors.

While European recovery rates hit some eye-catching lows in 2001 and 2002, long-term recovery values were still debatable. In previous studies conducted by Fitch, long-term recovery rates on defaulted US bonds ranged from 30% to 40% of par. These recovery values of course were realized in the context of US specific company structures and within the parameters of the US Chapter 11 Bankruptcy Code. The US Code generally tries to balance the interests of secured and unsecured creditors and affords companies the opportunity to reorganize. Another complexity surrounding recovery rates is that they are highly variable. As noted above, they generally move inversely with defaults and they also vary significantly by sector and by company depending on the nature of the defaults. In 2001, for example, even outside of telecommunication, a handful of US sectors facing systemic industry problems such as textiles and metals and mining, saw average recovery rates in the teens, while other industries experienced recovery rates of 30% to 50% of par.

MARK-TO-MARKET LOSSES LEAD DEFAULTS

The most troubling aspect of 2001 and 2002 defaults in Europe was the deep loss of par value accompanying the defaults. As noted above, the weighted average recovery rate on defaulted bonds through September 2002 was just 15% of par. But in step with a parallel development in the United States, most of the year's defaulted issues were already trading at deep discounts at the beginning of the year. In fact, the average trading price of defaulted bonds in Europe in 2002 was just 32% of par at the beginning of the year. In other words, on a mark-to-market basis, approximately 70% of the par losses on the year's defaults were absorbed by the market before the year got underway. This is an important but often overlooked consideration for investors pondering returns in a high default environment. The market had anticipated most of the defaults in 2002 and had already discounted them. Therefore while the total par loss on 2002 defaults was $13.6 billion, approximately $11 billion had been realized in 2001 or earlier.

The moral of the story is that in an efficient market a high default rate does not necessarily translate into equally dismal returns. The reality that many of the defaulted issues were trading at deep discounts at least six months before default confirms that the European high-yield market had achieved a meaningful level of sophistication by 2002.

CONCLUSION

Despite a painful start, the need for growth capital by noninvestment grade borrowers in an era of globalization, cross-border transactions, and privatization in Europe will drive the European speculative-grade bond market forward, albeit at a slower pace than that projected as recently as 2000. The 2001 and 2002 default storm may actually serve a greater good by fostering many of the changes needed to advance bondholder rights and hence enhance the market's appeal for investors, sponsors, and underwriters. If the United States is any guide, concentrated periods of high defaults are usually followed by long periods of average to below average defaults. This is due to the market's return to conservatism post defaults. For example, following the 1990–1991 recession, default rates in the United States averaged less than 2% per annum in the subsequent eight years. Given that new issuance in Europe in 2001 and 2002 had a strong conservative bias, it is safe to say that the European default model is likely to follow the US pattern, allowing the market to grow at a more moderate and profitable pace in the next decade.

CHAPTER 29

Analysis and Evaluation of Corporate Bonds

Christoph Klein
Portfolio Manager Corporate Bonds
Deutsche Asset Management

Permanent and independent credit ratings are key success factors for investments in corporate bonds. It is crucial to avoid future fallen angels and to be confident when investing in corporate bonds with weaker but improving credit profile. This chapter will present a quantitative sector credit rating model built and used by Deutsche Asset Management, based on discriminant analysis introduced by Edward Altman in 1968. The Swissair case is used as an example to illustrate this rating methodology. A brief relative value analysis concludes this chapter.

QUANTITATIVE RATING MODELS

Selecting individual corporate bonds with a favourable risk/return relation requires a precise analysis of risks and setting comprehensible assessment rules. For this reason rating models have been developed and presented here for various industries that help to evaluate the credit quality of corporations.

These models form an element within the investment process and are applied before taking an investment decision for every individual corporate bond. The overall investment process starts by analysing country risk, industry risk, and the special business and financial risks of individual corporations. Apart from qualitative factors, quantitative factors are used. After the assessment of credit quality, the terms of the bond, such as maturity, currency, liquidity, collateralisation, and seniority, are examined in order to decide whether the corporate bond's spread is relatively attractive in a peer group analysis and the bond can be recommended to buy.

Since the credit quality of a corporation may vary over time, permanent credit assessments are indispensable so that the bond can be sold in time before a rating downgrade or, respectively, to achieve the appropriate risk premium at any time. In credit assessments, investors fall back on data published in annual or quarterly reports, but also estimate future values based on extensive scenario analysis. These are factors such as debt ratio, liquidity, and profitability of the corporation that are of importance for credit assessment.

Selecting an appropriate methodology is of great significance. Widespread quantitative methods in the loan business are scoring models and discriminant analyses. After a brief description of scoring methods, the methodology of discriminant analysis is at first generally explained and then applied to a case study.

Scoring Methods

With a scoring model, several objects can be ranked by assigning utility values to their characteristics. When corporations are regarded as objects and their financial data, such as the debt/equity ratio, as characteristics, scoring methods can be used for credit assessment. This methodology is particularly useful when very complex objects with many characteristics have to be compared. A scoring model which is used for credit assessment requires that financial ratios are selected and weighted in advance. A scoring model for the assessment of corporations can only guarantee that corporations assessed on the basis of the respective model are judged on the same subjectively selected criteria and the overall assessment is established by an equable weighting of the criteria.[1]

A scoring model is established by selecting the characteristics for the assessment of corporations. For industrial corporations it is recommended to choose financial data providing information on the net worth, financial position, cash flows, and earnings. The weighting of the selected data is subjective. In the case of not metrically scalable data, such as management quality, a nominal scaling has to be defined. In this way, a partial assessment is established for each individual characteristic of an industrial corporation. For every characteristic an interval or a score can be unambiguously assigned to every corporation. The objects can thus be ranked according to one of their characteristics. Subsequently, the total assessment (total utility) of a corporation is the sum of

---

[1] Jörn Baetge, *Bilanzanalyse* (Düsseldorf: IDW Verlag, 1998).

the weighted partial assessments. Now industrial corporations can be valued according to their total scores. Whether this relation corresponds to the actual ranking of corporations with respect on their credit quality, primarily depends on the inclusion, importance, and plausibility of the subjectively selected data and their weights. The question which level of total assessment assigns good or bad credit quality to a corporation is once again decided in a subjective way.

Due to these methodological shortcomings, we now turn to an approach for selecting financial ratios and their weights in a more objective way.

Discriminant Analysis

Discriminant analysis is a statistical method for separating objects into two groups. The differences between these two groups are to be explained with the help of certain characteristics observed.[2]

This analysis is targeted at separating corporations of good and poor credit quality on the basis of a set of data (e.g. financial ratios). A discriminant function can, for example, be formulated as follows:

$$A(x1) + B(x2) = C$$

where A and B are coefficients, C is the discriminant score, and $x1$ and $x2$ are financial ratios

If the discriminant score, C, exceeds a certain threshold value (discriminatory value or cutoff value), the credit quality of a corporation will be classified as good, otherwise as poor. The estimation of the discriminant function requires a set of corporations that are already classified as solvent or insolvent (good or poor). Thus it is possible to assess the reliability of the function via the number of misclassified corporations.

In order to establish this function, a logical preselection of appropriate data is carried out safeguarding a sufficient representation of the net worth, financial position, and results of the corporation.[3] Here, it should be kept in mind that the financial ratios selected have to show only moderate correlations in order to avoid multicorrelation problems known from regression analysis.[4] With the help of multiple discriminant

---

[2] Klaus Backhaus, Bernd Erichson, Wulff Plinke, and Rolf Weiber, *Multivariate Analysemethoden* (Berlin: Springer, 2000)

[3] Edward I. Altman, "Financial Ratios, Discriminant Analysis and the Prediction of Corporate Bankruptcy," *Journal of Finance* 23, no. 4 (September 1968), pp. 589–609.

[4] Jörn Baetge, "Früherkennung, negativer Entwicklungen der zu prüfenden Unternehmen mit Hilfe von Kennzahlen," *Die Wirtschaftsprüfung* no. 22/23 (1980), pp. 651–670.

EXHIBIT 29.1   The Distribution of Corporations after a Discriminant Analysis

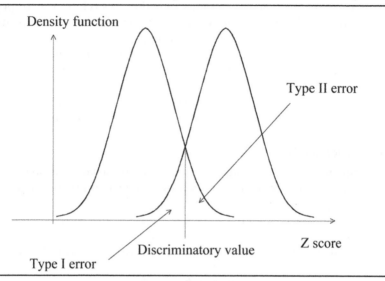

analysis, the coefficients of the discriminant function are estimated in such a way that the resulting means of the scores for solvent and insolvent corporations show a maximum difference. The larger the distance the more reliable the separation of corporations of good from poor credit quality. Generally, the discriminant function condenses several data into a discriminant score (labelled "Z score" in Exhibit 29.1).

Since, the distributions of both groups, even in the case of a successful separation, always show overlaps, type I and type II classification errors may occur. A type I error means that solvent corporations are classified as insolvent. A type II error refers to insolvent corporations which are classified as solvent. Since the rating methodology has been developed to serve investors as a means to assess risks, it is especially important to minimise the type II error. This can be achieved by setting the critical value for separating corporations of good and poor credit quality not in the centre of the overlapping zone, but closer to the mean value of corporations of good credit quality. The cut off value should be adjusted until the type II error has been reduced to an acceptable level, for example 1%.

All corporations left of the critical value are now classified as insolvent, and all those right of the critical value as solvent. A user can now also apply the discriminant functions to corporations that had not been included in the estimation of the function.[5]

---

[5] Baetge, "Früherkennung, negativer Entwickungen der zu prüfenden Unternehmen mit Hilfe von Kennzahlen."

Results in the literature and widespread practical usage suggest that discriminant analysis appears to be an appropriate method which is used for further model formation.[6]

The selection of data, formation, testing, and analysis of the discriminant analysis will now be discussed on the basis of a sector model.

The Selection of Financial Ratios for the Rating Model

Financial ratios are condensed data reporting quantifiable facts.[7] With their help, complicated facts, structures, and procedures of corporations are depicted in a simple way to permit a fast and comprehensive overview. Thus, financial ratios are appropriate for the complex task of comparative credit quality assessment. To simplify the methodology, the number of financial ratios used should not be too large, and every financial ratio must be economically plausible.[8] The selection of particularly appropriate financial ratios is a significant component of every rating methodology. These financial ratios should represent areas of relevance for creditors as exactly as possible, like debt/equity ratio, profitability, and liquidity. In this context, not only the level of these financial ratios is important but also their development over time.

Model Formation

In order to construct quantitative rating models, corporations are selected. These are randomly separated into two groups for model formation (training set) and model testing (test group). The data of the test group are *not* used for model formation. Subsequently, data required for the computation of the financial ratios are collected. Out of these financial ratios, the discriminant function with the highest hit ratio is now gradually formed. Further steps include testing and analysing the function.

As explained above, it is important for the formation of the discriminant function to know whether a corporation belongs to the group of "good" or "poor" credit quality before the analysis starts. This means that corporations must already be rated to be appropriate for building and testing the model. The requirement of an existing rating by at least

---

[6] Deutsche Bundesbank, "Die Untersuchung von Insolvenzrisiken im Rahmen der Kreditwürdigkeitsprüfung durch die Deutsche Bundesbank," *Monthly Reports of Deutsche Bundesbank* (January 1992), pp. 30–36.

[7] Karlheinz Küting and Claus-Peter Weber, *Die Bilanzanalyse: Lehrbuch zur Beurteilung von Einzel- und Konzernabschlüssen* (Stuttgart: Schäffer Verlag, 1993).

[8] Dietrich Köllhofer, "Moderne Verfahren der Bilanz- und Bonitätsanalyse im Firmenkundengeschäft der Bayerischen Vereinsbank AG," *Zeitschrift für betriebswirtschaftliche Forschung*, no. 11 (1989), pp. 974-981.

one of the rating agencies, however, significantly reduces the number of corporations in the database.

Further analysis requires detailed data from annual accounts of individual corporations. For this reason, only stock listed companies are selected as they are subject to particularly strict publication requirements.

However, rating is not the only criterion for the selection of companies. To analyse corporate credit quality in isolation, other risks such as country risk should be ruled out. Corporations should only differ in their credit quality. Otherwise, they should be as homogeneous as possible. For this reason, rating models for different industries (such as, for example, industrial, telecommunications or utility companies) have been developed as different industries may differ in terms of the competitive situation, profit determinants, and balance sheet ratios. This makes it necessary to analyse at first the business risks of an industry as well as to compare and assess the corporations within this industry on the basis of the criteria established.

Furthermore, only corporations with head offices located in AAA rated countries were selected so that potential country risks do not interfere with corporate risks.

Due to the poor availability of corporate data, the database is small for individual industry models. The industrial model was thus established on the basis of 153 corporations. The alternative of generating larger samples entails the major problem of making a distinction between industries impossible. Nevertheless, the goal to build further more detailed and homogeneous sector models like an airline model seems to be impossible due to insufficient data. For this reason airlines are rated with the industrial model.

Forming the Discriminant Function

On the basis of the selected appropriate financial ratios that show significantly different group means for industrial corporations of good and poor credit quality and are additionally fundamentally clear indicators, a quantitative rating model is developed with the help of discriminant analysis.

Apart from achieving the highest possible hit ratio (lowest misclassification), another objective is to include as few financial ratios as possible in order to make the function transparent and practicable. Since the literature has not yet decided which financial ratios are most appropriate for credit assessment, various combinations of financial ratios are tried and tested for their discriminatory power.

At first, every credit group of the sample is split up so that there are two groups of good and two groups of poor credit quality. As a first step one group of corporations of good and one group of corporations of poor credit quality are selected (training set) and the discriminant function is estimated. Subsequently, this function is used to classify the corporations of the two other groups that have not been used for model formation (test group). This second step controls the reliability of the model.

A statistics program (such as SAS or SPSS) computes the values of the group centroids on the basis of which the coefficients of the discriminant function are later established. Apart from the hit ratio, the names of the misclassified corporations are recorded.

Afterwards, calculations of a variety of parameter combinations are run. The objective is to find a discriminant function with the correct signs for the different coefficients. Only this permits the formation of a function where there is no exception to the rule: The higher the score, the higher the credit quality of the corporation. Incorrect signs may result in misclassifications and thus wrong credit assessments.

For the model of industrial corporations, the optimum discriminant function consists of the following four financial ratios: free cash flow to total debt (FCF/TD), inverse variation coefficient of operating cash flows (VACO), retained earnings to total assets (RE/TA), and total market value of the corporation (TMVD). An explanation of the financial ratios is given in the case study. The discriminant function is formulated as follows:

$$A \times (\text{FCF/TD}) + B \times (\text{VACO}) + C \times (\text{RE/TA}) + D \times (\text{TMVD}) = E$$

A, B, C, and D are coefficients computed with a statistics program. E is the discriminatory value (cutoff value) with a positive sign. If the financial ratios of a corporation are now entered in this function, a function value will be the result. If this value is above the discriminatory value, the credit quality of this corporation is assessed as good. The rough division of corporations into two classes of "good" and "poor" credit quality is refined in the following section.

Testing the Discriminant Function

Apart from the hit ratio (correct assignment to the groups of "good" and "poor" credit quality), whether the discriminant function established can provide a more precise assessment than good or poor credit quality is examined. For example, rating agencies use different rating classes from AAA to D which are further subdivided into so called "notches" (subclasses), a finer classification. For this reason, "credit quality scores" are computed for every industrial corporation with the discriminant function selected, which can be used for a more precise rating classification. These credit scores are then to be compared with the agency ratings. In order to

EXHIBIT 29.2   Credit Scores and Rating Classes of the Industrial Model

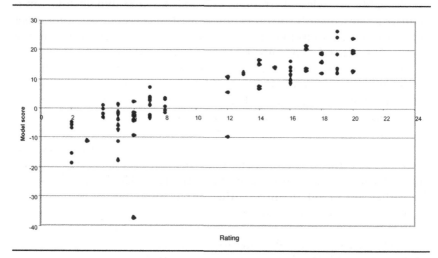

achieve a minimum difference between model results and agency assessments, the ranges of credit scores were optimised. A minimum difference should not only refer to the assessments of individual corporations, but also the sum of deviations should be minimised over all corporations. Since the correlation between credit quality and score is not linear, the ranges of the individual classes are also not equidistant.[9]

Exhibit 29.2 depicts the similarity of credit assessments of the industrial model and rating agencies. Here, a value of 24 on the abscissa corresponds with an AAA rating. The lower the value on the abscissa, the poorer the credit rating. The lowest value of 1 symbolizes a rating of D.

In the optimum case, a straight upward sloping line would be observed. This is not completely achieved here. There is, generally, quite a high similarity but there are some clear differences. It is not necessarily the objective of these models to exactly mirror the agency rating. This should be hardly possible with a quantitative model since important qualitative factors such as, for example, management quality, have not been included.

Analysis of a Discriminant Function on the Basis of a Case Study

The high hit ratios of the rating functions (96% for the industrial model) suggests that each of the selected four financial ratios (of the

---

[9] Manfred Steiner and Volker G. Heinke, "Rating aus Sicht der modernen Finanzierungstheorie," in Hans E. Büschgen and Oliver Everling (eds.), *Handbuch Rating* (Wiesbaden: Gabler Verlag, 1996), pp. 579–628.

industrial model) is complex enough to cover several areas such as liquidity, profitability, and equity/debt ratio and thus allows users assessing credit quality. The following applies to all financial ratios: The higher they are, the higher the credit quality of the corporation. Since the quantified rating method used here is based on only four financial ratios, they are described in more detail:

To this end, we use the figures of the Swissair financial statements for the year 2000. Swissair defaulted in 2001, but nevertheless this case should document the predictive power of the rating model. Furthermore, an airline is not exactly an industrial company, but due to the problems discussed above an airline model cannot be constructed and the industrial sector seems to have more similarities with the airline sector compared to the utility or telecom sector.

The four financial ratios included in the model—free cash flow to total debt (FCF/TD), inverse variation coefficient of operating cash flows (VACO), retained earnings to total assets (RE/TA), and total market value in US dollars (TMVD)—are computed on the basis of the Swissair financial statements and entered into the function. The discriminatory value of the function is E. If a higher score than E results, Swissair can be classified as a corporation of good credit quality on the basis of the quantitative analysis alone. For the total assessment apart from a quantitative rating, qualitative criteria such as the assessment of the business model, the competitive environment, regulation, and management quality are also relevant. Subject to the assessment of qualitative aspects, the quantitative rating is revised upwards or downwards using extensive scenario modeling. This section, however, describes the quantitative variables only.

Apart from the rough categorisation (good/poor credit quality), a finer grading to subrating classes (notches), such as A– or BBB+, can be carried out, but will not be documented here. If, for example, the discriminant score is between 10 and 12, this corporation will be assigned an internal rating of A3. The cutoff value between the "good" and "poor" credit quality group is 6. Due to confidentiality, the complete score-rating translation table cannot be presented here.

Free cash flow shows the residual payment flows available for debt redemptions. In the business year of 2000, this figure amounted to –€2,384 million for Swissair. The book value of total debt is taken from the balance sheet and amounts to €18,863 million. FCF/TD is computed by dividing FCF by TD:

$$\frac{-€2,384}{€18,863} = -0.126$$

The inverse variation coefficient of operating cash flows (VOCF) is an essential ratio of this function. Steadiness of payment flows appears to be an indicator of continuity. Reasons for a high steadiness of cash flows can be a stable economic environment or low competition within an industry, but also the quality of management who recognizes business risks in time and avoids them. For this ratio, the mean of operating cash flows of the last five years (€1,388 million) is related to its standard deviation (€657 million), measured over the same period. Creditors of a company are interested in positive stable cash. The lower the fluctuations of operating cash flows in the most recent past, the higher the rating of the corporation. For this reason, high positive scores of VOCF contribute to a high value of the discriminant function and thus to a good rating.

Using the data from the 2000 financial statements of Swissair, the result is:

$$VOCF = \frac{€1,388}{€657} = 2.11$$

The parameter retained earnings to total assets (RE/TA) includes the cumulative retained earnings of a corporation related to total assets. Retained earnings show both the profitability of the past and the historical dividend policy. High retained earnings increase the net worth of the corporation and thus the access of creditors to assets in the case of bankruptcy. It furthermore shows that a pure focus on shareholder value with high dividends is detrimental to the credit assessment of the corporation. For Swissair,

$$RE/TA \text{ is calculated as: } \frac{€283}{€20,215} = 0.014$$

Total market value in USD (TMVD) is the sum of the market value of equity and the book value of debt capital. The inclusion of this variable is justified by the observation that the probability of bankruptcy is smaller for large corporations than for small ones. If, for example, a larger corporation runs into trouble, the public interest in its further existence and thus in securing jobs might be stronger than in the case of a small company (especially in Europe). Furthermore, larger corporations tend to have easier access to the capital markets and find it therefore easier to bridge liquidity crises by short-term borrowing. Additionally, market assessments mirror expectations of future profitability.

Strictly speaking, using the market value of the corporation (TMVD) is an inconsistency of the model. All values except for the components of market capitalisation are ratios relating to the reporting date of the annual financial statements which we, however, estimate or adjust for the future. In contrast to this, the share price of the corporation changes daily. In an extreme case, this could mean that two analyses carried out on different days lead to different results. In the literature, there are approaches for quantitative rating models explicitly referring to the market value of the corporation so that the addition of TMVD introduces a component valued at market price into the model.[10] For Swissair TMVD amounted to roughly US $23 billion at the end of December 2000.

These financial ratios are now entered into the discriminant function

$$A \times (-0.126) + B \times 2.11 + C \times 0.014 + D \times US \text{ \$23 billion} = 2$$

The discriminant value is below the cut off value 6. This shows that according to the quantitative analysis, Swissair is classified as a corporation of poor credit quality. After a fine grading, the internal rating is BB2 and thus deviates from the rating by Moody's (A3 as of the end of 2000). Expecting a further downtrend for Swissair and assuming no backing by the Swiss government we calculated a model score of 0.85 in early 2001 which can be translated into a B2 rating. Moody's downgraded Swissair to noninvestment grade in June 2001 *after* the spread for Swissair bonds widened dramatically.

Many corporations are active in several industries. To assess the credit quality of such corporations, the credit quality of the different divisions should be rated separately with the discriminant functions appropriate for every industry sector. Subsequently, the ratings of the individual divisions are to be taken together as a rating for the total corporation. The weightings of the divisions within the corporations (e.g., as a percentage of total cash flow) should be taken into account here. Additionally, diversification features of the different business sectors should be integrated into the credit assessment. However, for such an approach ordinary financial statements are no longer sufficient. A detailed segment reporting is particularly required for companies, which is up to now sometimes unavailable.[11]

Furthermore, it has to be considered that the discriminant functions established may change over time. The combination of the most appropri-

---

[10] John B. Caouette, Edward I. Altman, and Paul Narayanan, *Managing Credit Risk* (New York: John Wiley & Sons, 1998)

[11] Rainer Husmann, "Segmentierung des Konzernabschlusses zur bilanzanalytischen Untersuchung der wirtschaftlichen Lage des Konzerns," *Die Wirtschaftsprüfung* 50, no. 11 (1997), pp. 349–359.

ate financial ratios might also change. For this reason, future permanent reviews of discriminant functions on the basis of updated corporate data are indispensable. This is the only way to avoid misjudgements resulting from structural ruptures of corporate reality or environmental conditions.

RELATIVE VALUE ANALYSIS

After assessing a bond with the help of credit analysis, the question arises to what extent the market price of this bond corresponds with the investor's judgement. The market price should compensate the investor for all risks connected with holding the bond. This market price (spread) is often referred to as the return differential between the analysed bond and the benchmark. Frequently, government bonds or the swap rate with matching maturities are used as benchmarks. Another standard reference are bonds of other issuers that are active in the same business field. Since one debt instrument is assessed relative to another debt instrument, this analysis is also called *relative value analysis*, the basic principles of which are described in this section.

As a first step in relative value analysis, it has to be decided which benchmark to use. The classic benchmark to calculate the spread is the government bond with the same maturity. As an alternative, the swap market gains importance.[12] An interest rate swap is an exchange of fixed against floating-rate payments (such as the plain vanilla swap). Counterparts are generally banks with a rating in the range of AA. Since they act as guarantors for the fulfilment of the parties' obligations arising from the swap, swap rates are used as indicators for risk premiums and thus the market rates of corporations of good to excellent credit quality. The swap market is very liquid and is therefore also used as a benchmark for relative value analysis. Later we will refer to both the government and swap market as benchmarks. As a case study, we focus on the Swissair bond with a coupon of 4.375%, maturing on 8 June 2006.

Historically, comparing the yield of the interesting bond with the benchmark yield may be a first step in relative value analysis. This allows one to examine the implications of events in the past on the spread of the bond. Exhibit 29.3 depicts the yield spread of Swissair and the matching Bund (German government bond) in the period from May 1999 to November 2001.

---

[12] Helmut Kaiser, Anja Heilenkötter, Markus Herrmann, and Werner Krämer, *Der Euro-Kapitalmarkt* (Wiesbaden: Gabler-Verlag, 1999).

EXHIBIT 29.3 Spread between Swissair 06 and Matching Bund (logarithmic scale)

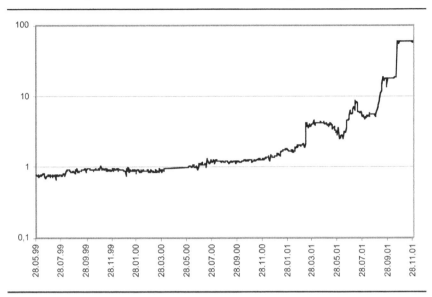

Source: Bloomberg, author computations.

After the reporting of rather weak company results in April 2000, the bond spread began to widen rather steadily. At the end of January 2001, Moody's added a negative outlook to their A3 rating. The following downgrades in April and June to Ba3 with negative outlook lead to a deterioration in the bond's price. These sharp price movements are quite common in comparable situations (especially in the European credit markets) as investors have strict guidelines to hold investment-grade issuers only. Thus the cliff to the noninvestment area tends to be extremely sharp due to the size of immediate forced selling. In this case, there was almost no bottom as bankruptcy fears started to spread out in August 2001 and it became evident that there would be no backing by the government.

Swissair was in very serious economic problems long before the attack on World Trade Center on 11 September 2001. This attack had a severe effect on the entire airline industry because travel volume declined significantly and increased security costs could not be fully transferred to customers and governments. Overall there might be more defaults coming ahead, leading to consolidation and in the long run to an overall healthier industry with higher margins and improved ratings.

This case shows the importance of independent and permanent buy-side research to be able to make investment decisions which avoid fallen angels sufficiently to credit deterioration. Furthermore, the models help to make fast decisions when new relevant information via Bloomberg/Reuters is published and can be used to adjust an asset management firm's internal ratings within a few minutes.

Credit default swaps used as a second source for spread measurement are derivatives for pricing and trading default risks. Buying protection pays a premium like a coupon to receive a fixed amount of money in an *ex ante* defined event like a default. With these instruments creditors like banks or investors can easily insure their credit risks or improve their diversification within the credit portfolio by transferring or exchanging sector or issuer exposures. For sophisticated credit investors, long/short credit strategies have become much easier to play. In Europe a lot of sizeable investors are not allowed to use credit default swaps. Thus overall we see more supply of credit default swaps (banks buying protection) than demand (investors selling protection). Furthermore, the issuer's cheapest-to-deliver bond is used as a reference to calculate the credit default swap. Sometimes, even convertible bonds can be used for this purpose. These effects tend to lead to higher credit default swaps as compared to corporate bond spreads for the same issuer with similar maturity (positive basis).

Exhibit 29.4 shows the substantial widening of the Swissair spreads compared to some competitors since the beginning of 2001 on a logarithmic scale. Before Swissair was downgraded to noninvestment grade in June 2001, the spread reached high-yield levels. Thus the investors have not really been protected by the rating agencies. On the other hand excessive downgrades might lead to self-fulfilling prophecies and an increased number of defaults as investors retreat or as covenants are triggered. In our opinion, higher transparency of the agencies' rating process which enables more investors to develop independent confident investment processes might lead to efficient investment decisions and sufficient and early discussions with the issuers' management helping to "turn the wheel around" in time. Thus bondholder value is a major area for improvement.

Depending on the corporation's operating sector, spreads differ. Sectors where risks are perceived as high—for example due to strong M&A activities—show higher spreads than sectors with lower risks. For example, firms operating in the automobile sector tend to be assessed as bearing higher risks than similarly rated companies of the service sector. This is also reflected by the fact that bonds issued by corporations with the same maturity and the same rating show different spreads because they belong to different sectors. Therefore it makes sense to develop industry specific rating models, as discussed earlier.

EXHIBIT 29.4 Comparison of Swissair 2006 and Peer Group Spread Over Swap

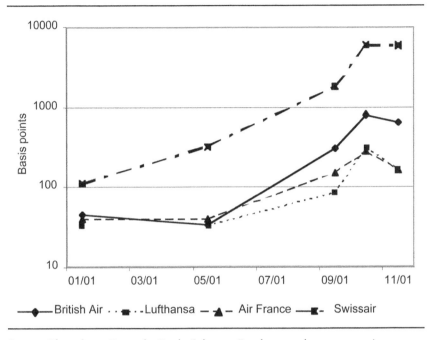

Source: Bloomberg, Deutsche Bank, Salomon Brothers, author computations.

Relative value analysis can be distorted by the "retail bid phenomenon:" Issuers with high name recognition (such as Deutsche Telekom in
Germany) are more heavily demanded by retail investors. This may lead
to spread narrowing and thus a price increase of the bond.

Issuance activities in a business sector are another factor to be taken
into account. If one sector has high borrowing requirements and the
corporations of this sector frequently tap the capital market, this will,
on the one hand, create a broad and liquid market. On the other hand,
new issues have to offer ever stronger incentives to win over investors.
Apart from higher returns, such incentives can also be covenants. Covenants could, for example, provide for coupon premiums to protect
against rating downgrades of the issuer (step-up coupons) or the assurance of a maximum debt/equity ratio. Additionally, investor relations
and a good information policy in the interest of creditors are becoming
an important element in valuation and relative value analysis.

SUMMARY

Crucial for the success in credit markets is to come to a timely, precise, and forwardlooking assessment of the creditworthiness of an issuer and its bonds. For this reason this chapter discusses credit assessment with the help of multiple discriminant analysis, a useful tool for identifying attractive issuers and avoid falling angels. Carefully selected ratios to analyze the profitability, capital structure, liquidity, and steadiness of a corporation are used in order to make a statement on its future credit standing. This method allows for a swift and effective fundamental assessment of an issuer's credit standing, which can also be used for scenario analyses, such as in the case of the corporation being taken over by another corporation.

The number and size of fallen angels in the recent past show the importance of independent buy-side research. Internal ratings might help investors to generate investment decisions which avoid fallen angels or to sell their exposure early enough before the corporate bond's price deteriorates. Furthermore, quantitative models have helped us to react very quickly to relevant information such as an announced debt financed takeover to adjust our internal ratings.

After getting a rating evaluation, a relative value analysis is performed to decide whether bonds are relatively cheap or expensive in comparison with other bonds. This assessment focuses on market technicals and should include factors like liquidity and optionalities such as coupon step-ups.

Legal Considerations

Five

Legal Considerations

CHAPTER 30

Legal and Documentation Issues on Bonds Issuances

Lourdes Villar-Garcia
Solicitor (England and Wales), Attorney at Law (California), Abogado (Spain)
Executive Director
CIBC World Markets PLC—DCM Advisory

Trusha Patel
Solicitor (England and Wales)
Director
CIBC World Markets PLC—DCM Advisory

The legal and documentation issues usually raised in a bond issuance are very diverse and, in some cases, very complex. This chapter is intended to introduce the reader to the most important issues, although a thorough analysis would probably require a book by itself.

We will start with a basic description of the documentation involved in the issuance of a bond to follow with a more detailed analysis of the main legal issues. We will finish with a case study describing one of the most common structures in the market and the legal and documentation matters involved.

We are assuming that the reader is a person with no legal background but who is familiar with bond issuances. This chapter is not meant to be used as a substitute for legal advice and is not intended to provide a complete coverage of the subject.

THE BASICS

One of the things that will surprise a "newcomer" the most is the rich terminology involved in the issuance of bonds. For example, people will call the same document offering circular, offering memorandum, and prospectus—or fiscal agency agreement and agency agreement.

In addition to the terminology used to describe the different documents, there is also a rich terminology to refer to the different parties involved in an issuance. Sometimes dealer, manager, and arranger are used to refer to the same entity. One could say that dealer is more commonly used to refer to the entity that underwrites a bond issued under an MTN programme to proceed on the same day or at a later stage to sell it to an investor. Manager is used to refer to the entity that purchases a standalone bond to proceed on the same day or at a later stage to sell it to the investor. Arranger refers to the entity that arranges the transaction for a third party (usually also acting as manager for the issuance). For purposes of this chapter, we will assume the arranger is both arranging and underwriting the bond.

The words "bond" and "note" are often also used synonymously, but more often than not when talking about a bond people refer to a standalone issuance, while when talking about a "note" they may refer to a bond issued under an MTN programme or on a standalone basis. When an issuer issues debt in a regular manner, it is usually more time and cost efficient to set up an MTN programme, where master agreements and terms and conditions are put in place (and are applicable to all the issues) and only the commercial terms need to be documented in a pricing supplement at the time of issuance. For more structured transactions, or when the issuer does not issue debt in a regular basis, a standalone bond is the usual form of issuance.

The legal and documentation issues raised when documenting a bond whether on a standalone basis or within the terms of an MTN programme are, in great measure, the same. In this chapter, we will refer to *bond* but, unless otherwise specified, the same could be said of a note issued under an MTN programme.

Documentation Involved in a Plain Vanilla Bond Issuance

The paragraphs below describe the documentation usually involved in a plain vanilla bond issuance. This should not be taken as an exhaustive list, additional documents may be needed depending on the structure of the bond.

Mandate Letters

The documentation process for the issuance of a bond starts when the arranger obtains a verbal mandate from the issuer. At this stage a mandate letter will need to be signed. Involving a lawyer at this time is important, as contractual obligations are already created for the parties in the mandate letter because, until a subscription agreement is signed between the issuer and the arranger or manager, the mandate letter will govern the relationship between such parties.

In sophisticated transactions involving an SPV,[1] mandate letters are usually signed between the investors and the arranger of the transaction.

The main points to keep in mind while drafting the mandate letter are set out below:

If one is an issuer or, in the case of sophisticated transactions involving an SPV, the arranger of the transaction, one will try to get a commitment from the counterparty—in the former case, the manager, in the latter case, the investor—to underwrite the obligation. One of the most negotiated clauses is the "walk-away" clause, which will contain a description of the cases in which the manager will be allowed not to perform its obligation to underwrite or to arrange or, in the case of the investor, to make the investment. Typical cases are if there is a material change in market conditions or the creditworthiness of the issuer.[2] On the latter point, for rated issuers it is advisable to include a rating downgrade clause, as a potential rating downgrade could be deemed not sufficient to trigger the walk-away clause based on a change in the creditworthiness of the issuer.

The mandate letter will also include a clause making the underwriting commitment conditional upon mutually satisfactory documentation. Care should be taken in this language, as this allows an easy way out to the counterparty. It is also important that the mandate letter clearly states that the arranger is not providing tax, legal, or accounting advice to the issuer or the investors. In mandate letters for transactions structured through an SPV and signed between the arranger and the investor, surprisingly many investors do not usually oppose a walk-away clause making the obligations of the arranger conditional upon internal approvals being obtained.

In the case of sophisticated transactions involving SPVs, it is important to address in the mandate letter who will pay the legal, rating agency, and other expenses if the transaction does not go through. Confidentiality undertakings should also be inserted to prevent the investors from using the information obtained to close parallel transactions.

Indemnity clauses in favour of the arranger should also be included in both the mandate letters and the subscription agreement. An indem-

---

[1] SPVs are described in more detail later in this chapter.
[2] The setting up of an SPV is explained later in this chapter.

nity clause allows the arranger to recover any loss without having to prove any breach of contract. If no indemnity clause is inserted, the arranger will have to prove that a breach occurred and that any loss it suffered was a foreseeable consequence of such breach.

After the mandate letter is signed, the process of preparing all the relevant documentation starts. The length of time needed from the mandate to the issuance depends on the specific circumstances of the transaction, market conditions and the experience of the issuer, it can take from three days in the case of a plain vanilla bond issued under an MTN programme to six or even more months for a structured transaction.

Subscription Agreements and Note Purchase Agreements

The subscription agreement is an agreement between the issuer and the manager. It includes an undertaking by the manager to purchase the bonds on the closing date, subject to certain conditions precedent.

The subscription agreement, like the mandate letters, usually includes "walk-away" clauses; as for example:

- Breach of representations, warranties and undertakings.
- Nonsatisfaction of any closing conditions. This will usually include matters such as the delivery of legal opinions, auditor comfort letters, no rating downgrade, listing of the notes, obtention of necessary governmental approvals, and the like.
- Force majeure event. IPMA recommends two force majeure clauses. The most common one is clause two which provides that the manager is entitled to terminate its commitment if, in his opinion, there is such a change in the national or international financial, political or economic conditions or currency exchange rates or exchange controls as would, in his view, be likely to prejudice materially the success of the offering, distribution or dealing of the bonds in the secondary market.

The subscription agreement will also include an undertaking of the manager to comply with the selling restrictions imposed by the issuer.

If there is more than one manager for the transaction, the commitments of the managers are joint and several. In other words, if one of the managers refuses to purchase the bonds, the issuer could oblige the other managers to purchase its share. In such cases an agreement between the managers allocating the amount to be purchased by each of them will also be signed.

A note purchase agreement is usually put in place when the notes are purchased by the investor from the issuer (i.e., the notes do not pass through any manager's book). The terms contained in this agreement are substantially the same as in the *subscription agreement*.

The Offering Circular

The offering circular, also referred to as the *offering memorandum* or *prospectus*, contains a description of the conditions of the bond and the issuer. It is usually the most important document for the investor (or at least the first he will ask for), as it is the document on which the investor will base its investment decision. The offering circular contains provisions on the following matters:

(a) *Terms and Conditions* of the bonds (the "Ts & Cs") which are the most negotiated terms are usually those dealing with the negative pledge, which is a commitment by the issuer not to create a security interest senior to the bond over any collateral or not to issue debt senior to the bond, in the case of unsecured bonds; description of the interest payable and redemption amount; early redemptions (e.g., for tax reasons, puts and calls); withholding taxes and events of default. If the bond is part of a repackaging or a structured bond, the Ts & Cs will also include a summary of the terms under which the security created for the benefit of the noteholders will be realised.
(b) Description of the issuer, which will include a description of the history of the issuer, it share capital, business strategy, current activities, management, and recent developments.
(c) Capitalisation tables, which will usually include the latest published audited accounts and, if more recent, the latest published unaudited accounts of the issuer.
(d) A statement indicating what the issuer is going to use proceeds for.
(e) Taxation language, this will usually include a description of the taxation environment in the jurisdiction of the issuer and could also include a description of the taxation environment in the main jurisdictions where the bonds are to be sold.
(f) Subscription and selling restrictions, which will usually include a description of the selling restrictions in the United States and those jurisdictions where the sale of bonds is more likely.

Global and Definitive Bond

Bonds may be issued in either bearer or registered form. In bearer form, ownership is evidenced by the possession of the bond. When in registered form, the owner is the person that appears on the register maintained by the issuer as the owner.

When in bearer form, the bond is the document that actually represents the issuance. A bearer bond can be in global form or in definitive form. Global bonds are held in a clearing system in the form of a single bond representing the whole principal amount of the issuance. While in global form, it can be a temporary global bond or a permanent global bond. Temporary global bonds are usually issued when sale of the bonds in the United States is likely.[3]

The permanent global bond can be issued on the closing date or can be exchanged for a temporary global bond. If the notes are to be held in permanent global form (as it is in most of the cases), the bearer of the bond and, therefore, the one who has any legal rights against the issuer, will be the common depository. (The final investor will be the beneficial owner only.) It is therefore necessary to create the legal link which will create rights in favour of the investors. Under English law, this creation of rights to entities that are not a party to any contract, as is the case of the investors here, is done by executing a deed. In the case of a trust deed being put in place, the investor can enforce its rights through the trustee. By contrast, in the case of a fiscal agency agreement being put in place, a deed of covenant creating rights in favour of the investors to enforce the terms of the notes will be needed.

The definitive global bonds are not usually issued except in exceptional circumstances due to their higher cost. The definitive notes are delivered to the bondholders, and the ownership is transferred by "hand" delivery of such definitive note.

Trust Deed/Fiscal Agency Agreement and Deed of Covenant

The legal obligations of the issuer under the terms of a bond are created pursuant to the signature by the issuer of a trust deed or a deed of covenant.

Under the terms of a trust deed, the issuer agrees to be bound by the terms and conditions of the bond and a trustee is appointed to represent the interests of the noteholders to whom it will have a duty of fiduciary care. Upon the occurrence of a default by the issuer, the trustee—and not the noteholders, except in exceptional circumstances—will be the one who can call an event of default. The trustee can usually agree to make amendments to the terms of the bond and can waive technical defaults.

---

[3] Under TEFRA D rule (enacted by the US government in order to reduce tax evasion by US tax payers), the issuer or manager of an issue is prevented from delivering notes in the United States during the 40-day period following the issue date. For this purpose, a temporary global note will be issued. After the lapse of the restricted period, the temporary global note is exchanged for a permanent global note upon certification of non-US ownership.

The appointment of a trustee also prevents the occurrence of conflicting interests between the different noteholders, as it will receive all the proceeds to be distributed among the noteholders on a pro rata basis (but taking into account any priority ranking). Having a trustee will also make possible the initiation of proceedings for the benefit of the investors. which might otherwise be impracticable due to the excessive cost. Also, the involvement of a trustee will protect the investor from the negotiations other more powerful investors may conduct with the issuer. In transactions where collateral is involved, the trust deed will have a detailed description of the creation of the security interest over such collateral and the procedures to follow when realizing such security interest.

For plain vanilla transactions, a fiscal agency agreement may be used in lieu of a trust deed. Under the terms of a fiscal agency agreement, a fiscal agent has no duty of care to the noteholders, as it is an agent to the issuer, not the investors. The fiscal agent will usually be appointed as paying agent in order to make payments to the noteholders against the presentation of the bond or coupons. The main advantage of having a fiscal agency agreement as opposed to a trust deed is, in addition to the lower cost of appointing a fiscal agent, that the investor can accelerate the obligations of the issuer on its own. If a fiscal agency agreement is signed, a deed of covenant will also need to be signed. In the event of default of the issuer, the deed of covenant will give rights to the holders of the note against the issuer.

Agency Agreement

Whenever there is an issuance under the terms of a trust deed, an agency agreement will be put in place. Under the terms of this agreement, the issuer will appoint a principal paying agent and, if necessary, other agents and paying agents to manage the payments due under the terms of the bond. On the issue date, the noteholders will give instructions to make the payment to the paying agent versus delivery of the notes by the paying agent to the noteholders. During the life of the bond, payments from the issuer to the noteholders will usually be made by the issuer to the paying agent who will deliver the due amounts to the noteholders through the clearing system (if the notes are in global form) or by cheque or transfer (if the notes are in definitive form).

Legal Opinions and Auditors Letters

When issuing a bond, an opinion from legal counsel in the jurisdiction of incorporation of the issuer and an opinion from legal counsel in the governing law jurisdiction are prepared. Even when the documentation is governed, for example, by English law, an English court would look to the jurisdiction of incorporation of the issuer to determine whether or not the issuer has the capacity to enter into the transaction (for which purpose constitutional documents and board minutes will need to be reviewed), to confirm the person executing the documents was duly authorised to do so, for which purpose board minutes and power of attorneys will need to be reviewed, and to confirm that the documentation has been duly executed (i.e., that any formal procedures have been followed). After the legal opinion in the jurisdiction of incorporation is issued, the counsel in the jurisdiction corresponding to the governing law shall issue a legal opinion confirming that the obligations created by the documentation are legally valid and enforceable against the issuer.

The auditor's comfort letter confirms that the financial statements included in the offering circular are accurate and that there has been no material change in the financial situation of the issuer since the latest audited financial statements.

Legal opinions and auditors comfort letters are documents very often overseen in the process of documenting a transaction. Professionals working on behalf of the arranger do not usually focus on this at an early stage of the documentation process. It is important to note that unsatisfactory legal opinions or unclear comfort letters may hold the closing of the transaction at the last minute. Therefore, it is advisable to request draft legal opinions and comfort letters at an early stage in the documentation process and in no case later than before the final draft is distributed to all of the involved parties.

In the case of notes issued under an MTN programme, the legal opinions and audit letters are usually prepared when the programme is set up and updated. If the programme has not been updated for more than one year, or if the note is a type of note for which the MTN programme was not designed, consideration should be given to whether or not a new legal opinion or comfort letter is needed. Also, in the case of new dealers who are not party to the MTN programme, attention should be paid to whether or not such new dealer can rely on the programme legal opinion and comfort letter.

Listing

The main purpose of a listing is to meet investment restrictions which have to be satisfied by many institutional investors due to regulatory or tax reasons. Also, listing usually makes bonds more liquid in the market.

The preferred exchanges for listing in Europe are the Luxembourg Stock Exchange, London Stock Exchange and the Irish Stock Exchange. The Luxembourg Stock Exchange and the Irish Stock Exchange are, in general, less stringent than the London Stock Exchange.

The Luxembourg Stock Exchange rules are contained in the Rules and Regulations of the Luxembourg Stock Exchange, the London Stock Exchange rules are contained in the Listing Rules of the UK Listing Authority, also known as the "purple book." The Irish Stock Exchange rules are contained in the Listing Rules of the Irish Stock Exchange.

The arranger of the bond issue would appoint a listing agent who is responsible for lodging all necessary documentation and acting as an intermediator between the arranger and the stock exchange in terms of ensuring all the necessary disclosure statements are in the documentation. Examples of such disclosure include the requirement for (a) any notices to noteholders to be published in the *Luxembourg Wort* in the case of the Luxembourg Stock Exchange, or with a daily newspaper of general circulation in London in the case of the London Stock Exchange; and (b) the filing of copies of certain documents (e.g., the constitutional documents of the issuer) in order to make them available for inspection at the specified offices of the paying agent.

Application Procedure for Listing

The arranger must submit a draft of the offering circular to the relevant exchange via the listing agent at least four calendar weeks prior to the proposed issue date of the bond. Some exchanges (e.g., Luxembourg) will require a form to be completed by the manager or arranger to state who shall be responsible for paying the fees.

As soon as the relevant exchange has approved the offering circular, the issue can be launched and the final offering circular published.

Deferred Listing

There are some situations where the arranger may wish to arrange the issue of a bond prior to getting it listed on the relevant exchange. In these instances the arranger would normally apply for a listing and arrange the issue of the bond, but the actual listing would be deferred. This is often driven by investors who do not have to buy immediately listed securities but are pressed to meet other timelines, for example, investments that have to be made by the financial year end and timing for listing is very tight.

The main disadvantages of deferred listing are twofold: (a) any comments/insertions required by the exchange where the notes are to be listed to the offering circular—and, in particular, the terms and conditions of the notes—could involve having to get noteholder's consent to amend the terms and conditions of the notes and the trust deed, leading to further time delay; and (b) for the period the notes remain unlisted, there may be less liquidity in the relevant market as any targeted purchasers will have to be those investors who can buy unlisted securities.

Therefore, it is good practice to avoid deferred listing wherever possible.

Due Diligence

While there will be disclaimers in the offering circular stating that none of the trustee or the arranger is responsible for the accuracy or information contained therein, in some jurisdictions the arranger owes a duty to the investors to ensure that the information included in the offering circular is accurate and not misleading. In such cases, if the offering circular is inaccurate or misleading, and an investor suffers loss as a result, the arranger may incur liability to the investor.

The level of due diligence undertaken by the arranger will depend on several factors such as (1) the quality of information supplied by the issuer, whether the arranger has a long relationship with the issuer and so has detailed knowledge of the issuer's business and financial condition; and (2) the structure of the bond. For example, a straight debt issue will require less due diligence than equity-linked issues as the risks assumed by the investor will be greater for the latter. Examples of some routine steps taken by the arranger include:

- Projections as to the future level of business, growth, or profitability of the issuer should be omitted on the offering circular, unless required by the rules of the stock exchange on which the issue is to be listed.
- Any statement by the issuer as to its position in the market relative to its competitors should be omitted on the offering circular, unless the source of the statement is independent.
- With respect to certain information in the offering circular, the arranger and its legal advisers should question the issuer and its accountants in relation to any unexplained changes in the historical information (whether financial or otherwise) made available by the issuer.
- The arranger should obtain a comfort letter from the auditors to the issuer confirming that all financial information presented in the offering circular has been correctly extracted from the audited financial statements and that there have been no adverse changes in specified financial items since the last financial year end, in the case of balance sheet items, or when compared with the corresponding period in the last financial year, in the case of profit and loss account items.
- The arranger should meet senior officers of the issuer on at least one occasion and have an opportunity to ask questions, designed to ensure not only that the offering circular is accurate but also that there are no circumstances or potential developments, which ought to be disclosed

but have not been. It is not uncommon for a list of questions to be submitted to senior management in advance of the meeting to enable it to consider its response. Typically, the questions asked to the issuer will deal with the following areas:

(a) General operational issues.
(b) Defaulted and problem loans.
(c) Funding and liquidity.
(d) Financial risk management.
(e) Investments.
(f) Capital.
(g) Off balance sheet assets.
(h) Premises, technology, management and employees.
(i) Competition.
(j) Legal and regulatory issues.

Selling Restrictions

The issue of bonds must comply with any securities laws in the jurisdictions targeted for sale. Generally, more onerous restrictions apply when securities are offered or sold to the public and these restrictions are more relaxed for issues to sophisticated investors and private placements.

A summary of such restrictions is usually included in the offering circular and subscription agreement. The restrictions are targeted to the jurisdiction where the issue is originated, the jurisdiction of incorporation of the issuer, the United States of America and the jurisdictions of the investors most likely to participate in the issue.

United States Selling Restrictions

Nearly all bonds documentation includes substantial provisions designed to meet the requirements of United States securities laws which are generally more developed than those applicable in any other country and breach of which can result in severe penalties. Furthermore, they can apply in certain situations to transactions which take place wholly or predominantly outside the United States.

The United States Securities Act of 1933 is administered by the Securities and Exchange Commission (SEC) in Washington. It controls the primary offering of securities to the public in the United States (i.e., new issues and not, in principle, subsequent dealings in the secondary market) and it does this by requiring that publicly offered issues must be registered with the SEC. The registration process involves a preclearance procedure with the SEC. Due to the process being quite burdensome, unless the bond issue targets the US market, the subscription agreement will usually contain a provision binding on the arrangers and the issuer, stating that the notes have not been and will not be registered under the Securities Act and may not be offered or sold within the United States to US persons (which essentially means US residents) except in certain transactions which are exempt from the registration requirements of the Securities Act.

There are four types of exception to this contractual restriction. The first is simply that sales can be allowed to US dealers who agree to the selling restrictions, normally by becoming syndicate members. The second and third exceptions both derive from the fact that private placements in the United States or to US persons are permitted under strictly controlled circumstances—in one instance to "foreign investors" of US banks and insurance companies and in the other to "sophisticated investors." The fourth type of exception and the one more widely used results from the SEC's Rule 144A which makes it considerably easier to do a private placement with very large US institutional investors.

Generally speaking, Rule 144A provides an exemption from US registration requirements for offerings in the United States that are made exclusively to qualified institutional buyers" as defined in the rule. These are basically large institutional investors that own and invest at least $100 million in securities. There are various other procedural requirements and conditions, but none that ought to be problematic. A Rule 144A offering in the United States can easily be made concurrently with an offering outside the United States and do not require approval of the SEC or any other regulatory authority.

There are also sales restrictions in the United States implemented in order to prevent tax evasion. For this purpose, under the TEFRA D Rule, the arranger will have to agree that it will not offer, sell or deliver the notes (i) as part of their distribution at any time; or (ii) otherwise until 40 days after the later of the commencement of the offering and the issue date within the United States or to US persons and that it will have sent to each dealer to which it sells any notes during the distribution compliance period, a confirmation, or other notice setting forth the restrictions on offers and sales of the notes within the United States or to US persons.

The 40-day restriction means the securities must be represented initially by a temporary global bond, i.e., one single bond for the whole issue. The investor can only obtain his permanent global bond on presentation of a certificate indicating that either (a) that the beneficial owner is not a US person; or (b) that the beneficial owner is a US person who falls within one of the limited exceptions available after the 40-day period has lapsed.

European Selling Restrictions

For the purposes of the discussion in this section, selling restrictions in those European countries where there is a wider investor appetite will be examined.

France In order for a sale of bonds not to be deemed to be a public offer and, therefore, subject to more stringent requirements, bonds should only be offered to qualified investors and a restricted group of investors. References to "qualified investors" mean legal entities such as credit institutions, investment companies, insurance companies and collective investment funds. References to "restricted group of investors" mean individuals other than qualified investors who are linked to the management of the issuer by a personal relationship of a professional or family nature. Offers to a restricted group of investors must be to no more than 100 such persons after which the entire issue is deemed to be a public offering and therefore subject to further requirements. Recent views from the Commission Des Opérations De Bourse suggest that any such individual persons should be able to demonstrate a link with the issuer.

Germany Under the German Securities Sales Prospectus Act, it is necessary to publish a prospectus prior to making a primary, public offer of securities in Germany unless an exemption can be relied upon. For bond issues, the most common exemption available is if the bond issues are "European Securities" that are not subject to public promotion. A selling restriction to this effect should be stated in the subscription agreement. Any German investor must buy notes that have an aggregate purchase price equal to at least €40,000, or as otherwise permitted under German law.

Luxembourg Selling restrictions may apply where the issuer is a Luxembourg-incorporated company or otherwise has connections with Luxembourg, but such selling restrictions will not apply if the issuance is through a private placement. In order for an issue to be deemed to be a private placement, the issuer must not offer or sell the notes to the public and no public offer must be made in the Grand Duchy of Luxembourg and such notes should not be subject to any advertisement.

The Netherlands Where the issuer is not a Dutch entity, there should be a selling restriction in the offering circular and subscription agreement indicating that the arranger agreed that the notes would only be offered or sold to persons who trade or invest in securities in the course of its ordinary profession or business. Such offering circular must be filed with the Netherlands Securities Board. If the issuer is a Dutch entity, additional restrictions may be applicable.

Italy All issues of any bonds to be offered or sold in Italy or to Italian investors must be notified to the Bank of Italy prior to issue. Public issues require prior clearance from the Italian Securities Exchange Commission (also known as CONSOB). Offers to sell bonds in Italy without such clearance can only be made (i) to professional investors, (ii) in circumstances that are exempt from the rules on solicitation of investments in Italy, or (iii) to an Italian resident who submits an unsolicited offer to buy the notes. Any offer or sale of notes must be made by a financial entity permitted to conduct such activities in Italy.

Spain Bonds and other debt securities cannot be offered or sold in Spain as a public offer without complying with prospectus filing requirements. However, exemptions to this include where securities are offered or sold (i) to institutional investors, (ii) to 50 or fewer investors, (iii) in an aggregate issue size of less than €6,000,000, or (iv) with a minimum denomination of €150,000.

United Kingdom The arranger will need to represent in the subscription agreement that in relation to notes with a maturity of more than one year, it will not prior to the expiry of six months from the issue date of the notes offer the notes to any persons in the United Kingdom unless their ordinary activities involve them in dealing in investments as principal or agent for the purposes of their business or in circumstances that will not result in a public offer in the United Kingdom within the meaning of the Public Offer of Securities Regulations 1995. Furthermore the arranger must comply with all applicable provisions of the Financial Services and Markets Act 2002.

IPMA Recommendations

The International Primary Market Association (IPMA) is an association that comprises of financial institutions that are heavily involved in the bond primary market.

IPMA is a self-regulatory body aimed at establishing good market practice in the primary market by publishing recommendations on an annual basis about the procedures for issuing debt and equity instruments to which its members are expected to adhere.

A brief outline below explains the nature of IPMA's recommendations. Some of its recommendations apply to every bond issue, while others only apply to comanaged deals.

Recommendations Applicable to Comanaged Deals

1. If issues are priced beforehand, final allotments should be made within the next business day following launch of the issue and any securities remaining unallocated should be retained by the lead manager.
2. A lead manager may offer comanagers a range of underwriting commitments and should grant protection to comanagers by guaranteeing a minimum allotment.
3. Lead managers should not offer participations in an issue with a view to repurchasing such commitments at a later date.
4. Final allotments of floating-rate notes denominated in US dollars or sterling should be in denominations of one million or multiples.
5. The lead manager should achieve price stabilisation such that the issue will create a secondary market and ultimately more liquidity.
6. All lead managers and colead managers must register as reporting dealers under the ISMA rules from the day after allotments and such registration should remain in place for a minimum of 12 months (and six months in the case of colead managers).
7. Each comanager must have the right of refusal on any additional issues which they are entitled to take based on a pro rata share of their original holding.
8. In deals involving a selling group, the lead manager should disclose to the other underwriters that there will be a selling group.

Recommendations Applicable to any Issues

1. The manager must advise all interested parties by screen or telephone of the basic commercial and noncommercial terms of an issue including, without limitation, information on ratings, guarantees, sales restrictions, negative pledge, governing law and cross-default. Copies of the dealer agreement and offering circular should be distributed for debt issues. Each participant in the issue must receive final drafts of the documents at least two business days prior to signing.
2. Underwriting fees should be paid either on the closing date in the case of prepriced debt issue or 30 days after the closing date in all other cases. Further, any legal and listing costs of the issuer should be borne by the issuer and not the lead manager, arranger, or syndicate.
3. 1% per month shall be the late payment interest rate for fees and commissions paid to managers, applicable to all currencies.
4. Definitive bonds should be available as soon as possible after the closing date but no later than 40 days after the closing date, except otherwise as disclosed in the offering circular.
5. All underlying sales restrictions must be observed.
6. The following should be conditions to closing:

    (a) Delivery of all appropriate legal opinions.

    (b) Delivery of a comfort letter from the auditor to the issuer and addressed to all the managers.

    (c) A certificate from a director or senior officer of the issuer stating there has been no change in the issuer's financial condition.

7. Arrangers should ensure that the ultimate holders of the relevant securities can exercise any rights they have against the issuer.

8. Arrangers of an issue should not be obliged to disclose names of potential investors in the issue or the level of interest.

9. The law firm representing the arranger and dealers should be free of any conflict of interest and should act as deal counsel and not represent any other party to the transaction separately in conjunction with the same deal.

Taxation

There are four main areas of taxation in relation to which the arranger ought to obtain appropriate tax advice.

Withholding Tax

From the investors point of view, it is important that an issuer should not be obliged by the law of its home jurisdiction to withhold tax on payments of interest to bondholders. Within Europe, there are many countries that benefit from double tax treaties which mean no income in the form of interest payments is subject to withholding tax. However, some treaties do impose a small levy.

There have been some recent European Union directives which may change the treatment of such income in the future. The Directive on the Taxation of Savings[4] aims to enable savings income in the form of interest payments made in one member state to beneficial owners resident for tax purposes in another member state to be made subject to effective taxation in accordance with the national laws of the latter member state. Under the directive, each member state is expected to provide information to other member states on interest paid from that member state to individuals resident in those other member states. For a transitional period, Belgium Luxembourg, and Austria would be allowed to apply a withholding tax instead of providing information. For this reason, language can be inserted into the offering circular to cater for this possibility if applicable to the relevant jurisdictions to the effect that "the issuer will ensure that it maintains a paying agent in a member state of the European Union that it will not be obliged to withhold or deduct tax pursuant to any such directive or law."

---

[4] The European Union has set itself the aim of ensuring taxation of savings income at the latest by 2010 through an automatic procedure of exchange of information.

Deductibility of Interest
An issuer will generally wish to ensure that all interest payments made on the bonds are deductible by the issuer from its profits in computing its net profits chargeable to income or corporation tax. This will be particularly salient if the issuer is a special purpose vehicle, as any deduction it is entitled to will usually benefit the most junior investors. For example, if the special purpose vehicle is based in Luxembourg, it must realise a minimum profit margin of three basis points of the company's indebtedness. According to general Luxembourg tax and accounting rules, any expenses, including interest expenses, are deductible from the total income of the company. Noteholders, in this instance, would benefit most if the taxable profits of the special purpose vehicle minus operating costs do not exceed the minimum profit margin of the company, which can be best achieved at the structuring stage, by ensuring the special purpose vehicle's income and expense cash flows balance at all times.

Inheritance and Capital Gains Tax
The arranger will generally take advice as to the extent to which, if a bondholder dies, his estate will be subject to any succession, inheritance or similar tax in the issuer's home jurisdiction and place of incorporation, if different. Advice should also be taken as to whether a bondholder who sells his bonds will incur any capital gains tax in that jurisdiction or place.

Stamp Duty
In certain jurisdictions a stamp or documentary tax may be payable on the issue of the bonds or the execution of documents relating to the issue. The issuer generally undertakes in the subscription agreement or note purchase agreement to bear any such taxes. In Italy, for example, stamp duty is payable by Italian issuers if they issue bonds and the relevant documentation is executed in Italy.

Government and Issuer and Approvals
At an early stage the arranger in conjunction with its legal counsel should establish whether any consents or approvals of, or any filings or registrations with, any governmental or regulatory authority are required in the issuer's home jurisdiction (or place of incorporation, if different) in relation to the issue. A typical example would be a foreign exchange approval. The arranger should also ascertain what internal approvals must be obtained within the issuer's and, if applicable, the guarantor's organisation in order to ensure that the issue has been properly authorised.

It is possible to sign the subscription agreement before all necessary consents and approvals have been obtained, but the obligations of the arranger must then be expressed to be conditional on their being obtained prior to closing and any representations given by the issuer of the same must be expressed to be effective as of the date such consents are obtained or the closing date, whichever is the later.

Setting Up an EMTN Programme

Euro Medium Term Notes (EMTNs) are bonds issued under EMTN programmes. An EMTN programme (the "Programme") is the framework under which the EMTNs are issued. Its purpose is to standardise the terms on which an issuer issues notes and consequently to minimise the documentation, time required for, and administrative costs of the issue of notes. It fixes the general terms for the issuance of EMTNs by the issuer. The terms of the EMTN Programme are usually agreed between the issuer, the dealers, the trustee and the agents of the Programme.

General features of an EMTN Programme

EMTN Programmes have the following features:

- They offer the issuer flexibility in raising funds, as the maturity and other issue terms can be structured to suit specific investor requirements and enables issuers to respond quickly to "windows of opportunity" in the market.
- EMTNs are usually offered continuously through a dealer group rather than issued in one tranche underwritten by a syndicate of banks.
- Issued tranches can be listed or nonlisted.
- Issued Notes can have a variety of different structures.
- Issuing method can be syndicated or via a single dealer.
- It offers the issuer flexibility over the amount of notes to be issued at any one time and EMTN documentation makes the issuance of small amounts economically viable.

Setting up an EMTN Programme takes approximately eight weeks depending upon the complexity of the Programme, the number of dealers, the cooperation of the parties involved and whether or not the EMTN Programme will be listed on a Stock Exchange.

Documentation Involved in the Setting Up of an EMTN Programme

The Programme documentation is to a great extent similar to the documentation put in place for a bond issue. Documentation applicable to all the issues under the Programme will be prepared when setting up the Programme, which will usually be updated once a year.[5]

Updating a Programme will typically involve amending the selling restrictions, currency restrictions and terms and conditions of the Programme to keep them up to market standard.

Typical Programme documentation will comprise principally:

(a) A "Programme Agreement," sometimes described as a dealer agreement, which contains the legal agreement between the issuer and the dealers in relation to the establishment and maintenance of the Programme and, subject to express variation in relation to any particular issue, the provisions which will apply whenever the issuer and one or more of the dealers agree on the terms for a specific issue under the EMTN Programme. The content of the programme agreement is substantially similar to the content of the subscription agreement previously described.

(b) The "Agency Agreement," which contains the legal agreement between the issuer and the agents (paying agent, calculation agent, and the like) appointed to service the EMTN Programme, to which will frequently be scheduled the forms of the notes which can be issued under the Programme.

(c) An "Offering Circular" describing the EMTN Programme, including the terms and conditions which, unless otherwise agreed between the relevant parties, will apply to the notes issued under the Programme; and giving descriptive information about the issuer. This document is substantially similar to the Offering Circular of a standalone bond described earlier in this chapter. The only difference is that, while the Offering Circular of a standalone bond will contain the commercial terms of the issuance, in the case of an EMTN note, the commercial terms will be contained in the pricing supplement.

(d) "Trust Deed" or "Fiscal Agency Agreement," as described earlier in this chapter.

(e) Other ancillary documentation, such as legal opinions, auditor's comfort letter, and so on.

Documentation Involved in the Issuance of a Note

When a note is to be issued, the following documents will usually be prepared:

---

[5] Unless the EMTN Programme is listed, there is no requirement for it to be updated. However, programmes which are listed on a stock exchange will require updating in order for the listing to be renewed.

(a) *Dealer's Confirmation*, by which the dealer agrees to underwrite the Notes.
(b) *Issuer's Confirmation*, by which the issuer agrees to issue the *Notes* to the dealer.
(c) *Pricing Supplement*, to be read in conjunction with the *Offering Circular*, which details the commercial terms of the issue.

If the dealer for the note is not a dealer under the EMTN Programme, the following documents will also be needed:

(a) *Dealer Accession Letter*, by which the new dealer accepts its appointment as dealer under the Programme. This will allow the new dealer to enjoy all the rights and obligations of a permanent dealer under the Programme. The dealer can be appointed permanently or just for a particular issue.
(b) *Issuer's Confirmation of Accession*, by which the issuer will appoint the new dealer as dealer.
(c) *Reliance Letter(s)*. For risk mitigation purposes, the new dealer may require to be allowed to rely on the legal opinion(s) of the counsel to the dealers.

COLLATERISED DEBT OBLIGATIONS AND ASSET-BACKED SECURITIES

Among the most popular structured products currently being offered in the market are asset-backed securities (ABSs) and collateralised debt obligations (CDOs).

There are many reasons why an investor may decide to invest in an ABS or a CDO, e.g., to exploit arbitrage opportunities targeting higher returns, to move assets off its balance sheet, to raise cost effective funding, to get exposure to a variety of risk profiles, and so on.[6]

An ABS is a bond issued by a single purpose vehicle (SPV) that is secured with a large number of assets (the "Assets") of one same type pooled in a portfolio. These Assets are usually the sole recourse the investors will have for repayment of the bonds.[7] Examples of Assets are residential mortgages, commercial mortgages, credit card receivables, aircraft leases, and the like.

---

[6] It should be noted though that the provisions of Basel II may reduce the efficiency of using this type of structures for balance sheet efficiency purposes.
[7] See "Nonrecourse to SPV, Recourse to Collateral" below.

EXHIBIT 30.1   Traditional Style of CDO or ABS Structure

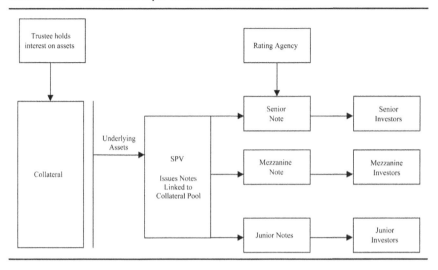

A CDO is a bond issued by an SPV that is secured by a pool of debt put by the issuer into a portfolio. As in the ABS, this pool is usually the sole recourse the investors will have for repayment of the notes. The pool may be composed of loans, securities, mortgaged backed securities or other ABSs.

The structure of an ABS or a CDO will usually look similar to the structure in Exhibit 30.1. This type of structure is usually known as "traditional structure" as opposed to synthetic structures, where the risk, but not the assets, is transferred.

In an ABS or CDO the SPV will issue notes and will use the proceeds to purchase assets, in the case of an ABS, or debt, in the case of a CDO (the "Collateral"). The SPV will receive a return from the issuer of the collateral and will use such returns to pay the investors a return on the bonds.

The balance sheet of an SPV issuing ABSs or CDOs will look similar to Exhibit 30.2.

In an ABS or CDO structure the issuer will usually issue different tranches of notes with different levels of seniority.[8] As losses occur in the portfolio, the most junior investors will start losing their investment. The mezzanine investors will only face a loss on their investment after the junior tranche has been lost, that is, the losses on the portfolio are greater than the junior tranche. The senior tranche investors will only face a loss on their investments when the losses on the portfolio are greater than the sum of the junior tranche and the mezzanine tranche together.

---

[8] See below "Security Issues."

EXHIBIT 30.2   Balance Sheet of an SPV Issuing ABSs or CDOs

Assets	Liabilities
If an ABS: Residential Mortgages Commercial Mortgages Credit Card Receivables Auto Loans Leases Whole Business Securitisation	Senior Tranche Super AAA AAA
If a CDO: RMBS CMBS ABS of Credit Cards ABS of Auto Loans ABS of Leases Bonds and Loans (Corporate Financials Sovereign High Yield Emerging Market) Credit Default Swaps Hedge Funds Private Equity CDO tranches	Mezzanine Tranche AA+ to BB- First Loss, Equity, Subordinated Tranche

Legal Issues

Confidentiality and No Conflicting Roles Clauses

The parties should consider putting in place a *confidentiality agreement* between the parties involved in a transaction until the time the transaction is made public. Also, in relation to collateral managers, the parties should consider whether or not the collateral manager should be prevented from acting as collateral manager for similar transactions while the Collateral for the relevant transaction is being ramped up.

Confidentiality issues will also arise when nonpublic assets are put into the portfolio. For example, if a loan is incorporated into the portfolio, the transferor of the loan should make sure all the authorizations of the borrower and any other party involved in the loan are put in place before disclosing information on the loan to the parties involved in the ABS or CDO. Likewise, if the risk is transferred to a portfolio through a synthetic instrument, (e.g., a credit default swap), care should be taken of any confidentiality obligation to the credit default swap counterparty.

Legal Due Diligence

One of the most time consuming tasks which is usually conducted in-house is the review of the documentation for the collateral to be put into the portfolio. Points to pay attention to are whether or not the assets are properly secured, transfer provisions,[9] which will be very important when the rating agencies look into the portfolio to determine the sale and insolvency clawback risks, governing law, and acceleration clauses.

Bankruptcy Remoteness

The issuer of the bonds under a traditional CDO or ABS structure or of credit-linked notes in a synthetic funded structure is a special purpose vehicle (SPV). The structure relies on the fact that such SPV is "bankruptcy remote," that is, the entity is unlikely to become subject to bankruptcy proceedings or claims by other investors. For these purposes, the constitutional documents of the SPV usually prohibit any merger, or consolidation, the SPV is prohibited from engaging in business other than those directly related to the transaction and is restricted from incurring any additional debt.

Nonrecourse to SPV, Recourse to Collateral

One of the most basic legal ideas in a transaction structured through an SPV is that the rights of the bondholders and other creditors involved in the transactions (e.g., swap counterparties, trustees, etc.), together the "Secured Parties" are intrinsically linked to the "Collateral" and any other assets and rights of the issuer under the terms of the transaction together the "Mortgaged Property," but not to any other asset of the SPV. Consequently, the Secured Parties will have a security interest in the Mortgaged Property, which cannot be secured in favour of any other party, but, if such Mortgaged Property is not sufficient to cover the amount owed to them, they will not have access to any other assets that the SPV may have. For this purpose, a clause is usually inserted in the documentation indicating that the secured creditors will have the right to realise the Mortgaged Property, but will not have the right to initiate insolvency or bankruptcy proceedings against the SPV.

---

[9] For further discussion on this, see below "Transfer of Assets and Perfection."

Transfer of Assets and Perfection

The Collateral needs to be transferred to the SPV. The transfer should be effected in a manner that shields the assets from the bankruptcy risk of the transferor.

When the Collateral consists of securities or other assets, a pledge of the assets to the SPV will not ensure the access of the SPV to the assets in a timely basis if the transferor goes bankrupt. As a matter of law, the creditor will probably be able to take the benefit of the assets, but time delays in payments often occur. Consequently, a true sale or absolute assignment of the assets is the preferred course of action. When making a true sale or assigning the asset, in order to isolate the asset from an event of insolvency of the transferor, the price paid for the asset should be paid at arm's length in order to minimise the risk of the sale being challenged.

In the case of loans to be incorporated into the portfolio, such loans may contain transfer restrictions or anti-assignment clauses. For example, in some cases, there is an outright prohibition of such transfer, in other cases transfer is only possible upon obtaining the consent of the borrower, or it could be that transfer is only to certain class of transferees. If the terms of the loan prohibit such transfer, it is possible to incorporate the loan in the portfolio by the creation of a participation, in which case the issuer will be bearing double credit risk, that is, the credit risk of the borrower and the credit risk of the transferor, or the creation of a trust. The loan could also be included in the portfolio by way of security, that is, the lender will remain the same person, but the SPV will get a security interest over the right of the lender in relation to such loan. Other key points to keep in mind when transferring loans to a portfolio is to make sure any set-off rights with the transferor are excluded, that there is no obligation to make further advances and that any security interest is properly transferred.

Tax Position

A structured transaction can raise a significant number of tax issues for all the involved parties. A detailed analysis of any potential income or wealth tax liability in the place of incorporation of the *issuer*, which will use funds that otherwise will be paid to the junior investors, potential withholding tax issues, which will make the investors receive their return net unless gross-up is provided for, and VAT issues for services received by the SPV should be made. Also, a complete analysis of the tax risks raised as a consequence of the relationship of the issuer with the collateral manager or collateral advisor is advisable.[10]

---

[10] See "Taxation" above and "Tax Aspects" below under the case study.

Netting Enforceability

Of special importance in synthetic structures involving total return swaps or credit default swaps, and where regulatory relief is being sought, is to ensure that the netting provisions of the credit default swap along with the netting against collateral will be enforceable in the case of a close out. Legal advice should be sought on this issue.

Also, when transferring credit risk to a portfolio through a synthetic structure, it is very important to make sure the transaction is not, unintentionally, converted into an insurance contract. Basically, the difference between an insurance policy and a credit default swap is that, while in an insurance policy the purchaser of credit protection has to suffer a loss in order to receive payment, in a credit default swap, the credit protection purchaser does not have to suffer a loss in order to obtain payment. Therefore, the incorporation of clauses indicating that that the protection buyer should hold a risk of loss in order to be paid any amount under a credit default swap should be scrutinise and seeking the advice of a legal counsel on this point is very important. If the credit default swap is deemed to be an insurance policy, regulatory and tax issues may arise. For instance, a bank selling protection under a credit default swap containing a requirement of loss before payment is made, would probably see this agreement recharacterised as an insurance policy. In such a case, such bank could be held to be in breach of the obligation to hold an insurance company licence.

Drafting of the Eligibility Criteria

The eligibility criteria are inserted to determine the parameters to be satisfied by new assets incorporated into the portfolio, during ramp up or after, for example, an early redemption, or when substitution of part of the assets in the portfolio is allowed. Sometimes overlooked by the lawyers is the drafting of the eligibility criteria, which is often left to the structurers. Bad drafting of the eligibility criteria could leave the purchaser of synthetic risk protection without protection, as many times the documentation indicates that if such asset does not meet the eligibility criteria, it shall not be deemed to be incorporated into the *Portfolio*.

Seniority

In structured ABSs and CDOs, the bonds issued by the issuer are ranked accordingly to the priority of claim it offers the investor in relation to the other noteholders for distribution during the life of the transaction and for purposes of distributing the proceeds from the realization of the Mortgaged Property in the case of acceleration of the bonds. The bonds issued in a transaction are usually divided into junior tranches (i.e., the first to suffer any loss), mezzanine tranches (which will suffer loss after the junior tranches), and senior tranches (which will be the first bonds under which payments will be made). The seniority ranking is described in the "Priority of Payment" clauses and is usually very heavily negotiated. The Priority of Payment clauses not only determine the order in which payments will be made to the different tranches but will also determine the order in which, among others, fees to trustees, agents and collateral managers, amounts payable to swap counterparties or repo counterparties, amounts payable to any liquidity facility provider and the like, will be paid.

Traditional vs. Synthetic: the Risk of Recharacterisation

Historically ABSs and CDOs were done on a real purchase basis with assets being purchased by the SPV and notes being sold to the investors.

More recently synthetic structures have become widely used as an alternative method. Many advantages can be found in the use of synthetic structures instead of traditional structures; (1) Synthetic structures are easier to execute as the assets need not to be actually transferred; (2) problems usually existing in traditional structures (e.g., transfer restrictions, tax and regulatory issues) can often be avoided by using a synthetic structure (stamp duty, for example, is not payable in relation to a synthetic structure); (3) a synthetic structure can also allow an entity to get regulatory relief without having to remove those assets from such entity's balance sheet from the accounting perspective; and (4) documentation is also very standardised, the starting point for the drafting being the 2000 ISDA Credit Derivatives Definitions and, for that reason, the legal costs are smaller than in a traditional transaction.[11]

An ABS or CDO structure can be structured as a synthetic ABS or CDO, through the use of swaps to transfer the risk (instead of transferring the assets). In an unfunded synthetic structure, an SPV (or another entity willing to intermediate) will usually sell protection to one or more entities on one or more names (being the resulting risk portfolio, the "Portfolio") through one or more credit default swaps and will enter into one or more credit default swaps with the investors under the terms of which such entity will pay a premium to the investors in exchange for the investors commitment to make payment in the case of default on any of the obligations held in the Portfolio. As in the traditional structures, there may be several tranches with different level of seniority.

A synthetic structure can also be funded. This is especially indicated for those cases where the investor wishes to get exposure to a portfolio

---

[11] At the time of writing, the International Swaps and Dealers Association is about to publish a new version of the ISDA Credit Derivatives Definitions.

EXHIBIT 30.3   Synthetic Partially Funded Structure

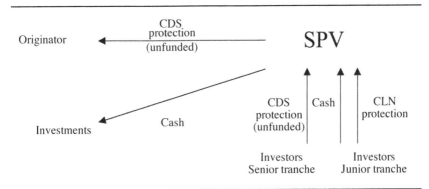

of risks but cannot invest on structures that are not securitised. In such structures, an SPV will sell protection to a third party (the "Originator") through a credit default swap and will hedge such protection through credit linked notes. The proceeds from the issuance of the credit-linked notes (the "Cash") shall be invested in highly liquid assets and pledged in favour of the Originator as collateral. Whenever a default occurs, the Cash shall be used to pay the protection amount to the Originator. At maturity of the notes, any residual cash is paid to the investors. The investors will receive during the life of the transaction a funded yield (which will normally come from the return paid on the Cash and the premium paid by the Originator on the credit default swap). A purely synthetic unfunded structure can be combined with a synthetic funded structure. A chart of such structure can be found in Exhibit 30.3.

CASE STUDY: EUROPEAN CDO OF MORTGAGE-BACKED SECURITIES

As a way of pooling together all the considerations explored in this chapter, the best way is to demonstrate the major issues through a case study. We will use for this purpose, a CDO of mortgaged-backed securities.

Facts

For the purposes of this discussion, the following assumptions about the structure will apply:

(a) Jurisdiction: The SPV is incorporated in Luxembourg.

EXHIBIT 30.4   Timeline for Case Study

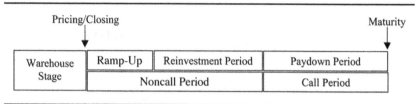

(b) Composition of portfolio: residential mortgages (RMBS), commercial mortgages (CMBS) and synthetic securities (i.e., notes issued by either a mortgage bank or special purpose vehicle, the repayment of which is linked to the performance of a portfolio of RMBS or CMBS). All RMBS and CMBS and synthetic securities (together, the "Collateral Debt Securities") are euro-denominated.

(c) Collateral Manager: a London branch of an investment bank that is also the Arranger.

(d) Collateral Adviser: a German bank, experienced in managing portfolios of RMBS and CMBS.

(e) Listing: Luxembourg for the final notes only.

(f) Interest Payment Dates: Semi-annual, based on EURIBOR plus a spread for the Senior Notes (as defined below). In the Junior Notes, interest will be paid semi-annual in amounts dependant on the proceeds from the Collateral Debt Securities.

(g) Tranching: Class A as the senior level, Class B as the second priority level (Class A and Class B being the "Senior Notes"). Class C-1 and Class C-2 at a subordinated level (together the "Junior Notes"), all of them denominated in euros.

(h) Rating: The final Senior Notes to be rated by Fitch Ratings Limited ("Fitch"), and Standard & Poors ("S&P," and together with Fitch, the "Rating Agencies") as "AAA."

(i) Governing Law: Predominantly English law.

(j) Investors: Senior Notes—a professional mortgage lender; Junior Notes—institutional investors with total return targets.

The timeline for this transaction is best explained into two tranches described below as the Warehouse Stage and the Final Closing Stage. Exhibit 30.4 describes the timeline for the discussed CDO.

Warehouse Stage

This stage does not require rating and merely aims to set up a facility whereby the portfolio can be ramped up partially. Warehouses can be structured in different ways, for example, the Collateral Debt Securities can be bought by the Junior Noteholders until an amount sufficient to launch the deal is bought, at which moment, the notes are issued by the SPV and the proceeds from such issuance are used to purchase the Collateral Debt Securities from the Junior Investor. In the case of this case study, the ramp-up was made by the SPV purchasing the Collateral Debt Securities directly from the market.

Once the SPV is incorporated and during the Warehouse Stage, the SPV shall issue an amount of €40,000,000 Class A Exchangeable Notes and €20,000,000 Class C-1 Exchangeable Notes (together the "Exchangeable Notes"). The initial proceeds from the Exchangeable Notes will be used to purchase Collateral Debt Securities for the portfolio with respect to which the SPV shall enter directly into purchase agreements with the seller of such Collateral Debt Securities. All Collateral Debt Securities to be purchased shall be identified on advice provided by the Collateral Adviser (described in more detail under "Collateral Manager and Collateral Adviser").

The Collateral Debt Securities will have to satisfy certain asset and portfolio criteria (the "Asset Criteria" and the "Portfolio Criteria" respectively and together known as the "Eligibility Criteria"). For example, the Asset Criteria will provide that the Collateral Debt Security will need to have a maturity shorter than the Final Notes. The Portfolio Criteria, will provide that the portfolio, as a whole, will not contain more than 5% of assets rated below BBB+.

At this stage, the Arranger, in addition to the usual Luxembourg and English legal opinions, will request a "True Sale" opinion confirming that the purchase of Collateral Debt Securities by the issuer is effective. Although this is usually a requirement of the Rating Agencies for rated notes, when rating the Final Notes, the Rating Agencies will request confirmation on this point for the Collateral Debt Securities purchased during the Warehouse Stage.

The issuer enters into a short term but renewable liquidity agreement (the "Liquidity Agreement") with a liquidity provider (the "Lender"). After exhausting the proceeds from the issuance of the above Exchangeable Notes, and as soon as more Collateral Debt Securities become available for purchase, the issuer will draw down under the Liquidity Agreement to fund such purchases. As soon as the aggregate amount outstanding under the Liquidity Agreement reaches a determined threshold amount, this will trigger a mandatory purchase by the holder of the Class A Exchangeable Notes of a tap issue Class A Exchangeable Notes in an amount equal to such threshold amount. The proceeds from such tap issue shall be applied in accordance with the relevant priority of payments but predominantly to the repayment of the

Liquidity Agreement. The issuer shall continue to issue taps of Class A Exchangeable Notes (each such tap shall be fully fungible with and form a single consolidated series with the initial Class A Exchangeable Notes) until at least 70% of the targeted total principal amount of portfolio is purchased (the "Exchange Trigger Event"). If by the first anniversary of the issue of the Class C-1 Exchangeable Notes, the Exchange Trigger Event has not occurred, the holders of Class C-1 Exchangeable Notes will, by a majority of votes, determine to (i) extend the period for such ramp-up for another six months; (ii) sell the existing portfolio and redeem all the issued Exchangeable Notes in accordance with a predetermined order of priority of payments; or (iii) close a smaller transaction. In the case of (ii), proceeds shall be distributed in accordance with the priority of payments (the "Priority of Payment") order described under the terms of the Exchangeable Notes for this case.

If, however, the Exchange Trigger Event has occurred, the Class A Exchangeable Notes shall be exchanged into the final Class A Notes and the Class A Noteholder shall purchase any additional Class A Notes to be issued on the day of such exchange (the "Final Closing Date"). Similarly, on the Final Closing Date, the Class C-1 Exchangeable Notes shall be exchanged into the final Class C-1 Notes and the Class B Notes and Class C-2 Notes shall be issued (the Class A Notes, Class B Notes, Class C-1 Notes, and Class C-2 Notes together, the "Final Notes").

From the Lender's perspective, the Lender will, at the time of negotiating the Liquidity Facility, wish to keep control on whether or not to extend the Liquidity Facility beyond the first anniversary of the issue of the Class C-1 Exchangeable Notes. In the Priority of Payments, the Lender will usually wish to be senior, or at least rank pari passu, with the most senior noteholders, in this case, the Class A Exchangeable Notes holder.

Interest is not payable on the Exchangeable Notes during the Warehouse Stage. The closing of the Warehouse Stage will trigger a distribution of (i) interest accrued on the Class A Exchangeable Notes up to but excluding the closing of the Warehouse Stage; (ii) the repayment of amounts outstanding under the liquidity agreement; (iii) the payment of any service costs such as trustee, custodian, paying agent, and collateral administration costs for the Warehouse Stage; and (iv) an amount equal to the interest paid on the portfolio (the "Warehouse Interest") during the warehouse stage minus the costs in (i), (ii), and (iii) above to the holders of the Class C-1 Exchangeable Notes on a pro rata basis, only to the extent funds are available. If the Warehouse Interest is insufficient to meet the distribution in (i), any shortfall will be funded by a further drawdown under the liquidity agreement and distributions or shortfalls to (ii) or (iii) will be funded from the proceeds of sale of the Final Notes.

The drafting of the "Priority of Payments" is probably the clause that will take the most time for the documentation of the Exchangeable Notes. In addition to the Priority of Payments clause determining what would occur if the Final Notes are not issued and the collateral needs to be realised, two additional waterfalls will be necessary, one to determine what to do with the interest paid in the Collateral Debt Securities during the Warehouse Stage on the Final Closing Date, the second to determine what to do with the proceeds from the issuance of the Final Notes (see below).

The Exchangeable Notes will not be rated or listed although if it seems that the Exchange Trigger Event will not occur at least two months prior to the anniversary date, the investors have required that the issuer will have to obtain a listing of the Exchangeable Notes.

Final Closing Stage

The gross proceeds of sale received by the Issuer from the issuance and sale of the Final Notes shall have the following fees and expenses deducted from it:

(a) The Arranger's structuring fee.
(b) The upfront rating costs.
(c) The upfront trustee costs.
(d) The amount outstanding under the Liquidity Facility if the Warehouse Interest is insufficient.
(e) The trustee, collateral administrator, the paying agent costs due under the Warehouse Stage if the Warehouse Interest is insufficient.
(f) A deposit of euros [€250,000] into the expense account of the Issuer (the "Expense Account") (discussed in more detail under the section "Trustee and Other Related Services").

The Ramp-Up

The net proceeds resulting after the application of the above waterfall will be used by the Issuer to purchase more Collateral Debt Securities. However, such investments can only be made up to the last day of the "Ramp-Up Period."

Although traditionally the Ramp-Up Periods used to be around 3–6 months from the Final Closing Date because the investors' interest is to have tight Ramp-Ups periods in order to maximise diversity and returns, nowadays we are seeing much longer Ramp-Up Periods (even Ramp-Up Periods as long as the Reinvestment Periods) so that only assets of the best quality are put into the portfolio.

Reinvestment on Collateral Debt Securities

After the termination of the Ramp-Up Period, the Reinvestment Period will start. This period has traditionally lasted around five years, but nowadays, we are seeing longer Reinvestment Periods. In this deal, the Reinvestment Period will last seven years from the Final Closing Date. During the Reinvestment Period, any proceeds received by the issuer upon redemption of any Collateral Debt Securities will be reinvested in further Collateral Debt Securities subject to compliance with any rating agency requirements.

No investment may be made in Collateral Debt Securities or Eligible Investments (as described below) after the termination of the Reinvestment Period or as a result of the suspension of such Reinvestment Period due to a failure of the overcollateralisation ratio test.

The Collateral Debt Securities purchased by the Issuer during the Ramp-Up and Reinvestment Period are required to have characteristics which will satisfy the Criteria agreed by the Arranger with the Rating Agencies (the "Eligibility Criteria"). In this case, such Eligibility Criteria will include, without limitation, the following:

Asset Criteria

- The obligation is a collateralized debt security.
- The interest paid will be floating either by way of an interest rate hedge or directly.
- The collateralized debt security is not subject to any other security arrangements.
- The collateralized debt security is not a defaulting or deferring security.
- The legal maturity of the collateralized debt security is less than the legal maturity of the notes, and the expected maturity is less than the expected maturity of the notes.
- The collateralized debt security pays interest at least semi annually.
- The collateralized debt security will have a minimum required rating.

Portfolio Criteria

- Overcollateralisation ratio test and collateral quality tests must be met.
- Various rating agency tests will be met.
- There will be constraints with regard to the minimum allowed diversity of the pool by obligation and servicer.
- There will be constraints with regard to the minimum required ratings of the pool as a whole.

In addition, to the extent that there is cash sitting in the Expense Account or any other account held by the SPV, if the Collateral Advisor determines that there are not suitable Collateral Debt Securities in the market, and pending investment in Collateral Debt Securities, the Issuer can invest such cash in liquid assets as, for example, (a) cash; (b) guaranteed obligations; (c) demand or time deposits; (d) unleveraged repurchase obligations; (e) short term debt securities; (f) commercial paper; or (g) any money market fund or similar investment vehicle (all together "Eligible Investments"). All such Eligible Investments shall be rated "AAA" by Fitch or "AAA" by S&P and shall be short term so that they can be liquidated easily.

The Collateral Advisor will also be obliged to proceed with the sale of Collateral Debt Obligations that fall below a required rating or are defaulted.

Form and Transfer of the Notes

Each Class of Final Notes will initially be represented by a Temporary Global Note, in bearer form, with coupons or talons (if any) attached. Each such Temporary Global Note will be deposited with a common depository (the "Common Depository") for Euroclear Bank S.A./N.V. as operator of the Euroclear System ("Euroclear") and Clearstream Banking, société anonyme ("Clearstream, Luxembourg") on or about the Final Closing Date. Interests in each such Temporary Global Note will be exchangeable not earlier than 40 calendar days after the Final Closing Date for interests in a Permanent Global Note, provided that written certification of non-US beneficial ownership by the relevant noteholders has been received. On the exchange of interests in the Temporary Global Note in respect of a Class of notes for interests in the Permanent Global Note in respect of such Class of notes, such Permanent Global Note will be deposited with the Common Depository. The Final Notes have not been registered under the laws of any jurisdiction.

Save in certain limited circumstances, notes in definitive form (the "Definitive Notes") will not be issued in exchange for Global Notes. For so long as Notes are represented by the Global Notes and held by the Common Depository, such Notes will be transferable in accordance with the rules and procedures for the time being of Euroclear and Clearstream, Luxembourg.

However, for ease, it may be better to issue the Exchangeable Notes on a Permanent Global Notes form (i.e., without issuing the corresponding Temporary Global Notes). This would eliminate the need to obtain temporary ISIN numbers and wait 40 days before fungibility occurs with the original Class A Exchangeable Notes each time there is a tap of such Class A Exchangeable Notes.

The Diverse Entities involved in the Transaction

The following is a brief description of the roles, rights and obligations of the different parties involved in this structure.

Collateral Manager and Collateral Adviser

Both the obligations of the Collateral Manager and Collateral Adviser will be set out in Collateral Management and Advice Agreement (CMAA).

The main distinction between the two roles is that, on the one hand, the Collateral Adviser will give advice and provide recommendations and to a certain extent make decisions regarding the portfolio, (for example, the selection, acquisition, and disposition of Collateral Debt Securities and the exercising rights and remedies associated therewith. On the other hand, the Collateral Manager will execute any decisions made in respect of the portfolio and generally look after the portfolio and take all actions necessary on behalf of the Issuer to progress the transaction. However, it is imperative to pay special attention on who actually is taking the decision of making a purchase as this will have some consequences from the tax point of view that are examined below in the section "Tax Issues."

The Collateral Manager and the Collateral Advisor are entitled to an annual fee to be paid on the Final Closing Date and on each anniversary thereafter. For US consolidation reasons, it is usually advisable to make sure that the payment of fees to the Collateral Manager and Collateral Advisor are not linked to the performance of the portfolio and rank senior to the Junior Noteholders.

Trustee and Other Related Services

There are several other administrative roles involved in the daily operation of the CDO and below is a brief outline of the various roles.

Calculation Agent

The Calculation Agent's main role is to determine the EURIBOR rate and calculate and notify all relevant parties of the interest amounts owing to the Noteholders on each Interest Payment Date. The Calculation Agent will be part to the Agency Agreement.

Collateral Administrator

Amongst other things, the Collateral Administrator is responsible for calculating certain amounts that are payable to the Noteholders, preparing the periodic reports (in this case, monthly reports) and carrying out any other duties in respect of the portfolio as instructed by the Collateral Manager. The monthly report will capture all details of the portfolio including number of defaulted securities, balance of each accounts, principal balance of the Collateral Debt Securities and whether each Collateral Debt Security meets the Eligibility Criteria or not. Such report is usually verified by the Collateral Manager before being distributed to the Noteholders, Trustee, and other parties.

Trustee

The Trustee will create security over the assets of the issuer (including, without limitation, the Collateral Debt Securities, Eligible Investments and cash accounts). Such security will be by way of first fixed charge and will be for the benefit of all the secured parties including the Noteholders. If there is an event of default under the Notes, the security will become enforceable and the Trustee will be involved in liquidating the assets in order to meet the claims of the various creditors in accordance with a predetermined order of priority of payments. The Trustee is also responsible for acting on behalf of the Noteholders in order to make sure any amendments to any documents and the like are not prejudicial to the Noteholders.

Paying Agent

The Principal Paying Agent is responsible for setting up and monitoring the various cash accounts on behalf of the Issuer. It is also responsible for transferring monies to the Payment Account in readiness for Interest Payment Dates. One of the accounts is the Expense Account, which will have monies on deposit which may be withdrawn to pay for the issuer's Extraordinary Administrative Expenses.

Extraordinary Administrative Expenses include fees incurred by the Issuer which are not already covered at the outset of the transaction and will usually include administrative fees, listing fees, accountants annual fees, legal fees of the Issuer, and Trustee or any other party and any indemnities.

The monies in the Expense Account will not be drawn until the share capitalization costs of the Issuer (equal to €124,000) are used up to cover such expenses. Thereafter as invoices become due and payable monies will be drawn and on each Interest Payment Date (and to the extent there are sufficient funds), to the extent that the Expense Account balance is below €25,000, monies will be applied from distribution to replenish to €50,000.

Since the notes are to be listed in Luxembourg it is a requirement of the Luxembourg Stock Exchange to maintain a paying agent in Luxembourg.

Custodian

The Custodian shall be responsible for holding the Collateral Debt Securities in a Euroclear Account.

Interest

The Senior Notes and Class B Notes will bear floating-rate interest plus a margin. The margin steps up after 12 years and this is designed to incentivise the Junior Noteholders to opt to redeem the Senior Notes and call the whole transaction, otherwise their returns will be diminished.

The Senior Notes are also "pickable," which means that if funds are not available on an Interest Payment Date to pay the full amount of interest owing to the Class A or Class B Notes, such amount will be deferred and therefore not due and payable on such Interest Payment Date but will be outstanding on the applicable Notes and payable with funds available in future Interest Payment Dates. The ratings by the rating agencies will therefore be based on ultimate payment of principal and interest and not timely payment of the same.

Payments of interest on the Junior Notes are subordinate to the payment of interest on the Senior Notes and therefore the holders of the Junior Notes are only entitled to the funds that are available for distribution after having made the payment under the Senior Notes. In this transaction, the Class C-1 Noteholders requested their Notes to be amortizing and so wanted their interest amount to be divided into a fixed interest portion. This will need some tax planning as described in the section "Tax Issues" below in order to prevent increasing the tax liability of the Issuer.

Redemption

The legal maturity of the deal is 99 years, but due to the optional redemptions described below, the deal is expected to be terminated in about 12 years.

The Senior Notes shall be redeemed (in whole but not in part) by the Issuer at the direction of the holders of more than 50% of the aggregate principal amount outstanding as at the Final Closing Date of the Junior Notes. Any such redemption is subject to the following conditions: (a) no such redemption may occur on any date other than an Interest Payment Date; (b) other than as a result of the occurrence of certain tax events, no such redemption may occur prior to the end of the Reinvestment Period; and (c) no optional redemption of the Senior Notes may occur unless there are sufficient proceeds to repay all the Senior Notes and any accrued and unpaid fees and expenses.

Any such redemption shall be effected from proceeds of sale of the Collateral Debt Securities and Eligible Investments and al other funds in the cash accounts.

On any Interest Payment Date on or after payment in full of the Senior Notes and any accrued fees and expenses, the Junior Notes shall be redeemed (in whole but not in part) by the Issuer at the direction of holders more than 50% of the aggregate principal amount outstanding as at the Final Closing Date of the Junior Notes.

You may have noticed that the above purposes, the Class C-1 Notes shall not be deemed to have been amortized (i.e., its voting rights will be in the same ratio as on the Final Closing Date). This is done so that the Junior holders keep the same controlling power, regardless of whether or not its note amortises. Also, distribution of principal among the Junior Noteholder at redemption shall be made taking into account the principal amount of the Class C-1 Note and Class C-2 Note as of the Final Closing Date so that the Class C-1 Note does not lose any participation in proceeds due to the early amortization.

Any such redemption shall be effected to the extent there are any remaining proceeds from the sale or other disposition of the Mortgaged Property.

The Junior Notes will be mandatorily redeemed if all the portfolio is sold as a result of defaults on the portfolio.

US Consolidation Rules

The Arranger is a bank listed in the New York Stock Exchange and, consequently, it is subject to US GAAP rules.

In January 2003, the US Financial Accounting Standards Board (the "FASB") issued a new interpretation on the consolidation of the Variable Interest Entities under US GAAP rules. The new rules are intended to tighten up the analysis in determining whether an SPV has to be consolidated and where. One could say that if the Arranger, the Collateral Advisor, the Collateral Manager, the Liquidity Facility Provider, or the holder of the Junior Note is subject to US GAAP rules, then such entity should examine whether or not it will have to consolidate the SPV into its balance sheet. In short, an entity shall be obliged to consolidate the SPV if that entity has a variable interest (or combination of variable interests) that will absorb a majority of the entity's expected losses if they occur, receive a majority of the entity's expected residual returns if they occur, or both . . . A direct or indirect ability to make decisions that significantly affect the results of the activities of a variable interest entity is a strong indication that an enterprise has one or both of the characteristics that would require consolidation of the variable interest entity.

The expected losses and expected residual returns of the SPV shall include (a) the expected variability in the entity's net income or loss; (b) the expected variability in the fair value of the entity's assets if it is not included in net income or loss (except as explained below); (c) fees to the decision maker (if there is a decision maker); and (d) fees to providers of guarantees of all of the values of the entity's assets (including writers of put options and other instruments with similar results) or payment of all of its liabilities.

Advice from the auditors of the involved entity should be sought when such entity is subject to US GAAP Rules.

The Setting Up of an SPV

When choosing the jurisdiction to incorporate the Issuer, there are three principal considerations that should influence the final decision.

Need for Double-Tax Treaty Relief

If a jurisdiction with a double-tax treaty network is not needed, one can consider one of the main three tax-free jurisdictions (namely, Cayman Islands, Gibraltar, or Jersey). Otherwise one must look to low-tax jurisdictions, for example, Ireland, Luxembourg, or Netherlands.

Investor Requirements

This is a key driver for where an SPV should be set up. Some European investors are restricted by their regulators and can only invest in securities issued by issuers outside of the European Union or the OECD up to a maximum threshold.

The other investor consideration may be the experience such investors have in a particular jurisdiction—whether they have dealt in one more than the other and it has worked well or whether they feel certain jurisdictions are perceived to be involved in money-laundering activities.

Availability of Service Providers and Running Costs

It is also important to ensure the service providers or administrators in the different jurisdictions are experienced and efficient. In maintaining any SPV, a transaction must factor in the costs of local legal counsel, accountants and the administration company.

The table in Exhibit 30.5 briefly outlines the three points discussed above as well as other jurisdiction specific points to notice.

In our case study, the SPV is based in Luxembourg. The following steps were taken in setting up the SPV.

EXHIBIT 30.5 Comparison Table for the Setting Up of an SPV

	Cayman Islands	Gibraltar	Jersey	Ireland	Luxembourg	Netherlands
Area	Not OECD or EU	OECD and EU	OECD only	OECD and EU	OECD and EU	OECD and EU
Minimum capital	US $1,000	£100	£10 paid up	€38,000	€124,000	€18,000
Incorporation fees	£2,000–£3,000	Approx £10,000	Approx £4,000	€38,000–€50,000	£1000–£1,500	£1000–£1500
Annual running costs	£3,000–£7,000	Approx £4,000	Approx £7,000	£2,800	£15,000	Approx £10,000–£20,000
Additional Information	Least regulated of all jurisdictions, but have a perception of being involved in money-laundering activities.	Perception of being involved in money-laundering activities.	Some disclosure may need to be made to the authorities on the beneficial ownership of the SPV.			
Taxation				25% Minimum profit of €5,000–€10,000. Not necessary to obtain advance ruling. No withholding tax on interest payments to any EU person from January 2003. From January 2003, interest on junior notes where rate depends on company's profits will be deductible for tax purposes.	30.38% Taxable basis is between 1 bp and 3 bp of amount of outstanding notes. Tax ruling is required but can proceed without ruling. Longest time to get ruling. No withholding tax on interest payments. There is a risk that company profit-related interest payments may not be tax deductible, but remains unresolved as at the time of writing.	30% Tax ruling is generally required on a "cost plus" (i.e., taking into account the management costs of the local administrator). No withholding tax on interest payments. Interest will not be deductible so long as it satisfies certain conditions related to the company's profit related nature of interest.

The arranger had to sign a mandate letter with the administrator, appointing them to carry out the day-to-day activities of the SPV. There was also a company domiciliation agreement between the SPV and the administrator setting out what the administrator's duties will be, the fees they will get paid and what the obligations of the SPV will be to aid the administrator in its duties.

A "Share Trust Deed" is entered into between the issuer and each trustee. The trustees hold the shares on trust for charitable purposes and this deed merely sets out the duties of the trustee to the relevant charities.

Once the "Articles of Incorporation" have been drafted for the SPV, the administrator will set up a bank account and as soon as the share capital is injected into the SPV, the SPV shall be incorporated. The share capital is equal to €124,000 and is usually funded by the arranger. However, due to the increasing concerns over consolidation, some arrangers may need to factor in a way of recouping such money through the structuring of the deal, particularly since the €124,000 can be used to pay down the issuer's costs and the arranger will not want to be seen to be supporting the SPV.

Tax Issues

The tax aspects relating to the place of incorporation of the SPV are diverse and should be looked into before proceeding to incorporate such SPV.

Corporate Tax Issues: The Issuer Being Taxed in Luxembourg

Under the tax regulations applicable in Luxembourg (place of incorporation of the SPV), at the end of each financial year corporation taxes at a rate of 30.38% are assessed on a taxable profit. The taxable profit is the higher of (a) the profit that appears in the commercial and tax accounts of the company at the end of the relevant financial year; and (b) a minimum percentage of the annual average book value of the notes issued by the company in connection with its securitisation activity (the "Minimum Profit").

According to administrative practice however, the SPV will not usually have profit in their commercial and tax accounts, as any profit is distributed to the Junior Noteholders and therefore the tax liability would be annually assessed a on the basis of a Minimum Profit margin. This Minimum Profit margin is calculated pursuant to a cost-plus method (which is one of the traditional transaction methods favoured by the OECD in order to implement the arm's length principle). In accordance with the cost-plus method the Minimum Profit margin is expressed as a minimum percentage (in general 3 basis points (0.03%)) of the value of the company's indebtedness, that is, the notes issued.

Usually, the applicable Minimum Profit margin will be cleared and accepted by the Luxembourg tax administration upon request. As the delivery of a written clearance (ruling) generally takes several months, in practice most structured transactions are launched with an oral confirmation only being the written clearance delivered at a later stage. Normally there is no formal requirement for the SPV to seek such clearance, but the rating agencies traditionally require having such clearance in order to rate the notes.

Any expenses, including interest expenses, are deductible from the total income of the company for tax accounting purposes (e.g., profits resulting from the investment of the company's share capital and retained earnings and profits resulting from its securitisation/repackaging activity minus interest due to noteholders, fees due to the domiciliation agent, the arranger, collateral manager, and so on). If a lower profit were to be realised, the declared profit will need to be adjusted to the Minimum Profit margin.

The terms of the Class C-1 Notes indicate that income produced by the investments may be used to repay part of the principal amount of the notes (i.e., to partially amortise the notes). If interest or any other income is indeed used to reimburse principal under the notes, there might be a mismatch resulting in a taxable profit, as no tax-deductible expense would offset this income (i.e., amortisation of the notes is not a deductible expense).

In order to avoid a taxable base in excess of the required minimum, the SPV's income and expense flows should balance at all times so that the taxable income generated will not be in excess of the Profit Margin plus operating costs of the SPV.

Also, care should be taken on the drafting of the distributions to the Income noteholders: the Luxembourg income tax (LIR) provides for the non-deductibility of the distribution of taxable income (i.e., the annual profits) or the liquidation proceeds of the SPV. Documentation should clearly state that the holders of the Junior Notes will receive the residual amount of the interest received by the SPV under the Collateral Debt Securities and not a residual amount of the overall profits of the SPV.

Corporate Tax Issues: The Issuer Being Taxed in the United Kingdom or Germany by Reason of its Relation with the Collateral Manager or Collateral Adviser

If the collateral manager of the transaction is a UK-incorporated entity, then care should be taken so that such collateral manager is not seen as actually taking the decisions and managing the SPV. If the SPV is deemed to be managed by a UK entity, there is a risk of the SPV being considered "resident" in the United Kingdom for tax purposes by the Inland Revenue. But even if the SPV is not deemed to be managed from the United Kingdom, the SPV may be charged taxes on profits in the United Kingdom if it is deemed to be acting through an agent or branch (e.g., if the collateral manager is located in the United Kingdom and is deemed to act as agent of the SPV).[12]

If the collateral adviser is a Germany incorporated entity, then in Germany the tax regulations indicate that the SPV will be deemed to be a resident in Germany for tax purposes if the management decisions of the company are taken in Germany. This will be determined not on the basis of the legal situation, but on the basis of the factual circumstances. In order to prevent the determination that the management decisions are taken in Germany, it is important to give certain scope to the issuer or the noteholders so that it does not have to follow the collateral adviser's advice in all the cases.

Wealth Tax Issues in Luxembourg

Wealth tax is levied on the net wealth of the SPV at a rate of 0.5%. A company's business wealth (*fortune d'exploitation*) is assessed by taking into account the estimated alienation value of its business assets. Debts are deductible provided they relate to taxable business assets. Thus, notes issued by an SPV are in principle deductible for wealth tax assessment purposes.

Accrued expenses will only be deducted from the wealth tax base (as provisions—*provisions pour risques et charges*), if it is certain at the time the provisions are accounted for that these expenses will actually be made in the future (although it may be impossible to determine their exact amount).

VAT-Related Issues

The collateral adviser and the collateral manager are, in fact, providing services to the SPV. Because the services provided by the collateral advisor and collateral manager are financial services, in Europe VAT is usually chargeable on the jurisdiction of the recipient of the financial services, i.e., in Luxembourg. Luxembourg tax law does not charge VAT for financial services and therefore to VAT will be charge on the fees payable to the collateral manager and collateral adviser. Nevertheless it should be noted that some law firms believe that there is, as a matter of law, some potential liability for VAT in the United Kingdom although, as a matter of practice, Customs and Excise are not currently requiring payment of such VAT.

---

[12] An exception could be available to the Collateral Manager if it were an investment management business.

Withholding Tax Issues in Relation of Payment of Interest Under the Terms of the Notes and Under the Terms of the Revolving Facility

With respect to the payment of interest to the noteholders under the terms of the Notes and to the Lender under the terms of the revolving credit facility, currently there is no withholding tax issue in Luxembourg as, in general, there is no withholding tax on interest payments coming out of Luxembourg.

Regulatory Issues Related to the Collateral Manager and Collateral Advisor

As the collateral manager and the collateral advisors are financial institutions domiciled in a jurisdiction other than the jurisdiction of incorporation of the SPV, they should make sure they are passported to render investment advice in the country where the SPV is set up.

CHAPTER 31

Trust and Agency Services in the Debt Capital Markets

Nick Procter
EMEA Structured Finance Services
JPMorgan Chase Bank

Edmond Leedham
EMEA Structured Finance Services
JPMorgan Chase Bank

This chapter is an account of trustee and agency services that are required to support proper functioning of the debt capital markets. A distinction will be made between responsibilities of a trustee, and the other services offered by trust banks, known as agency services, to support debt markets structured products. The purpose of this chapter is to give the reader a broad understanding of the work undertaken by trust banks and how these services relate to the structures themselves. It should be noted that while many of these services are offered globally, the focus of this chapter is primarily on the European structured finance market.

The authors would like to thank J. A. Carrington, Paula Jacobsen, and Ruth Kentish for review comments and assistance with preparing this chapter.

GENERIC TRUST AND AGENCY SERVICES

We begin by describing the functions required in all European capital market issues.

Trustee

The role of the trustee in a Eurobond issuance is to serve as a bridge between the issuer of the bonds and the bondholders throughout the life of the issuance. The scope of duties undertaken by a trustee in connection with any given issuance may vary from structure to structure, but the essence of the trustee's role is to hold and exercise as necessary, and as permitted by the trust documentation, the legal rights of each bondholder in the transaction.

Legal Background

A "trust" is an invention of common law and is particular to the law of England, the United States and other countries whose legal traditions have evolved from English law (although a few civil law jurisdictions recognise the concept of a trust in one form or another). The concept of trust flows from the common law construction that ownership rights in property may be divided into two distinct classes: legal ownership and beneficial ownership. A "legal owner" of property holds title to that property and is recognised in law as the owner of such property. A "beneficial owner" of property does not hold legal title to the property, but enjoys some or all of the benefits that normally would be associated with legal ownership of property. The recognition of different classes of ownership rights in common law allows one party to assume legal ownership of a piece of property purely for the purpose of holding that property "on trust" for the benefit of one or more third parties (the very essence of a trust).

A legal owner of property appears to all the world as the actual owner of such property. Thus, the rights of a legal owner in such property cannot be restricted by general operation of law. Where a legal owner holds such property on trust (i.e., as a trustee) for another party, the legal owner's rights in such property must be circumscribed by ancillary means. The common law, as well as statutory law, provides many principles and "default provisions" delineating the division of rights, liabilities, and responsibilities between parties to a trust. However, the specific relationship and division of rights between the trustee and the beneficiaries of a trust are regulated largely by the terms of the documentation establishing the trust (normally a "trust deed" under English law).

The terms of trusts created in support of Eurobond issuance are negotiated chiefly between representatives of the issuer (usually the arranger) and the trustee during the deal origination process (although outside parties, such as rating agencies, may have considerable input into the process). As is the case with most trusts, the beneficiaries of such trusts (i.e., the bondholders) have no input into the terms of the trust. However, any party who purchases a bond is deemed upon such purchase to be legally bound by the terms of the trust documentation executed in connection with the issuance. Thus, issuers and trustees are compelled to ensure that Eurobond trust structures meet certain market standards in order to induce investors to purchase the bonds being issued.

Use of Trusts in Eurobond Structures

The concept of trust is particularly well suited to Eurobond issuance because the concept supports an environment in which investors normally hold such bonds anonymously through a clearing system and actively trade such bonds on the secondary market.

The holder of a Eurobond is meant to benefit from a number of covenants, charges and pledges associated with the issuance. The most basic example of a "covenant" the issuer would be expected to grant the bondholder is the covenant to repay the debt. A classic example of a "charge" is a "first fixed charge" over assets meant to secure the debt. Such covenants, charges and pledges must be made in favour of a specific persons or persons to be effective. This is especially important in the case of charges over assets securing the debt. Beneficiaries of such charges must file a copy of the charge with the appropriate registry (which in England is "Companies House") in order to perfect (i.e., ensure the priority of its security interest in such assets against third parties) the security interest granted by the charge.

If the issuer were to grant the rights (e.g., covenants, charges, pledges) underlying such bonds directly to individual bondholders at the inception of the deal, the bonds might not be easily sold on the secondary market without modification of the original issuance documentation. Moreover, modification of the issuance documentation would be impractical in such circumstances because, in addition to cost and time considerations, it would be difficult to verify the identities of the parties to the secondary sale and many investors would not want to reveal their identity to the issuer.

Placing a trustee between the issuer and the bondholders at the inception of the deal eliminates the above problem because the trustee assumes legal ownership of the rights underlying the bonds (e.g., covenants, charges, and pledges) for the benefit of present and future bondholders for the duration of the issuance. Thus, bondholders, as the beneficial owners of the rights attached to the bond, which are held legally by the trustee, may freely trade the bonds without the need for modification of the original issuance documents, or fear that such transfer would compromise rights underlying the bonds.

A more obvious advantage of placing a trustee between the issuer and the bondholders of a Eurobond issuance is that so doing provides a constant point of contact between the issuer and a set of largely anonymous and often changing bondholders. The bondholders are able to speak to the issuer and other concerned parties with one voice and the issuer is provided a single point of contact with which it can consult as necessary on issues that might arise in the day to day operation of the transaction. Such an arrangement is useful not only in default, or potential default, situations, but for disposition of relatively routine or non-controversial matters that might arise throughout the life of the issuance.

Even in far less volatile commercial environments than that in which we now find ourselves, it may be beneficial to all parties to a transaction to modify the terms of issuance documentation and very often time is of the essence. In the absence of a trust structure, issuers would have to convene a meeting of the bondholders to sanction even the most mundane amendment to issuance documentation. Convening such meetings is a costly, time-consuming and generally arduous proposition that should only be undertaken when absolutely necessary.

The use of a trust structure in a Eurobond issuance can minimise significantly the need to consult bondholders on certain document modifications. The issuer and trustee typically craft the trust deed to empower the trustee to exercise discretion on behalf of all bondholders within specified parameters. Under current market standards, the trustee is normally permitted to agree to nonmaterial modifications of the terms of a Eurobond issuance and exercise very specific powers, such as the power to appoint or approve replacement agents within defined circumstances and criteria, without consultation of the bondholders. The ability of the trustee to agree to nonmaterial term modifications and exercise certain prescribed powers without consultation of bondholders benefits all parties to the deal both practically and economically because expensive and time consuming bondholders meetings are not necessary to deal with such issues.

Finally, in cases where convening a bondholder meeting is unavoidable due to the nature of the proposed amendment, the presence of a professional trustee in the structure is invaluable. The trustee, unlike most issuers, has well established contacts with paying agents and the clearing systems, and can play a crucial role in helping the issuer get word of the proposed amendment out to the bondholders and ensuring that the bondholders respond to such proposals. Moreover, an experienced professional trustee can be a useful resource to the issuer who often has no way of knowing in advance of the bondholders meeting whether the bondholders will accept its proposal. Drawing upon its experience, the trustee can advise the issuer of the likelihood of the proposal's success and recommend revisions thereby minimising the chance that the issuer will launch a costly exercise that is doomed to failure from the start.

Note Trustee versus Security Trustee

It is worthwhile to note that in addition to delineating the specific powers and duties of a trustee within a given trust structure, the issuance documentation is sometimes drafted to draw a distinction between the roles of "note trustee" and "security trustee."

A note trustee holds on behalf of the noteholders the issuer's covenant to repay the notes, as well as other related covenants. Accordingly, a note trustee is concerned mainly about whether the issuer is honouring such covenants and whether an acceleration of payment of the notes is in order. A security trustee holds the security interest, usually given in the form of a charge or pledge, granted by the issuer for the benefit of the noteholders and other secured creditors. The security trustee's focus is on enforcement of the security; although it is important to note that normally the security trustee would not enforce the security unless directed to do so by the note trustee.

In most Eurobond structures, the roles of note trustee and security trustee are combined and documented as a single trustee role (i.e., both roles will be documented in a single trust deed). However, some lawyers prefer to document the roles separately even though each role will be undertaken by the same entity. This is especially common in highly structured deals such as master trusts where the securitised assets are held by an entity other than the issuer of the overlying notes and the overlying notes are secured by intermediate loans. The logic behind this practice is that even in relatively straightforward structures, the note trustee and security trustee may come in conflict with one another in an enforcement action (note that a security trustee often holds the security for the benefit of other secured creditors as well as the noteholders). Should such a conflict arise, the entity undertaking the roles can simply delegate one role or the other to a neutral third party thereby eliminating the conflict.

Role of the Trustee while the Transaction Runs Normally

Under normal circumstances, the role of the trustee in a Eurobond issuance governed by English law, whether the role is cast as a note trustee, security trustee or both, is largely passive. In most Eurobond transactions, even highly structured transactions, the issuer is left to conduct its business, subject to limitations contained in the documents, without interference from the trustee. This is especially true in regard to cash and custody accounts over which the trustee holds charges. Normally, the issuer, again subject to limitations contained in the issuance documentation, is permitted to operate such accounts freely notwithstanding such charges (in which case such charges may be construed to be floating charges, that is, security interests that do not fully crystallise in terms of priority until enforced by the trustee.

In most trust arrangements, the trustee's main day-to-day duty is to monitor the issuer's compliance with its obligations under the deal documentation. Generally, such duty is limited to ensuring that the issuer generates the various certificates of nondefault and compliance and reports required by the issuance documentation. A prudent trustee will normally examine such certificates and reports to ensure they are in proper form and do not raise any specific alarms as to the status of the deal. However, the trustee normally will have no obligation under the terms of the trust or by operation of law to examine in detail or pass judgement on the substance of such reports. This limitation is entirely consistent with the purpose of placing the trustee in the transaction, which is to hold the legal rights of the bondholders on trust, not to serve as an auditor of or advisor on the performance of the transaction.

Depending upon the economic climate and the nature of a given transaction, the trustee may be compelled to take a more robust role in the transaction in certain areas. Usually such circumstances occur when the issuer believes that a modification of the issuance documents is in order. As mentioned earlier, a trustee may be asked at any point during the life of a deal to exercise discretion or certain prescribed powers to effect modifications to the terms of the deal documentation.

Normally, a request that the trustee exercises a prescribed power or duty will be clear-cut. For example, a highly structured transaction requires a number of agents, such as a custodian, cash manager and account bank, to help the issuer run the deal. Typically, the documents governing such roles require such agents to meet certain threshold financial and credit rating criteria and provide further that the trustee shall appoint a replacement agent should an agent's ratings fall below the stated criteria. While a prudent trustee would probably consult counsel and perhaps the rating agencies in dealing with such an issue, such requests, which are becoming more common in today's banking environment, should not pose too much of a problem for a trustee.

A request that the trustee exercise discretion is another matter. The general rule is that the trustee may only exercise discretion in agreeing to a modification if the proposed modification is not materially prejudicial to the bondholders. The underlying documents often provide concrete examples of what would be considered a material and prejudicial charge to the terms of an issuance. A change in the rate of interest is an obvious example. However, many requests fall into very grey areas.

Most trustees would prefer not to exercise discretion in agreeing to an amendment. In the real world, however, the issuer will be keen that the trustee exercise discretion and the trustee will be mindful that its ability to exercise discretion in a given instance could benefit all parties from a time and cost perspective. Such considerations cannot deter the trustee from its duty to act in the best interest of all bondholders. However, they do compel the trustee to take an honest look at the proposed modification.

In determining whether it can exercise discretion in a given situation, the trustee will normally retain counsel and the services of other experts as necessary to assist it with this exercise. The prudent trustee will also seek indications from the rating agencies as to whether the proposed modification will have any adverse effect on the ratings of the bonds.

During the process of reviewing the proposed amendment with counsel, the trustee may very well find that the modification would be more palatable (i.e., consistent with its duties to the noteholders) with minor or not so minor changes. Thus, many modifications made to the documents without consultation of the bondholders are the product of considerable negotiation and drafting by the trustee and the issuer and their respective counsels.

If the trustee determines that it cannot exercise discretion in dealing with a proposed modification or the modification is so material that the issuer would not ask the trustee to consider exercising discretion, the only alternative is to convene a meeting of the bondholders to consider the proposed modification. The process of convening such a meeting and preparing the necessary resolutions, which as mentioned above is a costly, time consuming and complex proposition, is governed by the issuance documentation.

The trustee's role in this process is to ensure that the issuer complies with notice provisions for bondholder meetings, conduct the bondholders meeting itself, certify/confirm the results of the meeting and resolutions and publish notice of the results of each meeting. At the beginning of the process and prior to the notices and resolutions being published, the trustee and its counsel will typically review and comment upon the proposed amendments and notice materials. The trustee's main concern is that the proposed amendments and notices are consistent with the spirit and letter of the issuance documentation and not prejudicial to the bondholders. However, this process also provides the issuer the opportunity to benefit from the trustee's experience in gauging how the bondholders will receive the amendments.

Once the notices and resolutions are agreed, the mechanics of publishing notices through the clearing systems and monitoring the responses of the bondholders through the clearing systems is largely the province of the principal paying agent. In the real world, however, the trustee often finds it necessary to take a fairly proactive role in the process.

As mentioned earlier, most investors hold Eurobonds anonymously through the clearing systems. To complicate things further, often such bonds are not held directly by their beneficial owners, but by custodians representing the beneficial owners. Professional custodians are charged to inform their clients promptly of all corporate actions affecting their holdings. In reality, however, the information flow from custodians to the beneficial owners of affected Eurobonds is less than first class. Consequently, beneficial owners of such bonds often do not become aware of bondholder meetings and resolutions until late in the process and often through other than normal channels. Even in cases where a bondholder receives meeting notices and proposed resolution through its custodian, the information can be garbled in transmission leaving the bondholder confused.

While a prudent trustee will not offer substantive advice to bondholders considering an amendment, trustees will spend a great deal of time during the notice period advising bondholders on voting mechanics and the meeting process. Also, if the trustee finds that a significant number of bondholders have received late notice of the bondholder meeting and resolution, the trustee may very well find it prudent to arrange an extension of voting. In short, the trustee can often play a large part in ensuring that the resolution receives maximum exposure to and consideration by the bondholders (hopefully to the benefit of all parties).

Depending upon the structure underlying the issuance, there are other areas in which a trustee may take on a proactive role during the normal life of the transaction. For example, in a real estate securitisation, the trustee may be asked to approve sales and purchases of real property in the securitised portfolio on a fairly routine basis. However, the foregoing should provide the reader with a feel for the most common activities undertaken by the trustee in connection with a smooth-running transaction.

Role of the Trustee when the Deal runs into Trouble

The main role of the trustee in the event of a default is to protect the interests of the bondholders to the extent the trustee is obligated or empowered to do so under the terms of the trust documentation. The degree of activity a trustee undertakes in a default situation can vary greatly depending upon the terms of the issuance documentation, the structure of the deal and the circumstances of the default. The basic mechanics of the trustee's role in a default situation are fairly uniform, however.

In keeping with the rather passive profile the trustee maintains while the transaction operates normally, the trustee bears no duty to make affirmative enquiries or investigations as to whether an issuer or an issuance is danger of default. Rather, the onus is on the issuer and its agents to report any circumstances that may constitute a default under the terms of the documents. Accordingly, the trustee normally bears no duty to act in regard to a default scenario until it has actual knowledge of the default. Most trust documents empower the trustee to respond to an event of default without consulting the bondholders. However, the trustee is normally not obligated to take any action unless affirmatively required to do by a vote of the bondholders and only if the bondholders indemnify the trustee to the trustee's satisfaction.

Generally, the trustee takes first priority in the post enforcement priority of payments scheme (i.e., the order by which monies in the structure are distributed to the bondholders and other secured creditors). However, the trustee cannot necessarily expect a transaction in default to produce sufficient cash flows to cover the fees, expenses and potential legal liabilities it might incur in dealing with a default scenario. Accordingly, most trustees will be reluctant to take action upon an event of default situation without the explicit mandate of the bondholders. The trustee will not only be looking to the bondholders for indemnification, but also for assurance that the requisite number of bondholders (normally a majority) agrees that acceleration of debt/enforcement of the security is prudent under the circumstances.

Whether the trustee acts with or without consultation of the bondholders, a prudent trustee will take great care in issuing a notice of default or enforcement notice. A prematurely issued default notice may lead to a general loss of confidence in the issuer and trigger cross defaults. However, if the trustee waits too long to issue the default notice, the amount of the bondholders' recovery could suffer greatly. Under most structures the trustee is entitled to accelerate the debt immediately or upon expiration of a specified cure period. However, it is not uncommon for the trustee and the bondholders to delay enforcement in order to explore workout options with the issuer.

In the event the decision to accelerate the debt/enforce the security is made, the trustee will issue the necessary notices and take control of the transaction. Any floating charges on accounts and assets will become fixed in favour of the trustee and existing agents of the issuer, such as paying agents, custodians, account banks, effectively become agents of the trustee and are bound by its instructions.

Most secured Eurobond structures are nonrecourse in nature (i.e., the bondholders' debt may only be recovered to the extent there is cash and assets in the structure). Accordingly, the trustee will move promptly to unwind the structure and distribute cash and assets to the bondholders and other secured creditors in accordance with the transactions' post enforcement priority of payments scheme. The trustee will often retain a liquidating or receiving agent to assist with this process. In some instances, the trustee will have no immediate recourse to assets to satisfy the bondholders' claims, due to the transaction's structure, some malfeasance by the issuer or where the transaction has become subject to insolvency proceedings. In such cases, the trustee will press the bondholders' claims through the applicable process or forum and serves as the bondholders' chief negotiator in any ensuing negotiations (while regularly consulting with the bondholders).

Paying Agent

All debt issuance in the Euromarkets requires a principal paying agent, or in the case of a programme of issuance (for example a Euro-MTN programme) an issuing and paying agent. The responsibility of the paying agent is to provide administrative support to the issuer throughout the lifetime of the issue, the primary one of which is to arrange for payment of the note coupon to investors via the clearing systems. The complete duties of a paying agent are:

- Issuing securities upon demand in the case of a debt programme.
- Authenticating definitive notes.
- Collecting funds from the issuer and paying these out to investors as coupon and redemption payments.
- In the case of global notes, acting on behalf of the issuer to supervise payments of interest and principal to investors via the clearing systems, and in the case of definitive notes, paying out interest and coupon on presentation by the investor of the relevant coupon or bond to the Paying Agent.
- Transferring funds to subpaying agents, where these have been appointed. For instance, a security that has been listed on the Luxembourg stock exchange must have a local subpaying agent appointed for it.
- Maintaining a bank account of the cash flows paid out on the bond;
- Arranging the cancellation and subsequent payment of coupons, matured bonds, and global notes, and sending destroyed certificates to the issuer.

A paying agent will act solely on behalf of the issuer, unlike a trustee who has an obligation to look after the interests of investors. For larger bond issues there may be a number of paying agents appointed, of which the *principal paying agent* is the coordinator. A number of *subpaying agents* may be appointed to ensure that bondholders in different country locations may receive their coupon and redemption payments without delay. The term *fiscal agent* is used to describe a paying agent for a bond issue for which no trustee has been appointed.

Common Depositary

The depositary for a Eurobond issue is responsible for the safekeeping of securities. In the Euromarkets well over 90% of investors are institutions, and so as a result issues are made in dematerialised form, and are represented by a global note. Trading and settlement is in computerised book entry form via the two main international clearing systems, Euroclear and Clearstream. Both these institutions have appointed a group of banks to act on their behalf as depositaries for book entry securities; this is known as *common depositaries*, because the appointment is common to both Euroclear and Clearstream. Both clearing firms have appointed separately a network of banks to act as specialised depositaries, which handle securities that have been issued in printed note or *definitive* form.

As at February 2003 there were 21 banks that acted as common depositaries on behalf of Euroclear and Clearstream, although the majority of the trading volume was handled by just three banks, JPMorgan Chase Bank, Citibank NA, and Deutsche Bankers Trust. The common depositary is responsible for:

- Representing Euroclear and Clearstream, and facilitating delivery-versus-payment of the primary market issue by collecting funds from the investors, taking possession of the temporary global note, which allows securities to be released to investors, and making a single payment of funds to the issuer.
- Holding the temporary global note in safe custody, until it is exchanged for definitive notes or a permanent global note.
- Making adjustments to the nominal value of the global note that occur after the exercise of any options or after conversions, in line with instructions from Euroclear or Clearstream and the fiscal agent.
- Surrendering the cancelled temporary global note to the fiscal agent after the exchange into definitive certificates or a permanent global note, or on maturity of the permanent global note.

A specialised depositary will hold definitive notes representing aggregate investor positions held in a particular issue; on coupon and maturity dates it presents the coupons or bond to the paying agent and passes the proceeds on to the clearing system.

Custodian

The custodian is the party that holds/safekeeps collateral, cash or other forms of security on behalf of the deal. The custodian takes into custody for safekeeping the assets on behalf of the deal. The securities that a custodian might be expected to take safekeeping of would include, sovereign debt, corporate debt, asset-backed securities, corporate loans, equity, distressed debt, repo, cash and any other form of collateral for which a third-party custodian is required. Given the pan-European and indeed global nature of many structured deals the custodian is often required to offer global capabilities. In order to achieve the required global reach a global custodian will often appoint a subcustodian. The subcustodian will perform the custodial duties for a specific local area.

The custodian/subcustodian is responsible for the following duties:

- Settlement of securities through the applicable exchange.
- Holding securities in clearing account or in physical form on site.
- Provision of corporate action information.
- Execution of corporate actions such as coupon payments.
- Collection of coupon and principal payments.
- Reclaiming tax on coupons paid net.

Custodial services are often performed by a third party to the deal. This is partly through necessity as in most cases, the deal participants do not have custodial capabilities. Additionally the third party involvement reinforces the off-balance sheet nature of the deal for the originator and clearly defines those assets associated with the particular deal. Finally the appointed custodian is generally, although not necessarily, the same entity as the appointed trustee. Hence, there is further protection provided to the investor in a default situation as the trustee effectively has control of the assets. This is a source of comfort for investors.

The traditional concept of a custodian as explained above is applicable to those deal types that hold the assets noted. This is usually the case for ABCP programs (although these deals may be set up to fund exclusively trade receivable assets), collateralized debt obligations (CDOs), and special investment vehicles (SIVs). With certain forms of CDO transactions, the proceeds of issued notes are sometimes invested in collateral. This is also held by the deal custodian. In addition ABS deals may also have a requirement for custodial services. Hence the custodian may be required to take possession of physical deeds and/or, pledges. These forms of security will be held in the custodian's vault for safekeeping.

Cash Manager and Account Bank

All structured finance deals have cash movements through the structure. Cash is continuously being generated by the assets whether they be residential mortgages, credit card receivables or high-yield bonds. Other cash movements may include monies moved through interest rate and FX swaps, third-party fees and expenses such as trustee, rating agency and legal costs, and payment of bond coupon and principal. The responsibility of the movement of the cash, which is distinct from the decision to move the cash, is the role of the cash manager. From a servicing perspective the cash manger does not have discretionary powers—the cash manager only acts on instruction from the originator or deal manager. In this respect the cash manager acts an investment agent, placing funds as directed into designated bank accounts or high quality assets such as Treasury bills.

Thus there is always a requirement for a cash manger. Crucial to the cash management function is the provision of bank accounts. That is, the deal will necessarily have a requirement for bank accounts (often multicurrency). It should be noted that the cash manager and account bank roles do not necessarily need to be performed by the same entity. Often the cash will be managed by the originator or servicer of the assets but the deal accounts will be held at a separate account bank provider. It is common for one agency provider to be appointed as both cash manager and account bank. Where a different party is appointed for the latter role, the cash manager will be required to liaise as required with the account bank.

Exhibit 31.1 is the transaction structure diagram for an hypothetical commercial MBS structure. It illustrates the complex nature of the cash management function. In this example the deal requires management of twenty one different cash accounts in multiple currencies. In addition to moving the cash between the accounts in the structure the cash manager may also be expected to maintain ledgers. In the example noted in Exhibit 31.1, the cash movements—including swap and hedge payments, principal and interest collections, interests due on the notes, principal due on the notes, third-party, eligible investments (suitably rated money market funds or GIC accounts for example)—must all be posted to the appropriate ledger. Given that each SPV in the example may have one or more ledgers this further serves to highlight the potential complexity of the cash managers duties.

EXHIBIT 31.1 Hypothetical CMBS Transactions Detailing Bank Accounts

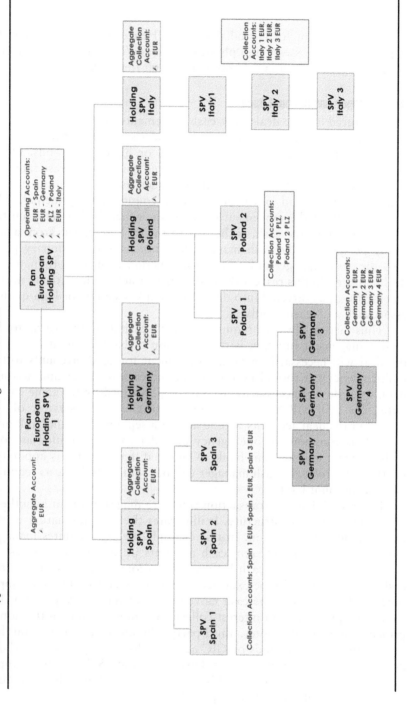

Listing Agent

Increasingly a requirement for many structured finance deals is to have the issued notes listed on a stock exchange. Listing raises the deal profile and indeed many institutional investors will not invest in a deal unless it is listed. In Europe the Luxembourg Stock Exchange has traditionally been the exchange that European deals have listed on, however the Dublin Stock Exchange is becoming increasingly popular for listing in Europe.

In order to list on an exchange firms use a listing agent. The listing agent facilitates the request to list with the exchange. This will involve:

- Assisting with the completion of the necessary documentation to list.
- Calculation and collection of exchange fees.
- Submitting the relevant documentation to the exchange.
- Liaising with the exchange to facilitate approval.

Backup Servicing

The concept of a backup servicer originated in the US market to appease investor and rating agency concerns in the mortgage-backed market. The appointment of a backup servicer on asset-backed and mortgage-backed deals in the US market is now widespread. Although the appointment of a backup servicer on ABS and MBS deals is not as prevalent in Europe the markets are increasingly seeking added protection through the appointment of the backup servicer.

The role of the back-up servicer is simple in principal. If the servicer of the assets breaches the covenants documented under the servicing agreement, and it is deemed that they are no longer fit or able to continue to service the assets, the back up servicer is then responsible for servicing the assets. There are different levels of responsibility depending on what type of backup servicer is appointed:

1. *Hot Backup Servicer.* The appointment of a hot backup servicer offers the most protection to the deal as the time window in which the servicer is replaced is smallest, usually the hot backup servicer agrees to be servicing the assets within 24 hours.
2. *Warm Backup Servicer.* A warm servicer ensures that the assets are serviced in the event of a servicer default usually within the period of 5–30 days.
3. *Cold Backup Servicer.* The appointment of a cold servicer offers least protection to the deal. The cold servicer undertakes to ensure that the assets are being serviced, not necessarily by themselves (most often not themselves), within a specified period, often a period of between 30–90 days.

As one moves down the spectrum from hot to cold the cost of appointing a backup servicer decreases significantly. The reason for this is because a hot backup servicer must effectively mirror the operations of the original servicer in order to be able to start servicing the assets within 48 hours. Depending on the extent of the operation this can be costly both in terms of staffing and technology. The cold servicer on the other hand has time to appoint a servicer capable of servicing the specified assets and assist in managing the hand over to the new servicer.

Although not all backup servicers are rated, increasingly both rating agencies and investor are looking for rated institutions to be nominated as the backup servicer.

The Appendix provides a quick reference guide of the trustee and agency roles offer by Trust Banks to support the Structured Finance Market.

CONCLUSION

The use of trusts and professional trustees within Eurobond issuance serves a number of legal and practical purposes. In the main, however, the essential service the trustee brings to the transaction is stability to the transaction and piece of mind for bondholders and issuers alike. Accordingly, the trustee is an invaluable element of a successful secured Eurobond transaction. Further to the role of trustee the Trust bank will offer a range of services to support the structured finance market place.

The range of services that the trust bank offers will vary depending on the sophistication and maturity of the trust business. Most if not all service providers will offer cash manager, account bank, paying agency, and custodial services in addition to trustee services to support their trust business. Other roles such as financial reporting may be offered in varying degrees depending on the banks experience and infrastructure.

Although some structures employ different banks to perform various roles in a transaction generally those services that are outsourced are performed by one entity. This is the most preferable solution as confusion regarding duties and responsibilities can arise when there are multiple service providers engaged in one deal. When a single service provider is appointed on all the roles they simply take responsibility for all the servicing and hence there is no confusion over responsibilities. Additionally investors might gain some comfort in the knowledge that the trustee has possession of the deal assets such as cash or securities should they deal default.

APPENDIX—QUICK REFERENCE GUIDE TO TRUSTEE AND AGENCY SERVICES

Account Bank—Bank with whom accounts are established.

Authentication Agent—Party that signs a security to authenticate the certificate, bond, or note.

Agent Bank or Calculation/Calculating/Reference Agent—This agent is responsible for making and publishing certain calculations that are used to assess security payments, risk determinants, voting rights, and/or to trigger events toward a financial transaction.

Collection/Collecting Agent—Party that receives/consolidates payments. Party may need to furnish reports summarizing activity.

Conversion Agent—Coordinates the surrender of securities by bondholders for the issuance of share certificates in lieu in a convertible bond issue.

Custodian/Subcustodian—Party that holds/safekeeps collateral, cash or other form of security for the benefit of a client or lender, as per underlying documentation

Escrow Agent/Depositary Agent—This agent assumes temporary possession of assets on behalf of two or more parties (one of which may be silent or third party) to a sale, conveyance or other transaction.

Facility Agent—Party that performs certain rate sets, acts as a conduit of information from a borrower to the lender(s) and vice versa, facilitates payments from a borrower to a lender and vice versa, acts upon majority lender instruction

Fiscal Agent—The agent prepares and authenticates the securities; arranges, if applicable, an international paying agency network; attends the closing; and delivers the securities to the underwriters as instructed by the issuer. There is no requirement to monitor compliance or pursue remedies upon default, since the agent is acting on behalf of the issuer. However, the agent carries out certain administrative duties, such as arranging for security holder meetings and issuing notices.

FX Agent—for the purchase of foreign currency pursuant to instructions from the customer and subject to receipt of funds.

Issuing and Paying Agent—The agent has responsibility for effecting the issuance, primary settlement and interest and principal payment of short term and continuously offered long term instruments (e.g., certificates of deposit, commercial paper, and medium term notes). (See *Paying Agent.*)

Paying Agent—The agent arranges the payment of principal and interest to bond holders upon behalf of the issuer. Also ensures that the relevant income tax on interest is withheld pursuant to local tax regulations. For US Issuers, the paying agent ensures that the relevant W-8 and W-9 Forms are circulated and received in order to withhold appropriately as per US Tax regulations. The paying agent will also facilitate relevant reporting to the IRS in the United States.

Principal Paying Agent—Party primarily responsible to claim funds due on security from an issuer/borrower and disburse same to paying agents, other agents, or investors. (See *Paying Agent.*)

Reference Agent—See *Calculation Agent.*

Registrar—The agent is responsible for registering exchanges and transfers and for maintaining bondholder records.

Registrar/Transfer Agent—Responsible for issuing and authenticating new securities for securities surrendered for transfer, for example, as a result of a sale, and maintaining ownership records.

Settlement Agent/Exchange Agent—On a private issue that switches to a registered issue with the Securities and Exchange Commission, (a public offering), the agent that coordinates the downposting of the private issue and issuance of the SEC registered issue. A settlement agent is also required when a company undergoes restructuring of existing debt (whether in the form of bonds or loans) and receives creditor approval to exchange old debt for new debt and/or shares/options and/or cash.

Trustee—The trustee has responsibility for any or all of the following roles dependent on the contractual obligations set out in the governing documents including; taking a security interest in any and all collateral and assets, and to receive and hold all certifications and/or notifications required from other parties. With regard to any amendments or supplements to the documents, the trustee would determine whether the proposed action is material enough to require noteholder consent; if noteholder consent is required, the trustee would obtain consent from the noteholders. In an enforcement situation, where the deal is in default and must be wound down, the trustee will liquidate the collateral and assets and make payments to the relevant parties, in accordance with the documents. Also, the trustee will generally monitor the activities of the Issue to ensure that the spirit of the document is followed and the interests of the noteholders are being looked after.

Warrant Agent—A warrant agent is responsible for the launch of an issuer's warrants (issue/programme) and to advise the issuer of subsequent warrants exercise details of investors. Duty may include calculation of number of shares to be delivered versus cash for fractional shares, if any.

Index

Printed and bound by CPI Group (UK) Ltd, Croydon, CR0 4YY

23/04/2025

14660924-0004